# Educational Dilemmas:
## Debate and Diversity    Volume One

**Educational Dilemmas: Debate and Diversity**

**Educational Dilemmas:
Debate and Diversity**   Volume One

# Teachers, Teacher Education and Training

*Edited by*
Keith Watson, Celia Modgil
and Sohan Modgil

CASSELL

Cassell
Wellington House
125 Strand
London WC2R 0BB

PO Box 605
Herndon
VA 20172

First published 1997

**British Library Cataloguing-in-Publication Data**
A catalogue record for this book is available from the
British Library.

ISBN 0-304-32893-6

Typeset by York House Typographic Ltd, London
Printed and bound in Great Britain by The Bath Press

# Contents

# Acknowledgements

The editors wish to express their gratitude to the following people who have made these volumes move from an idea into a reality: to Naomi Roth, for her unstinting support and encouragement; to all the contributors who have joined into the spirit of this venture; to the copy-editors who have worked so hard and speedily; but, above all, to Margaret King, for her labours in typing and sifting through the scripts, for her good humour in times of frustration and for her work in compiling a database for these volumes. To all of them we extend our thanks.

# Abbreviations and Acronyms

| | |
|---|---|
| AAU | Academic Audit Unit |
| ABE | adult basic education |
| ACEP | Australian Co-operative Assessment Programme |
| ACSET | Advisory Committee for the Supply and Education of Teachers |
| AGIT | Action for Governor Information and Training |
| AI | annual inspection |
| ALBSU | Adult Literacy and Basic Skills Unit |
| ANC | African National Congress |
| APEL | accreditation of prior learning from experience |
| APU | Assessment of Performance Unit |
| ASQC | American Society for Quality Control |
| ATO | area training organization |
| BD | Education Committee of the Board of Deputies of British Jews |
| BERA | British Educational Research Association |
| CAI | computer-aided instruction |
| CAPE | *certificat d'aptitude au professorat d'école* |
| CAPES | *certificat d'aptitude au professorat de l'enseignement du second degré* |
| CATE | Council for Accreditation of Teacher Education |
| CATS | credit accumulation and transfer system |
| CBI | Confederation of British Industry |
| CES | Centre for Educational Sociology |
| CNAA | Council for National Academic Awards |
| COSC | Cambridge Overseas School Certificate |
| COTU | Central Organization of Trade Unions |

| | |
|---|---|
| CPD | continuing professional development |
| CPR | *centre pédagogique régional* |
| CPVE | Certificate of Pre-Vocational Education |
| CTC | city technology college |
| CVCP | Committee of Vice-Chancellors and Principals |
| DES | Department of Education and Science |
| DEUG | diplome d'études universitaires générales |
| DFE | Department for Education |
| EBP | Education–Business Partnerships |
| EDSAC | Education Sector Adjustment Credit |
| EHE | Enterprise in Higher Education |
| EP | educational psychologist |
| EPF | education production function |
| EQUIP | education quality improvement programme |
| ERA | Education Reform Act |
| ERASMUS | European Community Action Scheme for Mobility of University Students |
| ERIC | Educational Resources Information Center [USA] |
| ERS | Education Renewal Strategy [South Africa] |
| ESOL | English as a second or other language |
| ESRC | Economic and Social Research Council |
| FA | faculty associate |
| FE | further education |
| FEFC | Further Education Funding Council |
| FEU | Further Education Unit |
| GCE | General Certificate of Education |

| | | | |
|---|---|---|---|
| GCSE | General Certificate of Secondary Education | LMS | local management of schools |
| GDP | gross domestic product | MDI | measure-driven instruction |
| GNVQ | General National Vocational Qualification | MNC | multinational corporation |
| GOK | Government of Kenya | MOTE | Modes of Teacher Education project |
| HE | higher education | NAGM | National Association for Governors and Managers |
| HEFCE | Higher Education Funding Council of England | NC | National Curriculum |
| HEI | higher education institute | NCC | National Curriculum Council |
| HEQC | Higher Education Quality Council | NCVQ | National Council for Vocational Qualifications |
| HMI | Her Majesty's Inspectors/ Inspectorate | NESIC | National Education Standards and Improvement Council |
| HRM | Human Resource Management | NFER | National Foundation for Educational Research |
| IAEA | International Association for Educational Assessment | NGO | non-governmental organization |
| IDA | International Development Assistance | NIER | National Institute for Educational Research |
| IEA | International Association for the Evaluation of Educational Achievement | NQT | newly qualified teacher |
| | | NTA | non-teaching assistant |
| | | NUT | National Union of Teachers |
| IFM | international faculty mobility | NVQ | National Vocational Qualification [UK] |
| IIEP | International Institute for Educational Planning | ODA | Overseas Development Administration [UK] |
| IIP | Investors in People | | |
| ILEA | Inner London Education Authority | OECD | Organization for Economic Co-operation and Development |
| ILO | International Labour Organization | | |
| INSEE | Institut National de la Statistique et des Etudes Economiques | OFSTED | Office for Standards in Education |
| | | OISE | Ontario Institute for Studies in Education |
| INSET | in-service training | | |
| IPPR | Institute for Public Policy Research | ORT | Organisation for Rehabilitation and Training |
| IQE | ideal quality of education | | |
| ISR | Institute for Social Research | OSCE | Objective Structured Clinical Examinations |
| IT | information technology | | |
| ITE | initial teacher education | PCET | Polytechnics' Council for the Education of Teachers |
| ITT | initial teacher training | | |
| IUFM | *institut universitaire de formation de maîtres* | PDP | Professional Development Programme |
| JEDT | Jewish Educational Development Trust | PEIP | Primary Education Improvement Project |
| JFS | Jewish Free Schools | PGCE | Post-Graduate Certificate of Education |
| KAL | knowledge about language | | |
| KCPE | Kenya Certificate for Primary Education | PRP | performance-related pay |
| | | PSLC | Primary School Leaving Certificate |
| KNUT | Kenya National Union of Teachers | QAD | Quality Assessment Division |
| LEA | local education authority | QTS | qualified teacher status |
| LINC | language in the National Curriculum | RE/I | religious education/instruction |
| | | RTL | reflective teaching lesson |

| | | | |
|---|---|---|---|
| SACRE | Standing Advisory Council for Religious Education | TSM | Teaching Service Management [Botswana] |
| SAT | Standard Assessment Test | TTA | Teacher Training Agency |
| SCAA | School Curriculum and Assessment Authority | TVEI | Technical and Vocational Education Initiative |
| SCE | School Certificate of Education [Scotland] | UCET | Universities' Council for the Education of Teachers |
| SCITT | School-Centred Initial Teacher Training | UDACE | Unit for the Development of Adult Continuing Education |
| SCOP | Standing Conference of Principals | UDE | University Department of Education |
| SEAC | School Examinations and Assessment Council | UFC | Universities Funding Council |
| SEN | special educational needs | ULIE | University of London Institute of Education |
| SENCO | special needs co-ordinator | | |
| SLD | severe learning difficulties | UN | United Nations |
| SNO | supranational organization | UNDP | United Nations Development Programme |
| SOED | Scottish Office Education Department | UNESCO | United Nations Educational, Scientific, and Cultural Organization |
| SRHE | Society for Research into Higher Education | | |
| SVQ | Scottish Vocational Qualification | UNICEF | United Nations (International) Children's (Emergency) Fund |
| SYPS | Strathclyde Young People's Survey | | |
| TA | teacher assessment | UPE | universal primary education |
| TAFE | technical and further education | UWC | University of the Western Cape |
| TEC | Training and Enterprise Council | WASC | West Africa School Certificate |
| TGAT | Task Group on Assessment and Training | ZFET | Zionist Federation Educational Trust |
| TQA | Teacher Quality Assessment | ZIMFEP | Zimbabwe Foundation for Education with Production |
| TSC | Teachers Service Commission | | |

# Contributors

**Beatrice Avalos** is currently a consultant for the Chilean Ministry of Education, co-ordinating the preparation and implementation of a programme of improvement of the quality and equity of secondary education (MECE Media). Previously, she was Professor of Education at the University of Papua New Guinea and, before that, Senior Lecturer at University College Cardiff. Her field of interest extends to matters concerning teachers and teacher training, especially in developing countries. In this respect, she has been a consultant for the International Development Research Centre, the Commonwealth Secretariat and the International Institute of Education Planning, and participated in international research in the field. Her publications include books, edited books and articles relating to education in developing countries.

**David Blake** is Dean of Education and Social Studies at Chichester Institute of Higher Education. He previously worked in primary schools before taking up a post in initial and in-service teacher education at New College, Durham. His research interests are higher education and teacher education policy.

**Mike Cole** is Senior Lecturer in Education at the University of Brighton. He has published extensively in the area of education and equality. With Dave Hill and Sharanjeet Shan, he is the co-editor of *Promoting Equality in Primary Schools* and *Promoting Equality in Secondary Schools*, both published by Cassell. With Dave Hill, he is a founder member of the Hillcole Group.

**Lotty Eldering** is a professor at Leiden University, and, since 1987, has been Director of the Centre for Intercultural Pedagogics at the university. She has written extensively on the education of ethnic minority children at home and at school. The Centre for Intercultural Pedagogics has recently carried out a major evaluation of a home intervention programme for ethnic minority children. Professor Eldering has been a member of several commissions advising the Dutch government on educational issues regarding ethnic minority children.

**Paul Ganderton** teaches at Queen Mary's Sixth Form College in Basingstoke, UK. He has a doctorate in land use planning and a master's degree in educational management. He has written in the areas of geography, environmental planning and educational management. He has been involved as an exchange teacher in Australia. He also examines for the Cambridge and London Examinations Boards.

**Alma Harris** is a lecturer in Education at Nottingham University. She has published widely within the field of teacher education and school improvement. Her most recent research has focused upon effective teaching and classroom improvement. Alma Harris is a Research Associate at the International Centre for School Improvement at the Institute of Education, London.

**Michael Heafford** is currently a lecturer at the University of Cambridge Department of Education. He has made visits to France since the 1970s to study the educational system and has been the guest of many institutions from nursery schools to the École Polytechnique. At Cambridge he has run courses on the French educational system and has published many articles about it. He is particularly interested in teacher education in France and in the career patterns of French teachers.

**Dave Hill** is Head of Initial Teacher Training (Crawley) and Course Leader of the Crawley BEd for mature and non-standard entry students run by Chichester Institute of Higher Education. Together with Mike Cole, he founded the Hillcole Group of Radical Left Educators in 1989. The Hillcole Group is a socialist think-tank which publishes books and booklets through Tufnell Press. In addition to many publications in books and journals, he is currently editing (with Mike Cole and Saranjeet Shan) two books on equality in primary and secondary schooling. He was a Labour parliamentary candidate in the 1979 and 1987 general elections and Labour group leader on East Sussex County Council through the mid-1980s. He has been active at local and national level in the NUT and NATFHE teacher trade unions. He is currently an adviser on teacher education to the Labour Party.

**Roger Homan** took his master's degree in government at the London School of Economics and his doctorate in sociology at the University of Lancaster. Since then he has lectured in various of the social sciences and is now Principal Lecturer in Education at the University of Brighton. His publications include journal articles in politics, the sociology of religion and pedagogical issues in religious and political education. His most recent work, *The Ethics of Social Research*, is published by Longman.

**A. G. Hopkin** has worked as a schoolteacher in England and Kenya, and in the University of the South Pacific, University College Cardiff and the University of Botswana, and has been a visiting professor in assorted countries and universities, including Nigeria, Cyprus, Chile, Egypt, Australia and Canada. Professor Hopkin's current position is Coordinator, Affiliated Institutions, in the Dean's Office, Faculty of Education, University of Botswana. Research and publishing fields have included developmental aspects of education in changing societies, development and multicultural education and, currently, qualitative aspects of teacher training.

**Eric Hoyle** has been Professor of Education at the University of Bristol since 1971. He had previously been head of English in two secondary schools and senior lecturer in education at the James Graham College, Leeds, and at the University of Manchester. He has published extensively in the fields of organization theory, educational management and teaching as a profession. His books include *The Role of the Teacher*, *The Politics of School Management* and, with Peter John, *Professional Knowledge and Professional Practice* (Cassell, 1995).

**Trevor Kerry** has taught in the primary, secondary and further education sectors. He was successively the Coordinator of the DES Teacher Education project, principal lecturer in educational research at Charlotte Mason College, coordinator of a Schools Council project on primary education and a senior manager in further education. In 1989, he became Senior General Adviser with Norfolk local education authority, then Staff Tutor with the Open University. He has written widely, is a Visiting Fellow in Education at the University of East Anglia and is a member of the academic board of the College of Preceptors.

**Lesley Kydd** taught history and guidance in secondary education in Scotland before moving to the Scottish Vocational Education Council. In 1991, she became a Staff Tutor with the Open University School of Education and is based in Edinburgh. Her research interests are currently concerned with two different areas: the professionalism of teachers in a managerial culture and post-compulsory education; in particular, the linking of education to its economic outcomes. Her most recent publication is a co-edited collection of case studies in educational management.

**Geraldine McDonald** began as a teacher of home economics. After the arrival of three children, she became involved in pre-school education. Following postgraduate work, she set up an early childhood research unit within the New Zealand Council for Educational Research and later became Assistant Director of the Council. Her research interests include the education of women, the demography of the classroom and the culture of learning. She has been awarded an honorary doctorate of literature by Victoria University and was made an honorary fellow of the New Zealand Educational Institute. She is now Honorary Fellow in the Faculty of Education at Victoria University of Wellington.

**H. James McLaughlin** is on the Faculty of Elementary Education at the University of Georgia. He formerly taught in middle schools and received a PhD from the University of North Carolina at Chapel Hill. He teaches courses in middle school curriculum and action research, and conducts action research with several teams of middle school teachers. The studies focus on questions that teachers wish to pursue and on his interests in multi-age grouping and the effects of long-term educational relationships between young adolescent students and their teachers. He is editor of *Action in Teacher Education*.

**Gaontatlhe Mautle** is from Hukuntsi, Botswana. He is currently Dean of the Faculty of Education, University of Botswana. Before becoming Dean he was head of the Department of Primary Education. Starting in 1971, after qualifying as a primary school teacher, he served for seven years in different parts of Botswana. He earned his BEd from the University of Botswana and Swaziland, and his master's and doctorate from Ohio University. He is an expert on social studies and curriculum development in primary schools and a member of the World Council for Curriculum and Instruction and the National Council for the Social Studies. He has been involved in curriculum review panels and the promotion of educational research. Since 1984 he has been active in the Botswana Educational Research Association and has served BERA in various capacities, including as Vice-Chair and Chair. He is currently researching Education with Production in Botswana.

**Sohan and Celia Modgil** studied at the Universities of Durham, Newcastle, Manchester, Surrey and London (King's College and the Institute of Education). In addition, Sohan Modgil spent a period of time at the University of Geneva. They have written, edited and co-edited books on Piaget, Kohlberg, Eysenck, Jensen, Chomsky and Skinner, on controversial sociologists such as Giddens, Goldthorpe and Merton, and in the fields of multicultural education, cultural diversity, and education and development.

**Celia Modgil** has served as Head of Initial Teacher Education as well as Deputy Head of the Department of Educational Studies at Goldsmiths College, University of London. **Sohan Modgil** is Reader in Educational Research and Development at the University of Brighton.

**Anne Murdoch** is Professor and senior manager responsible for staff and curriculum development at City College, Norwich, and Professor of Community Studies. Her work involves the management of staff and curriculum development and related research for the college, which has 1400 staff and 15,000 students. Her research interests and publications include the management and development of education and training and the concept of 'community'.

**William I. Ozanne** has held a range of teaching, departmental management, inspectorate and examiner appointments within the teaching of English and religious education, and has been a consultant for general education and management areas. He has convened a series of international conferences on the implementation of educational policies at national and regional levels, founded the *International Journal of Educational Development* and is Secretary of the first UK national Forum for International Education and Training, bringing together professional bodies in the fields of educational research, teaching and consultancy related to international or comparative education. He is convening a commission on language policies for the World Congress of Comparative Education Societies. He is a board member of the Multi-Faith Centre, Birmingham, and of the Church of England Diocesan Committee for Relations with People of Other Faiths.

**Alan Peacock** is Senior Lecturer in Primary Science at Exeter University School of Education. He has worked in teacher education for twenty years in Britain and in various developing countries, including Kenya, Botswana, Namibia, South Africa, India and Mozambique. His particular research interests are in the evaluation of in-service training of primary teachers and in the use of primary science text material by second language learners in developing countries.

**Anne M. Phelan** is an Assistant Professor in the Faculty of Education at the University of Calgary in Alberta, Canada. Her areas of specialization include teacher education, teacher socialization and curriculum studies. She has published in such journals as the *Journal of Teacher Education, International Journal of Teaching* and *Teacher Education and Curriculum Inquiry.*

**Rosalind M. O. Pritchard** is Senior Lecturer in Education at the University of Ulster, Coleraine, Northern Ireland. She trains teachers of English as a foreign language and pursues research in the areas of language teaching, British higher education and comparative education. She has a particular interest in German education and is currently involved in a large research project looking into problems arising from German reunification.

**Hilary Radnor** changed her career from head of department in a comprehensive secondary school to an academic career in education in 1984. After working as an educational researcher at the University of Sussex and the National Foundation for Educational Research, she joined the staff of Exeter University to teach curriculum studies, evaluation of curriculum programmes and assessment of students' learning to undergraduates and postgraduates. Her research interests are arts educational issues and the impact of educational curriculum and the change of assessment policy into practice from a political perspective. She has directed a number of research projects in these areas, funded by the Department of Employment, Leverhulme and the Joseph Rowntree Foundation, which have been disseminated through journal and book publications.

**Julia Johnson Rothenberg** is a professor at the Sage Colleges, teaching at both undergraduate and graduate levels in education and educational psychology. Her primary teaching interests are in preparing teachers for classrooms of diversity and in global education. Her research interests are in the area of memory and past experience of schooling, as well as in multicultural education and teacher preparation. She has consulted for the United States Agency for International Development and World Bank Primary Education Project in Africa.

**Ken Shaw**, after teaching in schools for nearly ten years, has worked in teacher education for over thirty years. His PhD is from a school of management. He has published widely in the fields of curriculum and management, and has taught in the USA, Australia and Africa. He has carried out funded research for the Schools Council and the Manpower Services Commission. His current interests are in government policy, together with the evolution of the secondary and higher education systems in the UK.

**Bill Taylor** is Senior Lecturer in Education, University of Exeter. He has taught in schools, colleges and higher education in Scotland, England, France and the USA, and in universities in Tanzania, Nigeria and India. He is currently examiner in matriculation examinations in Malaysia, senior validator of undergraduate BEd degree courses in Malaysia and senior validator of BPhil and MEd degree courses that are delivered partly in Kenya and Mozambique and partly in the UK. His published material is in both comparative and multicultural education.

**Elwyn Thomas** is a senior lecturer and formerly Chairperson of the Department of International and Comparative Education, Institute of Education, University of London. His first degree, from the University of Wales, was in biological sciences and he has higher degrees in educational psychology from the University of London. He trained as a science teacher and taught in schools, technical colleges and teacher training institutions in the UK. He also worked in industry in Britain and Europe for multinational organizations. He has been a teacher educator in Malawi, Nigeria, Egypt and Singapore. He has also spent time researching in Malaysia, Thailand, Burma, Japan, Korea and Taiwan as well as carrying out consultancies in teacher education in Uganda, Kenya and Gambia. His research interests are in cross-cultural dimensions to schooling and pedagogy, values and moral education, teacher appraisal and assessment, staff development in education organizations and social and emotional contexts to human performance. He has recently edited a volume on international perspectives on schooling and culture.

**Keith Watson** is Professor of Comparative and International Education at the University of Reading, where he is also Director of the Centre for International Studies in Education, Management and Training. After serving with the British Council in several countries, he moved to Reading in the mid-1970s. He is author of *Educational Development in Thailand* and *Education in the Third World*, and has numerous other books and papers to his name. He is currently Editor-in-Chief of the *International Journal of Educational Development*.

**Sheldon G. Weeks** is from New York City. He is currently Director of Graduate Studies and Research, Faculty of Education, University of Botswana. Between 1962 and 1974 he was involved in research activities in Uganda, Kenya, Tanzania and Nigeria, and resident in Uganda and Tanzania for over seven years. His doctorate in sociology of education is from Harvard University. He has worked at Harvard, Makerere University and the University of Dar es Salaam, where he was Associate Professor of Sociology. He was a Research Professor and Director of the Educational Research Unit, University of Papua New Guinea, and from 1988 to 1991, Professorial Research Fellow at the Division of Educational Research in the Papua New Guinea National Research Institute. He has published extensively on education and development in Africa and Papua New Guinea. The research reported on in this chapter was carried out at the request of the Ministry of Education, Gaborone, Botswana, and supported by US AID. The material was updated in 1995.

**A. Douglas Weir** is Professor of Education in the University of Strathclyde and currently Vice Dean for Postgraduate Studies and Research in its Faculty of Education. He has had a varied career including periods as a teacher, as a researcher and latterly as an academic. Throughout all of these, his major commitment has been to teaching and teacher education. The major focus of his professional activities, and the subject of most of his portfolio of over 80 articles and books, has been the issue of vocationalism. From that issue he has developed an interest in the vocational dimension of professionalism as it is particularly reflected in the control exerted by governments on professions.

**John Wilson** lectures in the Educational Studies Department at the University of Oxford. He has also written widely in the areas of philosophy and moral education. He is the author of numerous books in this field.

**Tony Wing** teaches mathematics teaching at the University of Brighton and is involved in developing approaches to practitioner enquiry with teachers of mathematics.

**Peter Woods** is Professor of Education at the School of Education, the Open University, Milton Keynes. He spent 11 years teaching before joining the Open University in 1972, where for a number of years he was Director of the Centre for Sociology and Social Research. He is the author of numerous articles and books, including *The Divided School*, *Sociology and the School*, *Inside Schools*, *The Happiest Days?* and *Teacher Skills and Strategies*. He has recently been researching 'creative teaching in primary schools'. His latest books, *Critical Events in Teaching and Learning* and *Creative Teachers in Primary Schools*, are the first products of this research.

# Should Teachers Be Educated or Trained? The Ongoing Debate

KEITH WATSON, CELIA MODGIL
AND SOHAN MODGIL

The present volume is one of a series of four which look at the educational dilemmas that face governments, professional educators and practising administrators in the light of debates, disagreements and diverse opinions regarding many current educational issues and reforms. As far as possible, examples and contributors give an international flavour to the debates.

The idea for the series began some years ago but to bring it to fruition has taken considerable time. In many countries of the world there have been, and still are, rapid and fundamental changes in society, the economy and education, both in terms of purpose and in terms of shape and delivery. Many of the problems faced by individual countries have resulted from global economic pressures and changes, often originating from the policies of multinational corporations and international agencies (Kennedy, 1993; Ilon, 1994; McGinn, 1994; Watson, 1995). Many of the educational solutions to perceived local problems are often remarkably similar, either in terminology or in effect (see, for example, Turner, 1993; UNESCO, 1993; World Bank, 1994, 1995).

As a result, governments throughout the world are faced with a series of educational dilemmas resulting from these pressures and changes. A few of these can be illustrated as follows: how to exert *greater government control* while at the same time allowing for local autonomy at institutional level and allowing for the individual development of pupils within the school system; how to spread the *burden of finance* for an ever-expanding and changing system within increasing resource constraints (in the richer countries the emphasis is on

diversification and training, in the poorer countries it is still on meeting the demand); how to *maintain political unity* in the face of growing ethnic and cultural diversity; how to reform *the curriculum* and assessment procedures while at the same time raising academic standards; how to improve the *management and efficiency* of education through greater parental and community involvement in the decision-making process. During the past few years, the British government, as one example, has introduced a number of apparently very radical proposals for educational reform: restructuring examinations, changing the balance of control between the central government, local government and the community, industrial involvement in the running of schools, new ways of financing schools and universities, the autonomous management of institutions, etc. These culminated in the Education Reform Act 1988. Many of the reforms have aroused strong opposition and heated debate. Yet how far these reforms are radical, and how far they are part of an ongoing *international debate* about resolving crucial education dilemmas, has never been adequately addressed.

It is interesting to note that the British government used *comparative educational studies* to justify loans at higher education level and the introduction of a common curriculum at school level, but it has chosen to ignore other lessons that could be learned from comparative studies, especially in the area of teacher training. The levy of an education tax on industry to pay for technical education, as, for example, happens in France and Sweden; the accountability of locally elected school boards, as happens in the USA and Canada;

community finance for all post-primary schooling, now being developed in many Commonwealth countries – these are all examples of where ideas could be borrowed and lessons learned from comparative studies. Ironically, the British government could have strengthened its arguments from such data. Equally surprising has been the reluctance to recognize the likely effects of a free European market on educational provision, especially in areas of the National Curriculum.

Yet Britain is not alone in seeking to improve the quality of educational provision by reforming nearly every aspect of the education system, from parental involvement on governing bodies to the reform of higher education, from an emphasis on technical and vocational studies to the restructuring of teacher education. It is frequently argued that these policies have come about as a result of the influence of the radical right (e.g. Chitty, 1989; Flude and Hammer, 1990) but many of the current changes are not unique to the UK. Japan is looking afresh at its teacher education, the role of parents in school and the place of testing and assessment. For some years, France has been seeking to devolve greater power to headteachers in schools while at the same time it has been modifying its national curriculum. In the USA, not only has there been a growth of 'magnet' schools and private schools, especially among religious groups, but there is growing concern that the push for multicultural education is likely to endanger the unity of the nation. While all the developed countries are concerned about how best to continue financing the ever-growing educational industry, many less developed countries have already begun experimenting with novel approaches: community finance, fees, loans, 'bonding' and the like (see, for example, Bray and Lillis, 1988; Watson, 1991). The point is that educational systems throughout the world are either in crisis or in ferment and there is no common agreement about how best to deal with the issues confronting governments and professional educators. These are exciting times and there are many legitimate disagreements and viewpoints.

The aim of this series of books, therefore, has been to explore these disagreements and debates in educational circles, as well as the dilemmas facing many governments and policy-makers from a variety of perspectives, and, wherever possible, incorporating an international and comparative perspective. There are thus single-authored overviews, joint chapters incorporating a general agreement on differing perspectives, joint chapters in the form of a dialogue between differing academic contenders and position papers leading to critical responses. Where possible, the last approach has been encouraged. The variety of presentations reflects the range of issues and approaches felt to be most appropriate by the different authors.

As far as possible the editors have sought to attract an international authorship providing international insights on the educational issues and dilemmas concerned. Interest in the series has been immense and the authorship, already large, could easily have been increased by another 50 per cent. Unfortunately it is a comment on our times that many interested academics simply felt that they did not have the time to contribute because of pressures of work and other commitments. The fact that so many have given of their labours to contribute is both a measure of their interest and enthusiasm and a result of some cajoling from the editors! But for all those who have contributed there is a united sense of gratitude that time has been set aside from already very busy schedules to become involved.

## Legitimate areas of debate

The broad areas of these four volumes – teachers and teacher education, the reform of higher education, the control of education and quality in education – were finally selected by the publishers as being perceived to be the most pertinent educational issues facing many countries during the 1990s. It is to these that we now turn.

Central to the debate in many countries have been legitimate concerns about the *purposes* of education. Should education be confined to school and college levels only, or should it involve adults learning throughout life? Should it be a training for specific employment opportunities, for survival in an increasingly harsh economic climate, or should it, as many of the great educational philosophers have argued over the years (UNESCO, 1994) and as most national statements of educational goals and purposes imply, be for the development of moral, social, intellectual, aesthetic and physical development of the *individual*, irrespective of his or her station in life? Closely linked with these concerns have been related debates about the *content* of education. These have ranged around whether or not there should be a common, or core, curriculum, such as has enveloped much educational argument in Australia, England and Wales and the United States, or whether there should be a nationally prescribed curriculum but with elements of local flexibility. In any case, who should have the ultimate say over the content of individual subjects on the curriculum – subject specialists, curriculum planners, teachers, businesspeople/industrialists, politicians or parents, or some combination of any or all of these – has also proved to be controversial. As several chapters in Volume Four, particularly, imply, there is considerable disagreement about individual areas of the curriculum.

While these debates have ranged from the heated and esoteric to the political and philosophical, by far the majority of the world's nations have neither the inclination nor the financial wherewithal to implement fundamental curriculum changes. Their concerns have focused on issues of *quality*: quality of provision, quality of teaching, quality in terms of efficient use of scarce resources, the quality of the graduates from the different levels of the system. As several authors in Volume Four highlight, this interest has spawned a whole new literature appertaining to quality in education, most of the original material emanating from an industrial or business environment.

Perhaps this is not surprising, since many governments have recognized both the financial costs of a national education system and the need to ensure that costs are kept under control, but there is also a belief that part of the quality issue is the efficient, and effective, use of increasingly limited resources. In a number of countries this has led to moves to decentralize educational administration,

ostensibly on the grounds of increasing parental and community involvement in local decision-making as well as participation in the running and administration of schools, but in reality it has been a backdoor way of encouraging, some would say of forcing, local communities to make a greater financial contribution to the education of their children. This is nowhere truer than in higher education. At the school level, however, it has been assumed that greater financial and administrative responsibility at local, and especially at institutional, level would lead to greater managerial efficiency, improved effectiveness of the process of schooling and 'ultimately' improved quality in the whole educational process (Lockheed and Verspoor, 1990). This has certainly been key to the thinking of the British and several Canadian provincial governments, as well as that of the Czech, Bulgarian and New Zealand governments. Some of these issues, and the fallacies lying behind them, are addressed in Volume Three.

For many politicians and educational theorists, however, quality improvement is measured not in terms of administrative reform or institutional management autonomy but in terms of outcomes. As a result, assessments, examinations and the place of testing in schools are put under the microscope, as a number of chapters in Volume Four highlight. But it is very clear that, in this area alone, there is considerable scope for professional disagreement and debate.

Curriculum control, raising academic standards through administrative and financial reforms and the extension of standardized tests and introducing criteria for a quality audit of both individuals and institutions are only a few of the educational concerns confronting most governments. For the majority, the bottom line is the amount of the national budget that is, or can be, made available for education, where savings can be made and where additional revenue can be raised. One major area is to allow the development of private institutions or even to encourage fee-paying in the state sector, as encouraged by several World Bank staff (see, for example, Psacharopoulos, 1990).

Probably in no other educational area have the issues of privatization and fee-paying been so acutely felt, and so hotly debated, as in higher education (see World Bank, 1994; Buchert and King, 1995). In nearly every country of the world higher education has come under scrutiny during the past few years. New types of institution have been developed, and debates about the place and purpose of higher education, whether as a training ground for specific areas of employment or as a training ground for the intellect alone, have been endemic. This is partly because of the rapid expansion of universities and other tertiary-level institutions since the 1960s, partly because many graduates are no longer guaranteed employment in the public sector, and have found it difficult to obtain meaningful employment for which they believe that their training and experience qualify them. As a result, increasing numbers of students clamour for the next, higher level of education at master's or postgraduate standard. This diploma escalation, and its knock-on effects on employment, has been critiqued elsewhere (Dore, 1976; Oxenham, 1984), but the cost of higher education, compared with both primary and secondary levels, especially in less developed countries, and more especially in sub-Saharan Africa (Hinchcliffe, 1985; World Bank, 1988), has more gradually been seen as a block on quality improvement because of the withholding of resources for primary education. Attempts at reforming the financial and administrative structures of higher education, government intervention in introducing new managerial techniques and quality audits, and the implications of these changes for both academics and administrators are addressed in Volume Two.

At the root of every education system, irrespective of level or type of institution, is the teacher. As a body, teachers' salaries consume between 75 and 95 per cent of the education budget. For each year of service they become more expensive. This principle applies in all societies, rich or poor, capitalist or socialist. The only problem is that in many poor countries neither the government nor the local communities can afford to pay them adequate salaries. In many parts of the world, therefore, there has been, and still is, a fundamental requestioning of the role of the teacher and the place and content of teacher preparation. There are widespread disagreements about both these broad areas, some of which are addressed in Volume One. In the Anglo-Saxon world the debate concerning the teacher's role and status has revolved around professionalism. How far is teaching seen as a 'profession' and how far, as a result of government intervention in the way schools are managed and financed, are teachers being deskilled and demotivated? In opening up schools, colleges and universities to market forces and treating them as business organizations, is there not a danger that commercial principles, as opposed to academic ones, become the predominant ethos? And if this happens, what effect will it have, or should it have, on teacher preparation? Much of the debate about teacher preparation has revolved around location and content, both in the industrial world and in the developing countries. Should training be prior to a teacher commencing his or her teaching in a school, or should it be inservice while teaching; should it be based firmly in higher or tertiary education, either through specialized teacher training institutions or through university departments of education, or should it predominantly take place in schools, as is being advocated in England and Wales? Should teacher preparation focus on pedagogical *training* or should there be a considerable input of general *education* and theory? There is considerable professional disagreement at both a philosophical and a political level over these quite legitimate questions, as the debates in Volume One highlight, but as the chapters showing some of the developments in differing countries also indicate, the issues that confront those involved in teacher preparation in the United Kingdom are mirrored elsewhere: teacher preparation is in a state of intellectual ferment.

So, of course, is the whole approach to the provision of education. For decades schooling was regarded as a public service to be funded by the state, with varying degrees of uniformity and cooperation. In many countries this is no longer the case, as chapters in Volumes One and Three illustrate. Principles of managerialism, market competition, parental choice and consumer (or customer?) rights have seen to that. Schools are being regarded as commercial propositions, business organizations, competing against one another for customers and clients – pupils and parents. No wonder there is such a heated debate; many people's long-held beliefs and assumptions about education are being forcefully challenged and they feel decidedly uncomfortable as a result.

The above paragraphs have only briefly touched upon a few of the debates and controversies that currently affect educational development in many countries of the world. Subsequent paragraphs highlight the more specific issues raised in the current volume.

## Teachers, teacher education and training

Part One focuses on the current position in relation to the professionalism and deprofessionalism of teachers. In the initial chapter, Peter Woods questions whether teaching is a science or an art, which is a crucial question, since policy, practice and training can be affected by the answer. The scientific conception has produced the 'behavioural objectives' model and a 'knowledge base' model. But such a viewpoint has not been popular largely because of social and political factors working against the emergence of a science of teaching since the nineteenth century. Woods considers this unfortunate, since science offers valid and reliable information, explanations for complex events, a defence against self-indulgence and a sound basis for action. However, science may not represent the better part of teaching, which, some argue, is more akin to art. For teaching consists of multiple forms of representation, is emergent, expressive and creative, has an 'emotional heart' and is risk-taking. Woods concludes that teaching is both science and art, a social construction, situated in time and space and imbued with values.

Douglas Weir's chapter gives an account of the interaction between states and professions. It takes as its focal point the actions of the British state, particularly during the unbroken period of Conservative administrations since 1979. One state profession – teaching – is the special focus of this chapter. Through an evaluation of the various

forms which the 'state' can take and the various ways in which it interacts with teaching, Weir tracks the shifts from social democratic to New Right philosophies. Weir concludes that the nature of the relationship between the state and professions has changed in a number of significant ways, that these changes are now under serious attack, particularly for their dubious 'business' orientation, and that without a redefined partnership between state, public and the professions it is doubtful whether all of society's goals can be reached.

Lesley Kydd reviews the nature of the current debate about the professionalism of teachers by drawing on two different education systems: those of England and Wales, and Scotland. She considers the context in which the education system functions and in particular how the ideology of the market place impacts on the management of schools and the selection and teaching of the curriculum. Kydd discusses the criteria – particularly those concerned with autonomy and knowledge bases – which have traditionally defined teacher professionalism, and examines ways in which the application of ideology to practice is changing the exercise of those criteria for teachers. The question of why the teaching profession is particularly vulnerable to the incursions of the state into arenas which have traditionally been within its control is also considered, suggesting that perhaps the internal structure of the profession itself is one of its inherent weaknesses. Kydd concludes that the professionalism of teachers is being restructured according to a different set of values and activities, which have less to do with important issues such as teaching and more to do with managing educational markets.

William Ozanne continues this theme by arguing that professionalism and market forces in education represent not so much optional models as separate value systems, destined to produce dilemmas for practitioners at all levels. Professionalism is linked to ontological essentials of humanity, market forces to pragmatic exchange balances between commodities. In all societies, plural value systems coexist. This is usually perceived as a struggle for dominance in which one value system strives for supremacy in a kind of discourse reducing the others to externalities. Ozanne draws on the OECD study of professionalism in teaching as well as the concept in business education and management consultancy. He also draws upon the role played by central government in relation to education, with the resulting models of partnership. He concludes by pointing to the ambivalence of educational economists over returns to investment and the relation between funding and the quality of teaching and learning. This suggests that committed teachers find ways of negotiating the dilemma in a kind of dialogue between the deep humanist culture of a country and the socio-economic styles and objectives of government. Where the dialogue is positive, both systems are enriched; where it is confrontational, both are dissipated.

Eric Hoyle identifies that it was the political right during the Thatcher years which imposed greater accountability – not least that of the market – on the professions. Hoyle considers to what extent recent policies have led to a deprofessionalization of teaching or to an alternative notion of professionalization. While accepting the need for greater accountability than in the past, Hoyle argues that the concept of a profession is being impoverished and reaffirms the importance of some elements in the older idea of a profession.

Alma Harris continues the theme of the steady undermining of teaching as a 'profession'. She argues that teaching is being systematically deprofessionalized and that teachers are being reduced to mere 'classroom technicians' by a 'competency-led' model of teaching. The chapter argues that a new professionalism is needed, based upon the epistemology of reflective practice. It suggests that deskilling and intensification will not be offset by an adherence to traditional notions of professionalism. Instead, Harris concludes that a redefinition of teacher professionalism is urgently needed to challenge and halt the current trend towards proletarianization.

The structures that facilitate teacher professional development and power are discussed by Beatrice Avalos. With examples from several country contexts, but thinking more concretely of developing countries, she attempts specifically to bring out the nature of what are called 'facilitative structures' of teacher professionalism, seen from the side of teachers and externally. Among the external facilitative structures Avalos considers are public opinion and policy changes, systemic factors such as salaries and work conditions, the gap between the power allowed to teachers and the power that is withheld from them and the role of institutional support mechanisms, such as teacher pre- and in-service training and professional support for teachers.

Part Two centres on recent policy directed to restructuring teacher education. Hilary Radnor and Ken Shaw's contribution takes the form of a dialogue which discusses the evolution of the teacher education system as it has striven to accommodate to changing demands. Both agree that the curriculum and approach to professional formation have moved to much greater concentration on school and classroom concerns.

Recent government policy in England and Wales, which has sought to control and curtail the part played by institutions of higher education in the initial preparation of teachers, is focused on by David Blake. He reviews the process of policy development, assesses evidence about the effectiveness of teacher education programmes, locates criticisms of the part played by higher education in teacher preparation and discusses the justifications advanced in favour of continued involvement. Blake argues that a resolution of this area of public policy will be influenced by the outcome of the campaign to establish a General Teaching Council for England and Wales. Meanwhile, there is likely to be continued interest, in schools and the teacher education community, as the Teacher Training Agency embarks on its objective of establishing more initial training in schools.

This impending increase of focus by policymakers on school-based training calls for a substantial consideration of the system of mentoring. Anne Murdoch, Trevor Kerry and Roger Homan debate the issues involved in the instigation of partnerships between schools and higher education institutions.

Anne Murdoch sets out a positive model of mentoring based on an argument that teacher education and development deserves appropriate resources, whether based on a model of school-based teacher education or on an ideologically oriented higher education model. Murdoch argues for a positive model of mentoring to support teacher education on the ground that good teachers have a great deal to offer their peers and those in training about the practices and ideologies underpinning education. While she recognizes that this must be managed and administered properly, she advocates a positive mentoring system throughout education, backed up by appropriate training for mentors. This includes those already in teaching as well as those who are in training to enter the profession. Murdoch emphasizes that the system must be set up to ensure that the best qualified enter the profession and those who are the best teachers remain in schools.

Trevor Kerry cites research findings to show that many experienced teachers are unlikely (without prior training) to possess the key skills required of a mentor, and highlights schools' procedures for appointing mentors, which lack rigour. Kerry explores motives for becoming involved in mentoring schemes and role conflicts for mentors (e.g. in assessing trainees). Kerry concludes that mentoring may not be as successful in achieving its purposes as its supporters claim.

Roger Homan argues that the new forms of advising and assessing the teaching practices of students have displaced the conventional intellectualism of academic staff with a new wave of instrumental professionals. Institutional managers knew that they had no option but to develop mentorship schemes and were left to sell these to their colleagues by means of their own choosing, despite some resistance to these arrangements from professionals who perceived their traditional role to be threatened and usurped. Drawing on observational field notes, Homan explores the tactics of management.

The issue of the relevance of educational theory to initial teacher education (ITE) in England and Wales is discussed by Dave Hill and Mike Cole. They question whether it is irrelevant or whether such a claim is indicative of a particular ideological position. In order to find an answer to this question, they refer to the views on ITE of various interested constituencies. They begin by outlining radical right perspectives on teacher education

and training, and then go on to assess data from headteachers, HMI/OFSTED, teacher educators and newly qualified teachers. To this they add a further piece of survey evidence on the attitudes of student teachers. The evidence, as a whole, controverts the stated opinion of the Conservative government and the radical right that there is widespread dissatisfaction with ITE courses and their theoretical content.

Part Three draws together a number of differing insights on teacher education. Geraldine McDonald examines the debate about where to train teachers within comparative and historical contexts. McDonald considers that this debate is bound up with debates about women's role and the effect of academic pursuits on their reproductive function. McDonald considers that the establishment of teacher training colleges created a structural barrier to a graduate profession which it has taken a long time to overcome. Further, the factors of gender and social class can be identified today in policies such as school-based training.

Anne Phelan sets out to rethink the discourse of reflection, which has reverberated in teacher education in North America, by analysing its Enlightenment assumptions, namely its faith in the power of a rational, conscious mind to decide on action, to control future principled practice and to be responsible for what one does and who one is. Drawing on contemporary post-modern critiques of the Enlightenment, she first examines epistemologies and practices within the reflection discourse, before introducing an alternative metaphor with a distinctly post-modern flavour, which she thinks might better direct our efforts in faculties of education.

James McLaughlin continues this theme by analysing further the forms and the operation of reflection. The chapter is framed as an analysis of Vygotskian and Bakhtinian theory, followed by a set of considerations that are intended to dig at the root of what reflection is, how one becomes a more reflective practitioner and how teacher educators might foster reflective action.

In continuation, Dave Hill argues for the retention and development of critically reflective teacher education and proposes principles for the development of teachers as critically reflective 'transformative intellectuals'. First, he provides an analysis of Zeichner and Liston's threefold categorization of different 'levels' or 'types' of reflection in (teacher) education: 'technical', 'situational/contextual' and 'critical'. Second, he evaluates the current, limited, state of reflection in ITE. Reflection is placed in the political context of the restructuring of teacher education in contemporary Britain and government attempts to prioritize 'technical' reflection in ITE and to inhibit the development of 'critical' reflection. Third, he discusses a number of problems with reflection. Finally, the chapter examines the effectiveness of reflective and of critical reflective ITE courses in affecting the ideologies and material practices of student teachers, and differences within the radical left over critical reflection and the development of teachers as transformative intellectuals.

Tony Wing utilizes Aristotle's distinction between technical and practical pursuits to analyse current developments within higher education approaches to 'teaching and learning'. In particular, a technical as opposed to practical mentality is seen to lie behind an increasing loss of distinction between 'education' and 'training', a continuing lack of attention to teaching itself and systematic deployment of the language of training for the regulation of teaching. Wing is of the view that the current dominance of technical thinking is related to the promulgation of a free-market ideology. He proposes that, contrary to current trends, a practical approach to education be taken and the teaching of areas of significant expertise, itself an area of considerable expertise, be recognized as crucial to 'teaching and learning' and substantially developed.

Part Four draws on international perspectives on reforms in teacher education. Rosalind Pritchard shows that the Education Act 1994, the move towards school-based initial teacher training (ITT) and the current emphasis on competences and mentors can all be subjected to criticism in the light of experience in some other countries, notably the USA, France and Germany. She expresses concern about the adverse influence that the recent reforms of British ITT is likely to have on British society in the long term.

While the UK government is advocating ever greater school involvement in ITT, the French government has just put an end to a school-based form of training secondary school teachers, which operated for forty years between 1950 and 1990. In its place, the French have created institutions which require much greater university involvement than before. Michael Heafford comments that although the reform had motives wider than the abandonment of the school-based model – in particular a desire to bring the training of primary teachers and secondary teachers into greater harmony – it is important to examine their evaluation of school-based training with a view to discovering why it was not incorporated into their reform plans. Heafford acknowledges that the involvement of schools in the training process is clearly essential. The crucial question concerns the percentage balance between the inputs of schools and training institutions which brings the maximum benefits and the minimum disadvantages. French experience shows that when students spend 80 per cent or more of their training time in schools, the course they experience is likely to be defective in important respects. In particular, it will probably lack coherence, be very dependent on the quality of individual mentors and promote narrow models of desirable classroom performance. Heafford reflects that if one proposes that the outcomes of similar policies in the UK will not be the same as in France, it needs much more persuasive arguments to justify such a claim than have so far been forthcoming.

Elwyn Thomas traces briefly the relationship between values, values education and interculturalism, and continues to examine values transmission as part of the current debate on cultures of training. A number of key cultural dilemmas are identified, including cultural adjustment to values old and new, individualism versus collectivism, consensus and diversity, contrived universalism versus relative values. Thomas discusses these dilemmas in the context of recent developments in the field in Japan, Malaysia, Singapore, Indonesia and elsewhere. In order to facilitate choice between the various dilemmas, Thomas puts forward a proposition for the development of a culture-sensitive pedagogy, which requires a rigorous cultural analysis to establish need and the development of an appropriate theoretical basis from which the problems of planning and implementation can be adequately addressed.

Bill Taylor and Alan Peacock centre on teacher education in developing countries, which continues to be problematic, in terms of funding, levels of entry and qualification, balance of emphasis between phases and delivery systems, and the role to be played by external aid donors. They focus primarily on the influence of such external inputs on policy and practice, addressing external and in-country provision and the constraints on the effectiveness of both strategies. They further highlight the tensions between policy appearances and practical actuality, between the demands of quality and relevance, between ethics and expediency and between instrumental adequacy and professional principles. Reference to case study evidence from Kenya, Botswana, Nigeria, Malaysia and South Africa gives support to the discussion.

Gaontatlhe Mautle and Sheldon Weeks focus further on Botswana when they consider some of the proposals to improve teacher incentives in Botswana from the perspective of the constraints faced by the state, and then the perspective of the key actors in the education system – the teachers.

Continuing in the context of Botswana, Tony Hopkin presents the thesis that university affiliation is an effective *modus operandi* for raising the quality of teacher training in developing countries, especially small countries. The model of affiliation that has been developed by the University of Botswana is used as a case study. Specific features of the Botswana model, such as the pattern of moderation that has been evolved and the procedures that have been installed to effect institutional improvement, are discussed, with particular attention paid to the 'political' context, the issues that generate tension, the role of the faculty of education in promoting quality in teacher training and how the system of affiliation could be made more effective.

Lotty Eldering and Julia Johnson Rothenberg centre on educational models associated with multicultural education – disadvantages or defi-

cit, enrichment, bicultural competence, collective equality or multicultural constructivism – drawing on anthropology and education and making reference to the USA and the Netherlands.

In a comparative study of New South Wales (Australia) and Hampshire (UK), Paul Ganderton surveys senior school principals to examine their ideas, pressures and reactions to training. Although they do the same job, there is considerable diversity of response between nations.

These chapters offer fresh insights, stimulating debates and differing perspectives on two central educational issues facing governments at the end of the twentieth century: how are teachers perceived by society – and governments – and how best should they be prepared for new tasks?

# References

Bray, M. and Lillis, K. (eds) (1988) *Community Financing of Education: Issues and Policy Implications in Less Developed Countries*. Oxford: Pergamon Press.

Buchert, L. and King, K. (eds) (1995) *Learning from Experience: Policy and Practice in and to Higher Education*. The Hague: CESO.

Chitty, C. (1989) *Towards a New Education System: The Victory of the New Right?* London: Falmer Press.

Dore, R. (1976) *The Diploma Disease*. London: Allen and Unwin.

Flude, M. and Hammer, M. (eds) (1990) *The Education Reform Act 1988: Its Origins and Implications*. London: Falmer Press.

Hinchcliffe, K. (1985) *Higher Education in Sub-Saharan Africa*. Washington, DC: World Bank.

Ilon, L. (1994) Structural adjustment and education: adapting to a growing global market. *International Journal of Educational Development*, **14** (2), 95–108.

Kennedy, R. (1993) *Preparing for the Twenty First Century*. New York: HarperCollins.

Lockheed, M. and Verspoor, A. (1990) *Improving the Quality of Primary Education in Developing Countries*. Washington, DC: World Bank.

McGinn, N. (1994) The impact of supranational organisations on public education. *International Journal of Educational Development*, **14** (3), 289–98.

Oxenham, J. (1984) *Education v. Qualifications*. London: Allen and Unwin.

# Part One

## Professionalism and Deprofessionalism of Teachers

# 1 Is Teaching a Science or an Art?

PETER WOODS

## Introduction: the issue

Is teaching a science or an art? Does it matter? The question, in one form or another, has long intrigued educationists. In essence, the debate is about whether teaching is an activity where some general laws or principles can be identified, which can be understood in scientific terms, facilitating planning or prediction; or whether it is largely an individualistic, intuitive, spontaneous process, involving so many factors that it is impossible to specify general lines of direction, and producing work of creative imagination. It is a small step from here to another popular, intriguing question: are teachers born or made? If teaching is knowable in scientific terms, it can be taught. We can build on knowledge, cumulate wisdom, get better and better. If it is to do chiefly with instinct, imagination, emotion, etc., then it might be argued that people either have these abilities or dispositions or do not.

The debate, too, might be identified, to some extent, with the progressive–traditional issue, which reveals some implications for teacher practice. The former outlook favours learning by discovery and through play, creative activity, learning through doing, holism and integration; the latter emphasizes instruction, factual knowledge organized by academic discipline, systematization, structured learning, clear objectives and formal testing (Bell, 1981). Inasmuch as the National Curriculum for England and Wales, instituted in 1988, and its accompanying assessment arrangements are founded on traditionalist thinking, it would appear that the current trend in central

policy is away from artistic teaching, which had its heyday in primary schools during the Plowden era of the 1960s and 1970s. In the debate leading up to the 1988 Education Reform Act, there were complaints about the loss of teachers' artistic qualities. Brighouse (1987) bemoaned the loss of spontaneity, while Barker (1987) now felt that 'visions were off the agenda'.

This, however, would be to take a very limited view of science. Educational theorists and social scientists are among the folk devils in the central government policy behind the reforms, while relatively popular among those of more 'progressive' persuasion. This issue is, of course, value-oriented, to do with the kind of society we wish to promote and the kind of education best suited to that aim. We might ask whether, over and above the values, there is a purer heart of education. Whatever the ends, are they best promoted by scientific or artistic means? I shall examine the cases for teaching as a science and as an art, before trying to draw a conclusion.

## Teaching as science

### The objectives model

To say that teaching is a science is to say that it is a rational activity, subject to general principles and laws, that are discoverable through research. As we come to know them, so teaching can become more systematic, structured and stable. Our aims are inevitably value-oriented, but, as J. S. Mill observed, we have to 'hand [our ends] over to science' for the best methods of achieving them. The more clearly we can specify our aims, the better. In one form, such thinking promotes the rational planning of a curriculum by objectives, which are harder-edged and more precise than general aims, and which, preferably, can be measured. This 'behavioural-objectives' model is the most prominent example of this approach, defining education as the 'changing of behaviour' (which includes thinking and feeling). As Sockett (1976, p. 17) points out, 'By eliminating the value aspect from the definition, the processes of education can be tackled by science. Furthermore, by making objectives measurable, you can see exactly what has been achieved, and what more needs to be done.'

Some have felt that these techniques are more appropriate for 'training' than for 'education', that they exert a constraining straitjacket on teachers and ignore the educational worth of processes as opposed to ends (Stenhouse, 1975). They are more about efficiency than educational quality. Nor can they so easily be separated from values. Specifying objectives is useful for teacher accountability as well as for assessing student achievement. The whole framework seems ready made for the marketing ideology that has informed government policy in the 1980s and 1990s (Ball, 1993). In short, the objectives model may represent a scientific means, but in respect of a highly specific and limited view of education.

## The knowledge base of teaching

In an attempt to conceive of teaching in a more comprehensive way and from the point of view of the teacher, for the purposes of teacher training, Shulman (1986, 1987) advances a 'knowledge base' model. The knowledge base, in summary, consists of content knowledge, general pedagogical knowledge, curriculum knowledge, pedagogical content knowledge, knowledge of learners, educational contexts, educational ends, purposes

and values. To take one example, pedagogical content knowledge includes

the most useful forms of representation of those ideas, the most powerful analogies, illustrations, examples, explanations and demonstrations – in a word, the ways of representing and formulating the subject that make it comprehensible to others. Since there are no single most powerful forms of representation, the teacher must have at hand a veritable armamentarium of alternative forms of representation, some of which derive from research whereas others originate in the wisdom of practice.

(Shulman, 1986, p. 9)

Shulman maps out the area rather like early cartographers, who knew where to look and could sketch outlines, though without precision. The next part of the enterprise will be for researchers to 'collect, collate and interpret the practical knowledge of teachers for the purposes of establishing and codifying its principles, precedents and parables' (Shulman, 1987, p. 12). Shulman is keen that the 'knowledge-base approach does not produce an overly technical image of teaching, a scientific enterprise that has lost its soul' (p. 20) – as perhaps it did under the objectives model. He clearly recognizes the circumstantial nature of teachers' knowledge. Some feel that, in practice, he has 'begun to build a new educational science, a new foundational knowledge-base for teaching' (Hargreaves, 1994a, p. 19).

## A socio-historical explanation

If Shulman points to the possibilities, why has it not been done before? Both teaching and science have been around for some time. Simon (1988) provides an historical answer. In an article entitled 'Why no pedagogy in England?' (where 'pedagogy' means 'science of teaching'), he argues that such a concept has become 'alien to our experience and way of thinking' (p. 336). He is critical, for example, of the now defunct Schools Council (1964–81), whose work he asserts was informed by no science of teaching, no theories of the child or learning, and was in consequence doomed. Why is the concept of pedagogy shunned in this way? It is not because of any intrinsic defects or inadequacies in science, or because of poor teaching, but, argues Simon, because of social and political factors. In the nineteenth century, the main factor was the influence of the dominant elite institutions – the ancient universities and the leading public schools – which saw the profession of teaching as a gentlemanly one, not requiring training as such, but learning through experience for those with the 'appropriate social origins' (Simon, 1988, p. 337). The main purpose of these schools was socialization and the formation of character. Teachers, students and parents of these schools formed a common, self-perpetuating culture. Moreover, in the two leading universities of Oxford and Cambridge, education, until recently, has had a low profile – low prestige, few resources for research, lack of quality output.

There was a great opportunity towards the end of the nineteenth century, with the publication of Alexander Bain's book *Education as a Science*, where a programme of study was laid out for the scientific study of such things as child development, the purposes and principles of curriculum, motivation and discipline. However, the early 1900s saw the demise of the elementary school (which might have made a good forum for the development of pedagogy) as a vehicle for mass education, and the rise of the local authority secondary schools, which required children to be differentiated at the end of elementary education. Elementary education became a matter of containment; and the emphasis on selection bred a preoccupation with mental measurement, and psychometric theories which laid stress on inherited ability.

Simon goes on to specify conditions for a science of teaching – mainly a recognition of the human capacity for learning, and a recognition that the process of learning is similar for all human beings, and that therefore there are some general principles that can be identified. This should be our starting point: identifying what children and teachers have in common (see also Galton, 1989). Unfortunately, we have been diverted in the past twenty-five years into concentrating on their differences. This has to a large extent been due to the overwhelming influence of the Plowden Report (1967), which stressed the uniqueness of every child. However, instead of revolutionizing teaching in the romantic way envisaged therein, 'child-centredness developed into an ideology which came to exert a constraining influence on teachers' careers and cultures' (Alexander, 1984, 1992). Alexander explains that 'Ideology – a group's array of central ideas, values and beliefs – is a key element in any culture because it serves to define, justify and control a culture's members . . . properly to belong one needed to accept and enact the ideology' (Alexander, 1992, p. 169). The grip of this ideology on primary teachers illustrates again the nature of teaching as a socially constructed activity. Many teachers felt that they had to pay it allegiance (careers and jobs depended on it), while practising pragmatically (and unscientifically) in their classrooms (Simon and Willcocks, 1981).

## Private troubles, public issues

Similarly, we have laboured under the idea that teaching is an individual activity. Until recently, autonomy in one's own classroom was a central feature of teacher culture (Hargreaves, 1980). Here one could develop the practices and strategies that marked one's own individual adaptation to the demands of teaching. We have a tendency, too, to celebrate the idiosyncratic, charismatic teacher. All the great teachers of the past were of this kind. Features in popular educational papers, such as the current 'My best teacher' series in the *Times Educational Supplement*, encourage this mode of thought. However, we need to look at what teachers have in common. What are the regularities and patterns in their behaviour that permit us to see them as members of particular groups? What forms of reciprocal interaction take place between the teacher and these groups? What is there in a teacher's background, such as upbringing, schooling, home life, peer groups and personal experiences, that helps to explain a teacher's behaviour?

The 'charisma' of exceptional teachers may then be demonstrated as something learned and acquired, and available to others. Similarly, it might be shown that teaching weaknesses that might seem due to individual traits have other, stronger explanations. Societal and institutional factors, for example, can contribute to discipline problems within classrooms, though they are experienced as an individual concern. Social science reveals that what is a private trouble is a public issue (Mills, 1959), and it is at that level that it has to be tackled.

In yet another scenario, a teacher might appear to be giving a highly skilful and artistic performance. He weaves a spell with words, takes up the pupils' spontaneous questions, puts disparate things together imaginatively, uses space, timing, cadences of the voice, creates a suspenseful atmosphere; most of the children seem to be enjoying the lesson and respond. However, systematic observation reveals that he has twice as many interactions with the boys as with the girls, that his examples and encouraged answers from the children in a multiethnic class are monoethnic, that the questions he asks favour middle-class pupils, that the pupils are not internalizing the teaching but engaging in coping strategies. This may be artistic teaching, but artistic for whom? The reality is less exciting, more uncomfortable and disturbing. We don't want to believe it. It threatens to take the edge off our own enjoyment. At worst, it threatens to undermine our own hard-won positions. These are all reasons why scientific explanations may be resisted. There are other reasons.

## Opposition to science

The social and educational sciences are still young, and much of their early history has been taken up with a struggle for status in the universities. Philosophical bases have to be explored, methodological development and refinement set in hand. They are imperfect sciences (though it might be claimed that they are improving as the search for rigour and relevance goes on) and the early years have raised questions about the failure or inconsequence of much educational research (see Woods and Pollard, 1988). There has also been a great deal of political opposition. Under the 'New Right' regime of the 1980s and early 1990s, 'educationists' have been branded as the villains in the alleged 'declining educational standards' saga. 'They've had their say, and they've had their day,' announced Prime Minister Major at the Tory Party conference of 1992. It is not difficult to account for such opposition. Sociology, for example, adopts a critical approach, and identifies as ideologies (such as that of the 'New Right') what politicians regard as truth (often expressed as 'common sense'). Sociology shakes received, unsubstantiated opinion, and identifies and exposes questions of value. The best way of teaching, good teaching, the purpose of it, what pupils should learn – these are all issues on which people hold strong views, sometimes as absolutes. That they are questions of value is not always appreciated where they are held as articles of faith.

If some object to the social sciences' debunking and demystifying tendencies, there are others who turn this claim against them. Thus Olson (1992, p. 91) has argued that science is often used to apply a dead hand to justify existing practices and policies, which are based on the 'best social science available'. Thus, the 'mystique of science is used to defend the reputation of the schools against criticism'. However, this will not work, for the simple reason that 'experts do not know the whole story; only a small part of it. Teachers know more.' This may be so, but it can be argued that it is still, in time, 'knowable' to others through scientific means. This kind of criticism is more, perhaps, of how science is used, rather than of science itself.

Above all, perhaps, is the so-called 'two cultures' mentality which continues to pervade society. Science, despite its enormous contributions and potential, remains the second culture. The public at large have little scientific understanding, more students still opt to study arts subjects at university, and the teaching of science itself in schools has a low reputation (*Guardian*, 25 September 1994, p. 23).

## *The promise of science*

What, then, are the gains of seeing teaching as science? As a complex and difficult activity, teaching generates a great deal of myth, mystery and homespun, pragmatic advice to new recruits. 'Never smile until Christmas' is a common recipe for coping through one's first term. Much rests on intuition and instinct which defies rational explanation. 'It just seemed right to do it that way.' However, social science demystifies and enlightens. It establishes the nature and purpose of myths like 'never smile', showing them to contain a kernel – but only a kernel – of truth, but to function as warnings and guides to action, appealing to emotional states. It offers to explain the apparently unexplainable. In some ways teaching may be not unlike primitive societies in the guarded mysteries of its culture, standing to gain in similar ways from systematic study:

> In arriving at an understanding of how such societies work, anthropologists have inevitably thrown a flood of light on general principles of social organization and have enabled us to see how, on the one hand, apparently exotic customs are simply ways of coping with common human problems that we handle in different ways.
>
> (Worsley *et al.*, 1977, pp. 30–1)

Similarly, sociologists show how the daily lives of individuals are connected to broader systems of organization in wider society, and how those lives are distinguished by order and regularities, rather than adventitious, unconnected events. As Worsley *et al.* (1977, p. 54) note,

> In order to understand these interconnections in the world 'out there', we need a body of theory which itself is systematic. We cannot, in social science, operate effectively with bits and pieces of ideas unconnected to each other, as we often tend to do in everyday life.

Science depoliticizes, identifying values, ideologies, the micro-political nature of school life and the strategies deployed in the furtherance of aims. It provides information, explanation and intellectual tools for understanding social action, for delineating and solving problems and for planning according to our preferred choices. Used in the service of human understanding it is a creative, imaginative activity that sometimes reveals something surprising, and can energize and inspire. There is nothing cold about the descriptions of warmth and care for their children given by primary teachers (Nias, 1989); or in the excitement and inspiration felt during particularly promising or rewarding teaching (Woods, 1993a); or in the analyses of humour as a teaching accessory (Stebbins, 1980). Science is not the only factor involved, since 'decisions, in the end, will be made as the outcome of sets of complex pressures from many kinds of people: idea-mongers, power-wielders, organized citizens, etc, not social scientists alone, and not only on the basis of knowledge or reason' (Worsley *et al.*, 1977, p. 69). But it provides a good basis, and offers a means of assessing the consequences of those decisions.

## Teaching as art: the inadequacies of science

The view of teaching as a rational and stable activity amenable to scientific methods is one that has been created by social scientists; but it is not one that has been recognized by teachers. Indeed, teachers' views have sometimes directly contradicted research, even that involving very large samples (see, for example, Denscombe *et al.*, 1986). Eisner (1985, p. 91) speaks of the 'yearning for prediction through control' and the 'drive to discover the laws of learning' in the quest for effective schools that has characterized many of the approaches to educational evaluation this century. He argues that this was based on a particular, nomothetic view of person. Science has undoubtedly made important contributions in education, but it has also had some bad effects. In particular, it has oversimplified complex situations; prioritized the future (in the form of objectives) over the present (process); objectified knowledge, seeing it purely as cognitively grasped and quantifiably measurable; and bred standardization and uniformity. However, teaching is a socially constructed activity (Adelman, 1988). Schooling itself is a cultural artefact, and education a process whose features may change from individual to individual, context to context (Eisner, 1985, p. 91).

Science is also, in large measure, a socially constructed activity. Consider, for example, the cold-eyed, disembodied, male-oriented scientism that characterized prominent approaches to teaching as during the 1960s and 1970s (Casey and Apple, 1989). These saw the improvement of teaching as being reliant on developments in technology, and held a deficit view of teachers. More recent studies of teachers, and particularly women teachers (for example, Acker, 1989; de Lyon and Migniuolo, 1989), have shown the barrenness of those approaches. But are not more modern attempts at scientific appraisals, like Shulman's, more promising? Not according to A. Hargreaves. For him, such attempts

> conjure certainty from uncertainty. They build a science from a craft. They answer a modern problem (threatened professional status and peripheralization from the university) with a modern solution (reinvention of scientific certainty as an aspiration to higher-order foundational knowledge). What we can claim to know about teaching becomes defined by what we wish to regulate and control.
>
> (Hargreaves, 1994a, p. 19)

Elsewhere, Hargreaves (1994b) heralds the demise of 'reason and purposive rationality'. Disillusionment with them has set in with 'the uncertainties, complexities and rapid change of the postmodern world, along with growing awareness of the perverted realizations of science in war, weaponry and environmental disaster' (Hargreaves, 1994b, p. 28). Science has made important contributions to our understanding of teaching, but in relation to current realities, it can only reach a small, and not necessarily the most important, part of the activity.

## Features of an artistic approach to teaching

What, then, does that activity consist of? The following sections detail prominent features.

## *Multiple forms of understanding and representation*

Eisner (1979, p. 264) argues that 'rationality has been conceived of as scientific in nature, and cognition has been reduced to knowing in words; as a result, alternative views of knowledge and mind have been omitted in the preparation of teachers'. Such alternatives exist in 'poetry and pictures, literature and dance, mathematics and literal statement'. Abbs (1989, p. 15) adds 'our quite remarkable abilities to sequence narratives, to construe analogically, to conceive figuratively, to consider tonally, to think musically, to construct maps and diagrams, to make signs and symbols with our bodies' (see also Gardner, 1983; Noddings, 1992).

Highet (1951, p. 243) points to the irrationality of some of this:

> Painters do not copy what they see, but select very carefully, and the elements which they choose to select carry a meaning all the more powerful for being sometimes irrational ... What visual artists like painters want to teach is easy to make out but difficult to explain. They can hardly ever explain themselves, because they put their experiences into shapes and colours, not words.

This seems to be at the opposite extreme to scientific certainty. It would appear, therefore, that an important part of teaching is 'not knowing'. Moloney (1994, p. xii) expresses this well in his treatment of a poem by Walter de la Mare:

> We had been reading 'The Listeners'. It's a wonderful poem to look into with children of any age. So much mystery. So many unanswered questions. And the eerie heart of the poem, the throng of phantoms ranged in tiers on the stairway of the empty house utterly unmoved by the mortal banging on the door ... It's an image to enrich the subconscious and stay with you for a lifetime.

Would it be useful to have the poet appear to clarify the mystery? No, because if he did 'explain the enigma, then he'd kill the poem stone dead'. 'Doubt, ambiguity, uncertainty, unspoken implication, innuendo, it's these imprecisions, these echo chambers which breathe life into literature ... leading us to the edge of what we know.' In these areas, explanation closes down, whereas it is important to convey to students' minds how much we do not know, leaving 'the imagination free to create and fill the dark spaces'. Perhaps the art of teaching here lies in the teacher's professional judgement in circumstances where there is no 'right answer' (Tripp, 1993), and where we 'get to know' through all our senses, not just mind. (On the more general application of 'poetic thinking', see Bonnett, 1991.)

## Expressive and emergent teaching

In describing teaching as an art, Stenhouse (1985, p. 105) said that he meant that it was 'an exercise of skill expressive of meaning ... It expresses in a form accessible to learners an understanding of the nature of that which is to be learned.' It is essentially a 'personal construction created from socially available resources and it cannot be imparted by others or to others in a straightforward manner' (p. 106). The teacher's art is expressed through performance:

> There is in education no absolute and unperformed knowledge. In educational research and scholarship, the ivory towers where the truth is neglected are so many theatres without players, galleries without pictures, music without musicians. Educational knowledge exists in, and is verified or falsified in, its performance.
>
> (p. 110)

Carr (1989, p. 5), discussing the work of Schwab (1969), elaborates on what is involved in performance:

> Teaching is primarily a 'practical' rather than a 'technical' activity, involving a constant flow of problematic situations which require teachers to make judgements about how best to transfer their general educational values ... into classroom practice. Interpreted in the language of the 'practical', 'teaching quality' would have little to do with the skilful application of technical rules but instead would relate to the capacity to bring abstract ethical values to bear on concrete educational practice – a capacity which teachers display in their knowledge of what, educationally, is required in a particular situation and their willingness to act so that this knowledge can take a practical form.

This is similar to Eisner's (1985) point about 'connoisseurship'. For Eisner, educational improvement comes not from the discovery of scientific methods that can be applied universally, or from particular personalities, but 'rather from enabling teachers ... to improve their ability to see and think about what they do' (p. 104), or in other words, their 'art of appreciation', a subtle ability to discriminate. This contributes to what Polanyi and Prosch (1975) describe as tacitly held practical conduct knowledge, or what Tripp (1993, p. 129) calls 'practical professionalism'. Tripp contrasts this with scientifically verified knowledge, which is still important, but cannot account for the expertise of all successful teachers. He writes, 'Is this not expertise which comes from intuition, experience and "right-mindedness" rather than scholarly disciplinary knowledge?' (p. 128).

Such teaching is expressive and emergent, and cannot be set up in advance through, for example, objectives. Some situations may call for this, but employed as a general framework it forecloses on so many possibilities and opportunities for educational advancement. Teaching requires ends to be created in process, in the 'course of interaction with students rather than preconceived and efficiently attained' (Eisner, 1979, p. 154). Stenhouse (1985, pp. 80–1) elaborates on why the objectives model is inappropriate in some areas. Objectives tend to be oversimplified and self-fulfilling; militate against teacher and student creativity; distort the intrinsic value of content and process; render problematic the investigation of exploratory areas; discount the possibility of teacher development. While objectives may serve the acquisition of skills and information, they 'do not work in respect of knowledge, which is the heartland of the school curriculum'. This requires teacher judgement, but the objectives model treats the teacher as a kind of 'intellectual navvy working on a site plan simplified so that people know exactly where to dig their trenches without knowing why' (Stenhouse, 1985, p. 85).

Tom (1988), in consequence, argues that the effective teacher needs to be flexible; that is, able to adapt his or her behaviour to the teaching situation, which is changeable and frequently unpredictable. In fact, 'the dynamic nature of teacher adaptability, mediating processes and the teaching situation itself means that we can recognize teaching effectiveness, if at all, only after the fact' (p. 49). There is not much hope here for identifying the general principles and regularities, which Simon thinks is such an essential task. Indeed, it is a misconceived idea since it applies a 'purely technical perspective to phenomena intimately connected to underlying human purposes'. Tom concludes that research-based prescriptions do not make an effective teacher, but rather this is one who

> is able to conceive of his or her teaching in purposeful terms, analyse a particular teaching problem, choose a teaching approach that seems appropriate to the problem, attempt the approach, judge the results in relation to the original purpose, and reconsider either the teaching approach or the original purpose.
>
> (Tom, 1988, pp. 49–50)

He quotes Dewey (1929, p. 6) in this context: 'Judgement and belief regarding actions to be performed can never attain more than a precarious probability ... Practical activity deals with individualized and unique situations which are never exactly duplicable and about which, accordingly, no complete assurance is possible.' Eisner (1979, p. 161) also notes that 'to say that excellence in teaching requires artistry implies that the teacher is able to exploit opportunities as they occur. It implies that goals and intentions be fluid' – in contrast to the single-mindedness and clarity of objectives required by rational planning.

## Creativity

Not all teachers are artistic in their practice. Those who are are reflective professionals who think deeply about their work, and discuss it among themselves at length. They are very articulate, both in speech and in actions; and they are creative. The 'I' part of the self, as defined by Mead (1934), the part that is the source of initiative, novelty and change, is well to the fore. They have a measure of the 'me', the agent of self-regulation and self-control, for without it the 'I' could not

operate. But it is from the 'I' that novel acts 'emerge'. It is the main ingredient behind social change and adaptation. Mead argues that people develop different propensities for using the 'I' or the 'me'. The conventional form of the 'me' may be reduced in some cases. Mead gives the example of the artist, where 'the emphasis upon that which is unconventional, that which is not in the structure of the "Me" is carried as far, perhaps, as it can be carried' (Mead, 1934, pp. 209–10). Creative teachers are like artists in this respect. They acknowledge the benefits, indeed indispensability, of a measure of routine, but for them, like Mead (1934, p. 213), the health of both self and society depends on the abilities and freedom of people to 'think their own thoughts' and 'express themselves', and 'be original'.

> What this means for students is not so much that they should know *about*, but that they should *know*, physics, mathematics, biology, history etc. And this will include developing a feel, a sensitivity, a grasp, and a love for a subject, entering creatively into the *spirit* of an area of enquiry ... In short, students ... should be creative scientists.
>
> (Best, 1991, p. 269)

Best, in consequence, recommends what he calls the 'personal enquiry' approach, which involves developing qualities such as 'curiosity, originality, initiative, co-operation, perseverance, open-mindedness, self-criticism, responsibility, self-confidence and independence' (p. 275). This is what makes a creative individual, imbued with the spirit of creative enquiry.

There are some who feel that teaching is far removed from this kind of activity. For example, Willard Waller (1932), in his classic and widely influential text, painted a grim, unrelenting, depressing view of 'what teaching did to teachers'. It 'deadened the intellect', 'devoured its creative resources' (p. 391), made teachers 'inflexible' and 'unbending' (pp. 381–2), 'reduced their personalities' (pp. 431–2). Though this text was written in the 1930s, there are echoes for some in current times, with the trend towards the intensification of teachers' work, and the deskilling and deprofessionalization of teachers (Apple, 1986). However, while this may represent the reality for some, it is wide of the mark for others (for example, Nias,

1989; Woods, 1993a). Jackson (1992) also does not recognize Waller's description from his experience. He is convinced that teaching has made a big difference in his, and in others', lives. He cannot verify this against some external reality or conventional indicators. In considering what teaching has done for him, Jackson relies not on scientific evidence, but on intuition, what 'feels right' to him. This is far from being a matter of guesswork, and involves a host of factors to do with such things as principles, knowledge and experiences. It is to do, in short, with the sort of person he has become. It is clear that this is one with distinct artistic leanings. We have much to learn, he feels, from the Romantics:

> They constantly sought to look past the world or through it, to see beyond the surface meaning of things. They strove to 'read' their surroundings much as one might read a complicated text or a piece of scripture. Lovers of nature they certainly were, but they also worshipped the human imagination, whose power to envision more than the eye alone could behold was looked upon as the ultimate source of artistic achievement.
>
> (Jackson, 1992, p. 85)

Jackson notes that we must guard against excessive sentimentality, just as against Waller's extreme cynicism and despair. If we think in terms of the sort of person we wish to be and the kind of life we wish to lead, scientific objectivity is completely the wrong approach. What is needed is 'something more like a kindly bias, a forgiving eye, an attitude of appreciation, a way of looking that promotes the growth of sympathetic understanding' (p. 88). We must look at the minutiae of school life through an interpretative frame, cultivating 'a heightened sensitivity to the nuances of schooling' (p. 90).

Thus equipped, we would be better able to appreciate the beauty of teaching. Lincoln and Guba (1990, p. 55), in elaborating 'the art of craftsmanship', write of the 'power and elegance of a narrative, its grace and precision'. The same kind of description can be used of teaching. Highet (1951, p. 79) argues that teaching 'demands a good deal of artistic sense, and those teachers who plan their teaching best are usually marked by strong aesthetic sensibilities'. He mentions one who 'cannot utter a sentence without shaping it beautifully' (*ibid.*). We can expand that idea usefully to a whole lesson, or part of a lesson, which, as observers, we can marvel at as an object of beauty. The way a lesson unfolds, how a teacher creates atmosphere, uses a range of tones (Jeffrey, 1994), orchestrates conflicting elements in her role (Lieberman and Miller, 1984; Woods, 1990), balances priorities, dilemmas, pressures and her own aims through exercising a complex and demanding skill (Nias, 1989), involves her whole self and her pupils likewise in situations where they realize their full identity – all of this involves teachers giving an 'aesthetic form to their existence through their own productive work' (Foucault, 1979).

## Emotional aspects

In contrast to the emphasis on rationality, teaching has an 'emotional heart'. Hargreaves (1994a, p. 22) represents this as 'desire', which is

> imbued with 'creative unpredictability' and 'flows of energy' ... In desire is to be found the creativity and spontaneity that connects teachers emotionally ... to their children, their colleagues and their work. Such desires among particularly creative teachers are for fulfilment, intense achievement, senses of breakthrough, closeness to fellow humans, even love for them ... Without desire, teaching becomes arid and empty. It loses its meaning.

Highet (1951, pp. vii–viii) makes a similar point. Teaching involves

> emotions, which cannot be systematically appraised and employed, and human values, which are quite outside the grasp of science ... 'Scientific' teaching, even of scientific subjects, will be inadequate as long as both teachers and pupils are human beings. Teaching is not like a chemical reaction; it is much more like painting a picture or making a piece of music ... You must throw your heart into it.

Some even feel strongly emotional about the issue. Carl Rogers (1983), for example, regrets that he cannot be 'coolly scientific' about the point, but 'can only be passionate in my statement that people count, that interpersonal relationships are important'. Better courses, curricula and technology can never release full human potential. 'Only persons acting like persons in their relationships with their students can ever begin to make a dent on this most urgent problem of modern education' (Rogers, 1983, pp. 132–3). Such an approach involves

> a transparent realness in the facilitator, a willingness to be a person, to be and live the feelings of the moment. When this realness includes a prizing, a caring, a trust and respect for the learner, the climate for learning is enhanced. When it includes a sensitive and accurate empathic listening, then indeed a freeing climate, stimulative of self-initiated learning and growth, exists.
>
> (p. 133)

This does not mean that the use of emotion is undisciplined. As in drama, artistic teaching and learning provides opportunities for a range and depth of emotional expression, and these are associated with the search for truth and sincerity (Stanislavski, 1972). Teachers must mean what they say and do, and be clear in the expression of their emotions, thus encouraging similar responses and emotional discoveries among their students (Collingwood, 1966).

The emotional aspect of teaching is thus important in its own right. But it is also important for cognition. Mackey (1993, p. 250) argues that 'there are occasions when the emotions cause the senses to be heightened such that sights, sounds, smells, tastes and the tactile send stronger images to the brain ... Our grasp on the real world is deepened by the intensity of these images.' She gives, as an example, her own experiences on reading William Golding's *Inheritors*, describing the intensity of her emotion, simultaneously sparking the insightful cognition as 'vision' and awareness, but which she could formulate in words only in subsequent reflection. Through his work of art, Golding had caused deep appreciation in this reader of basic faults in humanity because of her heightened emotionality. Similarly, she had been involved in a play that had generated an uncommon amount of community spirit, possibly unattainable in the real world, but casting new light upon it. 'It was during the "high" emotional points of the show that this cognition was reached, when you were

transfigured, most vulnerable and receptive to issues of universal interest' (Mackey, 1993, p. 253).

What Mackey was experiencing here has been described by D. Hargreaves as a kind of 'conversive trauma'. Teaching has tended to be dominated by incremental theories of learning, involving the gradual, cumulative acquisition of knowledge and skills. This is no doubt relevant for some learning,.but misses out a crucial aspect. Bolton (1994, p. 65) has referred to how art has 'always challenged the boundaries of our existence', how artists are prepared to suspend the 'conventional orderliness of their everyday systems of thinking'. Art is rule-breaking, and cannot be predicted by theory. Rather, art informs theory, which promotes sound practice until challenged again by artistic thinking. This is not an easy area to study, but Hargreaves has developed a 'traumatic conception of learning' which goes some way towards describing the cathartic experience involved. In studying adults' experiences of art, he found them to have experiences not unlike religious conversions. He detected four elements in 'conversive traumas': the powerful concentration of attention; a sense of revelation (a 'new and important reality is opened up'); inarticulateness ('feelings drown the words'); and arousal of appetite (i.e. for more of the experience). The last is the most significant for education, being a powerful motivator.

I have tried to develop these ideas and situate them within a theory of learning which combines the virtues of sudden traumatic change and gradualness (Woods, 1993b). Full educational benefit requires pre-trauma preparation in the form of confidence-building, sensitivity-sharpening, skill development and acquisition of control and powers of expression. During the trauma, personal change occurs with new discoveries about the self, realization of new skills and abilities, formation of new attitudes, and new levels of appreciation. There is also social development, leading to new knowledge and awareness of others, and a sense of community spirit rising above the restrictions of institutional roles and statuses. The 'critical events', which provided the data for this analysis, were all characterized by: a constructivist teaching style; charismatic personal qualities of teachers and others involved; naturalistic context; cooperation; and grounded and open enquiry (see Woods, 1993b, for details).

Though the above analysis was applied to arts subjects, there is no reason why it should not also apply to science. Scientists also experience the thrill of discovery or invention, marvel at the wonder of the natural world, experience the thrall of involvement, witness the dramas that are enacted in the chemical, physical and biological world, appreciate its beauty, work within naturalistic contexts – all essentially artistic accomplishments. That these might not yet have been realized in school teaching is more to do with levels of resource and tradition than the intrinsic nature of the subject.

*Courage*

Artistic teaching is risk-taking and potentially rule-breaking. It can question 'the boundaries of our existence' (Bolton, 1994, p. 65). Exploration involves freedom to try out new ways, new activities, different solutions, some of which will inevitably fail. It is important that education provides that kind of opportunity and disposition to play, and to take it to the limit, for 'to be able to play with ideas is to feel free to throw them into new combinations, to experiment, and even "to fail" ' (Eisner, 1979, p. 160). Play stimulates the educational imagination and increases the ability to see and take advantage of new opportunities.

Courage is required to adopt an initiative that might not work and to abandon unprofitable lines of enquiry in good time, and try a new tack, i.e. be flexible. It also takes some resolution to go against convention, seeking the expression of a truth in a performance, based on some cherished values. Finally, it is a brave person who puts his or her whole self into teaching with whole-hearted commitment. These are the teachers who are most at risk of stress and burnout at times of severe constraint (Woods, 1990, 1995).

The aim is to achieve 'breakthroughs' in learning, and to encourage the development of 'critical students', able to think their own thoughts and make up their own minds (Woods, 1994). But there can be no critical students without critical teachers. As noted earlier, such teachers have come under increasing attack in recent years. However, I have elsewhere (Woods, 1995) discussed how some teachers are involved in 'resistance' and 'appropriation'; how 'cultures of collaboration' (Nias *et al.*, 1989) have been intensified, and self-determination generated; how potentially alienative forces have been 'recognized', and how teachers' own philosophies and goals have been more clearly 'identified'; how the changes have been 'engaged with', and 'alliances' formed. I argue that these schools manage to integrate the subject-based National Curriculum around their own distinctive relational ideas (Bernstein, 1975; Maw, 1993); and that they generate a form of power that is positive and productive in the realization of their aims (Foucault, 1980).

## Teaching as science and art

Social scientists tend to see teaching as a rational and stable activity amenable to science. Artists tend to view it as more variously expressive. Both groups would probably agree that there is no such thing as 'real' or 'genuine' teaching. To say this, or that teaching is a science or an art (or anything else), would be to be guilty of essentialism (Cohen, 1992). Rather, it is a socially constructed activity, the product of a set of relationships, situated within historical time and particular conceptions of space (Hargreaves, 1994c). It is also a political activity, never more so than in the struggles in education over the past decade. Some (for example, Apple, 1986) relate these developments to theories of intensification and the proletarianization of educated labour, which result in teachers acting as little other than technicians, operationalizing other's requirements. Some (for example, Powell and Solity, 1990), however, feel that many teachers are still in control to some extent, and that pedagogy is a matter of individual resolution.

What is clear, however, is that teaching is a complex activity that defies any single form of characterization. We would be likely to find examples of science, art, technical and clerical work, intensification and many others in the course of a typical teacher's day. Teachers are faced with many problems and dilemmas; they have their own interests and beliefs; yet they are at the centre of a number of competing values and ideologies; they are situated within a network of interrelationships and expectations. Viewing teaching as a science represents a lifeline through these stormy waters, breeding a questioning spirit, seeking evidence for claims made, looking for explanations and for alternative explanations, for general applications and commonalities, protecting against self-indulgence. As the educational sciences develop, we can hope for improved understanding, and ultimately a better practice based on secure foundations. If 'some of the subtlest qualities of good teaching will always elude research' (Chanan, 1973, p. 7), this should not obstruct the attempt to discover and understand them. What is subtle in one generation may become common knowledge in another.

Moreover, some of the more generally recognized artistic aspects of teaching are becoming more amenable to scientific methods. Ethnography, for example, in some of its manifestations, is both a science and an art (see, for example, Denscombe, 1991). It is a science in its concern for rigorous procedures in collecting evidence, constructing categories and formulating concepts that have general applicability; in its concern for validity (through, for example, triangulation); and in its attention to sampling. It is an art in its ability to paint pictures in words, to tell stories, to evoke the spirit and feel of situations, to represent feelings, meanings and understandings. It meets Eisner's (1985, p. 92) requirements for 'educational criticism', which is striving to 'articulate or render those ineffable qualities constituting art in a language that makes them vivid'. The task of the critic is

to adumbrate, suggest, imply, connote, render, rather than to attempt to translate. In this task, metaphor and analogy, suggestion and implication are major tools. The language of criticism, indeed its success as criticism, is measured by the brightness of its illumination. The task of the critic is to help us to see.
(Eisner, 1985, pp. 92–3)

This may, of course, not square with some conceptions of science. It has different criteria of validity and generalization, a different focus of study, eschews standardization of form and publicly codified rules, is concerned more with the subjective than the objective, experiences rather than behaviour, explication rather than prediction, the creation of meaning rather than the discovery of truth (Eisner, 1985, pp. 191–8). Some conceptions of ethnography, however, see it as having the same epistemological basis as any research method, though having a different focus (for example, Hammersley, 1990). It may be able to reach the parts that other methods cannot reach, but it is still a science.

In the end, it has to be recognized that science and art is something of an artificial division. Abbs (1989, p. 15) traces back to Descartes this 'mental schizophrenia', which 'broke the world into the harsh polarities of objectivity and subjectivity, reason and unreason, cognition and affect, science and the arts'. Richardson (1990) points to the division between literary and scientific writing from the seventeenth century, which had become complete by the nineteenth (see also Clifford and Marcus, 1986). 'The search for the unambiguous was the "triumph of the quest for certainty over the quest for wisdom"' (Rorty, 1979, p. 61, quoted in Richardson, 1990, p. 14). Nisbet (1962), also, in discussing 'sociology as an art form', points to how myths formed in the nineteenth century, namely that art involved 'genius or inspiration' and was concerned with beauty, while science was concerned with rigorously controlled method and objective truth. However, both, he argues, are concerned primarily with reality and with understanding, and both depend upon detachment. But it is the artist, or the artist in the scientist, that provides the 'leap of the imagination'. Science and art, therefore, rely on the same kind of creative imagination. Where art is defined out of science, the latter loses a great deal of its creative stimulation. Equally, where science is defined out of teaching, teachers sacrifice a wealth of rigorously acquired and tested knowledge. This reveals the poverty of debating whether teaching is a science or an art – as with most dichotomies and polarized thinking (Alexander, 1992).

Gage (1978), in a book entitled *The Scientific Basis of the Art of Teaching*, agrees with this. He does not believe it possible that some day good teaching might be achieved by 'closely following rigorous laws that yield high predictability and control' (p. 17). But scientists, when doing research, are practising an art. They use 'judgement, intuition, and insight in handling the unpredicted – contingencies of the same kind that arise when a painting, a poem, or a pupil is the target of an artistic effort.' As far as teaching is concerned, Gage concludes,

> Scientific method can contribute relationships between variables taken two at a time and even, in the form of interactions, three or perhaps four or more at a time. Beyond say four, the usefulness of what science can give the teacher begins to weaken, because teachers cannot apply, at least not without help and not on the run, the more complex interactions. At this point the teacher as artist must step in and make clinical, or artistic, judgements about the best ways to teach.

In a similar way, Brown and McIntyre (1993, p. 19) predicted that the results of their investigation 'will not be a set of standardized teaching behaviours; they will be personalized to the individual teacher, but there are likely to be certain over-arching generalizable features which are common across teachers'. They prefer to see teaching as a craft, involving complex skills learned from both study and experience (see also Marland, 1975; Tom, 1988). However, it is not just about skills and knowledge, but also involves 'issues of moral purpose, emotional investment and political awareness, adeptness and acuity' (Hargreaves, 1994c, p. 6; see also Olson, 1992). This does not mean, to return to a question posed at the beginning of this article, that teachers are born, not made, as they 'learn through the critical practice of their art' (Stenhouse, 1980; see also Rudduck, 1985). Nevertheless, some of these issues identified by Hargreaves have hardly been touched on here, or indeed elsewhere. Clearly, teaching is both a science and an art – and more besides.

## References

Abbs, P. (1989) Signs on the way to understanding. *Times Educational Supplement*, 10 November, p. 15.

Acker, S. (ed.) (1989) *Teachers, Gender and Careers*. Lewes: Falmer Press.

Adelman, C. (1988) Looking at teaching. Unit C1 of Course EP228, *Frameworks in Teaching*. Milton Keynes: Open University.

Alexander, R. J. (1984) *Primary Teaching*. London: Holt, Rinehart and Winston.

Alexander, R. J. (1992) *Policy and Practice in Primary Education*. London: Routledge.

Apple, M. W. (1986) *Teachers and Texts: A Political Economy of Class and Gender Relations in Education*. New York: Routledge and Kegan Paul.

Ball, S. J. (1993) Education markets, choice and social class: the market as a class strategy in the UK and the USA. *British Journal of Sociology of Education*, **14** (1), 3–19.

Barker, B. (1987) Visions are off the agenda. *Times Educational Supplement*, 3 December, p. 4.

Bell, R. E. (1981) Approaches to teaching. Unit 15 of Course E200, *Contemporary Issues in Education*. Milton Keynes: Open University.

Bernstein, B. (1975) *Class, Codes and Control*, Volume 3: *Towards a Theory of Educational Transmissions*. London: Routledge and Kegan Paul.

Best, D. (1991) Creativity: education in the spirit of enquiry. *British Journal of Educational Studies*, **34** (3), 260–78.

Bolton, G. (1994) Stories at work: fictional-critical writing as a means of professional development. *British Educational Research Journal*, **20** (1), 55–68.

Bonnett, M. (1991) Developing children's thinking ... and the National Curriculum. *Cambridge Journal of Education*, **21** (3), 277–92.

Brighouse, T. (1987) Goodbye to the head and the history man. *Guardian*, 21 July, p. 11.

Brown, S. and McIntyre, D. (1993) *Making Sense of Teaching*. Buckingham: Open University Press.

Carr, W. (1989) *Quality in Teaching: Arguments for a Reflective Profession*. Lewes: Falmer Press.

Casey, K. and Apple, M. W. (1989) Gender and the conditions of teachers' work: the development of understanding in America. In S. Acker (ed.), *Teachers, Gender and Careers*. Lewes: Falmer Press.

Chanan, G. (ed.) (1973) *Towards a Science of Teaching*. Windsor: NFER.

Clifford, J. and Marcus, G. E. (eds) (1986) *Writing Culture: The Poetics and Politics of Ethnography*. Berkeley: University of California Press.

Cohen, P. (1992) 'It's racism what dunnit': hidden narratives in theories of racism. In J. Donald and

A.Rattansi (eds), *'Race', Culture and Difference*. London: Sage.

Collingwood, R. G. (1966) Expressing one's emotions. In E. W. Eisner and D. W. Ecker (eds), *Readings in Art Education*. Lexington, MA: Xerox College Publishing.

de Lyon, H. and Migniuolo, F. W. (eds) (1989) *Women Teachers: Issues and Experiences*. Milton Keynes: Open University Press.

Denscombe, M. (1991) The art of research: art teachers' affinity with ethnography. *Journal of Art and Design Education*, **10** (3), 271–80.

Denscombe, M., Szule, H., Patrick, C. and Wood, A. (1986) Ethnicity and friendship: the contrast between sociometric research and fieldwork observation in primary school classrooms. *British Educational Research Journal*, **12** (3), 221–35.

Dewey, J. (1929) *The Quest for Certainty: A Study of the Relation of Knowledge and Action*. New York: Minton, Balch.

Eisner, E. W. (1979) *The Educational Imagination*. London: Collier Macmillan.

Eisner, E. W. (1985) *The Art of Educational Evaluation: A Personal View*. Lewes: Falmer Press.

Eisner, E. W. (1993) Forms of understanding and the future of educational research. *Educational Researcher*, **22** (7), 5–11.

Foucault, M. (1979) *A History of Sexuality*. Harmondsworth: Penguin.

Foucault, M. (1980) *Power/Knowledge: Selected Interviews and Other Writings*, edited by C. Gordon. New York: Pantheon.

Gage, N. (1978) *The Scientific Basis of the Art of Teaching*. New York: Teachers College Press.

Galton, M. (1989) *Teaching in the Primary School*. London: David Fulton Publishers.

Gardner, H. (1983) *Frames of Mind: The Theory of Multiple Intelligences*. New York: Basic Books.

Hammersley, M. (1990) *Classroom Ethnography: Empirical and Methodological Essays*. Milton Keynes: Open University Press.

Hargreaves, A. (1994a) Towards a social geography of teacher education. In N. K. Shimahara and I. Z. Holowinsky (eds), *Teacher Education in Industrialized Nations*. New York: Garland.

Hargreaves, A. (1994b) Development and desire: a postmodern perspective. In T. Guskey and M. Huberman (eds), *New Paradigms and Practices in Professional Development*. New York: Teachers College Press.

Hargreaves, A. (1994c) *Changing Teachers, Changing Times*. London: Cassell.

Hargreaves, D. H. (1980) The occupational culture of teachers. In P. Woods (ed.), *Teacher Strategies*. London: Croom Helm.

Highet, G. (1951) *The Art of Teaching*. London: Methuen.

Jackson, P. W. (1992) *Untaught Lessons*. New York: Teachers College Press.

Jeffrey, R. (1994) The art of primary school teaching. Paper presented at CEDAR International Conference, 'Changing Educational Structures: Policy and Practice', University of Warwick, 15–17 April.

Lieberman, A. and Miller, L. (1984) *Teachers: Their World and Their Work*. Alexandria, VA: Association for Supervision and Curriculum Development.

Lincoln, Y. S. and Guba, E. G. (1990) Judging the quality of case study reports. *International Journal of Qualitative Studies in Education*, **3** (1), 53–9.

Mackey, S. (1993) Emotion and cognition in arts education. *Curriculum Studies*, **1** (2), 245–56.

Marland, M. (1975) *The Craft of the Classroom*. Exeter, NH: Heinemann.

Maw, J. (1993) The National Curriculum Council and the whole curriculum: reconstruction of a discourse? *Curriculum Studies*, **1** (1), 55–74.

Mead, G. H. (1934) *Mind, Self and Society*. Chicago: University of Chicago Press.

Mills, C. W. (1959) *The Sociological Imagination*. New York: Oxford University Press.

Molony, R. (1994) Heart of Darkness. *Times Educational Supplement*, 30 September, p. xii.

Nias, J. (1989) *Primary Teachers Talking: A Study of Teaching as Work*. London: Routledge.

Nias, J., Southworth, G. and Yeomans, R. (1989) *Staff Relationships in the Primary School: A Study of Organizational Cultures*. London: Cassell.

Nisbet, R. (1962) Sociology as an art form. *Pacific Sociological Review*, Autumn.

Noddings, N. (1992) *The Challenge to Care in Schools: An Alternative Approach to Education*. New York: Teachers College Press.

Olson, J. (1992) *Understanding Teaching: Beyond Expertise*. Buckingham: Open University Press.

Plowden Report (1967) *Children and Their Primary Schools*. Report of the Central Advisory Council for Education in England. London: HMSO.

Polanyi, M. and Prosch, H. (1975) *Personal Knowledge in Meaning*. London: University of Chicago Press.

Powell, M. and Solity, J. (1990) *Teachers in Control*. London: Routledge.

Richardson, L. (1990) *Writing Strategies: Reaching Diverse Audiences*. London: Sage.

Rogers, C. (1983) *Freedom to Learn for the 80s*. New York: Macmillan.

Rorty, R. (1979) *Philosophy and the Mirror of Nature*. Princeton, NJ: Princeton University Press.

Rudduck, J. (1985) The improvement of the art of teaching through research. *Cambridge Journal of Education*, **15** (3), 123–7.

Schwab, J. J. (1969) The practical: a language for curriculum. *School Review*, **78**, 1–24.

Shulman, L. S. (1986) Those who understand: knowledge growth in teachers. *Educational Researcher*, **15** (2), 4–16.

Shulman, L. S. (1987) Knowledge and teaching: foundations of the new reform. *Harvard Educational Review*, **57** (1), 1–22.

Simon, B. (1988) Why no pedagogy in England? In R. Dale, R. Fergusson and A. Robinson (eds), *Frameworks for Teaching*. London: Hodder and Stoughton.

Simon, B. and Willcocks, J. (eds) (1981) *Research and Practice in the Primary Classroom*. London: Routledge and Kegan Paul.

Sockett, H. (1976) Approaches to curriculum planning. Unit 16 of Course E203, *Curriculum Design and Development*. Milton Keynes: Open University.

Stanislavski, C. (1972) Emotional involvement in acting. In J. Hodgson (ed.), *The Uses of Drama*. London: Eyre Methuen.

Stebbins, R. (1980) The role of humour in teaching. In P. Woods (ed.), *Teacher Strategies*. London: Croom Helm.

Stenhouse, L. (1975) *An Introduction to Curriculum Research and Development*. London: Heinemann.

Stenhouse, L. (1980) Curriculum research and the art of the teacher. *Curriculum*, **1** (1), 40–4.

Stenhouse, L. (1985) *Research as a Basis for Teaching*. London: Heinemann.

Tom, A. (1988) Teaching as a moral craft. In R. Dale, R. Fergusson and A. Robinson (eds), *Frameworks for Teaching*. London: Hodder and Stoughton.

Tripp, D. (1993) *Critical Incidents in Teaching: Developing Professional Judgement*. London: Routledge.

Waller, W. W. (1932) *The Sociology of Teaching*. New York: Wiley.

Woods, P. (1990) *Teacher Skills and Strategies*. Lewes: Falmer Press.

Woods, P. (1993a) *Critical Events in Teaching and Learning*. London: Falmer Press.

Woods, P. (1993b) Towards a theory of aesthetic learning. *Educational Studies*, **19** (3), 323–38.

Woods, P. (1994) Critical students: breakthroughs in learning. Paper given at International Conference on the Sociology of Education, 'Pupils, Students and Empowerment', University of Sheffield, January.

Woods, P. (1995) *Creative Teachers in Primary Schools*. Buckingham: Open University Press.

Woods, P. and Pollard, A. (eds) (1988) *Sociology and Teaching*. London: Croom Helm.

Worsley, P., Mitchell, J. C., Morgan, D. H. J., Pons, V., Roberts, B., Sharrock, W. W. and Ward, R. (eds), (1977) *Introducing Sociology*, 2nd edn. Harmondsworth: Penguin.

# 2 Professions under Change

## A. DOUGLAS WEIR

Thus, when millions of people are jobless or can only find part-time low-paying work, we blame the school. Standards have fallen. Our teachers are poorly trained. Our students haven't enough work discipline. They too are technically unprepared ... Don't alter the economy; 'simply' change the schools.

(Apple, 1986, p. 18)

## Introduction

In the late 1970s there was a clear shift in thinking about public services among the major political parties in Great Britain. The shift was away from the post-Second World War consensus on welfare towards more competitive approaches to state services.

Within these changes there was a steady assault on the power of professionals to control services on behalf of the community, and a move towards control by managers and lay governing bodies, to whom the professionals were made accountable and through whom the status of professionals was diminished. Such tendencies could be observed in many Western democracies, even social democratic flagship states such as Sweden (Askling and Almén, 1993), and across many services, including health, employment and social work.

As the state is not, however, a single entity, the assault on the 'state professions' comes in a variety of forms. In the forefront are the government ministers who, if they show the energy and ideological commitment familiar in British Conservative governments since 1979, can promote and see on to the statute book almost any policies they choose.

Around them is the 'state apparatus' of senior civil servants and advisers (both inside and outside Parliament), whose support is required in the development of new policies and their implementation. And the state also has a 'local face', where elected local government can either obstruct or promote national policy (Lawn and Grace, 1987, p. 196). But around the 'political state' there are a number of other powerful groupings from whom, at the very least, assent is required if the political state is to affect change. Among them are the business community, consumer groups and the professionals themselves.

The business community is particularly influential when, as in recent years, economic considerations have dictated the social agenda. Consumer groups such as patients in health care and parents in education are influential because of their electoral power at general and local elections. Professional groups are highly experienced and have a power of association, through both of which they can ease or block the implementation of state policies.

The 'social democratic consensus' of the 1950s and 1960s was perceived by the New Right as having failed. They sought to replace it by policies which would improve the economic position of the major Western democracies. That social democratic consensus had set as its major criteria equality, protectionism and welfare, whereas for the New Right the principal objectives were excellence, choice and value for money (Knight, 1990, pp. 154–5).

As policy shifted towards the right, however, it had a number of conflicting representations. For example, the aspect of rightism described as 'post-Fordism' sought to develop flexibility and innovation in individual firms, while at the same time creating segmentation by status, gender and geographical location in society as a whole (Ball, 1990, p. 125), Similarly, in managerial terms, there was a differentiation between 'strong state' and 'weak state' philosophies, where in the public sector of social, educational and training policy the state increased its powers of centralization and control, while in the private sector of economic and industrial policy the state attempted to minimize government intervention (Esland, 1994, p. 4). And finally, rightism's influence varied across the regions of a country if the political balance of power was more fragile than prevailed at the centre. Taking Britain as one example of this, local government and national parliamentary representation in Scotland have both been dominated by the Labour Party in the 1980s and 1990s. The British state has accordingly been much more cautious in implementing rightist policies in Scotland or else has often found itself defeated by communities which prefer a form of social democratic consensus (Kydd and Weir, 1994).

As a large but vulnerable state service, education and its professionals have been the most vigorously attacked. The attack on education was consistent with the dominant ideologies of right-wing governments such as those led by Ronald Reagan and Margaret Thatcher.

Under a succession of Secretaries of State for Education, the Thatcher government in Britain introduced a series of legislative measures designed to bring public education under closer central control. While some of these changes were an attack on opposition local education authorities – typically described by Tories as the 'loony left' because of their progressive views on classroom behaviour, sexism and racism – most of the attack was made against teachers and teaching. The Conservative governments recognized that only by undermining teacher power and teacher status could they implement national testing and a national curriculum, take over the governance of schools and make the education service more publicly accountable.

The state succeeded in these transformations for a number of reasons. There had, for example, been considerable parental opposition to many pupil-centred, apparently *laissez-faire*, practices which were claimed to hinder the acquisition of skills of reading, writing and arithmetic. The education system in England was extremely diverse, including private-sector and grammar schools where the appeal of the New Right fell on fertile ground, unlike in Scotland, where the dominant school is still the neighbourhood comprehensive. The teaching profession itself was divided by competition among a variety of trade unions, again unlike in Scotland, where there is one dominant union. And, finally, the parliamentary majority of the Conservative Party, especially in the 1980s, was so large and the education policies of the Labour Party so ambivalent that there was no opposition to the New Right, no pluralism in debate. Not only had the Labour Party practised a very narrow form of 'statism' in the 1960s, but it had started the attack on the power of the 'educational experts' in the 1970s. By the 1990s its policy proposals owed more to the changes achieved by the Conservative governments of the 1980s and 1990s than to its own historic commitments (Lawn and Grace, 1987; Johnson, 1989).

Above all, society itself had changed and was ready for the New Rightist emphases which were introduced especially in Britain and the USA.

> The social democratic goal of expanding equality of opportunity . . . has lost much of its political potency and its ability to mobilise people. The 'panic' over falling standards and illiteracy, the fears of violence in schools, the concern with the destruction of family values and religiosity all have had an effect. These fears are . . . used, by dominant groups within society and the economy who have been able to move the debate on education (and all things social) onto their own terrain, the terrain of standardisation, productivity and industrial needs.
>
> (Apple, 1989, p. 38)

The role of education in Britain and other Western states and the role of the state itself has thus been recast so that the old social democratic, welfare consensus is replaced by the philosophy of a quasi-market place managed by central government. At the same time, however, the state has struggled to incorporate into its role in education the social capital dimension (human relations management) which is more characteristic of successful modern businesses than a narrower economic instrumentalism (Taylorism).

## Reconstructing public services

In Britain and other welfare-oriented states, the end of the Second World War saw two massive growth industries: state welfare or paternalism and excessive protection, often by legislation, for organized labour. These may have been necessary as part of post-war reconstruction but, by the 1970s, multinational corporations were arguing that this social democratic consensus inhibited both economic growth and individual initiative.

The corporate capitalists influenced Conservative policy-makers in particular and the first Thatcher government was elected in 1979 on a platform of 'rolling back the state'. The election legitimized a campaign of New Rightism which had three major strands (Newman and Clarke, 1994, pp. 21–2). These were that welfarism was too expensive by comparison with its returns, that state welfare demoralized and made dependants of its recipients, and that the welfare 'empires' gave too much power to professionals and bureaucrats who could even subvert the will of the people as expressed by the elected government.

The first and second of these have been represented in British education by policies such as reducing local authority control of individual schools, while the third has been represented by an attack on teachers and their professionalism. All three policies have been prevalent throughout Britain, but have taken a slower pace in Scotland.

## Attacking the professions

The attack on professionalism has been justified in a number of ways. A first justification has been double-edged in stating that professionals have to be accountable not to their own professional bodies but to society at large, while, as individuals, they must take more responsibility for their own actions and not shelter within collective action (Power, 1994, p. 15).

Within that justification we have seen the introduction of a whole range of auditors and managers in every public service. The creation of such groups of 'overseers' also acts against professionalism by offering alternative careers, which incorporate the professionals into the state, 'domesticate' them and make them less threatening opponents of the state's policies (Lawn and Grace, 1987, p. 222). In addition to controlling public services through managers rather than professionals, the state has used its fiscal powers to attack the professions. Under the excuse of austerity, and aided by labour market trends, governments have used funding devices to control access to and length of professional training (Murphy, 1990, p. 83).

With respect to education, a further justification for managerialism was advanced, namely that education had failed the national economy by not producing young people who were appropriately equipped or motivated to contribute to the nation's wealth. Accordingly, from 1976, when Prime Minister James Callaghan gave his Ruskin College speech, various business practices were imposed upon the education service. These included not only administrative devices such as performance indicators, development planning and management training for headteachers, but also curricular intrusions such as the Technical and Vocational Education Initiative (TVEI), Compacts and Education–Business Partnerships (EBP).

> School curriculum has been fashioned in the interests of an industrial psychology that attempts to reduce schools and learning to strictly economic and corporate concerns. Thus, in many countries, we are witnessing the development of school–business partnerships in which schools are adopted by corporate institutions and then organise their curricula so as to provide the skills necessary for domestic production and expanding capital.
>
> (Aronowitz and Giroux, 1991, pp. 89–90)

While it is common in many countries that headteachers should be obliged to undertake specific training, the issue in Britain has been not whether training is necessary, but what its nature should be. In education the notions of customers and products and clients are not amenable to the same interpretation as they would be in business. Therefore, the straight application of business styles of management to schools is resisted. Until such time as the academic and professional leadership roles of headteachers are more fully represented in training programmes, it is difficult to foresee any wholehearted commitment to training from them.

In keeping with the same business/management philosophy, the notion of people not professionally qualified in education running education services becomes ever more popular. In the reform of local government in Scotland, approved by Parliament in 1994, it is proposed that the local education service need not be headed by an educationist or even have its own director.

Although politicians since the late 1970s have clearly decided that the weaknesses of the public services are a major cause of national and international economic crises, it still remains possible that such a diagnosis is spurious, since 'when there is a serious crisis in the state ... by reducing state control and turning ... to a market, one deflects criticism' (Apple, 1985, p. 126).

## Education as a soft target

For any government seeking an easy scapegoat for its economic mismanagement, education is one of the first victims. Education is a highly expensive service, competing for resources against other spending departments. In addition, education is vulnerable because the public has developed a low opinion of teachers. One of the apogees of this trend was the proposal by John Patten, Secretary of State for Education, in 1993 that mature women could train for infant teaching in one year because their experience as mothers and homemakers compensated for any lack of formal training – the so-called 'Mum's Army' proposal (DFE, 1993a).

The gender balance in the teaching force also makes it vulnerable. Most primary (elementary) school teachers are women, as are at least half of secondary school teachers, with the proportions continuing to rise. States dominated by 'male' values consider female occupations to have lower status and see the wages earned by these women as a second income which is easy to reduce or excise (Apple, 1986, pp. 54ff). Moreover, the fact that everyone has been to school and does not see any 'mystery' in schooling, compared with, say, medicine or law, reduces the status and power of teachers and their organizations (Peters, 1977, p. 169).

Finally, education is vulnerable because the state controls salaries, staff : student ratios, and supply and demand from the primary all the way through to the tertiary sectors. Government departments and their agents, such as the Teacher Training Agency in England and Wales (DFE, 1993b) and the General Teaching Council in Scotland, determine the number in and the nature of teacher training. (Although the General Teaching Council for Scotland represents professional interests and has considerable control over those who are qualified to enter and fit to remain in teaching, it does not control access to training.)

For teaching to be a profession it must meet criteria such as performing an essential public service, ensuring standards of entry and behaviour, control of compulsory training and curriculum, and possessing a specialized knowledge base (Sayer, 1993, p. 119). When the state claims that 'parents know better than educational theorists and administrators and better even than our mostly excellent teachers' (DFE, 1992) it is difficult for teachers to claim professional status for themselves.

## Areas of action against education

The criticisms of teachers and schools in Britain have been turned into specific policy imperatives over the past twenty years. Among the particular policies have been:

1   Making the curriculum fit the needs of the economy. This has been achieved not only through the 'back to basics' thrust of National Curriculum prescriptions but also through the 'vocational impulse' of programmes such as TVEI and Compact, which often originated outside education (TVEI from the Employment Department) or outside Britain (Compact from the USA). That government felt it had to go outside the expertise of the teaching profession in order to achieve the improvements in schooling which it sought indicated a belief that teachers lacked commitment to change and was a further demotivator to teacher professionalism. Nevertheless, in examining a policy such as TVEI, 'one is struck by the extent to which an externally "imposed" policy was appropriated by the teaching profession for very different purposes to those intended' (Bowe *et al.*, 1992, p. 9).

2   Making schools more competitive by increasing parental rights of choice of school and freeing schools from the uniformity of local government control. Such policies as 'parental placing request' and 'opted-out schools', however, merely redistribute the available customers rather than increasing the customer base, and increase the unit cost of educating children in the schools which lose pupils (Jenkins, 1994).

3   Making schools more accountable by obliging them to meet specific performance indicators, often of a quantitative and financial nature. While it is essential that the community gets 'value for money', the new models of accountability divert teachers from securing quality learning towards 'book-keeping'. This process of 'intensification' (Apple, 1986, p. 44) is the opposite of professionalism.

4   Raising standards through testing of teachers and of pupils. While there has been much resistance to the testing movement (particularly from parents in Scotland), government is determined that only through testing pupils at various ages can teachers be shamed into improving the performance of their pupils, even when 'teaching to the test' will run the risk of routinizing both the teaching and the learning

and hinder the development of the 'enterprise culture' which politicians claim to value (Darling-Hammond, 1985, p. 210).

In this manner, and through policies of privatization, centralization, vocationalization and differentiation (Education Group II, 1991, p. 27), Western governments in the 1980s and 1990s have sought to bring teachers and schools into line with their ideologies. Although governments' intentions have not always been consistent and some have been overturned by other groups in society (parents, teachers, etc.), the commitment to change has been maintained.

## A wholesale reform of schooling

British Conservative governments since 1979 have been thorough in their reforms of schooling. These have been made easier by an unbroken period in office and by a lack of opposition from the Labour Party (Inglis, 1991). Indeed, the reform movement is now so well established that even the Labour Party has to endorse it if it wishes to regain power (Labour Party, 1991, 1994). These reforms have all increased the extent to which the state sets professional agendas.

### Supply and demand

Despite the acknowledged weakness of manpower planning, most states try to control the supply and demand for teachers. Such manpower planning is vulnerable to economic circumstances and so, in the 1980s and 1990s, high-unemployment areas such as Scotland have had little difficulty attracting applicants to teacher training, while low-unemployment areas such as southern England have had endemic teacher shortages. The same planning is also vulnerable to demographics. In the period 1985–95 there was a declining pupil population and a stable teaching force. But from the mid-1990s the pupil population will rise and many teachers recruited in the 1960s will retire from work. Consequently, English schools require an additional 20,000 teachers by the end of the century (*The Times*, 12 August 1994). In such circumstances, the government has sought ways of recruiting more teachers at a lower cost, through the Articled Teacher and Licensed Teacher programmes (OFSTED, 1993a, b) and proposed three- rather than four-year training programmes for primary teachers (DFE, 1993b).

Rather than economic expediency, governments have looked to intellectual justification for such moves, supported by their non-parliamentary allies (Lawlor, 1990) who claim that 'ability to teach is an aptitude and . . . formal qualifications do little in themselves to develop it' (Hillgate Group, 1987, pp. 35–6) and, ignoring the profession's own counter-arguments, that 'the emergency, temporary, and "alternate" licensing and certification programs hinder the development of strong teacher education programs and temper the development of teaching as a profession' (Wise, 1991, p. 7).

## Competence-based teaching

Not only has the state sought to control entry to teaching, it has also sought to make teaching a low-skill operation, by introducing various 'competency' systems of a bureaucratic nature (Wise, 1979, p. 96) where the tasks of a teacher are carefully specified and a narrow training provided, which requires little judgement or skill in the operatives (Darling-Hammond, 1985, p. 210).

A principal aim of British state policy in this regard has been the National Vocational Qualifications/Scottish Vocational Qualifications (NVQ/SVQ) movement, which presumes that every job can be reduced to an accumulation of pre-specified competences which produces a composite capability to discharge all the job functions (NCVQ, 1991). That strategy has been challenged (Collins, 1991), particularly in its application to education.

Programmes based on the functional analysis of work roles are likely to produce teachers who are 'competent' yet ill-equipped for further professional development, uncritical of educational change and largely ignorant of the wider cultural, social and political context in which the role of teachers needs to be located.

(Hyland, 1993, p. 130)

States have managed to introduce such models of teacher behaviour, however, partly because of public dissatisfaction over what they see as left-oriented, theory-loaded teacher training (Lawlor, 1990, p. 8) and because of disagreement among teacher educators over whether every teacher requires high-level capability as a 'reflective practitioner' or only a few teachers require such capability, with the rest being associate or auxiliary teachers (Soltis, 1987; Elliott, 1993).

## Curriculum and assessment

To produce such teacher behaviour, however, requires the state to control and package curriculum and assessment, hence the movements to impose a national curriculum and national testing (Apple, 1990, p. 530).

Outside the private sector of education, there is little which can prevent the state controlling curriculum and assessment. In the past, however, such control has often been achieved in partnership with the teaching profession. Throughout the 1980s and into the 1990s Conservative governments in Britain and elsewhere rejected that partnership in favour of central control through 'quangos' whose membership reflected government views.

While this happened in Britain across a number of public services, such as water and sewerage, electricity supply, and health, which all became increasingly 'privatized', it was most apparent in education. The government took it upon itself to determine the shape and content of the curriculum and the nature of the assessment. Not only were teachers not to be trusted, but they did not know as much about the curriculum as government or parents (Graham with Tytler, 1992).

Defining the curriculum is not a sufficient guarantee of what curriculum will be delivered. Teachers have become skilled in subverting the state's wishes (see above, p. 22). The British government therefore took further steps to control and make public teachers' and schools' behaviours, through systems of appraisal.

The appraisal of teachers is designed to judge their achievements for future salary enhancement or promotion, and to see how they adhere to the agreed development plan of the school. The appraisal of schools by government's inspectors or by the parents in their community is through scrutiny of published school plans and by visits from these 'externals'. Both are forms of control designed to achieve conformity rather than to respect autonomy.

While it is accepted that schools must be accountable, these forms of accountability have little to do with evaluating a school or a teacher's performance in qualitative terms (Power, 1994, p. 6). Indeed, they may hinder rather than advance standards of achievement, since 'recent studies of school effectiveness indicate the need to rest considerable responsibility for a school's instructional programme on the shoulders of the staff of a school. Over and over we find that without the commitment of the school staff, topdown mandates will fail' (Stedman and Smith, 1983, pp. 102–3).

## Continuing professional development

State action against teacher autonomy now extends to their continuing professional development. Until recently, teachers volunteered to attend relevant courses at minimal or no cost. Since the mid-1980s in Britain, the state has prescribed most courses and funded attendance at them. Courses which do not fit with government priorities or ideology are denied that funding and have become expensive.

To take but one example, the government wishes headteachers to be school managers rather than lead educators. Thus, headteachers will have vouchers which can only be spent on management training (Haigh, 1994), but will have to spend their own or their school's funds on any other training.

> While it is consistent with planning, appraisal, accountability, etc. that teachers should be retrained and updated on a regular basis, once again the state is prescribing what a teacher is and does, not from an educational perspective but from a bureaucratic and ideological perspective. In consequence, there is resistance from teachers who prefer to foot the cost of their own continuing professional development through substantial university courses with a sound academic element befitting their postgraduate status, rather than enrol for courses ... designed with more short-term and instrumental aims in mind.
> (Fergusson, 1994, p. 110)

## Managerialism

All these changes in the treatment of teachers stem from one simple ideology – managerialism – in which states see schools as businesses.

In many modern and successful businesses, forms of 'new managerialism' have been developed which depend upon 'people-centred' philosophies, where control is kept to a minimum and individuals are inspired towards excellence by managers who are first and foremost leaders rather than checkers (Newman and Clarke, 1994, p. 15). Western governments have tended not to favour such models for state industries, depending instead on 'neo-Taylorism', which is dominated by productivity, rigidity and control over detail. Education systems with national curricula, national testing, appraisal and performance indicators applied under constrained budgets are thus dominated by neo-Taylorism (Ball, 1990, p. 125).

Such managerialism is merely the culmination of a series of state interventions in education in the 1980s and 1990s. State views of 'education as business' are not only inappropriate on modern business criteria, but also irrelevant in educational terms, yet 'new teachers' capacities to act autonomously, work independently and, most of all, to mount well-grounded challenges to managerial diktat are likely to diminish, and their sense of membership of and solidarity with a larger body to be diluted' (Fergusson, 1994, p. 107).

## Conclusions

The phenomenon known as New Rightism has affected different Western democracies and emerging democracies in different ways. In all of them there have been various forms of state control exerted over the management, assessment and curriculum of schools. In Britain there has historically been a greater freedom for schools to determine their own curriculum than would have been the case in other countries, and no tradition of teachers being 'state servants', as in, for example, Germany. In that sense, the British government's attempts to bring teachers and the curriculum under closer scrutiny could be seen as merely bringing Britain into line with major international trends. Paradoxically, however, this is not only such a dramatic break with tradition (Fergusson, 1994, p. 113), it is also in conflict with a drift in the direction of less control over curriculum in countries such as Poland, Russia and France.

While the British state's intentions are not all wrong-headed nor have all been accepted without contest nor amendment, the major ideological drive of government policy has been successful, mainly because of a lack of concerted opposition (see above, p. 22).

In the late 1990s there are indications of more competition for political power between Conservative and Labour parties, which could lead to contests with which Americans are more familiar and which involve a shift in power from 'the state' to 'the public' (Carnoy and Levin, 1985, p. 47). That competition has long been apparent in Scotland, where teachers have not been reduced in status to the same extent as their English counterparts, where the Westminster government is effectively a minority government and has to behave more prudently and where the public values the democratic traditions of its schools.

Four particular areas of competition have been identified.

1   On the matter of curriculum and assessment the state has taken very obvious control of all but private schools.
2   As far as governance is concerned, schools are being given individual responsibility under direct links with central rather than local government.
3   Schools are being run by the 'value for money' standards of business, rather than the educational standards of teachers.
4   Teachers' notions of professional autonomy have been squeezed between parental pressure on the one hand and central government control on the other.

In all these the dominant motivation for the state since the 1970s has been a mistrust of teachers to the point where they are virtually being accused of disloyalty to society's interests (Lawn and Grace, 1987, p. 222; Knight, 1990, pp. 25–96).

Reconciling the paradox is therefore difficult. Without giving due recognition to professional expertise and without the partnership of government, public and the professions which was characteristic of the previous social democratic consensus, it is difficult to see how a state can emerge where success for individuals and for society can both be achieved (Newman and Clarke, 1994, p. 22).

> The language of efficiency, production, standards, cost-effectiveness, job skills, work discipline, and so on – all defined by powerful groups and always threatening to become the dominant way we think about schooling – has begun to push aside concerns for a democratic curriculum, teacher autonomy, and class, gender, and race equality.
>
> (Apple, 1986, p. 154)

## References

Apple, M. W. (1985) *Education and Power*, 2nd edn. London: Ark.

Apple, M. W. (1986) *Teachers and Texts*. London: Routledge.

Apple, M. W. (1989) The politics of common sense: schooling populism and the New Right. In H. A.

Giroux and P. L. McLaren (eds), *Critical Pedagogy, the State and Cultural Struggle*. Albany: State University of New York Press.

Apple, M. W. (1990) Is there a curriculum voice to reclaim? *Phi Delta Kappan*, **71** (1), 526–30.

Aronowitz, S. and Giroux, H. A. (1991) *Post Modern Education: Politics, Culture and Social Criticism*. Minneapolis: University of Minnesota Press.

Askling, B. and Almén, E. (1993) *Teacher Education as a Tool for State Steering*. Brighton: Society for Research into Higher Education.

Ball, S. J. (1990) *Politics and Policy Making in Education*. London: Routledge.

Bowe, R., Ball, S. J. and Gold, A. (1992) *Reforming Teacher Education and Changing Schools*. London: Routledge.

Carnoy, M. and Levin, H. M. (1985) *Schooling and Work in the Democratic State*. Stanford, CA: Stanford University Press.

Collins, M. (1991) *Adult Education as Vocation*. London: Routledge.

Darling-Hammond, L. (1985) Valuing teachers: the making of a profession. *Teachers College Record*, **87**, 210.

DFE (1992) *Choice and Diversity: A New Framework for Schools*. London: HMSO.

DFE (1993a) *The Initial Training of Primary School Teachers: New Criteria for Course Approval*. London: Department for Education.

DFE (1993b) *Government Proposals for the Reform of Initial Teacher Training*. London: Department for Education.

Education Group II (1991) *Education Limited*. London: Unwin.

Elliott, J. (ed.) (1993) *Reconstructing Teacher Education*. Lewes: Falmer Press.

Esland, G. (1994) *E817 Updating Notes*. Milton Keynes: Open University.

Fergusson, R. (1994) Managerialism in education. In J. Clarke, A. Cochrane and E. McLaughlin (eds), *Managing Social Policy*. London: Sage.

Graham, D. with Tytler, D. (1992) *A Lesson for Us All: The Making of the National Curriculum*. London: Routledge.

Haigh, G. (1994) Lights on for leaders. *Times Educational Supplement*, 8 July, p. 27.

Hillgate Group (1987) *The Reform of British Education: From Principles to Practice*. London: Claridge Press.

Hyland, T. (1993) Professional development and competence-based education. *Educational Studies*, **19** (1), 123–32.

Inglis, W. (1991) The Labour Party's policy on primary and secondary education 1979–89. *British Journal of Educational Studies*, **39** (1), 4–16.

Jenkins, S. (1994) Death of a profession. *The Times*, 5 January.

Johnson, R. (1989) Thatcherism and English education: breaking the mould or confirming the pattern. *History of Education*, **18** (2), 91–121.

Knight, C. (1990) *The Making of Tory Education Policy in Post-war Britain, 1950–1986*. Lewes: Falmer Press.

Kydd, L. and Weir, D. (1994) Managerialism versus professionalism. *Head Teachers Review*, Spring, 6–9.

Labour Party (1991) *Investing in Quality*. London: Labour Party.

Labour Party (1994) *Opening Doors to a Learning Society*. London: Labour Party.

Lawlor, S. (1990) *Teachers Mistaught: Training in Theories or Education in Subjects*. London: Centre for Policy Studies.

Lawn, M. and Grace, G. (eds) (1987) *Teachers: The Culture and Politics of Work*. Lewes: Falmer Press.

Murphy, R. (1990) Proletariarization or bureaucratization: the fall of the professional? In R. Torstendahl and M. Burrage (eds), *The Formation of Professions*. London: Sage.

NCVQ (1991) *A Guide to National Vocational Qualifications*. London: NCVQ.

Newman, J. and Clarke, J. (1994) Going about our business? The managerialization of public services. In J. Clarke, A. Cochrane and E. McLaughlin (eds), *Managing Social Policy*. London: Sage.

OFSTED (1993a) *The Articled Teacher Scheme, 1990–1992*. London: OFSTED.

OFSTED (1993b) *The Licensed Teacher Scheme, 1990–1992*. London: OFSTED.

Peters, R. S. (1977) *Education and the Education of Teachers*. London: Routledge.

Power, M. (1994) *The Audit Explosion*. London: Demos.

Sayer, J. (1993) *The Future Governance of Education*. London: Cassell.

Soltis, J. F. (ed.) (1987) *Reforming Teacher Education: The Impact of the Holmes Group Report*. New York: Teachers College Press.

Stedman, L. C. and Smith, M. S. (1983) Recent reform proposals for American education. *Contemporary Education Review*, **2**, 102–3.

Wise, A. (1979) *Legislated Learning: The Bureaucratization of the American Classroom*. Berkeley: University of California Press.

Wise, A. (1991) We need more than a redesign. *Educational Leadership*, **49** (3), 7.

# 3 Towards a Restructuring of Teachers' Professionalism

LESLEY KYDD

## Introduction

The teaching profession has traditionally based its claims to professional status on criteria similar to those which define the 'ancient' professions of medicine, the law and the Church. Thus professional status is derived from the exercise of professional judgement, professional autonomy, the right to self-regulation, expertise in a body of knowledge highly valued by society and a relationship with the 'client' based on common understandings of 'mutual' good (Humes, 1986). Although such explanations are deeply rooted in the psychology of professional behaviour, they can only be of partial use in shedding light on the complex ways in which the professions are acted upon by the broader political, social and economic context. In other words, 'The concept of the ideal profession does not fully tackle the question of state and political intervention in the process of professionalization' (Siegrist, 1994, p. 4).

A more helpful way in which to understand the professions is to consider explanations which include the context in which professional groups exist: the state and political ideology; the economy and the labour market; and the expectations which a society has of its professionals. In relation to the teaching profession we can, therefore, move on to ask questions about, for example, the role of political ideology in structuring and defining the professionalism of teachers; the role of the education system in the economy; and the aims and purposes of schooling in our society. In such ways it is possible to contextualize the relationship which

the teaching profession has to aspects of the societal fabric.

The *nature* of teachers' professionalism, however, is something which occurs at a point in time and can be described as happening at the confluence of political and economic ideology with traditional, historical notions of professionalism developed through comparison with other professions. This point of confluence is not necessarily a straightforward or uncontested space, since shifts in the political and ideological context in which the teaching profession interacts will change the nature of the professional activity, the ways in which professionals behave and how teachers view themselves as professionals.

The teaching profession, then, is part of a complex set of changing relationships which impact differently in different local circumstances. This chapter will examine the ways in which some of these relationships are restructuring teacher professionalism. Reference will be made to two different educational systems – those of England and Scotland. Although part of the United Kingdom, Scotland has retained its own distinctive education system, which is regulated through a separate legislative framework from that of England, Wales and Northern Ireland.

## Teachers and the state

During the 1960s and early 1970s, it is suggested, some kind of political consensus existed whereby education was accepted as being part of the 'national good' and, as such, the clear right of every citizen. Notions of partnership and the right of the teaching profession to participate in the policy-making arena were accepted and, furthermore, were seen largely as politically neutral. The strength of this model was partly based on the belief of the teaching profession that their authority as the 'experts' in the relationship was seen to be 'equivalent to authority derived from the political process' (McPherson and Raab, 1988, p. 268).

If it is accepted that the professions are linked to a broader societal context, then it is interesting to note that this situation of social democratic partnership endured during a period of expanding resources within the education system and an economy which seemed able to offer employment to most. The 1970s, however, saw the breakdown of the post-war social democratic consensus. This took place against a backdrop of economic recession, with increases in oil prices adding to the difficulties inherent in changes in the structure of the labour market, the decline of manufacturing and traditional industry and economic restructuring in world markets.

Against this background, the education system was singled out for criticism as failing in its contribution to the creation of economic wealth. The business community expressed concern that not only were schools expensive, they were also remote from the world of work and the culture of industry. As a matter of electoral expediency, politicians of both the right and the left added their voices to the criticism of teachers and teaching methods. Much of this criticism was drawn together in the speech made at Ruskin College in 1976 by the then Prime Minister, James Callaghan. This speech not only cast doubts upon the achievements of the education system, but also signalled that traditional forms of teacher professionalism, particularly curriculum autonomy, had 'failed' to produce the country's wealth creators.

From the perspective of the teaching profession one of the most influential outcomes of this criticism was the direct linking of the activities of schools to economic benefit. The general acceptance of such causation meant that for teachers there would, in the future, be an expectation that their professional activities would have economically tangible outcomes. Thus the 1970s provided a particular mind-set for the restructuring of teachers' professionalism in the 1980s. Teachers could no longer be considered the 'experts' in the policy-making partnership since government held that investment in the education system had failed to produce economic growth. More importantly, the activities of teachers and teaching were steered away from 'educational' outcomes towards 'economic' ones.

The election of a Conservative government in 1979 was to have a profound effect on the teaching profession. The most important aspect of Conservative Party policy has been the application of the ideology and practices of the market place to the organization and management of public services, including the education system. The 1980s illustrate not only the state's enhanced role as policy-maker but also the application of a particular and 'anti-professional' ideology to an occupational group which had struggled hard for recognition as a profession.

A succession of Education Acts have been passed to facilitate this. In summary, they encourage schools to opt out of local authority control and seek self-governing status, with funding supplied directly to the schools from central government. Where schools have remained with the local authorities, budgets have been delegated to them individually. As well as changing the way in which the system is organized, government has also been concerned to control the nature of the activities undertaken by teachers within schools. The 1988 Education Reform Act, which set up the National Curriculum in England and Wales, ensures that the curriculum is no longer a matter of professional autonomy for teachers. It is quite clearly the concern of the state.

It is interesting here to reflect on national differences and to note that these changes have impacted less severely in Scotland. To date, in Scotland, schools have not opted out of local authority control. In addition, the legislation prescribing the National Curriculum does not apply in Scotland. The Scottish Office has, therefore, been able to resist important aspects of the application of the market doctrine to schools. Although a national curriculum does exist in terms of a broad consensus over the shape and content of the curriculum, it is not regulated through legislation. Scottish teachers do, therefore, still exercise important roles in the policy-making community and curriculum change.

The 1980s also saw the link between education and the economy translated into 'vocationalizing' the culture of schools. This meant that schools were to be more closely associated with the culture and practices of business, and this provided the ideological focus for the introduction of many of the managerialist systems of the 1980s. Vocationalism appeals powerfully to notions of social justice and equity; to providing something worthwhile for the less advantaged. On the other hand, the system of vocational education adopted by policy-makers emphasizes outcomes and competence. This fits well with notions of a prescribed curriculum and the accountability models of the market.

The growing importance of vocationalism in the 1980s also led to the development of a complex system of vocational qualifications and the linking of these with academic qualifications in a national framework. Along with other factors, this has led to the rise of credentialism. More people now have more qualifications. This not only challenges the professionals' claims to possession of a body of knowledge highly valued by society, but for the teaching profession exacerbates an issue which has always been contested. That issue is, what is both the nature and the subject of the professional knowledge which teachers possess?

Thus aspects of the introduction of the market place into the education system and the rise of vocationalism challenge traditional notions of teacher professionalism. They also enable greater control by central government, since both are operationalized through management systems which make it possible to impose a greater uniformity on schools and the activities of teachers, and thus to redirect the activities of those working within the system. It can be argued that the ideology and structures of the market have replaced those of partnership and professionalism. Indeed, 'It was hard to reconcile the main impulse of the New Right policy (towards the market) with the legacies

of public education, the power of the LEAs, the autonomies of professionals' (Johnson, 1991, p. 47). Teachers are now at the forefront of the implementation of policy which they had no role in formulating and which ideologically and educationally many may not favour.

In addition, and more importantly, an enhanced role for the state and political ideology in shaping the nature of the school system and the expectations which society has of it shows quite clearly that the derivation of teachers' authority as 'experts' was more from popular belief than the political process.

The enhancement of the state's role has led to the disenfranchisement of local government and the teaching profession in shaping and participating in the policy-making process.

## Inside the teaching profession

As well as being part of a broader context, the professions have evolved as distinctive occupational groups. One of the features of the current debate is the apparent inability of the teaching profession to withstand the changes which are being made (Callahan, 1962). Part of the explanation for this may lie in the fact that teachers' claims to be a profession rest on comparison with the traditional professions, but part may lie in the internal structure of the profession itself.

One of the traditional criteria of a profession is that its members are given high status by society and are rewarded commensurately. The argument follows that professionals possess knowledge, skills and attributes not widely available, so in market terms their earning power is increased. The teaching profession finds itself in a position of ambivalence here. There are, as Lawton (1991) has said, 'simply too many teachers'. In addition, everyone has experience of the education system – the 'mystique' of teaching no longer exists. Teachers are no longer highly valued members of the 'elite' – a profession – in possession of a commodity which society is prepared to pay for. In other words, the success of teachers in raising universal standards of literacy and numeracy contributes to their difficulties in maintaining that distinctive expertise which separates a profession from an occupation. Teachers are poorly paid and their status is being steadily eroded.

In addition, the profession's participation in the governance of the system in which it works has been reallocated by the state to other groups. For example, teacher training in England and Wales has been relocated in a government quango, the Teacher Training Agency (TTA); the role of parents in the management of schools has been enhanced through school governors in England and Wales and, to a lesser extent, through school boards in Scotland.

If the state continues to remove the attributes and practices of a traditional profession from teachers, then teaching is unlikely to attract the most able graduates. Less critical recruits coupled with the 'ageing' of the teacher population may allow the state even greater control of the system.

Another area where the teaching profession shows considerable ambivalence in its claims to professional status is in the structure and nature of promoted posts. In general, a promoted post in education means a move away from the classroom – a move away from teaching. Thus advancement almost inevitably means management. The importance attached to the management role can be seen in the rapid increase in the number of management courses and degrees available. (At the time of writing there were 62 institutions of higher education in England offering forms of postgraduate degrees in educational management.) There is also a tendency to value management training over teaching professionalism in the appointment to promoted posts.

Perhaps, then, one of the real difficulties which the teaching profession faces is that the job of teaching is undervalued by the profession itself, and this is reinforced through the management orientation of the promotion structure. As Lawton (1990, p. 145) suggests, 'why should a good graduate join a poorly paid profession where [his or her] graduate status and professional training appear to count for little or nothing?'

There are other structural issues which tend to make the teaching profession vulnerable to central control. The majority of promoted posts are still filled by males, whereas the majority of teachers are female. For a large proportion of teachers the job provides a second income. Both of these factors point to structural conservatism. This is not to suggest that teachers lack the power or the will to organize collective action for higher salaries, better working conditions or over matters of excessive workload, but that the gender and economic imbalances in the structure of the profession make it susceptible to state intervention. One of the matters of greatest concern in the changing relationship between the state and public service professionals is the latter's apparent lack of resistance to redefinition by the state.

If some of the vestiges of traditional professionalism are to survive then it may be that the profession itself will have to reform its internal structures. For example, the Holmes Group – a group of deans of schools of education in the USA – suggested in 1986 that the profession should be restructured on three levels: career professional teachers, professional teachers and instructors. This has been echoed in the United Kingdom by Hargreaves (1990), who notes similar categories: the fully trained career teacher, the para-trained assistant teacher and the associate teacher, not necessarily trained at all.

## Managerialism

One of the most influential features of the 1980s has been the emergence of managerialism both as a political philosophy and as a set of systems and practices designed for the management of public services. Although it is couched in the language of effectiveness and efficiency, the central focus of managerialism is inherently political and rests on the state introducing mechanisms which support the rationale that 'value for money' is achieved only through the production of measurable outcomes.

The introduction of the market place as an organizational tool for the running of public services has led to an increase in the 'need for management'. Thus the activity of management has been elevated to become the linchpin for the newly marketized public services. It is therefore something which has a direct impact not only on schools and how they are run but also on the roles of the professionals within those institutions.

At the present time managers in schools are trained teachers, as are many of those who work in the education system in local authorities. Increasingly, however, the need to manage budgets and markets is leading to the appointment of 'lay' managers. There is considerable difficulty in conceptualizing the paradox between the professional teacher and the professional teacher as school manager. The outcome of this trend – whether schools will in the future be managed by those who are not trained teachers – will determine the nature of the professional role for teachers (Wise, 1990).

Managerialism, therefore, raises a whole set of issues which conflict with traditional notions of teacher professionalism (see Bowe *et al.*, 1992). One of the main points of conflict is ideological – that of the achievement of public goals through the private market (Darling-Hammond, 1988). As a way of managing public services, managerialism necessarily separates the formation of policy from its execution. These factors add to the tensions between the activities and values of traditional teacher professionalism and those of the market, even if the market is viewed as a device and as a neutral regulator. To many teachers, however, the operation of the market is a questionable organizational mechanism for the achievement of the 'educated' person.

One of the most important characteristics of managerialism has been the adoption in the education system (and other public services) of the ideology and discourse of some idealized notion of business. This is couched in the language of technical-rational management, which provides a discourse of order in a rapidly changing world (see, for example, Aronowitz and Giroux, 1991). Thus education is described as a 'commodity' which consumers 'purchase' through the medium of parental choice, and schools are funded accordingly on the basis of pupil numbers. The marketization of the system is based on a social Darwinist precept of the survival of the fittest (see Fergusson,

1994). In such a model the curriculum is the input, pupils are the throughput and success is designated by measurable outcomes. Such systems ensure that teachers 'deliver' the curriculum 'effectively' (Apple 1990).

Such a business-like discourse in schools is now not unusual. Talk about curriculum delivery is encouraged, as well as acknowledgement of the principles of line management in the introduction of appraisal systems. In all of this we are considering a kind of assembly-line view of students, whose failures can be explained through a failure in the implementation rather than in the conception of systems. This has led policy-makers to invest heavily in managerial systems rather than enhancing the preparation and professional development of teachers (Darling-Hammond, 1988).

In addition, management systems which involve the delivery of a prescribed curriculum with testable, measurable outcomes and the skills of financial regulation do not need to rely on teachers for their implementation. Also such notions do not necessarily rest on the intellectual and reflective skills of the professional teacher. They can as easily be delivered by a 'technician' trained in processes of delivery as by a teacher trained to engage with the knowledge base. Curriculum now tends to arrive in schools in neatly packaged portions, each complete with aims, objectives, tasks, worksheets, homework and assessment. It is standardized and off-the-shelf. Delivering this curriculum requires little creativity on the part of teachers and the exercise of professional judgement is confined to deciding which package to deliver next.

It requires little imagination to understand that delivery of a product to a client is not a process fundamentally concerned with the education of the next generation. In the market place the question about teaching methods becomes a technical one about its functioning in the production system. In other words we must begin to consider that 'Important issues about the purposes of schooling in our society are being thrown up by the implementation of LMS, but they are not being addressed in public debate. The assumption of the superiority of the market appears unassailable' (Bowe *et al.*, 1992, p. 81). The whole point of teaching is that it is not a passive activity which is delivered and automatically, and equally, received. Teaching is above all things a discourse of engagement with the knowledge base. It is about the uniqueness of the individual and the quality of the interactive process between teacher, student and knowledge.

> The idea that activities like teaching, any more than many of those of everyday life, can be undertaken as a technology is an error. The ends they seek are achievement in human beings which are brought about by reasons and not simply causes. They involve unique personalities in complex non-causal relationships, operating in what are often unique circumstances.
>
> (Hirst, 1990, p. 176)

The introduction of the discourses and practices of industrial market models into the education system therefore not only challenges but changes the precepts and values of traditional professional teachers.

Managerialism is also associated with new control systems concerned with attitudinal and behavioural compliance among staff. These systems can be loosely grouped together in the issue of accountability. There can be no doubt that teachers should be accountable; the education system consumes a large part of the public purse. Traditionally, teachers have been accountable to themselves, to their colleagues as professionals, to their students and to parents. Bearing in mind the ideology of the market place and the industrial management discourse which informs much of the debate, it is hardly surprising that we have come to describe accountability in fairly simplistic 'accountancy' terms.

This is illustrated in moves towards 'measurable outcomes' – in the introduction of systems of appraisal, line management, target setting, development planning and league tables. Not only are such systems paper driven and time consuming, but they clearly shift the focus of the debate from one of teaching to one of accounting for the *outcomes* of this activity; from one of intellectual engagement with the knowledge base to one of operating systems.

Thus what we are seeing is the disappearance of a 'form of intellectual labour central to the nature

of critical pedagogy itself' (Aronowitz and Giroux, 1991, p. 24). Taken even further, it can be suggested that accountability systems clearly devalue the means – teaching – used to achieve the measurable outcomes. Some would suggest, therefore, not only that the teaching profession is more technocratic but that its activity of teaching is largely irrelevant as long as students achieve the prescribed outcomes. Thus the job of the teacher is redefined. 'As responsibility for designing one's own curricula and one's own teaching decreased, responsibility over technical tasks and management concerns came to the fore' (Apple, 1988, p. 108).

Managerialism can also be seen as an alternative system to that of professional collegiality. One of the criteria traditionally used to distinguish the professions from other occupational groups is the possession of a self-regulatory body. There is a sharp contrast here between the parts of the United Kingdom. Scottish teachers have a General Teaching Council – enacted in 1965 – and English teachers do not. The existence of a regulatory body to which teachers are elected has contributed towards the way in which Scottish teachers see themselves as professionals and has, in addition, enabled them to maintain a role in the policy-making community. A General Teaching Council can therefore be seen as one of the important means by which professional interests can ameliorate the managerialist tendencies of the state.

All of this pushes the teaching profession away from its traditional concerns and activities towards a new direction. The intensification of management controls is replacing the wisdom, experience and self-monitoring of the practitioner and leading to the devaluing of capacities which are difficult to define but which make a difference between experienced and novice teachers. Therefore, the rise of managerialism and the emergence of the 'cult of efficiency' (Callahan, 1962) change the job that teachers do. For some, there are new career opportunities; for others there is the safety of systems; but for others there is a feeling of unease that schools are losing sight of their purpose – the education of young people.

What is clear is that the rise of managerialism calls into question the role of the autonomous professional and the rights of teachers to make decisions about what is taught and how it is taught. The debate is framed not in intellectual terms about what it means to be an educated person or even what kinds of educational experience the population should be entitled to; it is a debate couched in the economic language of industrial management. The profession's response to the management and operation of tightly regulated state systems is one of the major challenges facing teachers in the 1990s.

## Teacher training

Another way in which Scottish teachers retain a more clearly defined professionalism is in the area of teacher training. Teacher training in Scotland has remained firmly coupled with the universities, and all teachers must undertake either a BEd degree or a first degree followed by a one-year full-time course of teacher training. This situation contrasts sharply with recent developments in teacher training south of the border. Calls by the right (see the Hillgate Group, 1989; Lawlor, 1990) for the abandonment of teacher training altogether and attacks on university departments of education have resulted in the opening up of new routes to qualified teacher status, such as the articled and licensed teacher schemes.

The newly formed Teacher Training Agency removes the funding for teacher training from the universities and clearly separates the training of teachers from other university activities. Teacher training has, therefore, been disengaged from its intellectual knowledge base in the universities and become a school-based activity. This not only removes prospective teachers from an intellectual engagement with the knowledge base, but also isolates individuals in small numbers in particular institutions. In addition, it removes from the academic community a role in validating teacher education knowledge and, by implication, claims to professional status (Humes, 1986). There is an interesting ambiguity in current attacks on initial teacher training south of the border: 'on the one hand they argue that standards in schools are low

because teaching methods have become contaminated with the progressive theories of teacher educators. Yet on the other hand they propose to base teacher training on this contaminated system of schools' (Elliott, 1993, p. 21).

Entrants to teaching in England will be trained by their peers in schools. Schools may buy the expertise of the universities if they choose to do so. There is an interesting paradox here, in that making the profession solely responsible for training its own entrants can appeal powerfully to notions of the self-regulating profession. However, school-based training is likely to be highly subjective and concerned with the immediacy of everyday life in the classroom. No one would seek to argue that prospective teachers should not be engaged in learning these things, but by *only* learning these things teachers are unlikely to encounter any form of critical discourse which might direct them towards an interrogation of the purposes of education, the selection of knowledge and so on. In other words, on-the-job training *only* is the kind of model which is likely to encourage preservation of the status quo and compliance. It is also a model which is likely to be concerned that prospective teachers learn how to operate systems in the school rather than play a part in the selecting, planning and teaching of curricula.

In summary, it can be argued that teacher professionalism is being replaced by a kind of management professionalism which directs classroom teachers towards the operation of learning and assessment systems and away from the selection and teaching of knowledge.

## Conclusions

Throughout the 1980s two features dominated the education system: the emergence of managerialism and practical measures taken to link education to its economic outcomes. The education system was, therefore, reorganized in accordance with the ideology and principles of the market place. The discourse and practices of a politicized form of management based on outdated notions of industrial manufacturing was used to provide a technical-rational focus for these changes.

As a result, teachers have found both the practice and the discourse of their professionalism changed. They have been encouraged to make their subjects more relevant to the world of work and to become more efficient and effective in the delivery of the 'product' (the curriculum) to the 'client' (the student). If we set these changes against the traditional criteria of a profession then the teaching profession is being remade and restructured. Indicators of this are:

- A perception in the business and political communities that the professions are bastions of privilege and opponents of change. This has led to the state taking an enhanced role in controlling the governance, management and activities of the professions, such as education.
- The discourse of industrial management, which describes teaching as curriculum delivery and conflates quality with measurement.
- The assumption of a linear relationship between educational success and economic performance, which permits the state to deflect blame for poor performance towards teachers and teacher educators.
- The ways in which the traditional responsibilities, ideology and activities of the teaching profession are being rewritten in terms of management rather than pedagogy.

However, to accept that teaching is no longer (if it ever was) a profession is a dangerous step. It supposes that the autonomy of teachers is so limited that they are really technicians delivering a service in the educational market place and denies that autonomous professionals are a key part of the balance of powers through which a society imparts its values to the next generation.

## References

Apple, M. (1988) Work, class and teaching. In J. Ozga (ed.), *Schoolwork: Approaches to the Labour Process of Teaching*. Milton Keynes: Open University Press.

Apple, M. (1990) Is there a curriculum voice to reclaim? *Phi Delta Kappan*, **71** (7), 526–30.

Aronowitz, S. and Giroux, H. A. (1991) *Post Modern Education*. Minneapolis: University of Minnesota Press.

Bowe, R. and Ball, S. with Gold, A. (1992) *Reforming Education and Changing Schools: Case Studies in Policy Sociology*. London: Routledge.

Callahan, R. (1962) *Education and the Cult of Efficiency*. Chicago: University of Chicago Press.

Darling-Hammond, L. (1988) The futures of teaching. *Educational Leadership*, **46** (3), 4–10.

Elliott, J. (1993) The assault on rationalism and the emergence of social market forces. In J. Elliott (ed.), *Reconstructing Teacher Education: Teacher Development*. London: Falmer Press.

Fergusson, R. (1994) Managerialism in education. In J. Clarke, A. Cochrane and E. McLaughlin (eds), *Managing Social Policy*. London: Sage.

Hargreaves, D. (1990) *The Future of Teacher Education*. Frinton-on-Sea: Hockerill Educational Foundation.

Hillgate Group (1989) *Learning to Teach*. London: Claridge.

Hirst, P. (1990) The theory–practice relationship in teacher training. In M. Booth, J. Furlong and M. Wilkin (eds), *Partnership in Initial Teacher Training*. London: Cassell.

Holmes Group (1986) *Tomorrow's Teachers: A Report of the Holmes Group*. Michigan: The Holmes Group.

Humes, W. (1986) *The Leadership Class in Scottish Education*. Edinburgh: John Donald.

Johnson, R. (1991) A new road to serfdom? A critical history of the 1988 Act. In Cultural Studies, University of Birmingham, *Education Limited: Schooling and Training and the New Right since 1979*. London: Unwin and Hyman.

Lawlor, S. (1990) *Teachers Mistaught: Training in Theories or Education in Subjects?* London: Centre for Policy Studies.

Lawton, D. (1990) The future of teacher education. In N. J. Graves (ed.), *Initial Teacher Education: Policies and Progress*. London: Kogan Page.

Lawton, D. (1991) Problems of teacher education in the 1990s. In E. Jones (ed.), *Education, Culture and Society*. Cardiff: University of Wales Press.

McPherson, A. and Raab, C. (1988) *Governing Education: A Sociology of Policy since 1945*. Edinburgh: Edinburgh University Press.

Siegrist, H. (1994) The professions, state and government in theory and history. In T. Becher (ed.), *Governments and Professional Education*. Buckingham: Society for Research in Higher Education and Open University Press.

Wise, A. E. (1990) Six steps to teacher professionalism. *Educational Leadership*, **47** (7), 57–60.

# 4 Professionalism and Market Forces: With Special Reference to Education in the United Kingdom

## WILLIAM I. OZANNE

Professionalism and market forces can coexist, but ultimately constitute systems which are incompatible in values and in process. The best that they can achieve is a symbiosis in which each domain has due recognition but does not invade the other. This is not the same distinction as that between neo-classicism or neo-liberalism in the modelling of socio-economic dynamics; rather it is a conflict of value systems. It is clear that professionalism implies an overriding imperative to the service of other human beings *qua* human beings. As such, it is productive of professionalism in other activities than the immediate agent activity. Professionalism has an overriding commitment to the client and the professional reference group, while market values have an overriding commitment to what is ultimately a rate of exchange system for commodities between buyer and seller, leading to a shift of roles between trader and client and to a progressive 'commodification' of human beings in place of mutual service. In practice, all societies are in a state of constant change, and in the resultant 'mixed economies' and plural social structures both systems have little option but to coexist, as what is organic and indigenous to one system can appear an externality or accidental to another. Dilemmas arise for policy-makers, administrators and practitioners, who have to decide precisely how far each consideration should enter into their decision-making. In education, as in other fields, the tensions form a kind of dialogue or inter-subjective encounter, if not of words, certainly of confrontation between social groups, the result of which can be explosive or accommodating, creative of further professionalization or simply

of bargaining. Each group dominates the discourse in turn, but some ultimate inter-subjective balance has to emerge within the individual practitioner, between the imperatives of planner and implementer. Although there is a constant shift in the balance of dominance, the resultant direction probably determines what kind of society or culture is emerging.

At one time in Britain, it was considered that by a 'profession' was understood the law, the military, the Church and to some extent medicine. Education, like surgery, enjoyed a rather dubious status, largely because in an entirely private system of schooling (or surgery), qualification, entry requirements and code of conduct could be variable or non-existent. Professions indicated a 'public man' as distinct from a 'private man' and were one of the few ways of social mobility into the caste of ultimate status. In England, the tradition of 'liberal humanism' has tended to favour the model of the amateur rather than the professional in matters which are broadly cultural, and to distrust and subvert models which are absolute and centralist. Education, like architecture, has as a result been an easy prey to forces which have on the one hand expected the most professional of standards, while on the other found it easy to deprive practitioners of professional status, respect and remuneration. Currently, many members of the teaching profession in schools, or academics in higher education, feel deprofessionalized under the current 'neo-classical' model of socio-economic control; this begs the question of whether a professional identity was ever accorded them, or whether they have failed to take on board the balance of imperatives. Yet the experience described as 'deprofessionalization' indicates a real sense of the loss of integrity, if not of autonomy and the highest standards, in relation to the core of their work.

We are led to attempt to define what are the essentials which form a 'profession', and there are many bodies which currently claim under this title both a status and an independence from the judgement of the rest of the community. In the 'open' market, professionalism operates relatively spontaneously, no doubt led by the underlying 'liberal' culture. Bodies like the Institution of Civil Engineers or the Institute of Marketing talk of special knowledge and special skills put to the service of clients, to whom there is a priority of commitment, ensured by accountability to a self-regulating body. (The president of the Institution of Civil Engineers, Stuart Mustow, in one discussion added 'making money' to the professional criteria.) Delegated to local governing bodies, those elements of school planning and management which are not predetermined by central government controls over curriculum, testing and global budget limits oblige isolated individuals to seek consolidation and to formulate common objectives, which include the professional improvement of members, but also a share in policy-making for their field of activity. Associations of school governors (notably the National Association for Governors and Managers, or NAGM, and Action for Governor Information and Training, or AGIT), which have developed over some years, came together in October 1994 (*Times Educational Supplement*, 4 November 1994) to form a National Governors Council, relating to 10,000 governing bodies and covering a third of all the school governors in England and Wales. This body has a strong agenda for its own notions on reforms in schooling and was taken seriously enough for senior members of the Teacher Training Agency, the School Curriculum and Assessment Authority and the Funding Agency for Schools to be present. Indeed, the Department for Education itself provided some of the funding for the council. One might see a parallel in the political field, where associations of mosques are increasing in number in the Islamic community and the setting up of a (largely self-selected) national Islamic 'Parliament' caricatures central government. There is a curious pendulum-like swing here between the decentralizing elements of policy and the recentralizing urge from the community, which indicates a real politico-social dilemma over how to achieve partnership and equitable balance.

The OECD has been studying the question of 'professionalization' of teachers for a period of 15 years. Some of the findings emerged in the 1993 meeting of the Association for Teacher Education in Europe. The general conclusions were that, despite many signs of progress, professionalization as a principle had yet to extend to both the training and the socialization of the teacher. Teacher education should be balanced, one report states, in three types of knowledge: subject, pedagogy and practice; teaching needs a solid foundation of common theoretical and procedural knowledge together with explicit techniques, 'as well as clear ways of evaluating these things in teacher education' (Montané, 1994). Montané concludes that teachers need help in integrating the knowledge of educational scientists and teachers of long experience as well as the opportunity for contributing their own reflection and their own identity. Additionally, Montané sees the need for professional associations to set standards, keep teachers informed and provide a forum for discussion.

These conclusions are not new but they do represent a common experience among the countries whose systems were subject to descriptive or analytical case studies in the 1993 seminar referred to above, where interesting comparisons were drawn between the usage of the terms 'profession', 'professional' or 'professionalization', or even 'professor', in differing countries and languages. (The British Council, for example, used to employ 'professional staff' side by side with career administrators; a sportsperson or theatrical performer becomes 'professional' once he or she receives payment for performance.) Bourdoncle (1994) traces the distinction of, or movement from, trade to profession ('du métier à la profession'). One fair definition, from general experience, of a trade might be: 'doing the best job you can for the time and money available'. Profession is susceptible of more complex characteristics. Bourdoncle (1994)

claims that the principal distinction is in 'l'auto-
nomie et l'expertise':

> Une profession est une activité qui définit elles-
> mêmes ses conditions d'exercice, recrute et forme ses
> futurs membres, fait sa propre police, à l'aide d'une
> code et d'un conseil d'éthique professionelle, bref,
> une activité qui en appuyant sur son expertise qui la
> rend difficilement maîtrisable de l'éxterieur, arrive à
> échapper en large partie au contrôle de ses clients et
> même à celui de l'État.

Montané (1994), summing up the experience of
the 12 country studies, concludes:

> [Teachers] need help from the educational scientists,
> they need help from the practitioners – teachers with
> a long and wide-ranging experience; above all they
> need help in integrating the two sources of aid into
> their own practice, their own reflection and their own
> identity, all of which implies co-ordination between
> the subject faculties of the universities, the training
> institutions or pedagogy faculties and the schools.
> They also need professional associations to set stand-
> ards, keep teachers informed ... and provide a forum
> for discussion ... a wider range of responsibilities,
> more input into research and development, more
> contact with the world outside the classroom.

Bourdoncle is not alone in singling out the ambiguity or dilemma in the role of governments in
relation to schoolteachers, in making them at once
responsible for the children of a society, yet lacking power or financial status (being too numerous,
hierarchical and feminine in composition to command independent respect, as he puts it). Laderrière (1994), no less forcefully than Nóvoa (1994)
in the same volume, sees recent developments
throughout Europe to redistribute functions
between the centre and the periphery of policy-
making as using 'market competition' as a force
contributing to the disintegration rather than a
reinforcement of standards of teaching, not least in
generating the notion 'qu'on peut enseigner sans
avoir beneficié d'un minimum de formation pro-
fessionelle'. They are aware that their perception
is part of the political history of the French state, as
the situation of teachers in England is of the British political changes. It is clearly a dilemma for the
teachers in England and Wales in two respects:
'professional' in-service formation is still mainly
left to voluntary associations, or training undertaken at the teachers' own expense, while central

government funding is among pressures which are
used to impose the new centralized strategies.

There is no doubt that the concept of 'partnership' as a solution to the dilemma resulting from
such a polarity of interests has dominated the
rhetoric of British education. Chitty (1988) points
out that from 1944 onward this took the form of the
changing relationship between central government and local education authorities. He points to
the vagueness of the Conservative government's
'Butler' Education Act of 1944 over the curricular
content of education, or even of the duties and
powers of the collaborating bodies ('the local education authority, the governing body and the head
teacher': 'Rab' Butler, Minister of Education,
quoted in *Hansard*, March 1960, no. 620, cols
51–2), attributing it either to a fear of future
central control by a Labour government, or an
administrative oversight by which the Minister of
Education was left without specific powers of
intervention.

The desire to regain such control has always
been present, according to Whitty (1989), who
quotes Sir David Eccles (Conservative Minister of
Education 1959–62): 'Of course Parliament would
never attempt to dictate the curriculum, but, from
time to time, we could, with advantage, express
views on what is taught in schools and in training
colleges.' He goes on to refer (perhaps the first time
this image entered the debate) to 'a sally into the
secret garden of the curriculum'. From 1962 onward, there was a series of consultative groups
brought together by central government to tilt the
balance away from headteacher and teacher autonomy: first the Curriculum Study Group, then,
under Edward Boyle (Conservative Minister of
Education 1962–64), the Lockwood Committee,
which brought the Schools Council for Curriculum and Examinations into being. The work of
this council can be seen in the Curriculum Project
and research documents which survive it, and the
teacher resource centres which still give local support and dissemination of ideas. Historians of education dispute whether this was a time of teacher
autonomy and general consensus with the community and central government, or a time of strife
between central government and the 'profession'.
Vaisey (1983, p. 114) goes so far as to claim that the

Schools Council was 'sabotaged by the teachers unions'. The experience of the classroom teacher was, however, generally a sense of stimulus and innovation.

The 'Ruskin College' speech of 1976 presented by James Callaghan (Labour Prime Minister at that time), but generally thought to have been prepared by Bernard Donoghue and the Downing Street Policy Unit (Whitty, 1989), though it launched a 'great debate' in which Shirley Williams as Minister of Education toured the country to hold open meetings, was not in fact a consensus-creating exercise, though it was an effort to gain general support for government policies, especially the unversalization of comprehensive schooling. Whitty traces behind it the 'Yellow Book', *School Education in England: Problems and Initiatives*, prepared as a confidential report by the Department of Education and Science (DES) for the Prime Minister, concluding that the time had come to establish 'generally accepted principles for the compostion of the secondary curriculum for all pupils, that is to say a "core curriculum" ' (DES, 1976).

Whitty (1989) again points out that subsequent DES documents (the Green Paper of July 1977, *Education in Schools: A Consultative Document*, and *Local Authority Arrangements for the School Curriculum*, 1979) emphasized the governing role of the Secretary of State for Education, but with it the need for 'partnership': 'the Government must bring together the partners in the education service and the interest of the community at large'. Whitty sees the government methods from this point onward as an abandonment of the 'politics of persuasion' and a determination to pursue centralizing aims through examination reforms, testing and certification changes. This continuous movement from James Callaghan's speech of 1976 to some extent up to the present day is an interesting one, especially in view of the weight Callaghan gave to the Confederation of British Industry's (CBI's) views, encapsulated in Sir Arnold Weinstock's analysis that education was being conducted by 'unaccountable teachers, teaching an irrelevant curriculum to young workers who were poorly motivated, illiterate and innumerate' (*Times Educational Supplement*, 23 January 1976). The CBI has continued to be a powerful force in the background of education policy in England and Wales.

The end of consensus, as Vaisey (1983) points out, was not confined to education, but applied equally to the management of the economy and to industry. It is perhaps symptomatic of the old era that Kogan (1971, p. 94) quotes Boyle as saying that he agonized over decisions but, once a decision had been taken, had little worry about the responsibility of implementing it. This could hardly be said of Ministers of Education since that time (as central power has increased), for whom instant implementation has been a major political activity and direct oversight of the implementation not a suitable role for local authorities.

Behind the political swings, however, is a palpable dilemma for a politician in the conflict of the need to apply professional responsibility for leadership and government while struggling to retain control over a vast national resource such as education at a time when economics and world status made political leaders look for greater effectiveness and efficiency in the promotion of human resources, as they perceived it. In the process, the concept of partnership-like consensus has been a casualty, and education has become something of an easy scapegoat. Much of the struggle during the 1980s became an internal one between policy advisory groups, such as the Hillgate Group, or coteries such as that known as the 'New Right', where the contention was not so much over the centrality of government control of the curriculum as over the degree of autonomy to be allowed to parents, governors and teachers within its framework in order to achieve direct pressure upon teachers for the implementation of policies. It is difficult to know how much individual policymaking can be attributable to secretaries of state rather than to advisory bodies after Sir Keith Joseph. The Conservative Education Reform Act of 1988, building on the Education Acts of 1980 and 1986, allowed for varied interpretations of the expected outcome of the empowerment of governors, parents and, to some extent, teachers, in keeping with the notion of market forces, by which 'league tables' for schools were evolved and published. For the teacher in the classroom, the burden which regular and detailed testing imposed created a virtual denial of curricular autonomy (which some no doubt welcomed). When this was combined with centrally initiated and radical changes in the initial training of teachers, and suggestions of increased class size, it could not but be seen as a declaration that their professional standing was being devalued.

Recent pilot projects in Britain to employ untrained licensed teachers have demonstrated a measure of a kind of success within limited conditions. This is held up as some justification for overriding other professional qualities, such as the capacity for change and self-development in skills and perception. In the British situation (as Townshend, 1994, points out), the initial training of teachers is being weaned away from links with institutions of higher education, so that one aspect of professionalism, that of the socialization and acquisition of practice, is emphasized at the expense of the others (and the experience limited to one school and possibly one mentor) (see Crossley and Hall, 1993). This is in effect, if not in intention, a short-termism which may seem to carry a measure of success in control and recruitment, until major changes require flexibility, and wider professional skills are called into play. Most of all it removes the autonomous self-regulation of the teaching profession by acting without consultation: a kind of velvet fascism. It removes the dilemma of how to achieve partnership or consensus for the politicians, but creates a series of severe dilemmas for the teaching profession.

It may be useful, in looking at education, to take a parallel definition, from management consulting, of professionalism as a code of conduct or value system, to show that the case of education is not isolated because it is a public service. In the International Labour Organization's (ILO's) *Management Consulting* (Kubr, 1976), the 'profession' of management consulting is seen as a seminal activity towards the professionalization of other activities – in this case management. This is an important concept, because it at once identifies the nature of the relationship between differing professions and the emergent nature of professionalism.

'Professional awareness and behaviour come when the early juggling with a little knowledge gives way to skilled application of a generally accepted body of knowledge according to acknowledged standards of integrity' (Kubr, 1976, p. 45). In dealing with the aspect of 'a body of knowledge', Kubr sees as a 'major feature of professionalism, [that] a consultant must be able and willing critically to examine his own knowledge and skills when considering new assignments'.

One of the most detailed areas that Kubr deals with is that concerning professional associations and codes of conduct (the 'regulating body' referred to above). Regulating the profession is seen to include: developing and updating the common body of knowledge; determining the minimum qualification criteria for new entrants; defining and adopting a code of professional conduct and practice for its members; examining the various aspects of practice; organizing the exchange of experience; and making recommendations to members on improvements in method, organization, selection, development and remuneration.

Within the codes of professional conduct, which 'signify voluntary assumption by members of the obligation of self-discipline above and beyond the requirements of law' (Association of Consulting Management Engineers, USA, quoted in Kubr, 1976) are listed criteria which deal with the 'client' aspect of our parameters above:

- To place the client's interest ahead of their own.
- To keep information about the client confidential and take no advantage of its knowledge.
- To accept no commissions in connection with the supply of services to the client.
- To hold no directorship or controlling interest in any business competitor of the client without disclosing it.
- Not to invite an employee of a client to consider or apply for alternative employment.
- Not to calculate remuneration on any other basis than a fixed fee agreed in advance, which may be on a time rate.
- To inform clients of any relationships and interests which might influence the consultant's judgements.

- Not to work when their judgement might be impaired by illness, misfortune or any other cause.
- To refrain from seeking business by public advertising or by payment of commission for the introduction to clients.

These rules do not go as far as to outline methodological guidance or offer definitions of good practice, but they give some parameters to the concept of 'professional conduct'. There are certain codes which are specific to the kind of service management consulting offers. For example, in the last clause regarding advertising, the advertising or the marketing industries might view their own professionalism in a different light, since such bodies as the Advertising Standards Authority (Code of Advertising Practice Committee) or the Institute of Marketing in the UK cover many of the aspects of professional conduct insofar as their activities are seen as services to members of the public.

The dilemma of balancing control with self-regulation in education has, in Britain, several times produced the notion of a 'teaching council' as a regulatory body to work alongside government and to give a measure of disciplinary control over the profession and partnership in policy-making. Though one exists in Scotland, England and Wales have never agreed upon its creation. The model usually quoted as a parallel is the General Nursing Council, which has many regulatory functions within that realm of public health service, where the service–client relationship is an intimate personal one and the need for an intermediary body alongside financial and planning functions is clear. However, the history of the public health service in England and Wales in recent years has followed a sad parallel with that of education.

At all levels of education in the UK there are bodies which function as associations or unions, some of which would describe themselves as professional associations dedicated to mutual improvement and problem-solving as well as the sharing of good practice in relation to research or teaching. There are others whose declared task is to negotiate with the 'employers' for joint agreements and protection over conditions of employ-

ment and rates of remuneration. Within the associations there is a certain polarity between those which function as professional associations and those which function as, and align themselves with, trade unions. The latter have been more willing to act as disciplinary bodies over matters of professional behaviour, largely because employment and remuneration remain the ultimate weapons of control by employers, public or private, and disputes over competence or behaviour incur penalties in these dimensions. The English teaching profession has thus in practice lurched from a code of 'gentleman's agreement' to full-blown trade unionism, even though there are 15 'associations' involved. Many would argue that much the same process has occurred in higher education.

It suits the current political situation to treat education as a tool of economic policy, and professional associations which play this role allow themselves to be drawn from their professional roots and thrust into a totally other and, to education, 'accidental' value system. Rabbi Jonathan Sacks in his Reith Lecture of 1993 showed how it is possible to take a process which is derived from a community's value system (whether of altruism or idealism or any other ethic) and make it the servant of other values. Open University case studies have shown how the late Sir Keith Joseph and Lord Young picked up the notion which became the Technical and Vocational Education Initiative (TVEI, later just TVE) from its roots in the Jewish Organisation for Rehabilitation and Training (ORT), designed to help young people train to get back into employment, and thrust it into a secular system of education. Losing its religio-ethical roots, it became a mere tool of governmental economic policy within a limited notion of skills training as education. Its insertion into the system was deliberately made the initiative of the Manpower Services Commission, as having more power and influence than the Department of Education and Science, both financially and in terms of its ability to act outside the territory of local authorities. The conflicting power systems between these ministries and their clients are still reflected in questions involving the validation of Vocational Certificates, CPVEs or GNVQs by the

National Council for Vocational Qualifications in schools and further education, as distinct from the continuing evolution of the national schools curriculum-based credentialling.

When we return to the initial and post-experience training of teachers in the UK, we find a palpable loss of control in decision-making by the profession itself. One might even see a movement such as Sacks outlines, to take pedagogical interests such as diagnostic testing and the evolution of teaching plans out of the living context and make it the servant of a different value system. In 1973, P. H. Taylor argued:

> The impression has been gained that teachers face a complex of problems without the services of a well-developed technology. To help the teachers develop this technology further should be the aim of research. This means more research at the point where teachers actually engage in the process of planning and in the implementing of this planning in the classroom. Only in observing how teachers go about these tasks can we hope to help them refine their procedures so that they become not so much a matter of rule of thumb as a developed methodology.

If, other than the cheapness of informal training for teachers, it is still to be argued in 1996 that teaching offers no clear basis *per se* for a commonly agreed and teachable professional core of knowledge and skills, the response must be to look at the research which has been done over the past few years in both Europe and the USA. Eisenhart and Borko (1991), for example, report on a continuing research project which gives ample evidence for successful and useful identification of a professional core of knowledge. They judge that progress in the past towards such clarity has often been held up by the failure to give satisfactory analytical models of the teaching situation (and hence a clear model), and that this has been due to a lack of interdisciplinary collaborative research on the process of teaching, a system which would be anathema to the current approach to education planning.

In a situation as complex as teacher–pupil relations, workable models are lost unless that situation is treated holistically and methods are adopted which include psychological and social process, with both cultural and cognitive content,

since teaching and learning to teach include both knowledge acquisition and professional socialization. The methodology is to focus on critical incidents in the processes and produce a coherent account of the factors which interplay. Among the themes in cognitive psychological research on classrooms is, for example, the realm of schema theory, in which Shulman (1988) provides a theoretical model of components of teachers' professional knowledge. Teachers are seen as drawing on seven domains of knowledge: knowledge of major subject matter, general pedagogical knowledge, pedagogical content knowledge, knowledge of other content, knowledge of the curriculum, knowledge of learners and knowledge of educational aims.

Excellent models for self-regulation and professional development are also offered by the growing successful experience of and research evidence for qualitative and action methodologies in research (Vulliamy *et al.*, 1990; Hopkin, 1992; Walker, 1994). Part of the process of such research depends on participant observation, part upon the evolution of frames of reference from within the situation, taking into account the cultural context and permitting hypotheses to emerge from the fieldwork and data. The notion of the cultural context as a key determinant of parameters, of information and of policy has suffered from a lack of holism in approach. What is true of research is equally true of the conceptual centrism by which governments attempt to determine, for example, forms of teacher training, without reference to the interrelating focal centres of knowledge and perception which govern training institutions and schools. The training and the socialization of the teacher are of their natures intimately related and continuous.

One way in which this happens in research is when the notion of 'culture' is taken as an ethnographic or anthropological viewpoint only. It has in consequence tended to be regarded as applying to the 'cultural' externalities of the teaching situation. Davies (1990), looking at the response of teachers to change or innovation in a mainly Third World context, comments: 'I would claim that the central question for a teacher is always "How can I use work to maximise my rewards?" Even the most dedicated of teachers look for rewards — whether these are the satisfactions of watching pupils develop ... or the thrills and spills of curriculum delivery.' She goes on to point out that the culture of teaching in the UK seriously inhibits practical curriculum change at school and classroom level unless the material structures of work to which the culture of teaching is a response and on which it feeds are subject to structural redefinition in the areas of curriculum, staffing policies and teacher training. For Davies, this means giving teachers more influence over events in these areas. Hence the training, socialization and continued professional development of teachers call for situation-based research and independent self-regulation as a categorical imperative among many conflicting demands. The application of neo-classical economic principles of the 'free market' denies such a controlling role to teachers as a professional body, or at the very least crowds it out of consideration by other imperatives.

In schooling in Britain, the school and the micro-environment of the classroom (even the teacher–pupil relationship) have been opened up to public scrutiny in an effort to give accountability to central government's perception of its role as paymaster and *a fortiori* manager of the national economy and labour markets, often viewed in the light of the supposed performance of other countries. Here one can see politicians exercising their correct 'professional' judgement. In a semblance of creating a local market in which parental investment of child and opportunity costs and expectations are traded against good service from the school, central government has devised testing at 'key stages' of what has been taught, measured against a centrally devised curricular checklist. It is a poor basis for either partnership or consensus. It has also invaded the private professional world of the headteacher, by giving governing bodies, drawn from local communities, political, social and parental managerial powers to implement central policy. All this additional burden has been imposed on the delicate inter-subjective process of teacher and pupil interaction, with the dilemma of priorities and loyalties very much placed upon the teacher. Moreover, it is ironic that a monetarist government is prepared to give financial autonomy to headteachers and individual schools, even leaving it to the hands of often financially amateur governors, while depriving teachers of a reasonable measure of curricular autonomy, which is their professional field.

If we take the ILO model as a basis for comparison, the teacher, viewed as a professional person, has acquired particular skills and knowledge and has means of constant upgrading of them. The teacher has commitment to the well-being of the clients (pupils), with the subsidiary qualities which relate to this, such as confidentiality, non-exploitation and so on. In place of accountability to a professional institute or teaching council (like the British Medical Association or the Nursing Council), the teacher is bombarded with codes of conduct, which mainly relate to fulfilling administrative requirements and documentation, together with the images of teaching imposed by parents, governors, politicians and the press. As with the case of hospital trusts currently in vogue in England and Wales, there is a tendency for management to become separate from education, so that the headteacher, like the hospital trust manager, sees the production of a budget surplus (dare one say a profit?) as the key goal of financial management. Both the Secretary of State and the press have observed — and there is well documented evidence — that quite a number of British schools are accumulating substantial reserves under the local management of schools system, often by skimping on the purchase of more or better-qualified staff. They were expected to 'spend up' but not 'spend over'. In such a case the real 'client' is not the taught, but the government, the trust (or, in a private enterprise, the chief executive's salary and the shareholders' profits).

'Marketing' has, of course, itself developed into a profession, with codes of behaviour, skills, information and responsibilities to the client. However, even in this highly technical form, with psychological surveys, motivation analyses, product presentation packages, penetration strategies and a host of clever techniques, the well-being of the client through the provision of information and enabling of choice is quickly diverted into persuasion and exploitation where the value system is not the personal good of the buyer so much as the profit of shareholders and increased market share of dominant national and multinational organizations. Here efficiency forces upon the buyer a limited if not distorted set of choices, and the destruction of competition, even if it is, hypothetically, for the better service of the buyer. Recent legislation on Sunday trading in England and Wales has unveiled many of these effects, despite the gloss of greater freedom for individual choice. The inevitable surfacing of the market's profit- and commodity-based value system overweighs the effort to provide simply a service to the client.

It is easy to pretend that an activity is a simple market transaction, in which supply and demand find a balance. Even in a Keynesian ideal there is a need for external intervention from time to time. The fact is that any commodity in a complex, plural and industrialized society is subject to a palimpsest of interpenetrating markets. Means become ends and ends means, and in the service industries or professions, the concept of the client and the locus of control changes with the value systems. If money is the value system, the client becomes the lender, shareholder, banker, aid agency, not the beneficiary of the service. The money market, the labour market, the teacher training market and the political market all intersect with the development of the learner in education. In research, the pursuit of accurate information is conditioned by the same intersecting markets, added to the commerce of academic reputation and accountability. As Michael Young (1992) commented in a speech to a seminar of the National Commission on Education, 'The moral economy is always in tension with the market economy. The market economy is bound to value people more for what they do than what they are – for their efficiency, their productivity, their achievements – and to encourage people to compete against each other.' Halsey, quoted in the same volume, comments: 'We have seen teaching being turned into a cognitive relation between older and younger people: somebody else is responsible for the character, we just take care of the brains.'

In higher education, the Rockefeller Foundation, looking back on 22 years of higher education development, found that one of the major prob-

lems, especially in the Third World, was the tension between, or dilemma of, commitment to scholarship and the demands and offers of the financial market (Coleman and Court, 1993). While the quality, relevance and potential of research had, of its nature, to be determined by the scholarly community (increasingly an international scholarly community), pressures upon universities and departments to take on lucrative research produced a patchwork, often destroying the balance and cumulative programmes of a department or university. The reasons, pressing as they might be in the 'developed' world, were irresistible in Third World conditions: demonstrable productivity, public recognition, the retention or recruiting of able staff, considerations all valid in themselves, outweighed and destroyed the development of fundamental research or a coherent policy.

Similarly, in the realms of schooling and research, it is obvious that in Britain the real goals of education or of research are being distorted by a competing model of professional accountability and economic discipline as measures of performance. Where the national or local politics or the economy, local or global, become the dominant regulators, the professional skills survive more by the self-sacrifice and dedication of the educational practitioners than the policy of the government, and it is the ultimate client who ultimately suffers. The dilemma for the practitioner is an acute one in terms of relative responsibilities: the dilemma seems to have ceased to exist from the government's side.

In one major UK university, the professor of music, subject to financial controls and cost-centring development, is obliged to continue his research, write books and papers on musicology, teach a large group of students and conduct the university choir and orchestra, together with other musical groups. Under the current system of 'internal marketing', by which academic areas are designated 'cost centres', and having been reduced to an administrative factor of 2.5 per cent of his budget, he must also actively pursue the supply of materials and resources to his department in person. Who, except an academic, musicologist or creative musician, could judge at what point the time required for discipline of mind and sensibility crumbles under the other imperatives? Recently, a hospital trust in the south of England formally stated that it required its medical staff to show a prior responsibility to the trust and its financial viability, rather than to the patients, when medical services were required. It is difficult to see where the budgetary pressures produce improved motivation or quality; they certainly produce dilemmas of great severity as to where ultimate professional responsibilities lie and who shall judge. The most recent result of such policy, as regards research, is the current move of the British government since the Culyer Report (1994) to withdraw a substantial portion of free research funding from teaching hospitals and restrict such to projects approved by the government. On the advice of which 'profession' can such decisions be reached? It is clear what the Committee of Vice Chancellors and Principals (of universities) in Britain thinks, since it strongly opposes the work of the Higher Education Funding Council to judge quality assessment in research when allocating further funds, preferring the more academically linked Higher Education Quality Council (*Times Higher Education Supplement*, 13 January 1995).

Lest this should be thought to be mere neo-liberalism of the worst nineteenth-century variety, it might be relevant to quote from an internal document of the University of Central Lancashire's Business School. This business school is highly successful in relating to the labour market in producing commercial and industrial managers. It is innovative, and updates its courses and structures to meet the needs of the client students and their aims at reaching the labour market. In a study produced for a seminar on the upgrading of courses it says:

> BA Business Studies is part of a lifelong learning process for its students and as such it must fulfil two vital roles. It must equip them for this process with the essential skills of inquiry and scholarship, but it must also be immediately relevant to and useful in the real world. It is in this latter context that the course team regards as essential industrial placement for the sandwich students and on-going work experience for those on part-time degrees. There is no doubt that these ingredients enhance employment potential and prospects for all students.

In a previous passage the study says:

> The BA and BS courses attract large numbers of applicants and of good quality.
> The progression statistics are well within the norms attained nationally.
> The degree results are excellent.
> The career/career enhancement prospects excellent.
> This has been obtained against a background of continual change and disruption, additionally the BABS programmes have been revalidated in 1988, 1991, converted to MODCATS 1994 (stage 1) and revalidated in 1994 ...
> The additional workload imposed on the core department of staff of this continual change is debilitating and detracts from the real work of the department. The department is very fortunate to have a committed core of professionals whose expertise and teaching skills should be enhanced and developed to the longer term benefit of the university, not downtrodden by heavy and excessive administrative processes.

If this is the dilemma of professionalism under pressure in the face of 'market' imperatives in a highly successful 'market'-related university department, how much more in the primary school?

The high point of teacher autonomy was probably under Edward Boyle, when the Schools Council for Curriculum and Examinations formed some kind of partnership to identify good practice, centralize it and diffuse it. The curriculum development aspect progressed very quickly, fostered at the governmental level by Derek Morrell (Deputy Secretary of State in the Children's Department of the Home Office), and by university education departments of an innovative kind, such as that of the University of East Anglia. But it was the engagement of practising teachers who were able to share and develop 'good practice' which gave the driving force to the 'partnership'. At the administrative level, the Schools Council's committees consisted of academics and headteachers – the latter were always quoted as the 'teaching' element, but the experience suggested that their agenda, objectives and epistemology had changed from that of the classroom (see Shipman, 1974, for the misperception of objectives among participants in projects).

In a situation from which central government had been excluded in all but the provision of funds and adequate numbers of teachers, the age-old contest between curriculum and examinations was given a shift of balance by the sanctions given to the whole field of testing under structures devised initially by Professor Paul Black. The evolution of Key Stage tests, as they came to be known in the 1990s, was in itself a shift in the notion of testing and public examination, both in its age-grouping and in its objectives. Essentially the tests proposed by the School Examinations and Assessment Council (SEAC) (replacing in name and priority the Schools Council for Curriculum and Examinations) were proposed as 'mastery' tests, with an agenda for teaching and for testing what aspects of particular subjects had been taught and learned. It is true that in the early stages, pilot schemes were based on primary science teaching and learning and gave some weight to the judgemental aspects of learning. However, this very cognitive field made relatively easy the bringing together of subject field and some aspects of personal development.

Neither Black nor SEAC (later to be refounded and named School Curriculum and Assessment Authority, or SCAA) were to anticipate that the same 'mastery' approach would be applied across the affective objectives and then held up as measures of teaching and learning success, at micro and macro levels, of student, teacher, class, school or local authority, in measures which confused the aptness or background support of a child in development with the mastery of subject information. Most of all, the teaching profession found that the volume of testing crowded out the evolution of a student-centred learning process, with its important flexible or 'spiral' diagnostic elements. It was inevitable that a balance would be fought for in the dialogue between teachers, researchers and administrators. Though teachers found the clarity of programme and the opportunity for some testing in principle useful, they also found themselves mere commodity units in a competitive market-value system, where throughput of numbers, cheapness of younger staff and examination league tables dominated the market and the development of the child was reduced to 'value added'.

In a similar way, the effort to establish a dignified partnership was impeded by the encouragement of general press and public comment on issues which appear to the 'layman' as simple and commonplace matters of 'performance'.

Professionalism, as we have seen, is an emergent entity. It yet remains to be seen whether the deep culture of humanism and commitment to the client, which is typically British, can survive the onslaught of forces which, instead of encouraging practitioners to give their first priority to teaching and learning, expose them to servility and stress, thus destroying professionalism in a deep chain reaction. Clearly the intersecting 'professionalism' of the economist and the politician or administrator are affected by such action. That such concerns constitute a dilemma for the politicians is manifest in the committee set up in 1995 under Lord Nolan to establish guidelines for Members of Parliament over the relationship between their private business interests and their public duties. The fact that the field is a complex one does not mean that it is impossible to devise means by which imperatives can be negotiated and professional judgement of practitioners given due weight, alongside careful and responsible budgeting and accountability. To do this means to encourage a proper body to regulate, promote, protect and permit to emerge true professionalism in teaching and, in parallel, research, not least by cultivating a language of discourse less suited to a nation of shopkeepers ('delivery', 'customer' and so on). Such bodies would have a positive say in the entry requirements for prospective teachers, the socialization of teachers into work, their professional development throughout their career, innovations in curriculum or examination and professional codes of practice and their policing. The dilemma still remains of how such relative professional autonomy can relate to both economic and political policy-making.

Educational dilemmas lie at the core of many of the dilemmas facing societies in general: the whole nature of partnership, whether of equal professionals, of master and servant or of buyer and seller, concerns political no less than pedagogical style. The dilemma of equating fiscal and budgetary controls with concerns for investment and employment bears heavily upon education, whether it is seen as human capital development or human right. Many of the studies which seek to evaluate returns to investment in education, whether primary, secondary, tertiary or quaternary or 'higher' (excellently summarized in Sultana, 1992, pp. 287ff), suggest that the formation of personal qualities and social or learning attitudes in the foundational stages of a general education, and hence the quality of teaching and learning, rather than vocational direction, are the most significant factors. Questions of the relation between financial constraints and the quality of teaching and learning – broadly, whether more money or resources would improve the quality of learning – remain equivocally answered. This leaves unsolved the dilemmas of how to relate forms of education to socio-economic styles and objectives, and thus to control both educational investment and educational output. It is likely that the deep cultural values within committed teachers and within British society generally, perhaps more so in its multicultural development, will continue to provoke a dialogue of professional partners or of market antagonists for a really effective educational system. The dilemmas remain as acute, however: how such developments can be harnessed to produce the most productive harvest rather than a dissipating battlefield.

# References

Bourdoncle, R. (1994) La professionalisation des enseignants. *European Journal of Teacher Education*, **17** (1/2).

Chitty, C. (1988) Two models of a national curriculum: origins and interpretation. In D. Lawton and C. Chitty (eds), *The National Curriculum*. London: University of London.

Coleman, J. S. and Court, D. (1993) *University Development in the Third World*. Oxford: Pergamon Press.

Crossley, M. and Hall, V. (eds) (1993) *Research Training and Educational Management: International Perspectives*. Bristol: University of Bristol.

Culyer Report (1994) *Report on Medical Research Funding*. London: HMSO.

Davies, L. (1990) *Equity and Efficiency: School Management in an International Context*. London: Falmer Press.

DES (1976) *School Education in England: Problems and Initiatives*. London: HMSO.

DES (1977) *Education in Schools: A Consultative Document*. London: HMSO.

DES (1979) *Local Authority Arrangements for the School Curriculum: Report on the Circular 14/77 Review*. London: HMSO.

Eisenhart, M. A. and Borko, H. (1991) In search of an interdisciplinary collaborative design for studying teacher education. *Teaching and Teacher Education*. **7** (2).

*Hansard*, March 1960, no. 620, cols. 51–2.

Hopkin, A. G. (1992) Qualitative research methodologies: a cross-cultural perspective. *Compare*, **22** (2).

Kogan, M. (1971) *The Politics of Education*. Harmondsworth: Penguin.

Kubr, M. (1976) *Management Consulting*. Geneva: ILO.

Laderrière, P. (1994) Les politiques de quelques pays européens dans le champ de la professionalisation. *European Journal of Teacher Education*, **17** (1/2).

Montané, M. (1994) Editorial. *European Journal of Teacher Education*, **17** (1/2)

Nóvoa, A. (1994) Les enseignants à la recherche de leur profession. *European Journal of Teacher Education*, **17** (1/2)

Sacks, J. (1993) *Reith Lectures*, BBC Radio 4.

Shipman, M. D. (1974) *Inside a Curriculum Project*. London: Methuen.

Shulman, L. S. (1988) *Knowledge Growth in Teaching: A Final Report to the Spencer Foundation*. Stanford, CA: Stanford University.

Sultana, R. G. (1992) *Education and National Development*. Malta: Mireva Publications.

Taylor, P. H. (1973) *How Teachers Plan Their Courses*. Windsor: NFER.

Townshend, J. (1994) Developments in school-based initial teacher training. *European Journal of Teacher Education*, **17** (1/2).

Vaisey, J. (1983) *In Breach of Promise*. London: Allen and Unwin.

Vulliamy, G. *et al.* (1990) *Doing Educational Research in Developing Countries*. London: Falmer Press.

Walker, M. (1994) Professional development through action research in township primary schools in South Africa. *International Journal of Educational Development*, **114** (1).

Whitty, G. (1989) The New Right and the National Curriculum: state control or market forces? *Journal of Educational Policy*, **4** (4).

Young, M. (1992) *Insight*. London: National Commission on Education.

# 5 Teaching as a Profession

ERIC HOYLE

The idea of a profession has been under a sustained attack at the conceptual level for over thirty years and, in Britain at least, many of the attributes which might be considered to contribute to the status of teaching as a profession have been undermined by a whole raft of legislation which has been enacted over the past fifteen years. Is, therefore, the idea of a profession becoming an outmoded concept? Will the application of the term 'profession' to teaching eventually fall into desuetude? Or will the term remain in popular use but the institutions and practices which were its referent become radically changed?

It is the argument of this chapter that, despite predictions about the demise of the idea of teaching as a profession, it will be neither conceptualized nor politicized out of existence. The nature of teaching as a profession will certainly undergo change but, despite its current critics, the idea of a profession will continue to embody a set of principles which will be widely considered so worthwhile that they will persist. It would, however, be naive to claim that this prediction is based wholly on a value-free analysis of the likely future for the teaching profession. The present writer is of the belief that although the nature of teaching as a profession will, and should, undergo change, there is a case for defending some of the principles entailed in the idea.

## The semantics

The question of whether or not teaching is a profession is otiose. The term 'the teaching profession' is in widespread use and is likely to remain so. However, this usage raises two kinds of question. One is whether the term 'profession' can ever be wholly denotative. The other, related, question is whether a profession can be defined in terms of a particular set of criteria. These can be considered in turn.

The concept *profession* can be wholly denotative where those occupations labelled as professions have some legal or otherwise official status. In some countries professions have a legal status and responsibilities. In Britain, *profession* is not a legal concept, although, of course, occupations which are widely denoted as such have legal responsibilities. However, in some countries teaching has acquired the legal status of *profession*. Profession is also denotative where it is a term which is officially in use to categorize certain occupations. Beyond this, *profession* is used in a denotative way in everyday speech, although, as such, it is applied more widely than simply to medicine, law, teaching, etc., frequently being applied to any occupation. But *profession* is also used, and perhaps most frequently used, in a connotative way carrying different degrees of value-loading. Thus, when a mother tells a neighbour that her daughter is 'joining the teaching profession' or a teacher union leader reports that such and such is 'good for the profession', or a politician holds that 'no occupation which goes on strike can be regarded as a profession', it is reasonably clear that the term is used in those contexts in a value-loaded way. It therefore has to be recognized that the term is most often used with a symbolic or ideological intent.

This brings one to the question of whether professions can be designated as such on the basis of criteria which distinguish them from other occupations. There is a literature on the alleged criteria of a profession, which goes back at least to the second decade of the century (Flexner, 1915). The criteria which were usually invoked were the fact of being a crucial social service, the existence of a body of academic knowledge, the need for a lengthy period of training, autonomy of the individual and the professional group, self-government and a code of ethics.

This approach has been heavily criticized from the 1960s onwards on two main grounds. One was that these criteria were not objective but constituted part of an ideology of professionalism, whereby the elites of certain occupations sought to retain or extend their privileges, and sociologists of a functionalist persuasion sought to endow this ideology with a spurious objectivity. A second criticism, usually linked with the first, was that the various lists produced by sociologists had little in common. In fact, this alleged lack of consensus was a stick to beat a dog, since although the lists did vary, many of the crucial elements (e.g. knowledge, autonomy, self-regulation) were common to almost all.

As will be shown in the following section, the first argument was a very powerful one and cannot be readily dismissed. The 'characteristics' approach is somewhat circular, in that sociologists to a degree took the criteria from the ideological claims of the major professions. On the other hand, the significance of the criteria are evidenced by the fact that they are much discussed by those who otherwise would reject the idea of a profession. And, notwithstanding criticisms of the term, it is difficult even for the critics to avoid using it.

## Critical perspectives on the professions

The self-interested character of the professions has long been the subject of criticism. George Bernard Shaw called the professions 'a conspiracy against the laity'. A key work in debate countered the functionalist perspective with the alternative view that the professions had attained their rights and privileges not as a reward bestowed by a grateful public but by the exercise of power by certain occupational groups underpinned by an ideology of service (Johnson, 1972). A historical account of this process has been given by Larson (1977), who writes: 'I see professionalism as a process by which producers of special services sought to constitute and control a market for their expertise ... Professionalization is thus an attempt to translate one order of social resources – special knowledge and skills – into another – social and economic rewards.'

Although professionalization began when members of the professions were independent practitioners offering a service-for-fee, the process continued when the services offered by the professions became increasingly a matter of state provision, and until after the middle of the present century (Perkin, 1989). As, in different ways, the professions increasingly performed functions on behalf of the state-as-client as well as on behalf of individuals and families, they functioned as effective pressure groups in seeking to preserve their autonomy and their privileges within the state sector. Despite this change, the criticisms of the professions remained and perhaps became more strident. Moreover, as we will see, this led to political interventions to limit the power and privileges of the professions.

This broad critique of the professions embraced a number of more specific criticisms which were directed at the alleged criteria of a profession. Two instances can be given. One relates to the alleged knowledge base of the professions. It is argued that the knowledge claim has been greatly exaggerated and that the length and content of professional training was more concerned with the aggrandizement of the occupation than with improving the quality of service. Studies of professional practice have shown that the types of knowledge which practitioners use bear little relationship to the structure of knowledge acquired in the course of their training (Freidson, 1970). The other relates to the argument that professional practitioners require a high degree of autonomy in order to be free to make sound professional judgements in the interests of clients. This is criticized as being much more concerned with avoiding accountability to clients than with providing a service to them. Criticisms are also made of the other alleged criteria, such as self-government (again a device for avoiding accountability) and a code of ethics (held to be more concerned with protecting practitioners than protecting clients).

## The professionalization of teaching

The history of the teaching profession since it became organized in the latter quarter of the nineteenth century can be seen in part as the history of a quest for professional status. However, there are some crucial differences between teaching and, say, medicine or law in terms of their professional project. Although teaching as a fee-based activity had elements in common with the other professions as early as the eighteenth century (Holmes, 1982), it failed to create and control a market. Its emergence as a profession coincided with the introduction of a mass education system and it was largely a public service. Its professional project could, therefore, only be advanced with the support of the state. Early attempts, through the teachers' registration movement, for example, to establish a professional body for the advancement of professional status were, paradoxically, pursued by the teacher unions. A professional rhetoric was combined with a union strategy.

The relationship between the teaching profession and the state went through a number of stages in the nineteenth and early twentieth centuries (Grace, 1987). Ozga and Lawn (1981) have shown the symbiotic nature of the relationship, whereby state support for the professional project was mainly conditional on the support of the teaching profession for certain state policies. Largely, through the exercise of union influence, teaching in Britain increasingly met the criteria traditionally used to distinguish the professions from other occupations. Only qualified teachers could be employed in state schools. Qualification was ex-

tended to include training for graduate entrants. The minimum length of the teacher training course was extended from two to three and then to four years. Teaching became an all-graduate profession. The academic content of courses was increased and an infrastructure of research and development emerged. Teachers enjoyed a very high degree of autonomy and the organized profession had an influential role in what Manzer (1970) called 'the sub-government of education'. Teachers in England and Wales could have had a General Teaching Council in the 1970s, but the unions rejected the offer because of the strings which were attached. A GTC was established in Scotland in 1965. Thus, according to the usual criteria, teaching was in the process of professionalization, which reached its apotheosis in the late 1960s and early 1970s.

## Critics of the idea of teaching as a profession

One is concerned here with those critics who believe that the idea of a profession is an inappropriate lodestone for teaching, because it is unattainable and/or because the continuing pursuit of professional status is not in the interests of clients. Perhaps three perspectives can be identified, though there is considerable overlap between them.

The first perspective is that which sees the professional project as misguided because it is believed to be unattainable. Such critics point out that medicine and law should not be taken as models, since their structural and historical circumstances are different from those of teaching. This case is put most cogently by Kimball (1988), who holds that teaching can never achieve professional status because the profession would never be allowed full control over knowledge and practice.

A second, and related, perspective holds that the continued professionalization of teaching is not in the interests of clients. Contributions to this perspective can be ranged along a continuum of radicalism. At one end of the continuum could be placed the work of Illich (1971), who argued for deschooling on the basis that schools were run more in the interests of professionals than those of pupils, whose needs were subordinated to professional self-interest. While not dealing with teaching specifically, a similar, though perhaps less radical, case for deprofessionalization was put by Haug (1973) and Bennett and Hockenstad (1973). Their basic argument is that professionalization is a strategy for avoiding meeting the interests of clients by claiming more expertise than the professionals actually possess in order to dominate clients and refuse them a voice in the determination of their own needs. The excessive claims for autonomy and for a specialized knowledge base are identified as particular problems. Similar proposals have been made by educational professionals, e.g. Anderson (1987).

A third perspective takes the view that the idea of a profession is a misleading model for teachers to adopt in the face of what is seen as the increasing proletarianization of teaching. The proletarianization argument is usually associated with the labour process perspective of Braverman (1974), and has been developed in relation to teaching in Britain in a number of works by Ozga and Lawn (Ozga and Lawn, 1981; Lawn and Ozga, 1981). Basically, this view holds that economic, technological and political forces are so deskilling teachers that their work increasingly approximates to manual and routinized non-manual work.

## Recent trends in Britain

Ironically, although the criticisms of the idea of a profession and proposals for deprofessionalization were advanced in the 1960s and early 1970s from a radical left perspective, it was the influence of the radical right on the policies of governments of the 1980s and 1990s which actually led to legislation that challenged the practices of all professions, including teaching. The accountability movement is usually held to have been initiated by Callaghan's Ruskin College speech of 1976, but it was the Thatcher and Major governments that enacted the legislation which imposed greater political, bureaucratic and market accountability on all professions – but especially teaching – and reduced the degree of professional accountability, i.e. professional self-monitoring of effectiveness.

As there is now a substantial literature on these developments which implicitly deals with implications for teaching as a profession, a full account will not be given here (e.g. see Simon and Chitty, 1993). However, among recent policies relevant to the present argument are increased power of governors, local management of schools, grant maintained status, open enrolment, the National Curriculum, standard attainment tests, systematic inspection by OFSTED-approved teams, publication of inspection reports, institutional development plans, publication of exam results and other performance data, and teacher appraisal.

These strategies for increasing accountability have significant implications for teaching as a profession as defined by the key criteria, e.g. practitioner autonomy, knowledge base and the capacity to shape policy. The capacity to shape policy has also been reduced by legislation, limiting the influence and power of trade unions and the practice of excluding trade union representatives from making any input into policy.

## Implications of recent policies for the idea of teaching as a profession

It is undoubtedly the case that the radical right critique of the professions of the 1980s and 1990s has had a much greater impact on professional practice than the radical left critique of the 1960s, since there has been the political will and opportunity to transform the former into practice. The impact of these policies can be conceptualized in perhaps three main ways, which can be termed *reprofessionalization*, *proletarianization* and *professionalization*. These can be separately considered.

## Reprofessionalization

This position is rarely stated explicitly and is derived by inference from statements about teaching and other professions made by Conservative ministers and politicians. The position might be explicitly formulated as follows. It is the function of the professions, as components of a market economy, to meet customer expectations as efficiently as possible. Thus, as Ribbins (1990) has pointed out, there is a movement towards the concept of professional-as-deliverer. There has been a semantic shift in the connotation of *professional* – as both noun and adjective – a full consideration of which is beyond the scope of this chapter. Briefly, *professional* has become somewhat uncoupled from *profession*, and its connotations have increased in number, one of which is that of pragmatic efficiency. On this view, the professional task of the teacher is to understand and interpret government policies and consumer expectations and to translate them faithfully and efficiently into practice. At the same time, the attempt has been made to heighten the expectations of consumers of professional services via various 'charters', including the Parent's Charter.

This implicit conception is, of course, at odds with the traditional concept of a profession. Knowledge is reduced to technique, autonomy is replaced by the control of the consumer – parental and state control – and responsibility has been succeeded by a narrow concept of accountability.

## Proletarianization

This perspective regards the idea of a profession as having only a residual value in interpreting the current situation. It is seen as diverting attention from a process which is affecting many middle-class occupations in developed societies.

This perspective is usually associated with Braverman (1974). As indicated above, its main protagonists in the field of education in the UK are Ozga and Lawn (1981) and in the United States, Apple (1981). The basic argument is that under late-twentieth-century capitalism, changes in technology and forms of institutional power are transforming the work situation of technical and service occupations, including those traditionally considered to be professions, in ways which make it more akin to that of manual workers. Two processes in particular are identified as being of particular significance within the overall process of proletarianization: *deskilling* and *intensification*. The former entails a decline in the level of knowledge and competence required by members of the professions. The latter refers to the increasing demands made upon the time of professionals, particularly for routine activities.

Such changes as the introduction of a national curriculum and, particularly, the associated testing can be interpreted as constituting a deskilling of teachers, as can, more generally, the considerable inroads into teacher autonomy which were discussed above. Certainly, virtually half the teaching force believes that its professional strengths have been eroded by the National Curriculum (Pollard *et al.*, 1994). The intensification of teachers' work could be taken to include their increased involvement in the following activities: curriculum development, school management, examination and assessment, educational technology, links with the social services, responsiveness to parents, pastoral care, personal and social education, combating racism and sexism, and professional development. The question is whether the implications of these changes are best approached within the framework of *professionalization* (and *deprofessionalization*) or of *proletarianization*.

The problem with the concept of proletarianization is that its connotation in this context is far from clear. It carries too much political freight to be simply a descriptive collective term for a number of processes, including deskilling and intensification. The use of proletarianization in this context is perhaps less to do with the analysis of changes in the activity of teaching than with the long-running debate within social class theory about the structural location of the middle class, which has long been a problem in Marxist theory. However, there is a growing consensus among theorists of social class that the proletarianization thesis constitutes a dead end and should now be abandoned (Savage *et al.*, 1992).

Because proletarianization, as used in relation to teachers, carries both structural and ideological meanings and the relationship between the two is far from clear, it would appear that while the protagonists of the proletarianization thesis in relation to teaching are critical of the structural aspect, at the same time they are seeing it as a political opportunity for the ideological integration of manual and non-manual workers. However, this would be to ignore the current complexities of the political orientations of the middle classes as a whole and their separate components.

## *Professionalization*

This third perspective retains the idea of a profession, together with the alleged criteria, as the basis for the analysis of current issues in teaching. Since this preferred perspective informs the position taken in this chapter, it will be treated separately in the following, final, section.

## The uses of 'profession'

A number of telling criticisms of the idea of a profession were discussed earlier in this chapter. Perhaps the two basic and related criticisms are the irredeemably ideological character of the concept and the lack of analytic value and the alleged criteria of a profession seen as components of this ideology. While many of the criticisms are valid, the view taken here is that the idea of a profession, in T. H. Marshall's phrase, 'is not wholly the invention of selfish minds' and that it provides a valuable heuristic means of addressing current issues in education. This is not to take an essentialist view of the idea of a profession. The idea is a

social construct and, over time, it may well be replaced by a different set of concepts for handling key problems in education, but at the present time it continues to offer heuristic possibilities for understanding these issues and formulating policies with regard to them. Space does not permit an elaboration of the deployment of the idea of a profession in relation to current issues (see Hoyle and John, 1995, for a more detailed discussion). Thus the remainder of this chapter can only indicate some of the possibilities in terms of the traditional criteria.

## *Autonomy*

Complete practitioner autonomy is not practically possible, politically viable or morally acceptable. Yet some degree of autonomy is inevitable since, in the absence of some unforeseeable draconian means of surveillance, teachers will enjoy some degree of autonomy at the classroom level because of endemic uncertainties about the relationship between aims, methods and outcomes. Thus, professional autonomy leads one into a crucial set of issues in relation to teacher effectiveness, relationships with pupils and relationships between the expertise of the teacher and the expectations of parents.

Of particular interest at the present time is the nature of collaborative professionality. One of the ways in which it is suggested that the teaching profession needs to change is from autonomy towards what is variously termed collegiality, collaboration, participation, etc. Since some degree of autonomy is inevitable and desirable, the issue becomes one of how provision can be improved through greater collaboration. This, in turn, raises questions about the nature of teacher collaboration, the levels of collaboration, e.g. policy, planning and pedagogy, the voluntariness of teacher collaboration as contrasted with contrived (Hargreaves and Dawe, 1990) or enforced (Smyth, 1991) collegiality, and the stages by which collegiality can be achieved (Hargreaves, 1994).

## Knowledge

The legitimacy of the criticism that inert blocks of codified knowledge have very little impact on professional practice has for some time been accepted by teacher educators. There are thus continuing efforts to identify the nature of the knowledge which informs good classroom practice and how this can be developed during initial teacher education and subsequent professional development. This development is based on research on teachers' thinking and classroom practice. Following the approach of Schön (1987), there is a growing recognition of the role of reflection in professional practice and the accumulation of experience, and how this may be developed during training. The approach also gives priority to practice over knowledge acquisition. However, it rejects the position which has had much influence on recent policies in relation to education, which suggests that subject-matter knowledge is the only form of knowledge which teachers require, and that direct experience of teaching is, alone, sufficient for professional competence. This criticism is based on a wilful misrepresentation of the university-based element of teacher education as continuing to transmit bodies of abstract theory. The task of further identifying the relationship between cognition and classroom effectiveness is an important one for the enhancement of professionality. However, further success in this field is unlikely to enhance the professional status of teachers, which will, as far as can be foreseen, continue to be associated with conventional academic knowledge.

While it is right that the quest for further exploration between cognitive knowledge and classroom practice should be given priority, it should also be recognized that teachers have a wide range of professional responsibilities in addition to the transmission of knowledge and skill. Pastoral care, social education, curriculum development, departmental management, etc., are underpinned by forms of theoretical knowledge other than those relating to pedagogy, and require much further exploration.

## Responsibility

The idea of a profession focuses attention on the issue of responsibility. This is not to assume that there is a hard and fast distinction between the professions and other occupations, including the craft occupations of building, plumbing, car mechanics, etc., nor between professional service and business. Nevertheless, it is the notion of responsibility which is inherent in the idea of a profession that is the touchstone, and it is this notion which needs constant examination and reaffirmation.

Responsibility is frequently equated with accountability and, of course, in recent years there has been a growing emphasis on accountability in government policies. The appropriateness of different forms of accountability – political, bureaucratic, market, peer, etc. – to the professions needs continuing analysis. However, accountability does not exhaust the professional commitment to clients, since it is limited and extrinsic and entails accountability to, rather than responsibility for. Responsibility is an essential quality of the teacher as professional, since the uncertainties of teaching limit the scope of accountability. An exploration of responsibility takes one into the realm of ethics, which in recent years, with some exceptions (Langford, 1978), has been a neglected area – possibly because codes of ethics have been as often concerned with the protection of the practitioner as with that of the client.

## Influence

Influence refers to the role of a profession in shaping policy in the area of its practice. As noted above, the role of the teaching profession, as exercised by teacher unions, has been considerably reduced in recent years. The role of the profession in this respect needs reconsideration. Such a consideration would include the role of the unions in this process. The tension between the role of the unions in pursuing members' interests and clients' interests has long been debated and the need for such a debate to continue in changed circumstances is certain. Such a debate would need to consider the role of professional institutions other than unions in the formulation of policy, and especially the membership and functions of a General Teaching Council.

In conclusion, although the idea of a profession has been under attack from the political left and political right, the present chapter has argued that, despite the problems attaching to the idea, 'profession' remains a key organizing concept which helps us to explore a number of key educational issues, some of which have been listed above.

# References

Anderson, L. W. (1987) The decline of teacher autonomy: tears or cheers? *International Review of Education*, **33**.

Apple, M. (1981) Curricular form and the logic of technical control: building the passive individual. In L. Barton, R. Meighan and S. Walker (eds), *Schooling, Ideology and the Curriculum*. Lewes: Falmer Press.

Bennett, W. S. and Hockenstad, M. C. (1973) Full-time people workers and conceptions of the 'professional'. In P. Halmos (ed.), *Professionalization and Social Change: Sociological Review Monograph, 20*. Keele: University of Keele.

Braverman, H. (1974) *Labor and Monopoly Capital: The Degradation of Work in the Twentieth Century*. New York: Monthly Review Press.

Flexner, A. (1915) Is social work a profession? In *Proceedings: National Conferences of Charities and Corrections*.

Freidson, A. (1970) *The Profession of Medicine*. Chicago: University of Chicago Press.

Grace, G. (1987) Teachers and the state. In M. Lawn and G. Grace (eds), *Teachers: The Culture and Politics of Work*. London: Falmer Press.

Hargreaves, A. and Dawe, R. (1990) Paths of professional development: contrived collegiality, collaborative cultures and the case of peer coaching. *Teaching and Teacher Education*, **6** (3).

Hargreaves, D. (1994) The new professionalism. *Teaching and Teacher Education*, **10** (4).

Haug, M. (1973) De-professionalization: an alternate hypothesis for the future. In P. Halmos (ed.), *Professionalization and Social Change: Sociological Review Monograph, 20*. Keele: University of Keele.

Holmes, G. (1982) *Augustan England: Professions, State and Society*. London: Allen and Unwin.

Hoyle, E. and John, P. (1995) *Teaching: Professional Knowledge and Professional Practice*. London: Cassell.

Illich, I. (1971) *Deschooling Society*. London: Calder and Boyars.

Johnson, T. J. (1972) *Professions and Power*. London: Macmillan.

Kimball, B. A. (1988) The problem of teachers' authority in the light of the structural analysis of professions. *Educational Theory*, **38** (1).

Langford, G. (1978) *Teaching as a Profession: An Essay in the Philosophy of Education*. Manchester: Manchester University Press.

Larson, M. S. (1977) *The Rise of Professionalism: A Sociological Analysis*. Berkeley: University of California Press.

Lawn, M. and Ozga, J. (1981) The educational worker. In L. Barton and S. Walker (eds), *Schools, Teachers and Teaching*. Lewes: Falmer Press.

Manzer, R. A. (1970) *Teachers and Politics*. Manchester: Manchester University Press.

Ozga, J. and Lawn, M. (1981) *Teachers, Professionalism and Class*. Lewes: Falmer Press.

Perkin, H. (1989) *The Rise of Professional Society*. London: Routledge.

Pollard, A., Broadfoot, P., Croll, P., Osborn, M. and Abbott, D. (1994) *Changing English Primary Schools: The Impact of the Education Reform Act at Key Stage 1*. London: Cassell.

Ribbins, P. (1990) Teachers as professionals: towards a redefinition. In R. Morris (ed.), *Central and Local Control of Education after the ERA 1988*. Harlow: Longman.

Savage, M., Barlow, J., Dickens, P. and Fielding, T. (1992) *Property, Bureaucracy and Culture: Middle-Class Formation in Contemporary Britain*. London: Routledge.

Schön, D. (1987) *Educating the Reflective Practitioner*. San Francisco: Jossey-Bass.

Simon, B. and Chitty, C. (1993) *SOS: Save Our Schools*. London: Lawrence and Wishart.

Smyth, J. (1991) International perspectives on teacher collegiality: a labour process discussion based on the concept of teachers' work. *British Journal of Sociology of Education*, **12** (3).

# Response to Eric Hoyle

## ALMA HARRIS

In responding to Professor Hoyle's chapter, I want to take the debate further by focusing upon education and teaching in a post-modern society. In particular, I want to consider the role of the teacher in a society where political, organizational and personal life will be based on quite different principles from those which have underpinned education for most of this century. In doing so, I hope to reinforce the basis for my disagreement with Professor Hoyle concerning his notion of traditional professionalism.

Most writers on the theme of post-modernity agree that at the heart of the transition is the globalization of economic activity, information, communications and technology (e.g. Harvey, 1989; Giddens, 1991; Macdonald, 1991). These transitions will inevitably impact upon education, and whether they are described in terms of post-liberalism, post-industrialism or post-modernity, the net result is the same: widespread, unprecedented change. The post-modern condition is complex, paradoxical and contested but it is deeply consequential for education and teaching. If the current changes facing teachers seem confusing and disconnected, this is because the post-modern context is itself deeply confusing and unpredictable.

As I suggest in Chapter 6, the emergence of post-modern society is presenting immense problems and challenges for our modernistic school systems and the teachers who work within them. While Professor Hoyle and I agree that change has become a pressing and immediate feature of teachers' working lives, it is my contention that this change has resulted in intensification and proletarianization. It is my position that deep transformations have occurred at the very core of teachers' work, which have affected how teaching is defined and socially organized. Consequently, to adhere to notions of professionalism, as outlined by Professor Hoyle, seems to be somewhat idealistic.

One of the most immediate responses to the pressures of post-modernity has been the expansion of the teacher's role to take on new problems and new mandates. Teachers' responsibilities are now more extensive, their roles are more diverse and their workload is more diffuse. For instance, their increased workload can be construed as a proliferation of administrative and assessment tasks. Alternatively, it can be viewed as a steep reduction in the time and opportunity for teachers to show concern and care for their students' learning.

In an endeavour to explain the way in which such changes do not sit comfortably with professionalism, it is important to make the distinction between professionalism and proletarianism clear. Professionalism emphasizes changes in, and extensions to, the teacher's role that signify enhancement. Here teaching is viewed as becoming more complex, chiefly because teachers are involved more in leadership roles, partnerships with colleagues, shared decision-making and providing consultancy to others in their own areas of expertise. It is Professor Hoyle's view that teaching is becoming more complex and more skilled for these reasons. Furthermore, he advocates that this additional responsibility is not unwelcome but constitutes an 'extended professionalism'. It is on this point that we disagree.

It is my view that teaching has become deprofessionalized and routinized in the face of increased intensification and that there is a rapid move towards proletarianization. As Hargreaves (1994) has argued, intensification creates chronic and persistent overload, which reduces areas of personal discretion, inhibits involvement in and control over longer-term planning and fosters dependency on externally produced materials and expertise. Rather than producing 'extended professionals', intensification removes professional autonomy from teachers and deskills them.

I believe that the 'extended professional' argument is politically expedient, particularly because it encourages teachers to accept intensification voluntarily in the misplaced belief that it constitutes 'extended professionalism'. Furthermore, I would suggest that notion of an 'extended professional' is little more than a rhetorical ruse and a convenient strategy for getting teachers to collaborate willingly in their own exploitation.

The theoretical arguments for professionalism which Professor Hoyle has eloquently made in his chapter are not just matters of academic curiosity, but highlight an important area of debate. While we agree on the extent of the change experienced by teachers in recent years, we disagree about the net results of that change. Our two positions demonstrate the necessity for an ongoing dialogue about the nature of teachers' work and how it is evolving in a post-modern context.

It is my position that in order to meet the challenges of post-modern society teaching will need to undergo some restructuring and the role of the teacher will need to be redefined. If teachers are to function in quite unprecedented and unpredictable circumstances they will need to adopt quite different practices from those currently in use. In summary, while I share a common concern with Professor Hoyle regarding the effects of intensification upon teachers' autonomy, I feel that the greater threat is the move towards proletarianization, which even the most lofty and noble set of principles cannot prevent.

## References

Giddens, A. (1991) *Modernity and Self Identity.* Cambridge: Polity Press.

Harvey, D. (1989) *The Condition of Postmodernity.* Cambridge: Polity Press.

Hargreaves, A. (1994) *Changing Teachers, Changing Times: Teachers' Work and Culture in the Postmodern Age.* London: Cassell.

Macdonald, M. (1991) Post-Fordism and the flexibility debate. *Studies in Political Economy,* **36**, 177–201.

# The Deprofessionalization and Deskilling of Teachers

## ALMA HARRIS

### Introduction

The 1990s have witnessed an increasingly interventionist stance by the British government towards reform across the educational spectrum. Policies to control and manage the professional training and development of teachers have played a fundamental part in this process. There can be no doubt that both initial and in-service training have been subject to increased public scrutiny and that, as a result, a cyclical crisis of confidence has developed between teachers and the general public. Similarly, the recent moves by central government towards increased accountability of teachers have been largely construed by the teachers as an attack on the very core and substance of their profession.

It is not surprising, therefore, to find that teacher professionalism is once again on the agenda. The changes that have taken place within education in the past ten or fifteen years have been largely unprecedented in both scope and speed. The 1988 Education Reform Act heralded a series of reforms which subsequently altered both the conceptualization and the practice of teaching. The imposition of a National Curriculum, national testing and national league tables have all contributed to the removal of control from teachers, in favour of greater centralized control and increased accountability. Similarly, the range of roles and the power of local authorities have been significantly reduced and those of school governors substantially extended. This has marginalized teachers in the process of planning and managing whole-school

development. At the local, LEA and national levels, movements for strict accountability systems, competency-based education, testing, systems management, and mandated curricular content and goals are clear and growing (Apple and Jungck, 1992).

Within initial teacher training and at the in-service training level there is evidence of a similar trend. Both have experienced their own periods of change and relative instability. In-service training for teachers has, over the past five years, been delivered through various schemes which have changed at a bewildering pace. Initial teacher training has also been subject to radical change from a government intent on removing teacher training from higher education and keen to locate it unambiguously in schools (Talbot, 1991). Indeed, the government's pursuit of 'theory free', practical teaching skills has meant that the link between higher education and professional training has been seriously weakened if not, to a certain extent, broken.

Consequently, regardless of where, or how, change has taken place, the collective drift has been in the same direction. Despite all the rhetoric about enhancing teaching and professionalism, about enhancing teachers' powers and about raising pay and respect, the reality in schools is quite different. Rather than moving in the direction of increased autonomy, teachers have been subject to even tighter curriculum control and greater administrative burdens. As Apple and Jungck (1992) point out, in the UK and the USA, reductive accountability, teacher evaluation schemes and increasing centralization have become so commonplace that in a few years the two education systems will be largely indistinguishable.

## Proletarianization

The net result of this emerging framework of regulatory, legislative and structural change has been to redefine the manner in which education is carried out and, by association, to redefine the role of the teacher. Teaching as an occupation, with its associated skills and self-reflective actions, has been redefined. Important transformations have occurred within teaching which have collectively contributed to a reconceptualization of the processes and practice of teaching. With the curriculum increasingly planned and systematized at a central level, focused on competencies and measured by standardized tests, the role of the teacher has altered. These interventions have reduced the ability of teachers to control their own work and have largely separated conception from execution (Ozga and Lawn, 1988). Consequently, because of the centralization of authority and control, teaching has been deskilled and redefined. This redefinition of teaching is predominantly 'mechanistic' and can be characterized as utilitarian, positivist and ultimately competency led.

Furthermore, this 'proletarianization' has encouraged a redefinition of teaching which equates with the acquisition and practice of low-level, technical skills. Proletarianization follows from the removal of skill from work, the exclusion of the worker from the conceptual functions of work. As Ozga (1988, p. 87) argues, 'proletarianisation is a process which affects all work directly at the point of production but of necessity sooner or later at the points of realisation of value. If education is part of the creation of value, expressed as a trained work force, then this process will be analysed and restructured to increase its efficiency (productivity).'

In the sociological literature, the label attached to what is happening to teaching is the 'degradation of labour', which essentially means a rationalizing and standardizing of people's jobs. 'When individuals cease to plan and control a large portion of their own work, the skills essential to doing these tasks self reflectively and well, atrophy and are forgotten' (Apple, 1992, p. 22). The skills that teachers have built up over decades, such as individualized instruction, designing lessons and teaching strategies, and selecting content, are lost. In many ways, because of the centralization of authority and control they are simply no longer needed. In the process, however, the things that make teaching a professional activity, i.e. the control of one's expertise and time, are also dissipated. As a consequence, the very nature of that professional activity is, by implication, redefined.

## Redefining teacher professionalism

The chief ideological driving force behind this redefinition of the profession is what Elliott (1993) has termed the 'social market' view of teaching. This social market ideology is framed by certain basic assumptions which have been transferred from the economic to the social cultural sphere of human activity. Elliott (1993, p. 54) outlines these assumptions as follows:

1   That educational goals should be treated as 'product specifications' or production targets.
2   That 'production targets' in education should refer to learning outcomes, which must, therefore, be specified and standardized in advance of the educational process.
3   That educational processes should be viewed as production technologies for bringing about certain end states in pupils.
4   That the quality of an educational process lies in its instrumental value as a production function.
5   That evidence of the quality of an educational process should consist of data which are relevant to judging its effectiveness and efficiency.
6   That the rights and responsibilities of parents, employers and other social groups with an

interest in education should be defined as those of consumers of the products of education rather than those of participants in education.

7  That schools should be viewed as units of production whose performance is regulated by the mechanism of consumer choice based on the information about their relative effectiveness and efficiency.

In essence, the major characteristic of the social market model of professional learning is that it views appropriately trained teachers as products which may be valued by consumers (in the form of school managers, parents and governors). This valuing is informed by immediate short-term requirements to meet specific needs or through the appointment or provision of appropriately targeted training. As Elliott (1993, p. 17) argues:

> Products have to have markets and consumers. From a social market perspective, schools conceived as individual consumers of the products of teacher education are the market. And since these products are behavioural outcomes in the form of practical skills schools also become the main sites for training activities at all phases (from this perspective professional learning is an outcome of training rather than education).

The underlying principle entailed in this 'needs-driven' or 'social market' view is that of behaviourism. This basically assumes that required outcomes can be prespecified in performance terms and that knowledge can be defined in output terms. Within such a behaviourist application, theoretical knowledge in training takes on a purely technical, or instrumental, significance. It is not highly valued and, to a certain extent, is viewed as largely irrelevant in comparison with the acquisition of practical skills. At the core of this 'social market' perspective, therefore, is a desire to define with increasing accuracy those practical behaviours or competences which lead to successful outcomes.

The logic of the 'social market' model is premised upon a narrow definition of performance. Consequently, teachers' professional development simply becomes the acquisition of further practical 'know-how'. The 'social market' model conveniently ignores the value base and the situational knowledge base encompassed in professional practice. Instead, it offers a narrowly instrumental assessment of teachers, and teaching, which is wholly inadequate for reflecting the cognitive nature of professional activity. It is a model premised more on technical competence than intellectual development.

The consequence of the application of this 'social market' model to teaching has been to devalue teaching as a professional activity. Government policies have contributed to this by imposing policies which reflect a technical, rational model of teacher professionalism. They have effectively redefined teaching by adjusting the parameters of professional practice to fit the 'social market' model. Much of this redefinition has occurred through the changes imposed upon initial teacher education.

## Craft and apprenticeship

Within initial teacher education, the 'social market' model has found its most recent expression. The 1989 CATE criteria and 1991 NCC document on initial teacher training both signified an increasing shift in the behaviourist direction. Subsequently, Circular 9/92 firmly placed teacher training within a competency-based framework. The specification of 'competencies expected of newly qualified teachers' left teacher training establishments in little doubt about their future role.

Recent policies regarding teacher education seem to be firmly grounded in a 'craft' or apprenticeship view of teacher education. This emphasizes the development of competencies and certification linked to the demonstration of a predetermined set of discrete skills, and to extensive practice placement time. The move towards a corporate model of school-based training has placed greater training responsibility and control into the hands of schools. It has effectively devalued university work and conceptual work in favour of extensive time (80 per cent) in school, emphasizing instead apprenticeship as the most appropriate avenue for learning to teach (Barton *et al.*, 1992).

Most teacher educators would not dispute the fact that novice teachers can and should learn a great deal from the experienced teachers they observe in schools. Underlying this view is an acceptance that over a period of time experienced teachers have acquired substantial practical knowledge about teaching, largely through their classroom experience rather than their formal training. Implied in this is the notion that experienced teachers are similar to master 'craftsmen' or 'craftswomen' and that in the school-based components of their training they gain craft knowledge from experienced teachers.

While the craft metaphor has been used widely in relation to teaching and schooling (Lortie, 1975; Marland, 1975; Tom, 1980, 1984), there are wider implications from its usage. For example, the craft of teaching has been identified as an 'occupational technique' (Bensman and Lilienfield, 1973) which can be taught generally through modelling, rather than academically (Eisikovits and Becker, 1983, p. 266). In common with other crafts, teaching automatically conforms to Lortie's (1975) notion that 'craft is work in which experience improves performance' (p. 266).

The danger of such a craft-based or apprenticeship view of teaching lies in the assumptions that underpin it. For example, there is the assumption that learning to teach is primarily a matter of skill mastery and that skills are identifiable in advance by experts and are context free. In other words, teaching is telling or merely delivering prescribed packages of content (Stones, 1992). Similarly, there is the underlying assumption associated with the 'technical-rational' view of professionalism that learning is behavioural change and that standardized content and criteria will be wholly sufficient to ensure programme quality and guarantee levels of accountability. This matches perfectly with the requirements of the social market model.

The cumulative effect of recent government policy, therefore, has been to provoke a crisis in teaching. While a crisis in teaching is not new, this latest episode is quite unprecedented. It is acknowledged that a tension has long existed between teachers and the state depending on the government's need to exert control over the teaching force. As Ozga (1988, p. x) points out, 'in times of economic crisis, foreign competition and political dissensus, the central state tends towards strong directive management which imposes controls on teacher recruitment, training, salaries and status, and curriculum and examination content'. This has certainly been the case in the past decade. In response, teachers have attempted to construct a defence of their position by clinging to traditional notions of professionalism.

## The 'traditional professionalism'

While it has been most recently argued that the professionalism of teachers requires urgent reassertion (Kirk, 1988; Hoyle, 1990; Avis, 1991), it remains highly debatable whether the 'traditional' view of professionalism is an appropriate model to adopt. The well established 'traditional' view of a profession is that it is an occupation which is held to be distinguished from other occupations according to a distinctive set of criteria. The criteria listed in the extensive literature usually include the following: a crucial social service, a body of academic knowledge, a lengthy period of training, autonomy of the individual and the professional group, self-government and a code of ethics. Most importantly, however, the criteria would include knowledge, autonomy, self-government and client-centred ethics, which, it has been argued, are met in full by the professions of medicine and law (Hoyle, 1992).

Critics of this 'traditional' idea of a profession suggest that there is little consensus among those who have suggested such sets of criteria. Furthermore, they point out that even if there were a consensus, teaching only meets some of the criteria, unlike its medical and legal counterparts (Ozga and Lawn, 1981; Downie, 1991). Even alternative interpretations of professionalism still subscribe to a belief that the concept is hegemonic and consistent. As Ozga and Lawn (1988) point out, professionalism is a complex concept, involving contractions, groups and historically specific meanings. In essence, they suggest that the term itself can be used as a means of control and that the notion of a collective profession can lead to conformity and self-regulation.

Avis (1994) has recently argued that in order to reconstitute teacher professionalism in the 1990s, account must be taken of social difference and social antagonism. Any reconstitution of teacher professionalism, he suggests, cannot take comfort in a model of professionalism forged in different historical and political circumstances. The 'traditional' model of professionalism clearly runs this risk. Emerging at the start of the century as a means of demarcating different classes from one another, professionalism became the hallmark of privilege and position. Professionals were defined by the fact that they held rare skills and knowledge. They were not from working-class origins and it has been argued that professionalism was used as a petit bourgeois strategy for advancing and defending their relatively privileged position (Finn *et al.*, 1979, p. 170).

This defence also warranted the necessity for collective professional autonomy and control. As in the medical profession and legal profession, it resulted in the position that only fellow professionals could make judgements upon others, which required a means of self-regulation and professional accountability. It is no surprise, therefore, that the Conservative government regularly called for a General Teaching Council to oversee the 'profession'. In utilization of a traditional notion of professionalism, with its rare skills and knowledge, there is the danger that individual autonomy will be lost to collegiate pressure. In essence, teachers' autonomy will not be reclaimed but eroded, and individual deskilling will take place in the name of collective professionalism. Consequently, if the term 'professionalism' is to become meaningful and useful to teachers, it requires a new and alternative definition.

## The 'new professionalism'

The need for a 'new professionalism' has been widely acknowledged and it has been suggested that a 'new' professionalism, by definition, has to move beyond the boundaries of expertise embodied in social democracy (Avis, 1991; Mac an Ghaill, 1992). Most recently, Avis (1994) has argued that the 'new professionalism' has to be grounded in individual rather than collective autonomy. Elliott (1991) has similarly argued that the features of the new occupational images define a general view of professional practice which can be termed a 'practical science'. This 'practical science' view is characterized by the acknowledgement that professional practice in advanced modern societies needs to be responsive to unstable states of discontinuous and fragmentary social change.

Consequently, any new conception of professionalism has to embrace and encompass the potential for individuals to manage discontinuous and fragmentary social change. The model of 'traditional' teacher professionalism is clearly not suited to this purpose. With its emphasis on collective autonomy and accountability, it allows little scope for individual professional response or behaviour. In contrast, the model of the 'reflective practitioner' is one grounded in individual professional responsibility and, therefore, offers a more appropriate model of professionalism for the 1990s.

During the past ten years the broad field of professional education has witnessed a re-evaluation of traditional orthodoxies concerning the nature of the professional knowledge. At the core of this revised epistemology is the notion of reflective learning and the 'reflective practitioner'. The reflective practitioner has a critique of technical rationality as the defining characteristic of professional practice. This model of technical rationality is one where 'professional activity consists in instrumental problem-solving made rigorous by the application of scientific theory and technique' (Schön, 1983, p. 21). In Schön's view this is both a faulty and an inappropriate epistemology for professional practice. Even more damaging, the research paradigm itself has been seriously challenged as an adequate way to explain and guide teaching (Shulman, 1987: Richardson, 1990; Tom and Valli, 1990).

The critique of the 'technical-rational' mode of professional practice incorporates three domains: the forms of knowledge used in practice; the context of practice; and the nature of problem-setting. To take first the forms of knowledge used in professional practice, it is widely recognized that even good practitioners are often unable to give coherent accounts of their practice in terms of formal theory. In considering how professional practice takes place in any field, it would appear that the distinguishing characteristic is action orientation (Buchmann, 1984). This view of practice implies that professionals constantly make judgements about the appropriate course of action in a given situation or in a specific context. Wise action means making the best judgement in a specific context and for a specified set of ethical beliefs. This suggests that to improve practice, professionals' ability to make the best judgements needs to be facilitated (Cervero, 1988; Elliott, 1989). Indeed, it is clear from research evidence that what distinguishes expert judgement from the inexpert is not the ability to make rule-governed inferences from abstract problem representations. Instead, much of the practice knowledge is tacit and resides in action itself (Schön, 1983, 1987).

To turn to the context of professional practice, the traditional view of professional practice is as applied formal knowledge, which fails to recognize the context of practice as a formative influence in knowledge use and creation by practitioners. Professional knowledge is created and revealed through a range of media but only becomes personally owned through action in specific situations.

The third emergent line of critique of conventional epistemologies of practice has been to challenge the assumption that problems are predefined. Technical rationality suggests that qualifying professional education is a process through which practitioners are provided with alternative models, which can be drawn down into practice to map on to a pre-given problem. This represents what Schön has termed a view from the 'high ground', which is at odds with the practitioner's experience of life in the 'swampy lowlands' (Schön, 1987, p. 42)

In place of the technical-rational model of professionalism is the conception of the reflective practitioner, whose knowledge is directly constructed through engagement with problems encountered in the field and built through successive stages of hypothesizing, testing and reflection. This happens in real time through immediate engagement with practice (reflection in practice), and also subsequently, in a more detached opportunity to think back (reflection on practice). Within this model of professional practice, knowledge is taken to be provisional, contested and constructivist. It supplants the technical-rational model with a view of theory and research as providing a set of metaphors or frames through which problems of practice can be reviewed and reconstructed as part of the reflective process (Valli, 1992).

Indeed, developing the capacity to learn from experience and to reflect upon experience must be of central concern for professional development. It is within this context that the ideas of 'teacher as researcher' (Stenhouse, 1975), 'action research' (Carr and Kemmis, 1986) and 'experiential learning' (Kolb, 1984) have all been developed. More recently, Elliott's (1993) notion of a 'practical science' based upon a model of learning derived from practical experience extends this field. Elliott (1993) argues that it is the capacity to recognize the components of the situation and their relative salience which should be the goal of professional education.

This view of professional performance propounds a view of teaching as practical action informed by knowledge and judgement. It is incompatible with the development of identified behavioural competences and at odds with a technical-rational view of teaching. The model of professional development as practical science presented by Elliott (1993), like the model of the reflective practitioner, embodies the way forward. It is clearly more compatible with the demands placed upon professionals and their practice. Like the reflective practitioner, it stands in direct opposition to the technical-rational view of teaching and the increasing proletarianization of the profession.

## Conclusion

The strength of the reflective practitioner model lies in its potential to stand in the way of the proletarianization of teachers' work which the move towards a reductionist and technical-rational stance represents. As argued earlier, teachers' conditions of work have radically altered and their autonomy is gradually being eroded. The increased technical-rational interpretation of teachers' work is nothing more than a deskilling and reskilling towards proletarianizational ends.

As Schön (1987) noted, technical rationality is an epistemology of practice derived from positivist philosophy. It holds that practitioners are instrumental problem-solvers who select means best suited to particular purposes. Rigorous professional practitioners solve well informed instrumental problems by applying theory and technique derived from systematic, preferably scientific, knowledge. Medicine, law and business figure largely in this view as exemplars of professional practice. Consequently, if teaching is to avoid being distilled into mere technicism, it would appear that it cannot afford to subscribe to the 'traditional' notion of professionalism.

In order to defend their position teachers must move towards a 'new professionalism', and it is suggested here that despite the difficulties embodied in the notion of the reflective practitioner it provides a useful starting point. The reflective practitioner mode of professionalism raises questions about the notion of knowledge, power and expertise significantly absent in the powerful ideology of traditional professionalism. Yet, as Avis (1994) rightly notes, the reflective practitioner model is only partly an answer in the search for a radical and transformative professionalism. It has to be developed to move beyond individualism to accommodate notions of struggle and politics. But as Hargreaves and Fullan (1992, p. 5) argue, 'there is a need to return to the practices of educational research and enquiry whose primary

purpose is neither to support nor disguise political and bureaucratic control, but to engage in critical dialogue with the existing and collective wisdom of practice'.

There is clearly an urgent need for this, particularly as the government has placed itself in the position of determining the value base of the educational system and will no doubt continue to establish goals according to its ideological position. To accept the 'traditional' orthodoxy concerning teachers' professionalism, however, will not embrace the wider political struggle. Perhaps the greatest danger of accepting the 'traditional professional' view is that through a body like the General Teaching Council teachers may be persuaded to focus upon those things for which they are materially rewarded to the detriment of individual beliefs and values. In other words, under the guise of professional standards and competence, individual accountability and autonomy will be lost.

A model of professionalism premised on the reflective practitioner, or what Elliott (1993) has termed the 'practical science' model of learning, must therefore be a preferred alternative. Within this model there would be opportunity for ongoing professional training and far greater potential for self-determination. This 'new professionalism' offers teachers a continuum of learning from initial training to subsequent life-long practice, and is aimed at encouraging self-initiative, independence and autonomy among teachers. In this respect, it is clearly not a model of professionalism that the government would readily favour or immediately endorse.

As Elliott (1993, p. 85) concludes, 'it is naive to assume that government alone has the power to shape academic and practical cultures within society. Social change in democracies is usually in practice, if not intention, a matter of negotiated compromises and trade offs.' The trade-off between the 'traditional' orthodoxy and 'new professionalism' is one of political and professional significance. The former will move teaching even closer to becoming a low-status occupation concerned only with the rational application of knowledge or skills. The latter will offer teachers the opportunity to redefine their own practice and to emancipate themselves from the technical-rational stranglehold which the 'social market' model has created.

# References

Apple, M. W. (1992) *Teachers and Texts: A Political Economy of Class and Gender Relations in Education.* New York: Routledge.

Apple, M. W. and Jungck, S. (1992) You don't have to be a teacher to teach this unit: teaching, technology and control in the classroom. In A. Hargreaves and M. G. Fullan (eds), *Understanding Teacher Development.* London: Cassell.

Avis, J. (1991) Educational practice, professionalism and social relations. In Education Group 2 (ed.), *Education Limited.* London: Unwin Hyman.

Avis, J. (1994) Teacher professionalism: one more time. *Educational Review*, **46** (1), 63–72.

Barton, L., Pollard, A. and Whittly, G. (1992) Experiencing CATE: the impact of accreditation upon initial training institutions in England. *Journal of Education for Teaching*, **18**, 41–57.

Bensman, J. and Lilienfield, R. (1973) *Craft and Consciousness.* New York: John Wiley.

Buchmann, M. (1984) The use of research knowledge in teacher education and teaching. *American Journal of Education*, **92**.

Carr, W. and Kemmis, S. (1986) *Becoming Critical.* Lewes: Falmer Press.

Cervero, R. M. (1988) *Effective Continuing Education in Professionals.* San Francisco: Jossey-Bass.

Downie, R. S. (1991) Professions and professionalism. *Journal of Philosophy of Education*, **24**, 147–59.

Eisikovits, Z. and Becker, J. (1983) Beyond professionalism: the child and youth worker as craftsman. *Child Care Quarterly*, **12** (2), 93–100.

Elliott, J. (1989) The professional learning of teachers. *Cambridge Journal of Education*, **19** (1).

Elliott, J. (1991) A model of professionalism and its implications for teacher education. *British Educational Research Journal*, **17** (4).

Elliott, J. (1993) Three perspectives on coherence and continuity in teacher education. In J. Elliott (ed.), *Reconstructing Teacher Education.* Lewes: Falmer.

Finn, D., Grant, N. and Johnson, R. (1977) *Social Democracy, Education and the Crisis.* Working Papers on Cultural Studies 10. Birmingham: Centre for Contemporary Cultural Studies.

Glazer, N. (1974) The schools of the minor professions. *Minerva*, **12** (3), 346–63.

Hargreaves, A. and Fullan, M. G. (1992) *Understanding Teacher Development.* London: Cassell.

Hoyle, E. (1980) Professionalisation and deprofessionalisation in education. In E. Hoyle and J. Megarry (eds), *The Professional Development of Teachers World Yearbook of Education.* London: Kogan Page.

Hoyle, E. (1990) The teacher as a professional in the 1990s. *NUT Educational Review*, **4** (1).

Hoyle, E. (1992) An education profession for tomorrow: re-defining the concept of a profession. Paper given at the British Educational Management and Administration Society Annual Conference, Bristol.

Kirk, G. (1988) The professionalisation of teaching and its discontents. *Scottish Education Review*, **20**, 14–21.

Kolb, D. A. (1984) *Experiential Learning.* Englewood Cliffs, NJ: Prentice-Hall.

Lawn, M. and Ozga, J. (1981) The educational worker. In L. Barton and S. Walker (eds), *Schools, Teachers and Teaching.* Lewes: Falmer Press.

Lortie, D. C. (1975) *Schoolteacher: A Sociological Study.* Chicago: University of Chicago Press.

Mac an Ghaill, M. (1992) Teachers' work: curriculum restructuring culture, power and comprehensive schooling. *British Journal of Sociology of Education* **13**, 177–200.

Marland, M. (1975) *The Craft of the Classroom.* Exeter, NH: Heinemann Educational Books.

Martin, R. J. (1978) Craftsmanship and schooling. *Journal of Thought*, **13**, 187–95.

Ozga, J. (1988) Teaching professionalism and work. In J. Ozga (ed.), *Schoolwork Approaches to the Labour Process of Teaching.* Milton Keynes: Open University Press.

Ozga, J. and Lawn, M. (1981) *The Rise of Professional Society.* London: Routledge.

Ozga, J. and Lawn, M. (1988) Schoolwork: interpreting the labour process of teaching. *British Journal of Sociology of Education*, **9** (3), 289–306.

Richardson, V. (1990) The evolution of reflective teaching and teacher education. In R. Clift, W. R. Houston and M. Pugach (eds), *Encouraging Reflective Practice in Education.* New York: Teachers College Press.

Schön, D. (1983) *The Reflective Practitioner.* London: Temple Smith.

Schön, D. A. (1987) *Educating the Reflective Practitioner.* New York: Basic Books.

Shulman, L. (1987) Knowledge and teaching foundation of the new reform. *Harvard Educational Review*, **57** (1).

Stenhouse, L. (1975) *An Introduction to Curriculum Research and Development.* London: Heinemann.

Stones, E. (1992) *Quality Teaching: A Sample of Cases.* London: Routledge.

Talbot, C. (1991) Towards school based teacher training. *School Organisation*, **11** (1).

Tom, A. (1980) Teaching as a moral craft: a metaphor for teaching and teacher education. *Curriculum Inquiry*, **10** (3), 317–23.

Tom, A. (1984) *Teaching as a Moral Craft*. New York: Longman.

Tom, A. and Valli, L. (1990) Professional knowledge for teachers. In W. R. Houston (ed.), *Handbook for Re-* *search on Teacher Education*. New York: Macmillan.

Valli, L. (ed.) (1992) *Reflective Teacher Education: Cases and Critiques*. New York: New York Press.

# Comment on Alma Harris

ERIC HOYLE

There are many more points of agreement than of disagreement between the position taken by Dr Harris and my own. In particular, we are in close agreement in terms of the *analysis* of the impact of recent legislation on the role of the teacher, e.g. the processes of intensification and deskilling. We differ in terms of our respective semantics, our beliefs about the value of *profession* as an analytical and an evaluative concept and, consequently, our policy preferences.

One difficulty I have is with the linking of intensification and deskilling with proletarianization. I am well aware that such a link has been made at least since the work of Braverman (1974) and its application to teaching by Apple (1986) in the USA and Ozga and Lawn (1981) in the UK. I nevertheless find it misleading. If it is argued that *proletarianization* is deployed only as an analytical term to describe changes in working practices, it is otiose. Intensification, deskilling, the decoupling of execution from conception and a number of other changes are affecting the work of teaching and other professional occupations. But technological changes are affecting traditional manual and routine non-manual occupations. The use of a single social class term diminishes the complexity of changes in skill requirements. 'The professionalization of everybody?', a question asked over thirty years ago (Wilensky, 1964), might be nearer to the mark, though one would not wish to adopt this oversimplified position either. One must therefore assume that proletarianization is used with ideological intent. But, if so, is proletarianization a *bad* thing as the analyses of some writers suggest? Or is it a *good* thing in that it will even-

tually lead to the disappearance of the middle class, so long a problematic category for Marxian analysts, and lead to the long-predicted polarization of capital and labour? I must emphasize that I am not accusing Dr Harris of these, in my view, gross oversimplicities. I am arguing that in deploying *proletarianization* in this context she is running the danger of being misunderstood.

Dr Harris argues that the term *profession* is historically contingent and implies that its relevance as an analytical or as an evaluative category is passing if it has not already passed. This is perhaps the key point of difference between us. Although the concept *profession* has a long history and is still widely deployed in English-speaking countries, as is its equivalent in other languages, it does not constitute some Platonic ideal. I agree that it is contingent. The term would, no doubt, fall into desuetude if it ceased to have any referent in the real world. In the meantime it will be given different connotations as the circumstances of its usage change.

All that I can say is that I believe that it continues to be a useful heuristic concept because it enables one to link a number of substantive issues relating to knowledge, autonomy, political independence, etc. I concede that there may well be other ways of relating these concepts, but one notes that even critics of the idea of a profession find difficulty in avoiding the term and its related parts of speech. I accept that the term may cease to be of analytical value as circumstances change. One possibility is that it might succumb to the burgeoning language of managerialism, though it is perhaps just as likely that it will be incorporated into that language but given a very different connotation.

For this reason, and for other reasons which cannot be fully elaborated here, I am also willing to deploy *profession* as an evaluative term. Despite all the problems attaching to the term, not least in the role that it has played in sustaining an ideology which has been used to justify the privileges of medicine, law, etc., I believe that it embodies principles which relate to quality of service to clients and which, given some necessary reforms, ought to be sustained. Nevertheless, I concede that this view is based on a set of beliefs which are contestable (see Hoyle and John, 1995, for further discussion).

One of these beliefs is in the importance of the autonomy of the teacher. This is a belief which Dr Harris shares. She is clearly worried about the reduction of teacher autonomy, not only through political constraints but also through the constraints imposed by collegiality. However, one cannot dismiss the advantages of teacher collaboration. The balance between autonomy and collaboration at the school level is one which, as indicated in my own chapter, needs careful analysis and monitoring. It may be that 'the new professionalism' (Hargreaves, 1994) underplays the importance of autonomy.

Finally, I am surprised that Dr Harris sees the possibility of a General Teaching Council reducing teacher autonomy through the greater surveillance of teachers. I have to disagree very strongly with her contention that it has been the Conservative Party which has supported a council. The aspiration for a council goes back for the best part of a century but the closest that it has come to being instituted has been under Labour governments. It has been, and continues to be, the case that the Labour Party has supported the principle of a council and that the Conservative Party has rejected the idea. One is not too sanguine about the degree to which a General Teaching Council could influence government policy. One could not argue that the General Teaching Council for Scotland has exercised much political clout in the interests of teachers, but it has had some successes. There is nothing in the history of attempts to establish a council for England and Wales – including the constitution of the incorporated but as yet not formally recognized General Teaching Council – which suggests any policies that would undermine teacher autonomy.

In sum, Dr Harris and myself share a common concern about the effects of the intensification of teaching and the deskilling of teachers and with current threats to teacher autonomy. We differ in that I believe that despite the self-interest of the professions the concept still encapsulates a set of principles which one can invoke as a defence against not proletarianization but deprofessionalization.

# References

Apple, M. W. (1986) *Teachers and Texts: A Political Economy of Class and Gender.* London: Routledge.

Braverman, H. (1974) *Labor and Monopoly Capital.* New York: Monthly Review Press.

Hargreaves, D. (1994) The new professionalism. *Teaching and Teacher Education*, **10** (4).

Hoyle, E. and John, P. (1995) *Teaching: Professional Knowledge and Professional Practice.* London: Cassell.

Ozga, J. and Lawn, M. (1981) *Teachers, Professionalism and Class.* London: Falmer Press.

Wilensky, H. L. (1964) The professionalization of everyone? *American Journal of Sociology*, **70**.

# 7 Professionalism and Empowerment of Teachers: Views and Experiences

BEATRICE AVALOS

## Introduction

That the number of books and articles, specialized journals and other ways of bringing the subject of teachers (such as professional development projects and schemes) to the fore has grown in recent years can have a number of meanings. It may mean that the importance of the teaching profession is being reinstated; or it may mean that teachers are seen to be in need of changes in outlook, in practices or in their mode of contributing to educational policies. No major educational project in developing-country contexts ignores the role of teachers or neglects to consider sub-projects related to actions upon teachers. Equally, no projected change in curriculum orientation or practices can afford to ignore the position teachers may take towards the change, as has recently been shown in the case of Britain's new curriculum and assessment policies.

In the midst of all this – what one might call – 'literary' interest in teachers, there are two themes, not necessarily linked but constantly explored, that bring the discussion closer to the teachers' side rather than to that of the politicians, policymakers or educational theorists (meaning all those who write about what teachers should do and how they should do it). The words used to express these themes are professionalism and empowerment (or, as articulated in more radical positions, teacher emancipation). With examples from several country contexts, this chapter seeks to discuss the meanings behind these concepts and to do so joining them as part and parcel of one reality. It attempts more specifically to bring out the nature

of what is called the 'facilitative structures' of teacher professionalism and empowerment, and to conclude by indicating how these can be made more facilitative if the will is to recognize for teachers their professional status and support the development of their professional capabilities. In so doing the chapter seeks to place itself on the teachers' side of things.

## Professionalism and empowerment: the concepts

The relatively recent focus on teacher professionalism is linked not so much to its sociological connotations (the teacher profession in relation to other professions), as was the case in the literature of the 1960s and 1970s (e.g. Hoyle, 1969), but to discussions about the degree of autonomy teachers may have in relation to decisions and actions belonging to their specific sphere of concern: the classroom, the school and procedures of the educational system that affect their activity. There are different ways of referring to what it means for a teacher to be a professional, but in a nutshell one may say that it has to do with self-esteem and confidence that in turn is related to having enough knowledge about what must be taught and how such knowledge can be transformed into teachable knowledge – enough knowledge about how to deal with students and their different approaches to learning, enough understanding about how the educational system works, insight into the social context in which they and their students live,

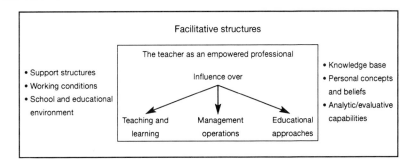

**Figure 7.1** Mode of operation of facilitative structures

insight into the manner in which the different types of administrative structures under which they work operate – to enable teachers to make judgements and decide on the procedures to be used within their various spheres of action.

Though teachers may have enough of the kind of knowledge and insight outlined above, the possibility that they will be able to act on the basis of their judgements does not necessarily follow – and therefore the issue of power is also a crucial one. Power can be seen, on the one hand, as the potential of a person to influence situations due to knowledge possessed and the capacity to judge how to apply it. On the other hand, it can be seen in relation to the opportunities provided to that person *actually* to influence situations. Thus, the power to act has a subjective side to it (the teacher's side) and an objective, external, component (the educational and socio-political system). Both the teacher's disposition to act professionally and the degree of freedom allowed by contextual factors constitute what we may call 'facilitative structures'. In this respect, the professional judgements of a teacher require facilitative structures for these to be changed into actions that can in turn be assessed by the teachers themselves or by others in relation to their value and effects.

## The facilitative structures of teacher professionalism and power

Teachers who make judgements as professionals and have the power to convert their judgements into actions grow into this capacity over a period of time: the time that goes between initial teacher preparation – becoming a novice teacher – and becoming an experienced teacher (or an expert, as the literature terms this condition: Tochon and Munby, 1993). During this process, a number of influences are at work that support or lessen professional growth and personal autonomy. These influences or facilitating structures operate from within the teacher and from without. The mode of operation looks as shown in Figure 7.1.

The situations that specifically require from teachers their professional judgement to make them more or less apt for the fulfilment of educational purposes are those related to: (a) what is taught and how it is taught to further relevant pupil learning; (b) the management of classrooms and the management operations of educational institutions to make these operations conducive to learning; and (c) thinking about education and decisions about which theoretical approaches and policies make sense for practical purposes and which do not.

The actual power that teachers may have to influence the above situations that are directly or indirectly within their sphere of action depends in the first place on their own perception of this power and the level of understanding they have of what needs to be done. This is what we may call the 'knowledge base'. Such knowledge base is of different kinds. There is knowledge that is part and parcel of the specialism of a teacher (be it a sphere of knowledge such as is required for teaching in the early grades, or a subject specialization for the higher levels of the school cycle). There is knowledge of students with their different characteristics and knowledge of how to transform subject matter or content specialism into knowledge-to-be-taught to a particular group of students ('pedagogical content knowledge', as explained by Shulman, 1987). There is also the practical type of knowledge that has to do with understanding how the contextual administrative structures (school and educational system bureaucracies) work and what they allow or do not allow.

Teachers, like all other persons, have beliefs and concepts about their tasks, about what counts as correct in educational activities and about their own capacity to exercise judgement or to carry out what they believe is right (Clark and Peterson, 1986). Many of these beliefs arise from teaching traditions, or what Hargreaves (1992) calls 'cultures of teaching'. Much is being researched at present about teacher belief structures and how to bring them to the consciousness of teachers in order to examine their validity or appropriateness in given contexts or situations. Lower levels of self-esteem or little trust in the power of education to be relevant to young people's needs can in fact affect the quality of the tasks performed.

The ability to look at oneself and what one does also affects the potential for improved practices. The literature on teacher reflection and the numerous projects aimed at enhancing pre-service or in-service teachers' analytic and reflective capabilities constitutes an effort to see how true the notion is that judgement and influence over situations requires the development of these capabilities. Rudduck (1992, p. 165) goes further, to suggest in this respect that it is the development of 'critical action research' that enables 'teachers to exercise the right to question the authority of past practice'.

All these aspects taken together – knowledge base, beliefs and analytic capabilities – constitute the facilitative structures seen from the side of the teacher, that work to enhance teacher competence and power.

Persons, however, are part of contexts and these contexts affect how they see their tasks, how they judge these can be performed and the actual possibility of acting upon those judgements. Thus, facilitative structures of teacher power and professionalism are linked to characteristics of out-side mechanisms and conditions. We call these the 'external facilitative structures'.

Important among these objective structures are the support mechanisms for teacher actions. Support can take many forms. It may be related to public opinion – how the public views the role of teachers. Support is also related to the existence of collegiate structures – locations and entities that make it possible for teachers to interchange views, to hear about what others are doing or are experiencing in terms of successes and frustrations, and to be able to voice personal experiences and concerns. Such support structures should also provide the opportunity for examining policies and suggesting change where change is perceived as needed. They have been described, among others, in two ways: as a 'collaborative culture' or as a 'contrived collegiality' (Hargreaves, 1992), depending on the degree to which they are bound in space and time, are regulated, allow for unpredictable or predictable results and are development- or implementation-oriented.

That teachers require minimum comfort in working conditions is obvious. In many countries these are far from adequate, in terms of both salaries and living quarters. Working conditions include minimal availability of teaching materials; teachers should not be criticized for using memoristic teaching procedures based on dictation and recitation if students have no textbooks, and schools have no books, maps or other equipment, as required, for example, for the teaching of science and technical subjects.

The school and educational system environment may also facilitate or hinder teacher power. The form of bureaucratic procedures affects the perception of what can be done and the self-assurance to try out new initiatives. In this respect, we know enough about the positive effects on educational climate that are created in democratic environments run with openness of procedures and space for initiative, versus what happens in authoritarian ones.

Outlining what facilitates or hinders the achievement of professionalism and power on the part of teachers provides only the framework within which to consider a variety of forms by which this achievement (which is a gradual process) may or may not take place. We therefore need to examine these forms more closely by providing examples, where possible, of how and when they may or may not constitute facilitating structures for teacher professionalism and increase teacher influence over the improvement of teaching and learning, management operations and the discussion of educational approaches and decisions over policies. The assumption in this is that teachers as persons stimulated by facilitating situations may enhance their ability to conduct their professional tasks; and equally, societies and organizations stimulated by facilitating situations may enhance the context which enables teachers to be real agents of educational development. In this next part of this chapter, I look at these two perspectives of implementation by way of examples or modalities of support for teacher professionalism and power, seen from the side of teachers and from the side of institutional contexts.

## Facilitative structures from the side of teachers: examples

The examples presented below are quite different and taken from different contexts. They are presented as an indication of a disposition on the part of teachers that serves to initiate reflection about practices, to develop thinking and judgement within a support context, to overcome contextual limitations and to form professional judgement and make it known despite opposition. Some are well developed and others represent mere sketches of what we might call the starting point of the process about which we are concerned.

### *The starting point: being able to look at oneself as an outsider would*

In connection with teacher development there is wonderful story that Philip Jackson (1992) tells, of a fellow who, having played double-bass for thirty years in the Metropolitan Opera, finally takes a

night off and goes to an opera performance. Having sat through the performance, he rushes full of enthusiasm to congratulate the conductor, who in turn asks him with astonishment what on earth he could have learned from a performance of which he had been part for so many years. The double-bass player's response is that for the first time he had distinguished in a section of the piece what the violins were doing when he was playing double-bass. The obvious lesson from this example is simple: that to see oneself detached from the situation in which one is continuously immersed gives the opportunity to examine not only what one is doing in such a situation, but also what others are doing, and how these actions affect the total production of a musical piece. The actions that were once routine and habit may never be that way again.

Teachers always think at some time or another about their teaching, whether in the solitary confinement of their classroom or their home, as they walk to and back from school or in a dialogue situation with a colleague, a friend or a wife or husband; but that thinking is not always systematic, enabling description and analysis of how and why things happen the way they do. The above anecdote is relevant, in that it illustrates the effects of temporary detachment and self-observation.

The example that fits the meaning of the above anecdote happened in a semi-urban technical-vocational secondary school in Chile. There was need to produce a video of classroom teaching for purposes of illustration for another audience, and three teachers of that school volunteered to have themselves recorded by others. The process by which this videotaping occurred, however, might well be likened to the situation described above. The teachers were told they had to re-enact a normal teaching situation in a different classroom context from their own (owing to the need to have appropriate lighting and equipment in place). Prior to filming, a discussion was held with all three of them, during which they were encouraged to visualize and briefly to describe the lesson they would teach. In thinking about this, the teachers took time to examine their normal teaching commitments, to select from their experience and describe what they would do in terms of class, context and the lesson content. The descriptions and later re-enactments of the lessons selected were different regarding what was emphasized – management procedures, the content of teaching or pupil–teacher relations. But generally speaking, the teaching approaches were not much different from what recent observational studies in Chile had shown to be the norm (Edwards *et al.*, 1993), an approach that could be subject to criticism. The teachers made no effort to alter their teaching pattern to teach what could be classified as a model lesson, although if required they would have been able to provide a perfect description of what a model lesson is. They responded to the request to teach as closely as possible to how they usually taught. That was also true of the students, who, during the actual filming process, behaved very much as they normally would.

After the teachers in the above example had concluded the filming, there was opportunity to discuss the experience with the three teachers involved. One of the teachers, a very young one, taught a tedious grammar lesson, and it was her pupils who had the strongest misbehaviour observed. Paradoxically, however, she was most articulate in attempting to explain her own and the class's behaviour in terms of the irrelevance of the contents of the grammar syllabus for her kind of students. Being a novice teacher, she saw herself as limited by curricular formats she did not feel free to change. The other two teachers also placed the lesson they had taught in the wider context of curriculum and student characteristics. One of them pointed to curriculum and examination demands that limited his desire to use local history (of events in the area where the school was located) in his teaching of ethics; and the other teacher explained how the special characteristics of the students he was teaching (good at maths and with families involved in business) determined their usually attentive and motivated classroom behaviour and reinforced his manner of teaching. This temporary detachment and the opportunity offered of explaining to others what they usually did in a non-evaluative context (as they prepared for the video and re-enacted their teaching) initiated these teachers into something they had not consciously done before: examining the 'why' and

'how' of their actions. They were beginning to have the experience of the double-bass player: seeing their ordinary practice in connection with what others were doing and learning from the experience. The lesson is simple. Without the will to accept detachment and enter into self-observation, there can be little possibility of generating conditions for growth or change.

## *Deciding to change and working with others to think and implement change*

Moving beyond the situation of initial awareness of one's usual practice, to that of investigating what is needed to improve, deciding to change and examining the outcomes of change actions, requires a longer process. In this connection, an increasing number of experiences are taking place whereby teachers, either on their own initiative or stimulated by outsiders, gather in groups to examine their practice and try out alternative forms of teaching, assisted with feedback and support from their group and the outsiders. The difference between these activities and formal in-service experiences is that they are less structured, with the agenda for discussion and work being generally developed by the group of teachers rather than an outside specialist. Although these activities always include some form of self-evaluation, it is not usual that teachers, who may record in a personal diary what happens to them and their students during the process, communicate their experience formally, and so we know little of the process of development and how it takes place. But there are exceptions, and one of these is presented below.[1]

The opportunity to organize a teachers' group in this school (Hymes, 1993) came when lecturers at the local university together with one of the teachers at the school invited others to take part in a group that would work on an action-research project aimed at improving student learning. Damien was an experienced teacher of geography and history, and was interested in the project because of the general feeling that the methods he had been using fell short of answering the questions 'Why does Johnny still make the same mistakes?', 'Why don't the Year 11 and Year 12 students show more initiative?' (Hymes, 1993, p. 21). As a member of this group, Damien resolved to use the strategies the group suggested for examining the learning difficulties of his students. What was not initially clear to him, however, was that the strategies assumed that the students themselves would be interested in improving their learning. When the strategies did not work as expected, Damien found himself needing to examine why this was happening and what was lacking. The turning point came, as he narrates, when he decided to test student reaction to the dictation of a set of two nonsense paragraphs. To his surprise the students asked no questions about the meaning of what they were asked to copy. Such a realization led Damien to the following conclusions:

> Firstly, I thought I had been teaching in a fashion that encouraged student involvement and initiative. I now realised that I had not been challenging the students enough. My reaction to these two classes was one of concern about my teaching methods.
>
> Secondly, I was surprised to see to what extent students expect teachers to dictate and dominate class situations. Students either believe that teachers should not be questioned or believe that it is much easier not to get involved in class discussion.
>
> Thirdly, that as a teacher I had an obligation to alter my teaching strategies. Even though I believed that I was using strategies that the ... project professed, I had to have a much closer look at the project and adapt it to my classroom methods.
>
> (Hymes, 1993, p. 23)

Damien's actions after he came to the above conclusions led him in two directions: the designing of strategies that required students to ask questions and the attempt to be receptive to student ideas and criticisms. The rest of the year was spent in this way, with experiences of success and some of failure; the latter made him realize that he had to simplify some of his assumptions about learning and implement new techniques. But the opportunity to compare what students understood as learning at the beginning of the year and what they said about it at the end of the year provided Damien with enough incentives to feel that it had been worthwhile to participate in the project and reflect

about and alter aspects of his teaching approach. Damien's words at the end of his narrative indicate the effect of both group support and support from students, as well as the extent of personal development (and increased confidence and empowerment) resulting from the year's experience:

> To embark upon a project like [this one] can and does leave one frustrated and insecure at times. Luckily, I was able to rely on two main avenues of support: a class assessment sheet that evolved from the concept of a [student diary] and the weekly meetings of those involved in the project ...
>
> As I became more involved in the project, I gradually began to perceive a difference in my teaching approach. I was not so much *telling* them to question thoroughly nor *telling them to think* about their learning, rather I was starting to *teach* them and help them think about their learning. The classroom should not consist of 24 students and one teacher but rather 25 people working together to enhance the independent learning ability of 25 people. I possibly learnt more than the students during the project.
>
> Although I have been a teacher of 14 years standing, I found this year one of the most enjoyable. On reflexion, the main reason was because my main energies were not spent in designing assignment and correction, but rather helping individual students understand what they were doing, helping them reflect on how they can improve, helping them research and find answers to their own questions and problems. Let's face it – I knew the answers to my questions before I gave them to the students.
>
> Hopefully, I will continue to learn and continue to help students become more independent thinkers. I believe if I do then I will enjoy teaching next year more than I did this year.
>
> (Hymes, 1993, pp. 29–30, 32)

## Being aware of environment limitations and thinking (with conviction) about how they can be overcome

The example here is of a teacher in a poor neighbourhood of La Paz, Bolivia, who was noticeably different in her teaching and relationship with pupils from most other teachers in similar circumstances (Avalos, 1986). Her pupils were mostly of

Aymara Indian extraction, had little Spanish linguistic skills before coming to school (because their parents were illiterate) and appeared destined, like most other children of their kind, to get very little out of school or to fail outright. But it did not happen to them. The children in her class not only did not fail but moved upwards to other classes, with other teachers retaining their interest in learning and their capacity to contribute to the lessons. The main reason for this success, it would seem, had to do with the teacher's sense of power drawn from observation, thinking and experience, which enabled her to build a constructive environment within the limitations of the poverty of the school, the prescriptive curriculum she was asked to observe and the view that Aymara children are doomed to failure. Below are some excerpts from her thinking that illustrate her reflections and her actions as observed by an outside researcher (de Crespo, 1986, pp. 95–107).

*On the curriculum and the pupils*:

> I think it is well conceived, but it does not relate properly to different environments. So we have to take from it what is needed, in accordance with what this area and its pupils requires. Of course, I know that not even 2% of the pupils here will reach the university, but that is why we take more care than needed so that they learn the basic four operations, so that they can survive if they have to sell potatoes, and we concern ourselves that they also learn to write and measure, and think and express themselves.

*Regard for and type of relationship with her pupils*:

> I like the kids a lot, because they are vivacious . . . and I like it if they scold me when I arrive late [*she lives very far away*]. I allow them to criticize me, to tell me that I cannot do this or that . . . Sometimes I tell them that they must stay on until one o'clock [*they normally leave at noon*]. They may say 'no' to this, 'we will leave when the bell rings'. I like it if the children are not afraid . . . if they respond . . . if they question.

*Are diplomas and prizes and indication of school success?*

> No, because the good pupil with prizes may have come with all that is needed to make him a good pupil: memory, intelligence. But the child without

prizes might be an excellent person, who thinks more but is not able to respond in examinations as we require him to, that is, by rote repetition; or it may be that we do not understand the way in which he understands things. Discipline in school is not just to form lines, to remain silent; it is not to have children sitting still without moving. I think that children's orderly participation, that they talk, that they converse among themselves – that is discipline – and I think we have attained a bit of that [*speaking of her experience in teaching*].

In fact, this last sentence 'I think that . . . we have attained a bit of that' points to an important trait of the empowered professional: thoughtfulness and knowledge of what is being achieved, but also confidence in being able to implement what is considered to be appropriate. Within a longer list of requirements for 'self-directed professional development', Clark (1992, p. 83) reminds teachers of the importance of being able to 'blow their own trumpet': 'Let others know what you are doing on your own behalf and how good you feel about it yourself.' Such, it would seem, was the personal disposition of this Bolivian teacher and, partly, the reason for her success.

## The courage to act and to offer the experience to others

A last example is the case of Chris, a young primary school headteacher in Papua New Guinea. Stimulated by a talk to the National Union of Teachers on the educational principles underlying the country's official philosophy of education document (the Matane Report, 1986) and the report on the future direction of community school teacher education (McNamara, 1989), this headteacher spoke about the experience of trying to create in his school a better learning environment for the children. The inherited educational system of Papua New Guinea prescribes that teachers in primary schools are generalists and that as such they move along with their children from grade to grade. Headteachers are required to observe this principle and to organize teaching in such a way that the principle is respected. The headteacher of this school in the East New Britain province noticed that among the factors associated with poor learning and dropout rates were teacher absenteeism and differences in knowledge of teaching subjects among teachers.[2] He also observed that the teachers in his school had different capabilities and felt more comfortable teaching some subjects than teaching others. Chris thus decided to organize the school teaching on the basis of teacher capability and interest. For this, while retaining the one-teacher practice for the first grade, he allowed all other teachers to teach what they felt more comfortable with, instituting a system of teacher horizontal mobility from class to class during the school year, rather than mobility upwards with one class from year to year. The effect, over a period of years of this system, was that a whole class of children no longer suffered for a day or more if a teacher was absent (i.e. other teachers were there to teach the different subjects of the timetable), and that the quality of the content taught and of teacher motivation increased retention and success in the final sixth-grade examination. That, in effecting this change, the headteacher risked being labelled as a rebel became evident when he was transferred to another school and tried to institute the same system. With a different authority over him, Chris was now requested to follow the rules and maintain the system as it was. However, his former experience had given him enough self-confidence to want to communicate its effects in writing to other teachers, and eventually to present them to an extraordinary meeting of the faculty of the University of Papua New Guinea, where national planners were able to hear and comment on the need to examine the policy of rigid generalist teaching at the community school level.

To have the courage to engage the support of an immediate authority to try out a new experience believed with good reason to be better in educational terms (as was the case in the first school where the headteacher worked), and to persist in trying to get it across to policy-makers despite the lack of support of immediate authorities (as was the case in the second school), is no doubt an indication of teacher personal power and professionalism. The example, together with the others noted above, considers, for individual cases, situations that trigger teachers into taking steps towards their professional growth that involve reflection and action – as was the case, in embryonic form, for the teachers who had their classes videotaped, and the Australian teacher who as member of a teacher group tried strategies out and reviewed them in the light of the real classroom situations he faced. The headteacher's example illustrates the power of the individual who thinks, observes and takes action based on these processes; such power is also noticeable in the case of the Bolivian teacher. These are what we call the facilitative structures, which lie largely with the individual teacher, his or her personal perceptions about the task of education and his or her commitment to undertake such actions as will further such perceptions. In the next section, I look at what might be called the broader, outside facilitative structures that have to do, among other things, with public opinion, the prevailing tenets of the culture of change and the systemic context.

## The external facilitative structures

While teachers are themselves potentially both the subjects and the motors of their power and professional growth, the actualization of this possibility is affected to a greater or lesser degree by structures in which their life and actions are embedded. The word 'structure' here is understood as a fabric that can be woven in different ways and either hides or suggests the shape of the person it envelops. The greater the transparency of the fabric, one would say, the greater is its facilitative power to let the teacher be. Two of these structures are noted here: the public concept of what teachers should do, which affects especially the view of their role as well as their status; and the systemic structure with its organizational rules. I look at these separately.

## The public's view of teachers

Teachers are perceived in a number of different ways by those who care about what teachers do. From the perspective of the public at large, a very common form of role ascription is to see teachers as having the power to transform children into the kind of adult they perceive to be useful for society. Not too long ago, an exercise was carried out in Chile among diverse groups in society (parents, teachers, students, business people, politicians and religious leaders), which was labelled a 'National Conversation' (Ministerio de Educación, 1993). The Ministry of Education invited groups of people around the country to get together and discuss a number of questions relating to education and the kind of problems that needed a solution. Among the objects of their perceptions were teachers and their role. All groups coincided in saying that teachers were the protagonists of the process of improving educational quality, and that the success or failure of educational activities would largely depend on what they did or did not do. However, these groups, which were representative of society at large, also noted that society, as represented by the political and administrative structures, in practice failed effectively to recognize the work of teachers, given their meagre salaries and the bureaucratic controls to which it subjected them. They considered, therefore, that the social status of teachers in Chile was low and that this affected their self-esteem and their behaviour as teachers.

Conservative Party educational policies in the United Kingdom turned, towards the middle and end of the 1980s, towards a concern for standards, 'back to basics', productivity measures and, in general, bringing education under more centralized control than it had ever been before. The move was foreshadowed by a strong turn in the opinion of sectors with power to voice it, which was expressed in the first Black Papers (alternatives to government official pronouncements), indicating that teachers were excessively influenced by the progressive theories of education, such as subject integration, discovery learning and child-centred teaching, and calling for a return to solid

subject-based teaching in its traditional form (Goodson, 1990). In this context, the reaction of one teacher, Rachel Pinder, was interesting as a professional's defence against the power of public opinion. In 1987, Pinder wrote a book with a very telling title: *Why Don't Teachers Teach Like They Used To?* Reacting to the 'back to basics' public view and the Black Papers, her position was to indicate, through concrete examples of integrated teaching and references to the history of education (Quintilian, Comenius, Bacon, Pestalozzi, Dewey and Montessori), that the child-centred approach practised by teachers was sound and effective; and that to blame teachers for embracing an approach they not only judged good but could prove to be so was contrary to the view that teachers as professionals may judge what is or not useful for achieving educational goals. Teacher knowledge and the capability to decide on forms of teaching suited to student needs was at the heart of the question. In that respect, Pinder's book was not only a defence of progressive education as best suited to teaching the primary education curriculum, but also a defence of teacher professionalism.

Another way of looking at the public concept of teachers is to examine what are considered to be teacher deviations (Davies, 1991). In all contexts, there are images of what teachers should be like that may or may not be relevant to the exercise of the profession. These images may be related, as Davies (1991, p. 149) says, to 'wider typescripts for action which sanction particular responses to the availability of power and resources'. For example, while in some country contexts teachers may be encouraged to work towards developing critical thinking and independence among their students, in others such an approach may be sanctioned for reasons of traditional culture (Lindstrom, 1990) or political pressure (Davies, 1991).

Public views, therefore, may or may not support the professionalism of teachers by putting pressure on the social and political structures to represent such views; they may define roles by establishing when and how teachers are deviant; and they may be changing to the point of supporting at one time positions that at another become contradictory and require that teachers be held accountable.

## Systemic factors

Views about teachers and what power they may have in the exercise of their profession vary according to the realities of socio-economic contexts and their political representations (Popkewitz, 1994; Riseborough, 1994). Below are recent examples, in the spheres of policies and of institutional control, of how these realities influence not only what is thought about teachers but also their actions.

### Policy changes

The effect in educational politics in the United Kingdom of the Black Papers, and other educational writings calling for a change of tide in relation to the power of teachers to frame the curriculum and to decide on teaching strategies linked to pupil realities, was reflected in national policy papers issued in 1983 by the Department of Education and Science and finally enshrined in the 1987 National Curriculum framework. These policies were criticized as supporting a diminished view of teacher professionalism and power to take active part in curriculum development and to judge the most appropriate forms of assessment (Goodson, 1990). They were also openly resisted by teachers, mostly because of the manner of their introduction without consultation (Cooper and Davies, 1993).

Policies during the period of military government in Chile in the 1970s and 1980s had the effect of altering the perception of teachers' roles and significantly eroding their status as persons and professionals (Cerda *et al.*, 1991). These policies included: (a) salary scales that placed them in positions lower than those of other state-employed professionals with university training; (b) the institutionalization of technical units within schools officially entrusted with the task of offering professional support, but in reality with little professional capability to do so; (c) attempts to lower the status of teacher training institutions to

non-university level; and (d) a system of school subsidies (controlled by school inspectors) based on numbers of pupils actually in school at any given time. The system required teachers, as they perceived it (Edwards *et al.*, 1993), to place more emphasis on having pupils sitting in classrooms than on how they were teaching and how their pupils were learning. Other policies of control included a transfer of teachers from central to local control (municipalities), with the effect of a massive dismissal of 8000 teachers in 1986, which still haunts current teachers. Even though the return of democracy to Chile has meant new policies and better possibilities for teacher professionalism and power, their status and self-esteem continue to be low.

### Power allowed and power withheld

Closely related to situations such as the British and Chilean ones described above, but also a permanent feature of educational systems, is the contradiction between what is expected of teachers in relation to results of schooling, implicit in the logic of rewards to teacher performance or excellency ('merit payment') which is openly espoused today in a number of contexts (*Times Educational Supplement*, 17 September 1993; Comité Técnico Asesor, 1994), and existing policies and structures that limit teachers' power to take responsibility for the quality of their teaching.

Looking at teacher professional development in the United Kingdom, Day (1993) argues that while much lip service is paid to the need for teachers to reflect upon their worth, and while recent legislation supports staff development activities focused on reflection, these activities are often channelled to the 'what and how' of education as expressed in government policy initiatives (the national curriculum, standard attainment targets, etc.), rather than to what teachers perceive to be the professional development needs relative to the task they understand they must perform.

In a very different country context, that of Papua New Guinea, the situation is similar. Despite the official version that teachers should be encouraged to apply the curriculum to local circumstances and make it relevant to the needs of the varieties of cultures and forms of life in the country (Matane Report, 1986), few teachers attempt to do so because the strategies of teaching have been strongly prescribed and will be inspected in those terms, and because of the pressure to prepare children for national examinations at the end of primary and secondary education.

Even if power to implement is supported, the power to generate knowledge may not be recognized in the same way. Kinchelow (1993) argues that while power to implement, apply and select among strategies is considered to be part of teacher entitlement, the power to take part 'in the active process of increasing and disseminating knowledge' is not generally accessible to them. Teachers are viewed more in the role of knowledge consumers of the predigested products of educational science; this meaning in practice that the empowerment of the higher orders of thinking is restricted. A clear example of this view of the role of teachers is the growing importance of provision of curriculum packages and commercially produced software or other teaching resources with a teacher-proof quality that is endorsed in reform programmes and attached as a strong condition to loans and aid programmes to developing countries. A way to reduce the impact of this type of influence is to allow space for institutionalized activities of reflective teacher professional development at school level.[3]

While it is expected that teachers will be key actors in the implementation of a reform, it is not often the case that policy-makers discuss with teachers on an equal basis what is needed to make education better – what sort of reforms should be undertaken and how teachers could actually carry these out. The difference between these perspectives – of the policy-maker and the teacher – was highlighted at a 1994 conference hosted by the University of Papua New Guinea that brought together teachers and policy-makers speaking about implementation of the current educational reform. As the policy-maker endeavoured to present what the reform was achieving and wanted to achieve – more children in all levels of schools by the beginning of the next century, with breadth of vision, development of mental capabilities and skills for

leading a useful life – a teacher asked: 'In framing what it is you expect, have you heard us? Have you considered that we are your implementers?' The thrust of the question was that while, on the one hand, the policy-maker (rightly so) had as his major concern increasing the quantity and quality of educational provisions, on the other, the teacher was thinking, 'How will I take on your task and your concerns and make them mine? We need to talk about this together.'

*Teacher training as a source of teacher empowerment*

The development of professionalism and empowerment needs to be at the root of the training system, and in this sense, the concept extends to the status of the system and to teacher educators. Experience with issues relating to teacher training in different contexts shows that despite views of its relative unimportance in relation to teaching quality (Lockheed and Verspoor, 1992), politicians and policy-makers perceive teacher training as an important factor in determining teacher power. From a negative viewpoint, this perception may have influenced the attempt (alluded to earlier) of Chile's military government to alter the university status of teacher training and so reduce the power granted to teachers by the academic quality of their training. Similarly, it may lie behind the move to transform teacher training in the United Kingdom into 'learning the craft' in schools, which, as Rudduck (1992) indicates, is a form of reducing the power of teachers through reducing the breadth of professional training.

The institutional structure of teacher training affects the format and content of training programmes as well as the professional status and autonomy of teacher educators. Initial teacher training is mostly delivered under two types of institutional structures: universities and tertiary-level colleges. While university structures provide a greater space for autonomy, this is less true of colleges that may be dependent on ministries of education or university faculties of education. These various forms of dependency affect the degree of autonomy of teacher educators to generate a curriculum that is responsive to the needs of student teachers and of the social and cultural context in which they will teach. While teacher training in a university setting seems to allow for independent development of relevant training curriculum and activities, in fact two situations often weaken the power of teacher educators to bring this about: (a) the subject departments or faculties that service the teaching programmes with their own views of what subject knowledge is and how it should be communicated; and (b) the isolated situation of teacher educators both within the university community and in relation to the educational world 'out there', which leads them to frame programmes that are not necessarily relevant to what schools and pupils require. Recent work done for a review of initial science secondary teacher training (Avalos, 1995) indicated examples, in diverse contexts such as Latin and North America as well as Asia and the Pacific, that science faculties providing specialized knowledge tend to operate in isolation from the concerns of teacher education. The effect of this situation is that science graduates who enter teacher training are in need of such training experiences as will help them reconstitute their science knowledge into more integrated and teachable science concepts. However, there is not always the time, or the possibility, in short one-year programmes, for this to occur. Teacher educators may not always be able to perform this task because of constraints resulting from their own knowledge background and from the fact that the one-year programmes seem to be organized as a pot-pourri of educational 'academic' knowledge or a Cook's tour of the school curriculum, and provide limited practical teaching experiences. What are needed here are university policies that make possible an examination of the teacher training programmes and their links with subject specialization, and that support the power of teacher educators to influence the framing of the whole curriculum.

College teacher education, generally focused on primary-level training, is more strongly controlled either by ministry of education policies (state or national) or by the universities to which the colleges may be attached. Recent conversations with lecturers of a college in India, affiliated to the local university, showed how profoundly immersed these lecturers were in the acceptance of the norms of what one might term a 'stultified' academic tradition, which formatted every subject and activity in the college into an examinable course with written examinations, for which, theoretically, much reading was needed, but which with limited library facilities was reduced to students learning from course handouts. Though unhappy about the university's control in bureaucratic matters, the teacher educators in that college did not question the curriculum straitjacket placed on them by the university faculty. In fact, not only did they not question it, they were proud of the status the arrangement provided both them and their students.

The situation of community school teacher training in Papua New Guinea is illustrative of the perception that is had of the importance of teacher education and of the struggle to exercise control over such training by different administrative departments within the Ministry of Education. The proposal to create a semi-autonomously functioning National Institute of Teacher Education offering professional support to teacher educators (McNamara, 1989) was at first strongly opposed by sectors within the Ministry of Education, which had exercised control over teacher training institutions since their establishment, having determined what was taught and how it was taught (within the behavioural framework, so influential in the early 1970s). However, the growth in awareness among teacher educators that other theoretical positions were relevant (in particular those related to reflective teaching and cognitive/constructivist learning) and the desire to have greater power in decisions about curriculum activities, coupled with support from an understanding ministerial head of department, paved the way for deciding on the establishment of the institute as proposed. Difficulties for its establishment reappeared, however, when another ministerial department, with a mandate to coordinate higher education institutions, realized the potential that the establishment of a semi-autonomous National Institute of Teacher Education might have over the power of teacher educators to determine the orientation of their institutions, and thereby lessen the control power of this department. Opposition to an independent institute was thus strongly voiced by the second department, and its power was used to oppose its creation as a semi-autonomous institution, favouring instead a coordinating body for teacher education.

The empowerment of teacher educators at college level in Papua New Guinea has nevertheless been supported at a different level, through a programme of professional development jointly implemented by the University of Papua New Guinea, the country's National Department of Education and an external body represented by an Australian university and partially funded by Australian government assistance. The programme involves upgrading teacher educators to degree level and continued professional support in the field, provided jointly by Papua New Guinea and Australian academic staff. The characteristics of the programme as an experience of continued professional development of teacher educators have been documented by Burke (1993) and Elliott (1993). Through a better grounding in subject knowledge and training strategies and confrontation with perspectives such as those of reflective teaching, the teacher educators have been able to become critical of the teaching formats experienced as student teachers, as teachers in the system and later as college lecturers. This awareness and professional expertise, as well as increased self-assurance, have enabled them to carry out what others might have deemed impossible: the development of a new curriculum for their colleges (which until then had been the curriculum nationally developed and determined by the Ministry of Education).

## Achievement of professionalism and power

As a way of concluding this chapter, some thoughts are given to ways in which structures can move from being less to being more facilitative.

## *Support for teachers*

Teachers' social recognition in terms of working conditions or salary structure is perceived differently depending on who is speaking: the teacher, a government representative or the public (parents, especially). As indicated earlier, at the level of public declarations teachers are generally accorded high status as persons responsible for children's learning and character development. In this respect, they are expected to be skilful in performing tasks leading to these aims and they are also expected to model what is considered to be appropriate behaviour. The reality of their status, however, is eroded by the particular conditions in which teachers in many countries have to work. These eroding conditions go from salaries that place them at the lower end of the salary structure of public employees (especially primary teachers) to working situations in isolated areas that have minimal facilities for professional development and action, let alone living facilities. Generally speaking, teachers take a long time before they complain strongly about these conditions. Within the constraints of their environment they attempt to carry out the socially expected role, but with diminished vigour as the conditions are experienced more negatively. Often politicians and administrators fail to understand the situation and resent teachers who make it known that their conditions are suffocating their capabilities and their practice (Rudduck, 1992). The solution to these problems is not easy in poorer countries with large school populations that also live in rural areas, but it must be tackled. Minimum support for teachers in their work requires that they have salaries and living conditions that allow them the freedom to improve the quality of their work.

Despite years of theorizing about how the success of reforms depends on the involvement in their planning of as many of the interested parties as possible, teachers continue to be left out of the process and its discussion. Much of this has to do with the notion of 'expertise' and 'technical know-how' that underlies the policy-maker's and aid agency's views of how to address the need for change. It is symptomatic, for example, that in the very visible higher education project in Papua New Guinea funded by the Asian Development Bank, a number of the consultants recruited were quick to offer advice without considering the opinion of the affected parties and their history of attempting to change primary teacher education in their country. Underlying the possibility of teachers' and teacher educators' empowerment within an education system must be the belief that they can be true partners in the process of educational reform.

While there is growing recognition of the need for teacher empowerment in relation to teachers' class- and school-level practice, such recognition is not as forthcoming when it comes to the power of teachers to influence policy. Fraser (1992) notes that the debate surrounding such scope of empowerment is not new, and that in the United States it was posed as early as the beginning of the century, with the proposal to create a Teachers' Council, where teachers could have a say in relation to matters of curriculum. John Dewey (quoted in Fraser, 1992) noted the concern about neglect of teachers' contribution in creating the council:

> There isn't a sinister interest in the United States that isn't perfectly willing to leave in the hands of the teaching body the ultimate decision on points of that particular kind which comes to be known as 'pedagogy' and 'pedagogical methods'. There is no certainty, there is no likelihood, however, that the views of the body of teachers, in most cities and towns of the United States, will at present time have any real positive, constructive influence in determining the basic educational policy of schools, of their communities, so far as a more general aspect of education is concerned.

There is a need, therefore, to support conditions through which teachers are able to exert greater influence in the framing and critique of policy.

In the light of the above considerations, it is possible to indicate support mechanisms through which the role of teachers as professionals and as generators and creative implementers of effective practice can become feasible and possible. Some of these are suggested in current literature:

● In teacher training, prepare student teachers for the hazards of school organization and provide them with some form of 'organizational literacy' (Tatto, 1992; Kuzmic, 1994).

● At school level, structure the school and its management in ways that support professional development and professionalization of teachers, and elicit support from peers, students, parents and the community (Tatto, 1992).

● At the level of the educational system, have an appropriate reward and incentive system, with reasonable salary and work conditions that provide stability for teachers to develop and act professionally (Davies, 1991; Tatto, 1992). This last condition is an underlying, *sine qua non*, basis for empowerment, but not a motive that leads to professional quality and the exercise of power.

## Teachers and collaboration among teachers

In reading the literature and policy declarations on teacher empowerment, one notices frequent reference to 'how teachers will be empowered'. Few articles address the teachers themselves, their own will to become empowered and how they can work themselves towards greater professional autonomy. The incipient literature in developing countries on teachers' ways of thinking,[4] their real and not the 'official' perceptions about their work, enables us to perceive a timidity to express feelings about their role in the profession, not because these are not there but because they might not be acceptable. Feelings about conditions of service are more frequently voiced at the times when these become intolerable and because teacher unions are ready to support them. Feelings about teachers' role in change are less likely to be voiced publicly unless they can be voiced in conditions that support the value of what they say. Hence arises the importance of institutionalized frameworks that make possible the collaboration of teachers and of teachers and administrators in the improvement of educational practices. For this to occur, teachers must want it and be committed not only to demand participation but also to engage in it with vigour. Such engagement in participation, and hence the use of professional power, requires the effort to develop analytic capabilities and, by discussion, reading and trying out, to look into teaching or administrative alternatives designed to improve educational practices. This is not an easy task, because in generating alternatives that may run counter to mainstream policies, practices and the views of 'experts', the next step, which is getting them across and acceptable, may require confrontation, with consequences that are not always foreseeable and may not be comfortable. These are the risks of empowerment and the risks of showing avenues for change. However, it is also true that teacher collaboration provides not only opportunity for reasoned confrontation but also conditions for negotiation, involving not only teachers as partners, but also schools and government (Day, 1993).

> Those of us who hunger for a different and better world must move beyond a pedagogy of resistance, powerful as that can be, and toward a pedagogy of engagement, in which to have our proposals and strategies for changing schools and schooling and specifically teacher education.
>
> (Fraser, 1992, pp. 11–12)

Empowering teachers should not be understood as yet another process that policy-makers engage in, such as providing in-service opportunities or improving working conditions. Teacher power necessarily means the capability and the opportunity of every teacher taken as an individual and of the body of teachers to think about their practice and the educational system, and to provide guidance for their improvement, be it through their own actions or wider reform policies. It also means thinking about the society to which educated people will contribute and the opportunity to provide guidance about the educational forms that will facilitate a more useful contribution of such educated people.[5] Teacher power and the manner in which it is actualized therefore has a two- or multi-way purpose. It involves growth and actions by teachers themselves, and policy frameworks and support by the system and society to make possible effective collaborative change experiences. Power transfer is not an easy process – and where such power has been more removed from teachers, the process will imply a degree of confrontation. But those of us who believe that progress requires confrontation and that teacher power will not come about without a degree of unsettlement and strife should also believe that in the end it will result if the parties in question are able to work out the grounds for agreement. The education of young people for a better society will be the gain in the process.

## Notes

1  We refer to publications about the Australian Project for Enhancing Effective Learning (PEEL), which originally started in a secondary school in the state of Victoria in 1985, but is now extended to other schools in Australia and to other countries (Baird and Northfield, 1992; Baird and Mitchell, 1993). These publications are rich in statements from the participants of teacher groups as well as from the Monash University facilitators, and include materials and strategies devised by the teachers to improve student learning.

2  Until recently, primary teacher training consisted of a two-year course after completion of tenth grade or lower secondary education, with little opportunity for teacher trainees to improve their subject knowledge.

3  This mode of accepting a World Bank loan to supplement a government reform programme aimed at secondary education in Chile (Ministerio de Educación, 1993) is enshrined in the establishment of teacher professional groups in all state-funded schools. These groups, constituted as teacher workshops using a reflection-in-action approach, may have the power to discriminate among products on offer, but, it is hoped, more than that, to develop their own ways of altering teaching to improve the quality of education.

4  See Joseph Pagelio's master's thesis for the University of Papua New Guinea (1994) on the thinking of secondary teachers in Papua New Guinea, where he reviews the literature and carries out an original study on the patterns of thinking among a group of teachers.

5  In relation to this point, Fraser (1992), referring to the implications of the Holmes and Carnegie reports on education in the United States, notes that it is crucially important to discuss these and to take a stand on the type of society for which young people and teachers are being educated. He says further that 'there are alternative visions of the potential of education available today. The visions offered by the civil rights movement, by generations of progressive educators, of a schooling that builds free citizens and a new sense of community rather than human resources for the maintenance of an economic hegemony in the world's market economy need to be nurtured and expanded' (p. 11).

# References

Avalos, B. (ed.) (1986) *Teaching Children of the Poor: An Ethnographic Study in Latin America*. Ottawa: IDRC.

Avalos, B. (1995) *Issues in Science Teacher Education*. Paris: IIEP.

Baird, J. R. and Mitchell, I. J. (eds) (1993) *Improving the Quality of Teaching and Learning: An Australian Case Study*, 2nd edn. Melbourne: Monash University Printery.

Baird, J. R. and Northfield, J. R. (eds) (1992) *Learning from the Peel Experience*. Melbourne: Monash University Printing Service.

Burke, C. (1993) From basic skills to reflective practice: a sustainable approach to professional development of teacher educators in Papua New Guinea. In C. Thirwall and B. Avalos (eds), *Participation and Educational Change*. Waigani: University of Papua New Guinea Press.

Cerda, A. M., Silva, M. L. and Nuñez, I. (1991) *El Sistema Escolar y la Profesión Docente*. Santiago, Chile: PIIE.

Clark, C. M. (1992) Teachers as designers in self-directed professional development. In A. Hargreaves and M. G. Fullan (eds), *Understanding Teacher Development*. New York: Teachers College Press.

Clark, C. M. and Peterson, P. L. (1986) Teachers' thought processes. In M. Wittrock (ed.), *Handbook of Research on Teaching*, 3rd edn. New York: Macmillan.

Comité Técnico Asesor (1994) *Los Desafíos de la Educación Chilena Frente al Siglo 21*. Draft Report of the Presidential Committee on Modernisation of Chilean Education. Santiago.

Cooper, P. and Davies, C. (1993) The impact of national curriculum assessment arrangements. *Teaching and Teacher Education*, **9** (5/6), 559–69.

Davies, L. (1991) Teachers as implementers or subversives. In J. D. Turner (ed.), *The Reform of Educational Systems to Meet Local Needs*. Manchester: Manchester University Press.

Day, C. (1993) Reflection: a necessary but not sufficient condition for professional development. *British Educational Research Journal*, **19** (1), 83–93.

de Crespo, M. (1986) Teachers can be different: a Bolivian case. In B. Avalos (ed.), *Teaching Children of the Poor: An Ethnographic Study in Latin America*. Ottawa: IDRC.

Edwards, V., Calvo, C., Cerda, A. M., Inostroza, G. and Gómez, V. (1993). *Prácticas de trabajo y socialización en los establecimientos de educación media* (research report). Santiago: Programa Interdisciplinario de Investigaciones en Educación.

Elliott, R. (1993) Principles, models and processes for professional development of lecturers in community teachers' colleges. In C. Thirwall and B. Avalos (eds), *Participation and Educational Change*. Waigani: University of Papua New Guinea Press.

Fraser, J. W. (1992) Preparing teachers for democratic schools: the Holmes and Carnegie Reports five years later. A critical reflection. *Teachers College Record*, **94** (1), 7–41.

Goodson, I. (1990) 'Nations at risk' and 'national curriculum': ideology and identity. *Politics of Education Association Yearbook*, 219–323.

Hargreaves, A. (1992) Cultures of teaching: a focus for change. In A. Hargreaves and M. G. Fullan (eds), *Understanding Teacher Development*. New York: Teachers College Press.

Hoyle, E. (1969) *The Role of the Teacher*. London: Routledge and Kegan Paul.

Hymes, D. (1993) Theory into practice. In J. R. Baird and J. J. Mitchell (eds), *Improving the Quality of Teaching and Learning*, 2nd edn. Melbourne: Monash University Printery.

Jackson, P. W. (1992) Helping teachers develop. In A. Hargreaves and M. Fullan (eds), *Understanding Teacher Development*. New York: Teachers College Press.

Kinchelow, J. L. (1993) *Toward a Critical Politics of Teacher Thinking: Mapping the Postmodern*. Westport, CT: Bergin & Garvey.

Kuzmic, J. (1994) A beginning teacher's search for meaning: teacher socialization, organizational literacy, and empowerment. *Teaching and Teacher Education*, **10** (1), 15–27.

Lindstrom, M. (1990) Local knowledge and the South Pacific classroom. *Papua New Guinea Journal of Education*, **26** (1), 5–17.

Lockheed, M. and Verspoor, A. M. (1992) *Improving Primary Education: A Review of Policy Options*. New York: Oxford University Press.

McNamara, V. (1989). *The Future Direction of Community School Teacher Education*. Waigani: PNG Department of Education.

Matane, P. (1986) *A Philosophy of Education for Papua New Guinea*. Ministerial committee report. Waigani: PNG Department of Education.

Ministerio de Educación (1993) *Informe Conversación Nacional sobre Educación Media*. Santiago, Chile: MECE Media.

Pinder, R. (1987) *Why Don't Teachers Teach Like They Used To?* London: Hilary Shipman.

Popkewitz, T. S. (1994) Professionalization in teaching and teacher education: some notes on its history, ideology and potential. *Teaching and Teacher Education*, **10** (1), 1–14.

Riseborough, G. F. (1994) Teachers' careers and comprehensive school closure: policy and professionalism in practice. *British Educational Research Journal*, **20** (1), 85–104.

Rudduck, J. (1992) Practitioner research and programs of initial teacher education. In T. Russell and H. Munby (eds), *Teachers and Teaching: From Classroom to Reflection*. London: Falmer Press.

Shulman, L. S. (1987) Knowledge and teaching: foundations of the new reform. *Harvard Educational Review*, **57** (1), 1–22.

Tatto, M. T. (1992) Policies for teachers in peripheral areas: a review of literature. Paper presented at the Seventh World Congress of Comparative Education: Education, Democracy and Development.

Tochon, F. and Munby, H. (1993) Novice and expert teachers' time epistemology: a wave function from didactics to pedagogy. *Teacher and Teacher Education*, **9** (5/6), 205–18.

# Part Two

## Restructuring Teacher Education

# 8 Re-reform of Teacher Education: A Dialogue

## HILARY RADNOR AND KEN SHAW

## Introduction

*Ken.* I came into teacher training in 1961, after teaching since 1954. At that time the two-year certificate course required students to study two main subject courses and three so-called 'curriculum' courses to a lower level. They also had to do religious education and physical education. And these were secondary students. This was the legacy of the elementary schools, which wanted staff prepared to teach several subjects to youngsters, most of whom left without any certificate into a buoyant job market. There were a few weeks' teaching practice in each year of the course, certainly not more than ten weeks altogether. In principle, students could elect to teach in primary or secondary schools. Specialization in science or physical education oriented many to secondary teaching, but there was a large specialized primary course, which emphasized the teaching of reading and number, in the second year. From that pretty low base undergraduate teacher education moved quickly to a three-year certificate course, then three-year BEd with qualified teacher status, and finally four-year honours BEd with sharply differentiated primary or secondary pathways and single subject specialization for the latter. So for me, what is happening just now comes at the end of a long development, and shows long-term openness to adaptation and change on the part of teacher educators.

*Hilary.* I made the move from being a teacher to a teacher educator in 1987 when I became a lecturer in education. It felt like moving from one side of the track to the other, for as a head of department from 1974 to 1985, I looked after students on their teaching practice. I experienced the lack of an established partnership and formal relationship with a teacher education institution. It did feel as if I and my department were carrying out a mentorship role with the student teachers. But officially there were no structures in place for discussion about courses, objectives, principles or aims with the university department. Moreover, we were only marginally involved in the evaluation of the student teachers' capacities to teach successfully. Therefore, it did not surprise me that this was a subject of debate when I entered teacher education in 1987.

*Ken.* At the beginning I did not have a lot to do with PGCE, since at that time it was oriented to preparing graduates to teach mostly in selective secondary schools, and carried on at another site. We rapidly developed a primary PGCE, though secondary was the big market for graduates. It was carried out by the individual subject lecturers, who also placed and supervised their students in schools of their preference. There was a course of general lectures, but it was very much a matter of 'me and my ten students'; PGCE tutors did their own thing in a very autonomous way, and up to a point still do, though with much more coordination and oversight. It was not difficult for untrained graduates to get into teaching in the sixties; the climate was quite different because of teacher shortages.

Don't forget, also, that there was a big programme of in-service courses to upgrade less qualified teachers and help to meet the needs of the still quite new comprehensive school for staff and for curriculum development skills; and, in addition, heaps of shortened courses for all sorts of mature entrants. To carry conviction we had to work closely with teachers and the LEAs.

*Hilary.* Well then, let us capitalize on our different perspectives and look particularly at four themes. There is the issue of the changing structures of teacher education from the sixties as it has striven to accommodate to changing demands. You have had first-hand experience of this. There is the issue of the changing balance between general education of intending teachers and the specific training in professional and vocational school/ classroom aspects of the courses, of which we both have a view. There is the contemporary situation that we are both now responding to in our different ways – another radical attempt at reform. Lastly there is the future, of which I have a particular vision that I should like to present to you.

*Ken.* Fine. Yes, we are caught up in a painful and fundamental restructuring of teacher education just now. It's a radical change of style. But it is not the first. There have been other periods of accelerated movement in the system. We are in a responsive business.

Remember that we ended the war short of about a third of the desirable teaching force, and soon faced a massive increase in births. Before the war there had been a major downturn in births and hence in the demand for schools and teachers. It took time for the post-war bulge of births to be appreciated. It was obvious that a major reconstructive effort would be needed. The conventional wisdom was that it would be a once and for all effort, since it was the taken-for-granted assumption that in developed industrial countries the birth rate was low, and the bulge was a passing event, after which the rate would fall back to the pre-war norm.

The adaptive response was the Emergency Training Scheme, which would take up the slack of groups who were willing to come forward to train as certificated teachers. For these the course was shortened to a little over a year for non-

graduates. The staff were mostly ex-schoolteachers, and the course was intensely practical. Some of the emergency colleges closed in the fifties. Births were higher than pre-war, and the school-leaving age had been raised to 15, so that others remained as permanent institutions, run by local authorities who invested heavily in improvements and rebuilding during the fifties and sixties. The LEA colleges decisively changed the balance between the denominational colleges and LEA colleges, which of course could count on support (as well as encountering those with an overdeveloped will to control) in county hall. There were no polytechnics to participate then. The university PGCE courses, though expanding, were often very small; but some universities offered a large number of places on evening courses for teachers to improve their qualifications.

*Hilary.* But what was the view about what teachers ought to be learning – who was deciding what? What about the courses? Did the influx of new people and the eventual lengthening of the course lead to a greater stress on what was directly relevant to teaching and classroom management skills?

*Ken.* Teacher education at that period was not the highly self-conscious activity it has now become. The great bulk of the research which survives is inevitably concerned with issues of access and growth of numbers in training, and was much influenced by the political arithmetic tradition carried over from the thirties. It bears no comparison, for sophistication, with the major researches carried out into 11-plus selection. There can be little doubt that the training methods and even the philosophy of teacher education in the emergency colleges during their heyday were very different from those in the older institutions. They were very much more practical and classroom-oriented perforce, given the short length of the course. There was a very intensive style of work, with less conventional, more mature entrants, who had in the main matured while carrying out their duties in the forces and other forms of national service during the war. More particularly, the staff of the emergency colleges tended to be different in origin and outlook from the staff who had been in the established colleges before the war and subsequently returned. Many of the small but influential emergency college groups who joined the staff in established colleges were much more concerned with transmitting up-to-date teaching skills and developing classroom insight.

*Hilary.* It sounds to me as if there were different approaches to teacher education between the emergency colleges' people and the more traditionally trained staff in the established colleges. How did the new people affect things?

*Ken.* The effect of the Emergency Scheme had been a matter of diffusion, which, along with other factors stemming from expansion and changes in the market for teachers and teacher educators, helped to create a revised culture and understanding of the nature of teacher training and how it could be implemented. A much deeper treatment of the older disciplines of education was possible. Some withered and were replaced by more thoroughly professional use of the wide range of social science disciplines and comparative education, and a greater reliance on the rapidly developing research of the day. Eventually the discipline of curriculum studies, which now occupies the centre of the stage, appeared, made possible by the increase in staffing and general growth. The undergraduate course moved from two years to three-year pass BEd and then honours and a four-year course, while the PGCE route expanded, increased in rigour and attention to classroom skills and became compulsory in the maintained sector. Just as these steady developments appeared to be moving on to a plateau that allowed for consolidation, the structural changes consequent on the end of growth began to be imposed. These were a second major change, and again affected the whole of the arrangements for teacher education (Alexander *et al.*, 1984).

*Hilary.* You talk about what was happening in England. I trained to be a teacher in Scotland. To teach in a secondary school you had to be a graduate except in the area of craft subjects. So the four-year training was three years for a degree and one year for a Secondary Schools' Teachers Certificate. Primary school teachers were educated in colleges of education but secondary school teachers in the main were university graduates. The notion of a three- or four-year BEd for secondary teachers was new to me when I came south of the border to teach. The emphasis for secondary teachers was clearly in the subject domain; professional studies was a very poor second. So that must be a problem for you, with the influence of the universities affecting teacher education in the colleges of education. Teacher education was trying to drive up the level of its teaching in the main subject courses to university level, and at the same time trying to give importance to the professional side of the work. Is that right?

*Ken.* In undergraduate work, yes; and the tension between the two clusters of aims must have been apparent to you when you came in, surely? PGCE work of course has to translate university knowledge in the subject to school- and classroom-relevant knowledge, as well as working on methods and approach to the teaching. Some strain was evident there too.

Summing up on the period from the late sixties to the late seventies, I want to stress two things. There was not anything like the present research interest in classroom activities and management. Because the curriculum was still very open, especially at secondary level, the emphases were more on understanding children, particularly stressing stages in child development and individual differences. Teaching techniques and classroom skills were more a matter of lore and tradition, with a lot of discussion and practical planning. It was less theoretically informed. The educational psychologists, then pretty powerful because their area was well developed compared with sociology of education or curriculum, were much concerned with theories of intelligence and testing because of the significance of 11-plus selection and all the controversies surrounding it.

Don't forget, either, that what we now regard as a professional specialism, educational studies, was seriously underdeveloped as a career. A lot of people taught history of education, philosophy, even history of educational ideas. Specialists in special educational needs were rather few, and multiculturalism, say, was still over the horizon. Most systematic and really professional empirical research in schools was confined to a smallish group of places like London and the famous Scots colleges.

*Hilary.* Yes, like the one I went to, Jordanhill College in Glasgow. What you say about the 'ologies is interesting. I was introduced to them when I went to do a master's course in the early eighties in curriculum development. It was taught really through sociology, with a touch of philosophy and history; but it was sociology that drove the course and underpinned the research on which much of it rested. It was part of a drive, I think, within the education department at that university to out-flank psychology as the leading discipline for understanding the educational context. As students, we loved it. We could relate to it. It helped to explain all sorts of problems we had experienced within the organizational structure of schooling and the difficulties in relationships in teaching and learning among teachers and with pupils. However, it was light years away from pedagogical studies directly prescribing good practice and how to get it in the classroom, and from researches into school contexts. It did not directly link with the development of professional practice. That was something we were left to do ourselves should we wish to, but it did provide us with a theoretical framework to help make sense of schooling, teaching and learning.

It seems to me that you were also interested in turning teacher education into an academic subject recognized by the universities. This seemed more important perhaps than having a professional impact directly related to pedagogical studies.

*Ken.* Yes, and I am unapologetic about it. For the times, I think we achieved a great deal. More youngsters had A-levels as a percentage of the cohort at the end of the seventies than had O-levels in the sixties. As a nation we were fully able to provide for the big expansion in higher education places post-Robbins. Teachers had a big hand in

that. They needed to be more educated in their subjects and learn through the disciplines.

## Becoming part of higher education

*Ken.* Strengthening of relationships with the university sector was important and was certainly not universally popular. Many in universities were rather condescending about teacher education and found it especially difficult to accept the wide spread of (by their standards) somewhat shallow courses which together constituted preparation for primary teaching as worthy of a degree. For some LEAs, their college of education was the flagship, a source of deep pride, and the churches had a keen proprietorial interest in some of the longest-established institutions. Deeply concerned with pressing issues of teacher supply, the DES was very anxious to keep tight control of numbers and strove continually to adjust them to needs. The crude factor of live births was only one of a cluster of others which complicated supply: wastage in a period when other occupational opportunities abounded; the pool of qualified teachers not actually teaching; shortage subjects; the balance of primary and secondary, and of concurrent three- or four-year courses as against PGCE courses; shortened courses for mature entrants; and no doubt plenty more. The institutions themselves, always carefully eyeing their competitors in the race for growth and resources, looked for an increasing measure of collegial self-government. They had achieved a small measure of this when college academic boards (at first in no sense democratic) were set up after 1966. They were not now looking for more academic control coming from the universities but a collegial relationship with them.

After all, the minority report of the McNair Committee had called for 100 per cent university control. With the publication of the Robbins Report (1963), major strides in the direction of collegial relationships could be made in academic matters. Administratively, of course, the DES and LEAs retained great powers; HMI were frequent visitors. The machinery in use was the Area Training Organizations (ATOs). These were large committees drawn at considerable expense from a wide area in some cases, but chaired and serviced by university personnel. They had general oversight of policy, and introduced a very wide range of LEA officials, advisers, teachers, college staff, HMI and teachers' unions representatives to the many and complex issues surrounding teacher education, especially where the ATO included a plurality of colleges with competing demands for teaching practice places in the schools, and conflicting interests in the provision of in-service education.

*Hilary.* There must have been a problem getting the college lecturers and the university people to reach an agreement about what the courses for teacher training should consist of.

*Ken.* It took time. Course development, all aspects of examining and, to a varying extent, the way that courses were delivered in the colleges were a matter for subject groups chaired by university professors, some of whom had almost no knowledge of the context of teacher education, but were understandably keen to improve the academic level of college work. There was widespread use of university staff as external examiners. Over time, well-established relationships grew up among the parties involved and working accommodations were arrived at among the vested interests.

The Council for Accreditation of Teacher Education (CATE) criteria were having an impact on the structure of teacher education courses and the curriculum for the student teachers was far more oriented to the practical issues of teaching and learning in the classroom. In stipulating the criteria for approval of courses the document states:

> Initial teacher training courses should be so planned as to allow for a substantial element of school experience and teaching practice which, taken together, should be no less than 15 weeks in a postgraduate course, a 3 year BEd or concurrent undergraduate course, and not less than 20 weeks in a 4 year BEd. Educational and professional studies should be closely linked with each other and with a student's practical experience in schools.
>
> (DES, 1984, Annex p. 24)

*Hilary.* The CATE criteria had become embedded as part of the culture of teacher training in 1987 when I came into teacher education. The students spent at least half of their time shared between developing practical skills of teaching through university-based preparation for teaching courses, teaching practice and educational studies courses. The other half was spent pursuing an academic subject at their own level. For the PGCE students, the course concentrated on subject tutors supplying them with ideas, models and resources for teaching their subject to pupils. This was interspersed with a limited amount of time spent on other, more general educational issues; for example, special educational needs, assessment and testing, tutoring and counselling and the way schools are governed. The culture of training predominated.

Students' greatest worry was the management of pupil behaviour. They wanted to be given a formula for success in managing a classroom full of 30 or so youngsters so that they could teach them something! It has been generally accepted that the best way to do this is through immersion in the school context and for students to be inducted into teaching by observing and doing, supported by expert practitioners in the field. Schools have therefore invested time and expertise in managing and supporting school experience visits by students, so that they can learn about the school's organization, culture, ethos, processes and practices before embarking on the more traditional teaching practice. It seemed to me to be a vocational degree.

*Ken.* The impact of CATE is crucial. Previously, because of the honours degree, most of the pressures were towards more academic courses, so that the final paper would raise questions and issues that would persuade external examiners that students were working at a genuinely honours level. Students could choose to follow fully developed courses in areas like history, philosophy, sociology or psychology of education, as well as curriculum studies, taught by specialists. Many staff were not keen on a teaching practice in year four because they wanted an uninterrupted run-up to the final examinations. But the courses were planned to provide a critical understanding of the system, of factors affecting educability of pupils, including special needs and multicultural aspects and a view of purposes, not merely processes. Students usually had to write a dissertation that was theoretically informed. The university culture of critical rationality and the striving for evidence was widely cherished; the accusations of zealotry and partisan, politically inspired, teaching were widely exaggerated. They were made by people who rarely, if ever, set foot in a training institution and regularly refused invitations. It is important to stress that the vocational aspect of the courses was powerful. Students worked in schools with main subject and education tutors for several terms, carried out the progressively lengthened teaching practices, which added six weeks to the PGCE working year, and were generally offered plenty of preparation for the classroom. Primary courses probably moved more quickly in the directions stressed by CATE. As secondary courses evolved, the more theoretical elements and options were reduced steadily as we all moved to prepare students to understand and carry out the requirements of the GCSE, the 1988 and subsequent Acts. A mass of classroom-oriented research had transformed knowledge about teaching and learning; the better students were becoming familiar with it and were quite capable of moving eventually to higher degrees involving research. Options were added in many cases to PGCE to deepen its professional content, and it became steadily more school based. CATE gave all this added impetus.

*Hilary*. It was also certainly the case that when I entered teacher education in 1987 there was recognition of what students could learn through experience. There have been ongoing serious debates about what constitutes the professional/ educational studies aspects of teacher education/ training courses, which have moved on apace. The perceived wisdom was that studying the 'ologies as such was no longer relevant to the developing emphasis on practical skills, and so there has been a general and genuine search for ways of engaging students in professional and educational issues that broaden their knowledge and understanding of how schools work and are managed as organiza-

tions, the way the curriculum had developed and changed, different theories of learning and models and styles of evaluation and assessment, to name but a few. There is also a feeling among many teacher trainers that the students should be able to articulate intelligently what they are doing in the teaching context and why they are doing it, and that they should be encouraged to exercise their capacity to develop their practice in a deliberate and thoughtful way. The notion of 'the reflective practitioner', as articulated by writers such as Schön (1983), is articulated as a way of conceptualizing a structure of educational/professional studies for student teachers. Hence at present there appears to be, broadly speaking, a twofold approach to training teachers: courses that generally follow the skill development, classroom teaching, how to teach your subject model; and courses (more often the longer four-year BEd courses) that favour the 'reflective practitioner' model with emphasis on students researching and analysing their own practice and that of others. Through studying action and interaction, the 'reflective practitioner' model encourages students to conceptualize principles of practice for themselves that meet the context in which they find themselves. Each student would therefore be engaged in the construction of her or his own knowledge about what it is to be a teacher, as opposed to the 'consumption' model, where they are given prescriptive formulaic knowledge about how to be a teacher generated from examples of good practice in certain kinds of educational research literature.

But we have not, as professionals, been allowed to develop changes in our own professional practices in the driving seat, so to speak. There has been a significant power shift, it seems to me, to political domination through government legislation. Having shaken up the curriculum in the schools, opened up educational systems to being more business- and market-oriented through such things as local management of schools, grant maintained schools, city technology colleges and the 1988 Education Act, the government was radically restructuring teacher education. The political right has had the ear of government and really set the agenda. This reached an apex in the 1994 Education Act.

*Ken.* Yes. It is worth looking at the debates in the Lords and Commons, which are especially significant for the 1994 Act for two chief reasons. First, there was no consultation about this measure other than on the floor of the Houses. Second, there was a very marked difference of atmosphere between the debate in the Lords, in which a very distinguished group of speakers with wide experience of education intervened, and in the Commons, where the government used its majority to overturn the Lords' amendments. The main debates took place in the Lords in December 1993 and in the Commons in June 1994.

The major themes that emerged were:

- the government's policies and intentions, and the likely consequences that these would have for central control and direction of the reformed system of teacher education, and the powers of the Secretary of State;
- the evidential or doctrinal/ideological basis upon which the proposed legislation rested;
- the issue of the future role of higher education in teacher education and in educational research and development;
- the question of standards of schooling as they were likely to be affected by styles in the education and training of teachers, and the future standing of teaching in relation to other professions.

In line with its general position in legislation for schools, the intention of the government was to assume closer central control of teacher education by replacing the Higher Education Funding Council (in England but not in Wales), CATE and the Teaching as a Career Unit of the Department for Education by a quango, the Teacher Training Authority (TTA). This was to be a small group of about 12 persons nominated by the Secretary of State to advise him or her on matters relating to teacher education. Its advice and work would not necessarily be public. It would be required to press for clarity, accountability and effectiveness in the arrangement eventually set up. It would accredit training institutions, whether partnerships

between higher education institutions and schools or schools alone, and oversee the allocation of funds. A sum of £4000 would be made available for each postgraduate student, of whom there were in 1994 about 16,500. It was expected that the first 450 places would be operating under the new arrangements by October 1994.

There is considerable opposition to quangos, which now administer about a third of all government expenditure in the UK, on the grounds that they are not publicly accountable in the way that the local authorities are. This system effectively leaves the power with the ministers and their departments. In the case of the 1994 Bill there was considerable opposition in the Lords to the fact that the minister had not drawn up and made available to Parliament the Regulations under which the new training arrangements would be administered. All teacher training institutions, whether schools or partnerships, would have to demonstrate, presumably to OFSTED and HMI, that they are committed to the criteria laid down by government and that they have systems in place to deliver quality in courses of training. The detailed Regulations would follow and have to be taken on trust. There can be little doubt that despite Mr Patten's remark about moving power from the hub to the rim in education (that is, to parents and governors), the real administrative, financial and curriculum power remains firmly with the minister. Speakers repeatedly stressed the dangers of the increase in central power. The government spokespersons affirmed that its aims were:

- to set standards;
- to define knowledge and skills that teachers require;
- to increase the time trainee teachers spend in schools;
- to ensure emphasis in primary courses on English, maths, science, reading and number work;
- to ensure a six-subject course for intending primary teachers;
- to bring the arrangements fully into operation by 1994 for secondary trainees and by 1996 for primary trainees.

The Conservative view expressed in the debates maintains that teaching has evolved rapidly and thus needs radically new training arrangements. Conservative speakers asserted that the ideas of the opposition have failed to keep up with this movement in teaching and that they remain stubbornly in the past, even, according to some, fixed in the ideas of the sixties. The objects of their new arrangements follow from the Conservative philosophy of providing choice, so that market forces may operate. Thus, instead of a higher education monopoly of the training of teachers, new providers will be encouraged to enter the market, notably through the various forms of partnership between school and higher education, or schools individually or in partnership or consortia, independently of higher education. All who do enter will be inspected on a 'no inspection – no funding' basis. Participation by schools will be quite voluntary. The decision about whether to participate in teacher training will be left to governors, as will the details of arrangements that will be called for within schools; that is, subject to the criteria and regulations to be published, who does the training, and how time, money and effort will be deployed. This will be a major extension of the responsibilities of governors in those schools which decide to participate. Monitoring such decision processes should offer a major research opportunity in the field of school administration.

The Conservative approach came under criticism and was described as an abdication of responsibility on the part of the Secretary of State; it is entirely consonant with the spirit of encouraging much greater independence and initiative as schools leave the LEAs and take grant-maintained status. The implication is that teacher training will only take place in 'good' schools, those with drive and an entrepreneurial spirit. These are the very ones, of course, likely to be under pressure from parents, as a result of their local reputation, to maintain standards of pupil achievement and skilled teaching. Given that the teacher training will call heavily on the skills and energy of experienced and successful staff in the school, the new task may lead to tensions and problems of priorities, which governors might find hard to allay. The hope is that the whole service would evolve

towards diversity, such that intending teachers, beginning with graduate entrants, would have a choice as to the kind of training they might wish to undertake.

Obviously, if the present higher education providers have to divert resources, particularly financial ones, to schools, they can only do so by losing staff. This process has, indeed, begun. The higher education institutions will inevitably be weakened. A few have already withdrawn altogether from training graduates. There is some risk that if schools later begin to withdraw from what speakers called 'an underfunded and underresourced system', the eventual number of providers may be reduced. Other speakers made clear their fears about an eventual two-tier system, where types of training perceived to be of different value were being offered within the differentiated system.

All trainees are required to have a mentor. Mentorship training proceeded during 1994 on a considerable scale. Speakers mentioned that they had evidence of attrition among mentors and students on the various provisional schemes being trialled. There were also cases of obvious plagiarism of higher education courses by other providers. Another possible scenario, which recalls the very limited scope of the city technology college initiative, is that the number of non-higher education providers might remain very limited, and yet disrupt existing arrangements, and that the course experiences eventually offered by such providers will converge towards and eventually differ little from that provided by present partnership arrangements. The latter would of course have been given an invigorating shake-up and more time would be spent in schools by trainees. It should not be forgotten that the licensed teacher scheme had to be wound down because of the very high costs it involved compared with conventional entry arrangements. The issue of costs is almost certain to play a very prominent part in determining the final operating arrangements now being set up. In sum, the new arrangements mesh with previous developments: opting out, the changing responsibilities of governors, the operations of a special sort of market, financial and resource issues, inspection and the availability of other employment opportunities for graduates made available by the economy. The PGCE arrangements are a test bed for the extension of the new system. Extending them to take in not simply the 16,500 graduates but the 60,000 teachers currently in training is clearly likely to raise problems of a quite different order of magnitude.

The opposition speakers pointed out that the commanding position of the Teacher Training Agency, and the decision that the lion's share of the training of graduates would take place in schools, after decades of steadily increasing cooperation, bids fair to reduce the higher education institutions, like the LEAs, to a marginal role in the system. They will be in danger of becoming little more than contractors offering services to schools, and certificating agencies. The assumption that a degree in physics, for example, is any guarantee that the trainee holding it is familiar with the selection of teaching content that makes up school physics is very contestable. There is a serious professionally led task of reconsidering degree subject content in PGCE training, alongside that of professional matters of teaching styles and classroom management alone. Higher education will evidently have a reduced opportunity to carry out assessment. Would it be appropriate for higher education institutions to certificate candidates on courses over which they have much reduced control?

While France is moving quickly to strengthen relationships between teacher education and the universities (Greaves and Shaw, 1992; Greaves, 1994), Britain is moving in the opposite direction. Speakers reminded the House of problems that might arise for teachers who wished to work in, for example, the Middle East or the Commonwealth. Government speakers expressed scepticism about educational research and theory. One of the speakers described the study of education as 'an immature discipline', adding that the dominant orthodoxy was suspect. It is doubtful, indeed, whether the government regards education as a discipline in its own right. Hence, in reply, critics charged that the government appeared no longer to regard teacher education as a genuine form of higher education, but rather aimed to train teachers as 'ask-no-questions' technicians by what amounted to an apprenticeship system – an enor-

mous step backwards. Deprived of a living and working relation with teacher education, the universities would find their educational research administered by the TTA and banished from the mainstream. It would be no longer truly independent, nor articulated at a deep level to the day-to-day education of teachers, including in-service courses and advanced study.

The general outcome was seen by the opponents of the Bill as pushing the whole education service down-market. School-based training is not, it bears repeating, a matter for objection. The Bill threatened to make it almost entirely school-centred – a very different thing, which meant watering down the intellectual and theoretical content of training and building on weakness rather than on strength. In June 1994, Mr Patten asserted 'the need for a structured consideration of pedagogy and theory of education. That is not an issue.' Opposition speakers were not reassured.

The debates in both Houses were characterized by government speakers reading departmentally prepared briefs, which simply reiterated their position against critics of the stature of Lord Annan, the former Vice-Chancellor of London University, Lord Blaug, Lady Plowden and Lord Dainton. The opposition amendments passed in the Lords were summarily reversed in the Commons and the Bill became law.

*Hilary.* So what are we left with? What can we do in the university sector? Where is our future?

The legislation over teacher training is significantly drawing student teachers away from any exploration of theory and thrusting them into the everyday life of the school, with an agenda for action based on a notion of competence. This is recognized as the meeting of specific predetermined criteria standardized for all teachers. Thus, the current model of teaching is explicitly competency based. Yet Hyland (1993), for example, articulates the faulty premise on which this notion of competence draws. He explains that it is ill-conceived and conceptually flawed, based as it is on outmoded and discredited behaviourist theories of learning.

> Generally speaking, there is a tendency for behaviourist strategies to stifle creative and imaginative

learning, gloss over individual differences between learners and, through the reduction of learning objectives to measurable outcomes and prespecified ends, to encourage a mechanical 'teaching to the test' approach.

He also reminds us that competency-based education has its origins in the performance-based teacher education movement that flourished in the USA in the 1960s. Moreover, there has been a rapid expansion in competency-based education through the work of the National Council for Vocational Qualifications (NCVQ), which has official endorsement by the Department for Education. Because such a model permeates the theory and practice of teacher education and is used in a variety of guises by CATE-accredited teacher education–school partnership schemes across the country, there is a strong possibility that this model will become the basis for a national curriculum for teacher training administered by the TTA. It is possible, using a CBE model, to set up a national scheme for teacher accreditation for teachers to be trained directly by practice in the schools without involvement of university departments of education. School staff have now been given the opportunity to have a twofold function: (a) to teach pupils the National Curriculum; and (b) to teach adults how to teach the National Curriculum to pupils. Graduate students with a National Curriculum subject will be able to go directly into a school and learn on the job.

The educational establishment, in making a concerted stance about the benefits of the present system, has not precluded more reasoned debate among educationists themselves about how the educating and the training of teachers could be improved. Development work among the teacher educators has been going on consistently, but owing to the formidable political attack on university departments of education, the argument has taken a rather defensive turn, which is understandable in the light of government insistence that schools can train teachers without recourse to any higher education involvement. It is foreseeable that many education departments in universities will be decimated. Many could prove not to be cost-effective for the universities to maintain and will therefore close. It is certainly a time of

radical change that calls for an intellectual vision on the part of those teacher educators who wish to foster the intellectual pursuit of critical inquiry in the next generation of teachers and who believe that government policy is engineering a wholly deficient model for educating teachers for the twenty-first century in a democratic country.

David Hargreaves (1990), Professor of Education at the University of Cambridge, has suggested a radical approach that does not view initial teacher training (ITT) in isolation. He states:

> My starting point is the title of the 1972 Report of the James Committee of Inquiry – Teacher Education and Training. ITT ought not to be reformed in isolation. The improvement of ITT, I assume, can be achieved only in the much wider context of teacher education as a whole, that is, the lifelong professional development of teachers and the process of school improvement. It is a system of teacher education that needs to be reconstructed. In this regard, my proposal parts company with both the more narrowly conceived reformist and Hillgate radical positions. Reformist and conservative radical positions begin with the question: how do we move from where we now are to an improved form of ITT? My proposal begins from the question: how, if we were able to start from scratch, would we design a system of teacher education as a whole, including ITT?
>
> (Hargreaves, 1990, p. 2)

He suggests seven principles to guide his design:

1 The setting up of a General Teaching Council.
2 High levels of qualification for teachers.
3 ITT should be largely school based.
4 The teacher as principal partner in ITT.
5 A national curriculum for ITT.
6 A national scheme for the continuing professional development of teachers.
7 Better research and development in education.

David Hargreaves has offered a radical solution to teacher education and training through the posing of his question, capitalizing on what he perceives as best practice within the teacher education movement and giving the university departments an intellectual role in development through engaging in high-quality research and development in the field of education. I would also like to respond to his question and take up his challenge of offering a radical solution. He says: if we were able to start from scratch, how would we design a system of teacher education as a whole? I would like to look at the very beginning of the process and conceptualize the way that university departments can enrich the experience of undergraduate students with an interest in being educators, which would directly feed into the education system and help to initiate a desire among teachers for lifelong professional development and the process of school improvement that he so rightly maintains as important.

My solution links with his second principle, concentrating on the issue of a high level of qualification for teachers, and I wish to do this by making a case that separates the notion of teacher education from the notion of teacher training. This issue has been well rehearsed and expressed cogently in the education literature on the curriculum for 14- to 19-year-olds, and from it we can perhaps learn something that has direct bearing on the teacher education/training debate. The central theme of this debate is the belief that children require an all-round education before embarking on vocational training for specific occupations.

The tradition of an all-round education written into the 1988 Education Act Section 1 places a statutory responsibility upon schools to provide a broad and balanced curriculum which promotes the spiritual, moral, cultural, mental and physical development of pupils at school and of society. The general phraseology in the Act describes a philosophy of education in the liberal tradition that has been the hallmark of the English education system and has survived from the turn of the century. The Secondary Regulations in 1904 suggested the type of education children should receive, and this does not differ wildly from the structure of subjects that make up the National Curriculum today – just replace manual work and domestic with technology and the rest of the subjects read much the same.

The main features of the liberal education philosophy, according to Pring (1991), are that what should be learned is firmly rooted in the intellectual disciplines and that to be educated is to be initiated into these disciplines. The subjects of the school curriculum are directly associated with these disciplines and should be studied for their own intrinsic worth. There is no reference here to education for economic wealth and the instilling of skills for occupations in the future. That is the philosophy of vocationalism, where the emphasis is on gaining knowledge that can be directly attributable to more effective performance in all walks of business, production and enterprise; educating for a highly efficient workforce through clearly defined objectives within the education programmes offered. As Pring states, in the philosophy of vocational education,

> the distinctive forms of knowledge which determine the logical structure of the process of learning, no longer provide the prime sources upon which the teacher should draw in the cultivation of the intellect. Instead these sources are also externally agreed competencies disconnected from the world of ideas which is the central concern of liberal education.

He goes on to make a particularly interesting point when he notes that within the vocational discourse personal development is supplanted by notions of personal effectiveness and that understanding and appreciation give way to skills and competencies.

This sounds to me very like the way that teacher education and training is going, as has already been discussed earlier in this chapter. So is there any way of reconciling these two competing philosophies of education? There has been an attempt at the level of schooling, with the introduction of the concept of pre-vocational education. The notion of pre-vocational education attempts to include a direction towards vocational education while at the same time being concerned with the personal needs of the individual learner. It is not about specific occupational vocational training but, in educating young people, raises their awareness of the economic needs of the society in which they live and enables them to find out what part they might play in their future life when they enter adulthood and have to provide a living for themselves. Within the pre-vocational philosophy there is an emphasis on acquiring personal knowledge and practical capacities to cope in real-life situations. The pupil is not perceived as an apprentice worker, but is acquainted with the world of work and, through various learning experiences, develops an increased understanding of how society works. There is an emphasis on practical 'know-how' as well as on propositional 'know-that'. So what about a pre-vocational education for would-be educators? Is it not important for them to learn about as well as experience the field of education? I would like to pursue this idea further and provide a rationale and curriculum for such a policy, which would enable the students to exercise their minds and to have the self-confidence that comes from the development of critical faculties to imagine the possibilities for evolution and change in the nature of schooling.

## A pre-vocational education for preparing adults to be the teachers of the twenty-first century

The central aim of the 'pre-vocational' education curriculum would be to equip students to engage in critical study and enquiry of educational systems, theories, processes and practices. Education as a field of study encompasses values and world views. Hence a vision would be communicated about what it means to learn and be educated as well as an understanding about the organizational contexts within which educative acts take place. The students would participate in both theoretical and applied study through a range of modules, involving both national and international dimensions, that could form a significant proportion of a modularized undergraduate programme.

Key components of such a 'pre-vocational' education curriculum would be as follows.

### Consciousness about educational contexts

Powerful educational ideas deal with cultures, environments and communicative relationships that extend beyond the face-to-face encounters that take place in 'classrooms', and thus go beyond the 5 to 14/14 to 19 scenario of closed institutions of schools. Education is about acquiring and constructing knowledge and about development and change of individuals and communities. A prerequisite for being a teacher in the fast-changing world of power shifts, complex interrelationships and high technology is having knowledge about education as well as gaining knowledge through education. It is no longer sufficient to educate the person without investigating the structures through which educative practices are realized. Toffler (1991) makes this point when he discusses the relationship between power and knowledge.

> Here then we glimpse one of the most fundamental yet neglected relationships between knowledge and power in society: the link between how people organize their concepts and how they organize their institutions. Put most briefly the way we organize knowledge frequently determines the way we organize people – and vice versa. (p. 20)

Therefore, fundamental debates about educational contexts would take place, including, for example, the purpose of schooling, the relationships between educator and students, the obligations of the educator to the wider community and recognition of different cultures.

### Learning about learning

The students would be facilitated in articulating and explicating their own learning styles. There would be an expectation that they would operate on two levels: at one level learning and at the other an awareness of how one is learning. Students would need to acquire concepts, frameworks and models to learn how to operationalize their knowledge and apply it to concrete situations, where emphasis would be on developing the ability to learn how to learn, to solve problems, to ask questions and to know where to look for the answers so as to be independent learners.

Moreover, they would engage in studying how others learn and recognize the opportunities and possibilities (or lack of them) that people have to learn in different ways depending on the social conditions in which they are learning. Such study would include observing, participating and evaluating learning taking place in different contexts and reflecting on the experience. Students would be encouraged to critique these teaching–learning encounters, making connections between the learning interactions studied and issues of social justice and equity. Zeichner (1993, p. 15) reminds us as educators that 'teaching cannot be neutral' and continues:

> We as teachers at whatever level, must act with greater political clarity about whose interests we are furthering in our daily actions ... because like it or not, and whether acknowledged or not, we are taking a stand through our actions and through our words. We should not of course reduce teaching only to its political elements, but we need to make sure that this aspect of teaching does not get lost as it often does.

Students would be encouraged to develop the concept of lifelong learners having the capacity to generate knowledge about education and learning as opposed to consuming it. Not just accepting, without thought, the strategies that have gained (for the time being) universal acceptance as being effective, they would be educated to engage in practice with an enlightened eye capable of adaptability, flexibility and evolutionary change. There is no surety about what constitutes 'good practice' when one is dealing with diverse learning contexts. What is important is the capacity for the individual to be able to evaluate what would constitute good practice and to have the knowledge, personal aptitudes and resources to put his or her ideals into practice.

## *Ways of knowing*

Education is about knowledge, so no 'pre-vocational' course on education would be complete without students studying epistemological questions. They would grapple with key notions about knowledge from philosophical, sociological, political, economical and historical perspectives. Such ideas would be introduced through active learning, where the students would be encouraged to construct their own meanings about knowledge so that they can apply them in a pro-

ductive and critical way to issues of curriculum organization and structure. The would-be educator reserves the right, in a democratic community, to be critical of current political and social policies that constitute the formal curriculum at the level of schooling, higher education and the workplace. The students would have the opportunity to dwell on ideas and principles and to develop practices unencumbered by the immediate concerns of survival and control within the formal schooling system. Students would engage in practical activities that involve designing, creatively and imaginatively, new curricular programmes for a variety of educational settings, recognizing the social, cultural, political and economic issues attached to implementing such programmes. The purpose would be to develop the potential in the students to create new structures of teaching and learning, within educational contexts that aimed at encouraging well-rounded, technologically capable, active and democratic citizens.

## Conclusion

Politicians claim to represent people in a democracy but take power to themselves in controlling the purpose and functions of the educational contexts in which people learn. Once they achieve this power – the National Curriculum and NVQs are examples – they are loath to give it up. This is manifested in the unprecedented rise in 'quangocracies'. So there is a sense of powerlessness in local communities, in the educational establishments. Just concentrating on the teaching skills for the future generation of educators (the competency movement) acculturates them into the prevailing orthodoxy. They get trapped into the cycle of arguments about standards. A standard is a conforming unit. In our future world do we really want standard people? We need unique, aspiring, creative and flexible individuals with the capacity to create different educational structures and learning webs. University departments of education need to seize the initiative, to be in the forefront of this educational revolution and to develop education as an academic and scholarly discipline, worthy of study in its own right and offering opportunities for young people to engage in concepts, ideas and paradigm shifts that energize them to seek alternative structures for educating others. Giving undergraduates the opportunity to engage in such ideas prepares them to take a productive, but also critical, stance towards the learning institutions. It gives them the capacity, through the perception of the overall structure of interactive relationships in educational contexts, to use their ability to communicate, to reform and to change the culture, ethos and character of learning contexts.

*Ken.* Among social institutions, universities are great survivors. They have not always changed as quickly as some would like, but they do learn, they are responsive, they can adapt. Relationships with the government have emerged as the key links throughout the sector, not just in schools of education. Criticism of some aspects of current government policy for teacher training does not mean there is unwillingness to change. It does mean that the professionals are unwilling to be marginalized without protest, and do not expect the results of decades of conscientious research and reflective experience to be ignored. Your visions of a future, and those of the authorities from whom it draws support, are indications that there are other possibilities, other alternatives, able to be developed within higher education. Our responses have to be positive, creative and feasible. They also have to link in some way with traditional good practice, rather than doctrine and ideology, so that there is constructive continuity in what we set out to do. There is a certain tension between professionalism and democracy. It shows in the health service as well as in education. The way to handle tensions is to manage them, to negotiate a more consensual position which gives a feeling of participation to those involved in implementing the policies. Recent Secretaries of State for Education have not shown much taste for that approach, but things may now be changing.

*Hilary.* I, too, believe that the university departments have a specific and necessary role to play in education for future teachers. They need to be central to the beginning process, as my 'pre-vocational' undergraduate course on education has exemplified. By following such a three-year 'pre-vocational' course, students would have a good foundation to become 'critical and reflective' practitioners when they proceed to more specific teacher training, following the model for graduates as articulated by David Hargreaves. Here the university departments of education are involved in partnership alongside expert practitioners in schools in a facilitating and supporting role. The university departments of education then come into their own, doing what they do best, undertaking and disseminating high-quality educational research in a broad context that is so desperately needed to meet the needs of our society in the twenty-first century.

## References

Alexander, A. J. *et al.* (eds) (1984) *Change in Teacher Education.* London: Holt, Rinehart and Winston.

DES (1984) *Initial Teacher Training: Approval of Courses.* Circular No. 3/84, Cmnd 8836. London: HMSO.

Greaves, A. E. (1994) The French educational system as a role model. *Cambridge Journal of Education,* **24** (2), 183–96.

Greaves, A. E. and Shaw, K. E. (1992) A new look at French teacher education. *Cambridge Journal of Education,* **22** (2), 201–14.

Hargreaves, D. (1990) Another radical approach to the reform of initial teacher training. Discussion paper for UCET conference.

Hyland, T. (1993) Professional development and competence based education. *Educational Studies,* **19** (1), 123–32.

McNair Report (1944) *Teachers and Youth Leaders.* London: HMSO.

Pring, R. (1991) Liberal and vocational education. Lord Callaghan Lecture, University of Swansea, November.

Robbins Report (1963) *Higher Education.* London: HMSO.

Schön, D. (1983) *The Reflective Practitioner: How Professionals Think in Action.* Aldershot: Avebury.

Toffler, A. (1991) *Power Shift.* New York: Bantam Books.

Zeichner, M. K. (1993) Connecting genuine teacher development to the notion of social justice. *Journal of Education for Teaching,* **19** (1), 5–20.

# 9 The Place of Higher Education in Teacher Preparation

DAVID BLAKE

## Background

Higher education's involvement in teacher preparation is long established, but its development has been neither smooth nor unproblematic. At a time when higher education's role is again being contested, it is instructive to note previous policy developments and debates, for there are clear resonances with the preoccupations of today.

Although Anglican training colleges began to be established in the mid-nineteenth century, at least in part so that the Church could exert ideological control over training, university involvement in the training of teachers is barely a century old (Thomas, 1990). Scotland was in advance of England, having established chairs in the theory, history and practice of education at St Andrew's and Edinburgh. In 1892, Professor Laurie of Edinburgh challengingly argued that 'the university trained schoolmaster imbibes some of the spirit of the university and goes forth as a scientific worker and not as a mere craftsman' (Thomas, 1990, p. 10). In 1886, the Cross Commission took evidence on the further development of teacher training, and Thomas argues that university involvement arose at least in part because of the perceived illiberal and anti-intellectual nature of what was going on elsewhere. In 1890, the universities established day training colleges. Eighteen were in place by 1900, with 1355 students against 4179 in the residential colleges.

Although much that went on in teacher training may have been routine and unremarkable, there were from time to time interesting experiments. At Manchester, for example, Professor J. J. Findlay established a demonstration school and began to articulate a view of the relationship between theory and practice, and of the role of the university in explicating it (Robertson, 1992). Findlay argued that mere time in school was not the main point. He considered that it was relatively easy for able students to master the largely practical strategies of class management, but 'the harder task, the real intellectual effort, is to get behind the mechanism and see the motive force behind it, to discern the interaction of ideas and results, of theory and practice' (Robertson, 1992, p. 370). Findlay wanted a training which would 'induce an outlook at once receptive to change, analytical and critical, and capable of relating untried ideas to the known needs of children'. He wanted training to provide guidelines for teachers through the rest of their careers and to encourage them to be independent. He believed that the function of the university within teacher preparation was to develop these qualities.

The McNair Report (Board of Education, 1944) established a post-war settlement in teacher training. Area training organizations (ATOs) were the means of local organization and control, bringing the local university into formal arrangement with training colleges. By 1963, the Robbins Report (DES, 1963) was proposing the redesignation of training colleges as colleges of education, the establishment of the BEd as the means of securing an all-graduate profession and arrangements for a new national validating agency (the Council for National Academic Awards) for the non-university higher education sector. The BEd was conceived as a professional degree for teaching, with undergraduate study a feature of both subject study and educational studies elements. There was an immediate response to Robbins's recommendations, so that by 1969, 21 universities were awarding the BEd degree (Ross, 1990, p. 59).

A change of mood was introduced by the James Report in 1972 (DES, 1972). Against a mounting tide of criticism of schools and colleges in the education Black Papers, Secretary of State Margaret Thatcher established a committee of inquiry into teacher education and training. The report contained a strong note of criticism of the colleges. The objectives of the colleges were said to be 'unhelpfully diffuse' and there was identified 'a hubbub of conflicting priorities'. The committee reported a widespread view that essentially relevant and practical matters, such as the teaching of reading, appeared to be neglected (DES, 1972, pp. 19–20). The conclusion was damning: 'It may be concluded that, with things as they are, the colleges are asked to do too much, are left with no rational basis for discrimination and are often unable to give enough time to aspects of training which they and the profession regard as central' (DES, 1972, p. 20). It was contended that the colleges' links with the universities had led them to strive for the wrong kind of academic excellence. In a search for academic respectability, colleges were said to feed students 'a diet of theoretical speculation, based on researches the validity and scholarship of which are not always beyond question' (DES, 1972, p. 53).

The solution, for James, was a pattern of professional development based on three cycles. The BEd was to be abolished. The first cycle, to diploma level, would involve two years' subject study in higher education. The second cycle would incorporate a two-year training programme, one year college based and one school based. In the school-based year students would be licensed to teach and attend local professional centres for a day a week. Teachers would be registered, and awarded the BA(Ed), at the end of the second cycle. Well-qualified mature students would qualify for direct entry to the second year of the second cycle. This second cycle would concentrate on practical preparation rather than courses in educational theory,

a rudimentary introduction to which was said to be all that should be realistically expected at this stage. It was doubted whether 'such studies, especially if presented through the medium of lectures to large groups of perplexed students, are, in terms of priorities, a useful major element in initial training' (DES, 1972, p. 23). Such matters would best be kept to the third cycle, which would comprise an entitlement to regular professional development for all teachers in post.

## Policy

DES policy on teacher education, presented in *Teaching Quality* (DES, 1983) and followed by Circular 3/84 (DES, 1984), led to the establishment of the Council for Accreditation of Teacher Education (CATE) in 1984. CATE then introduced a new process of individual course scrutiny against published criteria. Revised criteria were published in 1989 (DES, 1989d) and led to a reconstituted CATE from January 1990. In 1989, government policy initiatives established the licensed teacher and articled teacher schemes, starting up in 1989 and 1990 respectively (DES, 1989c).

At the North of England Conference (January 1992), the Secretary of State announced his intention of pressing ahead with the introduction of more school-based teacher training (DES, 1992a). He argued that schools should play 'the key influential role in a much closer partnership between the school and the teacher training institutions' (para. 20) and that college-based parts of teacher training should be 'fully relevant to classroom practice' (para. 21). The idea of the new partnership was one in which 'the school and its teachers are in the lead in the whole of the training process, from the initial design of a course right through to the assessment of the performance of the individual student' (para. 22). It was announced that the PGCE secondary route would be the first to be reformed, with four-fifths of the course being school based (para. 33). As responsibility for training shifted to the schools, so, it was argued, would the resources for that training (para. 39). As for primary training, the Secretary of State said he would review 'whether standard BEd courses needed to be as long as four years' and would consult on the proposition that 'the minimum amount of school-based work in four year courses should be ... the equivalent of at least one academic year' (para. 40).

Also in January 1992, HMI published a report, *School-Based Initial Training in England and Wales* (HMI, 1991b). The conclusion was clear:

> The success of school-based training depends on the quality of the relationship between the training institution and the school, the significant involvement of teachers in the planning, supervision and assessment of the students' training and the active involvement of tutors in supporting the students' work in schools.
>
> (HMI, 1991b, p. 3(iv))

But a significant number of practical problems were also pointed to, especially the multiple calls on teachers' time and the proposition that the primary purpose of schools is 'to teach pupils, not train students' (p. 4). It was concluded that a 'measured increase in the school-based element in initial training under the right conditions would pay important dividends' (p. 5).

The DES consultation document (DES, 1992b), *Reform of Initial Teacher Training* (January 1992), specified that four-fifths of the secondary PGCE and one-quarter of the secondary BEd should be school-based, postulated future performance indicators for the selection of partner schools, outlined 27 teacher competencies and detailed the way in which institutional accreditation would work. Circular 9/92 (June 1992) modified the initial proposals to 24 weeks of school-based work in the secondary PGCE and 32 weeks in the secondary BEd (DFE, 1992).

New primary criteria (DFE, 1993d) pursued the theme of developing partnerships between schools and higher education ('schools should play a much larger and more influential role in course design and delivery, in partnership as appropriate with higher education institutions': DFE, 1993d, p. 5). The criteria opened up the possibility of a three-year, six-subject BEd, identified the possibility of courses for specialists, semi-specialists and generalists, and required more at-

tention to be paid to the core curriculum. Not included in the new criteria was the proposal which had appeared in the Secretary of State's earlier draft circular (DFE, 1993a) for a new, non-graduate, one-year course for mature students with experience of working with children who wished to specialize in teaching nursery and infant pupils up to the end of Key Stage 1. This was the so-called 'Mum's Army' proposal, withdrawn in the face of vociferous opposition from all parts of the education service.

In September 1993, *The Government's Proposals for the Reform of Initial Teacher Training* was published in a Blue Book (DFE, 1993b). The key proposal was the abolition of CATE and the establishment of a new quango, the Teacher Training Agency (TTA), with responsibility for the control and funding of all courses of initial teacher training. With eight to twelve members appointed by the Secretary of State, it was proposed that the TTA would take responsibility for teacher training from 1995–96. Teacher education would be removed from involvement with the Higher Education Funding Council. New criteria for the accreditation of training courses would be established, with the intention of increasing the part played by schools in controlling and organizing training. The Secretary of State was said to favour a reduction in the length of BEd courses from four to three years, and those institutions which reduced average course length were to be rewarded. The intention of the proposals was to reduce the involvement of higher education in the training of teachers and to transfer more responsibility and funding to schools. In the Queen's Speech to Parliament on 18 November 1993, it was announced that legislation would be brought forward to establish the TTA. The Education Bill was published in November 1993 (DFE, 1993e), further increasing the proposed powers of the TTA. Heated discussions took place in both the House of Lords and the House of Commons over the powers of the agency, especially with regard to school-centred training, but the 1994 Education Act substantially confirmed the Blue Book's proposals.

The year 1993 also saw the inauguration of wholly school-centred teacher training within the School-Centred Initial Teacher Training (SCITT) scheme. This paid a fee direct to the school for each ITT student. There was no compulsion to use training provided by higher education, or to provide a course of training leading to the PGCE. The aim of the scheme was 'to give consortia of schools an opportunity to design, organise and provide school-centred ITT courses for graduates, leading to qualified teacher status' (DFE, 1993c). In 1994 an increase in the number of school consortia and city technology colleges (CTC) trust consortia offering school-centred training was announced. In total 450 places were available, 30 in primary schools (Teaching as a Career, 1994).

The direction of government policy is clear and consistent. It may be seen as a parallel development to changes in the school system put in place by the Education Reform Act in 1988, indeed as a logical underpinning of that reform. One strand is the provision of a market in initial teacher education, where services may be bought by the consumers from training institutions. Such a market was explicitly created in the training arrangements for the licensed teacher route (DES, 1989c), and an extension of it was clearly a part of the rationale for putting schools 'in the lead' in the proposals outlined at the North of England Conference in January 1992. The SCITT scheme represents a further development of the creation of a market. How far this market philosophy will be carried is as yet unclear, but already a substantial shift of resources from higher education institutions to schools is under way, leading to a new relationship between producers and consumers in the training process. A key element in the development of a market is the availability of a range of competing products; hence the emphasis in creating a diverse set of teacher training routes.

A second strand, also paralleled in arrangements for schools in the Education Reform Act, is the relationship between central government and local provision. For, although there is much emphasis on local autonomy in the arrangements between schools and training institutions, there is also a strong element of central control. It is clear that there is to be continuing supervision of teacher education from the centre through reformulated training and accreditation criteria controlled by the TTA. A further element of central control is retained through the power of inspection. As the furore about new arrangements for school inspections unfolded in 1992, and HMI numbers and responsibilities were transferred to OFSTED, HMI responsibilities for the inspection of teacher education were unchanged.

A third strand is the drive to make training more school based. The move was anticipated in the licensed and articled teacher routes. What is under way now is the adaptation of the perceived benefits of school-basedness in those routes to the PGCE and BEd. The expected benefits are that practising teachers will have more influence on training, that there will be more emphasis on classroom skills and that there will be less of the theory said to bedevil institutions providing teacher education. The implication is that college-based training was not fully relevant to classroom practice.

## International comparisons

As part of its contribution to debate, HMI brought forward reports of teacher education developments elsewhere. These were the training of secondary teachers in France in the Académie de Toulouse (DES, 1989a), the Provisional Training Program in New Jersey in the United States (DES, 1989b) and the initial training of teachers in two German *Länder*, Hessen and Rheinland-Pfalz (OFSTED, 1993a). The main focus of these reports was the way in which school-based training was working in other countries. In Germany, for example, training is in two phases, the first of which is university based and concerned with subject study. This phase takes at least three years and is followed by two years of professional training organized in regional training centres working closely with training schools. The professional phase, controlled by each separate *Land* ministry, was said to work smoothly and deliver 'good quality professional training' (OFSTED, 1993a, p. 3). Despite concern about the high cost of training, both *Länder* were reported to 'regard the length and depth of teacher training as an investment in quality' (OFSTED, 1993a, p. 2).

In the United States, a succession of reports on teacher education (Sarason *et al.*, 1962; Conant, 1963; Koerner, 1963; Holmes Group, 1986; Goodlad, 1990) opened up concerns about the preparation of teachers, many of them focusing on the role of the university. Departments of education were criticized as being distant from the concerns of classroom teachers, research has been seen as not useful enough to influence practitioners and not good enough to win the respect of other university academics, and there has been little success in developing durable modules of training (Sheehan and Wilson, 1994, p. 29). But the American drive was for reform and development of the university's involvement, based upon the view that teaching is a complex activity requiring sophisticated approaches to preparation (Holmes Group, 1986, p. 27).

Elsewhere, the direction of teacher education development is towards the involvement of higher education rather than away from it. In advance of a conference on teacher education in Europe in 1991, Judge noted 'a strongly emerging tendency to assign to the universities a more fundamental role in the education and training of teachers' (Judge, 1991, p. 257). In similar vein, Taylor observed that 'the education of all kinds of teachers is now fully integrated into university level studies in many countries', but identified a countervailing movement in England and Wales (Taylor, 1994, p. 50).

A general pattern in teacher education development is illustrated in the Netherlands (Wubbels, 1992). The training of primary teachers moved from an apprenticeship model, to normal schools run by teachers and headteachers, to the creation of teacher education colleges from 1935. In 1967, following moves to enhance the status of teacher education, the colleges were renamed pedagogical academies. In the 1970s, there were criticisms that the courses had become too theoretical and were giving too much emphasis to pedagogy and method and too little to subject knowledge. In the 1980s, courses were concentrated in larger institutions. By 1984, the number of teacher education centres had been halved, and almost all were in-

corporated within large institutes of higher vocational education (Wubbels, 1992, pp. 161–2).

In France, the foundation of the Institut Universitaire de Formation des Maîtres (IUFM) in September 1990 brought together the training of all teachers in institutions of university rank (Neather, 1993). Students are recruited at the level of licence, after three years' university study, to follow the two-year course of professional training. The first year of study is concerned with subject competence, observational skills, child development, educational technology, pedagogy and philosophy. At the end of this year there is a competitive examination for the particular branch of CAPES (*certificat d'aptitude au professorat de l'enseignement du second degré*) or CAPE (*certificat d'aptitude au professorat d'école*).

Sheehan and Wilson (1994) show how the control of teacher education by the universities is a comparatively recent development in Canada. It was secured in 1945 in Alberta, 1946 in Newfoundland, 1956 in British Columbia, 1964 in Saskatchewan, 1965 in Manitoba and only completed in 1970 in Quebec and Ontario. They argue that university involvement has raised the status of teaching in Canada. All teachers have degrees and this raises the esteem in which teachers are held. A focus on research in the universities has influenced teacher education programmes and policy decisions at ministry level, and led to the development of innovative curricular materials. Graduate studies in education have deepened the knowledge base of educational career professionals. Focusing specifically on British Columbia, they conclude that 'the theoretical knowledge base, professional understanding and skill development that teachers bring to their school and classroom practice ensure that teaching in British Columbia has attained a professional status recognized by parents and the public generally' (Sheehan and Wilson, 1994, p. 28).

## Evidence

A substantial evidence base about the effectiveness of initial teacher education is developing, allowing conclusions to be drawn about different training routes. A significant part of the evidence is supplied by HMI. Also available are the reports of research terms and individuals, such as the work of the ESRC-funded Modes of Teacher Education (MOTE) project.

In 1991, the overall judgement of HMI on the BEd and PGCE courses inspected was that there was 'an appropriate balance of theory and practice'. Of all the work inspected during 1989 and 1990, 85 per cent was satisfactory or better (HMI, 1991a). In 1992 the overall judgement was that 'most of the training of students observed in training institutions and schools was at least satisfactory' (HMI, 1992, p. 38), although problems of adapting course structure and content to prepare students for the National Curriculum were pointed to.

The report by HMI on school-based initial training (HMI, 1991b) drew the conclusion that students clearly benefit from 'skilful, well-organised and integrated school-based experience'. An argument is advanced for 'a measured increase in the school-based element of initial training', which would pay important dividends in the right conditions. Yet the qualification is made that there is not a uniform case for an immediate increase in all courses and all types of training. Whereas secondary training, and especially the PGCE, is 'well-placed for some further devolution of responsibility to schools', there are major constraints in the case of primary training (HMI, 1991b, p. 5). In reviewing the role of higher education, HMI concludes that 'higher education institutions provide an academic and professional expertise which is crucial in the support both of individual students and of schools' (HMI, 1991b, p. 4). It is argued that there is no straightforward or cost-effective way of transferring to a large number of schools higher education's responsibility for organizing and resourcing initial training and awarding qualifications to students.

In 1993, OFSTED reported on the training of primary school teachers (OFSTED, 1993b), the articled teacher scheme (OFSTED, 1993c) and the licensed teacher scheme (OFSTED, 1993d). The overall finding on primary training, based on visits to eight institutions, was that the work of students teaching in schools was generally at least satisfactory, although there was considerable variation in the proportions of students who were better, or less, than satisfactory among the institutions visited.

The findings on the articled teacher scheme are of particular interest. This well resourced, innovative scheme, offering a route to the PGCE through school-based training over two years, attracted much attention as a pilot for school-based development. HMI found that three-quarters of the articled teachers seen by HMI at the end of their training achieved 'at least a satisfactory level of teaching competence'. This is similar to the overall performance of students on conventional one-year PGCE courses, although around 10 per cent of articled teachers at the end of training were performing 'better than the best conventional PGCE students and as well as experienced teachers' (OFSTED, 1993c, p. 3). HMI found 90 per cent of the training which took place out of school satisfactory or better and over 50 per cent good or very good. The most successful schemes included a substantial period of out-of-school training early in the course. Insufficient attention was found to be given to monitoring the implementation of training, particularly in schools. There were 'few attempts to evaluate the overall coherence and effectiveness' of the training (OFSTED, 1993c, p. 4).

HMI found that a high proportion of the licensed teachers it saw were satisfactory or better. The scheme was successful in attracting good potential teachers, many of whom were qualified as teachers overseas. Of the licensed teachers performing poorly, many were in schools which HMI considered unsatisfactory for the training of teachers. Graduate licensed teachers tended to 'perform better than non-graduates, especially in secondary schools' (OFSTED, 1993d, p. 18). The training provided for the licensed teachers in schools was found to be *ad hoc* and rarely well structured. The courses provided outside schools were found to be variable in length and not always well matched to the training needs of the different categories of licensed teachers. Although the content of training courses was generally appropriate, the courses sometimes lacked a coherent structure directly related to licensed teachers' work in school (OFSTED, 1993d, p. 3).

The most recent evidence of HMI about the performance of new teachers in their first year of teaching provides a broadly encouraging picture (OFSTED, 1993e). This is not to say that the picture is uniformly rosy, or that modifications and renewal are not necessary, but in the main the picture is satisfactory and improving. HMI found a high level of satisfaction among headteachers about the quality of training. Some 94 per cent of secondary and 91 per cent of primary headteachers considered that the new teachers had been well prepared. High levels of satisfaction were expressed by headteachers about new teachers' professional competence, personal qualities and academic competence. Some 89 per cent of the new teachers considered that their training had been a positive experience which adequately prepared them for their new posts, with high proportions (more than 60 per cent) regarding that training as good or very good. When HMI graded the new teachers' lessons, using the same criteria as for more experienced teachers, it found 71 per cent of secondary and 73 per cent of primary lessons taught by new teachers to be satisfactory or better. This is a similar proportion to that found for the lessons of more experienced teachers, though HMI found that new teachers were teaching a higher proportion of very good lessons than experienced teachers. HMI found the subject knowledge of new teachers was at least satisfactory in 83 per cent of primary and 90 per cent of secondary lessons. Pupil behaviour was satisfactory in 84 per cent of lessons observed. When HMI awarded an overall performance grade to new teachers, based upon a range of professional competencies as well as the quality of lessons observed, 78 per cent of primary teachers and 80 per cent of new secondary teachers were found to be satisfactory or better.

The MOTE project team began its work by mapping the terrain of initial teacher education in England and Wales (Barrett *et al.*, 1992). The intention of the project is 'to characterise the nature of teacher education as a whole' and 'to compare the characteristics of the different types of course on offer' (Barrett *et al.*, 1992, p. 1). Its initial survey, undertaken in 1991, found that 72 per cent of primary and secondary ITT course leaders contended that the model of the teacher on which their course was based was that of the reflective practitioner, while only 6 per cent of courses explicitly subscribed to what they identified as a competency model of the teacher (Barrett *et al.*, 1992, p. 23). The MOTE team's findings on the extent of school-based work indicate that students on conventional PGCE courses spend an average of 50 per cent of their time in schools. For undergraduate courses, CATE required 100 days in school. All undergraduate courses reached this target, while a third offered substantially more (at least 30 per cent more) than this minimum. MOTE data support the findings of HMI of a move to increase significantly the extent of school-based work on conventional courses of initial teacher training.

During 1990–92 the MOTE team conducted a survey of the licensed teacher scheme (Barrett and Galvin, 1993). The survey was seen as significant because the scheme had established a non-graduate route to qualified teacher status, located responsibility for training with schools and based licensed teachers in one school for the whole of their training. It was found that the entry profile of the licensed teachers was crucial. A number of LEAs insisted on graduate status as a basic requirement, and the scheme succeeded in attracting mature candidates with high levels of commitment. The survey found considerable variation in the effectiveness of the training provided for licensed teachers and 'restricted notions of good practice' in the comments of some licensed teachers on their training. A heavy bias towards practical training was reported 'to inhibit the licensed teachers' skill at evaluating their teaching performance in order to develop their practice' (Barrett and Galvin, 1993, p. 91). The overall conclusion of the survey led the MOTE team 'to question the appropriateness of a general move to school-based training'. The licensed teacher scheme had attracted high-calibre individuals with particular life histories, and 'it would be unwise to assume that this mode of training would be appropriate for other population groups' (Barrett and Galvin, 1993, p. 94).

In December 1993, the Standing Conference of Principals (SCOP) undertook a postal questionnaire on primary initial teacher training. There were 1202 responses, all from headteachers. The results showed that the overwhelming majority of headteachers wanted to work in partnership with higher education but did not wish to take the lead in providing training. Only 12 respondents, for example, wanted to take major responsibility for ensuring the intellectual development and pedagogical progression of teachers in training. Only 42 heads wanted the major responsibility for assessing the quality of training and 20 major responsibility for setting objectives and devising training programmes for schools (SCOP, 1994).

A survey of the views of 440 primary headteachers, conducted by Carrington and Tymms and supported by the National Union of Teachers, had a similar outcome. In general, the heads were critical of attempts to give schools the main responsibility for training teachers. Only 11 per cent thought that more than half of primary training should be school-based and only 6 per cent of heads expressed dissatisfaction with the quality of trainee teachers they are already receiving (Pyke, 1993). Similar views were expressed by headteachers in surveys conducted by Hill in 1992 and 1993 (Blake and Hill, 1995).

The well-regarded Sussex University PGCE is often cited as a model for school-based training. Developed over twenty-five years, the scheme illustrates the importance of working with well-informed, committed schools and teachers. As early as 1977, Lacey looked at potential tensions between university and school cultures, leading students sometimes to indulge in a kind of 'strategic compliance' as a way of steering a course between the two ('I agree with the university tutor in principle and with the mentor in practice'). Dart and Drake (1993) argue that 'the government's move to widespread school-based training, unaccompanied by adequate resourcing or conceptualisation, will increase conservatism in education practice' (p. 176). They see success on the school-based PGCE as, to a considerable extent, based on fitting in, reflecting the school's practices and being rather compliant in meeting a school's expectations. Their fear about any substantial move to more school control of training is that there will be 'a national reinforcement of the status quo' (p. 189).

## Critical voices

A strong and influential voice of criticism of the part played by higher education in the initial preparation of teachers emerged in the 1980s (O'Hear, 1988; Cox *et al.*, 1989; Lawlor, 1990; O'Keeffe, 1990). The criticisms are philosophically coherent and amount to a campaign by the radical right to remove teacher education from the universities and to locate it wholly in schools. Many of the publications associated with the campaign are sponsored by the policy units of the New Right, the Centre for Policy Studies, the Social Affairs Unit and the Adam Smith Institute.

For Cox *et al.* (1989), the chief criticisms of teacher training are that the intellectual level is too low, content of courses is inappropriate and biased, and there is insufficient attention to classroom practice. An argument is developed for an apprenticeship model of training and for an extension of the promising licensed teacher route, which should not be limited to candidates over 26. The licensed teacher scheme puts proper emphasis on classroom skills rather than the 'pretentious pseudo-subjects, uncomprehended smatterings or shameless propaganda' (pp. 11–12) of higher education. The main repository of professional expertise and experience of teaching is the schools, so this is where training should be located. The prospect of unemployment for teacher trainers is one 'we would view with equanimity' (p. 18). Reform of teacher education is seen as a logical extension of the objective of undermining the power of the educational establishment: 'It is this establishment which, by neglect and design, has done so much to spread unreason in the name of enlightenment, to encourage ignorance in the name of equality, to put political agitation in the place of knowledge' (Cox *et al.*, 1989, pp. 19–20).

Lawlor makes similar claims about the low standards of teacher education courses, especially the BEd. The BEd fails to bring graduates to graduate status in the subjects prospective teachers will teach, and should be abolished. In any case, the claim that teaching is a graduate profession is a myth, since 'those trained in the old training colleges are now awarded degree status, without reaching the standard of a university degree and without the essential teaching of their subject' (p. 32). But the main strands of her argument are concerned with the nature of teaching and the poverty of educational theory.

Teaching is a practical activity, and Lawlor argues that its skills 'can be acquired only through experience, trial and error and careful, individual supervision' (p. 8). The reforms of the 1980s in teacher education had the sensible aim of ensuring that teachers know their subject, since subject mastery is the essence of effective teaching. But the reforms have been distorted by the universities and colleges of education, which introduce to the PGCE and BEd 'a dubious set of theoretical assumptions to be employed at every possible instance' (p. 32). The training courses demean the subject to being 'little more than a peg on which to hang modish educational theory', which has contributed much to the decline in educational standards (p. 42). The colleges and institutes of education 'should have no more to do with teacher training' and should be disbanded (p. 38).

O'Hear (1988), similarly, argues that the training process is misguided. The essence of good teaching lies in knowledge and love of the subject to be taught. It follows that many candidates are already qualified to teach and do not require a training course, certainly not one obsessed with questions of race and equality. In a campaigning piece in the *Daily Mail*, O'Hear (1993) called for a massive injection of new blood into the teaching profession, an infusion of teachers not indoctrinated by prevailing ideology. The seeds of education's anti-competitive ideology, of caring and cuddling rather than teaching and educating, are said to be sown in the training institutions. Solutions, for O'Hear, are to encourage a parents' army of experienced, mature people with common sense and experience of children to work with children at the infant stage after a short non-graduate training

course, and to turn the training of teachers over to the schools.

Berrill (1993, 1994) strongly supports the location of teacher education in schools, arguing that involvement in training will produce long-term benefits for pupils, students and teachers. Drawing on experience in training licensed teachers, Berrill and his colleagues 'learned that teachers can take a leading role in course planning and the delivery of initial teacher training (ITT) and that we should have every confidence in our ability as teachers to train new entrants to the profession' (Berrill, 1993, p. 17). The availability of good distance learning materials means that an 'initial lack of theoretical sophistication on training issues' can be quite quickly overcome. There are immense benefits for mentors in the 'focused professional dialogue' they engage in with students, leading to 'improved classroom practice and their enhanced professional awareness' (p. 17). Where a number of mentors are working in one school, 'it begins to have a profound effect on overall professionalism within the school'. Berrill (1994) is critical of the response of higher education to the new challenges. He attacks the idea that 'serious and sustained academic reflection can only take place within the hallowed walls of institutions of higher education' (Berrill, 1994, pp. 114–15). He regards the responses of teacher educators to moves to put ITT in schools as representing 'implicit elitism, a defensive conservatism and deep evidence of academic nervousness as the steady decline in the role of the intellectual in post-modern society continues' (p. 113).

From within teacher education, David Hargreaves has argued for some time that teacher training should be rooted in schools (Hargreaves, 1989a, b, 1990, 1992, 1994a, b). He believes that the BEd should be abolished, since 18 is too early an age for school leavers to commit themselves to a career in teaching. He argues in favour of the establishment of teaching schools, with training in the hands of selected practising teachers who will act as mentors. While many training institutions would disappear, those that remain would have a role in training mentors, establishing a national curriculum for teacher training, engaging in educational research and teaching advanced courses for experienced teachers. He argues for more flexibility in the length and construction of training as the logical consequence of a concentration on outcome competence. In his most recent publication, Hargreaves (1994b) continues to argue that 'substantial parts of initial training do not need to be located in universities' (p. 28) and denies that a consequence would be to distract schools from their principal purpose of teaching pupils. He attacks the notion that a reformed, school-centred teacher training would be harmful to the professional standing of teachers. For Hargreaves, it is pointless to justify lengthy training and the acquisition of a body of esoteric knowledge prior to entry to the profession, as in medicine and law, when such an approach is simply inappropriate for teaching. The skills and values of teaching, in Hargreaves's view, are best 'acquired, nurtured and matured largely in schools progressively over a period of continuing professional development, rather than off-site and before entry to the profession' (p. 29). He regards the universities' nervousness about the loss of teacher training as reflecting an understanding that it may be the thin end of a much larger wedge which threatens their educational credentialling monopoly.

## In support of higher education

Arguments in support of higher education's continued involvement with initial teacher education cluster around a set of interrelated ideas. In brief, these are the nature of the teacher required by the UK's schools as we enter the twenty-first century, the characteristics of the training and education which teachers need, the skills and knowledge of teacher educators, the attributes which the university brings to teacher education and ideas about teaching as a profession.

Ideas about the nature of the teacher contrast a model which emphasizes craft skills within a technicist or occupational culture with the model of the teacher as a critical and reflective practitioner. The value of the university is its recognition 'that teaching is not a simple craft based on the mastery of a limited repertoire of skills, but a task of extraordinary complexity requiring extensive and continuous study' (Turner, 1990, p. 73). Skilbeck (1992) develops these ideas further. For him a teacher in modern society is not simply a craftsman or technician, a bureaucratic functionary or a replicator or transmitter of established skills, techniques, knowledge and values. The teachers we need for the future will require more knowledge, both of their subjects and of pedagogy. Teachers will need to be more complete professionals, responding to their communities' needs and playing a role in meeting national social and economic objectives. In order to fulfil these functions, and to meet the requirements of an expanding knowledge base. teachers need to be critically minded and interested in reflective enquiry.

Furlong (1994) expresses astonishment that OFSTED's report on primary training approvingly notes how training has moved away from 'a focus on theoretical issues such as how pupils learn and develop, to practical matters such as classroom management and organisation'. In other words, there is a fashion to move away from, and to misrepresent or misunderstand, the intellectual, theoretical and conceptual characteristics of training and to dismiss everything which is not immediate and practical as irrelevant. There are serious misunderstandings here about the way a professional training occurs, about the nature of reflection in action and reflection on action, the way in which courses of training nurture students' critical abilities. Too much concentration on training in school can lead to idiosyncratic and narrow forms. Nichol (1993) points out the wealth of experience that higher education has had in devising forms of training and draws on his own experience to argue that there are certain inputs which are best supplied by higher education, such as specialized educational inputs and detailed pedagogical training. The development of models of training, according to Nichol, is a sophisticated area of activity, itself a kind of specialism influenced by a body of research, and most expertise in this area resides in institutions of higher education.

The characteristics of the teacher educator may be simply described. For Ruddock (1989), the teacher educator needs 'an analytic perspective that is fed by observations in a range of classrooms and sharpened by the evidence of research'. Alexander (1993) points out that university-based trainers have to prove themselves in three roles: 'as successful teachers or head-teachers in schools; as academics meeting the usual criteria of scholarship and research; and as trainers of teachers, a job quite distinct in its skills from that of teaching children'. At their best, for Alexander, teacher educators combine the dual perspective of knowledgeable insider and objective outsider, understand the challenges and dilemmas of teaching and through research build up analytical tools and insights which are needed to develop teachers' skills and improve classroom practice. Calderhead (1990) and Wilson (1991) show how the idea of helping students to become critically reflective is itself no straightforward or easy task. We have to pay attention to both the content of reflection (what we want students to reflect about) and the disciplines of thought which are relevant to reflection. Without some 'controlling procedures' of reason, according to Wilson, reflection may become 'no more than the airing of personal prejudice or fashionable ideology' (p. 117).

Kelly (1993) is not uncritical of the way in which teacher education has developed within higher education, and is fearful of the dangers posed by current policy. The university, for Kelly, is 'a politically independent centre for the fearless and impersonal pursuit of knowledge and understanding in all spheres' (p. 129). The training of teachers should introduce critical, intellectual challenge of the kind associated with university values. There should be no distinction between the training element of teacher education and the study of education, between 'learning how to practise the activity and critically reflecting on that practice' (p. 130). In a democratic society teachers cannot adequately fulfil their role without engaging in proper intellectual study of that activity. Teaching requires a critical apparatus to keep practice under review. A move to simplistic forms of relevance, in line with official pronouncements, holds significant dangers. Kelly sees government policy as moving 'to de-intellectualize the education of teachers and, thus, the teaching profession,

and to bring to a halt that critical, analytical study of educational policy and practice' (p. 134). Practical advice on teaching should be held up to 'the kind of constant challenge and critique which . . . is the essence of any form of academic study in a university setting' (p. 133). Shulman (1993), in similar vein, warns of the dangers of believing that teacher education will be improved merely by increasing the amount of first-hand experience. Too much experience and too little thinking might result in 'unwarranted confidence, uncritical habits of practice, and limits to pedagogical imagination' (p. 264).

Finally, how does teacher education's involvement with higher education contribute to the standing and development of teaching as a profession? Barber (1993) sees higher education's contribution as significant in providing certain aspects which cannot be provided by schools, namely access to research and debate about schools and education, a broader perspective than schools can provide, access to university-level libraries and learning resources, and the development of the kind of scepticism generated by professional education at university level, which is a healthy basis for professional development. McNamara (1994) identifies an all-graduate workforce and the location of vocational training within higher educational institutions as defining attributes of a profession. He is critical of any root and branch move to see professional learning simply as learning from experience, since such learning may be insufficient and may be limited to particular circumstances. There is a danger that such a form of professional development may be based on poor or inadequate practice and that beginners will fail to get a wider vision of their work or an appreciation of alternative practices. In sum, the value of higher education's contribution to teaching as a profession is to provide a wide frame of reference, to consider different ways of teaching well, to provide new teachers with research evidence and methods of enquiry relevant to developing professional skills and understanding, and to influence teachers to scrutinize ideas and practices with care (Institute for Public Policy Research, 1993).

## Conclusion

At the heart of the debate about initial teacher education's relationship with higher education lie conflicting views about the nature and status of teaching. On one side, there are those who criticize the influence of higher education, arguing that it has developed an over-academic, theoretical curriculum that is remote from the real needs of teachers in the classroom. On the other side, there are defenders of higher education's role and performance, who argue that substantial progress has been made in developing good training programmes characterized by intellectual bite and thoughtful approaches to professional development.

It is perhaps significant that high-status professional education (for example, in medicine and the law) is associated with the university and has traditionally resisted moves towards the wholly practical. Lower-status sub-professions, such as social work and teaching, on the other hand, have given more emphasis to the development of practitioner skills in the workplace, thereby perhaps confirming and perpetuating their status. It is, too, an international phenomenon in professional education in general for governments to seek increasing control of initial training programmes. Siegrist (1994) argues that when teacher education was secure in its place in higher education, the connection symbolized a kind of restraint on behalf of government, with control *de facto* being ceded to traditional sources in traditional institutions. In England and Wales in the 1980s, the New Right's interest in challenging traditional authority, especially professional authority, led to the identification of teacher education as an irresistible target for reform. The key to understanding the changes still under way is the redefinition of a new, restricted ideology of teaching practice encapsulated in the skill-based teaching competencies of the government's accreditation agencies. Powerful themes in the reform programme are an assertion of government control of the training of the state's teaching force and the creation of a market place of diverse training routes.

What is clear to the overwhelming majority of commentators is that the decoupling of teacher education from the university has severe implications for the status of the profession. It is significant that the existence of a General Teaching Council in Scotland has led to a quite different approach north of the border, with no challenge arising to the traditional place of Scotland's teacher education system within higher education.

There are dangers in downgrading the intellectual content within professional education. At one extreme there may simply be a collection of rules of thumb rather than a coherent conceptual framework for practice. Over-reliance on craft skills and tradition might 'stand in the way of much-needed changes to ingrained but out-dated practice' (Becher, 1994, pp. 164–5). Becher argues that a scaling down of professional programmes of preparation, without a higher education dimension, might lead to a perceived loss of status, a failure to attract candidates of an appropriate calibre and thus a direct threat to the healthy survival of the profession itself. Current policy development in teacher education in England and Wales makes such a danger acute.

## References

Alexander, R. (1993) Old myths die hard. *The Times*, 7 June.

Barber, M. (1993) The truth about partnership. *Journal of Education for Teaching*, **19** (3).

Barrett, E. *et al.* (1992) *Initial Teacher Education in England and Wales: A Topography*. Modes of Teacher Education Project.

Barrett, E. and Galvin, C. (1993) *The Licensed Teacher Scheme*. Modes of Teacher Education Project.

Becher, T. (ed.) (1994) *Governments and Professional Education*. Buckingham: Society for Research into Higher Education and Open University Press.

Berrill, M. (1993) He who dares. *Managing Schools Today*, **2** (6).

Berrill, M. (1994) ITE: crossroads or by-pass. *Cambridge Journal of Education*, **24** (1).

Blake, D. (1990) The teacher training debate: some parallels from health and social work. *Journal of Education Policy*, **5** (4).

Blake, D. (1993) Progress in the reform of initial teacher education in England and Wales. *Journal of Further and Higher Education*, **17** (3).

Blake, D. and Hill, D. (1995) The newly qualified teacher in school. *Research Papers in Education*, **10** (3).

Board of Education (1944) *Teachers and Youth Leaders* (The McNair Report). London: HMSO.

Calderhead, J. (1990) Conceptualising and evaluating teachers' professional learning. *European Journal of Teacher Education*, **13** (3).

Conant, J. (1963) *The Education of American Teachers*. New York: McGraw-Hill.

Cox, C. *et al.* (1989) *Learning to Teach*. London: Hillgate Group.

Dart, L. and Drake, P. (1993) School-based teacher education: a conservative practice. *Journal of Education for Teaching*, **19** (2).

DES (1963) *Higher Education* (The Robbins Report). London: HMSO.

DES (1972) *Teacher Education and Training* (The James Report). London: HMSO.

DES (1983) *Teaching Quality*. London: HMSO.

DES (1984) *Initial Teacher Training: Approval of Courses*. Circular No. 3/84. London: HMSO.

DES (1989a) *Initial Teacher Training in France: The Training of Secondary Teachers in the Académie de Toulouse. A Paper by HMI*. London: HMSO.

DES (1989b) *The Provisional Teacher Programme in New Jersey. A Paper by HMI*. London: HMSO.

DES (1989c) *The Education (Teachers) Regulations 1989*. Circular No. 18/89. London: HMSO.

DES (1989d) *Initial Teacher Training: Approval of Courses*. Circular No. 24/89. London: HMSO.

DES (1992a) Speech of the Secretary of State for Education and Science to the North of England Education Conference, Southport, 4 January.

DES (1992b) *Reform of Initial Teacher Training. A Consultation Document*. London: HMSO.

DFE (1992) *Initial Teacher Training (Secondary Phase)*. Circular No. 9/92. London: HMSO.

DFE (1993a) *The Initial Training of Primary School Teachers: New Criteria for Course Approval*. Draft Circular. London: HMSO.

DFE (1993b) *The Government's Proposals for the Reform of Initial Teacher Training*. London: HMSO.

DFE (1993c) Letter on second round of School-Centred Initial Teacher Training Scheme (SCITT), 29 September.

DFE (1993d) *The Initial Training of Primary School Teachers: New Criteria for Courses*. Circular No. 14/93. London: HMSO.

DFE (1993e) *The Education Bill: An Act to Make Provision about Teacher Training and Related Matters*. London: HMSO.

Furlong, J. (1994) Another view from the crossroads. *Cambridge Journal of Education*, **24** (1).

Goodlad, J. (1990) *Teachers for Our Nation's Schools*. San Francisco: Jossey-Bass.

Hargreaves, D. (1989a) Out of BEd and into practice. *Times Educational Supplement*, 8 September.

Hargreaves, D. (1989b) PGCE assessment fails the test. *Times Educational Supplement*, 3 November.

Hargreaves, D. (1990) Remission on a life sentence. *Times Higher Educational Supplement*, 21 September.

Hargreaves, D. (1992) On the right tracks. *Times Educational Supplement*, 17 January.

Hargreaves, D. (1994a) *The Mosaic of Learning: Schools and Teachers for the Next Century*. London: Demos.

Hargreaves, D. (1994b) Monopoly game must end. *Times Higher Education Supplement*, 24 June.

HMI (1991a) *Standards in Education 1989–90. The Annual Report of HM Senior Chief Inspector of Schools*. London: HMSO.

HMI (1991b) *School-Based Initial Teacher Training in England and Wales. A Report by HM Inspectorate*. London: HMSO.

HMI (1992) *Education in England 1990–91. The Annual Report of HM Senior Chief Inspector of Schools*. London: HMSO.

Holmes Group (1986) *Tomorrow's Teachers. A Report of the Holmes Group*. East Lansing, MI: Holmes Group.

Institute for Public Policy Research (1993) *Education: A Different Version. An Alternative White Paper*. London: IPPR.

Judge, H. (1991) Teacher education and the universities. *European Journal of Teacher Education*, **14** (3).

Kelly, V. (1993) Education as a field of study in a university: challenge, critique, dialogue, debate. *Journal of Education for Teaching*, **19** (2).

Koerner, J. (1963) *The Miseducation of American Teachers*. Boston: Houghton Mifflin.

Lacey, C. (1977) *The Socialisation of Teachers*. London: Methuen.

Lawlor, S. (1990) *Teachers Mistaught*. London: Centre for Policy Studies.

McNamara, D. (1994) *Classroom Pedagogy and Primary Practice*. London: Routledge.

Neather, E. J. (1993) Teacher education and the role of the university: European perspectives. *Research Papers in Education*, **8** (1).

Nichol, J. (1993) The Exeter school-based PGCE: an alternative initial teacher training model. *Journal of Education for Teaching*, **19** (3).

OFSTED (1993a) *The Initial Training of Teachers in Two German Länder: Hessen and Rheinland-Pfalz. A Report from the Office of Her Majesty's Chief Inspector of Schools*. London: HMSO.

OFSTED (1993b) *The Training of Primary School Teachers. A Report from the Office of Her Majesty's Chief Inspector of Schools*. London: HMSO.

OFSTED (1993c) *The Articled Teacher Scheme. A Report from the Office of Her Majesty's Chief Inspector of Schools.* London: HMSO.

OFSTED (1993d) *The Licensed Teacher Scheme. A Report from the Office of Her Majesty's Chief Inspector of Schools.* London: HMSO.

OFSTED (1993e) *The New Teacher in School.* London: HMSO.

O'Hear, A. (1988) *Who Teaches the Teachers?* London: Social Affairs Unit.

O'Hear, A. (1993) What Patten's tests tell us about teachers. *Daily Mail,* 7 June.

O'Keeffe, D. (1990) *The Wayward Elite.* London: Adam Smith Institute.

Pyke, N. (1993) Primary heads rally against Mum's Army. *Times Educational Supplement,* 16 July.

Robertson, A. (1992) Schools and universities in the training of teachers: the Demonstration School experiment 1890 to 1926. *British Journal of Educational Studies,* **40** (1).

Ruddock, J. (1989) Accrediting teacher education courses: the new criteria. In A. Hargreaves and D. Reynolds (eds), *Education Policies: Controversies and Critiques.* London: Falmer Press.

Ross, A. (1990) The universities and the BEd degree. In J. Thomas (ed.), *British Universities and Teacher Education: A Century of Change.* London: Falmer Press.

Sarason, S. *et al.* (1962) *The Preparation of Teachers: An Unstudied Problem.* New York: Wiley.

SCOP (1994) *Education Bill: Primary ITT Questionnaire. Commentary on Findings.* London: SCOP Teacher Education Group.

Sheehan, N. and Wilson, D. (1994) From normal school to the university college of teachers: teacher education in British Columbia in the 20th century. *Journal of Education for Teaching,* **20** (1).

Shulman, L. (1993) Conclusion. In M. Buchman and R. Floden (eds), *Detachment and Concern: Conversations in the Philosophy of Teaching and Teacher Education.* London: Cassell.

Siegrist, H. (1994) The professions, state and government in theory and history. In T. Becher (ed.), *Governments and Professional Education.* Buckingham: Society for Research into Higher Education and Open University Press.

Skilbeck, M. (1992) The role of research in teacher education. *European Journal of Teacher Education,* **15** (1/2).

Taylor, W. (1994) Teacher education: backstage to centre stage. In T. Becher (ed.), *Governments and Professional Education.* Buckingham: Society for Research into Higher Education and Open University Press.

Teaching as a Career (1994) *School-centred Initial Teacher Training Scheme. Information 5/94.* London: TASC.

Thomas, J. (1990) *British Universities and Teacher Education: A Century of Change.* London: Falmer Press.

Turner, J. (1990) Universities, government policy and the study of education in Britain. *Journal of Education for Teaching,* **16** (1).

Wilson, J. (1991) Teacher education. *Oxford Review of Education,* **17** (1).

Wubbels, T. (1992) Teacher education and the universities in the Netherlands. *European Journal of Teacher Education,* **15** (3).

# 10 Mentoring: A Positive Model in Teacher Education and Development

## ANNE MURDOCH

## Introduction

A mentor is defined as 'a wise counsellor or a person by whom we can confidently be guided' (*Oxford English Dictionary*). The role has evolved in the business world out of the notion of apprenticeships and the extended family, where the passing on of craft and managerial skills was seen as essential. In this context, much store has been placed on the role of mentor and in the 1970s it was stated that 'everyone who makes it has a mentor' (Collins and Scott, 1978). Mentoring has, however, undergone considerable change over the past twenty years, and the role itself may take many guises. Until the late 1970s, mentoring in business was arguably a matter of luck and relied on individuals being good networkers. Now, according to Clutterbuck (1994), one in three large UK companies have formal mentoring systems, many more are experimenting with them and formal mentoring is one of the fastest-growing strands of people development in business and government. However, Clutterbuck argues that informal mentoring is likely to be less beneficial to the organization. He cites the case of one chief executive who said that informal mentoring is likely to be bad for the organization, as it is likely to reinforce old habits and be used by those who perpetuate old cultures.

In other professions, such as social work, nursing, accountancy or the law, the roles of mentor and supervisor have for many years been seen as important, because these professions have a tradition of initial training or articled schemes in work. In education, however, the early introduction of mentoring in the 1970s tended towards an informal model and relied on those experienced teachers who made time to mentor new recruits (Williams, 1993). Teachers as mentors did not, arguably, become important until the late 1980s as a valuable resource to help students or newly qualified teachers and to encourage them to stay in the profession. The development of mentoring in initial teacher training has also not been without its difficulties, and it is important that this fact is not overlooked. The government's proposals in the late 1980s to move initial teacher training out of colleges and universities to schools, where the focus could be more readily on developing competence in the classroom, has been viewed with scepticism by many. The perception of government that those involved in initial teacher training should be suitably qualified and prepared for the task is sometimes seen as at odds with the view that student teachers should be immersed in the many theories and ideologies of education before entering the classroom. While there is insufficient scope within this chapter to do justice to either of these arguments, the HMI report (1993a) concluded that articled teacher training was most successful when trainee teachers had mentors who were well chosen and well trained themselves. It is only relatively recently, therefore, that mentoring schemes and approaches have been seen as important in initial teacher training, and the skills, abilities and personal qualities of mentors have exercised a range of writers who are referred to later in this chapter.

However, having come late to the debate about the value of a formal system of mentoring, educationalists soon became aware that there was a wealth of mentors, teachers and support staff who were willing to act as guides. Teacher mentoring was also seen as a way of increasing the personal commitment of experienced teachers and providing a school-based route to development. The selection of mentors, the quality and frequency of their support and the relationship of mentors to other forms of training which the mentee may be receiving at the same time are all issues which are now receiving considerable attention in educational research.

This chapter sets out the case for a positive model of mentoring in teacher education and development as a way of enabling the teacher in training and the new recruit, in particular, to learn 'on the job'. This model aims to enable learning to become a totally continuous activity. Mentors are expected to be people-oriented, to value their work and to want to help their less experienced colleagues (Clawson, 1980). Mentors are therefore expected to be nurturing, supportive, protective and knowledgeable, and at the same time to be able to 'make things happen' for their mentee in the workplace. When this relationship works well, it does, according to writers such as Kram (1983), Newstrom and Davis (1993) and Williams (1993), enable learning to become a totally continuous activity. Taken to its logical conclusion, mentoring can facilitate learner-centred development in a professional context in a way not possible in a teacher education system which pays high regard to theory building and less to the development of skills and understanding of self in the classroom context. With this background in mind, this chapter will outline the various facets of mentoring as both a training and a development tool and will draw conclusions about the value of these tools for the training and development of professionals in the service as a whole. The chapter will therefore work towards the building of a model of positive mentoring as a development tool in education.

Before we move to the position of 'positive mentoring', it is important to emphasize the wider context of mentoring in business as well as in education. Torrington and Hall (1991), in writing about human resource development, refer to mentoring as a 'training and development tool'. Men-

| Career-enhancing functions: | sponsorship |
| | coaching |
| | exposure and visibility |
| | protection |
| | challenging |
| Psycho-social functions: | acceptance and |
| | confirmation |
| | counselling |
| | role modelling |
| | friendship |
| Special attributes: | complementary |

**Figure 10.1**  Advantages of mentoring
*Source*: Torrington and Hall (1991)

toring is seen as offering a wide range of advantages for the individual. In this context there is much stress on career development, and individuals selected for mentoring are usually good performers (Kanter, 1977). The advantage for the mentor is not only recognition of this role but being seen as someone who is responsible for developing talent at work.

The advantages of mentorship relationships, according to Torrington and Hall, are in terms of three main areas as set out in Figure 10.1. Whether in business or in education, mentoring can be seen to facilitate two main processes: career functions (largely to do with career enhancement) and psycho-social functions (largely to do with a sense of competence, clarity of identity and effectiveness in a particular role). The career-enhancing functions of mentoring are important for both the mentor and the mentee. Torrington and Hall see these as opportunities for the development of supporters throughout the organization and the facilitation of the mentor's promotion by adequate training of a replacement. The psycho-social functions of mentoring relate to the support, guidance and trust relationship offered by one individual to another. The special attributes are the development of two individuals, with mutual respect for each other, who can often complement each other in the workplace.

Kram (1983) also identified the same two broad functions of mentoring as a career function and a psycho-social function. Mentoring, according to Kram, can include opportunities for information sharing, can provide the 'eyes and ears' for a new employee and may provide vital information exchange about career opportunities or career strategizing. All of these are important career functions for the new teacher. On the other hand, mentors can provide feedback on psycho-social activities such as behaviour, friendship, trust, opportunity for self-disclosure, emotional support or a chance to express personal and professional dilemmas, vulnerabilities or individualities.

## Mentoring as a development tool

This chapter attempts to build a picture of positive mentoring by looking at good practice in business and identifying how such models can help in teacher education. If one begins with the career function of mentoring, career development and accountability in education are made easier, according to Epstein (1993), by the use of a mentoring system. Accountability has become more appealing in the 1980s and 1990s as education providers and producers are accountable to consumers through the various charters which the government has encouraged and various organizations have produced. As the focus on accountability increases, the demands on teachers to ensure that they perform to standard increases more dramatically. This causes stress on teachers and those in training, but the development of a mentoring system has been shown to reduce some of that stress and to have a positive career development function (Kyriacou and Harriman, 1993). The most important element found by Kyriacou and Harriman in their study of teachers involved in school merger was that where individuals had a feeling of no control or lack of control over their own career development and therefore their destinies, teaching and school life, work became unbearably stressful. Those who had either career or emotional support were less stressed by the experience, as they could identify wider contexts of accountability and career development opportunities for themselves. In this sense, mentoring can provide information to allow career strategizing to

continue, even if organizational change has destroyed old expectations and networks.

The second function of mentoring where psycho-social activities develop is also important. Mentoring can, in this context, provide an important mechanism for self-reflection by both the mentor and the mentee. Biographies (Maclure, 1993), for example, are a vehicle for reflection on one's own behaviour and, with the help of a mentor, can be useful for ensuring professional accountability. There may also be, in a world more conscious of equal opportunities, pressure from outside organizations for senior managers to promote individuals from minority groups. In organizations where there has traditionally been an emphasis on individualist and analytical operations, often with high turnover of staff and a tendency to stifle creativity and caring, the use of mentors has been helpful as a way of preparing individuals with less experience to succeed in career terms, according to Hampden-Turner and Trompenaars (1994). Mentoring in this vein has also been seen as a very positive way of encouraging more women into senior management by providing opportunities for women managers to discuss vulnerabilities and individualities with mentors. The changing nature of organizations means that while mentoring in education management is still often seen as a gender issue, senior managers of either sex can be mentors to more junior female colleagues, according to Steve Shirley (1994). Shirley cites many examples of organizations with formal and informal mentorship programmes to encourage women into management.

Examining further the psycho-social functions of mentoring, Newstrom and Davis (1993) used data from a study of 887 industrial managers, examining role expectations, perceptions of their supervisors' expectations of them and their supervisors' actual expectations of them. They also considered where employees get information regarding their work-related roles so that they have accurate role perceptions. In addition to the traditional sources of information, such as job descriptions, many organizations have developed formal or informal mentorship programmes to help individuals reflect on their roles and behaviour. Newstrom and Davis found that mentors are used as role models to guide other employees by sharing valuable advice on roles to play and behaviours to avoid. Mentors therefore teach, advise and sponsor their protégés in order to expedite their career progress. The fairest method of assignment of mentors was seen to be when employees seek out their own role models. Newstrom and Davis also found that mentors are usually employees who are successful themselves and are respected by their peers. They must be willing to commit time and energy to helping others. In this way, the most successful mentors are often not direct supervisors and their detachment allows them to be more objective about the strengths and weaknesses observed in others.

When we look at mentoring as a development tool, however, some of the problems which Newstrom and Davis (1993) found in mentoring programmes are that some mentors are more effective role models than others, or are more interested in being good mentors. In other cases, mentors had provided information which had actually hindered new employees' development. In addition, if the mentor leaves, this can sometimes stifle the development of the individual employee who has come to rely on one individual. Despite well meaning attempts, Newstrom and Davis found in their 1993 study that the reliance of most mentoring programmes on individuals is a major weakness. They also cite an example of the problems created when the mentee has misinterpreted the advice and help of the mentor and the relationship has broken down. This leaves the mentor feeling rebuffed and the mentee feeling vulnerable, which is exactly what mentoring seeks most to avoid.

Another side of mentoring as a development tool is that, in a world of scarce resources, the question of who has access to a mentor may be restricted in some way. Cascio (1989) found that women and those from ethnic minorities are least likely to be offered mentors. This, Cascio argues, is because mentoring is frequently based on friendship, admiration and nurturing developed outside the typical working day. However, where the central goal of mentoring is to boost the self-esteem of the mentor as well as to help the mentee, the system seemed to work best. This has implications for who is recruited to the role of mentor and who

makes the best mentor. Cascio found that the best mentors must be bright, understand the dynamics and the politics of the organization and be willing to share that knowledge with a trainee or new member of staff. Cascio further argues that organizations should actively promote mentor relationships and provide sufficient time for the mentor and mentee to meet on a regular basis, at least initially. The mentor's role is then to teach 'the ropes' and to provide candid feedback on how an individual is progressing, as well as to serve as a confidential sounding-board for dealing with work-related problems. If successful, the mentor can help to reduce inflated expectations on the part of the trainee or new member of staff about the organization or the profession. This, in itself, has been shown to reduce stress and improve the chances of survival for the mentee, according to Cascio (1989), and supports the work of Kyriacou and Harriman mentioned earlier.

Harrison (1993) looked at the importance of a mentor in the induction of new teachers. He argues that a mentor can be allocated to each newcomer to act as a guide and counsellor and a catalyst of learning during the induction process, and, after this, to facilitate the improvement of performance once a satisfactory basic standard has been achieved. In addition, there may be guided experience with mentors to provide support and guidance or coaching by relevant others. This is probably one of the basic mentoring roles and one in which education, in particular, is arguably fairly good.

Peckett and Shepherd (1994) put forward a model of mentors as facilitators in their description of school-based mentors involved with students on a PGCE programme. In their research, they outline the responsibility for certain aspects of the students' school experience which is devolved to the mentors. They used a system of central and subject mentors. Central mentors were expected to ensure that the requirements of the student's learning contract were fulfilled: to monitor, discuss and help students to set targets and learning contracts. This means that time must be made available for professional dialogue between mentor and student. It also means that mentors must receive clear instructions and training as to their role and the learning programme or contract which the student is working towards. The conclusions of Peckett and Shepherd's study are that the mentor's perception of his or her role will have an overriding influence on the student's experience and that the mentor must be in tune with, and empathize with, both the learning requirements of the student and the culture and politics of the school. This is so that the mentor can be of help to the student. Where this is not the case, the student can be disadvantaged.

## The training needs of mentors

The difficulties of establishing a formal mentoring programme, the potential mismatch of individuals, unrealistic expectations on both sides and the time and effort involved sometimes make mentoring seem an impossibility in education. Quinn (1994) investigated the importance of a structured approach to the selection, training and assignment of mentors in five elementary schools in the USA. The study came about because it was noticed that mentors were often left to decide for themselves whether they would take a proactive or an advisory role. Quinn argues that unless the nature of the role is specified, the perceptions of mentors of their role will differ considerably, and this may not be helpful to the mentor or the mentee. This is particularly important if the mentor spends time observing the mentee and is therefore expected to take responsibility for informing the mentee of inappropriate behaviour as well as that which is going well. Quinn goes on to state that clear guidelines as to the role of mentors need to be laid down, which can then provide the scope for flexibility and practical responses in mentoring interaction in order to meet the needs of both the individuals concerned and the organization. As mentoring becomes more formalized, Quinn argues, specific outcomes and interactions will become more structured and focus more on practices and their consequences.

Williams (1993), however, in a study of teacher perceptions of their needs as mentors in the con-

text of developing school-based initial teacher education, provides a framework from which a positive model of mentoring can be built. Williams looked at how confident teachers felt in supervising PGCE students. These perceptions provided the basis for examining future needs of mentors and the preparation they need to perform their task. Williams argues that as PGCE courses have changed, more attention has been paid to the capabilities and training needs of mentors. It has been argued that the quality of school-based competence training depends very much on the capabilities of teachers in the role of mentor. Williams sees two different approaches to the training of mentors. The first is a focus on subject-specific issues and wider professional concerns. The second concerns the focus of the mentoring activity itself.

In the subject-specific approach, the mentor, and hence mentor training, will focus on the range of tasks and experiences to which the student teacher should be introduced in teaching his or her subject. In the mentoring activity approach, the emphasis will be on developing effective strategies with the student to induct him or her into the culture of the school, rather than focusing on teaching expertise. The first is a skills approach; the second is a political approach. Both may be necessary for the student or newly qualified teacher. Building on both of these approaches, Williams (1993) cites the model of the 'developed mentor' as a key figure in school-based learning. In this context, the mentor is a role model, facilitator, counsellor, adviser, teacher and assessor. This means that some of the mentor's role is organizational, some is as enabler, some is as observer or assessor, some is as experienced role model and some is as provider of emotional support.

The mentoring role within an organization is often very critical in terms of an individual's career, but the concept of mentoring and its different roles is quite complex, as can be seen from the discussion above. Mentors can be wise counsellors, teachers, coaches, trainers, talent developers, door openers, parent figures, protectors, sponsors, leaders or 'the positive role model'. Whatever the nature of the role taken, the impact for the individuals receiving the support is likely to be

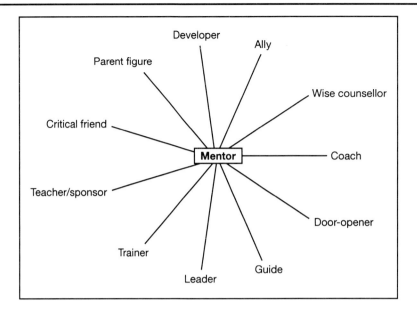

**Figure 10.2** The positive model of mentoring

positive but different, according to Tyson and Jackson (1992). While it is impossible in this chapter to look at all these roles in depth, it is important to realize that each has its own strengths and weaknesses as far as mentoring is concerned.

## Towards a positive model of mentoring

The study by Williams (1993) outlined the role of the developed mentor as one who can fulfil a number of functions for the student teacher, the new recruit or the teacher colleague who is in need of support at this time of great change in education. The developed mentor is regarded by Williams as a key figure in the development of school-based learning and of professional learning in schools. While this role may appear complex and very demanding for the mentor, if mentoring is to be used as a positive development tool then the mentor must be, or be able to become through training, a very flexible facilitator who can perform a number of supporting roles. Williams argued that mentors must be confident and want to take on the role for a number of reasons, not least of which may be the desire to ensure the

professional development of teaching. The mentor must also receive an appropriate payback, whether in the sense of professional recognition or in terms of time allocation to the job. Without this, which is often a key point of formal mentoring programmes in industry, the system could fail through lack of time. The significant point here appears to be that mentioned earlier by Tyson and Jackson, that whatever the nature of the role taken, the impact for both individuals must be positive.

The notion of the developed mentor can be expanded to encompass a number of functions within a positive model of mentoring, as set out in Figure 10.2.

The positive model of mentoring is developed from observations of mentoring undertaken with new recruits in a college of further and higher education and builds on the notion of the developed mentor outlined above. Data collected on those who are mentors and the evaluations of mentees suggest that the student in training or the new recruit will require the mentor to undertake different roles as he or she (the mentee) becomes more familiar with the professional demands of his or her role. Initially, the mentor may be required to act as information giver and friend, and later on to act as a coach or confidential sounding-board. The role undertaken by the mentor may also vary depending on the confidence of the mentee and the political context of the organization. What is clear, however, is that the mentor role is one which requires great professional skill, and not everyone has the ability to undertake this challenge. Some mentors appear instinctively through experience or empathy to be able to undertake the role necessary, while others can be very successful once they have received some formal training in the demands of the role. Others, usually those who are threatened by change or newcomers, should not be encouraged to undertake the role as their response is likely to be bad for the mentee and for the organization. While the weaknesses of this observational research, which is based on a single case study organization such as this, cannot be denied, these observations give rise to the need for further research in this field.

From research outlined above, the facets of the positive mentor model have emerged as follows.

*The positive mentor has:*
- an empathy for the position of the mentee;
- a willingness to act in a multiplicity of roles;
- a willingness to give time and to listen;
- an ability to make things happen for the mentee;
- a willingness to share information and positive insights;
- an ability to say when things are not going well and to suggest alternative action;
- a willingness to undertake training in the role;
- an ability to work to training guide-lines (with student teachers);
- a preparedness to pass on skills, knowledge and positive attitudes;
- an ability to differentiate between working and learning;
- a willingness to find a successor or substitute when appropriate.

*The positive mentor programme provides:*
- time for both mentor and mentee to meet, and other necessary resources;
- appropriate training where necessary to undertake the role;
- opportunity for the mentor to develop personally and professionally from undertaking the role;

- credibility in the role of mentor;
- choice of mentor for the mentee, if necessary;
- a formal structure to the total mentoring process;
- an opportunity for mentors to network.

Some successful mentoring schemes (Simco and Sixsmith, 1994) are supported by joint training programmes where the mentor and mentee attend together for a few days. This has been seen to be especially helpful in initial teacher training and induction programmes. The starting point, however, must be the full recognition of the training needs of both the mentor and the mentee. Mahoney (1994) also argues for the importance of mentoring networks, where experiences can be shared and information exchanged, and highlights an example of where mentorship programmes can gain the individual credits towards a master's degree. This kind of approach can only help to enhance the role of mentor and thereby increase the likelihood of satisfaction for the mentor and mentee.

## Conclusion

The success of any mentoring scheme is based on the two-way process in which the mentor and mentee work together to enrich the learning of the individual and the development of the profession. Mentees expect to gain confidence, support and competence in practice, while mentors expect to gain credibility, new ideas and further insights into the developing profession of which they are a member.

The development of mentoring in initial teacher training is therefore arguably a positive step forward for the profession. However, it would be inappropriate not to mention in this conclusion at least some of the dilemmas of this approach for teachers in training and for schools. For student teachers, there can be no doubt from research outlined above that the success of their 'training' lies at least in part in achieving the right balance of skill, ability and personal qualities in their mentor. The 'wrong mentor' can have disastrous consequences and leave all concerned feeling hurt and bruised as a result. For schools, the development of mentoring for articled teachers can also mean that the best teachers are taken away from the classroom to become mentors, that the system is very resource intensive and that the schools do not really see long-term benefit in the standard of education they can provide for their pupils. All of these issues are still very current in the debates around the development of initial teacher training in schools. However, as the development of a system of professional training for teachers moves towards the competence model already in existence for many other professions, the opportunities for colleges and universities to work with schools to improve the existing practices are immense and exciting. This is as true for the development of approaches to mentoring as for the development of initial teacher training itself.

This chapter has briefly attempted to highlight the role of positive mentoring as a two-way process and to suggest that the more formal the mentoring scheme, the more likely that mentor, mentee and the organization will gain from the relationship. However, what is clear is that while research in mentoring in education is growing, there is room for much more research which can quantify and qualify the positive outcomes of mentoring relationships for the individuals and for the profession of teaching. Only as research increases in this area will we know the true impact of this approach to the education and development of teachers.

# References

Cascio, W. (1989) *Managing Human Resources.* New York: McGraw-Hill.

CATE (1992) *The Accreditation of Initial Teacher Training under Circular 9/92 (DFE). A Note of Guidance from the Council for Accreditation of Teachers.* London: CATE.

Clawson, J. (1980) Mentoring in managerial careers. In B. Derr (ed.), *Work, Family and the Career.* New York: Praeger.

Clutterbuck, D. (1994) Business mentoring in evolution. *Mentoring and Tutoring for Partnership in Learning,* **2** (1), 19–22.

Collins, E. and Scott, P. (1978) Everyone who makes it has a mentor. *Harvard Business Review*, **56** (4).

DFE (1994) *Our Children's Education: A Parent's Charter.* London: HMSO.

Epstein, D. (1993) Defining accountability in education. *British Educational Research Journal*, **19** (3).

Garry, A. and Cowan, J. (1986) *Learning from Experience.* London: FEU/PICKUP.

Hampden-Turner, C. and Trompenaars, A. (1994) *The Seven Cultures of Capitalism.* New York: Doubleday.

Harrison, R. (1993) *Employee Development.* London: Cromwell Press.

HMI (1993a) *The Articled Teacher Scheme September 1990 to July 1992.* London: HMSO.

HMI (1993b) *The Licensed Teacher Scheme September 1990 to July 1992.* London: HMSO.

Kanter, R. M. (1977) *Men and Women of the Corporation.* New York: Basic Books.

Kram, K. (1983) Phases of the mentorship relationship. *Academy of Management Journal*, **16** (4).

Kyriacou, C. and Harriman, P. (1993) Teacher stress and school merger. *School Organisation*, **13** (3).

McIntyre, D., Hagger, H. and Wilkin, M. (1992) *Mentoring: Perspectives on School-Based Teacher Education.* London: Kogan Page.

Maclure, M. (1993) Arguing for your self: identity as an organising principle in teachers' jobs and lives. *British Educational Research Journal*, **19** (4).

Mahoney, M. (1994) Towards a UK network. *Mentoring and Tutoring*, **2** (1).

Newstrom, J. and Davis, K. (1993) *Organizational Behavior.* New York: McGraw-Hill.

Peckett, J. and Shepherd, C. (1994) An evaluation of learning contracts within the context of partnership in school-based training: implications for school-based mentoring. *Mentoring and Tutoring*, **2** (1).

Quinn, L. (1994) The importance of structure in providing uniform quality in mentoring/induction programs. *Mentoring and Tutoring*, **2** (1).

Shirley, S. (1994) Management: put the gender issue on the agenda. *Financial Times*, 10 January.

Simco, N. and Sixsmith, S. (1994) Developing a mentoring scheme in primary initial teacher education. *Mentoring and Tutoring*, **2** (1).

Torrington, D. and Hall, L. (1991) *Personnel Management.* London: Prentice-Hall.

Tyson, S. and Jackson, T. (1992) *The Essence of Organizational Behavior.* New York: Prentice-Hall.

Williams, A. (1993) Teacher perceptions of their needs as mentors in the context of developing school-based initial teacher education. *British Educational Research Journal*, **19** (4)

# Response to Anne Murdoch

## TREVOR KERRY

Murdoch's chapter is an interesting summary of received wisdom about mentors and the mentor process. My reservations about the views expressed there lie not with the models of effective mentoring which Murdoch describes, but with the mismatches between those models and what actually happens in mentoring schemes, especially schemes of initial teacher training (ITT). In this brief response I want to raise questions about some of the assumptions which underpin Murdoch's positive model.

First, Murdoch refers to commercial models, such as those promulgated by Clutterbuck. But these are predicated on two important principles:

- that the mentor's status in his or her 'company' will be enhanced through his or her protégé's successes;
- that such enhancement is valued in promoting the 'company's' image.

Where schools are the 'companies' of this model, there is no evidence for the former and little evidence for the latter belief, as an integral part of institutional philosophy in English schools.

Second, Murdoch refers to the traditional view of the mentor as the 'wise counsellor'. Wisdom is a quality which transcends both 'skilful performance' on the one hand, and 'knowledge and understanding about' teaching processes on the other. In the context of mentoring in ITT, I am unaware of any definition of wisdom which is applicable to mentors, any research into the individual or collective wisdom of mentors or any way of defining whether this quality – or the fruits of it – can be, or are, passed on to student teachers.

In the absence of such research, one is left to explore the key skills required of mentors. Of the array of skills identified by Murdoch, perhaps four are paramount:

- the ability to aid the learning of adults;
- the ability to observe analytically the teaching of students;
- the ability to reflect upon practice;
- the ability to feed back to the students those reflections in a way which can be accessed by them to improve their own practice through reflection.

Much of the research into so-called effective mentoring has concentrated on how students feel about the mentoring they receive. Few studies have tried to define what 'good' mentoring is and then to assess objectively whether it happens. In a paper to the BERA Annual Conference 1994, Anne Edwards (1994) reported interviews of primary and secondary school mentors. She concluded that in these narratives there was no evidence that schools are adapting to the mentor role. She appears to argue, rather, that the role is watered down and deprived of rigour so that teachers can create 'identities that allow them to cope without disrupting the existing equilibrium in their schools'. The grand ideals of mentoring as deep reflection and of mentors as guardians of a higher professional wisdom are shattered by Collison's (1994) research in primary schools as part of the same project. She concluded: 'opportunities do exist within primary classrooms for active mentoring. However, the majority of teacher mentors in this programme are not recognising them ... there can be little doubt that the dynamics of infant classrooms can militate against active mentoring'.

But if there are serious doubts about the value of mentoring in ITT at least, why is it so prevalent? In my chapter, I provide Bridges's (1993) answer: the issue is political and relates to the government's view of the value of school-based ITT. As a result, mentoring and school-based training seem to be inextricably linked in current ITT practice. If this school-based training is itself less than successful – for whatever reason – then mentoring, being so closely allied to it, must also be seen to contribute to, or result from, any failure of the school-based system. Empirical evidence continues to cast doubt on the effects of mentoring in practice. Thus, Edwards and Collison (in McBride, 1995) report a study of school-based partnerships in a pilot BA (QTS) (Early Years Scheme). Some of their conclusions are salutary:

- They found that teachers in this study drew a distinction between theory and practice and that primary school teacher-mentors were unwilling to risk discussion (i.e. with students) of areas which extended beyond the immediate task-setting and performance.
- They found that for secondary teachers theory was understood as subject theory, not pedagogy.
- They concluded that 'pedagogy as theory is not so much split from practice but *erased from the experience of the student*' (my italics).
- The study highlighted the tension teachers felt between teaching pupils and mentoring students, and the reluctance of senior managers in schools to grasp the concept of partnership, preferring purchaser–provider models which fitted the political context more directly.

These findings are of great importance, and they are not confined to the Lancaster project reported by Edwards and Collison. They lie at the root of the problem for defining and achieving mentor effectiveness. Even Rowie Shaw (1992), in a view from the schools, concluded that 'within schools there are issues of reflection and quality assurance to address' (p. 374). The view is echoed by Gore and Mitchell (1992) from an LEA perspective, who recognize how the issues of school-based training, mentoring and pedagogy hang together:

> The LEAs' experience of these two school-based schemes confirms both the benefits and pitfalls ... We are some way from understanding how teachers create practical theories; and some way from having models for promoting and supporting collaboration between all ... partners ... It is the failure to address principles and theories which has been the single most important reason why the Government's simplistic views on teacher education are insufficiently challenged.
>
> (Gore and Mitchell, 1992, p. 361)

# References

Bridges, D. (1993) School-based teacher education. In D. Bridges and T. Kerry (eds), *Developing Teachers Professionally*. London: Routledge.

Clutterbuck, D. (1994) Business mentoring in evolution. *Mentoring and Tutoring for Partnership in Learning*, **2** (1), 19–22.

Collison, J. (1994) The impact of primary school practices on the student experience of mentoring. Unpublished paper, BERA Annual Conference, Oxford.

Edwards, A. (1994) The impact of involvement in ITT on processes and procedures in schools: alternative narratives. Unpublished paper, BERA Annual Conference, Oxford.

Gore, L. and Mitchell, P. (1992) School-based training: a local education authority perspective. *Cambridge Journal of Education*, **22** (3), 351–62.

McBride, R. (ed.) (1995) *Teacher Education Policy: Some Issues Arising from Research and Practice*. London: Falmer Press.

Shaw, R. (1992) School-based training: the view from the schools. *Cambridge Journal of Education*, **22** (3), 363–75.

# 11 Mentoring: The Great Training Confidence Trick?

## TREVOR KERRY

Anne Murdoch (in Chapter 10) has drawn together the arguments currently fashionable to support the growing practice of mentoring. Mentoring is common in a number of contexts in education: in training new headteachers, in appraisal at various levels within the profession, as part of newly qualified teacher (NQT) induction training, and increasingly in initial teacher education. This chapter deals in the main with mentoring in the context of initial teacher training (ITT), but the ideas and objections raised here can be extrapolated to other situations too.

In the initial teacher education context, mentoring cannot be seen other than in tandem with the move towards school-based teacher education. There can be little doubt that successive Conservative Secretaries of State for Education have favoured the move to school-based training for initial teacher trainees because of a deep-rooted, and largely groundless, suspicion about the supposed left-wing attitudes and questionably 'progressive' educational philosophies held by trainers in traditional training institutions, such as the colleges of education and polytechnic and university departments of education. The underlying arguments for school-based training, which necessitates the use of classroom teachers as mentors, are themselves suspect.

David Bridges (1993) challenges the recent government-led position on school-based teacher education, and does so on three grounds. First, he looks at the hypothesis that the political, and to some extent professional, programme to strengthen the school as the unit of educational responsibility demands that initial teachers are trained on site. He makes a telling distinction between what he labels the 'strongly corporate model' and the 'collaborative professional model'. He notes that the articled teacher scheme, and the licensed teacher scheme in particular, have adopted a corporate model. This corporate model has a number of characteristics which differentiate it from a collaborative model and make it narrower in scope. For example, the school plays a significant role in determining which students it accepts, and the training itself is focused substantially on that school, with strong socialization into its own particular ways. Students may even be assessed by the training school on what amount to its own criteria, and are often employed within that school subsequent to obtaining NQT status. By contrast, in the collaborative model, the HE institution deals with a cluster or consortium of schools and is responsible for the interviewing and recruitment of initial trainees. Usually, students have a broad experience of a number of schools and are not socialized into the narrow ways of any particular school. Assessment is done against common criteria of success and students may be employed anywhere in the country following the successful completion of their course. So, Bridges concludes, 'many teachers in many schools continue to affirm their identity with a larger educational service and to recognise the regenerative benefits of communication and collaboration across a wider professional community' (p. 57).

But if the trend to school-based education limits professional vision in the way described, even for an initial trainee, there are also dangers inherent in school-based education, because giving up time and energy to the initial training of teachers distracts the school from its major concern with the education of its pupils. Inevitably, it could be argued, the best teachers in any school will be the ones identified to give attention to the process of mentoring initial teacher trainees; yet it is precisely these teachers from whom pupils potentially benefit most. The distraction of schools into the training field must be detrimental to the education of pupils.

Finally, Bridges argues, the ideologies which have driven politicians to support school-based education are grounded on a misplaced pragmatism. The idea that a hands-on approach to the classroom can, of itself, help students and mentors to articulate theoretical constructs is manifestly erroneous.

So it can be argued that the very foundations from which the edifice of mentoring has arisen – school-based training – can be seen to be built so significantly upon the shifting sands ideology that the whole issue of whether mentoring for initial teacher education should exist at all must be called into question. In the remainder of this chapter, I shall move on to explore a range of corollaries for appointing classroom teachers as mentors to oversee the initial training of teachers, and I shall draw attention to the weaknesses of a system based on such tenuous foundations.

We have seen that mentoring has come into its own substantially through the need to provide workplace learning for those undergoing initial teacher training, and for other (experienced) practitioners who need to learn new workplace skills. What most writers would agree upon is the mentors' involvement in providing a context in which trainees can reflect on practice: their own and (through observation) that of others. This is the view of Day (1993), for example: but he is very sceptical about whether it will work. He reviews the literature of reflective practice (for example, Ebbutt, 1985; Handal, 1990; Smyth, 1991) and concludes:

- classroom teachers may not be the most effective guardians of focused reflection on, and learning from, practice;

- the government, which controls training money, has low-level pragmatic, rather than high-level reflective, agendas;
- that as a precondition there needs to be revision in the definition of professionalism away from the emphasis on the teacher as content expert and towards the teacher as pedagogic expert.

For while the roots of educational mentoring may well exist in the concept of the reflective practitioner and in the engagement in action research, the workplace context is having the effect of redefining teaching activity in terms of competencies. What the mentor oversees and manages is the development of overall teaching competence: the route to which, for the trainee, is through the acquisition of individual competencies. It is for these reasons that Lunt *et al.* (1992, p. 50) conclude that 'mentorship is concerned with bridging the theory/practice gap'.

But, just as many would question the political motivation for school-based initial teacher training – on which ITT mentoring is predicated – so others have doubts about competence-oriented training in this sector. Thus Whitty (1992, p. 50), in a careful analysis, concludes:

> while there may be a firm philosophical basis for what critics discuss as the mystique of teacher education, both the competency movement and the capability movement offer positive scope for its demystification. But to recognize that is by no means tantamount to suggesting that quality should be measured, and funding allocated, purely on the basis of the number of competences demonstrated by students.

If one fails to absorb in significant measure the doctrine of competence as the key to training in teaching, then the rationale of school-based training – at least on Bridges's corporate model – is weakened, and with it the necessity for mentors of the kind now being widely advocated and appointed.

Despite the reservations expressed so far about the underlying rationale for mentoring, it remains true that the best-known approach to the mentor role is that of the experienced reflective practitioner, who encourages the growth of reflectiveness in the mentee. This approach was pioneered by Schön (1991) and also promoted by Tickle (1989). Gifford (1992) is right to suspect that many mentors may have embarked on that role expecting to be the 'friendly provider of practical help' rather than a guide into reflective practice techniques. But the question remains as to whether mentors in general actually have the skills of reflective practice and the ability to communicate those skills to a trainee.

In a piece of small-scale research, Kerry (1994) explored with a group of experienced teachers undergoing in-service training on pedagogy what the range of skills was that they shared. He hypothesized that, to be effective as a mentor, these teachers would need skills in observing another professional at work. He asked the teachers ($n = 29$) when they had last watched another teacher for a whole lesson. Only half of the respondents had done so within the past term (51.7 per cent). Of the remainder, their experience was two years old or more; and eight respondents said that their last observation was so long ago they could not remember precisely when it took place. Similarly, Kerry asked the teachers when they had last read a book devoted to pedagogy. Fewer than half (41.4 per cent) had done so within the past term. But 37.9 per cent of the respondents had not read anything concerned with pedagogy as such for at least two years and several commented that their last book was read 'years ago' or that they 'couldn't remember'. Asked to identify the book concerned, only half (55.2 per cent) were able to do so.

While direct observation of a colleague might be a useful skill for mentors to acquire, it might be suggested (in the absence of such experience) that being observed would be a useful experience in its own right as preparation for mentoring. From this group of respondents only a quarter (24 per cent) had been observed at work within the past term and a number claimed that they had never been observed, or had not been observed since their probationary period in the profession, or in one case had not been observed since 1974.

These findings call into question, among a group of experienced (and by definition keen) teachers attending a voluntary session on pedagogical skill, whether the skills necessary to undertake insight-ful mentoring are as widespread as those who champion the system would have one believe.

Clearly, the issues just described call into question the suitability of those people who are called upon to take on the mentor role. The question of suitability must exercise the minds of those who run initial teacher training schemes. In the scheme with which I am most familiar, the Open University PGCE, little initial guidance was offered to schools during the first year of operation about the kinds of people who were suitable to take on the role. The Open University offered a job description of mentoring, but failed to give anything other than basic guidance on the qualities required in a mentor in order to fulfil these functions. This guidance stated that the mentor should:

- be an experienced member of staff who can provide training in subject knowledge and application, as well as classroom teaching skills, that is appropriate for the student's subject or phase. In a primary school this would normally be a class teacher who would mentor the student on the school placement at each stage, and in a secondary school a class teacher who shares the student's subject specialism.

- be able to develop through training an ability to explain their own classroom practice, including strengths and weaknesses, and to support the student in developing the same ability to critically evaluate their own practice.

- be sympathetic and supportive to the needs of adult learners, including a sensitivity to their status during training.

These rubrics might be considered to be a minimal level of guidance to schools. The second and third are helpful to the extent that they explain the particular qualities required of mentors in an initial teacher training situation; the first is less helpful since it defines the mentor's activities rather than the qualities which he or she needs to bring to those activities. This lack of guidance was found to be a weakness of the scheme and plans are in hand to remedy the omission.

However, one has to remain sceptical about the effectiveness in practice of this kind of guidance when one talks to mentors about the ways in which they are, in turn, selected within the schools from among members of the school staff. Experience in operation of the Open University's PGCE scheme demonstrated that in many cases – too many cases – inadequate selection processes were operated by headteachers responsible for setting up school-based initial teacher training schemes. This is illustrated by the following piece of small-scale research.

During a training conference for mentors conducted by a university department of education, Kerry (1994) asked five teachers assigned to a particular training group to identify the means by which they were appointed to the mentor role. The mentors were drawn from schools across a wide geographical area, and had responded to a national advertisement offering this course of training. Each of the five teachers (who, in effect, formed a small opportunity sample) had a slightly different experience, but none of them appeared to have been selected against a suitable set of criteria:

- Teacher A was appointed by her headteacher of a middle school; that is, she was approached and asked whether she was prepared to do the job. She was given a choice about whether or not she undertook to do the role. She was told that her particular personal qualities fitted her, in the opinion of the headteacher, for the role, and that this was the reason for the invitation.
- Teacher B claimed to have been appointed because a mentor was needed within her two-person subject department. The university tutor attached to her school did not wish to work with her colleague and therefore asked her if she would act as the mentor to the HE institution's student.
- Teacher C was told by her headteacher that she had been appointed as mentor to a PGCE student. She was told that possible candidates for this role had been listed, and that she had been selected (presumably by the head and other senior staff) on the basis of being the most suitable person.
- Teacher D was simply informed by her headteacher that she was to mentor a PGCE student, but was not informed of any criteria by which she had been selected for this role.

- Teacher E was a new head of department in a secondary school. Some time after appointment she was informed that the school, prior to her appointment, had taken on a student in her department and that she would have to be the mentor to the student, since no one else in the department was competent to act in the role. She refused to be a mentor but was told that she had no choice. Subsequently, because of her feelings (which were based on an assessment of the school's current teaching in her newly acquired department), she failed to attend the briefing session held by her specific HE institution. However, when the student arrived for stage 1 practice, she was impressed by the student and by the course that the student was following, so she changed her mind and agreed to take on the mentor role.

These experiences appear to be a fairly typical cross-section of the ways in which mentors are appointed. In a trawl of appointments made in one Open University region, a number of the respondents claimed to have been appointed because they were nearing the end of their teaching careers and they were thought to be suitably experienced; a number of others identified their appointment as being because they were upwardly mobile within the profession. None of those questioned identified any specific criteria against which selection had taken place, least of all in a competitive mode within the school.

Why should anyone want to take on the mentor role? It could be argued (Watkins and Whalley, 1993) that the mentor role is a new route into managerial promotion. Certainly, as mentoring takes on an increased significance in school-based teacher education, in appraisal and in management training in schools, senior managers at least will have to demonstrate that they have experience of mentoring in order to gain promotion. But there are often conflicts of interest about taking on the mentor role. For example, from the point of view of the mentor, there is a significant time demand required, both in freeing up preparation time to work with the student through the exercises which he or she needs to complete, and in following up lessons which the student teaches within the school. These time demands cannot necessarily be accommodated within the teaching day, and inevitably teachers will find themselves mentoring at times when they are technically not contracted. Experience of the Open University PGCE scheme in one region showed that only a minority of mentors had the mentoring activity counted against their contracted 1265 hours. Furthermore, in most cases there is an expectation on the part of the validating HE institution concerned that mentors will attend initial training and follow-up briefing sessions during the student's course. In the case of the Open University, these briefing sessions take place on Saturdays – a cause of much dissent. With respect to other HE institutions, they may occur on weekdays, but this has implications for cover within the school. Thus, from a mentor's point of view, mentoring itself is a demanding occupation even when it is entered into without a full understanding of the reflective practitioner role. One would want to argue that, where the reflective practitioner role is carried out conscientiously, the time demands are even greater.

While the mentor may find the process demanding, and may be under pressures from the timetable and other commitments, as well as those of normal leisure and relaxation, the school may be motivated in the opposite direction to take on increasing numbers of students, and by definition to involve more and more people in the mentoring process. This is because there are financial incentives to be gained from accepting school-based initial teacher training students into the school. The thought of a lump sum of cash to be manipulated free of strings is one which is very appealing. And the argument can be even more compelling in the context of suitability, discussed above. A school which is looking to a significant cash injection into its budget may be less than fully selective about finding a suitable mentor and may be more motivated by the financial incentive than by the professional one. While this is probably true in only a very small minority of cases, and while HE institutions will do their best not to renegotiate contracts with schools found to fail in delivering initial teacher training effectively, the short-term

effects on individual students can be extremely distressing.

The cluster of problems associated with establishing the mentor process in school-based initial teacher education have been shown to be significant. But the list is still some way from being exhaustive. There is a second perspective on the issue of time and the demands of training for mentor activity. This is couched in terms of the quality of the preparation which is given by the HE institution in order to equip its mentors (who, as we have already seen, may not have been selected against any articulated criteria) for the arduous role which lies ahead of them.

Mentoring is a relatively new process in schools, and there is not a backlog of experience on which to draw. There is an increasing literature of mentor training (e.g. Haggar *et al.*, 1993), and some of these training opportunities have become formalized (for example, the Open University's MA module E830: Mentoring). But generally speaking, preparation for mentoring is given in a series of brief inputs by HE institutions to groups of mentors involved with their own initial teacher trainees. Given the extremely varied experiences and backgrounds of the mentors, as we have seen above, it is difficult for HE providers to know at what level to pitch this briefing and training process. For example, for teachers in primary schools there may be little or no experience of the kind of competency-based training now becoming the norm for initial trainee teachers. Equally, while secondary staff may be familiar with principles such as those in use with National Vocational Qualifications, they may be unskilled at dealing with peer-group learning. The underlying philosophy of the government, which was described in the early paragraphs of this chapter, makes the facile assumption that anyone who teaches in a classroom can by definition communicate those skills to another adult. Many (e.g. Bridges and Kerry, 1993) would challenge these assumptions. Peer-group learning requires different skills from teaching pupils in classrooms – skills which might well be acquired by teachers to enable them to work effectively as mentors, but skills which they will not necessarily have and which they have not as yet been trained for. The dilemma is this: to train effective mentors bites deep into the resources of the school in terms of time and energy, and not to train the mentors effectively condemns the initial training students to less than a fully effective experience of mentoring.

In a survey of Open University PGCE students in one region, Kerry (1994) discovered that the vast majority of students are in fact satisfied with the service which they receive from their mentors. And there is further research evidence to support this position (Rothera *et al.*, 1991; Baird, 1993). However, where a mentor failed, the failure was often quite spectacular. The following list epitomizes the characteristics of failing mentors according to the students' perceptions:

1   Failure to set aside adequate time to deal with the student's learning.
2   Poor organization, leading to a lack of learning opportunities in the school.
3   A lack of understanding of the training course itself, leading to the student's being disadvantaged in completing the activities required by the HE institution.
4   A failure to give advice, leading to the student's being unable to make progress.
5   A failure to follow up lessons, so that learning by the student was not promoted.
6   Failure to take an interest in the student, so that the student became alienated from the school and the training situation.

This issue in turn could, however, be turned on its head. Thus, a perfectly effective mentor might be unlucky enough to be assigned a student who subsequently fails. It is too early to answer with confidence the questions which will inevitably arise in this situation: about the HE institution's or the school management's perceptions of the mentor's own competence at mentoring; and about any negative effects such a 'failure' will have on the mentor's status in the school or even career prospects. In American business practice – which is probably where mentoring originated – mentoring was seen as an opportunity in a strongly corporate context for a talented manager to make a mark by bringing on a promising protégé for the good of the institution. Such a view is exemplified by Clutterbuck (1986), but it is not one which is tasteful to British susceptibilities, where a promising student is more likely to be seen as a threat than an asset.

Another significant area of debate, and one which is potentially extremely serious in its consequences, is whether or not the role of mentor should be combined with that of assessor. The arguments can be rehearsed as follows. The mentor is the person who gets to know the student better than anyone else, and is therefore in the best position to give advice to the student, to identify their strengths and weaknesses, to support them personally and psychologically during the course and to map out a ground plan for their improvement. In the process of watching the student at work, and in talking to the student in the follow-up sessions to lessons, the mentor above all will become privy to the most intimate knowledge of the student's abilities, attitudes, strengths and weaknesses. But for mentoring to succeed, all those things need to be true, and preferably to be true away from the context of assessment. Genuine trust and reliability can only be guaranteed where the person who is the object of the trust, in this case the mentor, is not part of the assessment process. Conversely, the mentor is the best-placed person to make any assessment of the student precisely because of the detailed and intimate knowledge which the mentor will have gained by the mentor process. Thus there is a Catch 22 situation here: the mentor can jeopardize a relationship with the student by being the assessor, or the student can be assessed on less than the full knowledge by some third party. This is a flaw in the system which has not been fully worked out by most validating HE institutions, who, in the end, compromise and combine the roles, at least in part.

Despite the negative tone of this chapter so far, it has to be admitted not only that there are many effective mentors mentoring initial teacher education students around the country, but also that many of those mentors take every aspect of their job seriously, prepare hard, produce effective advice to students and help students to be reflective about their own teaching. Some of those mentors carry out this role well despite the failure of HE institutions and schools to establish criteria for mentor choice, while others are selected according to what might be termed 'appropriate' criteria. The literature of mentoring is crammed with examples of good practice (e.g. Watkins and Whalley, 1993; Baird, 1993; Booth, 1993).

However, one has to take on board the Hawthorn effect. Whenever there is an innovation in education, inevitably most of the books and articles written about it are written by those involved, by those with a vested interest that it should succeed and those who are committed to the particular innovation. Mentoring may currently enjoy a good press, but it is difficult as yet to assess how much of that good press is a result of the Hawthorn effect. One would have to hypothesize that there is sufficient doubt to be cast over the process of mentoring, in the initial teacher education situation at any rate, that one might assume reasonably that time may well put a different perspective on the issue. It is, perhaps, appropriate to end this analysis of the drawbacks of mentoring in initial teacher education with the reflections of a mentee – one who had been well mentored and who nevertheless has clear-sighted views on the experience:

> My mentor was very good ... supportive, welcoming and egalitarian ... strong on subject expertise ... [But] I don't think the mentor really understood about drawing out learning ... There's a whole analytical thing here that the mentor was not fully in tune with. I feel this is the biggest single weakness in the system.

## References

Baird, J. R. (1993) A personal perspective on mentoring. In B. Caldwell and E. Carter (eds), *The Return of the Mentor: Strategies for Workplace Learning*. London: Falmer Press.

Booth, M. (1993) The effectiveness and role of the mentor in school: the students' view. *Cambridge Journal of Education*, **23** (2), 185–97.

Bridges, D. (1993) School-based teacher education. In D. Bridges and T. Kerry (eds), *Developing Teachers Professionally*. London: Routledge.

Bridges, D. and Kerry, T. (1993) *Developing Teachers Professionally*. London: Routledge.

Clutterbuck, D. (1986) Mentoring. *Industrial and Commercial Training*, November/December, 13–14.

Day, C. (1993) Reflection: a necessary but not sufficient condition for professional development. *British Educational Research Journal*, **19** (1), 83–93.

Ebbutt, D. (1985) Educational action research: some general concerns and specific quibbles. In R. Burgess (ed), *Issues in Educational Research*. Lewes: Falmer Press.

Gifford, S. (1992) Surrey new teacher competency project. *British Journal of Inservice Education*, **18** (3), 159–65.

Haggar, H., Burn, K. and McIntyre, D. (1993) *The School Mentor Handbook*. London: Kogan Page.

Handal, G. (1990) Promoting the articulation of tacit knowledge through the counselling of practitioners. Keynote paper, Amsterdam Pedagogisch Centrum, 6 to 8 April.

Kerry, T. (1994) Mentors: the new managers of initial teacher training. Motivation, effectiveness and problems. Unpublished MA dissertation, Open University.

Lunt, N., Bennett, Y., McKenzie, P. and Powell L. (1992) Understanding mentoring. *Vocational Aspect of Education*, **44** (1), 135–41.

Rothera, M., Howkins, S. and Hendry, J. (1991) The role of the subject mentor in FE. *British Journal of Inservice Education*, **17** (2), 126–37.

Schön, D. (1991) *Educating the Reflective Practitioner*. San Francisco: Jossey-Bass.

Smyth, J. (1991) *Teachers as Collaborative Learners*. Milton Keynes: Open University.

Tickle, L. (1989) On probation: preparation for professionalism. *Cambridge Journal of Education*, **19** (3), 277–86.

Watkins, C. and Whalley, C. (1993) Mentoring beginning teachers: issues for schools to anticipate and manage. *School Organization*, **13** (2), 129–38.

Whitty, G. (1992) Quality control in teacher education. *British Journal of Educational Studies*, **40** (1), 38–50.

# Response to Trevor Kerry

## ANNE MURDOCH

This response to the chapter by Trevor Kerry looks at the 11 fundamental points made about mentoring as a 'confidence trick'. It also notes the general concerns made about 'Mentoring: a positive model in teacher education and development' (Chapter 10) and attempts to reply, albeit necessarily briefly, to each of Kerry's points in turn. While the reply is based on a wish to promote the role of the mentor in schools, Kerry's chapter largely centres on a criticism of school-based initial teacher training, rather than the mentor role *per se*.

Kerry states that the underlying arguments for school-based training are themselves suspect. This argument assumes a position, based on the work of Bridges (1993), that on-site education is bad, that training is limited to the school context rather than the wider national picture and that the ideologies which support school-based education are grounded on misplaced pragmatism. There is much to support this line, but it fails to put teaching in context with other similar professions, such as nursing, social work and the legal professions. In these professions, a significant amount of 'training on the job' is seen as important to the development of professional values as well as professional competence. Indeed, Reid (1994) argues that this practical approach to initial teacher training provides 'better qualified entrants to the profession'.

Kerry also argues that school-based education limits professional vision. The basis of this argument appears to be linked to the debate that teachers in training should communicate with a wider professional community than just the school in which they are training. If this were the case then it can be argued that all initial teacher training fails

to encourage a professional vision by its very limitation to individual colleges, universities or school–college partnerships. However, as Woods (1993) states, the peaks (and troughs) within the teacher's career are the events which establish and sustain vision. These events are as likely to occur for teachers in training in schools as they are in the wider professional context.

Kerry also questions whether already qualified teachers are the most effective 'guardians' of learning from practice, and doubts whether competency-oriented, as opposed to ideologically oriented, training can provide the more effective entrance to the profession for the teacher in training. This argument again has much to support it, though it is based on an assumption that qualified and experienced teachers are not able to assist those in training to appreciate the ideological basis of education and that students only learn from those who 'train' them. The fact is, as Reid (1994) argues, that teachers in training, like any other students, learn from their own study, from experience and from role modelling, as much as from those who control access to information about ideological debate.

Another point raised by Kerry is the extent to which practitioners in schools have the skill to be reflective – a skill clearly required to mentor a trainee. This point has been raised many times in debates about mentoring, yet it is clear from research such as that of Woods (1993) and Waugh and Godfrey (1993) that if someone is deemed competent enough to teach, he or she must be competent enough to reflect on his or her own and others' practice. This is clearly where training for the role of mentor (Murdoch, Chapter 10, this volume) comes into play.

Training for the role of mentor does not, however, escape Kerry's criticism. In his own empirical research, Kerry found that the selection processes for the role of mentor are often wanting, and very rarely are appropriate criteria for the selection of mentors used. These points are no doubt major drawbacks in any mentor programme, but this is arguably more down to bad organization and planning on the part of the training programme managers than to a fundamental flaw in the mentor role. As Wiggins (1994) states, *ad hoc* arrangements leave too many students suffering the consequences of poor learning environments. In these circumstances, any training programme is only as good as those who manage and administer the processes.

A further concern raised by Kerry is the fact that financial incentives are to be gained from accepting school-based initial teacher training. This argument assumes that money, in some cases, will be diverted to the 'wrong' cause and have distressing consequences for the student. If this is the case, then undoubtedly Kerry's point is true, yet it cannot be argued that there is a direct relationship between the acceptance of money for training and the misuse of that money. It must be argued that it is the responsibility of those who administer the training contracts to ensure that any money associated with that contract, including that needed to support the mentoring process, is properly spent.

Kerry states that another problem with mentoring is when the mentor 'fails', in either the student's eyes or his or her own. This negative effect, if it occurs, cannot be anything but unsatisfactory for all concerned. However, a system which focuses on a student-centred approach to learning and development will not find the mentor or student in a situation which is likely to lead to failure because of the mentor's actions. If it does, that system places the mentor in an isolated position which is likely to lead to conflict. The positive model of mentoring ensures that the mentor, while playing a significant and pivotal role, is none the less only part of the learning experience of the student and can be replaced by mutual consent.

The mentor process, therefore, only becomes an expression of the self of the mentor if formally agreed with the mentee. It is, however, much more of a social process which facilitates development (Pollard, 1980) than a process which allows failure.

Other issues raised by Kerry concern the need to ensure that the mentor process is separated from the assessment process and also that sufficient doubt has been cast on mentoring to make it necessary to assume that there are still many issues to address with regard to initial teacher training. This cannot be doubted, and clearly the two chapters have given examples of how the system can go wrong if not managed properly. However, the essence of a positive model of mentoring is that time, resources, training, credibility and choice are available to the mentor and mentee to ensure that school-based initial teacher training is not a cheap alternative to an ideologically oriented higher education model of teacher education. In fact, as Reid (1994) has pointed out, it should be a partnership to ensure that, ultimately, those who are the best qualified enter the profession and those who are the best teachers remain in schools.

# References

Bridges, D. (1993) School-based teacher education. In D. Bridges and T. Kerry (eds), *Developing Teachers Professionally*. London: Routledge.

Pollard, A. (1980) Teacher interests and changing situations of survival threat in primary school classrooms. In P. Woods (ed.), *Teacher Strategies*. London: Croom Helm.

Reid, D. (1994) A philosophy of partnership. *Mentoring and Tutoring*, **2** (1).

Waugh, R. and Godfrey, J. (1993) Teacher receptivity to systems-wide change in the implementation stage. *British Journal of Educational Research*, **19** (5)

Wiggins, J. (1994) The conditions of work based learning. *Mentoring and Tutoring*, **2** (1).

Woods, P. (1993) Managing marginality: teacher development through grounded life history. *Mentoring and Tutoring*, **2** (1).

# 12 The Manager, the Mentor and the Marginalized Intellectual

ROGER HOMAN

## Introduction

In Eric Hoyle's conception, micropolitics consists of 'the strategies by which individuals and groups in organizational contexts seek to use their resources of authority and influence to further their interests' (Hoyle, 1982, 1986, p. 126). In his own interpretative studies of aspects of micropolitics in schools, Hoyle applies an X-ray vision to transactions between professionals. Things are not as they seem: they are seldom accidental or innocent. Those in control apply skills of which not all are aware. The basic requirement of certain forms of management is the naivety of the managed. Hoyle quotes as a keynote to his work an apocryphal conversation between two persons leaving an education committee meeting:

> *Committee member* : You didn't get your own way today, Alec!
> *Chief education officer* : You haven't read the minutes yet!
>
> (Hoyle, 1986, p. 125)

Accordingly, the basic qualification for the study of micropolitics is a suspicious mind: and it is there that the story begins.

The introduction of mentorship as a means of the supervision of students on teaching practice has profound implications for the professional role of the teacher educator. Influence, control and economic resources have passed from the higher education institutions to the schools. Tutors in the institutions who formerly made several advisory visits to their students in schools may now make two or three to each student over a period of a month or more. The function of the visit is now less advisory and tutorial, the time allowed being increasingly occupied with diplomatic liaisons and aspects of assessment. These shifts of control and changes in the nature of the tutorial role have happened at a time when teacher education has become increasingly buttoned down in terms of guidelines and consistent criteria. This has implied a diminution of the scope of professional judgement. In short, mentorship schemes have often been a painful innovation for tutors who have in the past valued the nature of the relationship with the student on school placement as a context in which to diagnose areas for personal development and to give support.

The introduction of mentorship schemes, therefore, provides a particularly observable case of innovation among a reluctant community of professionals and, in consequence, the testing of practised management techniques. This chapter is animated by a vested interest and a predisposition to conserve some of what were perceived to be the desirable features of the advisory role which obtained before mentorship gained ground.

## Methodology

The painter Beryl Cook writes of her painting *Ladies of the Watchtower* :

> I don't often paint from sheer malice but this was an exception. I grew to hate these two Jehovah's Witness campaigners who were always coming to the door and pestering me. After several reasonably polite requests not to call on me, I once again found them

there – side by side, leaflets extended. Slamming the door I vowed 'I'll get you' ... and I did!

(Cook, 1978)

Such a relationship with human subjects and subject matter is a theme of the research reported here and of the organization of data into essay form.

The data on which this chapter is based were collected by observation over a one-year period. They were not collected for the purpose of writing this chapter or for any other research purpose. That notes were made which were not directly useful for the conduct of the tutorial role was the function of a habit formed in the course of extensive observational research in other contexts and not easily discarded. Observation, once practised, serves the professional for other purposes than the collection of data. It occupies time in meetings when the business might otherwise be thought trivial; it structures and supports concentration; it is a coping strategy through periods of transaction when the business might otherwise be thought unsatisfying and through developments and innovations which would be found uncongenial. Observation is a way of distancing and dealing with experiences that have the potential of disturbing the professional but become welcome if they can be rendered as data and interpreted. Writing then becomes a cathartic process.

The meticulous collection of papers and recording of transactions was prompted by the self-interest of a disaffected party. Not only changes in local arrangements but also initiatives reported in the press had the effect of engendering on the part of some a deep-seated resistance to extrinsic interventions and on the parts of others a quiescent resignation to them: 'It's got to come.' 'I think it's only a matter of time.'

The expectations of intellectuals had included a place for rationality in policy-making, if not a personal involvement in the negotiation of decisions. During the 1980s there was an increasing tendency to signal policy intentions from the centre and to pursue these through a range of devices, including visits by inspectors and 'conferences' for senior staff. This had the effect of empowering a few with relevant knowledge and disadvantaging those who were not chosen, whose expressed views at meetings could be so easily

discredited: 'I hear what you are saying but I was at a very interesting conference last week and ...' Thereby local initiative was dissipated and the attitude of creativity gave way to a 'responsible' desire to know what was wanted by the centre, if possible with the privilege of advance notice. At management level, there was a sense of the inevitability of particular trends and an appreciation that economic controls by the centre would constitute the last word. In meetings, discussions of principle and quality were seen as at best redundant and at worst disruptive: papers were for information, not for deliberation. Debate was discouraged by the appeal to be 'businesslike', and those present were reminded of their place in the chain of decision-making: 'This paper has come down to us from senior management.' 'This really arises out of last week's HoDs' meeting.' 'Some of you will have heard what [the Dean] was saying at [faculty] board last week.' References were made to views held by senior colleagues chairing particular committees as though they were ultimate authorities, as though their opinions would in due course be affirmed as policy.

Such – at least according to this personal view – was the cultural milieu of the university as it moved into the 1990s. It is so described here not with the purpose of declaring a personal bias – though of course it has that function – but as a measure of the intellectual divide between the management and the managed.

If intellectual values were allowed to prevail, innovation would have been a more difficult or impossible course. In the institutions, as at central government level, the optimistic presentation of policies entailed the suppression of information: minutes of the meetings of managers were not available to their colleagues; more and more information was withheld from what came to be called 'the public domain'. Such debate as took place was based on selected sources. New contracts were introduced for academic staff, which made the breach of confidentiality a disciplinary offence, and there was on occasion much excitement when papers were found in photocopiers, in true Whitehall fashion.

If formerly there had been a taste for intellectual discourse and leadership in the profession, this now gave way to a mood of acquiescence. The active mind was rendered a misfit. It had been accustomed to order practice round principle. The new managerial type of personality, however, was distinguished by the willingness to receive rather than conceive, to take principles as read, to be flexible in its subscription to changing values, to deliver according to extrinsic prescriptions, to follow guidelines and submit to criteria, and to assess the worth of intentions not on moral or educational considerations but on the basis of the hierarchical position of those who initiated them or the material resources that would be likely to attach to them. This perception of a change of climate accords with an anomaly observed by other commentators upon mentorship: on the one hand the mentor's role in initial teacher training is seen as more 'politically sensitive and socially significant' than mentorship anywhere else (Monaghan and Lunt, 1992, p. 248), while on the other it is observed that 'there is almost no opposition for the principle of mentorship' (Jacques, 1992, p. 339).

Data collection was deployed as a response to the eclecticism of logical processes in the inauguration of change. It had been observed in the course of previous reforms that reasons were submitted not because they represented the intrinsic rationale of change but because they were likely to be persuasive with a particular constituency and in a specific moment. At least so it seemed to the fallible and vulnerable human memory: only comprehensive notes furnishing a full record would strengthen the hand of one who was not a manager. Anodyne and massaged minutes could not serve this purpose. So it was that the file that is the basis of this chapter came to be opened.

An ethical scruple is entered here. Had the year's observation been embarked upon not in the spirit of self-defence but with the conscious motive of research, it would have been appropriate, perhaps, to seek and inform the consent of all or selected parties, especially managers of the scheme or 'gatekeepers'. It would not be proportionate within this chapter to offer an expansive discussion of the ethics of the methods used. I have considered in a recent book (Homan, 1991, pp. 117ff) the conduct of research by retrospective analysis of routine experience, and have else-

where (Homan, 1992) challenged the righteous claim to openness in more conventional approaches. The long tradition of retrospective research includes the classic studies of the wartime experiences of Bettelheim (1943) in a concentration camp and Homans (1946) on a small warship. More recently, the illuminative work of Goffman (1971) has been achieved by observations of experiences in everyday circumstances in which the approach for consent would have been inappropriate.

There is, of course, a sense in which those who have ever done extensive observational research cannot exorcize themselves of the habit, and I have felt an affinity with those sociologists who, even when languishing in hospital beds, maintained their field books: 'Boredom suggested keeping a diary and habit and training prompted some very simple analysis' (Davis and Horobin, 1977, p. 143). The ethical problem, then, was not whether to observe and record, but whether to interpret and publish. This was much more easily conceived and resolved in terms of a moral obligation to offer an analysis of the power relations that exist in an institution of higher education, the control of information, the dominance of economic and political expedient and the marginalization of intellectual functions: these were phenomena which one felt no obligation to conceal.

It will be seen from this subjective scenario how deeply invested is the observer's perspective. The notion that changes imply a marginalization of the professional function heightens the awareness of those management skills which are used to introduce them. Others less sensitive to the implications of change for their own *modus operandi* may not recognize the account that follows: pain is a personal sensation but that does not mean that it is not real.

## Confidentiality and control

The intellectual expectation is that such discussion as occurs in the course of responding to new initiatives should have some impact upon outcomes and, even more, should be cognizant of all pertinent facts and conditions. However, both at local and at national levels, access to relevant information and research was being increasingly controlled in at least two ways. First, government departments and agencies sponsoring research have in recent years introduced clauses in research contracts claiming the ownership of data (Willmott, 1980; Boddy, 1988; Norris, 1988). Second, new conditions relating to the 1990–91 pay award to lecturers in colleges and polytechnics included clauses giving copyright status to the institutions' informal papers and restricting the use of data deemed confidential by heads of department. In the words of the advice issued in my own institution, ownership and copyright is assigned by the institution in respect of 'all records, documents and other papers pertaining to the finance and administration of the [institution] acquired by you during your employment'. Moreover,

> Confidential information must not be published or divulged other than to an authorised person. In cases of doubt about what is confidential or who is authorised, you should consult your Head of Department. Failure to adhere to this requirement may result in the appropriate disciplinary action, including dismissal, being taken.

It follows that this chapter was submitted for clearance by its author's head of department before being offered for publication in its present form. Meanwhile, some older-established universities are more relaxed about these matters than those institutions which have only recently achieved university status.

It is not difficult to speculate on the motives for the control upon the outward flow of information and the publication by researchers of their own findings. Both at government level and in the institution, the effective innovation of new arrangements depends upon a degree of faith and cooperation by the professionals affected. Acquiescence is sustainable only in conditions where early reports are favourable and significant parties well disposed. The myth that must prevail is, in Yevtushenko's phrase, 'that God's in his heaven and all's well with the world'. If central government wants to introduce city technology colleges, it cannot afford to acknowledge that anticipated

private sponsorship is not forthcoming; if it wants to empower parents over teachers through the annual school governors' meetings, it will be disinclined to publish research findings which show that parents are not turning up to these events; and if a teacher education institution is committed to introduce a mentorship scheme, it may want to secure confidential status for any data that show adverse responses by students on school placement. The consistent principle is the closure upon information that does not accord with policy intentions. There was an instance at a course board where the mentorship scheme was being reported by its manager in euphoric terms and the view of students was cited in its favour: one of the tutors then reported the experience of three students who had been ill-served by the scheme and the course leader interrupted this evidence (in the event unsuccessfully) to say that the tutor was in breach of confidentiality and the point could not be admitted. The pursuit of truth, which is an intellectual inclination, is as much concerned with data that are not released as those that are: to this extent the manager and the intellectual are not natural bedfellows.

Confidentiality, however, is in practice perceived as a one-way principle: the only direction in which colleagues disclose data at their peril is downward. There is little advertised objection to passing up to management level personal details of students which the students themselves might prefer to withhold, had they the capacity of heads of department to define what is and what is not confidential. The upward flow of personal information is encouraged, especially when there is a generalized reference in a meeting to a situation in which a student's performance in school was temporarily impaired by a domestic trauma. An example of advice that might be given is: 'It would be very helpful if you could let me have the details of that case afterwards.' This type of situation is revealing. There is in the use of the word 'afterwards' a sense that private data should not be made public: but there is also the sense of a right to know at one level what is going on at a lower level; this is not reciprocal, as the exercise of confidentiality principles demonstrates. The possession of personal information by managers enables them in due course to make public statements that may undermine the judgements and assessments of those most closely involved with the practice of the student, such as a comment like 'Yes, but there are special circumstances concerning that student which obviously I am not at liberty to reveal.'

## The hierarchy, the trump card and the *fait accompli*

Mentorship arrived on the scene of this study during a period said by its managers to be one of economic privation. The institution was having to provide for salary increases from inflexible resources and there were several aspects in which the domestic budget needed to be reviewed if ends were to be met. At the same time, schools were coming to terms with new forms of local management and were receptive to ways in which they could supplement their own resources and receive cheap or free in-service training. The cost of staff making frequent visits to schools to advise students was a heavy financial burden for the institution. To this were added the costs of hours spent advising, which might otherwise be given to teaching in the institution. The economic argument for reducing the number of visits made by tutors and paying the schools to take some or all of the responsibility for advising appealed to both institutional managers and headteachers.

In the summer of 1990 a senior member of one institution's teaching staff held meetings with school heads in each of two neighbouring local authorities. These were reported to colleagues in the institution not at the stage of planning but *post hoc*, when the outcome was represented in the form of an overwhelming demand by local headteachers. Within the institution there had been no discussion of mentorship schemes below the level of management. The first engagement of the project by those accustomed to operate as advisers was when the desire of heads to pilot mentor schemes was reported to department meetings and

course boards. If the willingness of the institution to cooperate in such a scheme had been signified at the meetings with headteachers, it could have been assured only on the basis of discussions at management level.

The familiar politician's turn of phrase was used to allay fears: 'No final decision has yet been made.' The purpose of the working party which was then set up was to 'explore' and 'pilot' a scheme, and there were appointed to it 17 persons, of whom none were students. The majority of these had been party to the initiative in its earlier stages, and new recruits were intellectually well disposed to the scheme. The pilot scheme which was devised was rationalized in terms of the desirability of a closer 'relationship' or 'partnership' with schools. In retrospect, these terms are curious, as tutors are now in schools much less than previously, but the contact of schools with the managers of the scheme is much closer: what has happened is that the relationship which always existed has been cornered by an element of the institutional management. It is not a cultural relationship but a bureaucratic partnership.

Under the pilot scheme schools were to receive payments for taking on three of the five visits or observations normally made during the course of a student's second and third school practices. In October 1990, schools received letters giving details of these arrangements for the practices which were scheduled for the spring term of 1991. In the following month these details were circulated to tutors within the institution, among whom a meeting was held. By this time the pilot scheme had been set up. It was introduced on the basis of outside pressures and the practice already adopted in other institutions.

A striking feature is the sense conveyed that the initiative is indigenous. Financial factors operating at local levels are seen to weigh heavily in its favour. Support is found in one constituency and conveyed to another. Participants are made aware of innovations in other places that have passed them by and rendered their local environment a relative backwater in educational change. But it was not a coincidence that mentorship was arriving simultaneously in many other places. Indeed, it was a directive from central government, the introduction of which needed to be thought of by those who took part in it as their own idea, or at least their own choice. The desirable way of conveying this kind of directive was to allow participating professionals what is called 'ownership'. This was particularly important in a situation in which the phrase 'knee-jerk reaction' was being widely used to draw attention to the unthinking compliance which critics of government policy felt their senior colleagues were showing towards it. When participants could not be inveigled into wishing it, they were advised of the inevitability of change: 'It has to come.'

Misgivings expressed by tutors included concern for the continuity between the students' course and their school practice. Even at this early stage it was foreseen that an element of assessment would attend school experience and that tutors would be disadvantaged in delivering an effective course if they were less involved in the observation of students' practice. These concerns, and the sense that the decision had already been taken, elicited an assurance of the experimental status of the scheme, with phrases such as: 'It's a pilot scheme and if anybody says "I don't like it", the answer is that it is only a pilot.' The paper that had been sent to schools similarly entertained the possibility that the scheme might not prove 'successful':

> It is proposed that the pilot scheme would be monitored and evaluated very thoroughly and, providing that it is successful, will be extended across the four years of the BEd degree and across the two primary PGCE courses from October 1991.

The appeal to pilot or experimental status of course proved to be a hollow assurance. Since there were prevailing pressures from the centre to introduce a mentorship scheme and resources were being redirected accordingly, the institution could hardly allow the pilot scheme to result in an evaluation that was other than favourable. This meant that all responses should be privatized, so that only the official monitor would know what the balance of opinions was. In the event, several problems were reported: the intention of collab-

orative evaluation by students and mentors on occasion gave way to unilateral reports sent to the student by post; students informed tutors that they had not been observed by class teachers and mentors, although reports had been written; some schools submitted very short and anodyne reports on students and others returned none at all; there were cases in which the placement of a student had allowed the school to send the class teacher on a course or other mission and the student was not receiving the customary advice. In a number of institutions it was felt that students were being used as free supply teachers and were in some cases giving a service but not getting one. No objective or independent summary of feedback in these circumstances could be risked. The summary given was much more optimistic and the idea that it had been an experiment was not recalled. As one administrative colleague asserted, 'I think we always knew that there would be teething problems but now we have got this far there can be no going back.'

## Division and conquest

The late stage at which the majority of tutorial staff were engaged in the consultative process and the low priority given to educational considerations were significant factors in the persistence of dissenting views. Had participating tutors been persuaded at an early stage that mentorship was an economic expedient, they would perhaps have been better disposed to work for it. In the event, their exclusion from the early stages of consultation engendered a sense of disownership and left them reluctant to comply. That the scheme was as late as November 1990 being carried forward, and only upon the explicit assurance that it was conditional upon 'success', put the onus on the scheme's managers to avoid, privatize or deny all unfavourable noises. Monitoring and evaluation had so to be conducted that there could never be seen or heard a general view that the scheme was unsatisfactory. If at any meeting a contrary voice was expressed, this needed to be isolated or coun-teracted, if not in the meeting then at least in the minutes. One strategy was to discredit or under-value those who opposed the scheme and to dig-nify and honour those who favoured it. It was not uncommon for the following remarks to be ex-pressed: 'I think we all know his view.' 'You're always going to get one or two people … ' 'In-cidentally, it was good to hear some of the very interesting things that were being said about our mentorship scheme.'

Throughout the year the communities that were party to the pilot scheme met separately. There were meetings for mentors conducted by the scheme manager or course leader, but other tutors were not invited. After the second- and third-year practices, course leaders held feedback sessions with the students on their respective courses: no other tutors were involved. Similarly, meetings of tutors were not attended by any colleagues from the schools: such was the concept of partnership in which relations were to be fostered. Tutors were told by the scheme manager that there had been feedback sessions with students at which 'one or two little niggles' had been expressed; however, they were told by students that these meetings were very lively and that serious criticisms had been made of the scheme in principle and in prac-tice. At one of the tutors' meetings there were 16 tutors present and the scheme manager dispersed those attending into three rooms 'to allow discus-sion': reports from each of these small groups were then collected in a feedback session at the end of the meeting, for which 5 minutes was allowed.

The segregation of meetings and the fragmenta-tion of groups had a number of strategic effects. So many points of view were generated that the sum-mary could not be comprehensive, allowing the scheme manager as rapporteur to select the themes and tones to be registered. The procedure left little opportunity for the emergence of opinion leaders or the generation of a common view. Dissent is not a problem if it remains private or isolated, but it threatens evaluation and monitoring procedures if it breaks through from one compartment to an-other. It is the insulation of these compartments that the code of confidentiality protects.

## Conclusion

The practice of excluding intellectual activity from the course of change comes from the top and works downward. Political resolution and eco-nomic expedient have for some time been the legitimizing principles of educational and social change. Research is commissioned and findings are cited according to convenience, but they are not allowed to embarrass policy intentions. Prime Minister John Major expressed his view of in-tellectuals in an unambiguous way when address-ing his 1992 party conference: 'The educational experts have had their say and, Mr President, they have had their day.'

## References

Bettelheim, B. (1943) Individual and mass behavior in extreme situations. *Journal of Abnormal and Social Psychology*, **38**, 417–52.

Boddy, A. (1988) *DHSS Research Contracts*. London: Society for Social Medicine.

Cook, B. (1978) *The Works*. London: John Murray/ Gallery Five.

Davis, A. and Horobin, G. (eds) (1977) *Medical En-counters: The Experience of Illness and Treatment*. London: Croom Helm.

Goffman, E. (1971) *Relations in Public: Microstudies of the Public Order*. London: Allen Lane.

Homan, R. (1991) *The Ethics of Social Research*. Harlow: Longman.

Homan, R. (1992) The ethics of open methods. *British Journal of Sociology*, **43** (3), 321–32.

Homans, G. C. (1946) The small warship. *American Sociological Review*, **11**, 294–300.

Hoyle, E. (1982) Micropolitics of educational organiza-tions. *Educational Management and Administration*, **10** (2).

Hoyle, E. (1986) *The Politics of School Management*. London: Hodder and Stoughton.

Jacques, K. (1992) Mentoring in initial teacher educa-tion. *Cambridge Journal of Education*, **22** (3), 337–50.

Monaghan, J. and Lunt, N. (1992) Mentoring: person, process, practice and problems. *British Journal of Educational Studies*, **40** (3), 248–63.

Norris, N. (1988) The contractual control of social inquiry: the terms and conditions of funded research. Paper presented at the British Educational Research Association conference, Norwich.

Willmott, P. (1980) A view from an independent research institute. In M. Cross (ed.), *Social Research and Public Policy: Three Perspectives*. London: Social Research Association.

# 13 Initial Teacher Education and the Irrelevance of Theory: Mainstream Thinking or Ideological Dogma?

## DAVE HILL AND MIKE COLE

## The political context: initial teacher education and the radical right

The context of this chapter is the British government's commitment to restructuring the education system – in schools, further education and higher education (HE), as well as teacher education. This is based upon the application of both a market ideology and what is, in effect, a centrally controlled prescriptive national curriculum (Whitty and Menter, 1989; Hill, 1990, 1993a, b, 1994a, b; Hartley, 1993; Whitty, 1993; Cole and Hill, 1995; Hill *et al.*, 1996). The justifications accompanying the policy, often expressed in rhetorical and populist terms, emphasize parental choice, specialization, diversification, efficiency, a return to basics and higher standards. The clearly stated claim is that standards are too low, and that this is caused, first, because teachers, teacher educators and the educational establishment are seen as representing producer interests which have been too dominant in the past, and, second, because of the malignant ideologies they espouse.

The emphasis on low standards and failure in the education system is a key contextual point. Across the variety of educational arenas, it is the deficient performance of practitioners which is routinely identified as the main problem. In teacher education, the context of policy development has been denigration of performance, a 'discourse of derision' (Ball, 1990; Wallace, 1994) and 'a discourse of treachery' (Hill, 1994c), accompanied by rhetoric about improving quality. There

is general disapproval of both liberal, 'child-centred' progressivism and egalitarian approaches (Cole, 1996; Hill, 1996). The radical right, in and outside of government, calls for a return to 'basic' educational values, attacks 'trendy', 'dangerous' and 'theoretical' teacher education, asserts that good teaching is mainly a matter of subject knowledge and recommends that teaching is best learned 'on the job' as a form of apprenticeship.[1]

The essence of the argument is that teacher education institutions contribute to low standards in schools and should be reformed or even abolished (Hillgate Group, 1989; Lawlor, 1990, 1992; O'Hear, 1988, 1993). Hence, since 1989, there has been a proliferation of new routes into teaching and a clear preference stated for school-based 'teacher training' (Hill, 1989, 1990, 1991a, 1994b).

The agenda has been taken up by government. The 1988 version of *The New Teacher in School* (HMI, 1988) (which, in 1987, surveyed the performance of 300 newly qualified teachers (NQTs), both undergraduate and postgraduate trained) was said to have 'disturbed' the then Secretary of State, Kenneth Baker (*The Times*, 1988). Margaret Thatcher's disquiet at initial teacher education (ITE), expressed in her memoirs, was made clear to Baker (Thatcher, 1994, pp. 597–8). The subsequent 1989 requirements for ITE courses demanded by Circular 24/89 of the (government appointed) Council for Accreditation of Teacher Education (CATE) were intended to meet such criticisms of ITE courses, but, apparently, did not go far enough in focusing ITE more exclusively on the 'delivery' of the National Curriculum for schools, in particular the Core Curriculum basics.

At the North of England Education Conference in January 1992, the Secretary of State for Education at the time, Kenneth Clarke, asserted that much college-based work was irrelevant; that college-based training was offering inappropriate models of teaching; that colleges were remote from the real world of the classroom and that they peddled dogmas about methods and organization (Clarke, 1992, para. 2.1). These allegations originate in, and have been repetitively promulgated by, radical right-wing ideologues.

At the 1992 Conservative Party Annual Conference both John Major and Secretary of State for Education John Patten launched scathing attacks on ITE. In Major's words:

> I also want reform of teacher training. Let us return to basic subject teaching, not courses in the theory of education. Primary teachers should learn to teach children to read, not waste their time on the politics of gender, race and class.
>
> (quoted in Chitty and Simon, 1993, p. 144)

In September 1993 the government presented its proposals for the reform of primary ITE as part of a consultation process (DFE, 1993a). The central justification for the reform proposals was the criticism of the performance of new teachers said to be drawn from *The New Teacher in School* (OFSTED, 1993a).

School basing of ITE, and the accompanying reduction in time for 'education studies' courses and theoretical analysis, has been substantially implemented as a result of Department for Education Circulars 9/92 and 13/93 (DFE, 1992, 1993b). At the time of writing (July 1996) this policy is continuing, with proposals for further prescriptions for the primary ITE curriculum.

# Initial teacher education and the educational community

Are the radical right/government views representative of mainstream thinking? Available evidence suggests otherwise. Notwithstanding the utterings of those few individuals who openly identify themselves with radical right thinking, there appears to be a general distancing from such views by headteachers and by the Inspectorate. In addition, there is negligible support from teacher educators (but see, for example, David Hargreaves in many works). Finally, and perhaps most significantly, neither NQTs nor student teachers seem to associate themselves with the radical right position.[2]

While all of these groups have some criticisms of the current and recent state of ITE, there is very widespread agreement that both theory and practice need to be retained in ITE and that ITE courses validated under the CATE criteria of 1989, prior to the revisions of 1992 and 1993, were working well.

## Headteacher opinion surveys

Do headteachers think there is too much theory and too much college-basing on the BEd and PGCE courses? Do they think there is too little time in schools?

Between them the Hill (1993a, b) and Blake and Hill (1995), Carrington and Tymms (1993) and Standing Conference of Principals (SCOP) (1994) surveys received the responses of 1737 headteachers. While some headteachers may have been included in more than one survey, the cumulative response, from across the country, covering, respectively, 95, 440 and 1202 respondents, out of a total of 25,000 headteachers in England and Wales, is clearly important.

*Two local surveys of headteacher opinions*
In spring 1992, 95 West Sussex and Hampshire headteachers (of whom 80 were primary) responded to a postal questionnaire sent out following the announcement by Kenneth Clarke of proposals for basing secondary ITE in schools.

Of the 80 primary headteachers, only 12 were favourable to basing ITE on an apprenticeship scheme. Some respondents called the idea 'laughable', and thought it would 'deprofessionalize the profession' and 'lower the intellectual calibre of teachers' (Hill, 1993a).

Not one of the 80 primary heads dissented from the view that 'teachers in training need educational theory as well as practice'. Typical comments were that 'the teaching profession only maintains high standards and full understanding with a solid theoretical background', 'educational theory is a form of evaluation of current practice and needs to continue', 'practical training should be placed in a theoretical context', 'colleges/ universities can more effectively than schools provide foundations in psychology, sociology, child development and the political contexts and aspects of schooling and education' (*ibid.*).

Only 7 per cent of primary heads described the quality of primary BEd students when in school as 'not very good' or 'poor'. There was a similar low rate of dissatisfaction with secondary BEd and secondary PGCE students, though the number rose to a 30 per cent dissatisfaction rate for students on primary PGCE courses.

In June 1993, 51 primary headteachers responded to an identical questionnaire sent at the time of the Patten–Blatch proposal for basing primary ITE in schools. The results are remarkable and similar to those of the previous year's survey.

Thirty headteachers wrote comments on teacher apprenticeship training, the role of theory and the role of colleges. Twenty-seven headteachers were strongly opposed to apprenticeship-style training, using such phrases as 'attack on the teaching profession', 'typical lack of government thinking', 'it assumes all teachers are capable', 'would produce a narrow and pragmatic workforce', 'the children would suffer', 'essential to maintain breadth of training – students need time for their own intellectual subject development, as well as philosophy of education.'

Forty-two headteachers wrote comments supporting the view that teachers in training need educational theory as well as practice. Not one headteacher disagreed. Sample comments include: 'students need awareness of theory to reduce becoming puppets of state "propaganda"', 'theory forms a basis for new teachers' philosophy', 'theory helps make students deeper thinkers on educa-

tional issues', 'which other profession would be expected to train "on the job"?', 'theory and practice are inseparable; otherwise there will be lower standards and shallowly trained teachers – as in private schools'.

### The 1993 Carrington and Tymms survey

An overwhelming majority of 440 primary headteachers surveyed by Carrington and Tymms for the National Union of Teachers rejected the then Secretary of State for Education, John Patten's, 'Mum's Army' proposals for a non-graduate one-year totally school-based training route for infant (Key Stage 1) teachers.

The research also highlighted disquiet about other aspects of Mr Patten's consultation document on primary training. The heads were critical of the government's attempts to give schools the main responsibility for training teachers. Only 11 per cent thought that more than 50 per cent of primary training should be based in schools, and only 6 per cent of heads were not satisfied with the quality of trainee teachers they were already receiving (Carrington and Tymms, 1993; Pyke, 1993a).

### The 1994 SCOP survey

The Standing Conference of Directors and Principals of Colleges and Institutes of Higher Education (SCOP) surveyed 1202 primary headteachers in England and Wales. SCOP showed that an overwhelming number have strong reservations about accepting a major share of the responsibility for the training of teachers.

The questionnaire asked headteachers if they would wish to take a major, equal or minor responsibility (in partnership with the higher education institutions) for the various aspects of teacher training. The only areas in which headteachers preferred a major responsibility were in guiding and supervising students within the school and in assessing the students' professional competencies – areas in which they already undertook a major role.

Only 12 headteachers (1 per cent) wanted to take the major share of responsibility for the intellectual and pedagogical development of the trainee teacher; 1038 (86 per cent) favoured only a minor responsibility in providing student welfare support; 900 (75 per cent) wanted a minimal involvement in course design; 840 (70 per cent) preferred a minimal involvement in monitoring the quality of course provision. More than 70 per cent expressed a preference for a shared or major responsibility in developing the students' competence in curriculum content, planning and assessment.

Fewer than 25 per cent wanted a share of major responsibility in improving the students' subject knowledge in relation to the curriculum in primary schools.

The results from these various surveys of headteachers show overwhelming opposition to major aspects of the restructuring of ITE post 1989.

## HMI and OFSTED opinions

Do HMI and OFSTED think there is too much theory and too much college basing on BEd and PGCE courses? Do they think there is too little time in schools? The 1988 HMI Report, *The New Teacher in School*, did not see much of a problem with NQTs – their classroom performance was judged to be about the same as that of more experienced teachers. Moreover, those NQTs from BEd and PGCE courses had been virtually unaffected by the CATE 1984 and CATE 1989 improvements to ITE courses – improvements such as regular classroom teaching 'refreshers' for ITE 'professional/curriculum studies' and 'education studies' lecturers. As stated above, in some respects, the 1993 OFSTED report gave a cleaner bill of health to ITE courses, and to 'education studies' components, than did the 1988 report. Similarly the OFSTED report, *The Secondary PGCE in Universities 1991–92*, reported that 45 of 48 subject courses seen were good (16 courses) or satisfactory (29 courses) (OFSTED, 1993b).

Since the introduction of licensed and articled teacher schemes, various types of school-based ITE have also been criticized in official reports (DENI, 1991; HMI, 1991; NFER, 1991), in the wide-ranging topology of ITE, in the Modes of Teacher Education (MOTE) Interim Report (Barrett *et al.*, 1992) and in evaluative reviews (such as Jacques, 1991).

These reports have criticized school-based models of ITE on grounds of lack of consultation with teachers, lack of teacher education about the nature of the school–college partnership and who does what best, the general unpreparedness of schools to take the lead in ITE, and the general limitations of school-based training. Writing with other members of the Hillcole Group, we have summarized these as follows:

> Evaluative evidence of the current school-based training has pointed out weaknesses that need to be remedied. Where schools have taken a major role in the professional aspects of training (i.e. the Articled Teacher Scheme), evaluation reports have shown some serious limitations both in terms of resources and expertise in training postgraduate students. Articled Teachers themselves expressed a strong wish to spend more time at college at the onset of the course.
>
> Trainees on this route develop a dependency culture and, in comparison with postgraduate trainees on the normal route, are more anxiety-prone. We disregard to our cost the immense amount of peer group support and the value of shared experience that takes place in the normal route, but which is denied to those on the heavily school-based training programmes.
>
> (Hillcole Group, 1993, pp. 10–11)

## The views of teacher educators

While many teacher educators were relatively unforthcoming over the licensed and articled teachers schemes on their introduction in 1989, they commented numerously and vociferously in reaction to both the 1992 DES criteria for secondary ITE courses, Circular 9/92 (DFE, 1992)(e.g. Bennett, 1992; Bines, 1992; Elliott, 1992; Gilroy, 1992; the 'letters pages' in the *Times Educational Supplement*, February to April 1992) and the 1993 Circular 14/93 (DFE, 1993b) criteria for primary ITE, and its preceding consultation documents. These included the subsequently dropped proposals for a 'Mum's Army'. Notwithstanding support from right-wing sources, this 'Mum's Army' scheme was almost universally criticized by teachers as well as by teacher educators, by the Labour Party and the Liberal Democrats, and by parents and governors organizations, as well as being savaged in the House of Lords on a cross-party basis (e.g. Hill, 1992a, b, 1994a; PCET, 1992, 1993; Abbott *et al.*, 1993; Association of Metropolitan Authorities, 1993; Barber, 1993a; Campaign for the Defence of Teacher Education, 1993; Labour Party, 1993; McLure, 1993; NAHT, 1993; NUT, 1993a, b; Pyke, 1993a, b, c; Santinelli, 1993; UCET, 1993; and the 'letters pages' of the *Times Educational Supplement*, June to July 1993).

General opposition to government plans for ITE has been expressed in academic journals (e.g. Gilroy, 1992; Whitty, 1992); in journalistic articles (Barber, 1993b; Wragg, 1993; Price, 1994); at conferences such as those of the British Educational Research Association (BERA); through the Universities' Council for the Education of Teachers (UCET) and the Polytechnics' Council for the Education of Teachers (PCET). It has also been expressed by organizations such as the Labour Party (1991, 1993, 1994) and the Institute for Public Policy Research (IPPR) (Barber and Brighouse, 1992; IPPR, 1993). Radical left groups have added to this opposition and critique (e.g. Hillcole Group, 1991, 1993, 1996).

## The views of newly qualified teachers

The evidence presented here derives from both official reports (HMI, 1988; OFSTED, 1993a) and our own surveys (Hill, 1993a; b; Blake and Hill, 1995).

### The New Teacher in School *reports of 1988 and 1993*

Newly qualified teachers' evaluation of their ITE courses in the 1988 report showed that half the sample thought too much time was spent on courses in education studies: 'Substantial propor-

tions of new teachers felt that education studies had received too much emphasis while the more practical aspects such as teaching method, classroom observation and teaching practice had received too little' (HMI, 1988, p. 4). In the 1993 Report, however, NQTs were satisfied that the range of their previous teaching experiences had prepared them suitably for their first post. Eighty-nine per cent of the new teachers considered that their 'training' had been a positive experience, which adequately prepared them for their first post. A high proportion (69 per cent secondary and 61 per cent primary) considered their training 'good' or 'very good'. Only 9 per cent of secondary and 13 per cent of primary teachers described this training as 'unsatisfactory' or 'poor'. A major difference, as compared to the 1988 report, is the higher rating for the 'education studies' components of courses.

The government's 'news management' of the findings of this 1993 OFSTED report was significant. The report's findings were presented in a highly selective way and used to justify subsequent government claims that one-third of lessons taken by new entrants to teaching were unsatisfactory (DFE, 1993a). The report itself, however, stated: 'The teaching of the 300 new teachers seen in England and Wales was at least satisfactory in almost three-quarters of cases. This proportion closely matches that of teachers in general' (OFSTED, 1993a, p. 8). The report did not indicate that ITE was failing its students. Nine out of ten new teachers regarded their training positively (see Blake and Hill, 1995).

However, within this global total differences between the views of one-year trained PGCE NQTs and the views of four-year trained BEd/BA (QTS) NQTs are apparent. Primary BEd 'trained' NQTs were far more satisfied with their 'training' (with 74 per cent expressing themselves 'very satisfied' or 'quite satisfied' with their ITE course) than PGCE trained NQTs. Only 44 per cent of these expressed themselves as 'very satisfied' or 'quite satisfied' with their ITE course. Only 8 per cent of BEd 'trained' NQTs were 'less than satisfied' with their 'training', compared with 20 per cent of PGCE trained NQTs.

As far as the college-based elements of their courses were concerned, NQTs were well satisfied, with two-thirds of them finding 'education studies' useful. This is in marked contrast to the view in the 1988 report that excessive weight had been given to this element. There was a widely shared view that college courses were well coordinated, with individual components relating well to each other. Links between college and work in school were considered to be well established. However, it should be pointed out that a number of the aspects of higher levels of satisfaction may be due to the changes in ITE courses implemented in accordance with the 1989 CATE criteria.

The new teachers valued their school experience very much. They praised the excellent preparation and support received from both college and school, valued having taught a range of classes in different school settings and were appreciative of opportunities to observe experienced teachers. New teachers were well satisfied by the quality of college supervision, though secondary teachers more so than primary (72 per cent of secondary teachers graded supervision 1 or 2 compared with 59 per cent of primary).

Overall, although primary BEd trained NQTs rated their ITE courses much more highly than did primary PGCE trained NQTs, the NQTs surveyed by OFSTED during 1992 showed clearly that they were, in general, satisfied with their ITE courses.

*Unofficial surveys of NQTs*
Hill (1993b) and Blake and Hill (1995) present data on 355 undergraduate and postgraduate NQTs who graduated or certificated in summer 1990, 1991 or 1992. These findings were gained from postal questionnaire surveys carried out during the NQTs' second term of teaching in 1991, 1992 and 1993. This number of respondents is larger than that presented by OFSTED in *The New Teacher in School* report (OFSTED, 1993a), though the balance between course types is different and the breadth of selection of colleges is narrower.

Very broadly, the results of this unofficial survey are similar to those found by OFSTED (1993a). Detailed responses from the 355 NQTs are pre-

sented in tabular form later in the chapter alongside data for student teachers.

## Survey of student teachers

### Introduction
This survey of student teachers from three institutions and one off-site outpost was carried out in spring 1994 at the time of the controversy surrounding ITE, school basing and the role of theory in ITE in connection with the Education Bill/Act of 1994. The institutions are all in the south of England.

### Methodology
The questionnaire we are reporting on here used the questions of the 1988 HMI *New Teacher in School* survey, with extra questions added (see Hill, 1993b; Blake and Hill, 1995).

There are a number of problems with the methodology. First, the size of the 1994 sample of student teachers breaks down into relatively small groups. The same is also true of the OFSTED (1993a), the Hill (1993b) and the Blake and Hill (1995) NQT surveys. The respective numbers are 185 in our survey, 300 NQTs in the OFSTED 1993 report and 355 NQTs in the Hill (1993a, b) and Blake and Hill (1995) surveys. The result is that some of the material presented in percentage form rests upon very small numbers of respondents in some categories. The OFSTED report, too, acknowledged that sample sizes are small in some cases (OFSTED, 1993a, para. 4.20).

Second, the new teachers' assessment of aspects of their training was determined by self-complete questionnaires, inviting responses on a 1 to 5 satisfaction rating against a list of categories. The problems are those of validity of the selected items, their match to the particular course elements undertaken by students, the possible exclusion of significant additional items, possible factors influencing responses at a given moment in time and the robustness of a self-reporting five-point scale. In the OFSTED report, for example, it is acknowledged that 'while individual views can be reported accurately, these are essentially per- ceptions which may or may not be an accurate reflection of the nature or quality of the matters about which the views were expressed' (OFSTED, 1993a, Appendix 1, para. A1.6). This same criti- cism may be made of our survey. While we do not believe in uncritical acceptance of 'voice' (see Cole and Hill, 1996), be it student or any other, we do consider that voices should be heard.

Finally, there is the problem of drawing too confident a set of conclusions about the effective- ness of an ITE system on the basis of a sample from four institutions. In the OFSTED report of 1993, there is no indication which courses of training are represented in the report, or how wide is the vari- ety of responses between and within institutions. As we have noted elsewhere, the use of the blanket category of BEd and PGCE conceals huge varia- tions of practice, which more local studies could investigate with benefit (Blake and Hill, 1995).

In our survey, the institutions remain an- onymous. The undergraduate courses may or may not be representative of such courses nationally, and their student intakes may or may not be sim- ilar to national intakes. However, we have no reason to believe, from our participation in the wider national teacher education community, that the courses or the student intakes vary markedly from courses nationally.[3]

Furthermore, there are differences within each primary course (for example, between primary lower years (or first school) and primary upper years (or middle school)) and within each second- ary course (for example, between the different main subjects). However, some evaluative conclu- sions about particular courses could be made in a follow-up study using a methodology of curri- culum analysis and student and staff interviews, together with quantitative data such as are pre- sented here. Additional local reports, such as this student teacher survey, can serve to minimize these methodological problems by building a big- ger database drawn from a wider variety and num- ber of institutions.

Another problem with our survey is the weight- ing given to the responses from one of the three institutions surveyed, Institution A, which pro- vided 98 responses. The off-site outpost B pro-

vided 17 responses, Institution C 43 and Institu- tion D 27.

### The questions

The questions in the student teacher survey (and in the Hill NQT surveys) replicate those used in the *The New Teacher in School* reports of 1982 and 1988. The 1993 OFSTED report asked fewer questions.

The Hill NQT survey, the Blake and Hill survey and this student teacher survey asked additional questions in recognition of the limited nature of the HMI and OFSTED questions. These limita- tions, even more apparent in the 1993 report, chiefly concern questions of social justice, of 'crit- ical reflection' (Zeichner and Liston, 1987; Adler, 1991; Hill, 1991a, b, 1992b, 1994b; see also Chap- ter 17, this volume) and of the weight given in ITE courses to issues of anti-racism, anti-sexism, anti- classism and critical theory ('critiquing the rela- tionship between teachers, schools and society'). Questions were also inserted on whether courses had facilitated discussion on such issues as 'the teacher as a political or as a non-political class- room practitioner', critical evaluation of current practice and developments in education, demo- cratic participative pedagogy, teachers as political activists and teachers as 'transformative intellec- tuals' engaged in transforming children's views of society.

These questions were added since they are par- ticular foci of criticism of ITE and of schooling by government and by radical right 'think tanks', po- lemicists and politicians (Hillgate Group, 1986, 1987, 1989; O'Keeffe, 1986, 1990a, b; O'Hear, 1988, 1991, 1993; Lawlor, 1990, 1992; Major and Patten, quoted in Chitty and Simon, 1993).

The Hill, and Hill and Blake, surveys of NQTs and our survey of student teachers contain two types of questions, as in the OFSTED and HMI surveys.

1   The first type asked respondents to rank course elements or aspects on a five-point scale.
2   The second type of question asked respond- ents to evaluate the balance of various dimen- sions within their courses.

Elsewhere (Hill, 1993b; Blake and Hill, 1995) we have identified problems associated with the two types of questions in the OFSTED and Hill surveys of NQTs. The rating of 'how well prepared' NQTs felt by their ITE courses (e.g. 'well prepared to teach socially deprived children' [*sic*], 'well prepared to teach mixed ability groups', 'well prepared to promote equal opportunities for boys and girls') will have been answered in relation to ex-students' and NQTs' opinions of how important, or how pressing, they felt their individual needs were in the light of their present circumstances, after about a term of teaching. For example, if an NQT is not engaged in teaching mixed-ability classes, then there are no pressures on him or her in this respect and he or she might well feel adequately prepared through the ITE course. On the other hand, an individual NQT respondent might be placed in a school where the issue is prominent in the school's or his/her own class(es)' agenda, demanding considerable response, expertise and commitment. Faced with a considerable pressure, such a respondent might feel that he or she has been inadequately prepared.

Contemporary government and media pressure ('back to basics', 'back to formal reading methods') might raise the profile of various aspects of and styles of preparation for teaching, causing NQT anxiety and dissatisfaction with one or more aspects of their ITE courses. Similar considerations might apply to the second type of question. For example, changes in the wider educational climate in the late 1980s and early 1990s evidenced a shift from Plowdenite progressivism as a dominant discourse in primary education, towards an official delegitimation of child-centredness, relevance[4] and an integrated curriculum towards a more traditional model of teaching. This *might* serve to suggest to NQTs that they had rather too much 'theory', too much 'egalitarianism' in their ITE courses and too little emphasis on 'teaching methods'.

Having raised these various methodological problems, we feel that a clear strength of our survey is the large-scale response, which irons out and averages individual respondent peculiarities and particularities. Furthermore, we consider that our quantitative survey is given depth by the

**Table 13.1** Degrees of satisfaction by student teachers and by NQTs (percentages well satisfied, satisfied and moderately satisfied for each area)

| | Student teachers | NQTs (undergrad. trained) |
|---|---|---|
| The promotion of equal opportunities for boys and girls | 92 | (96) |
| The planning of a programme of work over a period of time | 87 | (89) |
| Teaching mixed-ability groups | 88 | (88) |
| Assessing the effectiveness of (their) own teaching | 79 | (84) |
| Classroom management | 77 | (78) |
| Understanding the place of their main subject in the whole curriculum | 94 | (75) |

breadth, range and number of questions answered.

*Data presentation: the views of student teachers*
What do student teachers actually think? Do they think there is too much theory and too much college basing on their BEd/BA (QTS) courses? Do they think there is too little time in schools? Do they think their courses are too 'political'? In the presentation of results in Tables 13.1 to 13.5, data from the Hill (1993b) NQT survey are set out in parentheses alongside the main body of data.[5]

Of the 34 ITE course aspects surveyed, the highest levels of satisfaction ('well satisfied', 'satisfied' and 'moderately satisfied') were as shown in Table 13.1.

*Results: degrees of satisfaction with the balance and emphasis of 21 aspects within ITE courses*
Were their courses dominated by political or educational dogma? Was there too much emphasis on anti-racism and equal-opportunities issues in general? The results of this part of the survey are remarkable.

There were very high levels of teacher satisfaction with the emphases on education studies and theory (see Table 13.2) and with a range of con-

**Table 13.2**   Balance of courses (percentage results)

| Emphasis on | Much too much | | Acceptable/right amount | | Much too little | |
|---|---|---|---|---|---|---|
| | Students | (NQTs) | Students | (NQTs) | Students | (NQTs) |
| Education studies | 3 | (5) | 67 | (63) | 0 | (2) |
| Theory | 3 | (8) | 64 | (55) | 3 | (3) |
| Critique of the current education system | 1 | (1) | 62 | (59) | 7 | (6) |
| Child development | 1 | (2) | 58 | (55) | 10 | (9) |

**Table 13.3**   Level of preparation (percentage responses)

| | Very well or well prepared | | Acceptably prepared | | Not very well or poorly prepared | |
|---|---|---|---|---|---|---|
| Teach children with special educational needs in ordinary schools | 30 | (30) | 27 | (32) | 43 | (39) |
| Liaise with community | 29 | (23) | 33 | (29) | 39 | (48) |
| Teach pupils for public examinations (secondary only) | 22 | (12) | 11 | (18) | 66 | (70) |
| Perform administrative duties | 23 | (16) | 34 | (22) | 43 | (62) |

textual and political issues covered, such as anti-racism, anti-sexism, social egalitarianism, the critical evaluation of the relationships between teachers, schools and society and the critical analysis of current practices and developments in education (see Table 13.2).

The lowest levels of satisfaction are set out in Table 13.3. The figures presented relate to those respondents who felt 'less than satisfied' or 'dissatisfied' with aspects of their courses. The four aspects of teaching which respondents felt least well prepared for were teaching children with special educational needs in ordinary (mainstream)

**Table 13.4**   Balance of courses (percentage responses)

| Emphasis on | Much too much | | Acceptable/right amount | | Much too little | |
|---|---|---|---|---|---|---|
| | Students | (NQTs) | Students | (NQTs) | Students | (NQTs) |
| Special needs | 1 | (0) | 31 | (31) | 18 | (30) |
| Information technology | 1 | (1) | 27 | (31) | 34 | (28) |
| Teaching practice | 2 | (0) | 43 | (45) | 17 | (23) |
| Teaching methods | 1 | (1) | 49 | (56) | 10 | (8) |
| School–college links | 0 | (1) | 49 | (48) | 14 | (17) |
| Child development | 1 | (2) | 58 | (55) | 10 | (9) |

schools, liaising with the community, teaching pupils for public examinations (this question applied to secondary teachers only) and performing administrative duties.

The second type of question used to elicit degrees of course satisfaction is the type of question about 'balance of courses'. Of the 21 aspects tested for 'balance' or 'amount within the ITE course', the following aspects were among those viewed as having too little emphasis: special needs, information technology, teaching practice, teaching methods, school–college links and child development (see Table 13.4).

The data in Table 13.5 indicate that student teachers (and NQTs) demand or would like more, rather than fewer, 'political', 'egalitarian' and 'contextual' courses – precisely those aspects of ITE which have been emasculated by the latest government sets of criteria for ITE, Circulars 9/92 and 14/93.

## Conclusion

In instituting this student teacher comparative survey, we were very aware of student teacher (and NQT) objection to what is widely felt by them to be the patronizing government view that they are likely to be duped and indoctrinated by left-

**Table 13.5** Balance of courses and contextual/political issues (percentage responses)

| Emphasis on | Much too much | | Acceptable/right amount | | Much too little | |
|---|---|---|---|---|---|---|
| | Students | (NQTs) | Students | (NQTs) | Students | (NQTs) |
| Democratic education | 1 | (1) | 64 | (56) | 8 | (6) |
| Critiquing the current education system | 1 | (1) | 62 | (59) | 7 | (6) |
| Anti-racism | 3 | (11) | 53 | (58) | 14 | (3) |
| Anti-sexism | 4 | (11) | 56 | (62) | 11 | (3) |
| Egalitarianism | 2 | (5) | 57 | (58) | 9 | (6) |
| Critical theory (critiquing the relationship between teachers, schools and society) | 2 | (6) | 54 | (51) | 8 | (3) |
| Becoming a teacher who is a 'transformative intellectual' (wishing to transform children's view of society) | 1 | (4) | 69 | (67) | 7 | (3) |
| Theory | 3 | (7) | 64 | (53) | 3 | (3) |
| Teacher as a political activist | 4 | (10) | 56 | (53) | 9 | (4) |

wing and/or liberal progressive teacher educators. Many students – and many NQTs – are bewildered that the radical right has what appears to them to be a nonsensical stranglehold on ITE policy (and indeed on education policy in general). In a sense, therefore, we are carrying out and reporting this research on behalf of ITE students and NQTs.

The student teacher (and NQT) responses indicate a substantial degree of support for courses as constituted prior to the school-basing Circulars 9/92 and 14/93. They also point to concerns, although they indicate a need for the modification of courses as structured prior to 1992–93, rather than the wholesale restructuring being undertaken by the Conservative government.

Even within the limited terms of the questions asked of student teachers (and, indeed, of NQTs), some improvements in courses validated under the 1989 CATE criteria are clearly required. Our report on student teachers, like those on NQTs (such as the 1993 OFSTED *New Teacher in School* report), indicate the areas of the teacher education curriculum where NQTs consider that improvements are necessary. These include preparation for the teaching of reading, teaching the foundation subjects, assessing pupils' work and planning for differentiation. These last two are areas where experienced teachers also have difficulties (Blake and Hill, 1995).

Hence, prior to the 1992 and 1993 criteria, there were already moves on various courses to increase the number of days spent in school beyond the requirements of CATE (DES, 1989). These are reported by the Modes of Teacher Education project report of 1992 (Barrett *et al.*, 1992).

However, the data reported in this chapter do not indicate student teacher or NQT dissatisfaction with college-based courses in education studies. In general, student teachers find themselves satisfied with the elements contained in their ITE courses and the balance between different course elements. In this, their responses are very similar indeed to those of NQTs.

The above data lead us to the following conclusion. While there is critical evaluation of ITE courses, there is no widespread dissatisfaction with theoretical aspects or aspects which deal with equal opportunities or with education components. On the contrary, the BEd/BA (QTS) trainee teachers surveyed in the studies reported here – and the NQTs, headteachers and teacher educators – are generally well satisfied with these aspects of teacher education courses. If anything, they show a desire for *more* courses dealing with equality issues rather than fewer.

From the available evidence it seems that the radical right is virtually alone in its view that ITE is too theoretical, too liberal and/or too egalitarian, and that it should be divorced from higher education. All of the empirical evidence presented in this chapter shares a general consensus with the schooling and teacher education communities, one of overwhelming opposition to the salient detheorizing and school-basing aspects of government policy.

We believe that the student teacher survey analysed in this chapter highlights student teacher demand for BEd/BA (QTS) courses not only to develop certain of the technical skills of teaching, but also to develop an understanding of equality and equal-opportunities issues and their relevance to and importance for educational theory and practice. This necessitates space in the ITE curriculum for these issues to be discussed and developed, not the constriction of such opportunities that is apparently one of the major aims and effects of Conservative policy on ITE.

Suggestions as to what might constitute a radical left, critically reflective ITE curriculum which takes full cognizance of equality and equal-opportunities issues are set out in 'Critical reflection in initial teacher education', Chapter 17 in this volume (see also Cole *et al.*, 1996; Hill, 1991a, 1994d; Hill *et al.*, 1996).

## Notes

We thank Ian Clemence for programming the questionnaire data, Naomi Hill for inputting them, Imelda Gardiner for her collaboration and Pat Ainley for his helpful comments.

1  For this reason, competency-based approaches, already in place in further education and in youth service training, are now being implemented in ITE through Circulars 9/92 and 14/93. In this way, learning is apparently reduced to the acquisition of a set of primarily technical competencies.

2  The views of parents on changes in ITE have been little researched. However, one example of parental opposition to the changes was the Exeter University survey of 250 Devon school governors, teachers and parents, 96 per cent of whom opposed the move to schools taking over responsibility for teacher education. Two-thirds of the respondents to the project, set up to examine the public view of government ITE reforms,

stated that student teachers need two or three months in college before they are ready to take charge of a class of children, even under supervision. The survey also found strong opposition to any plan to reduce the four-year BEd to three, largely because of the risk to standards. However, half supported an extension of the school-based element (of undergraduate ITE courses) to over one year, provided the overall course length was not cut. With respect to postgraduate ITE courses, two-thirds of respondents opposed students' spending more than half their PGCE course in schools. This was because there would then be too little time for main subject study, learning about education and discipline and learning how to teach a second subject. The respondents' view was that these areas cannot be adequately covered in 12 weeks as intended by the government (*Times Higher Education Supplement*, 31 July 1992). It is not clear, though, how many of the 250 respondents to this survey were parents, and whether or not their responses differed markedly from those of other groups of respondents. This survey does, however, demonstrate nearly unanimous opposition to schools taking over responsibility for teacher education.

3  One exception is a primary BEd course for 'mature and non-standard entry students', which publicly claimed to be aiming at the development of 'critically reflective teachers'. While there was a more than 50 per cent response rate from members of this course, at 17 respondents this will not have skewed the overall pattern of the 185 student teacher responses.

4  Whereas 'relevance' in the 1960s and 1970s related to children's interests and to an education serving *all* children, not just the children of the middle class, it has shifted so that it now refers to relevance with respect to the (so-called) needs of industry.

5  The Hill survey NQT data published thus far do not differentiate between undergraduate and postgraduate trained teachers. Neither, in their published data, do the HMI (1982, 1988) and OFSTED (1993a) reports, whereas Hill (1993b) provides raw data to facilitate such a distinction and thereby enable a comparison to be made

with the undergraduate student teacher responses.

# References

Abbott, L. *et al.* (1993) *Articled Teachers Respond to the Government Proposals to End the All-Graduate Status of the Teaching Profession.* Manchester: Manchester Metropolitan University.

Adler, S. (1991) The reflective practitioner and the curriculum in teacher education. *Journal of Education for Teaching,* **17** (2).

Association of Metropolitan Authorities (1993) Letter on early learning enquiry: teacher training to Sir Christopher Ball. London: AMA.

Ball, S. (1990) *Politics and Policy Making in Education.* London: Routledge.

Barber, M. (1993a) Till death us do part. *Times Educational Supplement,* 28 May.

Barber, M. (1993b) Reform by envelope. *Journal of Education,* 2 July.

Barber, M. and Brighouse, T. (1992) *Partners in Change: Enhancing the Teaching Profession.* London: IPPR.

Barrett, E. *et al.* (1992) *Initial Teacher Education in England and Wales: A Topography.* London: Goldsmiths' College.

Bennett, N. (1992) Never mind the sophistry: primary schools must absorb reform before they are ready to train new teachers. *Times Educational Supplement,* 14 February.

Bines, H. (1992) Quality or survival? The consultation document on the reform of initial teacher training for secondary education. *Journal of Education Policy,* **7** (5).

Blake, D. and Hill, D. (1995) The newly qualified teacher in school. *Research Papers in Education,* **10** (3).

Campaign for the Defence of Teacher Education (1993) *Crisis in Teacher Education.* Birmingham: CDTE.

Carrington, B. and Tymms, P. (1993) *For Primary Heads, Mum's Not the Word.* Newcastle: School of Education, University of Newcastle upon Tyne.

Chitty, C. and Simon, B. (eds) (1993) *Education Answers Back: Critical Responses to Government Policy.* London: Lawrence and Wishart.

Clarke, K. (1992) Speech to the North of England Education Conference, 4 January.

Cole, M. (1996) Equality and primary education: what are the issues? In M. Cole, D. Hill and S. Shan (eds), *Promoting Equality in Primary Schools.* London: Cassell.

Cole, M. and Hill, D. (1995) Games of despair and rhetorics of resistance: postmodernism, education and reaction. *British Journal of Sociology of Education,* **16** (2), 165–82.

Cole, M. and Hill, D. (1996) Postmodernism, education and contemporary capitalism: a materialist critique. In O. Valente, M. Barrios and V. Teodoro (eds), *Values and Education.* Lisbon: University of Lisbon Press.

Cole, M., Hill, D., Soudien, C. and Pease, J. (1996). Critical transformative primary teacher education: some suggestions for the new South Africa. In J. Lynch *et al* (eds), *Innovation in Delivering Primary Education.* London: Cassell.

Department of Education for Northern Ireland (1991) *Teachers for the 21st Century: A Review of Initial Teacher Training.* Bangor: DENI.

DES (1989) *Initial Teacher Training: Approval of Courses.* Circular 24/89. London: HMSO.

DFE (1992) *Initial Teacher Training (Secondary Phase).* Circular 9/92. London: HMSO.

DFE (1993a) *Draft Circular: The Initial Training of Primary School Teachers: New Criteria for Course Approval.* London: HMSO.

DFE (1993b) *The Initial Training of Primary School Teachers.* Circular 14/93 London: HMSO.

Elliott, J. (1992) Defeat the defeatists: surrender is the wrong response to Kenneth Clarke's training proposals. *Times Educational Supplement,* 7 January.

Gilroy, D. P. (1992) The political rape of initial teacher education in England and Wales: a JET rebuttal. *Journal of Education for Teaching,* **18** (1).

Hargreaves, D. (1992) On the right tracks: the Education Secretary's teacher training reform should be welcome. *Times Higher Education Supplement,* 17 January.

Hartley, D. (1993) Confusion in teacher education: a postmodern condition? In P. Gilroy and M. Smith (ed.), *International Analyses of Teacher Education.* Abingdon: Carfax.

Hill, D. (1989) *Charge of the Right Brigade: The Radical Right's Attack on Teacher Education.* Brighton: Institute for Education Policy Studies.

Hill, D. (1990) *Something Old, Something New, Something Borrowed, Something Blue: Teacher Education, Schooling and the Radical Right in Britain and the USA.* London: Tufnell Press.

Hill, D. (1991a) *What's Left in Teacher Education? Teacher Education, the Radical Left and Policy Proposals.* London: Tufnell Press.

Hill, D. (1991b) What's left in teacher education? In Hillcole Group, *Changing the Future: Redprint for Education.* London: Tufnell Press.

Hill, D. (1991c) Seven ideological perspectives on teacher education in England and Wales. *Australian Journal of Teacher Education,* **16** (2).

Hill, D. (1992a) The Conservative government and initial teacher education: a critique. *NUT Education Review*, **6** (2).

Hill, D. (1992b) What the radical right is doing to teacher education: a radical left response. *Multicultural Teaching*, **10** (3).

Hill, D. (1993a) What's it all about? Training teachers in school and educating them in college. What 95 West Sussex and Hampshire headteachers think of school-based work, theory and what colleges do well and badly, and who should do what. Paper delivered to the British Educational Research Association Annual Conference, Stirling University, 27 August.

Hill, D. (1993b) *What Teachers? School-Basing and Critical Reflection in Teacher Education and Training.* Brighton: Institute of Education Policy Studies.

Hill, D. (1994a) Teacher education and training: a left critique. *Forum*, **6** (3).

Hill, D. (1994b) Primary teacher education and cultural diversity. In G. Verma and P. Pumfrey (eds), *Cultural Diversity and the Curriculum,* Volume 4: *Cross-curricular Contexts, Themes and Dimensions in Primary Schools.* London: Falmer Press.

Hill, D. (1994c) Britain today: capitalist (teacher-) education or postmodern (teacher-) education? Paper delivered to the Annual Conference of the British Educational Research Association. Oxford University, 10 September.

Hill, D. (1994d) A radical left policy for teacher education. *Socialist Teacher*, **56**.

Hill, D. (1996) Conservative education policy reforms: putting the national curriculum in context. In M. Cole, D. Hill and S. Shan (eds), *Promoting Equality in Primary Schools.* London: Cassell.

Hill, D., Cole, M. and Williams, C. (1996) Equality and primary teacher education. In M. Cole, D. Hill and S. Shan (eds), *Promoting Equality in Primary Schools.* London: Cassell.

Hillcole Group (1991) *Changing the Future: Redprint for Education.* London: Tufnell Press.

Hillcole Group (1993) *Whose Teachers? A Radical Manifesto.* London: Tufnell Press.

Hillcole Group (1995) *Education and Democracy: A Socialist Perspective for the 21st Century.* London: Tufnell Press.

Hillgate Group (1986) *Whose Schools? A Radical Manifesto.* London: Hillgate Group.

Hillgate Group (1987) *The Reform of British Education: From Principles to Practice.* London: Claridge Press.

Hillgate Group (1989) *Learning to Teach.* London: Claridge Press.

HMI (1982) *The New Teacher in School.* London: HMSO.

HMI (1988) *The New Teacher in School. A Survey by HM Inspectors in England and Wales 1987.* London: HMSO.

HMI (1991) *School-Based Initial Teacher Training in England and Wales: A Report by HM Inspectorate.* London: HMSO.

IPPR (1993) *Education: A Different Version. An Alternative White Paper.* London: IPPR.

Jacques, K. (1991) The articled teacher scheme. Paper delivered at BERA National Conference, Nottingham Polytechnic, Nottingham, UK.

Labour Party (1991) *Investing in Quality: Labour's Plans to Reform Teacher Education and Training.* London: Labour Party.

Labour Party (1993) *Opening Doors to a Learning Society: A Green Paper on Education.* London: Labour Party.

Labour Party (1994) *Opening Doors to a Learning Society: A Policy Statement on Education.* London: Labour Party.

Lawlor, S. (1990) *Teachers Mistaught: Training in Theories or Education in Subject.* London: Centre for Policy Studies.

Lawlor, S. (1992) Touch of class for teachers: plans to train teachers on the job should be welcomed. *The Times*, 6 January.

McClure, S. (1993) Fight this tooth and nail. *Times Educational Supplement*, 18 June.

Major, J. (1993) Extract from speech to the 1992 Conservative Party Conference. In C. Chitty and B. Simon (eds), *Education Answers Back: Critical Responses to Government Policy.* London: Lawrence and Wishart.

National Association of Head Teachers (NAHT) (1993) Press release. Haywards Heath: NAHT.

National Foundation for Educational Research (1991) *Evaluation of the Articled Teachers Scheme.* London: NFER.

NUT (1993a) *Response to the June 1993 Draft DFE Circular on 'The Initial Training of Primary School Teachers: New Criteria'.* London: NUT.

NUT (1993b) *Qualified to Teach: Teacher Education under Threat.* London: NUT.

OFSTED (1993a) *The New Teacher in School: A Survey by HM Inspectors in England and Wales, 1992.* London: HMSO.

OFSTED (1993b) *The Secondary PGCE in Universities 1991–92.* London: HMSO.

O'Hear, A. (1988) *Who Teaches the Teachers? A Contribution to Public Debate.* London: Social Affairs Unit.

O'Hear, A. (1991) Putting work before play in primary school. *Times Educational Supplement*, 10 October.

O'Hear, A. (1993) The unsuitable leading the untaught. *Daily Telegraph*, 8 July.

O'Keeffe, D. (1986) *The Wayward Curriculum: A Cause for Parents' Concern.* London: Social Affairs Unit.

O'Keeffe, D. (1990a) *The Wayward Elite.* London: Adam Smith Institute.

O'Keeffe, D. (1990b) The real lesson to be learned in our schools. *Daily Mail*, 9 March.

Patten, J. (1993) Extract from speech to the 1992 Conservative Party Conference. In C. Chitty and B. Simon (eds), *Education Answers Back: Critical Responses to Government Policy*. London: Lawrence and Wishart.

Polytechnic Council for the Education of Teachers (PCET) (1992) Letter to Secretary of State re ITT changes, 28 January.

PCET (1993) *Response to the June 1993 Draft DFE Circular on 'The Initial Training of Primary School Teachers: New Criteria'*. London: UCET.

Price, C. (1994) A new vice anglaise. *Times Educational Supplement*, 14 January.

Pyke, N. (1993a) Into combat after a year for the Mum's Army. *Times Educational Supplement*, 11 June.

Pyke, N. (1993b) Primary heads rally against Mum's Army. *Times Educational Supplement*, 16 July.

Pyke, N. (1993c) Unions fire at Mum's Army plans. *Times Educational Supplement*, 30 July.

Santinelli, P. (1993) Teacher trainers call halt to reform. *Times Higher Educational Supplement*, 23 July.

SCOP (1994) *Education Bill: Primary ITT Questionnaire. Commentary on Findings*. London: SCOP.

Thatcher, M. (1994) *The Downing Street Years*. London: HarperCollins.

Tytler, D. (1988) New teachers lack proper training, inspectors find. *The Times*, 25 October.

UCET (1993) *Response to the June 1993 Draft DFE Circular on 'The Initial Training of Primary School Teachers: New Criteria'*. London: UCET.

Wallace, M. (1994) Discourse of derision: the role of mass media within the education policy process. *Journal of Education Policy*, **8** (4).

Whitty, G. (1992) Quality control in teacher education. *British Journal of Education Studies*, **40** (1).

Whitty, G. (1993) Education reform and teacher education in England in the 1990s. In P. Gilroy and M. Smith (eds), *International Analyses of Teacher Education*. Abingdon: Carfax.

Whitty, G. and Menter, I. (1989) Lessons of Thatcherism: education policy in England and Wales 1979–1988. In A. Gamble and C. Wells (eds), *Thatcher's Law*. Oxford: Blackwell.

Wragg, T. (1993) Ruled by the free market Stalinists. *Times Educational Supplement*, 5 February.

Zeichner, K. and Liston, D. (1987) Teaching student teachers to reflect. *Harvard Educational Review*, **5–7** (1).

# Part Three

## Differing Insights on Teacher Education

# 14 Gender, Social Class and the Debate about Where to Train Teachers

## GERALDINE McDONALD

For most of the time that teachers have been formally trained, a degree has not been required in order to teach at the primary school level. Although there is a long tradition of allowing or encouraging prospective teachers in training to gain a university degree, the conditions under which this could be achieved have varied by country and over time. Today, a high proportion of students recruited to primary teacher training courses take a four-year course of study leading to a BEd. In 1990 in England and Wales, of 14,331 students recruited to primary teacher training courses, 9524 were enrolled for a BEd and 4807 for a PGCE (Straker, 1991, p. 21). In the United States, academic requirements differ according to state, but a survey by the National Center for Education Statistics in 1987–88 showed that 39 per cent of teachers had majored in general education for their bachelor's degree (or associate's degree if they did not have a bachelor's degree) and about half of all teachers had earned an advanced degree. In Australia in 1988, the former colleges of advanced education which had the major responsibility for teacher training were transformed into universities by national legislation. In New Zealand, the colleges of education do not have the right to grant degrees, although it is possible for them to apply to the New Zealand Qualifications Authority for degree status for particular programmes. The colleges have all embarked on (sometimes fragile) arrangements with their local universities. At the present time about 80 per cent of students are studying for a four-year BEd awarded by a university.

Until recently, it might have been assumed that there was a kind of natural progression from school-based pupil teaching, to normal schools, to training colleges, to institutes and colleges of education and, finally, to some form of training in a university leading to a degree (Niblett *et al.*, 1975). However, in view of the time it has taken, the restrictions placed on university study by universities and by teacher training institutions alike and the long haul to establish professional degrees for teachers, we cannot be too sanguine about the permanency of any arrangements. In England and Wales, there have been moves to return to a form of apprenticeship in the articled teacher scheme (DES, 1991), a scheme which took its inspiration from provisional licensing arrangements in the state of New Jersey (Beresford-Hill, 1993). School-based teacher training is being discussed in the United States (for a review see Roth, 1994) and in Australia (Knight *et al.*, 1993; Australian National Board of Employment, Education and Training, 1994). Even in Scotland, where there is as yet no suggestion that the control of teacher training should be taken away from institutions of higher learning, mentoring is being discussed and there is a strong move to more school-based training (Brown, 1996).

In what kind of institution should training for school teaching take place? In a school, in a specialized teacher training institution or in a university? The debate was set off by the demand, in the nineteenth century, for large numbers of elementary school teachers, the consequent recruitment of young women and the need to train them.

Following Grace's (1991) advice, the policy issue of where to train teachers will be examined in terms of structural, political and historical facts. Evidence will be drawn from several countries and the focus will be on the professional preparation of teachers for schools, mainly, but not exclusively, at the elementary or primary level.

The desire of governments to curb public expenditure, the contemporary conceptualization of education as an industry with economic outcomes and the enthusiasm for competency-based training may all have contributed to the current promotion of school-based training, but it is hard to imagine that similar forces would dislodge training for medicine, law, business or engineering from their niches within the university system. These are traditionally male-dominated occupations with considerable social prestige. The long time it has taken the primary school profession to attain graduate status, and the insecurity once training within degree-granting institutions has been attained, can be attributed to the origins of mass education following the industrial revolution and the creation of a teaching force with a substantial proportion of young women, often from working-class backgrounds.

Purvis (1981, p. 227), in her study of the nineteenth-century Working Men's College movement, comments that gender ideologies, especially that of the bourgeoisie, determined access to particular forms of education and relegated representatives of the less advantaged sections of society to training and apprenticeship. With this in mind, the words 'teacher training' will be used in preference to 'teacher education'.

## Gender and social class

According to Halsey (1991), before education became free and compulsory in the latter half of the nineteenth century, it was intended for 'workmen and servants'. The English public schools and ancient universities, on the other hand, 'were vehicles for the preservation, transmission and renewal of the styles of life rather than the occupations of the elevated strata' (Halsey, 1991, p. 11).

In both England and Scotland, the churches were responsible for the instruction of the children of the poor. The pupil-teacher system, introduced before the establishment of formal institutions of teacher training, selected the brightest of the students in the elementary schools and educated them as apprentices. Thus the pupil-teacher system imported the class position of the pupils into the occupation of elementary school teaching. Public elementary education was not the usual route to secondary education, but the pupil-teacher system began to provide a post-elementary education for children from less well-off sections of society. Until the latter half of the nineteenth century, academic secondary schools were provided only for boys.

Teacher training in Scotland illustrates the themes of gender and social class very clearly (Cruickshank, 1970). In Scotland, the arts degree was long associated with the profession of teaching. The image of teaching was of a highly respected, university-trained dominie in every parish. Cruickshank explains that this picture is somewhat distorted. Many of the teachers were hoping to become ministers and, if university trained, and not all were, might have spent only a brief time at university. By the early nineteenth century the system was breaking down. There were at that time about 50,000 children in Scotland who attended no school. As the need for elementary education grew, women were recruited into what had previously been regarded as a male profession. By 1835 the need for training had been recognized, and 1837 saw the establishment of training in normal schools in Scotland. Similar developments had been taking place in England. When women had been trained as teachers they often took positions previously filled by men, causing the principal of Aberdeen University in 1887 to express 'the prevailing prejudice when he spoke of certain local schools having "descended to a female teacher"' (Cruickshank, 1970, p. 87).

The most important and distinctive feature in the training of teachers in Scotland was the development in the 1870s of the concurrent system. Pupil-teachers could combine their professional training with study in the Scottish universities.

This did not at first apply to women. They were excluded from the universities by policy or by custom.

## Training college meets the university

The nineteenth-century debate over the right for women to be admitted to universities became part of the debate about where to locate the training of teachers for the first level of schooling.

At McGill University in Montreal, Canada, the entry of women was a major issue for several decades (Gillett, 1981). Among the arguments marshalled to prevent their entry was the claim that higher education would lead to uterine disorders and hysteria and, if educated women were indeed capable of bearing children, that there was a strong chance that the children would be abnormal. The McGill Normal School for the training of elementary school teachers was opened in 1857. Although operated by McGill College (later McGill University), it was not an integral part of the college's academic programme. J. William Dawson held the two positions of principal of McGill College and director of the normal school. He also taught natural science at both institutions. The normal school trained both men and women. The university would not admit women, let alone allow them to share classes with men, but there were mixed classes at the normal school. Dawson directed the normal school for over a dozen years and there is no evidence that he found the women students wanting or that he had any problem with classes containing both men and women.

Dawson argued in public for the right of women to receive higher education, yet the records of McGill University show that he consistently blocked their entry. Gillett (1981, p. 40) explains as follows:

> The acceptability of co-education at the normal school was probably more related to the low status of teachers generally than to any liberality of viewpoint on [Dawson's] part. The Victorian ethic which Dawson upheld was clearly class-related. It placed

women of the upper echelons on pedestals while it consigned lower class women to factories and mines – and schools.

Dawson did not send his own daughters to university. As ladies they were to be protected. The admission of women to the Faculty of Arts at McGill occurred 27 years after the establishment of the normal school. At first, women could attend only the separate classes arranged for them.

When the Montreal Girls High School was established, its pupils studied for the examination for entrance to the university. Before long, girls were heading the lists. However, Dawson's concerns were driven not by women's capacity to cope but by his notion of the proper activities of women.

## Training college enters the university

A further example of how gender and class fuelled a debate on where teachers should be taught can be found in the relationship between Teachers College and Columbia University in New York (Cremin *et al.*, 1954; Lagemann, 1979). Teachers College had its beginnings in the Kitchen Garden Association formed in 1880. This was a kindergarten movement with the added objective of training very young children in domestic occupations in order to relieve the chronic servant shortage. Following the theme of education for 'workmen and servants', the children were given little kitchen utensils and spades to play with.

The movement was at first conducted by volunteers: women who were well placed in society. The association then began to offer training in its methods. Classes were arranged for practising teachers. However, the women teachers' aspirations for academic and career advancement were not shared by the 'ladies' on the governing board.

In 1884, the Kitchen Garden Association was reorganized as the Industrial Education Association. Its aim was now to introduce manual training and industrial arts into the public schools, in the hope that this would engender in pupils a respect for manual labour and proper habits of work. This resulted in a great expansion of the training courses and the acquisition of a training centre.

Meanwhile, developments in Germany had turned the practice of teaching into scientific pedagogy. As early as 1864, the president of Columbia College, then situated in downtown New York, wanted to include the principles and art of education in the college's course offerings. He proposed a chair of education. For over twenty years the trustees of Columbia College rejected plans for a course in pedagogy on the grounds that it would bring women into the college.

The training facilities of the Industrial Education Association developed into the New York College for the Training of Teachers. In 1892, its trustees offered Teachers College to Columbia College, which refused on the grounds that it would commit the university to a policy of coeducation, which would be a mistake. An agreement of 1893 started the gradual development of a formal but tense relationship between the two institutions. In 1894, Columbia College was looking for a new location. The Teachers College, getting wind of the fact of the proposed move to Morningside Heights, bought adjoining land on 120th Street. Teachers College continued to argue for professional degrees for teachers, while Columbia University objected to the Horace Mann demonstration school, which was part of Teachers College. In 1915, Teachers College finally became a faculty of the university, ending a series of collaborative relationships that fell short of full membership. There remained a hostile attitude on the part of some members of the university staff to Teachers College, towards all courses in education and towards the presence of women in higher education.

Although Teachers College included both men and women, 120th Street was disparagingly referred to as 'hairpin alley' (Cremin *et al.*, 1954, p. 70). That Teachers College was a graduate school was significant for its acceptance. Rossiter's (1982) study of the role of graduate schools in getting women into American universities showed that this was much less controversial than getting them accepted into undergraduate coeducation.

## Teacher training in New Zealand

In 1840, New Zealand became a colony of Great Britain. The settlers were predominantly from the British Isles. Until very recently, virtually all teacher training in New Zealand has been publicly provided, non-residential, coeducational and located in university centres.

Before the Education Act of 1877, which established a national system of education, New Zealand teachers had either been already trained in their country of origin or were trained by means of the pupil-teacher system copied from England and Scotland. Formal training first began in the Scottish Presbyterian settlement of Otago, where a pupil-teacher system was set up in the late 1850s and was formalized by ordinance of the provincial council in 1864. The first normal school/training college was also established in Otago, at Dunedin. By 1881 all four main cities in New Zealand had a training college for teachers. The first university was established in Otago in 1869. 'As early as 1868 a member of a select committee on the establishment of a college (i.e. a university) had suggested that university training could be given to schoolmasters as well as other professions' (Johnston and Morton, 1976, pp. 6–7). However, applications for entrance to teacher training in the Otago province turned out to be from prospective schoolmistresses rather than prospective schoolmasters.

During the planning for the university, the Presbyterian fathers saw the institution as mainly for the education of clergy:

> There was little role for women in the plans for university education discussed by the Presbyterian Church and the provincial council. The Church was concerned with training men for the ministry; the provincial council found the idea of a local university preferable to the alternative of sending young men on scholarships to British universities.
>
> (Page, 1992, p. 100)

Acceptance of women by the early Otago University owed much to the continued efforts of a Scottish settler called Learmonth Dalrymple. She circulated a petition, which was signed by 149 prominent women. It asked for a degree for those 'ladies and others preparing themselves for teaching'. The petitioners regarded the degree 'as nothing more nor less than a certificate', meaning by this a certificate for teaching. This reflects the Scottish expectation of an arts degree as the appropriate qualification for teaching. The council of the university voted unanimously to admit women to classes, but turned the petitioners' message around by permitting women 'to compete for all certificates, equivalent to degrees'. Page says that the council probably meant to award women certificates rather than full degrees, as was the practice in the University of London at the time. In 1871, Otago University opened all its classes to women, although it did not at this time play any role in the training of teachers.

In 1873, the Otago provincial council considered establishing a normal school or a training college. Again it was suggested that the academic subjects could be taught at the university. The principal argument for this appears to have been cost containment, in that it would reduce the number of staff required (Johnson and Morton, 1976, p. 7).

Although Otago had started the first university, the University of New Zealand, founded in 1870, developed as a federal system linking constituent university colleges situated in the four main centres of population. Further discussions took place on the relationship between the university and the training of teachers.

> The BA degree, first established in 1874, was ... closely related to the needs of the teachers which the growing colony required. It was a general degree, including arts and science subjects, characterised by breadth rather than depth.
>
> (Parton, 1979, p. 23)

When a university college for the city of Wellington was being discussed, the Wellington education board recommended the abolition of its normal school in order to found a chair of psychology and education (Beaglehole, 1949, p. 11). The offer was refused.

There was no logical reason why teachers could not have been trained in the colony's university colleges, which were, at first, and indeed for many years, basically undergraduate institutions. Academic lectures given in the university might be replicated in the training colleges and, as in Montreal, the same persons might lecture at both sites.

Despite concessions to the needs of primary school teachers, the University of New Zealand took the British universities, especially the ancient ones, as its model, and while it was only too glad to admit teachers' college trainees as university students, it was not about to train them to teach.

As already noted, there had been debate over the inclusion of teacher training at the time of the founding of the University of New Zealand. However, following the establishment of the national system of education, teacher training became the responsibility of the central Education Department, which 'curtailed all but the most trivial local action: the minister of education enjoyed a theoretical right of approval over almost all college activities' (Carter, 1993, p. 77).

A fresh approach was taken in 1905, when the Education Department began to pay the fees of training college students who attended lectures at their local university colleges. In return, the principals of the training colleges were to become honorary lecturers in the history and theory of education at their local university (Carter, 1993, pp. 77–8). When, following the First World War, the universities began to establish chairs of education, the training college principal might become the professor.

The teacher training colleges were closely guarded by the Education Department. They existed at a psychological distance from the universities and were not accorded the same prestige. The result was that over the years the system drew off from the training colleges academically able student teachers. What explanations were given for two different institutions with overlapping functions and, to a large extent, a shared student body? The institutional difference came to be attributed not to the historical effects of gender and class but to 'philosophy' and purpose. Issues of autonomy were stressed. An academic distinction between theory and practice was made by the university. This did not seem to apply to other university courses, such as law and accountancy. Such perceptions then contributed to maintaining the distance. University departments of education stayed free from the contamination of practice teaching for either primary or secondary schools. Education remained within the faculties of arts.

## Women and the university

Otago University, discussed above, was the first university in Australasia or the United Kingdom to admit women, and the University of New Zealand did not specifically exclude women. However, the attitude of the university and indeed of society can be gauged from the tentativeness with which women applied for admission. Kate Edger, the first woman to graduate, was admitted in 1874 on the understanding that she entered classes with eyes modestly downcast (Hughes and Ahearn, 1993). Although the province of Otago was the first to establish the pupil-teacher system, a teacher training college and a university, it was not the first to have a woman graduate. Sixteen years after the founding of the university, a local teacher, trained under the pupil-teacher system, gained a bachelor's degree.

The number of women entering the colleges of the University of New Zealand was not at first very great. There was open hostility to women from some male students. Nor were academics free from prejudice. Various devices were used to control the entry of women. For example, arts students were required to study the classics and there were dire warnings about the danger to women's sensibilities of certain classical works, such as the plays of Terence.

Despite the ideological barriers to women's access to the university, by 1893 more than half the students were women (New Zealand National Archives, 1993). This increase was mainly due to the enrolment of teachers and teachers' college students on the concurrent system and the timetabling of university courses after school hours. In the early years of Auckland University College, for example, 'a fair number were students from the teachers training college. Even in chemistry, of forty students in 1887, fourteen were student teachers. Such students were to assume a greater

role in later years' (Sinclair, 1983, p. 33). These students almost certainly included women.

## The eugenics movement

Even when women were entering the university colleges in considerable numbers there were continuing objections, particularly from the supporters of the eugenics movement. What women had earlier heard in Montreal about the effect of higher education on women's reproductive functions, they heard now in New Zealand.

In 1906, a wealthy landowner, who was himself an Oxford graduate, offered to provide the money to set up a chair of domestic science which would relate to women's proper station in life. In his proposal he stated:

> Thousands of cases of stunted vitality, of ruined digestions, of structural malformations, could be annually prevented by the systematic and universal teaching of the general laws of health and the proper feeding, clothing and handling of infants – all of which are among the subjects included in the term 'Home Economics'.
> (Studholme, quoted in Thompson, 1919)

Studholme, the benefactor, offered to make a special visit to Columbia University (he was obviously referring to Teachers College, which now had a thriving department of domestic science) in order to obtain a suitable professor. Otago University College eventually accepted Studholme's money and set up a School of Home Science. According to the foundation professor, a woman not from the United States but from England, students were to learn about 'heredity and natural selection so essential to the well-being of the race' and, among other things, study 'the life histories of some of the household pests, e.g., the house fly and clothes-moth' (Thompson, 1919, p. 247). The school offered a three-year degree and a two-year diploma. The latter was specifically intended as a training for teachers. Teacher training had entered the university through its association with women's traditional role.

It has been established (Fry, 1985) that at the turn of the century secondary schoolgirls in New Zealand were studying mathematics, physics and chemistry just as the boys did. The position changed once the School of Home Science began to furnish the girls' high schools with science teachers. Following regulations promulgated in 1917, which required that all girls should be taught home science, physics for girls disappeared and chemistry became applied chemistry, with an emphasis on cooking processes and laundry materials. The myth then developed that girls could not cope with 'hard' subjects like physics and inorganic chemistry, when, in fact, they had had little opportunity to study them.

## Working-class women

Most commentators say that at first it was girls from the working classes who were trained to teach. This must certainly have been true where working-class children were given instruction and the most able of these were selected as teachers. However, this may not be the whole story, or if generally true in the first half of the nineteenth century, may not have been true after the establishment of national systems of education. Cruickshank (1970) records that the women recruited to the teacher training colleges in Scotland were the daughters of shopkeepers, clerks and the manse. Further, the women paid fees for their training whereas the men did not, suggesting again that the men and women might come from different strata of society.

The issue of the social class of the entrants to teacher training is an important one. It may be that contemporary judgements by representatives of the ruling class do not match the views of the entrants themselves, or that they do not match objective evidence from other sources. There are also hazards in trying to determine the social evaluation of occupations at a time different from our own. The method adopted here is to compare contemporary comment from the middle-class viewpoint with what can be shown by historical research to be the social position of some women teachers and pupil-teachers of the same period.

On 19 September 1893, the governor of New Zealand gave his assent to an Electoral Act which gave New Zealand women the right to vote. The general election was only six weeks away and a campaign was mounted to ensure that women registered as voters. An anonymous pamphlet containing a 'sketch' was published (Eve Adams, [1893]). The pamphlet is undated but publication was probably in October 1893.

The author of the sketch imagines a tea party attended by a group of young ladies. They engage in conversation and arguments are presented for women's suffrage and the need for women to exercise their vote. The topics discussed are not confined to suffrage issues. The young women discuss compulsory education and women as teachers. Some quotations will give the flavour of the discussion:

> But I do wonder why the working classes are too proud to be servants because one can at once tell what their position ought to be when one sees them in the telephone exchange, or typewriting or teachers.

The term 'working classes' is hardly surprising at a time when some women worked for money and many others did not. With this definition it was relatively easy in the nineteenth century to determine who was in the working class. However, the young women appear to assume that working women who are not servants are servants *manqué*, and to be socially evaluated in the same way. This is another comment from the sketch: 'she had to earn her living, and as she was not clever at teaching ... she much preferred cooking to being a "lady help" '. The picture that emerges is that free education has given young women ideas above their station and that teachers are clever girls who would otherwise have been servants. The 'ladies' thought that free education ought not to go beyond the fifth standard.

That these are not unrepresentative middle-class opinions can be seen in a quotation from an article written by William Pember Reeves, a former politician, and member of a prominent New

Zealand family. The article was published in 1898. Pember Reeves wrote:

> Most New Zealand women are engaged in domestic duties. Those who go out to work do so to work unassumingly as school-teachers, factory hands or household servants. As school-teachers they are usually efficient, as domestic servants civil and hard working, as factory hands, neat, industrious and moral.

## A New Zealand primary school

The records of a New Zealand school established about ten years before the Eve Adams pamphlet was published have been studied (Shramka, 1985). Shramka looked at the age, gender, social class, qualifications and training of the teachers over the period 1882 to 1918. No publicly provided secondary schooling was available for girls in the area until 1883.

In this primary school, women teachers always constituted a majority of the staff. Women had to resign upon marriage and so the women were of two kinds: those who were pupil-teachers and who might serve four or five years until marriage, and some older single women for whom teaching was a career. Shramka found that the young women pupil-teachers were from the local district and were spread across the social scale. They included the daughters of the economically most secure families living in the best streets. Some came, for example, from families in which other daughters helped at home. A comparison of the views of Eve Adams and Pember Reeves with the facts of this school suggests that the opinions expressed by the two former were little more than conventional ideology. According to Shramka (1985, p. 266), teaching was considered a suitable occupation in which the young ladies of the town might engage until they were married.

Similar comments have been made about teachers in the USA: 'It was appropriate for the educated young woman to occupy her time until she married and began her family' (Clifford, 1991, p. 119). A study in the USA in 1929 showed that the

working class, middle class and upper class all sent some of their daughters into teaching. It would seem that teaching attracted young women from a wide range of backgrounds, but that the middle classes did not consider being a teacher as a step up the social ladder (Bergh, 1982).

## Some other interpretations

It has sometimes been argued that by accepting low wages and poor working conditions women blocked the aspirations of men for a professional career. But a modern profession implies a university training. Women were not kept out of a professional occupation, they were kept out of universities.

Another familiar theme is that for women teaching has been but 'a short sojourn between school and marriage' (Watson, 1966). It is difficult to see how most women teachers could have interpreted their position as anything else, since for much of the history of teaching only single women were trained and they were required to resign from training or from teaching upon marriage. In New Zealand, not until the early 1960s were married women permitted to train as teachers, and to be accepted they had to assure the authorities that their family responsibilities would not be neglected.

While the 'working-class' label characteristic of the nineteenth-century evaluation of women teachers has disappeared, another evaluation has surfaced. As married women continue to teach or return to teaching, 'there are those of course who are simply seen or see themselves as "second wage" earners' (Bingham, 1991). Does this apply to men teachers too?

When women were first recruited to teaching they were valued for qualities of goodness, docility, malleability and compliance, none of which depends upon a degree. These qualities sound like competencies which could be appraised, and perhaps in the present policy climate they will be revived!

To what extent do gender and social class influence current policy? The apprenticeship implied in school-based training echoes the early days of pupil-teaching and the education of the poor. Since school-based training is enthusiastically supported by conservative political groups, it can be suggested that these groups do not view teachers and pupils in state schools as their social equals. The return to apprenticeship systems also recalls the idea that women have a natural ability to teach, not requiring a foundation of theoretical training, because teaching is an extension of the mothering role. Indeed, McBride (cited in Brown, 1996) criticizes the articled teachers and licensed teachers schemes on these very grounds: that they create a 'so-called mum's army'.

Gender and social class have affected policy decisions about where teachers should be trained. The effects come from their historical origins, from the ideologies of the time and from the structures for training which emerged. The debate about the entry of women to the university is also a debate about teacher training. The influence of gender and class can be seen not only in historical perspective but continuing to influence policies on teacher training today. The debates of the past about the role of women as professional teachers and as university graduates have returned in a different guise. The dilemma facing women in the past was how to achieve equality and justice. The dilemma now is that deskilling and degrading of teaching by taking it away from the universities applies just as much to men as to women.

# References

Australian National Board of Employment, Education and Training (1994) *Workplace Learning in the Professional Development of Teachers*. Canberra: Australian Government Publishing Services.

Adams, Eve (pseudonym) [1893] *Women's Franchise: A Short Sketch*. Pamphlet.

Beaglehole, J. C. (1949) *Victoria University College: An Essay towards a History*. Wellington: New Zealand University Press.

Beresford-Hill, P. (1993) Teacher education, access and quality control in higher education: lessons from America for Britain's policy-makers. *Oxford Review of Education*, **19** (1), 79–86.

Bergh, B. H. (1982) Only a schoolmaster: gender and class and the effort to professionalise elementary teaching in England 1870–1910. *History of Education Quarterly*, **22** (1), 1–21.

Bingham, C. (1991) Teachers' terms and conditions: a view from the schools. *Evaluation and Research in Education*, **5** (1/2), 49–55.

Brown, S. (1996) School-based initial teacher education in Scotland: archaic highlands or high moral ground? In R. MacBride (ed.), *Teacher Education and Policy*. London: Falmer Press.

Carter, I. (1993) *Gadfly: The Life and Times of James Shelley*. Auckland: Auckland University Press.

Clifford, G. J. (1991) 'Daughters into teachers': educational and demographic influences on the transformation of teaching into women's work in America. In A. Prentice and M. R. Theobald (eds), *Women Who Taught: Perspectives on the History of Women and Teaching*. Toronto: University of Toronto Press.

Cremin, L. A., Shannon, D. A. and Townsend, M. F. (1954) *A History of Teachers College, Columbia University*. New York: Columbia University Press.

Cruickshank, M. (1970) *A History of the Training of Teachers in Scotland*. London: SCRE and University of London Press.

DES (1991) *School-Based Initial Teacher Training in England and Wales*. London: HMSO.

Fry, R. (1985) *It's Different for Daughters: A History of the Curriculum for Girls in New Zealand Schools 1900–1975*. Wellington: New Zealand Council for Educational Research.

Gillett, M. (1981) *We Walked Very Warily: A History of Women at McGill*. Montreal: Eden Press.

Grace, G. (1991) The state and the teachers: problems in teacher supply, retention and morale in England and Wales. In G. Grace and M. Lawn (eds), *Teacher Supply and Teacher Quality*. London: Multilingual Matters Ltd.

Halsey, A. H. (1991) An international comparison of access to higher education. *Oxford Studies in Comparative Education*, **1**, 11–36.

Hughes, B. and Ahearn, S. (1993) *Redbrick and Bluestockings: Women at Victoria 1899–1993*. Wellington: Victoria University Press.

Johnston, C. M. and Morton, H. (1976) *Dunedin Teachers College: The First Hundred Years*. Dunedin: Dunedin Teachers College.

Knight, J., Lingard, R. and Bartlett, L. (1993) Re-forming teacher education: the unfinished task. In J. Knight, L. Bartlett and E. McWilliam (eds), *Unfinished Busi-*

*ness: Reshaping the Teacher Education Industry for the 1990s.* Rockhampton: University Publishing, University of Central Queensland.

Lagemann, E. C. (1979) *A Generation of Women: Education in the Lives of Progressive Reformers.* Cambridge, MA: Harvard University Press.

New Zealand National Archives (1993) *The Undersigned Women.* Pamphlet.

Niblett, W. R., Humphreys, D. W. and Fairhurst, J. R. (1975) *The University Connection.* Windsor: NFER.

Page, D. (1992) The first lady graduates: women with degrees from Otago University, 1885–1900. In B. Brookes, C. Macdonald and M. Tennant (eds), *Women in History 2.* Wellington: Bridget Williams Books.

Parton, H. (1979) *The University of New Zealand.* Auckland: Auckland University Press.

Purvis, J. (1981) 'Women's life is essentially domestic, public life being confined to men' (Comte): separate spheres and inequality in the education of working class women, 1854–1900. *History of Education,* **10** (4), 227–43.

Reeves, W. P. (1898) Five years reform in New Zealand. *The National Review,* p. 842.

Rossiter, M. W. (1982) Doctorates for American women, 1868–1907. *History of Education Quarterly,* **2,** 159–83.

Roth, R. A. (1994) The university can't train teachers? Transformation of a profession. *Journal of Teacher Education,* **45** (4), 261–8.

Shramka, J. E. (1985) Petone School and its teachers 1882–1918. Thesis for degree of Master of Arts in Education, Victoria University of Wellington.

Sinclair, K. (1983) *A History of the University of Auckland 1883–1983.* Auckland: Auckland University Press.

Straker, N. (1991) Teacher supply in the 1990s: an analysis of current developments. *Evaluation and Research in Education,* **5** (1/2), 17–33.

Thompson, G. E. (1919) *A History of the University of Otago (1869–1919).* Dunedin: J. Wilkie.

Watson, J. E. (1966) Marriages of women teachers. *New Zealand Journal of Educational Studies,* **1** (2), 149–61.

# 15 When the Mirror Crack'd: The Discourse of Reflection in Pre-service Teacher Education

ANNE M. PHELAN

Throughout the past decade, the discourse of reflection has reverberated in the field of pre-service teacher education in North America. The discourse resounds with promises of greater insight, sharpened self-awareness, ethical and political sensitivity and more balanced and reasoned self-analysis skills for prospective teachers (Zeichner, 1987). The teacher education literature is littered with descriptors such as 'teacher as action researcher', 'teacher scholar', 'teacher as change agent', 'teacher as participant observer', 'self-monitoring teacher', 'teacher as moral craftsperson', 'teacher as researcher', 'reflective teacher' and 'reflective practitioner'. Despite the odd cautionary note (Zeichner, 1987; Smyth, 1992), the discourse of reflection appears to have been embraced wholeheartedly (perhaps uncritically?) by teacher educators; 'reflective practice' has become the unquestioned contemporary standard of the good teacher. One would be hard pressed to find someone disputing that standard. 'For', as Donald Schön (1987: xiii) states, 'how else are practitioners to gain wisdom except by reflection on practice dilemmas that call for it?'

In this chapter, I want to rethink Schön's adage by analysing its Enlightenment assumptions, namely its faith in the power of a rational, conscious mind to decide on action, to control future principled practice and to be responsible for what one does and who one is (Giroux, 1991, p. 11). I am particularly concerned about what the discourse does to pre-service teachers. How are they inscribed by the rationalist discourse-practices of reflection? In what ways are they rewarded and indulged or deprived and sanctioned relative to

the exercise of reasoned analysis? In Lyotard's (1989) terms, 'how does the discourse influence what [pre-service teachers] must do in order to be heard, what they must listen to in order to speak ... what role they must play to be the object of the narrative of reflection in institutions of teacher education?' Drawing on contemporary postmodern critiques of the Enlightenment, I first examine epistemologies and practices within the reflection discourse. I then identify three deceptions in the discourse which I believe to be problematic for the pre-service teacher. Finally, I introduce an alternative metaphor, with a distinctly post-modern flavour, which might better direct our efforts in faculties of education.

My practice as a teacher educator has been, and continues to be, informed by the discourse of reflection. As such, I find myself writing against the grain of my own practice to produce what Lather (1992) called 'an awareness of the complexity, historical contingency and the fragility of the practices we invent' in the name of teacher preparation. My exploration begins with and leads back to the epistemologies and politics of our various institutional practices.

## Epistemologies and practices in pre-service teacher education

The discourse of reflection is highly complex, and encompasses a variety of approaches and practices (Tom, 1987; Zeichner, 1987; Grimmett *et al.*, 1990). Approaches within the tradition can be differentiated from one another in terms of their theoretical positions, the degree of specification of the reflective process, the extent to which the notion of reflective practice dominates the teacher education programme in question and, finally, the extent to which the strategy promotes change of teaching practice and context (Zeichner, 1987). I wish to differentiate between approaches on the basis of their underlying epistemologies – the technical, the practical and the critical (Habermas, 1974; Van Manen, 1977).

The technical orientation finds its roots in instrumental rationality and advocates that teachers take privileged knowledge (generated by university researchers) and apply it to instrumental problems of practice. Reflection becomes a vehicle for promoting research-based practice (Cruickshank, 1984). In teacher education, 'reflective teaching lessons' (RTLs) are used to help prospective teachers gain an understanding of theory and how to apply it. RTLs include peer teaching of faculty-developed lessons followed by small and large group reflection sessions.

The practical perspective draws on the work of philosophers of practical action such as Gauthier (1963), Polanyi (1967), Schwab (1971) and Van Manen (1977), who view teaching as 'consisting of practical problems, requiring deliberation and action for their solution' (Calderhead, 1988, p. 44; see also Bolin, 1988; Clift *et al.*, 1991; Munby and Russell, 1994). In this view, knowledge about teaching has 'a relativistic quality' (Grimmett *et al.*, 1990, p. 25). Teachers must strive to understand the particular contexts of their practice before deciding how to act. If external knowledge is used, it is always mediated through the particular context. In this way, teachers begin to develop their own practical theories of teaching (Sanders and McCutcheon, 1986; Connelly and Clandinin, 1988). The goals are student learning and teachers' own professional development. In the teacher education context, practices such as journal writing and supervision conferences are used to encourage pre-service teachers to develop their own practical theories.

Finally, in the critical perspective, 'reflection is viewed as a process of becoming aware of one's context, of the influence of societal and ideological constraints on previously taken-for-granted practices, and gaining control over the direction of these influences' (Calderhead, 1988, p. 44). Teachers are to take charge of the content and processes of their teaching and school affairs in the name of what they deem decent, humane and just (Greene, 1978). Pre-service teachers develop the tools and skills of critical enquiry by engaging in action research, ethnographic studies and curriculum analysis projects (Zeichner and Liston, 1987). Student learning and the construction of a democratic society are fundamental goals.

Despite the obvious differences in emphases and claims among perspectives – variegated promises of thoughtful mediated action (Cruickshank, 1984), the unsilencing of the teacher's voice (Richert, 1987) and the promise of future self-determination (Habermas, 1974) – all three perspectives rely on the Enlightenment assumption that 'being able to establish reasons for one's action, to deliberate in accordance with these reasons, and to act on one's deliberation are essential aspects of responsible, autonomous action' (Calderhead, 1988, p. 44). Zeichner (1983, p. 5) cites Harvey Siegel, who describes a liberated person as one who is 'free from unwarranted control of unjustified beliefs, unsupportable attitudes and the paucity of abilities which can prevent that person from completely taking charge of his or her life'. It is this metaphor of liberation through reason that gives the discourse its coherence and renders it seductive.

My contention is that the discourse's reliance on reason, while neither essentially liberating nor oppressive (Sadwicki, 1988), is in fact deceptive to ourselves and to our students. The discourse belies the complexity of practice while it ignores the relations of power which discourse-practices, such as action research and journal writing, actualize. First, it creates the illusion that it is possible to free oneself from unjustified beliefs. Second, the pre-service teacher is led to believe that the volatility and ambiguity of practice, once identified, can and should be contained. Finally, having freed him- or herself from unwarranted beliefs and ambiguity, the pre-service teacher learns that principled action is by definition improved, or more just, action. In what follows, I want to examine these deceptions at close range by exploring the particular experiences of one pre-service teacher, Lou. It is not my intention to equate Lou's experience with that of all pre-service teachers. My hope is that in reading his story, and that of his supervisors, we might begin to read our own practices more critically.

## The power of reason to deceive: practitioner, practice and principle

> To tell the truth, I am not really sure what else to put down in the journal. The 'I think ...' and 'I feel ...' concept has me confused, so I put in what I think seems to fit.
>
> (Student teacher, Lou, in Bolin, 1988, p. 51)

In her article 'Helping student teachers think about teaching', Frances Bolin (1988) analyses the reflective journals of a student teacher named Lou. Bolin is concerned about Lou's reluctance to 'explore issues' or 'thoughtfully weigh alternatives' to practice (p. 51). 'For Lou, teaching is active; it is something you do, not something about which you deliberate,' she writes. Bolin suggests that in order to foster more reflection on Lou's part, his supervisor needed to model 'a more mature level of thought' (p. 52). The author concludes that journal-writing in the supervisory context may be an effective tool to help students like Lou become more deliberative about their teaching. Lou, however, seems less certain.

## Deception 1: Liberating the self through reason

> Sometimes I'm not sure how 'strict' I should be with the kids as a student teacher. Max said he wants me not to be so timid. My timidity comes from not knowing the disciplinary boundaries at [the school]. Since I didn't know, I didn't really react. I am by no means timid, as the kids [I have worked with every summer] will attest. Now that I know what the system of discipline is I can implement it.
>
> (Lou, in Bolin, 1988, p. 51)

The assertion that one can free oneself from unjustified beliefs assumes a unified subject whose consciousness is within immediate grasp, while it denies the social construction of the self. The process of learning to teach itself contradicts this assertion. Learning to teach is, in part, a tacit cultural process which begins when we are children in classrooms, continues on to our apprenticeships in colleges of education and beyond to our experiences as teachers (Phelan, 1993). Throughout the learning to teach process, prospective teachers are immersed in multiple discourses – ways of thinking and talking about teachers and teaching. Some discourses are institutionally and culturally sanctioned and as such are dominant. The individual's ability to negotiate those dominant educational discourses is contingent upon his or her own biography, personal and institutional. We are at once active, knowing subjects and objects being acted upon – products of discourse (Marshall, 1990, p. 14).

Lou is a case in point. His journal entry attests to the multiple discourses which he must negotiate to succeed as a student teacher. Lou has to learn how to negotiate the framing discourses of his cooperating teacher, Max, and his supervisor. To one, he must appear strong and assertive; to the other, he must appear thoughtful about his choice of disciplinary procedure. His tendency to talk in terms of 'knowing' and 'applying' reflects the long history of instrumental rationality in teacher education. As Lou writes, his gaze on himself and his practice has already been encased by discourses such as those embodied by the cooperating teacher and the faculty adviser; such discourses define his axis of vision. Bolin's researcher-gaze doubly frames Lou in the act of looking.

It is the practices of journal-writing and supervisory conferences which facilitate Lou's framing. Both practices serve to expose certain aspects of the pre-service teacher's self and provide those in authority (supervisor) with the knowledge they need to regulate the subject further in particular ways. For example, Lou's focus on methods of teaching leads Bolin to conclude that he has so far only developed a 'craft knowledge' of teaching and must be helped to develop more 'mature levels of thought' – 'the conscious rationale that enables one to go beyond specific [teaching] methods' (Bolin, 1988, p. 51). Quoting Bruner (1966), she explains how Lou can be moved to such rational deliberation in the context of the supervisor–supervised relationship:

> It is not so much that the teacher [supervisor] provides a model to imitate. Rather, it is that the teacher [supervisor] can become part of the student's internal dialogue – somebody whose respect he [or she] wants, someone whose standards he [or she] wishes to make his [or her] own. It is like becoming a speaker of a language one shares with somebody. The language of that interaction becomes a part of oneself, and the standards of style and clarity that one adopts for that interaction become a part of one's own standards.
>
> (Bolin, 1988, p. 124)

The individualizing tendency in the discourse of reflection is clear in the model Bolin proposes (Gore, 1991). Students like Lou are given an opportunity to write their own journals and do their own action research projects according to their own interests. Each one is subsequently evaluated according to the level of mature thought reached. In the process, each student is normalized into a particular notion of what counts as valid knowledge, a particular rationality. In Lou's case, given his supervisor's practical orientation, personal theorizing is validated. If he were Zeichner's student, then socially critical thinking would be validated. Students are rewarded with grades or teacher certification for styling themselves accordingly. In some sense, prospective teachers become 'mimic men', pretending to be real, to be learning, to be reflective, turning themselves into what they think we want them to be (Bhabha, 1989, p. 128); Lou writes what he thinks 'fits'. Meanwhile, he continues to carry on the charade that his becoming a teacher is the 'autonomous preserve of free-will' (Clark, 1989, p. 166). He writes, 'Who says that a teacher in a typical, traditional school can't be creative and try new things. I hope that no matter what type of school I work in I will be creative and not fall into a mold' (Bolin, 1988, p. 51).

Practices such as journal-writing assume the existence of a unified self capable of knowing itself and expressing that knowledge accurately and unambiguously to others (Young, 1990). For example, according to Yinger and Clark (1981, p. 570), journal-writing allows pre-service teachers to learn at least four important things about themselves: (a) what they know; (b) what they feel; (c) what they do (and how they do it); and (d) why they do it. We find the same faith in the critical orientation, where Smyth (1992) asserts that when teachers describe and analyse their practices in diaries and journals they are beginning to answer such questions as: what do I do; what does this mean; how did I come to be like this? The self-knowledge which results from such questioning amounts to 'higher levels of thinking and increased awareness of personal values and implicit theories through which one approaches experience' (Zeichner, 1987). As one teacher put it, 'I'm getting right to the core in understanding why I act the way I do' (Canning, 1991, p. 21).

This concept of self-knowledge retains the Cartesian understanding of subjectivity basic to the modern metaphysics of presence; it assumes 'the unity of consciousness and its immediate presence to itself' as well as the self as 'the same starting point of thought and meaning, whose signification is never out of its grasp' (Young, 1990, p. 303). This notion of the self has been called into question by contemporary philosophers, such as Kristeva. She asserts that because the subject is not a unity (that is, it does not arise from some ego as origin), it cannot know what it means, needs, wants and desires (Young, 1990). 'Subjects all have multiple desires that do not cohere; they attach layers of meanings to objects without always being aware of each layer or their connections. Consequently, any individual subject is a play of differences' (Young, 1990, p. 310). Lou's immersion in multiple and often contradictory discourses ensures such an incoherent self. The adage 'know thyself' has found new proportions in the discourse of reflection. In the face of the highly complicated world of practice, pre-service teachers are offered self-knowledge and self-control as teaching tools.

## *Deception 2: Containing the ambiguity of practice*

> The conflict that Lou encounters places him in the position of having to deal with the inexplicable by denying the conflict, in effect backing away, or choosing between opposing good actions. A third alternative that Lou may not be ready to discover alone is engaging in the kind of dialectical mental process that allows one to synthesize opposing views under new thought and belief categories.
>
> (Bolin, 1988, p. 52)

Bolin is anxious that her students experience ambiguity but that they must then resolve their dilemmas and base their actions on resoluteness. Bolin's willingness to embrace dialectical thinking is reminiscent of John Dewey's influence on the discourse of reflection. Dewey (1933) pointed to the quality of responsibility as a prerequisite of reflection. Responsibility is defined as 'the desire to synthesize diverse ideas, to make sense of nonsense, and to apply information in the aspired direction' (Goodman, 1986, p. 20). This willingness to synthesize is problematic on two levels: first, the two dominant forms of dialectical thinking, the classical dialectic of Plato and Aristotle and the modern dialectic of Hegel, both display gender bias (Phelan and Garrison, 1994); second, the effort to reconcile contraries reflects an urgency to avoid tension and contain the ambiguity which pervades practice. I will begin with the latter.

> When Lou's supervisor invites him to be more analytical, he writes, 'I feel bad because I really can't think of any problems I am having. I've tried to think about it but all is really going fine ... The problem kids (Tim and Andy) at the start are doing much better. I feel really accepted by the kids, and Max always tells me he really appreciates me and has told me that he feels confident in me as a "teacher." But more importantly, I feel good about me as a "teacher." '

When students refuse to identify ambiguity in their practices, we are concerned because they haven't learned analytic discourse yet, and are reluctant to because they don't see the purpose of it. However, Lou, like many of his peers, has already experienced many years of 'a passive and uncomplicated reception of the truth, facts or reality that some authoritative figure has discovered'

(Schwartz, 1989, p. 61). It is no wonder that teaching is seen as a relatively closed system where things are the way they are for good reasons. Moreover, our efforts to encourage students to interpret practice more problematically do not always make the situation any clearer. Reflecting on practice has 'the potential to confuse things by introducing too many possibilities for meaning' (Schwartz, 1989, p. 62). Having established that there are many possible interpretations of a given problem, we then expect our students to act simply with singularity of purpose. We encourage them to examine how their actions reflected their initial intentions. Our attitude tends to be 'Do what you set out to do.' It is ironic that we ask them to see so much but expect them to act straightforwardly. McDonald (1988, p. 482) reminds us of the non-linear, non-rational mode that teaching calls for:

> Teaching requires wilder images ... [that encapsulate] three of our culture's villains: ambiguity, ambivalence, and instability ... the wildness helps explain why, despite so many exhortations to do otherwise, teachers tend to orient their work towards activities rather than goals, and to guide their planning by means of mental images of routines rather than by means of specific objectives, strategies and assessments

The problem is clearly related to the first deception – the model of an autonomous self – which the discourse and Western culture itself propagate. It speaks to a need to order the complex, disordered, unstable, uncertain and conflictual world of practice by exercising a certain kind of knowledge (Schön, 1987). This singular emphasis on rationalizing practice in pre-service teacher education forgoes a deeper understanding of teaching and learning. Control is often achieved 'only by ignoring or failing to see what cannot be controlled' (Schwartz, 1989, p. 63). Deborah Britzman (1991, p. 64) discusses the 'unleashing of unpopular things' in educational settings. As one high school student read her 'slasher' story aloud, her peers responded with encouraging screams; violence and misogyny seemed to pervade the classroom. Typically, the student teacher would be encouraged to calm the group, move on with the lesson and later reflect on the incident. However, such excessive moments constitute unexpected detours, whose ambiguity teachers are accustomed to; they have no rational explanation and must be explored on other terms.

It seems important, then, that pre-service teachers learn the art of constructed knowing (Belenky *et al.*, 1985) so that they can begin to

> show a high tolerance for internal contradiction and ambiguity ... recognize the inevitability of conflict and stress, and, although they may hope to achieve some respite, they also, as one woman explained, 'learn to live with conflict rather than talking or acting it away.' They no longer want to suppress or deny aspects of the self in order to avoid conflict and simplify their lives.
>
> (Belenky *et al.*, 1985, p. 137)

The capacity to live with detours and ambiguity may well be gender-related. Such a view opens up a different notion of practice and of the reflective practitioner. In her book *Maternal Thinking*, Sarah Ruddick (1989) writes, 'Thought-provoking ambivalence is a hallmark of mothering.' She goes on to describe 'protective thinking' as an alternative to reflective thinking. While the latter relies on a division between an inner self and an outer world, protective thinking relies on the connection between the self and other.

> In maternal thinking, feelings are at best complex but sturdy instruments of work quite unlike the simple and separate hates, fears and loves that are usually set aside and put down in philosophical analyses ... Rather than separating reason from feeling, mothering makes reflective feeling one of the most difficult attainments of reason.

Perhaps Ruddick's work points to the importance of knowledge 'about being mothers and being mothered' to teacher preparation. Without wishing to essentialize the 'maternal', we might wonder why 'the rationalist concept of teaching handed down to us by contemporary analytic philosophers of education' is so authoritative (Laird, 1988, p. 456). Why doesn't their concept of reflective teaching include any 'maternal' dimension? This leads us to our third and final deception: principled action is improved, or more just, action.

## Deception 3: Principled action – new and improved

> The point is when I am teaching, how can I tell my students something that I think is false unless I tell them what I think is true. In good conscience, how can I teach kids that we come from Apes or that the universe was made from a 'Big Bang'? ... I guess I'll have to decide when I get to the situation, but I plan to tell the school I will be working in what I believe and find out if I am free to voice my opinions in class.
>
> (Bolin, 1988, p. 52)

There are two questions which need to be addressed in relation to the third and final deception. First, whose principles will drive Lou's practice? Second, does the possibility of unprincipled action exist for him within the discourse of reflection?

The belief that we can build a better world of practice is endemic to the discourse-practices of reflection. In the above excerpt from Lou's journal, he is beginning to formulate a principle of practice, a rule of action that can guide his future practice. Honesty, for Lou, is the best policy when it comes to sharing his beliefs with students. Bolin (1988) describes this entry as one of the most reflective that Lou produced. The equation of reasons for practice with more reflective and, hence, better practice is clear and, to my mind, far too simple. What if Lou had concluded that dishonesty was in fact the best policy? Are some principles for practice more adequate, and more acceptable, than others? The answer to this question is related to the source of such principles. In the practical orientation, the answer is practical experience. So experience emerges as the essential truth for Lou, the teaching subject. Lou becomes what he knows, and he knows from subjective experience. In the technical orientation, Lou's principles would be drawn from university research. In this sense, 'his' principles of practice and his teaching self are bounded by notions of objective truth. In the critical tradition, it is clearly the grand narratives of truth and justice which provide insights. In each scenario, the principles of practice are drawn from 'cultural scripts written by white males whose work is often privileged as a model of high culture informed by an elite sensibility that sets it off from what is often dismissed as popular or mass culture' (Aronowitz and Giroux, 1991, p. 58). The grand narrative of the progressive march of history and the belief that we can build a better world has been shown not to work (Rorty, 1991), yet the narrative lives on in the discourse of critical reflective practice.

Second, what about practice that remains unprincipled? Traditionally, such 'irrational' behaviour has been associated with women. One wonders if the discourse of reflection is part of an effort to 'rationalize' teaching, to make it more male-oriented and, hence, professionalized. For example, the Holmes Group Report on teachers and teacher educators in the United States 'argues for the importance of having reflective teachers if schooling is to improve and the economy is to undergo the supposed necessary revitalization' (Smyth, 1992, p. 286). Susan Laird (1988) points out that such reports have implicitly juxtaposed two conceptions of teaching: 'feminized occupation' and 'professional work'. She writes of the Carnegie report, 'The people attracted to teaching until now have been women, one paragraph reports; "the people who must now be attracted to teaching" are professionals, the next paragraph then declares' (p. 458). The implication is, according to Laird, that the traditional values associated with and defined by men – rational autonomy – must replace those 'feminine' values associated with child-rearing and heretofore with teaching. There is no discussion of personal and emotional attachment in Lou's case. When the student teacher does express empathy for his cooperating teacher, whom he feels he is pushing out, Bolin gives little comment; the qualities of loyalty and empathy warrant little attention in her discourse. Bolin's article reflects the synecdochial tendency in the discourse of reflection to reduce the teacher to one aspect of the person – the mental, rational self.

David Jardine (1994) writes about student teaching as a liminal zone, a deeply pedagogic space full of possibility. His concern is that we limit the possibility of the experience when we transform it into 'the hurried accumulation of skills and techniques' (p. 17). The danger is that action research, journal writing and supervisory conferences can become a new 'bag of tricks' with which we stifle the possibilities of learning in pre-service teacher education. In support of Jardine's position, I offer a different metaphor, a different epistemology, for our practices.

## Exchanging 'reflection' for 'conversation'

It is time to rearticulate the challenge of educating teachers: how do we help our students to gain the ability to read practice with 'interpretive and critical acumen' and to teach with 'clarity, power and grace' without being deceived by the supposed power of reason (Scholes, 1990, p. 99)? One answer lies in a pedagogy of conversation. Conversation offers a different kind of relationship between pre-service teachers and other players in teacher education. The relationship is best described by Nina Schwartz (1989, p. 63):

> 'Exchange' is an important idea for our students to understand because it implies a giving up of one thing for a substitute or alternative. What is given up in the exchange is not necessarily a particular opinion, to be substituted by someone else's. What I give up is a *kind of closure or certainty*: no exchange occurs without some risk, however minimal, to my ideas and opinions. And the substitute I receive in exchange is a new role, one constituted by a *responsibility to another*. In this role, I take on the responsibility for my own views ... And I take on as well the responsibility for interpreting and understanding the views of the other. I must recognize that I have a world view and that not everyone shares it; that I am like others, in short, not necessarily because we all think alike but because my view, like any other, makes good sense only within *a particular and limited context*.

The metaphor of conversation helps us overcome the three deceptions outlined above and fosters a post-modern turn in teacher preparation. First, it casts the self not as autonomous agent but as a subject configured at the intersection of discourse. Second, it reframes practice as text and as such irreducibly plural, 'an endless play ... which can never be finally nailed down to a single centre, essence or meaning' (Eagleton, 1983). Finally, it emphasizes responsibility to the other rather than to rational principles of action. Let us examine how the practitioner, practice and principle are reconfigured in conversation.

Rather than 'self-control' or 'liberation', I want to invoke 'irony' and 'parody' to characterize a different pedagogy of conversation. As Clark (1989, p. 166) writes, 'These terms do not mark ideological positions but rhetorical attitudes that pitch one discourse against another and constitute the "subjectivity" of the author in – or even as – this discursive conflict.' Pre-service teachers do not teach in a style of their own, no matter how reasoned and justified their practices are. The aim of the teacher educator is to help the students understand how their practice has been framed by particular discourses they have 'absorbed unconsciously as monologic authority or – as one hopes – consciously as dialogic strategies'. Agency, in this case, refers to the ability of the practitioner to analyse subjectivity. As pre-service teachers' sense of themselves becomes increasingly complicated, fluid, moving and under constant reconstruction, so must their notion of practice honour that complexity.

Reading practice complicatedly means acknowledging that there is no singular interpretation of practice. Relying instead on the performance of meaning, the inexhaustibility of practice becomes evident; so too its ambiguity. We let go any effort to reduce practice to singular meanings. Recognizing this, teacher educators must then turn to the students', as well as their own, interpretations as the central text in the conversation. Enquiry into practice is no longer seen in terms of levels of reflectivity or mature thought but rather as an activity which both teacher and students engage in collaboratively, with no sense that one interpretation is better or more thoughtful than any other. 'Knowing' is recognized in all its uncertainty, obstacles, anxieties, resolutions, complications: teacher educators and pre-service teachers together come to recognize their uncertain beginnings as makers of meaning (Schwartz, 1989). So, if we are to read practice complicatedly, we cannot continue to act simply, managing ambiguity and striving for synthetic solutions to practical dilemmas. We must begin to draw our students' attention to the excessive moments in our practice which refuse synthesis.

A pedagogy of conversation emphasizes our responsibility to the other, rather than to principle, in conversation. Schwartz (1989) emphasizes the difficulty in living with other people because it involves 'turning ourselves around, sometimes inside out'. This means that we must be willing to enter the pedagogical conversation with a certain intellectual humility, ready to give up certainty, to recognize the particularity of our positions and to take Rorty's advice that 'the best way to find out what to believe is to listen to as many suggestions and arguments as you can' (Rorty, 1991, p. 31).

## Conclusion

So we end as we began – in the epistemologies and politics of our institutional practices. The mirror has crack'd and we have walked through the looking glass to find a maze of questions. 'The point is not a set of answers, but making possible a different practice' (Kappeler, 1986, p. 212).

## References

Aronowitz, S. and Giroux, H. (1991) *Postmodern Education: Politics, Culture and Social Criticism*. Minneapolis: University of Minnesota Press.

Belenky, M. F., Clinchy, B. M., Goldberger, N. R. and Tarule, J. M. (1985) *Women's Ways of Knowing*. New York: Basic Books.

Bhabha, H. (1989) The other question: difference, discrimination and the discourse of colonialism. In F. Barker *et al.* (eds), *Literature, Politics and Theory*. London: Methuen.

Bolin, F. S. (1988) Helping student teachers think about teaching. *Journal of Teacher Education*, March/April.

Britzman, D. (1991) Decentering discourses in teacher education: or the unleashing of unpopular things. *Journal of Education*, **173** (3), 60–79.

Britzman, D. (1992) *Practice Makes Practice*, New York: SUNY Press.

Bruner, J. S. (1966). *Toward a Theory of Instruction*. Cambridge, MA: Harvard University Press.

Calderhead, J. (1988) Reflective teaching and teacher education. *Teaching and Teacher Education*, **5** (1), 43–51.

Canning, C. (1991) What teachers say about reflection. *Educational Leadership*, March.

Clark, M. (1989) Afterword. In P. Donahue and E. Quandahl (eds), *Reclaiming Pedagogy: The Rhetoric of the Classroom*. Carbondale, IL: Southern Illinois University Press.

Clift, R., Veal, M. L., Johnston, M. and Holland, P. (1991) Restructuring teacher education through collaborative action research. *Journal of Teacher Education*, **41** (2).

Connelly, M. and Clandinin, M. (1988) *Teachers as Curriculum Planners: Narratives of Experience*. New York: Teachers College Press.

Cruickshank, D. R. (1984) *Models for the Preparation of America's Teachers*. Bloomington, IN: Phi Delta Kappa Educational Foundation.

Dewey, J. (1933) *How We Think*. Boston: D. C. Heath.

Eagleton, T. (1983) *Literary Theory: An Introduction*. London: Redwood Burn.

Flax, J. (1993) *Disputed Subjects: Essays on Psychoanalysis, Politics and Philosophy*. New York: Routledge.

Gauthier, D. P. (1963) *Practical Reasoning*. Oxford: Oxford University Press.

Giroux, H. (ed.) (1991) *Postmodernism, Feminism and Cultural Politics: Redrawing Educational Boundaries*. New York: SUNY Press.

Goodman, J. (1986) Teaching preservice teachers a critical approach to curriculum design: a descriptive account. *Curriculum Inquiry*, **16** (2).

Gore, J. (1991) On silent regulation: emancipatory action research in preservice teacher education. *Curriculum Perspectives*, **11** (4).

Greene, M. (1978) The matter of mystification: teacher education in unquiet times. In M. Greene (ed.), *Landscapes of Learning*. New York: Teachers College Press.

Grimmett, P., MacKinnon, A., Erickson, G. and Riecken, T. (1990) Reflective practice in teacher education. In R. Clift, W. R. Houston and M. Pugach (eds), *Encouraging Reflective Practice in Education*. New York: Teachers College Press.

Habermas, J. (1974) *Theory and Practice*. London: Heinemann.

Holmes Group (1986) *Tomorrow's Teachers: A Report of the Holmes Group*. East Lansing, MI: The Holmes Group.

Jardine, D. (1994) Student-teaching, interpretation and the monstrous child. *Journal of Philosophy of Education*, **28** (1).

Kappeler, S. (1986) *The Pornography of Representation*. Cambridge, MA: Polity Press.

Laird, S. (1988) Reforming 'woman's true profession': a case for 'feminist pedagogy' in teacher education? *Harvard Educational Review*, **58** (4).

Lather, P. (1992) Critical frames in educational research: feminist and post-structuralist perspectives. *Theory into Practice*, **31** (spring).

Lyotard, J. (1989) *The Postmodern Condition: A Report on Knowledge*. Minneapolis, Minnesota: University of Minnesota Press.

McDonald, J. (1988) The emergence of the teacher's voice: implications for the new reform. *Harvard Educational Review*, **89** (4), 482–3.

McKay, A. (1994) The implications of postmodernism for moral education. *McGill Journal of Education*, **29** (1).

Marshall, J. D. (1990) Foucault and educational research. In S. Ball (ed.), *Foucault and Education: Disciplines and Knowledge*. London: Routledge.

Munby, H. and Russell, T. (1994) The authority of experience in learning to teach: messages from a physics methods class. *Journal of Teacher Education*, **45** (2).

Phelan, A. (1993). Unmasking metaphors of management. *Teaching Education*, fall.

Phelan, A. and Garrison, J. (1994) Toward a gender sensitive ideal of critical thinking: toward a feminist poetic. *Curriculum Inquiry*, **24** (3).

Polanyi, M. (1967) *The Tacit Dimension*. London: Routledge and Kegan Paul.

Richert, A. (1987) Reflection and pedagogical caring: unsilencing the teacher's voice. Paper presented at the annual meeting of the American Educational Research Association, Washington, DC.

Rorty, R. (1991) *Philosophical Papers*, Volume 1: *Objectivity, Relativism, and Truth*. Cambridge: Cambridge University Press.

Ruddick, S. (1989) *Maternal Thinking: Towards a Politics of Peace*. Boston: Beacon Press.

Sadwicki, J. (1988) Feminism and the power of Foucauldian discourse. In J. Arac (ed.), *After Foucault: Humanistic Knowledge, Postmodern Challenges*. New Brunswick, NJ and London: Rutgers University Press.

Sanders, D. P. and McCutcheon, G. (1986) The development of practical theories of teaching. *Journal of Curriculum and Supervision*, **2** (1), 50–67.

Scholes, R. (1990) Toward a curriculum in textual studies. In B. Henricksen and T. Morgan (eds), *Reorientations: Critical Theories and Pedagogies*. Urbana, IL: University of Illinois Press.

Schön, D. (1987) *Educating the Reflective Practitioner*. New York: Basic Books.

Schwab, J. J. (1971) The practical: arts of eclectic. *School Review*, **79**, 493–543.

Schwartz, N. (1989) Conversation with the social text. In P. Donahue and E. Quandahl (eds), *Reclaiming Peda-*

*gogy: The Rhetoric of the Classroom.* Carbondale, IL: Southern Illinois University Press.

Smyth, J. (1992) Teachers' work and the politics of teacher reflection. *American Educational Research Journal*, **29** (2), 267–300.

Tom, A. (1987) Inquiring into inquiry-oriented teacher education. *Journal of Teacher Education*, **36** (6).

Van Manen, M. (1977) Linking ways of knowing with ways of being practical. *Curriculum Inquiry*, **6**, 205–28.

Yinger, R. and Clark, C. (1981) *Reflective Journal Writing: Theory and Practice.* East Lansing, MI: Institute for Research on Teaching.

Young, I. (1990) The ideal of community and the politics of difference. In L. J. Nicholson (ed.), *Feminism and Postmodernism.* London: Routledge.

Zeichner, K. (1983) Alternative paradigms of teacher education. *Journal of Teacher Education*, **34** (3), 3–9.

Zeichner, K. (1987) Preparing reflective teachers: an overview of instructional strategies which have been employed in pre-service teacher education. *International Journal of Educational Research*, **2**, 567–75.

Zeichner, K. and Liston, D. (1987). Teaching student teachers to reflect. *Harvard Educational Review*, **57** (1).

# Response to Anne M. Phelan

## H. JAMES McLAUGHLIN

Anne, I want to express my admiration for your chapter. (Our two chapters have resulted from various conversations between us, so I will write as if talking with you.) You tend to write 'against the grain', in this case by questioning our long-held assumptions about the claims and meaning of reflection. Your writing always challenges me to think more clearly and often to consider how I might reshape radically what I do. In this response to your writing I want to critique the metaphor of reflection and attend to how your idea of a 'pedagogy of conversation' might be extended.

## Critiquing the metaphor

The metaphor of 'reflection' is troublesome, as we both state in our chapters. Any concept that attempts to capture the complexity of how humans interpret experience needs to connect the individual and the collective, to consider thought and action jointly, to examine differing forms of speech and communication, and to incorporate a negotiation of multiple discourses (your phrase) that surround educational ideas. Most of the writing and research about reflection does little or none of that.

I agree with you that rationality is a cultural creation and that controlling practice is an illusion. We should be careful not to overstate any claims for the efficacy of reflection. Fundamentally, action is meaningful not simply because re-

flection may help to make it more intelligible, but because its consequences have meaning for our lives and others'.

I would question your depiction of 'deceptive discourses' and of student teachers 'pretending to be real'. This phrasing smacks of conscious duplicity and neatly personifies the concept of 'discourse'. My experience with teachers is that they are struggling with others' expectations and are *trying* to be real. Theirs is not a pretence but an act or a performance, in Vygotsky's terms (see Newman and Holzman, 1993, pp. 150–1, 172–3, for further explanation of the difference between acting and performing).

Rather than deceptions, I find it helpful to think about 'illusions' (somehow fitting because, like reflection, this is a metaphor of light). Our illusions about education and life are not necessarily destructive, and there is certainly a thin line between illusion and ideal. However, we are obliged as educators to cast light upon our often illusory assumptions and beliefs, perhaps, as I state in my chapter, by using different forms of individual/collective speech to 'dis-illusion' ourselves. I want students in teacher education programmes to question their experiences, not as solitary subjects acting in front of a closed curtain, but as people performing within a collective endeavour. (Metaphorically, we must not let 'reflection' connote seeing oneself more clearly against a backdrop of blurred figures.) I also want pre-service teachers to act responsibly, and by that I mean that they should *be able to respond* to students, parents, administrators and other teachers. I concur with you that we must not act as if we can construct a fully rationalized world, as if pre-service teachers' major task was to learn how to control what is in many ways not controllable. Yet to strive for greater consciousness and clarity of intention does not require us to deify rationality or to inculcate an individualized, instrumental form of 'self-control'.

Another point on which I agree is that reflection, whatever we may take it to mean, should certainly not provide material for others' critique of pre-service teachers' faulty reasoning or their means of expression. There are no defensible standards to evaluate how someone interprets experience – though there are questions to pose in our pedagogy.

## A pedagogy of conversation and collective performance

You are right that we should not ask pre-service teachers to wander down a hall of mirrors, but should instead engage in a 'pedagogy of conversation'. Extending the ideas presented in your two concluding paragraphs, don't we also need a 'pedagogy of collective performance'? Reflection is not just about conversation and language, because languages of practice encompass action.

How, then, do our pedagogies relate to the necessary process of dis-illusioning, which I conceive as an imperative for learning to teach? The discursive process may begin a 'baring of belief' (in my terms) and a challenge to the 'discourse of certainty' (Phelan and McLaughlin, 1996) pushed upon teachers. I would argue that the long-term goal should be to help to dis-illusion one another, to establish a pattern of constantly shedding ourselves of illusions about who students are, about the naturalness of school environments and policies, and about the growth potential of different instructional strategies and curricula.

What forms might a pedagogy of conversation and a pedagogy of collective performance take? We might address this question by reconsidering

the purposes, limits and forms of journal-writing. I agree with you that what someone presents in writing is not a 'unitary self' (your phrase), *the* answer to *a* question. But what is wrong with trying to determine what we believe? Understanding that 'the subject is not a unity' (your words, again) does not imply that we should not seek to see ourselves within the field of collective experience. Journals reveal that writing as a form of speech both expands and limits one's experience, just as oral speech does. How might journals reflect conversation and collective performance? Can dialogue journals reflect a 'reading of our own practice' (your felicitous phrase) and a willingness to examine grand educational discourses?

What if we reconceived *supervision* as 'collective learning' by teaching together and examining what happened, and the implications of what happened? Our job as teacher educators would not be to assume the role of 'objective' observer in order to ascertain how well a student teacher performed a predetermined task defined by the teacher educator. Instead, we would try to learn how student teachers reorganize and reinterpret what happened in the flux of classroom interactions, and how they analyse afterwards what might have been possible during the preceding class session.

In our discussions of reflection, we might think about the difference between 'societization' and 'socialization' (Newman and Holzman, 1993):

> To Marx, *socialization* is the process of the human species becoming more social, that is, producing more varied and complex relations of cooperation in the remaking of its life … The need to adapt to an existing society, what we call *societization*, is both a product of and produces socialization.
>
> (p. 117)

It is the interplay between adapting to and remaking the world that we must heed – along with the 'complex relations of cooperation'. In the course of this collective interpretation of experience, it is our task as teacher educators to ask questions about purpose, to set certainty aside and to nurture a sense of multiplicity and possibility. Anne, though we express it in differing ways, I believe we are both working towards this end.

# References

Newman, F. and Holzman, L. (1993) *Lev Vygotsky: Revolutionary Scientist*. New York: Routledge.

Phelan, A. and McLaughlin, H. J. (1996) Educational discourses, the nature of the child, and the practice of new teachers. *Journal of Teacher Education*, in press.

# 16 The Nature and Nurture of Reflection

H. JAMES McLAUGHLIN

'*Reflection*' is a term that has been tossed around loosely; how one addresses the idea of learning to be a reflective teacher depends on how one interprets the concept. In this chapter I analyse the forms and the operation of reflection. Five considerations about the nature of reflection in teacher education frame the discourse. My purpose is to challenge other teacher educators to re-examine their notions of reflection and to strengthen their commitment to create better conditions for reflection to occur.

## Conceptual framework

Others have found it useful to categorize reflection in heuristic ways as a flexible series of actions akin to the scientific method (Dewey, 1933), as three levels that differ according to interests and means of enquiry (Habermas's ideas, explicated in Van Manen, 1977), as varying forms and interests (Weiss and Louden, 1989) and as three dimensions that might be used to classify differing conceptions of reflection (Tom, 1985). This chapter is framed instead as an analysis of Vygotskian and Bakhtinian theory, followed by a set of statements to consider. The five considerations address these fundamental aspects of reflection: its relationship to action and intention, its social genesis, its role in enquiry, its conditionality and its emotional and ideological characteristics. I offer a brief theoretical discussion of each consideration followed by a section providing examples of how teacher educators foster reflective action.

## Forms of speech and the nature of reflection

Vygotsky's (1987) theories are premised on his studies of three forms of speech: oral speech, inner speech and written speech. Examining the forms gives us a deeper understanding of the genesis and the nature of reflective action.

According to Vygotsky, speech has individual and social characteristics; it is monologic and dialogic. But *oral speech* is a precursor to inner and written speech – in dialogue we find the genesis of monologue. Oral speech may be abbreviated, particularly if there is shared knowledge of a subject or situation (what Vygotsky called 'intersubjectivity').

*Inner speech* is a theoretical construct that cannot be directly studied. Vygotsky was clear that inner speech did not consist simply of verbal memory, of simple abbreviations of normal sounds and words ('speech minus sound') or of the internal processes that occur before the act of speaking (pp. 256–7). Its origins lie in socially constructed oral speech: 'Inner speech is not merely what precedes or reproduces external speech ... External speech is a process of transforming thought into word; it is the materialization and objectivization of thought. Inner speech moves in the reverse direction, from without to within' (p. 257).

Vygotsky further explained inner speech in terms of its function: 'Inner speech is not meant for communication. It is speech for oneself ' (p. 278). Inner speech is abbreviated and its purpose is self-regulation. It 'acts as an internal rough draft in oral as well as in written speech' (p. 273).

*Written speech* is quite another bird. 'While the development of external speech precedes the development of inner speech, written speech emerges only after the development of the latter. Written speech presupposes the existence of inner speech' (p. 204). Written speech is expanded and formal, and 'it requires a child who is capable of extremely complex operations in the voluntary construction of the fabric of meaning' (p. 204). This construction of meaning entails a greater consciousness and intentionality. 'Written speech is the algebra of speech. The process of learning algebra does not repeat that of arithmetic. It is a new and higher plane in the development of abstract mathematical thought that is constructed over and rises above arithmetic thinking' (p. 203). If a teacher writes down her thoughts about a class in order to enquire about some aspect of it, this speech can be more precise and more easily expanded (less abbreviated) – and certainly more structured – than inner or vocal speech.

Vygotsky was quite concerned with the development of will or motive in human actions, but as with all psychological constructs, *will* ('volitional action' in Vygotskian terms) was tied to social interactions and the form of speech.

> Dialogue is speech that consists of rejoinders. It is a chain of reactions. In contrast, written speech is connected with consciousness and intentionality from the outset ... The rapid tempo of oral speech is not conducive to the development of speech activity as a complex volitional action, that is, as an action characterized by reflection, the conflict of motives, and selection.
>
> (p. 272)

At this stage of the chapter, a working definition of 'reflection' is in order, because the meaning is linked with the preceding analysis and subsequent questions. The important considerations here are: what is 'reflection' and how does a reflective consciousness emerge?

'Reflection' involves conscious thought. At its core, reflection is a process of becoming more conscious: about purpose, about action, about conditions and about social consequences of actions. I propose that we consider how the development of

reflection in prospective teachers may recapitulate the development of speech. Like inner speech, reflectivity – a propensity to be reflective – may develop from social action and dialogue. Perhaps it begins with being conscious of events and of one's part in those events, and is raised to higher levels through reinterpretations of the events in oral, inner and written speech. There would then be qualitative differences in how one 'reflected' while using the different speech forms, and we should take those differences into account as we promote increased reflectivity in teacher education.

To provide several examples related to the final point above, I would note that reflecting in oral speech differs from reflecting in writing or to oneself. We are presented with a paradox: while oral speech may not be conducive to complex reflective activity, particularly within the fast-paced social interactions of a classroom, its dialogic nature is necessary for challenging and transforming the content of inner or written speech. Inner and written speech bereft of external dialogue would suffer from a lack of competing interpretations of events. Oral speech cut off from inner and written monologues would abandon much of its intentionality, because the dialogic without the monologic may lack internalized reflection.

The following section offers five considerations derived from a Vygotskian analysis of speech forms, and my budding understandings of reflection in light of that analysis. I use the term 'consideration' because there is no claim that the statements are 'postulates' or 'propositions' or some other universalistic artefact. Instead, I am merely trying to suggest some matters to consider when reflecting about reflection.

## Five considerations about reflection

*We might consider how to initiate reflective activities by retelling actions we have experienced.* Reflection is inextricably bound up in action, and a consideration of past action is fundamental to reflection. 'To become consciously aware of an operation, it must be transferred from the plane of action to the plane of language; it must be recreated in imagination such that it can be expressed in words' (Vygotsky, 1987, p. 183). Vygotsky did not contrast imagination with reality, because any recollection of past events involves imaginative reinterpretation. We move from 'direct' to 'indirect' memory as we learn how to reformulate direct perceptions through linguistic mediation (Bruner, 1987, pp. 9–10). Memory in the service of reflection is more intentional than automatic, and is subject to multiple interpretations.

Bakhtin (1981) thought along these lines when he contrasted 'retelling' and 'reciting' as means of reporting from memory. During the past decade there has been an explosion of ideas about how best to help pre-service teachers to 'retell' prior experiences as students and as teachers. For example, teacher educators have used written speech in journals and free writing; autobiographies or life histories; 'reaction' papers to a particular situation; case studies created from observations and experiences; written self-evaluations; and metaphorical analysis or development.

*We might consider that reflection, no matter the form or the action in which it is instantiated, is constituted through social interaction.* The discourse about *reflection* has largely centred on the self. Yet, I would not be alone in arguing that reflection is a social construction, or perhaps more accurately, a social *reconstruction* of practice. Teaching is predicated on responses to novel situations. Routines of action can be planned and begun, but the outcomes of action are socially created probabilities. The literal view of this process would perhaps portray people conferring after a teaching episode, thus reflecting in an explicitly social way. Bakhtin (1981), however, advanced the subtler and quite powerful notion that multiple voices are involved in one's internal discourses. This idea of *heteroglossia* may at first seem antithetical to Vygotsky's ideas of inner speech as monologic, but Bakhtin really complements and broadens Vygotskian theory. Oral speech is the reflective medium of social interaction, and teacher educators should consider how dyads, small groups or large groups engage students in retelling and reflecting. Because Bakh-

tin's theories are tied to ideological concerns, they will be explained further in a consideration of politics and reflection.

*We might consider how reflection operates as part of enquiry and research.* It would make sense to follow the traditional pattern of talking about 'form and function' with regard to reflection, since the opening discussion in this chapter dealt with forms of speech. *Function*, however, has assumed a constricted meaning; I want to focus on the *operation* of reflection, which I take to mean the purposes, processes and consequences of reflective acts. The operations of reflection are a part of everyday enquiry as well as the more formal concept of research. I will use Schön's (1983, 1987) treatment of reflective enquiry and several writers' conceptions of action research to discuss this issue.

Schön's major interest lies in determining how to define and resolve problems that arise in practice. In this scheme, a 'problem' originates from a discrepancy between expectations and reality. The problem cannot normally be solved by routines; it requires reflective action that includes recollecting a situation, defining what constitutes a problem, asking questions and discussing the problem, and arriving at possible reactions to the problem.

Schön advanced the notion that there is 'reflection-in-action' and 'reflection-on-action'. 'Reflection-in-action' is essentially inner speech (to use a Vygotskian analysis) and thus not subject to public display or validation, except as observed and interpreted action. 'Reflection-on-action', as explained by Schön, is a process of reconstructing experience, primarily through discussion. It is clear how Vygotsky's ideas can enrich this perspective, if we consider the intertwining of written and oral speech, and the social dynamics of reflective action in problem-solving.

Schön's problem-solving approach may seem a bit antiseptic and value-neutral. Rather than talking of gaps in 'expectations', Canning (1991) believes that questioning may result from a conflict between what one states and values, and what one practices (p. 21). Reflective enquiry about one's own values and the consequences of one's actions is at the heart of action research. There are many varieties of action research, but all emphasize reflective action for the purpose of changing one's practice and enhancing students' learning.

Articles in a recent issue of *Educational Action Research* illustrate the range of reflective operations in action research. Such writings expand the traditional talk about 'problem-solving', which often sounds abstracted and removed from the messy business of emotion, conflict and action. Arnold (1994) wrote, as an individual teacher conducting a study, about students bullying one another in her school. Her purpose was to learn how students interpreted the social situation: was bullying even a problem? Arnold interviewed and observed students, and engaged in informal conversations with students about her questions and theirs. One of the consequences she raised was the conflict she sometimes perceived between teaching and researching, and her need for 'time for reflection and a wider forum for discussion' (p. 21). Laidlaw (1994) detailed the process of her dialogue with one student during a pre-service practicum. Her purpose was to 'democratize the educational process'. The dyadic study involved reading the student's write-up of an action enquiry and then discussing the project. A consequence of the reflective action was Laidlaw's tension about balancing her respect for the values and ideas of the pre-service teacher, and her strong belief in certain values and practices that she wanted to be promoted. Friesen (1994) reported a triadic study of an internship involving a pre-service teacher, a cooperating teacher and the university researcher. The author's purpose was to foster increased participation by all three parties. Interviews and journals were analysed, and the consequence was that while the nature of status and authority within the triad did not change (the pre-service teacher was not afforded the same status as the other two), the 'pedagogical relationships' were enhanced.

The groupings were individual, dyadic or triadic; the researcher's values were openly expressed or more implicit; and the processes and consequences differed across the studies. Yet, in each of these reports of action research, reflective action was central to the authors' understandings.

*We might carefully consider the conditions of reflection.* 'Conditions' are composed of the socio-historical and environmental contexts in which one acts. Cannot someone be quite reflective in one context and much less so in another? On a localized level, let's say that the one who is reflecting happens to be a pre-service teacher in the midst of a practicum who is alone in a room, in the late afternoon, after a tumultuous day in which a sixth-grade student broke into tears because of others' teasing. Perhaps this pre-service teacher is discussing a certain cooperative grouping arrangement with a mentor teacher, between mouthfuls of food, while sitting with other teachers in a noisy cafeteria. Or the pre-service teacher is talking with classmates in a university classroom. The process and content of reflection are clearly shaped by the social and environmental contexts, and we must consider contexts carefully in thinking about how to encourage reflection by pre-service teachers. Different reflective actions could well work under one set of conditions and not another. The conditions of pre-service teacher education can certainly constrain reflective action, as Goodman (1988) found.

Lave (1988) took the matter of conditions further afield by studying experiential learning beyond school walls and traditional worksites. Cultural and historical conditions are examined in her work. Lave's research with apprentice tailors in West Africa and with supermarket shoppers doing everyday mathematics problems indicated that it is more meaningful to imagine experience as holistic activity than to consider discrete techniques or behaviours. We should 'focus on whole-person activity rather than on thinking as separate from doing' (p. 171), and on '"problem-solving" as a culture-specific vision of mental activity' (p. 172). Lave went on to characterize a Western cognitivist view of experience and, obliquely, the idea of reflection: 'The only "good" experience [is] distanced and generalized, removed from the debilitating influence of immediate time and place in the form of abstract accounts of action.' But for Lave, the problems we face cannot be understood apart from conflict. 'A problem is a dilemma with which the problem solver is emotionally engaged; conflict is the source of dilemmas. Processes for resolving dilemmas are correspondingly deprived of their assumed universalistic, normative, decontextualized nature' (p. 175). 'I do not conclude from this [her studies of people's everyday maths activity] that people fail to meet some rational standard of conduct, but rather, that a psychology drawn from an ideology of rationality cannot adequately account for practice' (p. 176).

*We might consider that reflection always involves emotion and ideology.* To recapitulate the argument so far, I believe that becoming more reflective means achieving greater consciousness through some form of speech that is embedded in, and generated through, action. However, to desire greater consciousness is not to deny the power of subconscious and affective influences. Reflection cannot be wholly rational, and rationality is a cultural construct anyway, as Lave (1988) pointed out. 'Thought has its origins in the motivating sphere of consciousness, a sphere that includes our inclinations and needs, our interests and impulses, and our affect and emotion. The affective and volitional tendency stands behind thought' (Vygotsky, 1987, p. 282).

On a theoretical plane, both Vygotsky and Bakhtin were concerned with creating a social interpretation of psychological processes and human development. Vygotsky was interested in semiotic mediation but did not overtly address the relationship between social institutions and mental processes in the individual. Bakhtin was interested in novelistic discourse that incorporated 'other utterances and voices, each with its ideological perspective' (Wertsch, 1985, p. 64). Inner speech for Bakhtin was not monologic, but dialogic. Consciousness was conceived as an operation of *becoming*, 'an ideological process characterized by a gap between the authoritative word ... that does not know internal persuasiveness' and the 'internally persuasive word that is denied all privilege' (Bakhtin, 1981, p. 342).

Munby and Russell (1994), in a similar vein, spoke of 'learning from the authority of experience' rather than from the 'authority of reason' or the 'authority of position' (p. 92).

> There is a competing authority in long and short conversations with other teachers in the school, conversations expressing perspectives and practices shared by many teachers in the school. This competing authority may restrict the ability of the beginning teacher to listen to personal experience, including the responses of students ... In the absence of any clear delineation of the epistemology of practice and the nature of the authority of experience, they understandably look for the familiar and trusted authority of position and reason associated with propositional knowledge rooted in the experience of those who have been successful teachers.
>
> (p. 93)

Please note the cultural boundedness of these ideas, in line with Lave's (1988) thinking. Reason may seem authoritative in one culture, while age or family position may be authoritative in another culture.

To place these ideas squarely in the realm of teacher education, I believe that pre-service teachers in classrooms and field experiences are constantly dealing with the authoritative discourses (Bakhtin) or the authorities of reason and position (Munby and Russell) generated from university faculty, mentoring teachers and memories of past school experiences. Then, when pre-service teachers become the sole adult in a classroom, they must in some way continue to 'struggle with another's discourse' (Bakhtin, 1981, p. 348).

It seems to me that reflecting through the forms and operations that I have been discussing offers a way to deal with this struggle to develop internally persuasive discourses or to understand the authority of experience. We need to involve pre-service teachers in 'retelling their experiences in their own words', to paraphrase Bakhtin. Written speech may allow them more clearly and fully to reflect on their experience, but oral, directly dialogic speech can challenge them to consider the conflict among discourses.

The central point is that political ideology is always implicated in reflective action. According to Zeichner and Liston (1987), 'reflection is primarily a political act, an act related to our understandings of justice'. The purposes of reflection should be to further an ideal of communication and to foster action that is ethical and just. O'Hanlon (1994) asserted that even the usually formulaic dissertation process ought to be conceived as an example of reflective action. If enquiry or research of any sort is truly reflective, then the enquirer will experience some alteration of consciousness and the development of 'phronesis' or practical wisdom. 'How will we influence the world as a result of a process of altered consciousness, or how do we validate the true meaning of the investigation in the real world if we do not embrace the moral imperative to act intentionally as a result of educational research?' (pp. 288–9).

## Nurturing reflective action in teacher education

How can teacher educators use these ideas about the forms and operations – the *nature* – of reflection? Next, I will describe two teacher educators' approaches to nurturing reflective action that incorporate an explicitly Vygotskian perspective. That will be followed by a concise summary of seven other examples of what teacher educators do to encourage reflection in different settings (university classrooms and field experiences), with different people (pre-service and in-service teachers), using different processes (written and oral, individual and social).

Two possible ways to proceed are to consider seriously the social structures of reflection and the links between different forms of speech. Bayer (1990) described how she developed a 'scaffolding structure' to enhance the conceptual development of pre-service teachers. Bayer initially spent time 'engaging students in joint activities designed to make public their knowledge and interest in topics and helping them build on what they already know' (p. 9). 'Focused free writing' was used as a starting point: 'I ask my students to write what they already know about a very broad, core concept in this field (literacy), such as, "How do individuals learn something new?"' This form of writing encourages 'expressive' or conversational language. Students *reflect* on what they know, while writing, and then they read to peers in small groups to 'make public the individual student's knowledge' while beginning 'peer collaboration' and fostering the idea of 'pooled knowledge' (p. 10). Bayer, as the teacher, then uses this 'shared

knowledge of the class participants as an anchor for negotiating the meaning of new knowledge about topic *x*' (p. 10). In part, this entails the teacher acquainting students with the conceptual language of the topic at hand. In line with Vygotskian theory, the students are being asked to internalize (as inner speech) what they have learned socially, and the teacher is ascertaining what the students already know and how they have come to know it, in order to determine how much 'scaffolding' or further direct teaching is needed.

I would note that Bayer's method of beginning with written speech allows students to reflect in a more structured and expansive way before entering into the social milieu. The students move from written to vocal to internalized reflection, though this is not an invariable sequence. Throughout the course, students increasingly take the initiative for directing their own learning. After reflecting initially about what they already know, and collaborating with others to determine collective knowledge, the students reflect by enquiring about their own questions. 'They are encouraged to find answers for the questions and to challenge the "received definitions" of existing knowledge' (Bayer, 1990, p. 20). Students write more formally for an audience (Bayer refers to this as 'transactional writing'), lead discussions and make dramatic or musical presentations to represent what they are learning.

Notice in Bayer's approach to enacting Vygotskian theory in teacher education the emphasis on combining different forms of speech, on individual and collective reflection and on moving from teacher-directed to student-initiated activities.

Manning and Payne (1992, 1993) have taken another tack: they have worked to unite inner speech and oral speech through the development of 'self-guiding speech' as a means of furthering reflection among pre-service and in-service teachers. Their work is founded on Vygotskian principles of will and self-regulation. 'Will' involves the ability to talk oneself into an action (Bruner, 1987). Manning and Payne have found that pre-service teachers are more likely to engage in self-regulation – that is, to have the conscious will to take action – if they utilize written speech and learn ways to enhance their inner speech during teaching episodes. Self-guiding speech is predicated on determining what questions to ask oneself and one's students that will lead one to reflect more frequently while teaching.

Seven other examples of reflective action will be ample to show the scope of current initiatives. As a general example, the University of Wisconsin-Madison elementary teacher education programme has long emphasized reflective action. Through action research projects, seminars, journals and supervisory conferences, pre-service teachers have engaged in reflective action, with a strong social reconstructionist philosophy (Zeichner and Liston, 1987; Gore and Zeichner, 1991).

Some teacher educators centre on university classrooms. Munby and Russell (1994) described a university course in the teaching of physics that placed reflection at its core. In Salvio's (1994) classroom, pre-service teachers develop autobiographical scripts and create theatrical improvisations to embody reflection.

There are many examples of reflective actions in field experiences. Posner (1989) advocated using self-questioning protocols and structured logs during pre-service teachers' field experiences. Pultorak (1993) outlined a structured approach to working with student teachers where he conducted reflective interviews in dyads, gave written feedback about the lesson observed and established through dialogue a prescriptive focus for future observations.

Finally, there are reflective activities reported not by teacher educators but by practising school-teachers. For example, Ballenger (1992) told the tale of her efforts to learn how to teach children who were recent Haitian immigrants to the USA. She engaged in a series of conversations with a teacher-researcher group, with non-Haitian teachers and parents in a day-care centre and with Haitian teachers in a child development class. Her choice of multiple settings, diverse participants and varying topics of conversation is instructional for teacher educators who want prospective teachers to learn about community and culture.

## Concluding comments

In this chapter I have examined the nature and the nurture of reflective action. Reflection cannot be nurtured unless we understand:

- its forms of speech and discourse (reflecting through mental thoughts is markedly different from writing reflective comments in the pages of a journal);
- its relationship with action and experience (reflecting about what one does as a student teacher differs from reflecting about practice from the vantage point of twenty years as a teacher);
- its social genesis (reflecting on one's own differs from reflecting with one's interdisciplinary teaching team);
- its part in enquiry and research (reflecting on how to do a team-wide survey of student attitudes about intramural sports differs from conducting a series of interviews with a 10-year-old non-reader);
- its conditions (reflecting in the calm of a studio differs from reflecting in the midst of 30 13-year-olds);
- its affective and ideological characteristics (reflecting about the best way to prepare students for an upcoming standardized test differs from reflecting about the educational and social consequences of the in-school suspension programme in one's school).

I ask teacher educators (at any level of schooling) to join me in considering the nature of reflective action, and then considering the consequences for our own actions as we try to nurture reflection in our future teachers.

## References

Arnold, F. (1994) Bullying, a tale of everyday life: reflections on insider research. *Educational Action Research*, **2**, 183–94.

Bakhtin, M. M. (1981) *The Dialogic Imagination*. Austin: University of Texas Press.

Ballenger, C. (1992) Teaching and practice. *Harvard Educational Review*, **62**, 199–208.

Bayer, A. S. (1990) *Collaborative-Apprenticeship Learning: Language and Thinking across the Curriculum, K-12.* Mountain View, CA: Mayfield Publishing.

Bruner, J. (1987) Prologue to the English edition. In *The Collected Works of L. S. Vygotsky*, Volume 1, trans. N. Minick. New York: Plenum Press.

Canning, C. (1991) What teachers say about reflection. *Educational Leadership*, **35**, 18–21.

Dewey, J. (1933) *How We Think.* Lexington, MA: Heath.

Friesen, D. W. (1994) The action research game: re-creating pedagogical relationships in the teaching internship. *Educational Action Research*, **2**, 243–58.

Goodman, J. (1988) University constraints to reflective teacher education. Paper presented at the Conference on Reflection and Teacher Education, Orlando, FL, January.

Gore, J. M. and Zeichner, K. M. (1991) Action research and reflective teaching in preservice teacher education: a case study from the United States. *Teaching and Teacher Education*, **7**, 119–36.

Laidlaw, M. (1994) The democratising potential of dialogical focus in an action enquiry. *Educational Action Research*, **2**, 223–42.

Lave, J. (1988) *Cognition in Practice.* Cambridge: Cambridge University Press.

Manning, B. H. and Payne, B. D. (1992) A correlational study of preservice teachers' reported self-talk reactions to teaching dilemmas. *Teacher Education Quarterly*, **19** (2), 85–95.

Manning, B. H. and Payne, B. D. (1993) A Vygotskian-based theory of teacher cognition: toward acquisition of mental autonomy. *Teaching and Teacher Education*, **9** (4), 361–71.

Munby, H. and Russell, T. (1994) The authority of experience in learning to teach: messages from a physics methods course. *Journal of Teacher Education*, **45** (2), 86–95.

O'Hanlon, C. (1994) Reflection and action in research: is there a moral responsibility to act? *Educational Action Research* **2**, 281–90.

Posner, G. J. (1989) *Field Experience: Methods of Reflective Teaching*, 2nd edn. New York: Longman.

Pultorak, E. G. (1993) Facilitating reflective thought in novice teachers. *Journal of Teacher Education*, **44**, 288–95.

Salvio, P. M. (1994) What can a body know? Refiguring pedagogic intention into teacher education. *Journal of Teacher Education*, **45**, 53–61.

Schön, D. (1983) *The Reflective Practitioner.* New York: Basic Books.

Schön, D. (1987) *Educating the Reflective Practitioner.* New York: Basic Books.

Tom, A. (1985) Inquiring into inquiry-oriented teacher education. *Journal of Teacher Education*, **36**, 35–44.

Van Manen, M. (1977) Linking ways of knowing with ways of being practical. *Curriculum Inquiry* **6**, 205–28.

Vygotsky, L. S. (1987) *The Collected Works of L. S. Vygotsky,* Volume 1, trans. N. Minick. New York: Plenum Press.

Weiss, J. and Louden, W. (1989) Images of reflection. Paper presented at the annual meeting of the American Educational Research Association, San Francisco, March.

Wertsch, J. V. (1985) *Vygotsky and the Social Formation of Mind.* Cambridge, MA: Harvard University Press.

Zeichner, K. M. and Liston, D. P. (1987) Teaching student teachers to reflect. *Harvard Educational Review*, **57**, 23–48.

# Revisiting Bakhtin: A Rejoinder to H. James McLaughlin

ANNE M. PHELAN

In his chapter, Dr McLaughlin outlines five considerations which address the fundamental nature of reflection: its relationship to action and intention, its conditionality, its social genesis, its emotional and ideological characteristics and its role in enquiry. By way of response, I explore the interrelated concepts of *self, consciousness* and *experience* which undergird Jim's discussion of the nature of reflection, yet remain in the shadows of his text. These concepts are central to a re-articulation of the discourse of reflective practice. Jim's use of Mikhail Bakhtin's work provides a promising starting place for such a rearticulation.

## An/other(s) story

> 'How many books may I borrow from the library, Miss Yaeger?' asked Veronica. Carolynne considered the question and answered, 'One.' 'I want to take two home tonight,' Veronica insisted. 'I'm afraid that we'll just be borrowing one for the moment,' reminded Carolynne. Veronica, now highly indignant, retorted, 'I'm going to ask the *real* teacher!' The second-grader turned and stalked away in the direction of the 'real' teacher.

Carolynne Yaeger was a student teacher completing her semester-long practicum in a second-grade classroom. I was her practicum adviser. Carolynne's empathy for children trying to survive in the world of school was striking. Then came Veronica! Before long, the questions were swimming about in Carolynne's journal: 'How did she know that I'm not the full-time classroom teacher? What am I doing which seems to give that impression?'

Carolynne concluded that she hadn't been assertive enough; she hadn't disciplined the children sufficiently; she must be 'meaner', as her cooperating teacher put it playfully. Carolynne believed that if she could establish herself as a disciplinarian, then her problems would be solved. Next day, she sent a child into the time-out area. The questioning in her journal began again: 'Why did I do this? Why do I feel so uncomfortable with this?' Instead of feeling that she had at last asserted herself as the teacher, she felt angry and undermined. In a conversation, Carolynne remarked, '[The children] make you do these things. They have learned already that teachers discipline and they bring that expectation with them into the classroom. If I do not fulfil it, then what?'

## Heteroglossia, the dialogic subject and the problem of 'greater consciousness'

> I believe that becoming more reflective means achieving greater consciousness through some form of speech that is embedded in, and generated through, action.
>
> (McLaughlin, Chapter 16 this volume, p. 186)

To view reflection as a vehicle for achieving greater consciousness, as Jim seems to, is to assume a pre-existent, stable consciousness and a substantial self. However, Jim's subsequent discussion of 'consciousness as an operation of becoming' in a heteroglossic world, as per Bakhtin, is a welcome contradiction of this assumption.

In the student-teaching experience we find Bakhtin's heteroglossic world, and in Carolynne his dialogic subject! Carolynne's experience of learning to teach situated her at the intersection of multiple educational discourses, confounded by her own biography, personal and institutional. The questions she explored in her reflective journal did not presuppose an end point, an identity, monological or dialectical, which Carolynne would ultimately achieve. Nor were the questions indicative of a consciousness which existed *prior* to her experiences as a student-teacher, a core-like entity which might guide her intentions. For Bakhtin, both 'subject and intention are positional and interlocutive terms' (Holquist, 1990, p. 155). Carolynne was a subject in process, a dialogic subject who must 'answer with her life'. Her experiences are seen as events and her consciousness an invention, a *constant* social negotiation among discourses.

So if we are to borrow from Bakhtin, as Jim would have us do, the stability of consciousness is no longer tenable; it is constructed in the very context of reflection.

## Retelling, experience and the problem of social expression

> During the past decade there has been an explosion of ideas about how best to help pre-service teachers to 'retell' prior experiences ... in journals ... autobiographies ... and metaphorical analysis.
> (McLaughlin, Chapter 16 this volume, p. 184)

If we continue to borrow from Bakhtin, we must consider the implications of a heteroglossic world for the way in which our student-teachers talk about their experiences. Absent from the literature's valorization of reflection is an investigation into the dynamics of social expression in the first instance. If we are to take Jim's point seriously – that people speak and act as subjects from within discursive fields that they do not set up (Ellis, 1989) – then we must help our students to explore the discourses which frame their retelling of classroom experiences.

There is little doubt that 'the category of experience is key to the dynamics of teacher education and the process whereby one becomes a teacher' (Britzman, 1992, p. 29). However, our tendency in teacher education, Britzman reminds us, has been to objectify experience like a map, in written forms such as journals and autobiographies. She reminds us further that 'experience has no independent reality outside the cultural codes that deploy knowledge. We do not see or feel experience, we understand it' (Britzman, 1992, p. 29). Volosinov (1986) is helpful here:

> there is no such thing as experience outside the embodiment in signs. Consequently, the very notion of a fundamental, qualitative difference between the inner and outer element is invalid to begin with ... It is not experience that organizes expression, but the other way around – expression organizes experience. Expression is what first gives experience its form and specificity of direction.
>
> (Volosinov, 1986, p. 85)

In reflective practice, we have tended to encourage our students to reflect on experience naively. For example, Carolynne reflected on her experience with Veronica; however, her retelling of the event was left unproblematized. So Carolynne's classroom experience as recounted in her journal organized her view of what occurred. Absent was any discussion of how her *particular* retelling of the experience – as an issue of classroom management – shaped the experience itself in a particular manner.

In a pedagogy of conversation, Carolynne would begin to consider how she perceived the world 'through particular epistemological commitments and symbolic systems and how [her] meanings [were] organized and produced within the positions [she] inhabit[ed]' (Britzman, 1992, p. 31). Student teachers need to reflect on the discourses which shape their interpretations of events and experiences. For example, Carolynne might ask:

- What are the dominant discourses that frame my thinking about my classroom experiences?
- What are some of the discourses that I find internally persuasive?

- How am I answering the polyphony of discourses with which I'm faced?
- Who am I in the process of becoming?
- Which social languages will continue to inform my teaching self?

Because of its ambivalent nature, the student teaching experience is a fertile ground for the exploration of meaning-making, the processes by which student-teachers come to know. The meanings our student-teachers make when they reflect are central. They are not simply answers to problems; they are the problems themselves (Cherryholmes, 1988).

In closing, if we accept that learning to teach is in fact dialogic, then our teacher education programmes ought also to be dialogic. In a pedagogy of conversation, we might help our student teachers to recognize the coexistence of multiple discourses and encourage them to participate in and value the struggle for meaning.

## References

Britzman, D. (1992) The terrible problem of knowing thyself: toward a poststructural account of teacher identity. *Journal of Curriculum Theorizing,* **9** (3).

Cherryholmes, C. (1988). *Power and Criticism: Poststructural Investigations in Education.* New York: Teachers College Press.

Ellis, K. (1989) Stories without endings: deconstructive theory and political practice. *Socialist Review,* **19** (2), 37–52.

Holquist, M. (1990) *Dialogism: Bakhtin and His World,* New York: Routledge.

Volosinov, V. N. (1986) *Marxism and the Philosophy of Language,* trans. L. Matejka and I. R. Titunik. Cambridge, MA: Harvard University Press.

# 17 Critical Reflection in Initial Teacher Education

DAVE HILL

## Three levels of reflection: the work of Kenneth Zeichner and Daniel Liston

In this chapter I seek to clarify Zeichner and Liston's three different levels of reflection. For each level of reflection, I examine one aspect of structural inequality, that of 'race', and suggest:

1    What *content* of ITE courses is typical.
2    What *ideology* is adopted and promulgated.
3    What *theory* is necessary for each level of reflection.

'Race' is selected as one of the three major structural inequalities in society and in education. Social class or gender inequality could have been selected instead. It is suggested that this analysis and amplification of the three levels of reflection has clear implications for the critique and development of ITE courses.

## Reflection level 1: technical reflection

This can be defined as unproblematic technical proficiency at achieving ends which are predetermined.

For Zeichner and Liston, 'at the first level of *technical* rationality, the dominant concern is with the efficient and effective application of education knowledge for purposes of attaining ends which are accepted as given. At this level, neither the ends nor the institutional contexts of classroom, school, community, and society are treated as problematic' (Zeichner and Liston, 1987, p. 24; cf. McIntyre, 1993, p. 44). Commentators such as Adler and Rosaen, Roth and Lanier succinctly summarize this as follows.

Adler describes Zeichner and Liston's first level of reflection as the *technical*.[1]

> At this level the emphasis is on the efficient application of professional knowledge to given ends; goals and objectives are not a subject for scrutiny, nor are long range consequences. Teachers and prospective teachers need to learn to reflect upon the effectiveness of their teaching strategies; have the learners achieved the given set objectives?
>
> (Adler, 1991, p. 142)

### *Technical reflection, 'race' and racial inequality*

With regard to 'race' education, the *technical* level of reflection is 'colour blind', ignoring issues of racism, discrimination, prejudice and stereotyped curriculum materials. It is essentially an *assimilationist* and individualistic approach. It is also a teacher-based approach. Where respondents (children) fail to give correct responses to teacher stimuli, then those individuals or groups of children 'failing' to give anticipated or desired responses (in Standard Assessment Tests (SATs) or in behaviour relationships with the teacher) are deemed deviant. They are deemed to be in need of compensatory assistance or relocation to special units or schools. This is to say, within the parameters of this technical form of reflection, if the teacher is doing her or his job to technical perfection, and the pupil is not responding as desired by the teacher, then the pupil can be justly marginalized, or even pathologized, as defective in terms of domestic culture, child-rearing patterns, intelligence, home language 'correctness' or complexity, or whatever. Such technical competencies form the basis of the 'competency-based' approach to teacher 'training'.

In some respects, similar pathologizing, or hierarchical differentiation in terms of superiority–inferiority, can be applied to social class and to gender. By definition, contextual, institutional or societal factors are excluded from this technical level of reflection.

This technical level of reflection dominated many BEd and PGCE courses in the 1970s, with the education of 'ethnic minorities' being placed into 'special needs' courses. It is contended here that it is this type of reflection which the radical right is increasingly attempting to enforce on initial teacher education (ITE). Their view appears to be that achievement in schooling is a matter of individual merit, with 'merit' (ability) being the sum of 'intelligence plus effort'. This individual merit is socially decontextualized. And merit-worthiness and ability are determined and defined by a dominating and dominant ideology. That is, 'anyone who is like us can get on', 'anyone who isn't and doesn't is defective'.

## *Technical reflection and theory*

How do ITE students and teachers get to the three different levels of reflection? What type of theory is necessary for each level or type of reflection?

For technical reflection, trial and error and mimicry based on an apprenticeship competence-based approach, such as the licensed teacher system or pupil-teacher system, could be enough. Hence, no theory would, at first sight, be required. Rather like an apprentice butcher, the apprentice teacher could learn her or his cuts and strokes by copying the 'master butcher', and by having a go, getting better through practice. This is the 'tips for teachers' approach, the tips being primarily re-

lated to execution and presentation within a teacher-dominated stimulus–response framework, with no development or understanding of the 'why' of teaching, only of the 'how to'.

This is also the NCVQ approach that is being applied to further education lecturers and to youth workers. Desired outcomes are specified as precisely as possible via units of competencies, range statements and underpinning knowledge (Wolf, 1994).

## Reflection level 2: situational or contextual reflection

This level of reflection looks at the theoretical and institutional assumptions behind, for example, curriculum and pedagogy, and looks at the effects of teaching actions, goals and structures.

For Zeichner and Liston, the

> second level of reflectivity [is] based upon a conception of practical action whereby the problem is one of *explicating and clarifying the assumptions and predispositions* underlying practical affairs and assessing the *educational consequences* toward which an action leads. At this level, every action is seen as linked to particular value commitments, and the actor considers the work of competing educational ends.
>
> (Zeichner and Liston, 1987, p. 24)

Rosaen *et al.* (1990) summarize this as *reflecting on theory and practice*. 'The starting point for learning to be a "reflective teacher" ,' they claim, is learning to analyse carefully pedagogical issues, using programme and course concepts as conceptual tools for analysis, which then guide one's classroom teaching. 'Reflection about consequences of pedagogical action is often facilitated by using particular strategies such as having students conduct action research, ethnographic studies and case studies accompanied by discussions, journal writing and written cases' (Rosaen *et al.*, 1990).

For Adler (1991, p. 142),

> a second level of reflection places teaching within its *situational and institutional contexts*. Teachers are expected to be able to reflect upon why certain choices of practice are made. How are these choices

constrained and influenced by institutional, social and historical factors? What hidden curricula may be embedded in their practices, in the norms of the institution? This level of reflection goes beyond questions of proficiency at achieving particular ends towards a thoughtful examination of how contexts influence teaching and learning, and a consideration of the work of competing educational goals.

McIntyre is even more succinct. For him, the second, or *practical*, level is where 'the concern is with the assumptions, predispositions, values and consequences with which actions are linked' (McIntyre, 1993, p. 44).

## Situational/contextual reflection, 'race' and racial inequality

With regard to 'race' education, the second level of reflection, the *situational* or *contextual*, enables students and teachers to depathologize subaltern (subordinate group) non-elite behaviour (dress, accent, language, clothes, body language, cultural and sub-cultural behaviour, food, religion, family structures) and to become aware of, and accept and value, ethnic and cultural diversity. Within the classroom, such teachers are aware of the danger of stereotyping, of under-expectation, of micro- and macro-level discrimination and prejudice (within small groups and the classroom, and within the school). Such teachers are also aware of macro-level, societal-level, prejudice and discrimination. Their classroom behaviour is non-racist. It is not simply colour-blind, it is aware of, and welcoming to, the diversity of colour and culture, and seeks to represent this in a multicultural approach to teaching, or an approach welcoming ethnic diversity or cultural pluralism. It is aware of and challenges, within the classroom and school, racist name-calling, negative images and inter-ethnic group hostilities. It can, however, exoticize and patronize cultural diversity (Sarup, 1986; Hessari and Hill, 1989, Chapter 2; Cole, 1992).

For contextual/situational reflection, teachers and ITE students need some data input, some facts about attainment levels of different ethnic (and

class and gender) groups, to become aware of differential attainment, i.e. that there *is* a problem. They then have to become aware of the ways in which teachers' and schools' open and hidden curricula, peer group, domestic and societal pressures can alternatively demean and constrain or enhance and encourage the development of pupils' interests, security and attainment. They then, within their own classrooms, and within the school environment, seek to engage in non-stereotyping, non-culturally exclusive individual and school-wide practice and behaviour.

Smyth (1986, pp. 79–80) suggests that teachers need

> a preparedness to reflect upon one's own history and how it is embedded in current practice, to speculate about the likely causes of relationships, but also to follow through into action whatever informed decisions to change are deemed desirable.

He proceeds to set out a number of questions which reflective teachers (teachers engaging in a critical form of 'clinical supervision') should ask themselves:

- how do our professional histories, individually and collectively, affect the way we teach?
- what are the taken-for-granted assumptions in our teaching?
- where do these theories come from?
- how do the ways we choose to teach lock us into certain kinds of relationships with our students?
- in what ways does the structure of schooling determine our pedagogy, and how might we begin to change those structures?
- what are the unintended outcomes of our teaching?
- how can we create 'new' forms of knowledge about teaching through discourse with our colleagues?

Although Smyth advances these as part of 'a collaborative, reflective and critical mode of clinical supervision' (p. 59), these questions are equally appropriate for levels two and three of reflection. In order for them to be utilized in a socially just and critically transformative manner, then such a metanarrative needs to be explicit. Hence I have included them as exemplars of level two (contextual/situational) rather than level three (critical emancipatory) reflection.

## *Situational/contextual reflection and theory*

The theory required for the second level of reflection is that relating to teacher and school effects and cultural difference. At this level of reflection, theory about societal and educational stratification and about its relationship to power structure and ideology is not necessary. Indeed, although not by the likes of Smyth, it can be seen as dangerously provocative.

## Reflection level 3: critical reflection

This level of reflection involves a consideration of the moral and ethical implications of pedagogy and of school structures (see Bourdieu's notion of 'rational pedagogy' in Ainley, 1994).

For Zeichner and Liston (1987, p. 23),

> the third level, *critical reflection*, incorporates moral and ethical criteria into the discourse about practical action. At this level the central questions ask which education goals, experiences, and activities lead toward forms of life which are mediated by concerns for justice, equity, and concrete fulfilment, and whether current arrangements serve important human needs and satisfy important human purposes. Here both the teaching (ends and means) and the surrounding contexts are viewed as problematic — that is, as value-governed selections from a large universe of possibilities.

For Rosaen *et al.* (1990), this becomes 'reflecting on issues of schooling and society', where prospective teachers consider the moral implications of pedagogical actions and the structure of schooling as a major reflective activity. They are encouraged to confront the moral dilemmas of instruction and conditions of schooling in a deliberate fashion, and to examine ways in which the structure of schooling influences classroom learning (e.g. tracking, ability grouping, curriculum selection practices).

Adler's summary of this third level of reflection is that it introduces *moral and ethical* issues. For Adler,

> Reflection at this level asks that teachers become, in Henry Giroux's (1988) terms, 'transformative intellectuals', who are capable of examining the ways in which schooling generally, and one's own teaching specifically, contribute or fail to contribute to a just human society. It is expected that in reflection, teachers would be able to transcend everyday experience, to imagine things as they ought to be, not simply accept things as they are. And it is expected that such images would shape the teacher's practice and their thinking about their practice.
>
> Critical inquiry, as Zeichner, and others, see it, involves questioning that which is otherwise taken for granted. It involves looking for unarticulated assumptions and seeing from new perspectives. The area of the problematic moves beyond the immediate situation into an awareness of ethical and political possibilities. It involves learning to make decisions about teaching and learning based upon perceived ethical and political consequences and an awareness of alternatives. The pedagogy utilised to promote critical inquiry must be designed to encourage students to question, analyse and consider alternatives within an ethical, political framework.
>
> (Adler, 1991, p. 142)

For McIntyre (1993, p. 44) the third level is the *critical* or *emancipatory* level, where 'the concern includes wider ethical, social, and political issues, including crucially the institutional or societal forces which may constrain the individual's freedom of action or limit the efficacy of his or her actions'. Tabachnik and Zeichner (1991) use identical terms and similar definitions.

## *Critical reflection, 'race' and racial inequality*

At the *critical level of reflection*, teachers, while incorporating the aspects of multiculturalism listed above, would extend beyond them, seeking to enable their pupils to develop an awareness of, an understanding of and a commitment to oppose structural and structured inequalities in society, such as discrimination based on 'race', class, sex, sexuality and disability. Such teachers go beyond the cultural relativism and political pluralism characteristic of liberal democracy. They take a political stance based on egalitarianism, the need for political action and a deliberate exposure *within the curriculum* of racism and the development and promotion of anti-racism. They represent an egalitarian activist democracy, as opposed to authoritarian quietist democracy. Such teachers deliberately and knowingly engage in, for example, anti-racist history, anti-racist mathematics and, in varying circumstances, democratic participative pedagogy.

At this level, macro-sociological theories of the role of schooling in a capitalist society are necessary. Teachers and students need to appraise major analytical theories of power in society critically. These include the following.

1  Structural-functionalist, conservative, 'meritocratic' (e.g. British Prime Minister John Major's view of a 'classless' (*sic*) society, by which he presumably means socially mobile rather than socially egalitarian). This theory involves social mobility but eschews positive discrimination.
2  Liberal-democratic pluralist analyses of power and of the neutrality of state institutions in, for example, questions of access and performance in relation to different ethnic, sex and social class groups.
3  Marxist analyses of the class nature of power in society and the relative functionalism of state apparatuses/structures, such as schooling, in the reproduction of existing structuring of power in society along lines of 'raced' and sexed classes.

Students need to become aware of and critique these three major sets of responses, ideologies and policies regarding 'race': (a) assimilationism/monoculturalism; (b) cultural pluralism/multiculturalism; and (c) anti-racism, in terms of explaining and responding to the racialized structuring of opportunity and academic and job attainment.

If multiculturalism is seen as an essential part of anti-racism and not as an end goal, then both multiculturalist and anti-racist strategies are necessary as means to an anti-racist end. If, however, multiculturalism stops at celebrating ethnic diversity and does not see itself as a development of a metanarrative of anti-racist social egalitarianism and justice, then multiculturalism can be viewed as, in essence, conservative, failing to challenge the status quo.[2] Apartheid is one form of 'pluralism'.

In sum, if teachers and ITE students are more effectively to attack racism (and classism and sexism) in the interests of a socially just system of distributing power and rewards in society, then they need to question the above ideology or policy responses to ethnic diversity and racism by asking, 'Whose interests are served by this policy, theory or level of reflection? Who wins (if only by legitimation of the status quo) and who loses (who has to deny identity in order to join the winners, if this is at all possible)? Who is likely to have to continue accepting a subordinate and exploited position in society (by virtue of membership of oppressed groups)?'

## The political context and the need for critical reflection

Much has been written about the detheorizing, decritiquing and deprofessionalizing of ITE in Britain (Hill, 1989, 1990a, b, 1991, 1994b; Whitty and Menter, 1989; Gilroy, 1992; Barber, 1993; Whitty, 1993; Hill and Cole, 1996; Whitty and Barton, 1987) and in the USA (Apple, 1979, 1982, 1989, 1991, 1993b; Giroux, 1983, 1988; Aronowitz and Giroux, 1986, 1991; Giroux and McLaren, 1989a, b). In Britain, one salient characteristic is the contemporary (mid-1990s) change in the self-proclaimed aims and rationale for ITE courses from a model of the teacher based on 'reflection' to one based on technical competencies. This clearly follows new DFE guidelines for primary and secondary initial teacher 'training' (DFE, 1992, 1993), and is apparent from the Secretary of State for Employment and Education, Gillian Shephard's, proposals in September 1996 for an official National Curriculum for Teacher Training (DFEE, 1996).

Whereas the 'reflective' model for undergraduate and for postgraduate ITE courses was the norm in the early 1990s (Barrett *et al.*, 1992), technical, competency-based ITE courses have become far more widespread as courses have been rewritten to conform to the requirements of ministerial circulars 9/92 and 14/93 (DFE, 1992, 1993).

Many radical left teacher educators have recognized the 'conservatization' and 'conforming' of teacher education in states such as the USA, Britain, Australia and New Zealand. In Michael Apple's words, 'There is immense pressure not only to re-define the manner in which education is carried out, but what education is actually *for* ... [The conservative restoration] has altered our definition of what counts as good teaching and what counts as an appropriate education for our future teachers' (Apple, 1991, p. vii; see also Apple, 1979, 1982, 1986, 1993a; Beyer, cited in Liston and Zeichner, 1991, p. 32).

This chapter, then, engages in the 'ideological culture wars' (Shor, 1986; Giroux, 1983, 1988; Giroux and McLaren, 1989b; Hill, 1990a) surrounding the purpose and nature of teacher education. It seeks to stimulate and participate in a debate within the radical left and the 'left in the centre' (Hill, 1992, 1994b) over issues such as the role of a teacher and teacher educator as 'transformative and public intellectual' (Giroux, 1983, 1988; Giroux and McLaren, 1989b; Hill, 1990a, 1994a) engaging in critical moral utopianism inside, as well as outside, the classroom. Such a debate, of course, needs to be carried out within the constituencies of teachers, student teachers and the wider community, as well as within the academic community.

## How much critical reflection and egalitarianism was there in ITE in England and Wales?

During the 1970s and 1980s, many ITE courses (and schools) developed egalitarian curricula, pedagogies, management styles and relationships, relationships with local and ethnic communities, and anti-racist, anti-sexist, anti-homophobic policy and practice.

Following the course criteria and development demanded by the Council for Accreditation of Teacher Education (CATE) in its circular 10/84, many BEd degree and PGCE courses in the mid-1980s became 'permeated' by issues such as anti-racism and anti-sexism. In many institutions each constituent course module or unit of the four-year BEd degree or the one-year PGCE had to show permeation of these issues. Geoff Whitty describes this process – the compulsory and essentially collaborative whole-team review and development of BEd and PGCE courses – as opening a space for the left (Whitty, 1993; see also Hill, 1994b; Reid, 1993).

Thus the 1980s saw the sporadic development within ITE courses of attempts to develop egalitarianism and critical reflection and to transform students', and thereby pupils', perceptions of the social, sexual and racial inequalities and injustices within curricula, pedagogies and structures. This critical analysis underlay a specific commitment to struggle for a more socially just, caring, compassionate and egalitarian system of schooling and society. Such courses affected a considerable number of students over a number of years.[3]

## How much anti-racism was there in ITE in England and Wales?

The following section examines one aspect of critical reflection and egalitarianism in ITE, that concerned with 'race' education. The purpose is to show the limited nature of the egalitarian advances.

In 1985, the Swann Report suggested that very few institutions offered a core course on anti-racism, let alone any cross-curricular permeation (Swann, 1985). This was, however, before the CATE criteria and the CNAA criteria for validating college and polytechnic ITE courses had had much time to take effect. But it does point to the lack of radicalism, or even of multicultural celebration of cultural diversity, which was actually voluntaristically being developed without these bodies' external demands. It is contended that such anti-racism and multiculturalism as did happen in ITE courses was the result of the efforts of individuals, rather than of coherent overall course planning.

By 1989, the Commission for Racial Equality (CRE) suggested that 'What is apparent is that compared with schools, universities and polytechnics have been relatively untouched by the debate on racial equality in education and have not, on the whole, seen the need to develop specific policies in this area' (Swann, 1985, quoted in both Siraj-Blatchford, 1992, and Clay and George, 1993). Clay and George (1993) criticize the lack of specificity in CATE guidelines, which allowed institutions to implement the criteria in ways that closely mirrored their own levels of consciousness, prevalent beliefs and levels of competence of staff employed. They cite a limited survey of ten HEIs:

> All ten had stated rationales in their courses that committed them to the study of issues relating to cultural diversity. Although, as with the EOC survey, they expressed recognition of the importance of studying 'race' and culture issues, there was considerable variation. The survey found that only two institutions out of the ten stated a clear anti-racist rationale. The rest expressed rationales that were clearly multicultural/multiracial, or as part of a general equal opportunities programme. The survey also found that less than a third of the course (8 out of 26) had a core input. Four courses offered an option model, whilst the rest relied on permeation.

With regard to school-based teaching practice, Crozier and Menter (1993) note that:

> Even on courses where there is a strong expression of commitment to equality issues, there is evidence that this very rarely leads to effective treatment of these concerns within the teaching practice triad. Research carried out at two institutions indicated a 'stasis' within these relationships. Potentially contentious issues, especially if they might challenge the professionalism of the teacher, were invariably avoided. (pp. 97–8) ... What has been most striking, though, is how often there is a very direct contradiction between the espousal of liberal anti-sexist and anti-racist positions by college staff and the lived experience of students and staff. (p. 100)

Blair (1992) and Blair and Maylor (1993) make similar comments.

## 'Reflection' in teacher education: its lack of meaning

Having sought to establish the existence and the limited extent of egalitarianism within British ITE in the 1980s and early 1990s (at least with regard to 'race' education), this chapter now turns to examine the concept of 'reflection' in teacher education.

The view that all practice is an expression of personal theory underpins the 'reflective practitioner/teacher' model (Griffiths and Tann, 1992, p. 71, following Carr, 1986; Carr and Kemmis, 1986; Elliott, 1987, 1989; Schön, 1983, 1987). However, without clarification and exemplars, the term 'reflection' is meaningless (Adler, 1991; Calderhead, 1988; Giroux and McLaren, 1991; Smyth, 1991; Tabachnik and Zeichner, 1991; Calderhead and Gates, 1993; McIntyre, 1993). Liston and Zeichner (1987) call it an 'education slogan'. Reflection manifestly does not constitute a unified discourse. For Giroux and McLaren (1991, p. 52), 'As a term it is useless, unless amplified to locate it within one of a number of competing discourses of teacher education.' They contrast 'reflection' with 'critical reflection' thus:

> While hardly constituting a unified discourse, 'critical pedagogy' nevertheless has managed to pose an important counterlogic to the positivistic, ahistorical, depoliticized discourse that often informs modes of analysis employed by liberal and conservative critics of schooling, modes all too readily visible in most [US] colleges of education.

This may be relatively true of critical pedagogy, but it is not true of 'reflection' in teacher education and in teaching *per se*; that is, the terms 'reflection' and 'reflective teacher' impose no logic or counterlogic to current discourses.

This lack of consensus about the term 'reflection' was particularly evident at the 1991 Bath University Conference, 'Conceptualising Reflection in Teacher Education', organized by James Calderhead, in the various contributions to the resulting book (Calderhead and Gates, 1993), in Calderhead's previous work, such as *Reflective Teaching and Teacher Education* (Calderhead, 1989) and in Liston and Zeichner's (1991) latest formulation and categorization of US traditions of reflective practice.

Teacher reflection can be related to the New Right dogma of 'free marketeering', 'in the rhetoric of autonomy and devolution ... in a context in which there has been a vicious attack on person rights and the social, political and economic infrastructure that has traditionally supported them' (Smyth, 1991, p. 2). Smyth argues that 'the rhetoric of devolution and the attempts to acknowledge "the wisdom of the practitioner" ' are occurring in contexts in which there have been 'substantial thrusts to centralisation'; that this is related to the contemporary 'crisis of the state' and of late capitalism; that 'particular' (though not all) forms of reflective practice are far from being emancipatory or liberating for teachers. He goes on to explore the dimensions of 'a more socially, culturally, and politically reflective approach to teaching and to teacher education' (pp. 2–3).

He accepts that 'in some respects Schön has become a rallying point for ... liberal progressive educators' (p. 7) besieged by international conservatism, but argues (in a classic Marxist functionalism) that growth of reflective approaches allows

> what appears to be a freeing up of control mechanisms by allowing schools, parents, local communities and teachers to engage in participative, locally based and reflective approaches [but these] have to be set in the context of the policy of western capitalist governments world-wide to strategically withdraw from certain areas of education, while bolstering and fortifying their central policy making powers.
>
> (Smyth, 1991, pp. 11–12)

## Some problems with the threefold classification of reflection

### The effectiveness of critical reflection in ITE courses

There is no guarantee, of course, that any type of ITE programme will achieve its various objectives, ideological, transformative or otherwise. There is ample research on the ineffectiveness of ITE courses failing to impact on the classroom behaviour of either student teachers or novice teachers.

McDiarmid, working within the very large-scale NCRTE programme at Michigan State University, investigating characteristics and effects of teacher education programmes in the USA, reported on 11 different teacher education programmes (including pre-service, induction, in-service and 'alternate route' (school-based) courses. He examined teachers' beliefs about students and pupils as learners and found that their views seemed to change very little as a result of their courses (McDiarmid, 1993). Griffiths and Tann (1992, pp. 71–2) report 'serious doubts about the extent to which this is happening' after five years of course development attempts to enable student teachers 'to build and refine their personal theories of action'. Blair (1992), Blair and Maylor (1993), Clay and George (1993) and Crozier and Menter (1993) make similar points about the limited efficacy of 'race' equality in ITE courses. This is discussed further in Hill (1996).

### Collaborative and individual reflection

Zeichner and Liston (1987) suggest that reflective practice requires a supportive environment, that in order to develop as reflective practitioners novice teachers require a supportive collaborative staff culture. Tabachnik and Zeichner (1991) make similar comments. For Smyth (1986, p. 77), 'one of the major limitations of' what he terms 'clinical supervision as it is generally conceived' is that 'it is frequently construed ... as a means by which teachers can "turn a blow torch on themselves" '. For Smyth (1985, p. 9), acting critically refers to 'collaboration in marshalling intellectual capacity so as to focus on analysing, reflecting on, and engaging in discourse about the nature and effects of practical aspects of teaching and how they might be altered'.

### Three levels of reflection: concurrent or consecutive development?

One way teacher educators differ is in their view of which of these levels, or 'arenas', is an appropriate starting-point for reflection in the learning-to-teach process, with commentators as diverse as Calderhead and Gates (1993), McIntyre (1993) and the DFE circular 9/92 all assuming or arguing that the three levels of reflection need to be developed in sequential order, i.e. that contextual, not situational and critical, reflection is more appropriate for teachers who have attained technical and practical skills and skills of reflection.

Calderhead and Gates, introducing the papers in their edited collection, suggest that

> there appears to be a developmental process in becoming reflective. In the early stages of pre-service education, student teachers need to develop a vocabulary for talking, writing and thinking about practice and, at this stage, simply being able to describe practice may well be a significant achievement. Thereafter, reflection may develop into making explicit underlying beliefs and assumptions and also using other public knowledge such as research evidence and academic theories or teaching principles by which to appraise classroom practice and its context.
>
> (Calderhead and Gates, 1993, p. 9)

Unlike some commentators (O'Hear, 1988), and unlike the clear implication in Circular 14/93 (DFE, 1993), Calderhead and Gates assert that such processes appear to apply not only to experienced teachers but also to student teachers, though, like McIntyre (1993), they note that

> when teacher educators expect student teachers to conduct insightful and analytical evaluations of their lessons . . . this may well be a very high level demand to which few students are able to respond since changes in student teachers', and even experienced teachers' levels of reflection appear to occur only over fairly lengthy periods of time.
>
> (Calderhead and Gates, 1993, p. 9)

My own view is that a three- or four-year undergraduate ITE course provides just such a lengthy period of time. The increase in the school-centred and school-based component of undergraduate ITE courses (from 100 days minimum under the 1989 CATE criteria to 150 days minimum under the 1992 and 1993 criteria) may well provide a more appropriate immersion into the practices of teaching, learning and schooling and facilitate, with appropriate support, organization and encouragement, the application of theory to practice and practice to theory. Prior to the CATE 1992

secondary and 1993 primary criteria, such students had been spending too little time in schools. This is *not* to accept the over-reliance and over-emphasis on school-based and school-centred ITE characteristic of Conservative government rhetoric and policies in the late 1980s and early 1990s (see Hill, 1991, 1994b).

McIntyre (1993, p. 45) develops an argument 'that reflection is a much more central means of learning for experienced practitioners, than it can be for novices', but he does assert the necessity for student teachers to engage in *critical* or *emancipatory* reflection:

> It is certainly of fundamental importance that beginning teachers should learn to see how their efforts as teachers, and the effects of their efforts, are shaped by the institutional and societal structures within which they work, and by the ideologies which support these structures. In particular it is important that they should understand how their own work, shaped by these structures and ideologies, can serve interests different from, and sometimes in conflict with, those of the pupils whom they are teaching; and that they should be helped to begin to search for strategies through which, individually and corporately, they can contest the processes and the ideologies of schooling.
>
> (McIntyre, 1993, pp. 45–6)

## Radical reflective content and/or process? Predefined or negotiated content?

Calderhead and Gates (1993) and Russell (1993) mention a number of problems in the development of reflective (and, by extension, of critically reflective) teachers. These include questions such as 'should a truly reflective teaching program have predefined content or should it be negotiated? How does one reconcile the aim of developing particular areas of knowledge, skill and attitudes with the aim of encouraging autonomy and professional responsibility?' (Calderhead and Gates, 1993, p. 3). Should reflective courses concentrate on teaching and learning *processes* or on course *content*? In order to develop, or facilitate the development of, 'teachers as radical left critical transformative intellectuals', should 'democratic participative pedagogy' typify the course, as championed, for example, by Giroux (1983, 1988), Shor (1986) and Giroux and McLaren (1989a, b, 1991)? To what extent does a heavy reliance on and use of discussion-based and own-experience-based small-group collaborative work, typical of much primary schooling and primary teacher education in Britain in the 1970s and 1980s, militate against the development of the broad span of critical theoretical insights argued for later in this chapter? Have Maureen Stone (1981) and some readings of Gramsci concerning the desirability of hard study and the criticisms of 'liberal progressive' pedagogy (Sarup, 1983; Brehony, 1992; Epstein, 1993; Hill and Cole, 1996; Hill *et al.*, 1996) got a point?

Calderhead and Gates (1993, p. 4) also question the compatibility between assessment and concern for reflection, pointing out that 'if student teachers know they are to be assessed by their tutors or supervising teachers, they may be much more reluctant to confide in them and discuss their concerns and difficulties openly'. In other words, they tend to give what they assume to be 'ideologically correct' answers. In my own experience of some years of marking essays on contextual and ideological issues in education, the percentage of radical right-wing answers has been infinitesimal, but the percentage of liberal-democratic answers has been pronounced, although my own radical left position has been known to students.

## Where to start: reflection on self or reflection on context?

McIntyre (1993) questions the value of starting by reflection on one's own practice, and describes how 'the Oxford Internship scheme' parallels courses in classroom teaching with theoretical studies of such matters as 'special needs, social class, race, gender, assessment, education and industry, and environmental education', and relates them to investigation of the practices and policies of the school in which the students are placed. McIntyre (1993, pp. 46–7) concludes that

> tensions found between practices found in the schools and the abstract analyses and theoretical ideals studied at university and in the literature are deliberately exploited so that both theory and practice can be critically examined. It is thus through theorising about others' practices that student teachers are helped to gain a critical perspective on the contexts within which they are working; and it is on the basis of such an understanding that they are encouraged to introduce this level of reflectivity into their reflection on their own practices.

Another way teacher educators differ, of course, is in the extent to which they consider the third arena, the moral, socio-political arena, should be included in the teacher education curriculum at all. In Britain, for example, there do exist various 'reflective' teacher as researcher, action-researcher and initial training–in-service education for teachers (IT–INSET) movements. Each of these not only has a radical left, but also a non-critical, liberal-democratic, individualist, interpretation. IT–INSET, for example, is essentially collaborative and non-elitist, but is also often non-critical (see Everton and Impey, 1989).

## Differences over teacher education within the radical left

This chapter does not assume that there is a monolithic radical left perspective. On the radical left there are differences of opinion, interpretation and project over the possibility and nature of a transformative, egalitarian, critical, utopian movement in teacher education. It is to such differences of opinion and interpretation and project within the radical left, and the development of a radical left discourse about teacher education and schooling in Britain, that this chapter now briefly turns.

Some of the differences within the radical left relate not to the theoretical analysis of these three types of reflection associated with Zeichner, nor to recognizing the existence of these three levels, arenas or layers of reflection, but to different concepts and strategies regarding the *scope* of critical reflection and egalitarianism within ITE and schooling in two respects: (a) the appropriate *site* of political action; (b) the *space* for effective resistance and proselytizing within those sites.

An attempt has been made elsewhere (Hill, 1992) to differentiate between the three distinctive variants of radical left socialist, Marxist and neo-Marxist positions on teacher education.[4] Teachers can be seen variously as:

1   Transformative intellectuals or public intellectuals, whose belief in social justice and egalitarianism inform teaching *within* as well as *outside* the classroom (for example, Giroux, his associates such as Aronowitz and McLaren, and Hill).
2   Transformative teachers *outside* the classroom, committed to the autonomy of intellectuals and of students within a pluralistic discourse within the classroom (e.g. Zeichner, Liston, Popkewitz).
3   Social reproductivist/deterministic teachers, who see little space for contesting the dead hand of capitalism (in some respects, Smyth).

Radical left or left critical theory, teacher educators and theorists differ over the *scope* for critical (level three) reflection – the moral and ethical. To explain the difference between the first two categories above by taking one instance, Zeichner explicitly rejects Giroux's call for teachers to be 'transformative' intellectuals *within* the classroom. And there is a third category of radical left critics, 'the social reproductionists' so criticized by Giroux in various articles and books, who, in effect, do not see much possibility for going beyond critique (Giroux, 1993).

First, let us examine the similarities and agreements between their analyses and policy. Together with Ira Shor (1986), Liston and Zeichner accept many dimensions of what Shor has called 'egalitarian teacher education' (Shor, referred to in Liston and Zeichner, 1987, p. 127), which would include dialogic teaching, cross-cultural communication and critical literacy. And Liston and Zeichner accept many aspects of Giroux's and McLaren's passionately and vibrantly argued 'conceptual apparatus for thinking about teacher edu-

cation as a democratising and counter-hegemonic force' and, at one stage, teachers as 'transformative intellectuals'. Liston and Zeichner (1987, 1991) and Zeichner and Liston (1987) detail a radical agenda for teacher education.

There are two major differences on ITE within the radical left. In Zeichner and Liston's words,

> Beyond the common desire to prepare teachers who have critical perspectives on the relationships between schooling and social inequities and a moral commitment to correcting those inequities through their daily classroom and school activities, there is a great deal of variation among these contemporary proposals of social reconstructionist teacher educators ... At various times the focus has been on the content of programmes, the skill of critical analysis and curriculum development, the nature of the pedagogic relationships between teachers and pupils, and between teacher educators and their students, or on the connections between teacher educators and other political projects which seek to address the many instances of suffering and injustice in our society.
> (Liston and Zeichner, 1991, p. 33)

## An ITE core curriculum and organization

What follows is a series of principles for ITE course content, which, it is suggested, are appropriate for the development of critically reflective teachers. The following four principles should underlie the organization and curriculum of ITE courses.[5]

1   The development of macro and micro theory regarding teaching and learning, in which the socio-political, economic, ideological and cultural contexts of schooling and education are made explicit.
2   The development of effective, skilled classroom teachers able to interrelate and critique theory and practice – their own and that of others. In addition to a deep knowledge of core subjects, student teachers need to develop reflective skills on pupil and student learning, on teaching and classroom management and on stimulating all the children in their classes to learn. They also need to de-

velop skills in monitoring standards and demanding or facilitating the best from their pupils and students.

3   The development of teachers as critical 'transformative intellectuals' and democratic participative professionals and citizens committed to a particular morality of social justice based on an interrogated and critical cultural diversity (social class, racial, gender, sexuality, disability). Such teachers are committed to a radical democratic egalitarian political project.[6]

4   Resistance to totally or overwhelmingly school-based teacher education, i.e. retaining a substantial college-based and higher education role.

In Troyna and Sikes's (1989, p. 25) words,

> Training students to be mere functionaries in our schools rather than educating them to assume a more creative and, dare we say it, critical role is precisely the name of the game at the moment. But should we abandon pre-service education courses entirely and hand the reins over entirely to practising teachers? We think not.
>
> Research evidence suggests that many teachers continue, consciously or otherwise, to make important decisions about the organisation, orientation, and delivery of the formal and informal curricula on grounds which are racist, sexist and discriminatory in a range of significant ways. Should we, therefore, succumb to a system of teacher education/training in which these practices could well be reproduced systematically? Or should we, instead, develop pre-service courses geared towards the development of a teaching force which reflects in a critical manner on taken-for-granted assumptions, which can articulate reasons for contesting some of the conventional wisdoms about pupils, their interests and abilities, and which, ultimately, might influence future cohorts? In short, shouldn't we be encouraging students to be intellectual about being practical?

In addition to being planned as discrete units (such as units on the social contexts of schooling), such issues should also permeate the rest of the ITE experience (both the overt and the 'hidden' curricula). Permeation is not enough in itself. Egalitarian issues and critical reflection must be put firmly on the ITE agenda, not just slipped into myriad spaces within other sessions.

Links between anti-racism, anti-sexism and anti-classism have been drawn, suggesting that anti-racism and multiculturalism can lead to and be informed by anti-classism and anti-sexism. Many teachers can, and could, substitute the word and concept 'class' (or 'sex') for 'race' in checklists for stereotyping, policies concerning equal opportunities, appointments policies, classroom activity choices or subject option choices in secondary schools (ILEA, 1983; Hessari and Hill, 1989; Hill, 1994a, b; Cole *et al.*, 1996). Many other writers examine the interconnections between race, class and gender (e.g. Miles, 1989; Williams, 1989; Cole, 1990; Brah, 1992; Cole *et al.*, 1995).

## Conclusion

The particular perspectives in this chapter from a radical left position are based on a belief that teachers must not only be skilled, competent, classroom technicians – they must be much more than that. They must also be critical and reflective and transformative and intellectual; that is to say, they should operate at level three reflection. They should enable and encourage their pupils and students not only to gain basic and advanced knowledge and skills. They should enable and encourage their pupils and students to question, critique, judge and evaluate 'what is', 'what effects it has' and 'why', and to be concerned and informed about equality and social justice; not just in school, but in life beyond the classroom door.

Such a perspective is clearly at odds with the intentions behind the current Conservative restructuring of initial teacher education in England and Wales. It is a challenge to it.

## Notes

1   Pat Ainley has pointed out, in his comments on this chapter, that some forms of technical proficiency do not necessarily involve any reflection at all (for example, riding a bike or swimming). Some reflection

(for example, when typing) can actually inhibit task accomplishment.

2 Leicester (1992) and Cole (1992) continue this debate in the UK, as do Gill *et al.* (1992), Braham *et al.* (1992) and Donald and Rattansi (1992). United States responses to cultural diversity are set out in Sleeter (1989, 1992).

3 Some British egalitarian/critical initial teacher education courses are referred to or described in Clay *et al.* (1991), Cole (1990), Cole *et al.* (1990), Hill (1989) and Troyna and Sikes (1989). The last article describes the BA and QTS (qualified teacher status) at Warwick University based on biographical life histories 'in the conviction that personal experiences and understanding provide an ideal basis from which to begin to explore why we, and others hold particular beliefs and values and why we, and they, do things in certain ways'. The PGCE course at Sheffield University attempts an innovative approach to the formation of the reflective, critical teacher. The 'schools and society' unit of the BEd course at West Sussex Institute of Higher Education in 1988–89, and the optional 20-hour Year 1 and 2 BEd units 'Contexts for learning' at Brighton Polytechnic in 1989–90, are set out in Hill (1989). The Crawley Primary BEd course for mature students (1990–5) was a further attempt at a 'critically reflective' course (see Hill, 1993a, 1996).

4 Elsewhere, together with Mike Cole, I have criticized post-Marxist 'resistance postmodernists' (and other postmodernist analysis), referring (though not uncritically) to the work of Althusser (1971). See Cole and Hill (1995, 1996), Hill and Cole (1995, 1996) and Cole *et al.* (1997).

5 Zeichner and Liston (1987) describe the curricular plan for the student teaching programme at the University of Wisconsin, Madison, instituted in 1979, designed to stimulate reflection about teaching and its contexts at all three levels. They set out the aims of elementary student teaching in relation to a view of knowledge, a view of the role of the teacher, the form, epistemology and scope of the curriculum, teacher–student social and authority relationships. These criteria clearly develop the third level of arena of reflection, the 'moral and ethical', where (a) knowledge and situations are viewed as problematic and socially constructed and value-governed selections as opposed to certain; (b) the institutional form and social contexts of teacher and schooling are viewed as problematic rather than unproblematic; (c) the teacher is viewed as a moral craftsperson as opposed to a technical craftsperson; (d) the form of the curriculum is seen as reflexive as opposed to received, i.e. the curriculum is not non-negotiable with student teachers being relatively passive recipients of predetermined knowledge (there is (some) space for the self-determined needs and concerns of student teachers as well as the creation of personal meaning by students); (e) the epistemology is viewed as practical as well as theoretical knowledge, not just theoretical; (f) student–teacher authority relationships are enquiry-oriented, not hierarchical. Radical left principles and proposals for the ITE curriculum are suggested in Hill (1991, 1994b, c), Hill and Cole (1995), Cole *et al.* (1996) and the Hillcole Group (1991, 1996).

6 It is suggested in this chapter that all three levels of reflection are necessary but that it is the critical level of reflection alone that is capable of enabling teachers to act as transformative intellectuals (Giroux, 1983, 1989a, b; Aronowitz and Giroux, 1986; Giroux and Simon, 1988; Liston and Zeichner, 1987; Giroux and McLaren, 1987, 1989b; Sarup, 1983; Cole, 1988; Hill, 1991, 1992, 1993b).

## References

Adler, S. (1991) The reflective practitioner and the curriculum in teacher education, *Journal of Education for Teaching*, **17** (2).

Ainley, P. (1994) *Degrees of Difference: Higher Education in the 1990s.* London: Lawrence and Wishart.

Althusser, L. (1971) Ideology and state apparatuses. In *Lenin and Philosophy and Other Essays*, London: New Left Books.

Apple, M. (1979) *Ideology and Curriculum.* London: Routledge.

Apple, M. (1982) *Education and Power.* London: Routledge & Kegan Paul.

Apple, M. (1986) *Teachers and Texts.* London: Routledge.

Apple, M. (1989) Critical introduction: ideology and the state in educational policy. In R. Dale (ed.), *The State and Education Policy*. Milton Keynes: Open University Press.

Apple, M. (1991) Series introduction. In D. Liston and K. Zeichner, *Teacher Education and the Social Conditions of Schooling*. London: Routledge.

Apple, M. (1993a) What post-modernists forget: cultural capital and official knowledge. *Curriculum Studies*, **1** (3).

Apple, M. (1993b) *Official Knowledge: Democratic Education in a Conservative Age.* London: Routledge.

Aronowitz, S. and Giroux, H. (1986) *Education under Siege: The Conservative, Liberal and Radical Debate over Schooling.* London: Routledge and Kegan Paul.

Aronowitz, S. and Giroux, H. (1991) *Postmodern Education: Politics, Culture and Social Criticism.* Minneapolis: University of Minnesota Press.

Barber, M. (1993) Till death us do part. *Times Educational Supplement*, 28 May.

Barrett, E., Barton, L., Furlong, J., Galvin, C., Miles, S. and Whitty, G. (1992) *Initial Teacher Education in England and Wales: A Topography.* London: Goldsmiths College.

Blair, M. (1992) Black teachers and teacher education. *Education Review,* **6** (2).

Blair, M. and Maylor, U. (1993) Issues and concerns for black women teachers in training. In I. Siraj-Blatchford (ed.), *'Race', Gender and the Education of Teachers.* Buckingham: Open University Press.

Brah, A. (1992) Differences, diversity and differentiation. In J. Donald and A. Rattansi (eds), *'Race', Culture and Difference.* London: Sage.

Braham, P., Rattansi, A. and Skellington, R. (1992) *Racism and Anti-racism.* London: Sage.

Brehony, K. (1992) What's left of progressive primary education. In A. Rattansi and D. Reeder (eds), *Rethinking Radical Education: Essays in Honour of Brian Simon.* London: Lawrence and Wishart.

Calderhead, J. (ed.) (1988) *Teachers' Professional Learning.* Lewes: Falmer Press.

Calderhead, J. (1989) Reflective teaching and teacher education. *Teaching and Teacher Education,* **5** (1).

Calderhead, J. and Gates, P. (1993) *Conceptualising Reflection in Teacher Development.* London: Falmer Press.

Carr, W. (1986) Theories of theory and practice. *Journal of Philosophy of Education,* **20** (2).

Carr, W. and Kemmis, S. (1986) *Becoming Critical: Education, Knowledge and Action Research.* London: Falmer Press.

Clay, J. and George, R. (1993) Moving beyond permeation: courses in teacher education. In I. Siraj-Blatchford (ed.), *'Race', Gender and the Education of Teachers.* Buckingham: Open University Press.

Clay, J., Cole, M. and Hill, D. (1991) The citizen as 'individual' and nationalist or as social and internationalist? *Critical Social Policy,* **30**.

Cole, M. (ed.) (1988) *Bowles and Gintis Revisited.* London: Falmer Press.

Cole, M. (ed.) (1990) *Education for Equality.* London: Routledge.

Cole, M. (1992) British values, liberal values or values of justice and equality: three approaches to education in multicultural Britain. In J. Lynch, S. Modgil and C. Modgil (eds), *Cultural Diversity and the Schools, Volume 3: Equity or Excellence? Education and Cultural Reproduction.* London: Falmer Press.

Cole, M. and Hill, D. (1995) Games of despair and rhetorics of resistance: postmodernism, education and reaction. *British Journal of Sociology of Education,* **16** (2).

Cole, M. and Hill, D. (1996) Postmodernism, education and contemporary capitalism: a materialist critique. In O. Valente, A. Barrios, V. Teodoro and A. Gaspas (eds), *Teacher Training and Values Education.* Lis-

bon: Faculty of Science, Department of Education, University of Lisbon.

Cole, M., Clay, J. and Hill, D. (1990) Black achievement in initial teacher education – how do we proceed into the 1990s? *Multicultural Teaching,* **8** (3).

Cole, M., Hill, D. and Shan, S. (1996) *Promoting Equality in Primary Schools.* London: Cassell.

Cole, M., Hill, D. and Rikowski, G. (1997) Between postmodernism and nowhere: the predicament of the postmodernist (a reply to Nigel Blake). *British Journal of Education Studies,* forthcoming.

Cole, M., Hill, D., Soudien, C. and Pease, J. (1996) Critical transformative primary teacher education: some suggestions for the new South Africa. In J. Lynch *et al.* (eds), *Innovations in Delivering Primary Education.* London: Cassell.

Crozier, G. and Menter, I. (1993) The heart of the matter? Student teachers' experiences in schools. In I. Siraj-Blatchford (ed.), *'Race', Gender and the Education of Teachers.* Buckingham: Open University Press.

DFE (1992) *Initial Teacher Training (Secondary Phase).* Circular 9/92. London: DFE.

DFE (1993) *The Initial Training of Primary School Teachers: New Criteria for Course Approval.* Circular 13/93. London: Sage.

Department for Education and Employment (DFEE) (1996) Shake up of teacher training and new focus on leadership skills for headteachers – Shephard. *DFEE News,* 302/96, 18 September.

Donald, J. and Rattansi, A. (1992) *'Race', Culture and Difference.* London: Sage.

Elliott, J. (1987) Educational theory, practical philosophy and action research. *British Journal of Educational Studies,* **35** (2).

Epstein, D. (1993) *Changing Classroom Cultures: Antiracism, Politics and Schools.* Stoke-on-Trent: Trentham Books.

Everton, T. and Impey, G. (1989) *IT–INSET Partnership in Training: The Leicestershire Experience.* London: David Fulton.

Gill, D., Mayer, B. and Blair, M. (1992) *Racism and Education: Structures and Strategies.* London: Sage.

Gilroy, D. (1992) The political rape of initial teacher education in England and Wales: a JET rebuttal. *Journal of Education for Teaching,* **18** (1).

Giroux, H. (1983) *Theory and Resistance in Education: A Pedagogy for the Opposition.* London: Heinemann.

Giroux, H. (1988) *Teachers as Intellectuals: Towards a Critical Pedagogy of Learning.* Granby, MA: Bergin and Garvey.

Giroux, H. (1989a) Schooling as a form of cultural politics: toward a pedagogy of and for difference. In H. Giroux and P. McLaren (eds), *Critical Pedagogy, the State and Cultural Struggle.* Albany: State University of New York Press.

Giroux, H. (1989b) *Schooling for Democracy: Critical Pedagogy in the Modern Age*. London: Routledge.

Giroux, H. (1993) *Border Crossings*. London: Routledge.

Giroux, H. and McLaren, P. (1987) *Critical Pedagogy, State and Cultural Struggle*. Albany: State University of New York Press.

Giroux, H. and McLaren, P. (1989a) Teacher education and the politics of engagement: the case for democratic schooling. *Harvard Education Review*, **56** (3).

Giroux, H. and McLaren, P. (1989b) *Critical Pedagogy, the State and Cultural Struggle*. Albany: State University of New York Press.

Giroux, H. and McLaren, P. (1991) Radical pedagogy as cultural politics: beyond the discourse of critique and anti-utopianism. In D. Morton and Mas' Ud Zavarzadeh (eds), *Theory/Pedagogy/Politics: Texts for Change*. Chicago: University of Illinois Press.

Giroux, H. and Simon, R. (1988) Schooling, popular culture and a pedagogy of possibility. *Boston University Journal of Education*, **170** (1).

Griffiths, M. and Tann, S. (1992) Using reflective practice to link personal and public theories. *Journal of Education for Teaching*, **18** (1).

Hessari, R. and Hill, D. (1989) *Practical Ideas for Multicultural Learning and Teaching in the Primary Classroom*. London: Routledge.

Hill, D. (1989) *Charge of the Right Brigade: The Radical Right's Assault on Teacher Education*. Brighton: Institute for Education Policy Studies.

Hill, D. (1990a) *Something Old, Something New, Something Borrowed, Something Blue: Schooling, Teacher Education and the Radical Left in Britain and the USA*. London: Tufnell Press.

Hill, D. (1990b) Initial teacher education and the development of teachers as reflective transformative intellectuals. Paper presented at the British Educational Research Association Annual Conference, Roehampton Insitute of Higher Education.

Hill, D. (1991), *What's Left in Teacher Education: Teacher Education, the Radical Left and Policy Proposals*. London: Tufnell Press.

Hill, D. (1992) Seven ideological perspectives on teacher education today and the development of a radical left discourse. *Australian Journal of Teacher Education*, **16** (1).

Hill, D. (1993a) *What Teachers? School Basing and Critical Reflection in Teacher Education and Training*. Brighton: Institute for Education Policy Studies.

Hill, D. (1993b) Book review of Stanley Aronowitz and Henry Giroux, *Postmodern Education: Politics, Culture and Social Criticism* (University of Minnesota Press, 1991). *Journal of Education Policy*, **8** (1).

Hill, D. (1994a) Current developments in teacher education in England and Wales: post-modernism in action or ideological and repressive state apparatuses in

force? Conference paper to the CEDAR International Conference, Warwick University, April.

Hill, D. (1994b) Teacher education and ethnic diversity. In G. Verma and Pumfrey (eds), *Cultural Diversity and the Curriculum*, Volume 4: *Cross Curricular Contexts, Themes and Dimensions in Primary Schools*. London: Falmer Press.

Hill, D. (1994c) A radical left policy for teacher education. *Socialist Teacher*, **56**.

Hill, D. (1996) Ideological value added: course ideology and the ideology of students and newly qualified teachers. British Educational Research Association Annual Conference, Lancaster University.

Hill, D. and Cole, M. (1995) Marxist state theory and state autonomy theory: the case of 'race' education in initial teacher education. *Journal of Education Policy*, **10**(2), 221–32.

Hill, D. and Cole, M. (1996) Materialism and the post-modern fallacy: the case of education. In J. V. Fernandes (ed.), *Proceedings of the Second International Conference of Sociology of Education*. Lisbon: Gulbenkian Foundation.

Hill, D., Cole, M. and Williams, C. (1996) Equality and primary teacher education. In M. Cole, D. Hill and S. Shan, *Promoting Equality in Primary Schools*. London: Cassell.

Hillcole Group/ Chitty, C. (ed.) (1991) *Changing the Future: Redprint for Education*. London: Tuffnell Press.

Hillcole Group (1996) *Education for Democracy: A Socialist Perspective*. London: Tuffnell Press.

ILEA (1983) *Race, Sex and Class*. London: ILEA.

Kirk, D. (1986) Beyond the limits of theoretical discourse in teacher education: towards a critical pedagogy. *Teaching and Teacher Education*, **2** (2).

Leicester, M. (1992) Anti-racism versus new multiculturalism: moving beyond the interminable debate. In J. Lynch *et al.* (eds), *Equity or Excellence: Education and Cultural Reproduction*. Lewes: Falmer Press.

Liston, D. and Zeichner, K. (1987) Critical pedagogy and teacher education. *Boston University Journal of Education*, **169** (3).

Liston, D. and Zeichner, K. (1991) *Teacher Education and the Social Conditions of Schooling*. London: Routledge.

McDiarmid, G. (1993) Changes in beliefs about learners among participants in eleven teacher education programmes. In J. Calderhead and P. Gates (eds), *Conceptualising Reflection in Teacher Development*. London: Falmer Press.

Macintyre, D. (1993) Theory, theorising and reflection in initial teacher education. In J. Calderhead and P. Gates (eds), *Conceptualising Reflection in Teacher Development*. London: Falmer Press.

Miles, R. (1989) *Racism*. London: Routledge.

O'Hear, A. (1988) *Who Teaches the Teachers? A Contribution to Public Debate.* London: The Social Affairs Unit.

Reid, I. (1993) The last opportunity? The relative failure of British teacher education in tackling the inequality of schooling. In G. Verma (ed.), *Inequality and Teacher Education: An International Perspective.* London: Falmer Press.

Rosaen, C., Roth, K. and Lanier, J. (1990) Becoming a reflective teacher of subject matter. Paper presented at the American Educational Research Association Annual Meeting, Boston, MA.

Russell, T. (1993) Critical attributes of a reflective teacher: is agreement possible? In J. Calderhead and P. Gates (eds), *Conceptualising Reflection in Teacher Development.* London: Falmer Press.

Sarup, M. (1983) *Marxism/Structuralism/Education.* London: Falmer Press.

Sarup, M. (1986) *The Politics of Multi-racial Education.* London: Routledge.

Schön, D. (1983) *The Reflective Practitioner.* London: Temple Smith.

Schön, D. (1987) *Educating the Reflective Practitioner: Toward a New Design for Teaching and Learning.* San Francisco: Jossey-Bass.

Shor, I. (1986) *Culture Wars: School and Society in the Conservative Restoration 1969–1984.* London: Routledge and Kegan Paul.

Siraj-Blatchford, I. (1992) Social justice and teacher education in the UK. In G. Verma (ed.), *Inequality and Teacher Education.* London: Falmer Press.

Sleeter, C. (1989) Multicultural education as a form of resistance to oppression. *Journal of Education,* **171** (3).

Sleeter, C. (1992) How white teachers construct race. In C. McCarthy and W. Crichlow (eds), *Race, Identity and Representation.* New York: Routledge.

Smyth, J. (1985) An alternative and critical perspective for clinical supervision in schools. In K. Sirotnik and J. Oakes (eds), *Critical Perspectives on the Organisation and Improvement of Schooling.* Boston: Kluwer Nijhoff.

Smyth, J. (1986) Towards a collaborative, reflective and critical mode of clinical supervision. In J. Smyth (ed.), *Learning about Teaching through Clinical Supervision.* London: Croom Helm.

Smyth, J. (1991) Teachers' work and the politics of reflection, or reflections on a growth industry. Paper presented to conference, Conceptualising Reflection in Teacher Development, Bath University.

Stone, M. (1981) *The Education of the Black Child in Britain: The Myth of Multiracial Education.* London: Fontana.

Swann, Lord (1985) *Education for All: The Report of the Committee of Inquiry into the Education of Children from Ethnic Minority Groups.* London: HMSO.

Tabachnik, B. R. and Zeichner, K. (1991) Introduction. In B. R. Tabachnik and K. Zeichner (eds), *Issues and Practice in Enquiry Oriented Teacher Education.* London: Falmer Press.

Troyna, B. and Sikes, P. (1989) Putting the why back into teacher education. *Forum,* **32** (1).

Whitty, G. (1993) Education reform and teacher education in England in the 1990s. In P. Gilroy and M. Smith (eds), *International Analyses of Teacher Education.* Abingdon: Carfax.

Whitty, G. and Barton, L. (1987) Ideology and control in teacher education. In T. Popkewitz (ed.), *Critical Studies in Teacher Education.* Lewes: Falmer Press.

Whitty, G. and Menter, I. (1989) Lessons of Thatcherism: education policy in England and Wales 1979–88. In A. Gamble and C. Wells (eds), *Thatcher's Law.* Oxford: Blackwell.

Williams, F. C. (1989) *Social Policy: A Critical Introduction, Issues of Race, Gender, and Class.* Cambridge: Polity Press.

Wolf, A. (1994) *Competence Based Assessment.* Buckingham: Open University Press.

Zeichner, K. (1991) Reflections on reflective teaching. In B. R. Tabachnik and K. Zeichner (eds), *Issues and Practice in Enquiry Oriented Teacher Education.* London: Falmer Press.

Zeichner, K. and Liston, D. (1987) Teaching student teachers to reflect. *Harvard Educational Review,* **57** (1).

Zeichner, K. and Liston, D. (1990) Traditions of reform in US teacher education. *Journal of Teacher Education,* **41** (2).

# 18 Teachers, Teaching, Learning, Education and Higher Education 1994 (or 'Sleep Faster, We Need the Pillows')

TONY WING

## Nationally

The proverb of the sub-title amuses (if it does, any more) because of the absurdity that anyone could think we might be able to sleep faster. Note that it is common to be told to sleep *less*, i.e. to take less time over it, but that is different; no one seriously supposes sleeping to be something we might be able to speed up.

I use the proverb at the beginning of this chapter because it has become fashionable in recent times to presume that any end may be achieved, if only we devote enough energy and concentration to inventing a means. And the dominance of the disposition that treats ends as unproblematic, the disposition the Greeks called *techne*, currently characterizes educational structures and change throughout England and Wales, and beyond that throughout most of the English-speaking world. Not surprising, you might think, that in 'a techno-logical age' *techne* will predominate, but before presuming that the problems to be faced in education today are all purely technical it is worth recalling that Aristotle distinguished a more re-flexive *practical* thinking from technical thinking (partly) on the very good grounds that in contexts involving human interaction ends are just as prob-lematic as means.[1]

The predominance of a technical mentality today conditions the terms in which problems are articulated and set before us to solve. *Learning to Succeed*, the recent report of the National Com-mission on Education (1993), is a classic example of the framing of an educational situation in tech-nical terms, terms which through their imman-ence pre-empt examination of the practicality of the ends being taken for granted. There is heavy emphasis in the report upon *training*, an activity undertaken when it is presumed that the problems to be faced by individuals will not be new, unique or possibly insoluble, that satisfactory techniques are available (or can be invented) for responding to any situations that will arise and that trainees will not need, fundamentally, to think out anything for themselves beyond the possible refinement or de-velopment of rehearsable techniques. (Few would speak of *training* as an adequate preparation for tomorrow's mathematicians; who knows what problems they will invent for themselves?) There is also an almost exclusive concentration in the report upon *learning* (as opposed to *thinking*), a preoccupation entirely consistent with a predilec-tion for training, and there is much optimism about opportunities for innovation in learning *methods* through *new technologies*, the develop-ment of new *media* for something called 'distance' learning and pleas for the support of expansion in higher education through the funding of research into new *methods* of teaching and learning. Fi-nally, there is in the report continuous emphasis upon the training of *skills*, a term taken from the context of sport and manual activity and applied metaphorically (and carelessly) these days to an extraordinary range of complex human intellec-tual and emotional functioning. At one point the report speaks quite unselfconsciously of 'life' skills – working in teams, effective communication, problem-solving, personal 'effectiveness' and self-discipline – as if these complex personal experiences can all readily be understood as and reduced to routine and practice. The whole picture is painted in terms of unquestioned techniques employed to *given* ends, as if problems in teaching and education were all purely matters of method. But *'learning to succeed'* at what, and why? Neither the ends nor the means presumed for this vision of education are treated as problematic.

Other instances of the current tendency to cast education in purely technical terms are easy to find. The National Curriculum for England and Wales began to be introduced in 1988 as a set of given ends for teachers and pupils to reach by whatever means they could. School teachers were accorded the privilege of being allowed to 'deliver' the curriculum however they chose (and isn't *that* still a peculiar notion, 'delivering' a 'curriculum'? Like a smart blow to the head?), but the ends themselves (called 'targets') were to be looked after by the Secretary of State. The practice of teaching is cast in this as a problem purely of means. Art education is being recast nowadays as 'art and design', with critical emphasis placed upon the design challenge of inventing means to given ends. The now technically conceived practice of teaching is thought to be comfortably held in a set of preordained *competencies* for the purposes of teacher *training*, and learning is everywhere thought *manageable* as sets of limited and predictable *outcomes*. The list could go on.

The origins of this exclusively technical mentality are manifold and complex, and have been much written and thought about.[2] I am not trying to examine them here. Whatever the origins, the consequences are evident. A national curriculum is rewritten several times (at immense human and financial cost) before even one cohort of children has reached its secondary schools, because no one questioned whether the end as conceived by the Secretary of State was even possible. Fine-arts courses are marginalized and design courses (as a consequence) impoverished because 'design' (that is, 'making') is now thought to be much more important to the nation than whatever it is 'artists' do (whatever that is, it isn't considered *produc-*

*tive*). Teaching is treated simply as the application of techniques for the 'delivery' of learning packages, and learning itself is understood as a behavioural and, like training, morally inert phenomenon.

It is important to note as well that the current dominating technical mentality lies alongside (or within, or around) an accompanying, mutually reinforcing preoccupation with *administration*, in particular with the methods and practices of the administration of production. Education is now overwhelmingly 'managed' through such things as 'learning outcomes', 'competencies', 'performance indicators', etc., as if measurable control of every aspect of education is possible, highly desirable and fundamental. *Learning to Succeed* (p. 59) puts it succinctly: 'Curriculum requirements will be framed on the basis of outcomes, that is to say that they will make clear what those following the curriculum will be expected *to know, to understand, and to be able to do*.' Thus education is to be judged against entirely (and unquestioned) utilitarian values, and the distinctly limited performance-oriented conceptions of knowing and understanding enshrined in the TGAT Report of 1987 are adopted unseen. The curriculum is to be limited to that which is thought both useful and measurable; it is understood as that which leads to particular outcomes; it is a means to an end.

Yet Aristotle's classification of forms of knowledge and enquiry into theoretical, productive and practical follows from a recognition that the disposition appropriate for 'making' things (*techne*) is quite different from the disposition appropriate for 'doing' things within a society (*phronesis*). When I am engaged in 'making', I look no further than the self-contained project of 'making' itself; when I am engaged in 'doing', I need to ask what I am doing or making this for, whether it is possible or desirable to do or make this for that, and what the value of all that I do might be. I cannot enter into 'making' without first presuming making is possible; *techne* presupposes making is possible and is concerned with only 'making' itself, never mind the consequences. *Phronesis* is the disposition which allows both ends and means constantly to interrelate and to influence each other and recognizes that the rightness of any 'doing' within a society is always problematic.

The problem with adopting a 'making' mentality for 'doing' things is that 'making' takes ends for granted and leaves ethics aside. Making a bomb requires only a technical disposition; asking what the bomb is *for*, asking whether it is quite *right* to be obtaining these detonators by deception, are practical questions, requiring that the ethics of both the making and threatening or exploding be judged. In Aristotle's terms, educating is a practical, not a productive, activity. *Learning to Succeed* is not a 'radical' look at education, as it claims; it is a technical look. The radical move came somewhat earlier, when ministers and their advisers decided to root national discussion of education in the terms and practices of production.

## At the new University of X

A recent Division of Quality Audit (DQA)[3] report on the new University of X (note the term *audit* – in our new productive understanding we no longer 'inspect' educational institutions) made evident to its readers the fact long known to those with experience of higher education, that teaching was not being accorded a high institutional priority. Let us be clear, the University of X is simply typical of a wider higher and further education culture in England and Wales which has traditionally valued scholarship, erudition, research and technical excellence more highly than the practice of teaching its students. Evidence of how little importance has been attached to teaching institutionally at X was readily apparent in academic staff appointment and promotion criteria and staff development reviews and practices; succeeding as a lecturer as far as higher education institutions are concerned is about what you have published, managed or produced, not about how well you teach your students.

Recently, owing to the rapid expansion of higher education and an accompanying widening of access, concern is increasingly being expressed

in places both high and low about something usually run together in speech and thought as 'teaching-and-learning'. ('Sex-and-violence' are commonly and equally automatically run together in the same way, as if the two have some necessary and symmetric relation.[4]) It has been recognized that we cannot simply increase student numbers and widen access without developing new arrangements for student learning, particularly since the increase in numbers has been rapid and massive and teaching resources to match have not been forthcoming. Responses to the concern about 'teaching-and-learning' are to search for techniques to promote 'student independence', 'distance learning', 'action learning', 'resource-based learning', and, within many institutions, to adopt 'modularity'. What is interesting in this development is that the recently awakened concern for 'teaching-and-learning' follows from the rapid increase in student numbers and widening of access without commensurate resources, not from any newly discovered concern about the low priority previously given to the teaching abilities of academic staff. The technical mentality is again clearly evident: *given* the ends of expansion and wider access without commensurate resources, how can we find a means? And as is equally clear in the example of health service 'reforms', administrative investment increases significantly while front-line (in the case of education, teaching) resources are pegged.

It is important to note in this that the concern, energy and resources currently focused upon 'teaching-and-learning' in higher education are not being directed at all towards the *teaching* of the arts, the sciences, the humanities, engineering, etc. *per se*, but to administratively inspired coping strategies for conditions in which there are not enough teachers for the numbers of students taken on to courses. Teaching in higher education is still not itself considered problematic; resourcing is. 'Independent learning', 'distance learning', 'action learning', 'self-directed learning', 'supplemental instruction' and 'resource-based learning' (to name but a few) are being advocated across the board as ends in themselves, not as responses to educational problems arising within the idiosyncratic contexts of teaching art, mathematics, pharmacy, civil engineering or podiatry. All students and teachers, regardless of subject, discipline or practice, are being asked to develop means whereby students can learn anything without teachers. 'Independent' learning means learning independently of the teacher; 'distance' learning means learning distanced from the teacher; 'action' learning means learning from 'experience', not the teacher; 'self-directed' learning means learning without the benefit of guidance from the teacher; 'supplemental instruction' means senior students teaching junior students; 'resource-based' learning means learning from anything so long as it is not a teacher. This is patently not about 'independent learning', for no learning can be 'independent' at all; it is about teacher-free learning.

The dominating technical and administrative mentality determines that 'teaching-and-learning' problems are conceived as essentially administrative and technical, and are, as a consequence, thought susceptible to solution through the application of administrative methods and techniques developed within a culture of production. 'Teaching-and-learning' is understood in administrative and technical terms, its 'problems' are produced in these terms and proposed solutions are tested against administratively determined criteria.

Now it is possible to discern two interrelated assaults upon prior, normative use of the terms 'education' and 'teaching' woven in among these current developments. On the one hand an administrative conception of a 'process' (a further metaphor from the culture of production) being called 'education' is controlling both the conditions and the terms in which 'teaching' is permitted to occur, and on the other a technical conception of 'education' is being promulgated as opposition to 'traditional teaching' through new initiatives such as Higher Education for Capability[5] and through new techniques for 'facilitating learning', such as action learning.[6]

The administrative assault is conducted as follows: in order to 'manage' the imbalance in resources, students must find ways of working on their own, and those who used to teach students can consequently be directed to developing strategies and devices for students to cope with their absence. But if students are to work on their own, how can their work adequately be 'managed'? When there were enough teachers, teaching guided student effort significantly and (by and large) students arrived at their examinations suitably prepared. If teachers are not to be on hand to guide studies, students might now waste time pursuing unproductive lines of enquiry, might learn the wrong things, might not learn enough things or might learn too many. A further complication is that widening access has exacerbated the problem of insufficient teachers being available simply for the numbers of students because it has created high demand for much greater variety of provision. If there were sufficient teachers available, variety of provision would not be a problem, for we could just increase the variety of courses to match. Without sufficient teachers, however, variety is difficult to provide.

The administrative response to this 'management' problem is to make courses more 'manageable', and by this is meant susceptible to a sufficient degree of administrative control. Administratively this is approached in two ways: first, by ensuring that we concern ourselves only with *learning* (since behaviourism has allowed us to believe that learning is an eminently measurable and manageable thing); second, by presuming that learning is not only measurable but also *containable*. If learning is containable it can be 'managed' as variable sets of discrete learning packages, and what used to be called 'courses' can be reinterpreted as individually 'tailored' subsets of learning packages 'built' and 'delivered' as 'programmes of study'. (Since individualized programmes of study are being 'built' from discrete units we may as well call these units *modules*; the term has a technically respectable home within the laudably productive activity of building.)

The administrative conception in all this is evident: beginning with an administratively conceived problem of resourcing, several educational presuppositions are taken for granted (that all courses both can and should be restricted to a 'learning' that may be treated as measurable and containable) and an administratively acceptable response to the problem of resourcing is adopted.

Note, importantly, that in these moves teaching itself is still accorded a low institutional priority. The problem has been understood as 'not enough teachers', and consequently there is no point in raising the status of teaching; effort must be directed, and status given instead, to 'facilitating independent learning' – learning independently of the teacher, that is.

The second contemporary assault upon understandings of 'education' and 'teaching' is being conducted through apparently 'educational' initiatives. The Higher Education for Capability initiative has adopted a 'mission statement' (a clear signal they mean 'business'), which reads as follows:

> There is a serious imbalance in Britain in the full process which is described by the two words 'education' and 'training'.
>
> Individuals, industry and society will all benefit from a well balanced education concerned not only with academic excellence in the acquisition of knowledge and skills of analysis but also with excellence in using and communicating knowledge, doing, making, designing, collaborating, organising, and creating.[7]

Note several aspects of this statement. The 'serious imbalance' being deplored is presumably at the moment in favour of an 'academic' excellence wherein the 'excellence' involved is caricatured as 'acquisition' of 'knowledge' and 'skills of analysis'. 'Creating' is apparently not presently part of academic work, and neither is 'collaborating' or 'communicating knowledge'. And if we haven't got the message yet about the inadequacy of the current, 'traditional' academic higher education experience, we are next told that: 'Spoonfeeding information for subsequent regurgitation is an inadequate preparation for a world in which self reliance, inter-dependence, individual and collective initiatives ... [etc.] are essential requirements.' Well of course it isn't adequate, yet whoever suggested it was? Somehow or other, redressing a perceived imbalance between 'education' and 'training' is expected to result in much less 'spoonfeeding' and 'regurgitation', and much more 'self reliance', etc. The caricature of 'teaching' and presumed benefits of 'training' in this are really quite farcical. There is no sense in which

teaching requires students to be passive, nor any likelihood that training will result in self-reliance; quite the opposite, in fact.

Knocking over the same educational Aunt Sally is at the heart of another current initiative called 'action learning'. According to some recent proponents of this *technique* for facilitating learning (McGill and Beaty, 1992), action learning is a *process* centred on 'learning from experience', with an intention of 'getting things done'. It caricatures an 'academic world of theory' opposed to 'the practical world of work' (academics don't *work*, apparently), and higher education seminars as to do with some distant world 'out there', opposed to action learning in which that 'academic' world is *related* to particular individuals' contexts. Prior, 'well prepared material for group discussion', such as an academic 'expert' might think relevant, is specifically excluded from the action learning process, and 'traditional' teaching is characterized (despite an explicit acknowledgement that this may not always be the case) as 'didactic', 'hierarchical', as having a cognitive 'bias', as giving students a 'dependent, passive' role, and as utilizing exclusively 'lecture/tutorial' methods. Action learning is explicitly contrasted to a model of teaching which mistakenly (it is thought) emphasizes an unequal relation between teacher and student consequent upon the teacher having more 'expertise' than the learner. Action learning recognizes the 'student' as 'the world expert' on the problem he or she is facing (and also, presumably, therefore in the best position to make up a solution).

What Higher Education for Capability and action learning share is their attack upon a thoroughly limited conception of teaching. Both initiatives portray higher education teaching as an appalling mixture of 'spoonfeeding' and 'regurgitation' of abstract and uselessly distant 'academic' theory. Both also claim that traditional higher education teaching accords too little respect to learners and their immediate 'situations'. Note that in both these initiatives particularly poor methods of teaching are singled out for attack in order that no teaching at all can seem like a good idea. Although it is only poor methods of teaching which are in fact pilloried, the solution that is presumed to follow from this technical analysis is the removal of the teaching function from higher education entirely: because poor teaching may regard learners as passive, all teaching must somehow be inadequate. It is a happy accident indeed that just as we find we don't have enough teachers, teaching turns out to be a thoroughly useless pursuit anyway.

Through these twin contemporary attacks upon earlier understandings of 'education', teaching remains the lowest of higher education institutional priorities. Prior to expansion, research, scholarship, technical achievement and (among the new universities) administration took precedence over teaching. Subsequently, a thoroughly administrative and technical conception of higher education is again ensuring that teaching comes after everything else. It is because 'education' itself is nowadays so thoroughly technically conceived and administratively managed that only after the ends of student 'independence' and 'modularity' have been agreed administratively are those who used to be teachers allotted the task of inventing the means of 'delivering' administratively conceived learning packages. When technical solutions are called for, technical responses are produced. Asking whether any of this is worthwhile is most likely to be interpreted as a question about 'quality' systems, audits and procedures.

## Being practical

The argument that education requires a practical (not technical) disposition because of what it is was made by R. S. Peters (1966) long ago (during that other period of rapid expansion in higher education this century), when he pointed out that the notion of education has built into it the condition of being worthwhile, and further that whatever education is judged to involve is to be approached in morally acceptable ways. Note, importantly, that education is *intrinsically* worthwhile; its worth does not lie in any further instrumental function it may contingently serve. If an educated population happens to prove useful

to an economic project, so well and good; but that accident is not what makes education valuable, for it is valuable in itself. And it is no good responding, 'Well that's just his view of education, mine is something else', because what Peters's argument showed is that simply asking, seriously, what education might involve commits one in some senses, if one is to be rational, to following certain ethical principles of procedure and to being initiated into particular forms of knowledge. The ethical principles include, he argues, respect for persons, fairness, consideration of interests and freedom to do what there are good reasons for doing, and the forms of knowledge are precisely those which one would need to come to understand in order to answer the question 'What is worthwhile?'

Of course, as Peters points out, it is possible to accept the logic of the argument about what education means and respond, 'Well, I am against education then. We have no time for such luxuries. We must equip people for suitable jobs and train enough scientists and technicians to maintain an expanding economy.' As he says, 'This is an arguable point ... Arguable, that is, in certain limited contexts, but difficult to defend to the last ditch; for presumably an expanding economy is a necessary base for a way of life that is thought desirable. And what is to be done about handing *that* on?' (Peters, 1966, p. 29). A practical disposition (*phronesis*) is necessary to educating in order to recognize the normative aspects that education necessarily entails. Being practical (not technical) involves recognizing, reflectively, both ends and means as interrelated and continually problematic, and that there is an obligation always to act wittingly in ethically defensible ways. It becomes easier to see now, in the light of these points, how the prevailing technical conception of 'education' is much better described as a conception of training, and that there is a much more radical and significant conflict between 'education' and 'training' than the announced mission of 'education *for* capability' acknowledges. Apart from anything else, education *for* anything misses an essential point. Educating is a practical pursuit; it is training that is instrumental.

There are related points to be made about teaching. Teaching is contrasted to 'training', 'indoctrinating', 'conditioning' and other approaches to the intentional bringing about of learning by the conditional expectation that teaching respect learners' capacities for rational thought and deliberation, and aims at their witting involvement in coming to understand what is before them to learn. Training does not necessarily require that trainees understand what they do, merely that in the end they do it efficiently; teaching necessarily involves awareness and understanding on the part of those who are taught. Pavlov's dogs were not taught to salivate at the sound of a bell, they were trained. Thus teaching too, in requiring students' witting engagement in their own coming to know, is a practical pursuit involving commitment to at least those minimal procedural ethical principles identified in the arguments put forward by Peters. Teaching, although intentional, is not wholly instrumental; it cannot be reduced to the mere deployment of technique. It matters, in teaching, that students come to understand actively *for themselves*, and in this important respect that students are accorded as thinkers in their own right lies the implicated risk they will come up with ideas to be preferred to those with which their teachers began. Teaching, unlike training, involves genuine *dialogue*, the outcome of which may not always be presumed or predicted or (worse) decided in advance; it cannot, in practice, become solely instrumental. It is training that denies self-reliance, not teaching; the Higher Education for Capability 'mission' has stood these ideas on their head.

Attempting to regulate the activity of teaching through the terms of (supposedly) predictable and measurable 'outcomes' of 'competencies' and 'learning' denies the importance of dialogue and negotiation upon which the activity depends. The essential distinction between teaching and training, that in teaching students come wittingly to understand what they learn, requires that students think, deliberate, enquire, experiment and come in their various ways to know (also wittingly) for themselves. It is both ridiculous and mistaken to believe that the highly complex experiences involved in coming, wittingly, to understand for oneself can be constrained within the purely instrumental task of producing 'learning outcomes' and 'competencies' that anyone could both measure and predict. The language of predictable, instrumentally determined 'learning outcomes' and 'competencies' is that of training, not teaching.

With these central points about education and teaching before us it is now interesting to enquire further why teaching continues to be accorded such low priority in higher education today. The administrative problem of 'not enough teachers' that motivates today's 'modularity' and 'teacher-free learning' does not by itself explain why 'teaching' has had to be pilloried and passed over. Teaching expertise may be scarce, but why is it not valued? Why take the administrative view?

An important part of the explanation begins to appear if we step back from the concern of educating and examine recent wider movements in the social and historical context of our nation's affairs. We live in times when in the Anglo-Saxon economies successful promulgation of a particular free-market ideology (not that of Adam Smith by the way, for he wrote of *enlightened* self-interest) depends upon marginalizing all expertise that is not purely technical. A technical mentality thoroughly adopted by nations would be doubly useful to today's free-marketeers, for it would both ensure that much is produced and leave the presumed ultimate 'good' of unbridled wealth creation unquestioned. It would ensure that people 'lower their heads to pull the cart instead of raising their heads to look at the road'.[8] The clergy are left well alone today until their concern with moral values is felt to impinge upon 'political' life, at which point they are attacked and told they have strayed beyond the bounds of their legitimate expertise. Medicine and teaching (both practical, involving ethical concerns) are systematically cut down to matters solely of technique, and the practice of law (sometimes practical, in relation to 'justice'; sometimes technical, in relation to the exercise of power) is sometimes attacked and sometimes approved. The single (and purely technical) expertise elevated today is that of 'business', and the methods of 'business' are made obligatory for all on the grounds of their supposedly superior instrumental efficiency alone.

I want to argue that the methods and language of business, being purely technical, are inadequate on moral grounds for the conduct of a practical pursuit. *Techne* is not *phronesis*; *poietike* not *praxis*. Medicine, teaching and the practising of law and religious ministry cannot be reduced to technique or the unquestioned pursuit of anything, since all of them involve continually challenging ethical concerns. In education, in particular, the concern is with approaching what is worthwhile through respect for individuals' capacities to reason and think for themselves.

It is most important to make this point clearly: there is interest today in reducing teaching to training, in reducing witting understanding to learning, in reducing practical pursuits (especially teaching) to the restricted technical limitation of 'competencies'. There is interest in control of the very thinking of the nation, and the strangling of teaching through imposition of the language of production serves that interest very well. Allotting school teachers the task precisely of *delivering* a curriculum was no accidental slip of the tongue; it presaged the wholesale intentional corruption of the language of teaching for ideological 'free-market' ends.

If we do not defend, in particular, the terms in which teaching is regulated and understood, we conspire to submit to an amoral, technical abuse of our selves and our various professions. This is a not unimportant point. Yet I want to argue further, on quite other grounds, that the culture of business with its prevailing mythologies is inadequate for the teaching or practice of mathematics, of science, of the humanities, of the arts, or for initiation into any professional practice which involves considerable, legitimate, reliable and valuable expertise. The culture of business is inadequate, in particular, precisely for its systematic devaluation of established expertise (a feature which of course serves today's free-market interest well).

There is a prevalent myth within business today that continually changing conditions demand continuously novel responses, that in their very nature today's and tomorrow's conditions will demand ever more innovative strategies and responses. It is a myth that devalues any, however legitimately, established expertise (note, incidentally, how often a mythical 'educational *establishment*' has been the object of ministerial bile). The

myth within business is perpetrated through an instrumentally blinkered and excitable preoccupation with rapidly developing technologies, through the uncritical adoption of organizational models such as 'The learning company' (Pedler *et al.*, 1991) and in an excited rediscovery of 'multiple intelligences' (Gardner, 1983). 'Intelligence' and 'learning' are exactly what is required for situations in which no one knows what to do because nothing similar has happened before. (Note that there is potential for contradiction here; we need to rely on intelligence because this problem is new, yet we must also learn from *our* (not 'expert') experience in case we meet it again. Yet if all our problems are new, how can we meet them again? The contradiction is apparently avoided by stressing that all our learning very rapidly becomes obsolete.) The myth is no doubt significantly supported by the failure of economics to 'deliver' anything like successfully on its promise to predict (Ormerod, 1994) – the likelihood that business will some day be able to rely upon an empirical 'science' seems to diminish day by day. Of course, there are areas of expertise that business is prepared to exploit, such as mathematics and psychology, and successful areas developed for itself, such as marketing and public relations, but the prevailing role model of 'action-man' taken to be legitimated in Donald Schön's interesting *The Reflective Practitioner* (1983) is of one who is continually obliged to act largely in the dark of the new. Significantly, Donald Schön also chose to oppose his 'reflection-in-action' to the by now familiar caricature of a uselessly distant, 'theoretical' academic. It is clear how little regard is shown within 'business' for any expertise found useful before this morning; easy to see how short-term immediate interests prevail.[9]

Such technically inspired scepticism about established expertise hardly translates well to circumstances in which there are substantially reliable and developing bodies of knowledge. Not all knowledge becomes obsolete overnight; space shuttles do not return guided to their impressively unpowered landings solely on the basis of mathematics invented last week. I want to argue that it is time to recognize, to develop and to value forms of reliable practical and theoretical expertise, not to suffocate them uniformly in the locally appropriate terms and practices of business. Even if economic concerns do seem pressing, that is no reason for denying our students the respect they deserve and shackling them in their crucial task of going *beyond* what we know. And in particular, if there is expertise to be used (and there most certainly is), it is teaching expertise that will serve the task of initiating the young most effectively.

If we face the full challenge of educating (and don't tell me we haven't the time), we will find that we need first to support, to encourage, to value and to develop the practice of higher education teaching, not throw it away with the books. If we face the full challenge of educating we will find that we remember (from long ago now) that becoming a good mathematician, a good chemist, a good engineer, a good historian, a good painter, even a good manager, takes much more than acquiring a set of (supposedly) measurable, soon-to-be-obsolete 'competencies' and 'skills'. Thinking is necessary, and courage important; imagination, responsibility and coming to care are involved. To think that such qualities are adequately captured in trite descriptions of 'skills', 'competencies' and 'capability' and trained into people like habits is patently absurd. We fail to respect our students when we face them with these pitiable conceptions. Reducing their 'education' to administrative and ideological conveniences effectively retards initiation into their complex and dynamic fields of concern. We fail to respect our students' minds when we pretend that 'learning' is containable, packageable as bricks; some learning might be treatable that way, but only very limited kinds and not those they will need to lead whole *and* productive lives. We fail to respect our students when we keep them from the challenge of active and live dialogue with those who presently know more than they do. We fail to respect our students when we fob them off with so called 'independent' teacher-free learning, when we give them instead of knowledgeable, thinking experts to share the struggle of their enquiring, machines programmed to respond only to questions we thought of in advance of their asking. We fail to respect our students when we ignore the work to be done on the teaching of mathematics as opposed to the

teaching of science, the teaching of art as opposed to the teaching of history, the teaching of the practice of law as opposed to the practice of podiatry. We fail to respect our students when we pretend that these challenges are effectively the same, when we speak glibly of 'learning' as if it doesn't make any difference what is to be learned. We fail to respect our students all the time in these things, because, through our preoccupying administrative, technical and ideological concerns, we have no respect for their teachers.

## Reading the book

It was Aneurin Bevan who asked, 'Why gaze into a crystal ball when you can read the book?' We have been here before, of course. Not exactly here, but close enough to see what will happen. In the USA,

> Around 1912 ... a heroicizing [*sic*] view of the businessman, positivism, and social darwinism, combined to produce a utilitarian ideology of rare blatancy. Its catchword was 'efficiency'; a 'cult of efficiency' pervaded all areas of social life, including the school system. The ideology of efficiency ... [was] both strengthened and instrumentalized by three very consequential achievements: F. Taylor's 'scientific management', Thorndike's behaviouristic learning theory, and the development of standardized tests.
>
> To adapt the principle of efficiency to the educational system means to subject the school to the logic of economics ... Viewing the school by analogy to a factory/plant, the student is the raw material, the adult the end product, the teacher is the worker, and the curriculum is everything that brings about the change from raw material to end product. The curriculum is conceived as a series of stimulus–response acts accompanied by continuous testing.
>
> (Keitel, 1986)

In England by this time a technical, instrumental obsession had produced 'payment by results', a system doomed to 'collapse under its own administrative weight' (Gipps, 1990, p. 104). One Edmond Holmes, Chief Inspector for Elementary Schools, published in 1911 a reflection on education over the previous fifty years:

The State, in prescribing a syllabus which was to be followed, in all the subjects of instruction, by all the schools in the country, without regard to local or personal considerations, was guilty of one capital offence. It did all his thinking for the teacher. It told him in precise detail what he was to do each year in each 'Standard', how he was to handle each subject, and how far he was to go in it; what width of ground he was to cover; what amount of knowledge, what degree of accuracy was required for a 'pass'. In other words it provided him with his ideals, his general conceptions, his more immediate aims, his schemes of work; and if it did not control his methods in all their details, it gave him (by implication) hints and suggestions with regard to these on which he was not slow to act; for it told him that the work done in each class and each subject would be tested at the end of each year by a careful examination of each individual child; and it was inevitable that in his endeavour to adapt his teaching to the type of question which his experience of the yearly examination led him to expect, he should gradually deliver himself, mind and soul, into the hands of the officials of the Department – the officials at Whitehall who framed the yearly syllabus, and the various officials who examined on it.

What the Department did to the teacher, it compelled him to do to the child. The teacher who is the slave of another's will cannot carry out his instructions except by making his pupils the slaves of his own will. The teacher who has been deprived by his superiors of freedom, initiative, and responsibility, cannot carry out his instructions except by depriving his pupils of the same vital qualities . . . As profound distrust of the teacher was the basis of the policy of the Department, so profound distrust of the child was the basis of the policy of the teacher.

(Holmes, quoted in Gipps, 1990, pp. 104–5)

The dominating nineteenth-century technical mentality culminated in the obscenity of the First World War, and in all the horrors that continued remorselessly in its train. That is the trouble with technical thinking: no sense of perspective, 'no time other than now' (comment by Neil Kinnock in a speech to the Labour Party Conference, 1988).

We don't have payment by results today; we have instead performance by outcomes. We in higher education are all free to determine our own syllabus, to teach in our own ways, to examine our own work. Just provided, that is, we have first carved up our 'intended learning' into self-contained packages, reduced humanity's hard-won expertise to specious 'competencies' and (paradoxically) increased our limiting control of student effort by denying students their right to our time. We don't have *payment* by results today. Just management.

Being practical would not be easy. It would involve acknowledging that all who act to educate are committed to acting thoughtfully, reflectively, prudently and rightly; that giving teachers ends to strive towards unquestioningly in itself prevents them from acting to educate. If teachers are to educate they must be in a position to judge their actions and to act upon their judgements; this is only possible to the extent that their actions are not constrained by others in advance as a precondition of their acting. It is impossible to act either morally or reflectively in conditions where there is nothing to decide.

Being practical would involve conceiving courses as educational, not administrative, challenges, and in this recognizing that not all 'outcomes' can (or should) be known in advance. Students (all students, whatever their abilities and backgrounds) would need to be respected and encouraged as thinkers, not patronized and constrained as the subjects of training. Teaching would have to be developed, not replaced. And of course there would be need for organizational change (from bureaucratic structures towards model 'thinking companies' perhaps?); teachers *qua* teachers would need to be involved more fully and considerably earlier in the formulation of institutional and national educational policies.[10] That last idea is rather controversial. 'Teachers would never agree about anything.' 'They couldn't be relied upon to see the need for administrative priorities.' 'It would take too long to involve everybody in making decisions.' Don't they understand that teachers are the most expensive of all?' 'We can't just fly in the face of government restrictions.' 'Come out of your clouds.' 'Be *realistic*.' 'Sleep faster!'

Yet when the last teacher has gone, or been brought to his or her knees by the unceasing grind of reducing what is worthwhile to 'skills', 'competencies' and 'outcomes', who will be left to *inspire* the young? Who will speak to their *hearts*?

# Notes

1 Aristotle's discussion on this is to be found in his *Nicomachean Ethics*, and an interesting introduction to these distinctions in Carr and Kemmis (1986). In this chapter I do not follow their path into being 'critical'; I think enough is perhaps to be gained by being practical, without moving that significant step further into Marxist critique.

2 Notably in this century, Martin Heidegger's work developed a perceptive analysis of Western thinking since Plato and Aristotle, tracing the essence of our most unfortunate relationship to technology and science to influences grounded in their positions. More recently, many influenced by aspects of his thinking have related his idea to Marxist critique, in particular the work of the 'Frankfurt School' and Jürgen Habermas.

3 The Division of Quality Audit is part of the current Higher Education Quality Council and is charged with reviewing the 'mechanisms' and 'structures' used to 'monitor, assure, promote and enhance academic quality and standards'.

4 There is much to be studied concerning the coining and subsequent life of terms such as 'teaching-and-learning'. It happens so often that a term is coined in particular circumstances which give that term a meaning significantly different from meanings more generally (and perhaps previously) available. This is the case with 'teaching' and 'learning'; 'teaching-and-learning' is currently a sign of a particular concern within many higher education institutions, and refers specifically to a contemporary context of rapid, underfunded expansion. As I later show, 'teaching-and-learning' thus has very little to do with *teaching* at all, even though one might think it would. The easy use of catch-phrases such as these also diminishes the complexity of that to which they would otherwise refer; thus 'teaching-and-learning' is dealt with glibly and smoothly in a manner quite inappropriate to the complexity of either teaching or learning. The practised unity of the phrase also tends to conceal the fact that teaching is about more than learning, and learning about more than teaching, the single unitary phrase seeming to suggest that they are but 'two sides of the same coin'. The practice of 'nouning the unsayable' has been discussed by W. M. Brookes (e.g. 1993).

5 Higher Education for Capability is 'a National Initiative of the RSA based at Leeds Metropolitan University and the University of Leeds'.

6 For a recent exposition of what 'action learning' involves, see McGill and Beaty (1992).

7 The 'Capability Mission' and its supplementary 'Educating for Capability' statement are to be found on all publicity papers published by HEC to announce forthcoming conferences. The quoted mission statement is taken from one such document in circulation during early 1994.

8 This is a Chinese proverb, used by Mike Bottery (1992) as a subtitle. I refer later to his discussion of educational institutions and the requirement for particular forms of administrative organization.

9 Of course, the belief that everything is nowadays changing so quickly that no established expertise can 'keep up' is also part of a wider cultural and historical phenomenon frequently referred to as postmodernism. Andy Hargreaves (1994) has published an interesting discussion in which he interprets the difficult circumstances of contemporary teaching as a product of conflict between the pressing of postmodernism and lingering modernist structures found in the educational institutions of today. In a fascinating book, he describes today's conditions for practising teachers accurately in sensitive and harrowing detail. There is no doubt that yesterday's technically inspired bureaucratic forms of organization are totally unsuited to the conduct of education, but I cannot share a belief in *irresistible* postmodernist forces which continually invalidate all expertise. Dignifying today's amoral behaviours as inevitable concomitants of an irresistible, technologically driven race to 'keep up' with the consequences of our inventions seems to me to miss the point that we always have choice, each one of us, in how we *use* the technologies made available each day. The fact that information travels daily much more quickly and freely does not entail either that we should use that rapid availability of information to stupid or immoral ends, or that everything now becomes rapidly obsolete. Mathematics does not become obsolete in the way that marketing strategies do; much older knowledge of the physical world remains valid even if our explanations for physical phenomena may change and help us to see more; the challenge of living a life rightly, and with integrity, does not change because we now have incessantly new means of relating to others. The belief in some irresistible force called post-modernity seems to me eminently suitable folklore for lemmings to explain their behaviour to each other, but hardly appropriate for human beings. That said, Hargreaves's book is a thoroughly insightful description of the lives led by teachers today in totally unsuitable institutions.

10 See Bottery (1992) for a full and interesting argument concerning the need for educational institutions to adopt appropriate, non-bureaucratic forms of organization, and Hargreaves (1994) for a rather different perspective on the unsuitability of bureaucratic 'modernist' forms of organization for the 'management' of education in 'post-modernist' times. For an

interesting discussion of rather different perspectives on 'education' enshrined in the differing organizational structures of the older and new universities, see Adelman and Alexander (1982). Their account of the cultural clash that occurred between CNAA technical traditions and those of older university-inspired colleges of education as the latter were taken over by polytechnics remains instructive today to anyone seeking to understand the current ethos and ambitions of the new universities.

# References

Adelman, C. and Alexander, R. J. (1982) *The Self-evaluating Institution*. London: Methuen.

Bottery, M. (1992) *The Ethics of Educational Management*. London: Cassell.

Brookes, W. M. (1993) Some thoughts on sustainable design. *Chreods*, **6**, 11–12.

Carr, W. and Kemmis, S. (1986) *Becoming Critical*. London: Falmer Press.

Gardner, H. (1983) *Frames of Mind*. New York: Basic Books.

Gipps, C. (1990) *Assessment: A Teacher's Guide to the Issues*. London: Hodder and Stoughton.

Hargreaves, A. (1994) *Changing Teachers, Changing Times*. London: Cassell.

Keitel, C. (1986) Social needs in secondary mathematics education. *For the Learning of Mathematics*, **6** (3), 27–33.

McGill, I. and Beaty, L. (1992) *Action Learning*. London: Kogan Page.

National Commission on Education (1993) *Learning to Succeed*. London: Heinemann.

Ormerod, P. (1994) *The Death of Economics*. London: Faber & Faber.

Pedler, M., Burgoyne, J. and Boydell, T. (1991) *The Learning Company*. New York: McGraw-Hill.

Peters, R. S. (1966) *Ethics and Education*. London: George Allen & Unwin.

Schön, D. (1983) *The Reflective Practitioner*. New York: Basic Books.

TGAT (1987) *Report of the National Curriculum Task Group on Assessment and Testing*. London: DES.

# Part Four

## International Perspectives on Reforms in Teacher Education

# 19 Some International Perspectives on British Teacher Training

ROSALIND M. O. PRITCHARD

## British education through the eyes of others

British education has long commanded admiration in other countries.[1] It arouses interest for several reasons: its child-centred orientation, the easing of the clear lines of demarcation between the provision of teachers for primary and secondary schools, the establishment of an all-graduate profession, the tradition of research in education and the freedom enjoyed by teachers from excessive state intervention. The British cult of child-centredness is intriguing, if somewhat alien, to continental European educators, and is being cautiously emulated in, for example, some areas of Germany. The author of this chapter was once ushered into a German primary classroom of which the ministry official was particularly proud because of its child-centred methods. He paused for a moment, however, when he suddenly remembered that she came from the United Kingdom, and wondered aloud whether the visit would be worthwhile; he supposed with some regret that if she was familiar with the inside of a typical British primary school (which she was), then she would have 'little to learn from one in North Rhine–Westphalia'.

In Britain, the rigid barriers between primary and secondary teachers have been abolished and both kinds of teacher are educated at universities or university-level institutions. This is widely regarded as a progressive move in European terms, and Britain is seen as a trailblazer. Bourdoncle (1994, p. 15), in an article on the professionaliza-tion of teachers, refers to the movement, now sweeping Europe, of locating the education of trainees in universities (*universitarisation*) and awards the credit for starting this trend to the England of the 1960s. A corollary of the location of teacher education and training in universities is the development in Britain of a fine body of education-related research. Most European countries regard research in education as actually and potentially important (see Coolahan, 1992), but believe that they have a long way to go in developing a research basis. Askling and Almén (1993), for example, in an article about Swedish initial teacher training (ITT), complain that the research foundation of teacher education in their country 'is still weak'. The process of building up British education research to its present degree of breadth and depth has been a long one. O'Hara (1991, p. 26) harks back to the time when the area did not have a strong or developed literature, and Simon (1990) shows how the dominant preoccupations of British educational research have varied over the decades. Now, however, the British research tradition in education is rich and well established. Barber (1993, p. 261), in a paper about university–school partnerships, asserts that 'Britain is an international leader in educational research', but feels it necessary to add that 'it would be tragic if, through short-sighted reform of initial teacher education, the research community was significantly weakened or even destroyed'. In a number of European countries teachers are civil servants, and this close relationship to the state can result in excessive interventionism or even intrusion from state officials. Foreigners look to Britain as a country where the relationship between the state and the education sector is overwhelmingly positive, since they believe it to be free from excessive governmental interference. Thus Bourdoncle (1994, p. 19) can still write unproblematically that because the state is not allowed excessive control of social and commercial life in Anglo-Saxon countries, the role of professional groups is enhanced.

Abroad, Britain is still seen as the possessor of certain virtues. The truth is, however, that many of these are currrently under threat; in the past decade and a half, hostility has developed between the British government and professional educators, with the result that foreigners' favourable view of the relationship betweeen the two parties no longer corresponds to reality; it obviously takes a certain period of time before such major changes are perceived internationally.

## Initial teacher training stands indicted

British teacher training has been subject to a process of continuous change since the Second World War (see Galvin, 1993). *Inter alia*, it has had to cope with significant fluctuations in demographic trends, the ensuing closure of some institutions, the raising of the school-leaving age and the decision to move to an all-graduate profession. Teachers, the product of ITT, have been the target of damaging criticisms, the most fundamental of which are that they have failed to achieve universal basic literacy and numeracy, and to equip the nation's youth for well-conducted civic life and for wealth creation. Yet if we inspect some of the key documents in policy-making, we find that ITT is by no means the Augean stable its detractors claim it to be. Even the sharply critical HMI booklet *The New Teacher in School* conceded that three-quarters of the teachers in a survey were 'well' or 'very well' equipped for their task and that some were impressive; few demonstrated weaknesses that were irremediable, given suitable conditions for teaching (HMI, 1982). The two-year

survey (1983–85) of 'quality in schools', based on a sample of 30 institutions – 45 per cent in the public sector – had many proposals to make for the improvement of ITT, but nevertheless the authors were able to write that 'The majority of the students at work in schools were teaching satisfactorily' (DES, 1987). More important still, the survey revealed that the whole system was neither static nor entrenched in mediocrity. On the contrary, it was on the move: by 1985, most of the institutions surveyed were offering a 36-week PGCE. There was growing evidence of partnership agreements between HEIs and practising teachers, and in response to Department of Education and Science Circular 3/84, many HEIs had radically changed the structure of their courses; they were also appointing lecturers with recent and relevant experience of teaching (DES, 1987).

Nevertheless, the situation was patchy and there were so many variations countrywide that it was difficult to speak of a teacher training system. If the time allocated to subject studies in the BEd could vary dramatically from 22 to 50 per cent (quoted in HMI, 1979), it would be idle to pretend that all was well: some lecturers were out of touch with school life and emphasized theory too much at the expense of practice; there were serious deficits in students' subject knowledge; some students did not have the requisite personal qualities for teaching, thus raising questions about the selection procedures used to admit them; some had not achieved a satisfactory level of professional skill. There was a need to raise standards and above all to ensure consistency in teacher training across the country. With the demise of the area training organizations (ATOs) as the bodies responsible for recommending students for qualified teacher status, there was a vacuum which left the university departments of education and the Council for National Academic Awards effectively in charge of the recommendation process (Taylor, 1994, p. 51). After the abolition of the ATOs, which had been advocated by the James Report, the executive powers of the Secretary of State for Education steadily increased, and the Advisory Committee for the Supply and Education of Teachers (ACSET) recommended that he should establish criteria which would be taken into account when deciding whether or not to approve courses.

## CATE to the rescue

The Council for the Accreditation of Teacher Education (CATE) was set up in 1984 as a government agency to monitor whether institutions conformed adequately to the criteria for the approval of teacher training courses promulgated by the Secretary of State for Education. During its lifetime, CATE made a major impact on British ITT. It tightened the relationship between schools and universities by insisting that they work in close long-term partnership and that university lecturers gain first-hand recent and relevant experience of classroom teaching; it influenced the selection procedure for entry to teacher training courses by involving serving teachers in interviews and briefing sessions; it lengthened students' periods of teaching practice during ITT courses and ensured that certain set periods of time were spent on core subjects such as English and mathematics for primary school teachers (who also had to have O-level passes in these subjects).

CATE worked hard to improve British ITT, and its members gave their time freely to do so. It was, however, in a very real sense an agency on the cheap, and this was the cause of some of its shortcomings. CATE did not have the resources to visit institutions and carry out a first-hand survey of the proposed courses. For its input data, it was dependent on Her Majesty's Inspectors' perceptions of what was actually happening. Sometimes these were out of date and had to be revised; sometimes the judgement of CATE members differed significantly from that of the HMI, and this lack of congruence had to be resolved – usually by CATE falling into line behind the HMI, on whom it depended for input data and for the face validity of its work. The author of a book on CATE, himself a member of one of its working groups and an admirer of its achievements, admitted that 'at times the line between [inspectors'] advice and intrusion became a little blurred' (McIntyre, 1991, p.

35). There were suspicions that inspectors exerted covert pressure on CATE to conform to their judgements, and these suspicions reached the point where one CATE member felt that the Inspectorate was using CATE as a front to cover its own exercise of power (McIntyre, 1991, p. 34). The authoritarianism of one staff inspector was clearly demonstrated in her statement, 'if you don't like [the criteria], you can get out of teacher training' (McIntyre, 1991, p. 33), and a DES assessor's prescriptivism was reflected in an equestrian metaphor: he admired CATE's reporting groups for their prowess at 'coaxing [higher education institutions] *into the box*' (p. 49)!

CATE suffered from certain operational difficulties. The three different reporting groups experienced problems in holding the same standards, and one of them had the unenviable reputation of being too soft (though this might have been because it tended to deal with PGCEs, which were on the whole more straightforward). The volume of paperwork was overwhelming, and initially CATE fell badly behind. Some of its members felt that the criteria's concept of 'recent and relevant' school experience for university lecturers in education was too narrow, but by then CATE had dug itself into an entrenched position from which it would have seemed weak to retreat in an attempt to reach greater flexibility. It had no authority to exercise discretion or to deviate from the official accreditation criteria. If a university department of education formally satisfied them, then that had to be the end of the matter, even if CATE had serious reservations about the way in which it did so. This was the case for the University of Oxford's practice of 'interning' each trainee teacher in one school virtually to the exclusion of other school-based practice. CATE doubted the wisdom of such a narrow experience but was powerless to do anything about it. CATE did not 'discuss philosophical issues such as the relationship between educational theory and the practice of teaching' (McIntyre, 1991, p. 228). It was no real help to higher education institutions (HEIs) which were trying to reconcile the two. CATE was powerless to reinstate aspects of teacher training which had been excluded (some believed wrongly) from the curriculum: educational psychology, sociology and philosophy. In the end, CATE was widely perceived as being too prescriptivist and mechanistic, and the accusation that accreditation was the mere application of a checklist gained currency.

## Developments after CATE: some international perspectives

In this section, an attempt will be made to compare British developments in ITT with those in other countries, and to use foreign experience to reflect critically on British policy initiatives after CATE. In recent years, the British government has shown more than usual interest in educational experience elsewhere, notably in France, Germany and the United States, and has commissioned numerous reports by HMI on their practices and structures (HMI, 1989, 1993a, b, are three of many such). It is therefore not the case that recent British reforms have been undertaken in ignorance of what is happening in the education systems of other countries. Despite Britain's geographical and political closeness to continental Europe, it has borrowed more from the USA than from the continent of which it forms part. Strangely, this borrowing has gone ahead notwithstanding well known shortcomings in American institutional structures which have been 'transplanted' to British soil. In 1984, the American report *A Nation at Risk* (NCEE, 1984) listed a whole series of serious educational weaknesses which challenged its preeminence in the world and asserted that 'If an unfriendly foreign power had attempted to impose on America the mediocre educational performance that exists today, we might well have viewed it as an act of war. As it stands, we have allowed this to happen to ourselves.' Most of the British appropriations of US education and training policies took place in the final years of the Thatcher government (1986–90) and may have had something to do with the fact that Margaret Thatcher felt close ties with the USA (and its president) but had severe reservations about Britain's ties with Europe. The common UK/US emphasis on market values and voluntarism – leaving training to the

market – no doubt also promoted the process of reciprocal influence on policy (see Finegold *et al.*, 1992/3).

## *ITT and higher education: combining theory and practice*

CATE had many shortcomings. Nevertheless, the government had by 1989 made a decision that CATE must have a successor (DES, 1989) which would have a much wider remit and a strengthened secretariat. That successor was the Teacher Training Agency (TTA), for which the basis was laid in the 1994 Education Act – passed only after passionate parliamentary and public debate. While not excluding HEIs from involvement in teacher training, the 1994 Act enabled schools or indeed any other body designated by the Secretary of State to provide it without reference to HEIs if they wished. The TTA made it legally possible for teacher training to be entirely school-based and divorced from HEIs. It allowed the Higher Education Funding Council to make payments for that purpose to schools, further education corporations or consortia, thereby shifting resources away from university departments of education (UDEs) and potentially making their survival questionable (Paine and Sedlak, 1994, pp. 232–4).

Not only was the passing of the 1994 Education Act a great blow against UDEs; it also set Britain on a course of development which ran completely contrary to that in other European countries. The EC *Memorandum on Higher Education* (1991) called for greater involvement of higher education in ITT in its member states, and welcomed such involvement as a means of reinforcing teachers' status, strengthening their morale and achieving the renewal necessary to prepare young people for life in a complex society. The memorandum stated that, ultimately, the intention is to create a single labour market for highly qualified personnel. In this market, higher education and advanced training will be regulated and planned in a European frame of reference. Since recognition is crucial to the mobility of students and graduates, special attention must be devoted to promoting mobility in the teaching force; it is asserted that teachers are important multipliers of knowledge and experience and can make a significant contribution to European understanding and cohesiveness. This confidence in teachers and desire to promote their professionalism contrast markedly with British governmental attitudes.

## The role of research and theory

A particularly hard-fought clause in the battle to get the 1994 British Education Bill through Parliament was that pertaining to research. Originally the intention was that the TTA would have the power to fund all research into the theory, practice and management of education. If this clause had stood, UDEs would have lost large tracts of their research to schools or to commercially based consortia. Some Conservative Members of Parliament were virulently opposed to higher education maintaining a role in teacher training; in the Upper House, Lord Pearson of Rannoch referred to HE's 'stranglehold' or 'malign monopoly' on ITT, thus prompting an allusion on the part of Lord Beloff to Pearson's 'hatred of higher education'.

Notwithstanding Lord Pearson's strictures, many parliamentarians in both Houses recorded their opposition to the Bill. Bodies such as the Society for Research into Higher Education (SRHE), the Universities Council for the Education of Teachers (UCET) and the *Journal of Education for Teaching* mounted campaigns to have the clause amended, and eventually it was redrafted to the effect that the agency could carry out limited research for its own functions and objectives but would not have generalized control over all research in education:

> A funding agency may carry out or commission such research as they consider appropriate with a view to improving
> a) the training of teachers, or
> b) the standards of teaching.
> (Education Act 1994, para. 11)

In the House of Lords at the end of the Third (and final) Reading, Earl Russell proclaimed that 'The concession we have had on research today ... prevents the dismemberment of research in universities. That is something of great importance for which we are truly thankful.' Lord Judd castigated the Bill as one that 'should never have been'; it was 'a wretched enterprise with which the Minister [Baroness Blatch] should never have allowed herself to be associated'. He recalled that at the Second Reading there had been more than 30 speeches with barely three in full support of the Minister, and went on to spell out the Act's negative implications for democracy: these will be discussed in the last section of this chapter.

The bitterness of the British debate is very different from the European stance, which views institutions of higher education in a positive light. According to the 1991 European Memorandum on Higher Education, research – and not only that of an applied nature – is important in ITT. It states (para. 24) that the range and type of research conducted in HEIs must accommodate the pursuit of knowledge for its own sake, and should not always be dominated by economic considerations. The memorandum's comments about teacher training are reinforced by the Commission of the European Communities (CEC, 1993). While admitting the diversity of approaches among its member nations, the CEC still has no hesitation in discerning 'a growing involvement of higher education institutions ... particularly universities, in the academic and professional training of teachers'.

An examination of experience in France and Germany – countries in which the British government has shown a special interest – reveals a stark contrast with British policy on ITT. Germany is often held up as a example of a system with predominantly school-based teacher training (led by the *Seminar*), and is cited as such by Lawlor (1990).[2] It is insufficiently realized that before *Seminar*-based ITT begins, future teachers have already done an extensive programme of educational studies at university concurrently with their subject studies for their first state examination (their equivalent of a British first degree). They do not, therefore, begin their ITT courses ignorant of all theory, as British entrants to PGCE do; moreover, their training courses last much longer than do British ones and they study theory in the *Seminar* as well as during the first phase of their training. Their written plans for formally assessed lessons are very different in style from those of their British counterparts, since they are required to give a theoretical justification of their practical classroom pedagogy; this may involve, for example, relating choice of a work of literature to a particular stage of child development or gender psychology. References to the scholarly literature are usually provided at the end of a lesson plan for an assessed lesson. Naturally the lesson plans turn out much longer than pragmatic British ones, but the German tradition of using theory to guide practice militates against superficiality and helps to make teachers flexible and creative (see Pritchard, 1992).

Of course, the German system has its weaknesses as well as its strengths. One shortcoming is that the university lecturers and professors in educational studies who teach students for their first state examination are theoreticians rather than practitioners. They are usually very productive in terms of research but they do not, nor are they normally expected to, take upon themselves the duty of going out into schools to supervise their students on school experience. The exception to this statement was the One Phase Teacher Education Model pioneered at the Universities of Oldenburg and Osnabrück, which removed the division between the academic and professional stages of teacher training and set up a concurrent course aiming to produce qualified teachers at the end of five years (see Pritchard, 1993, for a descriptive analysis). It was a revolutionary model in German terms and, despite favourable reports from external experts, was eventually defeated by a coalition of vested interests and the fact that it was not put on a proper legal footing until it was too late. The kind of course which was attempted in Germany, but failed, was very similar to what has already been achieved in Britain but is under threat. The great reproach against German professors of education is that they are too remote from practice, and the fact that they have tenure

makes it easy for them to resist any pressure to undertake recent and relevant school teaching. In British UDEs there are lecturers and professors who are qualified teachers, who have been recruited from the teaching profession, who have gained the highest academic degrees, who have recent experience of practical teaching, who have many years' proven track record as teacher trainers and who embody the synthesis of teaching and research in their own persons. In European terms, this is something of a rarity and has eluded the much-vaunted German academics who, at university level, are heavy on theory and light on practice. How ironic, then, that the British government wishes to remove responsibility for initial teacher training from competent staff in its universities and hand it over instead to school teachers.

Structures for ITT in France are very different from those in Germany. Traditionally the French have worked on a subject-based model of preparation for teaching, especially at the highest levels, and pedagogy as a discipline has been underdeveloped. The importance attached to competitive examination (*concours*) is part of the Napoleonic heritage: a pursuit of *égalité* on the basis of meritocracy open to talent (Vaughan and Archer, 1971). France has recently given much thought to the reform of its teacher education and has established the somewhat controversial *instituts universitaires de formation de maîtres* (IUFMs), which are an attempt to introduce new ITT structures into the existing landscape. A number of clear purposes, principles and values underpin the IUFMs (see Marchand, 1992). Teacher education is to be located in university-level institutions, even for primary teachers, and the rigid divisions between school types are to be somewhat diminished by requiring that 10 per cent of the course is to be delivered to primary and secondary trainees studying jointly. It is hoped that this will contribute to a common culture among French educators. Verbally symbolic of this aspiration is a change of nomenclature: the primary school teachers, formerly called *instituteurs*, have been renamed *professeurs d'école* – a term more redolent of prestige (Blondel, 1991). The French wish to raise the professional status of teachers and upgrade their professionalism, and they view the association of initial teacher training and higher education as essential to this effort. In developing new courses, they are seeking permanent dialogue between theory and practice, a synthesis which in Britain has been dismissed contemptuously by Lawlor (1990) (writing for the influential Centre for Policy Studies set up to contribute to the formation of Conservative policies). The balance in the IUFMs between the academic and the school-based parts of the course is about two-thirds to one-third (and very different from the 80 per cent demanded by a British Secretary of State for Education; see Gilroy, 1992, pp. 6–7).

The quality of the debate in France about the IUFMs is reminiscent of that in 1960s Britain (see Kerviel, 1992, in which Finkielkraut and others complain that future teachers may be downgraded under the pretext of professionalization and that subject disciplines may be marginalized). Holyoake (1993) asserts that France is in the vanguard of a general movement in Europe to lengthen and upgrade the quality and status of professional training and to foster closer relationships between teacher training and HEIs. The truth is, however, that Britain got there first; in recent years Britain had bonded the two closely and productively but is on the point of doing away with what has been achieved. Continental educators are very conscious of the polarities of choice. Buffet (1993), in an article about harmonization of initial and continuing education in the European Union, formulates two opposing possibilities: does one design a course enabling the trainee to adapt immediately to the present needs of the employment market or does one equip the trainee to adapt to long-term social change? The French have now very deliberately chosen the latter alternative: they want teachers who can think and act creatively, not just apply ready-made methods and solutions (Bériot *et al.*, 1992). This is the diametric opposite of present-day British short-termism, which may culminate in newly qualified British schoolteachers being regarded as underqualified to teach in certain European countries (Hill, 1991, p. 32).

## Competencies

The work of CATE had been based on the criteria promulgated by the Secretary of State for Education. A worrying feature of its work was the gradual realization that even when the criteria were satisfied, a course could *still* be bad because the necessarily formalistic measures were only a proxy for the reality. Even McIntyre (1991), who is something of an apologist for CATE and subtitles his first chapter 'Our heroine is born', is obliged to admit that: 'if, for example, a student devoted at least 100 hours to studying the teaching of mathematics in primary schools, she was likely to have a firmer grasp than if she spent less time on it, but there was still no guarantee of any particular standard being reached.'

This problem is a common one in the social sciences. Essentially it is a lack of validity: the putative measures do not really 'measure' what they are supposed to measure. A remedy lay conveniently to hand. Instead of concentrating upon student selection and what HEIs were putting *into* students' education, it was decided to focus on *outcomes* – what skills and understanding the trainees had acquired at point of exit. This harmonized well with National Vocational Qualifications (NVQs) and with the government's desire to make teacher training even more practical and less 'theory-ridden'. The competency movement and the 'output' approach reached their apogee in official documents: Circular 9/92 (England)/Circular 35/92 (Wales), 'Initial teacher education (secondary phase)', and Circular 14/93, 'The initial training of primary school teachers'. The main principles which underpin Circular 9/92 are: (a) that schools should play a much larger and more influential role in course design and delivery; (b) that the accreditation of ITT courses should require HEIs, schools and students to focus on the competencies of teaching. For example, newly qualified teachers should be able to:

- create and maintain a purposeful and orderly environment for the pupils;
- devise and use appropriate rewards and sanctions to maintain an effective learning environment;

- maintain pupils' interest and motivation (Circular 9/92, para. 2.4);
- produce coherent lesson plans;
- ensure continuity and progression within and between classes and in subjects;
- present subject content in clear language and in a stimulating manner (Circular 9/92, para. 2.3).

No one would wish to maintain for a single moment that any of the skills specified above is inappropriate for a teacher to possess. They are all conducive to good teaching. However, by themselves they constitute an inadequate, impoverished model of what it is to be a teacher. Competencies are necessary but not sufficient, and long use of them in the USA shows clearly what their weaknesses are. At school level, minimal competency examinations have been deemed a failure because the 'minimum' tends to become the 'maximum', thus lowering educational standards for all (NCEE, 1984, p. 63). Their empirical, mechanistic quality derives from behaviourism and from the spirit of positivism which Schön (1991, p. 34) asserts is 'at the very heart' of the American university. He actually argues that because of the complex nature of professional practice – be it of medicine, psychotherapy, town planning, agronomy or engineering – techniques derived from positivist doctrines are often useless (and competencies are one such technique). Schön blames positivism and its progeny for an inadequate epistemology of practice in American universities; it is this inadequacy which leads him to develop his highly influential 'reflective practitioner' model.

The notion of competency is based on an atomistic rather than a holistic analysis of human functioning, and owes much to crude enumeration. Norris (1991) reminds his readers that, back in the 1920s, Ralph Tyler collated the answers from two million questionnaires to develop competency-based teacher education, and Johnston (1984) quotes the prodigious industriousness of Charters and Waples, who in the late 1920s collected 235,000 'activity statements' about teachers, which they reduced to 1001 teacher activities for checking by administrators; they also found 798 trait actions, which they distilled to a mere 83 basic traits, eventually boiled down to a master list of 25 teachers' traits. Such work formed the empirical basis of competencies. Yet a serious problem remains: a teacher may demonstrate many competencies but still fail to motivate, inspire and stimulate the young. The humanistic dimension is missing and, because competencies are supposed to be the same for everyone, so is individualism. As Van Manen (1984, p. 157) eloquently puts it, 'Exactly because pedagogy is fundamentally unfathomable, it poses the unremitting invitation to the creative activity of pedagogic reflection which brings the deep meaning of pedagogy to light.'

The status of knowledge and creativity in relation to competencies arouses much debate. An extreme view of competence would imply that if you can demonstrate it, you need not follow a course at all, since the whole emphasis is upon 'can do' as opposed to 'know'. Some people maintain that 'competence' can include the reflective practitioner approach by incorporating the underpinning knowledge and understanding: the thinking is embedded in the ability. This, however, evoked Wilkin's (1993, p. 43) assertion that ITT is a case of post-modernism in which the primacy of reason is replaced by utility, and intellectual levels become blurred. Others maintain that competence is an anti-intellectual approach which downgrades the importance of knowledge and circumvents the issue of what people need to know; knowledge is taken account of only in so far as it can be demonstrated. Barnett (1994) argues that competencies can in fact be formulated to allow for the ability to cope with the unexpected and even to allow for creativity, but for him this begs the all-important question: 'Whose competencies are they?' They are of course drawn up by certain interest groups and organizational cultures; if these are unsympathetic to the profession, the competencies may be the very opposite of emancipatory; they may lend themselves to assertion of social control because good practice is determined by the authorities. Because competencies are usually the product of conventional orthodox thought, they are essentially conservative and ill-suited to preparing for change. Whitty and Willmott (1991, p. 313) point out that 'such a strategy places the entire burden of assuring the attainment of the required standards on the assessment process'. Competences, assessment and social control seem to form a somewhat unholy trinity in the current British climate of almost obsessive quality assurance and accountability.

The relationship between competences and professionalization has been the subject of much scholarly attention. Apple (1984), writing of the United States, states that deskilling involves the separation of conception from execution: the authorities conceive and the workers execute. Although he does not intend any reference to the British situation, one cannot help but think of the demand of the British government that teachers should 'deliver' the National Curriculum, which is determined elsewhere. In the sphere of ITT, there can be no doubt that by reducing trainees' contact with the scholarly basis of education, 'know-how' is championed over knowledge. O'Hear (1988), a right-wing British Conservative, explicitly rejects any intellectual meta-perspective in education: for him, explicit verbal knowledge about teaching skills is unnecessary; knowledge ought to be knowledge *how* rather than knowledge *that*, let alone knowledge of *why*. The opportunity is removed for future teachers to synthesize theory and practice, and they are demoted to being mere executors of objectives determined by others (i.e. state officials). This does not *deskill* them – on the contrary, they may 'deliver' the curriculum with consummate skill. What it does is to *deprofessionalize* them. Professionals have an input into the conception, as opposed to the mere execution, of their work. They contribute to setting standards, as distinct from enforcing standards set by others. To divorce a profession from its scholarly knowledge base is to demote those who practise that profession. This is not a direction in which many European countries, apart from Britain, intend to proceed. Indeed, an Irish professor writing for the Association for Teacher Education in Europe succinctly expresses his aversion to such a course of action: 'Teachers should not be just efficient functionaries slotted into a status quo system' (Coolahan, 1992, p. 9).

## Mentors

The greater part of the British PGCE course must now be spent in school rather than in higher education, even if it is university-based. The major responsibility for developing competencies is placed in the hands of mentors: experienced teachers in the school where the trainees are located for teaching practice. Finance is shifted from UDEs to schools, with the result that some UDEs are becoming unviable (Paine and Sedlak, 1994, p. 33). These school-based courses, which may be conducted entirely independently of UDEs, rely on good mentoring for their success.

American research reveals the weaknesses of ITT based on mentorship. At its heart lies the relationship between the mentor and the trainee teacher, a relationship which is often problematic and which, because of its intensive nature as compared with the more episodic contact between trainee and university tutor, bears down much more heavily on the trainee. Hollingsworth (1989) indicates that when mentor and trainee are similar, rote copying can result and matched pairing can therefore 'hinder growth'. Yet when mentor and trainee are very different in their approaches to education, the result can be interpersonal tension. Fullan (1991, pp. 294–5), writing about the USA, quotes research to show that mentors are extremely variable in quality, and that teaching practice under this arrangement is often narrow, routine, mechanical and short term. Usually trainees try hard to satisfy their mentors, and this can have its own intrinsic shortcomings. In Germany, where the student–mentor relationship is at the heart of teacher training, this is very much the case. In a paper entitled 'German classrooms observed', Pritchard (1992) describes how a trainee being assessed on classroom teaching in a West German grammar school behaved in a way quite contrary to his natural judgement in order to please the mentor on whom so much depended; in doing so, he was perfectly conscious of the cognitive dissonance which his behaviour created for him, but tolerated it as a means to an end. In a UK study conducted by Corbett and Wright (1993), articled teachers focused on pleasing their mentors at the expense of engaging in a professional dialogue about how children learn. Some mentors found it hard to listen to their trainees and had ready-made answers to other people's problems. The fact that they were not good at letting the trainees develop their own individual style led to tensions which became particularly pronounced as the trainees grew in confidence and experience. Mentoring is not on the whole conducive to creative practice, and the limited experience of schoolteacher mentors contrasts unfavourably with that of typical university tutors, many of whom will have visited dozens of different types of school and seen literally hundreds of teachers (pre- and in-service) in action. Dart and Drake (1993) believe that mentors carry out their supervision in the way they themselves were mentored, thus merely conserving existing practice and reducing the time available for innovative pedagogy, and Hill (1991, p. 16) calls for modes of ITT which will produce a teaching force able to reflect in a critical manner on taken-for-granted assumptions and articulate reasons for contesting some of the conventional wisdoms about pupils.

In British Columbia, a variant of the conventional institutional approach to mentoring has been in operation for over twenty years at the Simon Fraser University (Croll and Moses, 1990). Here, experienced school teachers (called faculty associates (FAs)) function as mentors on short-term secondment to the faculty of education; the fact that they work alongside university lecturers gives the faculty a profile of differentiated staffing which brings student teachers into close contact with excellent practitioners and at the same time gives lecturers more space to engage in research. The Professional Development Programme (PDP) is by now thoroughly established and much can be learned from it about the advantages and disadvantages of using mentors. The greatest single problem faced by the FAs is the tension between their nurturing role and their judgemental role: they find it emotionally very difficult to fail people (Croll and Moses, 1990, p. 86). This contrasts with the traditional British model, in which there used to be a clear role division between the schoolteacher's formative judgement of a trainee and the university teacher's summative one (though this

model is changing). In the present author's experience, most practising teachers are uncomfortable at having to assume ultimate responsibility for passing or failing a trainee, and are only too glad to pass it on to the supervising UDE tutor. Schools often take the line of least resistance if hard verdicts have to be delivered, and back off from unpleasantness or difficulty.

It is interesting to note that the PDP's centre of gravity shifted from the school to the campus, and that the FAs came to attach importance to theory; however, they held conceptions of 'theory' which differed radically from those of the mainstream faculty members. The FAs believed that theory consisted of articulating their personal philosophy of education and of reflecting on personal practice, whereas the faculty lecturers held a model of theory which was more conceptual, propositional and conducive to empirical investigation. This contrast again calls to mind the work of Wilkin (1993) on ITT as a case of post-modern development. Wilkin argues that the boundaries between high and low intellectual culture have collapsed, leaving relativism and instrumentalism in which the trainee's (or mentor's) personal experience enjoys equal status with that of public disciplinary enquiry.

From what has been said above, it is obvious that there have been many debates regarding the best way forward for ITT, both in the UK and in Europe. Dilemmas have arisen as a result of the government changes (a) for those involved in ITT at UDEs, (b) for teachers in schools, especially if they are mentors, and (c) for the government as a whole regarding closer links with Europe. Many European countries are moving towards a greater emphasis on theory, whereas the British tendency is to repudiate it to a large extent.

Regardless of what view one may hold of 'theory', it was obvious that by the 1990s British ITT was no longer at all 'theoretical' – even CATE members admitted that was the case – thus at least one goal of the government had been achieved. Moreover, international comparisons indicated that English pupils' school performance, far from being at the bottom of the league table, made quite an honourable showing (OECD, 1993, pp. 145–66). Many of the faults which had been diagnosed in the 1980s in ITT had been rectified. A report entitled *The Secondary PGCE in Universities* (OFSTED, 1993) examined 48 courses covering all 10 subjects of the National Curriculum and rated all but three of them satisfactory or good. Most university departments of education had established long-standing, amicable, effective relationships with schools. Most students were teaching well and found their university supervisors to be supportive, constructive and helpful in enabling them to set realistic, individual, professional objectives. Yet the very next year after the favourable OFSTED report, the government enacted the Education Act 1994 making it possible to exclude UDEs altogether from teacher training. Because of its seizure of power from local education authorities (see Wallace, 1990) and its ability to have legislation passed, it was able to exert central domination[3] of the educational system much more effectively than could ever have been done in the United States where joint involvement of federal, state and local governmental systems is required in the reform process. Its action had, and will continue to have, implications for the climate of democracy in Britain.

It is essential to consider why the authorities insisted on overkill after CATE had done its work. At its most fundamental level, the rationale was based on political dogma. The Conservative government desired to eliminate progressivism from ITT. Many progressivist ideas had arisen in the 1960s, and Edgar (1986/88) notes the New Right's tendency to demonize the 1960s because they were socially radical; the first Black Papers in education, many of which originated in the Labour Party, were motivated by the student revolt and lit a fuse leading eventually towards the Education Reform Act of 1998 and the National Curriculum (NC). The NC was very much in line with practice in other European countries and had good effects as well as less good. It had, for example, the necessary and beneficient effect of homogenizing the school curriculum across almost all school types so that most pupils received a balanced offering of subjects. The public schools were exempted from the NC (although in practice most of them adopt it as their core) and, this being so, it is a misnomer to call the NC 'National'. It is sig-

nificant that historically both of the main political parties had actually wanted an NC but for different reasons: socialists had called for an NC as long ago as 1957 because the nature of comprehensive schooling seemed to require it (Simon, 1952, 1982); Conservatives wanted one for educational reasons, but also as a means of exerting social control over teachers and teacher trainers. Hill (1991), while agreeing that the National Curriculum has a number of laudable characteristics, insists that its underlying political aim is clear – it is ideological – intended to produce a nation of Thatcherites'.

The desire to assert control is the reason by deprofessionalization is an important feature of the governmental agenda. It has taken (and is continuing to take) measures to bring all professionals, not just educationalists, under its control. NVQs and competencies are a major tool in this enterprise. The ultimate intention is to develop centrally set criteria for accrediting all sorts of jobs, including professional qualifications and middle management (DES, 1991, p. 18). Burrage (1994) emphasizes that these NVQs are based on survey research – the minute analysis and ranking of distinct competencies – and that their effect will be to downgrade universities. Levitas (1988), in her study of the Adam Smith Institute's Omega Files (OF), recounts how the OF's proposals in initial teacher training call for the destruction of the professional status of teaching. Hargreaves (1990) in fact envisages the future stratification of the British teaching body into career, assistant and associate teachers, just as in the social domain neoconservatives routinely call for the reestablishment of a more hierarchical order. Thus O'Hear (1991, p. 23) insists that British society before 1914 was in many ways better than that of today because it 'had not yet taken on the manners of egalitarian democracy, the lack of deference to one's betters so characteristic of collectivism, or the denial of authority in every area of life' (it may be to some extent a reflection of the government's educational values that O'Hear was appointed to CATE by the Secretary of State). The legal measures which have now been taken in the 1994 Education Act and in other legislation are calculated to ensure the acceleration of the trend towards deprofessionalization. Lord Judd, in a speech reported in *Hansard* (12 April 1994), denounced these measures in ringing tones:

> We must have teachers who understand what they are doing and its interrelationship with the whole development of the pupil as a person – not simply conveyor belt operatives. That is why the self-perceived and externally perceived significance and status of the profession is so vital ... The positive engagement of the profession in responsibility for the provision and development of education rather than merely the application of concepts designed by others is long, long overdue if we are to do well by our children ... In effect, she [the Minister, Baroness Blatch] has been asked to start a retrograde movement towards classroom instructors in place of teachers, with all the fullness that professional title should imply.

The neo-conservative strand of the New Right's thinking is strongly authoritarian, and authoritarianism brooks dissent only with difficulty. The removal of most of the intellectual content from ITT and its relocation from universities to schools will have the effect of discouraging critical thought in a sector of the population where it might normally be expected to exist; these changes will make educationists more conformist and more amenable to state control. Educationists' fear of unemployment, heavy work burdens and subjection to the dual pressures of performance indicators and appraisal all absorb energies which might otherwise be used to express critical judgements about societal developments – to the ultimate health and well-being of that society. Enlightened observers regard with misgiving the withering of the civic courage inherent in dissent. Barnett (1994) writes, 'Blatant resistance [to the pervading culture] will be avoided: it leads to death', and Christopher Price (1994, p. 282) expresses his misery at the decline of English nonconformism; he deplores people's 'desire to please, to be in the mainstream, not to be against the grain'. It is important for the climate of freedom in Britain that thought, even of the anti-authoritarian variety, should not be suppressed. The recent changes in British ITT will contribute to such suppression and may have long-term adverse consequences for the country.

## Notes

1 This chapter uses the term 'Britain' to refer predominantly to England and Wales. Northern Ireland and, more especially, Scotland have their own distinctive structures and traditions. See Kydd and Weir (1993) for recent developments in Scotland.

2 Lawlor does include a factual account of German practices in an appendix but fails to interpret them correctly and treats them very selectively in the body of her text, ignoring the aspects which do not support her position. She condemns British postgraduate courses for failing to provide subject education, and in so doing confuses the 'operational' with the 'substantive' (see Skilbeck, 1992).

3 Mention should be made here of Turner's (1990, p. 55) article about the area training organizations, which 'were devised for distancing the academic control of teacher education from the direct influence of government', a move which succeeded admirably because 'the government also believed that academic independence was an important route to the development of high quality teacher education'. How times have changed.

## References

Apple, M. W. (1984) Curricular form and the logic of technical control. In E. C. Short (ed.), *Competence: Inquiries into Its Meaning and Acquisition in Educational Settings*. Lanham, NY: University Press of America.

Askling, B. and Almén, E. (1993) *Teacher Education as a Tool for State Steering*. Society for Research into Higher Education Conference, University of Sussex, December.

Barber, M. (1993) The truth about partnership. *Journal of Education for Teaching*, **19** (3), 255–62.

Barnett, R. (1994) *The Limits of Competence*. Buckingham: Open University Press.

Bériot, A.-M., Cayol-Monin, A. and Mosconi, N. (1992) *La Mise en place des IUFM-pilotes et le débat théorie/pratique. Recherche et Formation No. 11*. Paris: Université de Paris X.

Blondel, D. (1991) A new type of teacher training in France: the IUFMs. *European Journal of Education*, **26** (3), 197–205.

Bourdoncle, R. (1994) La professionalisation des enseignants. *European Journal of Teacher Education*, **17** (1/2), 13–23.

Buffet, F. (1993) L'harmonisation des actions de formation initiale et continue entre pays de la Communauté: principes théoriques et réalisation pratique. *European Journal of Teacher Education*, **16** (2), 137–45.

Burrage, M. (1994) Routine and discreet relationships: professional accreditation and the state in Britain. In T. Becher (ed.), *Governments and Professional Education*. Buckingham: Open University Press.

Commission of the European Communities (1993) *The Outlook for Higher Education in the European Community: Responses to the Memorandum*. Brussels: European Commission.

Coolahan, J. (1992) Teacher education in the nineties: towards a new coherence. Keynote address in proceedings of a conference of that title, Limerick.

Corbett, P. and Wright, D. (1993) Issues in the selection and training of mentors for school-based primary initial teacher training. In D. McIntyre *et al.* (eds), *Mentoring*. London: Kogan Page.

Croll, P. and Moses, D. (1990) The involvement of teachers in initial teacher education: a study of the Simon Fraser University professional development programme. *Research Papers in Education*, **5** (1), 73–92.

Dart, L. and Drake, P. (1993) School-based teacher training: a conservative practice? *Journal of Education for Teaching*, **19** (2), 175–89.

DES (1987) *Quality in Schools: The Initial Training of Teachers*. London: HMSO.

DES (1989) *Future Arrangements for the Accreditation of Initial Teacher Training*. London: HMSO.

DES (1991) *Education and Training for the 21st Century*, Vol. 1. London: HMSO.

Edgar, D. (1988) The free or the good. In R. Levitas (ed.), *The Ideology of the New Right*. Cambridge: Polity.

European Commission (1991) *Memorandum on Higher Education*. Brussels: European Commission.

Finegold, D., McFarland, L. and Richardson, W. (1992/3) *Something Borrowed, Something Blue? A Study of the Thatcher Government's Appropriation of American Education and Training Policy*. Wallingford: Triangle.

Fullan, M. G. with S. Stiegelbauer (1991) *The New Meaning of Educational Change*. London: Cassell.

Galvin, C. (1993) Higher education in initial teacher education: a promotion of teacher professionality. Society for Research into Higher Education Conference, Brighton, December.

Gilroy, D. P. (1992) The political rape of initial teacher education in England and Wales: a JET rebuttal. *Journal of Education for Teaching*, **18** (1), 5–22.

Hargreaves, D. (1990) The future of teacher education. Lecture for Hockerill Educational Foundation.

Hill, D. (1991) *What's Left in Teacher Education: Teacher Education, the Radical Left and Policy Proposals*. London: Tufnell Press.

HMI (1979) *Developments in the BEd Degree Course: HMI Series Matters for Discussion No. 8*. London: HMSO.

HMI (1982) *The New Teacher in School*. London: HMSO.

HMI (1989) *The Provisional Teacher Program in New Jersey*. London: HMSO.

HMI (1993a) *Aspects of Vocational Education in France*. London: Department for Education.

HMI (1993b) *Aspects of Full-time Vocational Education in the Federal Republic of Germany*. London: Department for Education.

Hollingsworth, S. (1989) Prior beliefs and cognitive change in learning to teach. *American Educational Research Journal*, **26** (2), 160–90.

Holyoake, J. (1993) Initial teacher training: the French view. *Journal of Education for Teaching*, **19** (2), 215–26.

Johnston, H. C., Jr (1984) Teacher competence: an historical analysis. In E. C. Short (ed.), *Competence: Inquiries into Its Meaning and Acquisition in Educational Settings*. Lanham, NY: University Press of America.

Kerviel, S. (1992) Comment on forme les futurs enseignants. *Le Monde de l'Éducation*, **192**, 28–40.

Kydd, L. and Weir, D. (1993) Governments and the higher education curriculum: international trends in teacher professionalism as seen in the Scottish and English context. Society for Research into Higher Education Conference, Brighton, December.

Lawlor, S. (1990) *Teachers Mistaught*. London: Centre for Policy Studies.

Levitas, R. (1988) Competition and compliance: the utopias of the New Right. In R. Levitas (ed.), *The Ideology of the New Right*. Cambridge: Polity Press.

McIntyre, D. G. (1991) *Accreditation of Teacher Education: The Story of CATE 1984–89*. London: Falmer Press.

Marchand, F. (1992) *Devenir professeur: l'IUFM*. Paris: Vuibert.

National Commission on Excellence in Education (1984) *A Nation at Risk*. Cambridge, MA: USA Research.

Norris, N. (1991) The trouble with competence. *Cambridge Journal of Education*, **21** (3), 331–41.

OECD (1993) *Education at a Glance*. Paris: OECD.

OFSTED (1993) *The Secondary PGCE in Universities 1991–1992: A Report from the Office of Her Majesty's Chief Inspector of Schools*. London: HMSO.

O'Hara, M. (1991) Teacher education: back to the future. *Irish Journal of Education*, **25** (1/2), 25–41.

O'Hear, A (1988) *Who Teaches the Teachers? A Contribution to Public Debate of the DES Green Paper*. London: Social Affairs Unit.

O'Hear, A. (1991) *Education and Democracy: The Posturing of the Left Establishment*. London: Claridge Press.

Paine, L. and Sedlak, M. (1994) England. In H. Judge, M. Lemosse, L. Paine and M. Sedlak (eds), *The University and the Teachers: France, the United States, England*. Wallingford: Triangle.

Price, C. (1994) Teacher education in Britain: a JET symposium with politicians. *Journal of Education for Teaching*, **20** (30), 261–300.

Pritchard, R. M. O. (1992) German classrooms observed. *Oxford Review of Education*, **18** (3), 213–25.

Pritchard, R. M. O. (1993) The struggle to democratise German teacher education. *Oxford Review of Education*, **19** (3), 355–71.

Schön, D. (1991) *The Reflective Practitioner: How Professionals Think in Action*. London: Temple Smith.

Simon, B. (1990) The study of education as a university subject. In J. B. Thomas (ed.), *British Universities and Teacher Education: A Century of Change*. Lewes: Falmer Press.

Skilbeck, M. (1992) The role of research in teacher education. *European Journal of Teacher Education*, **15** (1/2), 23–31.

Taylor, W. (1994) Teacher education: backstage to centre stage. In T. Becher (ed.), *Governments and Professional Education*. Buckingham: Open University Press.

Turner, J. D. (1990) The area training organisation. In J. B. Thomas (ed.), *British Universities and Teacher Education: A Century of Change*. Lewis: Falmer Press.

Van Manen, M. (1984) Reflections on teacher competence and pedagogic competence. In E. C. Short (ed.), *Competence: Inquiries into Its Meaning and Acquisition in Educational Settings*. Lanham, NY: University Press of America.

Vaughan, M. and Archer, M. S. (1971) *Social Conflict and Educational Change in England and France 1789–1848*. Cambridge: Cambridge University Press.

Wallace, R. (1990) The Act and the local authorities. In M. Flude and M. Hammer (eds), *The Education Reform Act 1988: Its Origins and Implications*. Basingstoke: Falmer Press.

Whitty, G. and Willmott, E. (1991) Competence-based teacher education: approaches and issues. *Cambridge Journal of Education*, **21** (3), 309–18.

Wilkin, M. (1993) Initial training as a case of postmodern development: some implications for mentoring. In D. McIntyre, H. Hagger and M. Wilkin (eds), *Mentoring*. London: Kogan Page.

# 20 Teacher Training: Some Lessons from France

MICHAEL HEAFFORD

Even in a climate where educational change is often celebrated for its own sake, most forms of educational experiment in Britain, as in other civilized countries, remain morally reprehensible and administratively foolhardy – and therefore unjustifiable. Those which are not usually have to be carried out within a tight budget, over a short period of time, and involve a small proportion of the target population. As a result, findings tend to be vague and doubtfully applicable to the relevant population as a whole. There is all the more reason, therefore, to seize the opportunity to examine closely the educational practice of other countries, not with a view to importing uncritically structures or methods, but in order to predict better the possible outcomes of particular policy decisions. Academics within the field of education have all too often dismissed comparative studies as superficial and unrigorous. In so doing they have left the field open for government and others to use comparative data, often superficially and uncritically and always selectively, to bolster criticisms of British national practice or to support their own agenda for change. It is of interest to note, for instance, that whereas HMI has recently reported separately on teacher education in France, Germany and the United States (DES, 1989a, b; OF-STED, 1993),[1] the National Curriculum was introduced in England and Wales without any official appraisal of the workings of national curricula in the countries of our European neighbours, in spite of the fact that many of them had had well over a century of experience in operating such curricula. Similarly, in the quest to bring British education standards into line with those of our European neighbours, attention seems almost deliberately not to have been focused on our atrocious record in the provision of nursery places. One wonders, too, at a time when educational powers are being relentlessly gathered into the centre, how much thought has been given to the consequences, both desirable and undesirable, of unfettered centralization. Here especially, continental experience, particularly that of France, has much to teach us.

Before we consider teacher training in France, the necessary preliminary cautions need to be made. Even in a country with which our historical and cultural links are so strong, traditions, perceptions and presumptions can be very different from our own. Even the most common words in the field, 'education', 'school' and 'teacher', cannot be translated easily into French. Different evolutions in the past have played decisive roles in shaping the present. English schools still hold to the nineteenth-century belief, promoted by Thomas Arnold and others, that they should seek to build the character and to have regard for the bodies and souls of their pupils as well as to develop their minds. The revolutionary and republican traditions in the French system led early to a focus on the development of cognitive skills as being the almost exclusive aim of formal education. Religious education was quite explicitly excluded from the curriculum of all state elementary schools. While remaining aware of such fundamental differences which manifest themselves in all sorts of ways, both obvious and subtle, within the two systems, we need also to recognize how much we have in common: both large and prosperous Western industrial countries recognizing the importance of maintaining economic prosperity and political stability. To do so requires strategies to ensure a population in which a range of high-quality, yet adaptable, skills are widely diffused. Technical and technological skills must be accompanied and supported by communication and social skills. A failure to maintain excellence in all these various skills will lead to a decline in the quality of life; a failure to diffuse them adequately not only disenfranchises individuals but threatens the unity of society. When so much is at stake, both countries have a clear obligation to ensure a teaching force of high quality, in terms of both subject knowledge and professional training. Not surprisingly, therefore, both countries have, in recent years, been paying particular attention to teacher training. What makes a study of French reforms particularly interesting is that they seem to be moving, in several important respects, in the opposite direction to the British.

As far as teacher training is concerned, both countries have a similar historical legacy manifested in two quite different systems: training for elementary school teachers and training for grammar school teachers. Historically, in both countries, the former was characterized by instruction with a prescribed academic content limited to what was necessary for the teaching task. Methodological techniques figured large and were carried out in a rigid and prescriptive manner. The training was carried out under a regime designed to ensure that the largely lower middle-class students who underwent it did not get ideas above their station, e.g. a full timetable which included many domestic duties. By contrast, the future grammar school teacher received a loosely structured academic education to a high level in a single discipline. Even though this study would have usually been well beyond the level required for grammar school teaching, and may have had little relevance to it, no pedagogic training was considered essential. The academic preparation, with or without an added training component, was, of course, carried out within the comparatively free and indulgent atmosphere of a university. Some of the sharpest differences in the two forms of training gradually began to disappear on both sides of the Channel, especially in and

after the 1950s. In England and Wales, college of education courses were gradually extended from two to four years and ultimately culminated in the award of a university-validated BEd degree. For specialist graduates, a PGCE course was undertaken by an increasing number of graduates before satisfactory completion became a requirement for obtaining qualified teacher status. In France, ever higher qualifications were required for entry to teacher training colleges, the *écoles normales*: first the *baccalauréat*, then the DEUG (*diplôme d'études universitaires générales*) and increasingly the *licence*.[2] For secondary school teachers, the creation of the *centres pédagogiques régionaux* in 1950 provided some structured induction into teaching in an almost entirely school-based year of training. A small, but increasing, number of days was allocated to theoretical inputs. Nevertheless, right up to the beginning of the present decade, some important and unresolved differences between the two systems remained. These were strongly reinforced in France through different conditions of service and pay structure, and formalized through a different nomenclature, primary schoolteachers being designated as *instituteurs*, secondary ones as *professeurs*.

The gradual merging of the primary and secondary systems of teacher training has helped to draw attention to the central organizational question: what is the optimum balance of input between the three main providers of initial teacher training, university, training institution and school, and how can they optimally share out and integrate their responsibility to deliver to the trainee sound subject knowledge, appropriate professional expertise and a solid grounding in the working of schools, both within and outside the classroom? It will be noted that the proportional input of these three providers has varied considerably in the past, not only between the two countries but also, especially in relation to primary–secondary differences, within them. An important subsidiary question has also arisen: how can the professional requirement for job-specific training be reconciled with the demands for a personal multivalent education? Precisely because it is so profession-specific, difficulties have arisen most sharply in the concurrent training model. In France, students in the *écoles normales* found themselves, financially and contractually, locked into the primary school network of their *départements*, and, in England and Wales, BEd students found that their degrees held little currency outside the educational world. Worse still, those who failed the teaching practice element of the course could find themselves, even after four years in higher education, with no qualification whatsoever. It is with the resolution of these key questions that the French, as well as the British, have been grappling over the past few years. I therefore turn now to give some account of their deliberations and measures in the hope that such an account may help to clarify our thoughts on the same questions.

The obvious starting point must be the creation, on a pilot basis in 1990, then generally in 1991, of the so-called *instituts universitaires de formation de maîtres* (IUFMs). In a nutshell, these new institutions offer a two-year training programme for all prospective teachers at both primary and secondary level. A *licence*, i.e. a minimum of three years of university study, was laid down as the minimum entry requirement. Year 1 of the course is essentially university taught and prepares students for one of the *concours* (competitive examinations)[3] giving access to Year 2 of the training. The two main examinations are the CAPES (*certificat d'aptitude au professorat de l'enseignement du second degré*) for secondary school teachers and the CAPE (*certificat d'aptitude au professorat d'école*) for primary teachers. The ministry, having regard to national needs, lays down the numbers who will pass the examination. Year 2 of the course provides the main induction into classroom practice and educational theory. In the setting up of the new institutions, the abandonment of a 'concurrent model' as exemplified in the old *école normale* was confirmed and the essentially school-based model of the *centre pédagogique régional* was rejected. Second, the inclusion of the word *universitaire* in their name made it clear that higher education was henceforth to play a key role in teacher training. As it is these features which point for point contradict government policies in Britain, it is worth examining them more closely.

As far as the gradual abandonment of concurrent training is concerned, it is not possible to

point to a single moment when a policy was proposed or a decision made. Certain trends, once initiated, largely brought the change about. Until some 20 years ago, the majority of primary teachers were recruited at about the age of 15 into *écoles normales*, of which there was one for *instituteurs* and one for *institutrices* in each department. Entry was by competitive examination. Those who were successful were prepared for the *baccalauréat* in the *école normale* and subsequently continued with a further two years of concurrent training. Pre-*baccalauréat* students were supported by scholarships, post-*baccalauréat* students by salaries. In the 1970s, pre-*baccalauréat* recruitment was gradually phased out and the *écoles normales* came to recruit solely after the *baccalauréat*. The fact that the *baccalauréat* entitles holders to a university place, along with the perceived need to increase the academic quality of primary teacher training, led to the creation of a special DEUG for *école normale* students. The students quickly challenged the currency of this qualification, dismissing it as a *DEUG-bidon* – a 'rubbish DEUG' – because, unlike a real university DEUG, it did not form a stepping-stone to higher academic qualifications within the university sector. As a result, an ordinary university DEUG was required as a prerequisite for entry to primary training. Increasingly students stayed on at university to take the *licence* before entering the *école normale*, a trend confirmed in the new IUFM regulations requiring the *licence* as standard of entry.

Two other factors encouraged these developments. The first was the value placed by the French on intellectual prowess. Confinement to a narrow department-based *école normale* seemed increasingly isolating for the future teachers of a modern industrialized country: teachers needed to be better educated than most of the parents of the children they would teach, not worse. An upgrading of academic standards and a broadening of minds could best be satisfied by university study. Second, and in tandem with this development, came the demands of the strong primary teachers' union for greater parity in pay and conditions of service between primary and secondary school teachers. As the quality of entry qualifications to primary and secondary teacher training approached parity, the different recognition given to the two groups of teachers became increasingly unjustifiable.

Turning now to French secondary teacher training before 1990, we find a most interesting set of arrangements under which trainees spent an academic year on an essentially school-provided course. In other words, if we want to glimpse the future of school-provided training, we do not have to rely on the UK's fleeting experiences of the articled and licensed teacher schemes, but can examine a programme developed nationally over a forty-year period. The format of the programme grew manifestly from the grammar school tradition of training already outlined. The most important criterion by which a prospective secondary teacher was selected was academic ability. Access to a training year lay, therefore, through two types of *concours*, the CAPES and the *agrégation*, for which the ministry set quotas for each subject of the curriculum. Successful candidates were then, for their year of training, allocated to a *centre pédagogique régional* (CPR) run by an inspector. Although the name might seem to imply some similarity with a British university department of education, this was not the case. The CPRs were essentially offices from which the inspector in charge allocated students to schools and made arrangements for minimal parts of the course which were taught to groups of trainees outside the school. During the CPR year, trainees were based in two or three different schools, one of which was a *lycée* and one a *collège*. Classroom practice was of two types. All students took over responsibility for one class throughout the year. Students could receive guidance from a mentor, but none from the class's regular teacher, because the class was not allocated a teacher apart from the student. Alongside these so-called *stages en responsabilité*, students also had a more structured and supervised form of practice where they worked alongside regular teachers. Complementing this practical introduction to the classroom, the student was also supposed to attend some 20 to 30 days of sessions devoted to various aspects of education. Some of these were about subject methodology, some about the psychology of adolescence, some about the workings of the French

school as administrative institution. The sessions were organized by the inspector in a number of different venues.

Before we consider why the system was much criticized and ultimately abandoned, it should be pointed out that the scheme was carried out under extremely favourable conditions. First, it had the full powers of control and coordination of the French ministry behind it; schools and mentors could be carefully chosen and the whole scheme was integrated by regulation into the legal framework of the national educational system. Second, the traditional French focus on the development of cognitive skills as the key ingredient in school education meant a narrower definition of the role of the teacher and, in turn, a much simpler induction task. Mentors in France were free of almost all the pastoral and administrative load which bog down all British teachers. Weekly hour allocations for staff were in any case generous, because it has always been recognized that at secondary level the preparation and follow-up of lessons require time if quality is to be provided.

In evaluating the training programme as carried out in the former CPR, we can do no better than base our comments primarily on the report written by Nelly Leselbaum of the Institut National de Recherche Pédagogique in 1987. Her findings derived from an analysis of the training programme in 17 of the 26 CPRs, of structured observation of 16 training days organized by six of the CPRs and of data gathered by questioning trainers and trainees. The serious weaknesses in the training scheme underlined by the report can be summarized under three main headings: administration, content and rationale.

In their administrative role, the CPRs had to bring together the different people who were required by regulation to contribute to the training programme: inspectors, headteachers, classroom teachers and education specialists, usually university-based. These people operated within quite different professional spheres. They also understandably had very different professional allegiances, none of which included teacher training as a major one. It is scarcely surprising, therefore, that the Leselbaum report pointed to a serious dislocation between the elements of the course. In particular, the content and timing of the training days did not integrate with the teaching practice experiences, and the training days themselves failed to bring together general pedagogy and subject methodology in a coherent way. The general lack of coherence was often aggravated by the poor and belated information about the programme passed on to the students. Finally, the logistical difficulties encountered by the students expected to travel to sessions at a variety of venues often resulted in poor attendance at the training days.

The content of the CPR year also gave rise to a number of areas of concern. On teaching practice, students felt that the *stage en responsabilité* was placed too early in the year – it was seen as an experience to survive rather than one to learn from. On the other hand, working alongside a classroom teacher was generally welcomed, though students recognized that the benefits were closely related to the quality of the teacher to whom they had been assigned and to the support they received. Several were given the impression by their mentor that their presence was resented and was an interruption to the work of the class.

In the CPR programme itself (the 20 to 30 days), students most valued sessions where they could openly exchange experiences and discuss methodological questions. They disliked sessions which seemed too prescriptive. They stressed the need for a careful ordering of elements, in particular suggesting that subject methodology should be placed early on in the course, even before the start of their first teaching practice. They also condemned insufficient time allocations to some parts of the course, e.g. information technology.

Finally, the course seemed to lack unity of purpose. The division of responsibilities in the provision of the course resulted in a lack of coherence not only in delivery, but also in rationale. In particular, the contributors, for none of whom it was a major responsibility in relation to their other duties, failed to accord their role as trainers the importance it deserved. This was particularly true of the school subject mentors:

> Our study has shown that the great majority of mentors [*conseillers pédagogiques*] chosen and designated by the system to provide the professional pedagogic training of future teachers paradoxically do not see themselves as 'trainers' but as 'mere teachers to whom a teacher trainee has been allocated'.
> (Leselbaum, 1987, p. 59)

Mentors were considered not to have reflected sufficiently on the theory of their own practice and were thus not in a position to give explicit advice to those in their charge. In addition to the uncertainty of whether mentors really perceived themselves as 'trainers' rather than as 'teachers', there was also ambivalence in their training role brought about by their responsibilities for giving support and advice on the one hand and contributing to the assessment process on the other. The fact that the mentors were chosen by the *inspecteur*, i.e. by the hierarchy, emphasized the ambivalence for both mentors and students. The basis of their being chosen, their own high-quality teaching skills, all too easily obscured the importance for them to be able to stand back from their own practice and view it objectively; similarly neglected was the need to give mentors training in both situation analysis and the means of effective intervention into the trainees' learning – all essential if they were to be able to give considered advice to trainees.

These inadequacies and unresolved ambiguities in the mentor role contributed to and compounded a fundamental weakness in French secondary teacher training – its dependence on the model lesson. Students, in order to please inspectors who controlled grades and would therefore influence their pay, and teachers who played a part in assessment and with whom, in any case, they understandably wanted to establish a good working relationship, inevitably tended to imitate what was presented to them as good practice, rather than exploring ways of adapting methodology to their own aptitudes and to the different conditions they might find in other classes and schools. While challenging the system when opportunity allowed,[4] in self-interest they conformed to it.

Two years after the Leselbaum survey, a government report by Daniel Bancel (1989), Recteur of the Academy of Rouen, proposed the creation of the *instituts universitaires de formation de maîtres*, a proposal which the minister put into immediate effect in the *Loi d'Orientation* of 1989.

The aim was broad and ambitious, to improve the quality of recruitment and training. In a key sentence, the document stated that:

> in order to reorganize the types of training and to offer all teachers a professional training combining basic knowledge, didactics, the acquisition of pedagogic methodology and an introduction to research, the institutional involvement of the universities is essential.

Thus the new law substantially increased the involvement and responsibilities of universities in the training of both primary and secondary teachers.

The introduction of the IUFMs has not occurred without controversy – controversy which was inevitably inflated when a government of one political persuasion took over the legislation of another. In 1993, the socialist government led by Pierre Bérégovoy was replaced by a right-wing government led by Edouard Balladur, and Lionel Jospin was replaced as Education Minister by François Bayrou. As a result, the infant institutions were particularly closely scrutinized and evaluated from their very inception onwards.[5] The sharpest criticisms arose from concern over academic standards; the requirement that candidates for secondary school teaching should not only acquire some experience of school but be judged on their suitability for teaching was regarded as incompatible with the high level of concentration they needed to take the CAPES. In similar vein, a requirement for some joint teaching of primary and secondary groups was considered to be often inappropriate, especially when a handful of secondary school students found themselves in a large group of primary students. A further major concern has centred on the relationship between the IUFMs and the universities. Because the new institutions were sited in former *école normale* buildings and because of the tenure of teaching staff, a large number of primary trainers were kept on. Their presence, above all the somewhat hasty involvement in research of some of them, brought demands for the exclusion of research from the IUFM remit and for tighter financial control to be exerted by universities. It has also been suggested that a specialist *licence* is not suitable for primary school teachers and that a more generalist *licence*

should be set up for them. It remains to be seen exactly how these various tensions between the traditions of the primary and secondary sectors and between the demands for academic excellence and for professional aptitude will ultimately be resolved. At the same time, it is important to note that in spite of their great experience of a school-based training mode, there has been no challenge to the new balance between school-based and institution-based components and no calls for the re-creation of the CPRs. Adjustments and improvements to a range of administrative features are being called for, but *not* any radical change to the new structure, let alone its abolition.

Let us now try to bring French ideas, perceptions and experience to bear on teacher training in the hope that we can evaluate more critically the changes which are occurring in Britain. The French would argue that education is essentially about the transmission of knowledge. As it is teachers who have to transmit this knowledge, it is essential that they are selected on the degree to which they themselves have acquired it. Thus we find that, at secondary level, the French have long used purely academic criteria to make the first and most important selection of their teachers. Changes over recent years have increasingly required primary teachers to acquire a solid academic background as a precondition to entering the profession. The latest legislation maintains the view that primary teachers should not be fobbed off with any sort of pseudo-diploma, but should join in university study along with other students holding a *baccalauréat* and continue to do so for three years, i.e. until obtaining the *licence*. It should, incidentally, be noted that nursery school teachers are subject to the same regulations as primary teachers. There is one parallel to the idea of a 'Mum's Army', the special dispensation given to mothers with three children. But the dispensation applies to entry requirements, not exit ones; that is, to acquire the status and tenure of a *professeur*, the mother of three will still have to pass the *concours*. What has no parallel in Britain is the importance attached by the French to using academic excellence in teachers as a means of selecting and rewarding them. It is interesting to note that the recent UK government proposals for the reform of ITT make no mention of the quality of entrant or how high-quality applicants can be encouraged to apply for and then to remain in the teaching profession. The French would argue further that the knowledge which teachers have to transmit is subject to constant change. As it is universities which create and process this change, it is self-evident that they should participate in the preparation of teachers, not only academically, but also professionally. A fundamental weakness in school-provided training is that it promotes imitation of a model – a model which is necessarily anchored in the past. If universities can be successfully persuaded to participate in coordinating and delivering teacher training, the teachers who emerge should prove not only academically competent, but much more flexible and forward-looking.

So much for the broad principles behind the recent changes. Alongside these can be seen one pressing practical concern, the need for the existence of an institution whose prime responsibility would be to harness and coordinate all the contributors to a teacher training programme: university academics, education experts, educational administrators, headteachers and classroom teachers. The most important lesson learned from the old system of secondary teacher training in France was that a system which is owned by no one, for which no one takes full responsibility, will lack coherence and a sense of direction. The IUFMs were created in order to put an end to this serious deficiency. It is important, at the same time, to note that, for all their great experience of top-down models of management, the French did not opt for a centralized controlling agency run by politically selected nominees but for regionally distributed institutions controlled by professionals and judiciously located between the universities and the schools.

The irony which will escape no one is that while the French have found it necessary to create such institutions, the British are in serious danger of abolishing them in favour of a system very like the one which the French have abandoned as unsatisfactory. There are further ironies: some of the teething problems of the IUFMs are undoubtedly caused by lack of experience and expertise in producing a programme which effectively combines theory and practice. In particular, they lack the experts in 'applied education' who form an essential group in university education departments in Britain. We have to hand much experience on which the French could, at this precise moment, usefully draw, experience which our own administrators seem in danger of devaluing and even dismissing.

For all the disagreements which exist in France over the precise structure of the new IUFMs, discussions seem to be focused firmly on how to bring about real improvements in teacher training. In Britain, we need to stress our own professionalism by doing the same. When questioning the merits of school-based training, it is not, of course, the importance of schools in the training process which is being challenged, merely the degree of control and proportion of student time schools should take over. There is no doubt that courses have benefited as student involvement in schools has increased from some 30 to 50 per cent of their period of training. In particular, the greater participation of schools has enabled them to regard themselves as real partners in the training process, not merely the short-term hosts of guest students from an outside institution. The key problem is, therefore, to determine at which point above the 50 per cent mark the school/training institution balance reaches its optimum position. French experience unequivocally suggests that as a course approaches the 80 per cent school-based mark, it will fragment into as many courses as there are participant schools. Furthermore, in any conflict of time or energy, schools will quite rightly neglect their subsidiary role (teacher training) in favour of their main role (teaching in the classroom). The universities will, because of their low input, regard their involvement as tangential to their main research and teaching responsibilities. The students will resent their isolation, their lack of opportunity to discuss their progress on neutral ground with their peers and with neutral tutors, their lack of supporting facilities (especially libraries and educational technology/IT provision) and the pressure put on them by mentors, consciously or unconsciously, to conform to a particular teaching model. This fragmentation occurred in the French

CPR in spite of the strong and centralized administration seeking to coordinate it. In the UK, where, under present legislation, central government cannot control school participation and where schools can pull out of teacher training from one year to the next, the threat of fragmentation in a school-provided form of training is all the greater.

Any evaluation of heavily school-based schemes operating in Britain needs to take account of the fact that they have been able to draw freely on the valuable experiences built up over decades in universities and colleges. If the latter were to withdraw their coordinating force, such success as the former had achieved would prove evanescent. To adapt the words of a famous Frenchman, if university departments of education did not exist, it would be necessary to invent them. The French have discovered the truth of this. It would be extremely sad if we had to destroy the tradition of high-quality professional training in a real university–school partnership, only to have to rediscover the truth in ten years' time. By then the expert personnel would have dispersed or retired and the traditions would have vanished. It would also be extremely unhelpful if the open-minded search for the optimum balance between school and institution inputs into training were frustrated by prior and general imposition of over-prescriptive funding-led regulatory frameworks which rigidly described content, siting and duration of courses or which laid down precise percentages for the inputs. Similarly, it would be unfortunate if partisan funding encouraged schools to participate in training for the wrong, i.e. financial, reasons, while suggesting to universities that their involvement in teacher training was no longer essential.

English teacher education, which surely would be rated 'excellent' in any international assessment exercise, needs full governmental support in terms of both encouragement and resources to achieve maximum benefit from its present structure based on a genuine university–school partnership. To replace the partnership model by a school-provided one would represent a step backwards into the unknown – to us, but not to the French, who have had long experience of such a model, found it wanting and abandoned it. In the introduction of the National Curriculum, the failure to take account of and build on the experiences of our European neighbours cost us dearly in terms of time, effort and money.[6] Failing to learn lessons on teacher training will have similarly serious repercussions, threatening at the same time both teacher supply and teacher quality.

## Notes

1 These reports based on lightning visits, although well edited and quite perceptive, stand like sixth-formers' essays against PhD theses when compared to the Board of Education reports of ninety years ago. For instance, when Mr Cloudesley Brereton produced his report on the rural schools of north-west France for the Board in 1902, it was based not only on wide and clearly referenced reading (a five-page bibliography was included), but also on a tour of 600 miles, 300 of them on bicycle, during which over 60 primary schools were visited and some 120 people interviewed. Perhaps even the DFE has something to learn from its Edwardian predecessor about what a return to traditional standards really involves.

2 The *baccalauréat* is the examination taken at the end of secondary school; passing it traditionally entitles pupils to a university place. The DEUG was introduced in 1973 as an intermediate examination to be taken after two or three years of university study. Successful candidates can move on to the *licence* after one further year of study and, if successful again, on to a *maîtrise* after another year.

3 The *concours* is regarded by the French as a republican device which ensures equality of opportunity to all citizens seeking to enter the service of the state. It comprises formal examinations which are assessed by examiners who have no knowledge, personal or professional, of the candidates.

4 See, for instance, the article written by a group of former CPR trainees in *Le Monde de l'Education*, October 1989, pp. 33–4.

5 Attention is drawn to two particular critiques. The first is that maintained by the Société des Agrégés, which, in particular, expresses great concern about any measures which threaten the academic standards required of future teachers. The views and interventions of the society are described in its journal *L'Agrégation*, especially numbers 322 (1989), pp. 159–65; 326 (1990), pp. 17–23; 330 (1991), pp. 254–66; 332 (1992), pp. 9–22; 338 (1992), pp. 1–8. The second is to be found in the report of André Kaspi,

which resulted from a ministerial request, after the election of a new government in 1993, to evaluate the IUFM (see *Rapport sur les Instituts Universitaires de Formation de Maîtres*, 1 July 1993).

6 According to the Education Editor of the *Daily Telegraph* (11 November 1994), the lesson took seven years to learn, disrupted schools and cost up to £750 million.

# References

Bancel, D. (1989) *Créer une nouvelle dynamique de la formation des maîtres*. Rapport du Recteur Daniel Bancel à Lionel Jospin, Ministre d'Etat, Ministre de l'Education Nationale, de la Jeunesse et des Sports, Paris.

DES (1989a) *Initial Teacher Training in France: The Training of Secondary Teachers in the Académie de Toulouse. A Paper by Her Majesty's Inspectorate*. London: HMSO.

DES (1989b) *The Provisional Teacher Program in New Jersey. A Paper by Her Majesty's Inspectorate*. London: HMSO.

Leselbaum, N. (1987) *La formation des enseignants du Second Degré dans les Centres Pédagogiques Régionaux*. Collection Rapports de Recherches, no. 4. Paris: Institut National de Recherche Pédagogique.

OFSTED (1993) *The Initial Training of Teachers in Two German Länder: Hessen and Rheinland-Pfalz. A Report from the Office of Her Majesty's Chief Inspector of Schools*. London: HMSO.

# 21 Teacher Education and Values Transmission: Cultural Dilemmas with Difficult Choices

ELWYN THOMAS

## Introduction

A dilemma describes a situation which is perplexing, in that choices have to be made between alternatives that may be equally undesirable. This chapter is about dilemmas originating mainly through social, political, economic and technological change, which are seriously challenging core values held by members of many societies in the developing world. The adherence to these values hitherto has provided order and considerable social stability. This order and stability has underpinned a predictable and often enriching way of life which has been handed down to successive generations. In the main, it has been the function of the school, and the role of teachers in particular, to ensure that harmony exists between what is taught in school and the accepted values of a certain community in which the school functions.

Values and their transmission through education are certainly a fruitful area from which cultural dilemmas are likely to arise, especially in times of marked social change. Most societies see the need to have a value system in order to give meaning to people's lives, and to ensure some measure of stability and predictability in their relationship with other persons and the environment. The problem is, however, that values and their transmission have often been used by those in authority, such as governments, heads of industry and commerce or religious leaders, as a means of controlling the lives of others.

The proximity of values with culture and the commonality which both have with education as an agent of transmission provide the underlying argument for this chapter. That is, the transmission of values through education needs to be seen as part of a larger process of intercultural transmission, from which a series of cultural dilemmas arise challenging educators to explore the need for a more culture-sensitive pedagogy.

Culture is viewed as a set of transient or enduring encounters between individuals or groups of individuals (Thomas, 1992a) and an intercultural process as one which provides an active interface between different sets of encounters, providing a possible substratum for cultural exchange. As a working statement, values will be considered to be centrally held sets of enduring predispositions which can determine both deep-seated and peripheral attitudes that have the propensity to motivate a person's behaviour. Education, for the purposes of this chapter, is viewed as being mainly synonymous with schooling.

The chapter addresses four key issues relating to the cultural dilemmas likely to influence values education, and especially the training and education of teachers in the process of values transmission. The first issue relates to examining briefly the nature of values, and the case for having values education as part of the school curriculum in the context of interculturalism. The extent to which recent research into cultures of teaching can throw light on the process of values transmission in the context of interculturalism is the second issue that will be addressed. A third issue is the nature of some of the key cultural dilemmas that arise in values transmission with reference to schooling. The fourth issue tackles the problem of how values can become part of a cultural pedagogy, sensitive enough to address some of the cultural dilemmas inherent in values transmission.

## Values, values education and interculturalism

### *What are values?*

When one is addressing the case for values education and the question about the nature of the subject, as far as the school curriculum is concerned, it is worth reminding ourselves that in the first place there are different approaches to the study of human values. Second, there are differences in approach to the place of human values in the educational process. There is considerable variability in the way different authors interpret what they mean by values.

To social psychologists, the nature of values is a central core of generalized attitudes which have a salient role in motivating and thereby directing a person's behaviour. Peripheral to centrally held values would be one's specific attitudes to more contemporary and less enduring events and situations. Human values can be perceived at a series of levels. At the highest level we have *value orientations*, which guide behaviour (Kluckholm and Strodtbeck, 1961). At the next level we have the construct of attitude, as an expression of our value systems, and sometimes called *attitudinal syndromes* (Yang, 1986). At the third level, we have the extent to which an individual perceives that he or she is able to control his or her environment, believing either that he or she can be mainly responsible (*internality*), or that factors such as luck and people power are the determinants (*externality*). This level psychologists call *locus of control* (Rotter, 1966).

Milton Rokeach (1960, 1967), producer of seminal work on the nature and understanding of human values, has provided a classification which distinguishes between *terminal* values such as love of freedom and *instrumental* values like trust and obedience. For a more detailed account of the nature of values the reader is referred to the work of authors cited above and to Thomas (1994a).

The developmental approach to the study of values taken by Piaget (1932), Dewey (1963) and Kohlberg (1976) suggests that our understanding of values, and the decisions we take which involve judgements about values, go through a sequence of phases from childhood to adulthood.

A more philosophical approach to the study of values and values education is that of McPhail (1972, 1982), who focuses on moral values in the context of others and how they interact with one another. McPhail sees moral education solely in terms of consideration for others. The essence of moral behaviour is consideration, care and mutual respect. McPhail works on the assumption that moral behaviour is a direct consequence of what we take from our environment and the people who make up this environment.

The work of Wilson (1977; Wilson *et al.*, 1967) also provides an interesting philosophical framework for introducing moral values into school. Rather than using indoctrination to teach a particular set of values or moral code, he uses a problem-solving approach to the inculcation of values. For Wilson there are four basic components to moral education: consideration of others in the light of valued moral principles, awareness of people's emotions as well as one's own, knowledge of facts relevant to moral education and an ability to make moral decisions and act upon them.

### *Why values education?*

There have been many attempts to introduce values into the formal educational process in most countries and, in the main, the results have not been very successful. Moral values have been the most targeted values, owing to the fact that moral values are sometimes identified with national goals and, where applicable, to the aims and objectives of an established national religion, as in the United Kingdom.

This becomes reinforced especially where national goals are closely associated with a religion or national philosophy that predominates in a particular country. For example, Islam in Malaysia and Pakistan, Christianity in many Western countries, Pancasila in Indonesia, Buddhism in Thailand and Myanmar and Confucianism for overseas ethnic Chinese, as in Singapore and Taiwan, are all instances where national governments have identified the school curriculum as the place for the learning and inculcation of values.

In many countries, the school curriculum embraces not just moral values but a whole spectrum of secular values (e.g. thrift, obedience, hard work ethic) which are systematically taught, not only for the purpose of inculcation, but to reinforce national aims and a national identity. In the case of multicultural and multireligious societies, the introduction of programmes of values education or values learning has often been planned with the aim of promoting national cohesion. These programmes make a selection from different cultural values and belief systems represented in a population; this selection then becomes part of a moral education or values education curriculum.

An example of a particular response by government to the awareness of values erosion and what role education might play is provided by Singapore. The Singapore government introduced Confucian ethics into moral education for ethnic Chinese students in the secondary schools of the republic in the mid-1980s (Tu, 1984; Sim, 1992). This is an example of an injection of traditional values into the school curriculum. The Confucian approach to values recognizes that although cognitive structures shape the kind of feelings an individual has, the factors that eventually determine moral conduct are fundamentally affective, not cognitive. Confucian morality is not just about sentiments but about carrying out life in terms of good conduct. To promote Confucian values, the role of education is seen as providing an atmosphere of learning through example and ample opportunities for teachers and pupils to reflect upon.

Moral education programmes that make pupils and teachers think and talk about issues of right and wrong, and are concerned with how people behave in real situations, are what the Confucian values programme in Singapore attempted to provide. It tried to address the erosion of traditional values by putting education in the forefront of reinforcing an ethnic Chinese value system which was perceived to be under threat by the secular and intensely materialistic effects of modernization. The jury is still out on the result. However, the example does show that attempts are being made to emphasize how education could play its part as a broker in the transmission of values, especially values that are held to be part of a greater cultural identity which is in danger of being eroded.

It is clear from the various approaches to the study of values that a distinction is made between a general value system and morality. This is because values tend to be an individual's preference from a spectrum of human goals, described as secular, while morality relates mostly to an *a priori* human view and is in many cases strongly linked to a religion like Christianity or Islam or a humanistic philosophy like Buddhism.

## Values education and interculturalism

The values dichotomy discussed above should be seen to be part of a dynamic intercultural matrix, of which language, religion, customs and traditions are also a part. One may need to add to this matrix cultures of entrepreneurship, economic success, empowerment and greening (environmental awareness). Education has an important role in intercultural transmission of values, in not only maintaining a balance between the retention of desirable traditional values, but promoting conditions for acceptance of new and alternative ones. The task of embedding values education into an intercultural system which allows for a straddling of different cultural, linguistic and religious influences will not be an easy one. A totally new way of thinking about values education will be required by the architects of this approach and by its users. This applies especially for those responsible for implementing any intercultural values programmes. Recent attention given to the process of teacher development, and research on teaching as a culture or constellation of cultures, points to ways in which both balance and transmission of values may be achieved. This is discussed below.

## Transmission of values and cultures of teaching

A discussion about values transmission in education is really a discussion about cultural transmission, which is closely related to the act of teaching, and which is increasingly being perceived as a culture or set of cultures. Values transmission in education not only involves teachers and their pupils in a one-way process, but also invariably involves interaction between significant others, such as teachers with administrators, teachers with parents and other community members and pupils with pupils. To date, there has been little research on teacher education which focuses on all these intercultural relationships.

It is interesting to note that in the third edition of the American Educational Research Association *Handbook on Research on Teaching*, edited by Merlin Wittrock (1986), space was given to the subject of the culture of teaching. Since then, although not necessarily related to this event, interest has intensified in the subject and there has been a considerable amount of research generated on teaching as a culture or set of cultures.

The research on teaching as a culture should also be seen against a universal need to improve teacher quality through provision of better opportunities for teacher development. During the 1980s the work of Schön (1983) and others on the concept of the reflective teacher fuelled further interest in the debate on viewing teaching not just as an activity but as a culture.

The recent ideas put forward on the subject of teacher development by Hargreaves, Fullan and others, and the outcome of current research into the cultures of teaching, are steadily emerging as closely related activities. The outcome of this relationship could form a valuable basis to an under-

standing of how teachers transmit their skills and knowledge, and at the same time further their own personal development. This duality of purpose on the part of the teacher would be an important factor in the effective transmission of values in education, as it would probably lead to improved teacher motivation and commitment.

The extensive review by Feiman-Nemser and Floden (1986) of teaching cultures indicates a growing number of research studies which identified a variety of such cultures. These authors came to the conclusion that it is no longer tenable to hold the view that teaching has a uniform culture. They cite the work of Metz (1978), Little (1982) and Zeichner and Tabachnik (1983). Teaching, it appears, is a complex and varied process and not just a uniform set of encounters and traits. For these workers, teaching has a richness and diversity about its character, so that cultures of teaching rather than a culture of teaching would be a more appropriate description.

This is contrary to the early work of Waller (1932) and later that of Jackson (1968) and Lortie (1975), who perceived teaching to have a uniformity which is typified by a certain number of generic features. More recently, David Hargreaves (1983) has spoken of the term 'teacherish' being used as one of several universal descriptions of teacher behaviour. Individualism and teacher territoriality, the need for pedagogical space and even professional possession could also be included as pervasive and generic features of a teaching culture.

It is probably better to consider teaching as having a set of universal generic features, while at the same time sustaining a variety of cultures which interrelate with each other, including those labelled generic. Teaching is a very contextual activity, which should be flexible and adaptable. Pervasive features like individualism might be necessary at some times and more recessive and adaptable behaviours at others.

Andy Hargreaves (1992) takes the line that teaching cultures might be better explained if we distinguish between the *content* of a culture of teaching and its *form*. The *content*, according to Hargreaves, includes substantive attitudes and values, habits and ways of doing things shared within a particular group. Academic cultures, pastoral cultures and subject cultures therefore predominately reflect the content of a diverse teacher culture. *Form* includes pervasive features like *individualism*, which emphasizes the isolation of teachers in the classroom; *Balkanization*, in which teachers work in separate groups, often in competition with one another; *collaborative cultures*, which emphasize professionality between teachers and tend to include compatible initiatives to improve practice: and *contrived collegiality*, binding teachers in time and space to meet certain demands by their superiors.

From the above, it appears that teaching is a suspension of cultures occupying a common matrix characterized by individualism, a need to have pedagogical space, to develop collaboration with peers and to meet the needs of a contrived collegiality. This profile of teaching could be seen as part of a process of intercultural transmission, which is characterized by the existence of active interfaces. Values which make up so much of people's cultural identity are an obvious interface that may be affected by intercultural transmission. Teaching, and for that matter the learning which invariably accompanies it, is essentially part of an intercultural process. The transmission of values, alongside the various cultures of teaching, enables a rich cultural exchange to take place between significant others, such as pupils, parents and other members of the community. This is likely to result in individuals being exposed to new values, and the reinforcement of traditional values which they may wish to preserve but which they may also want to discard.

## Cultural dilemmas and the transmission of values in education

Before we discuss the role teachers and teacher education might play in the process of values transmission, which may be influenced by various cultural dilemmas, it is necessary to identify what these dilemmas are, their nature and how they might relate to the process of values transmission.

As the literature worldwide in the field of values and moral education over the past ten years indicates, a number of dilemmas exist for educators when governments draw up a blueprint for attempting to maintain or improve the 'moral health' of the nation. From personal research and literature surveys carried out by the author in this field over the past eight years, mainly in South, South-East and North Asia (Thomas, 1990, 1992a, b, 1994a), at least four key cultural dilemmas can be identified. The first cultural dilemma relates to adjustments that have to be made by societies to cope with the pressure to retain older values, while at the same time having to accept, sometimes forcibly, new ones. Let us call this a dilemma about *old and new values* which require cultural adjustments to be made by most members of a society. A second cultural dilemma that influences values transmission is the way in which the individual has to compete against the collective will, the latter often being heavily ingrained. This dilemma might be labelled a conflict between *individualism and collectivism*. A third dilemma is how to balance the need for a national identity while ensuring a *modus vivendi* for the diverse cultural groups that make up the nation. This is a particular problem in plural societies that have recently emerged from the yoke of colonialism and wish to show the world that they have a national identity. This is a dilemma about a choice between achieving some form of cultural or national consensus while allowing cultural diversity to flourish in some form. It is essentially a dilemma between *consensus and diversity*. This is a sensitive dilemma for any government to handle, especially when it overspills into language policy, religion and, of course, values education.

A fourth dilemma is the emergence, in the past decade or so, of the need felt by certain nations to share their problems and ideas about making values education more effective. There is a trend in different regions of the world, e.g. South-East and North-East Asia, for nations to identify certain pan-cultural characteristics embracing religious and linguistic origins. Once identified, these apparently common features could form the basis for a core set of values, and provide a basis for an interculturalism specifically related to a region. These trends are the result of at least two factors.

The first is a perceived threat (real or apparent) to a particular nation's cultural heritage from the forces of modernization and the impact of technological advance. The second factor is the noticeable movement in several parts of the world towards nations sharing economic and political interests (e.g. in Western Europe) in order to improve their understanding of each other by finding out what common values they might share. This may result in the search for universals or general principles (Thomas, 1994b). Set against this search for universals is the suspicion felt by some countries that unwarranted outside interference may not be such a good thing in the end for a national programme of values education, which in some countries is already a national dilemma. Fears are also raised by many nations that even if there is a partial agreement on a pan-cultural philosophy of values education, implementation is likely to be problematical and certainly sensitive. This fourth dilemma we will call *contrived universalism versus relative values*. Each of the above four dilemmas will now be discussed in more depth.

## Cultural adjustments to values old and new

The case of Singapore has been cited elsewhere in this chapter, showing how and why Confucian ethics was introduced into the secondary school curriculum. The introduction of a value system such as Confucian ethics is part of a number of attempts by the Singapore government, since independence, to provide its pupils with a programme of values education (Eng, 1989). The economic success of the country, while enabling it to flourish and achieve full employment and an improved standard of living for its citizens, was perceived by the government to have attendant detrimental effects which could lead to the erosion of family values, less filiality and lack of consideration for

others. Programmes of values education entitled 'Being and Becoming' and 'The Good Citizen' were meant to counteract the more undesirable effects of modernization for all ethnic and religious groups in the republic. They also pre-dated the introduction of Confucian ethics.

For the Singapore government, values, be they old or new, Western or Eastern, should have a place in the school curriculum. The move towards including Confucian ethics and the introduction of religious teaching of Christianity, Islam and Hinduism aimed at specifically targeting cultural and religious diversity, which 'Being and Becoming' and 'The Good Citizen' did not and were not meant to do.

In Japan, despite the secular profile of public and official institutions, religion is a pervasive undercurrent which affects moral education in both the home and the school (Luhmer, 1990). In very different ways, Buddhism, Shintoism, Confucianism and latterly Christianity, coupled with the influences of Western values mainly from North America, provide an interesting and complex system of intercultural exchange. The nationalism of the period from 1872 to 1945 influenced, sometimes in the extreme, a system of values which eventually led to a radical reappraisal of the Japanese value system after the Second World War. This period was marked by a deliberate policy of secularization, which was typified by the introduction of social studies emphasizing citizenship but without extolling nationalist values.

Introduction of moral education into the curriculum of primary and secondary schools in Japan has always been a very controversial affair, especially where the programme makes reference to national pride, self-respect and discipline. These values are for many too closely associated with the past. However, the *Rinkyoshin*, an *ad hoc* committee set up by Premier Nakasone in 1987, suggested that these older values be included in the new moral education programme alongside newer values, including 'understanding and appreciation of foreign cultures and an awareness of the responsibility of Japan toward the rest of mankind' (Luhmer, 1990, p. 178). The programme is now being used in schools, and measures have been taken for the training and education of teachers to help its implementation.

The Japanese case is an interesting one, and is the reverse of what is happening in Singapore. In Japan, the inclusion of older values into the school curriculum was specifically avoided for historical reasons, while newer and often very different values, such as internationalism, were identified for schooling the younger generations of Japanese youth. However, recent developments in curriculum development in Japan show that older values are gradually taking their place in the school curriculum in primary and secondary schools. This, Luhmer hints, is something of a gentle return to the past. In both Japan and Singapore, the old and new values are now included in the curriculum; therefore at least three key issues will need to be addressed in the near future. The first concerns priority and balance in terms of time and space given to both categories of value in the curriculum. The second issue is how the old and new values will be taught alongside one another. The third is what type of teacher education programmes will be available to implement these changes and adjustments. It goes without saying that tackling the third issue is a top priority if an acceptable meld between old and new is to be achieved in the future.

## Individualism versus collectivism

A dilemma that does not emerge very often in the rhetoric, and certainly in print, associated with programmes of values education is the issue of one's own personal values and how they relate to a public system of values which are reflected in the curriculum of the school, in the college and frequently within the group norms of the community. One usually comes across this dilemma in private discussions with teachers, pupils and often parents, for they are at the working interface of most values education issues. There are a number of problems which are associated with this dilemma. One problem is that while teachers and pupils may agree with much of what a programme

of values education is trying to achieve, they find the subject difficult and its presentation boring. This was certainly the case for most of the Singapore programmes (Eng, 1989; Thomas, 1992b). The teaching of, and the teacher training for, most programmes was generally inadequate and usually highly unimaginative.

Another problem may be labelled 'perceived dissonance' on the part of pupils and probably teachers. This entails a situation in which a pupil is supposed to uphold value A, which is also emphasized by the school. However, it is clear to the pupil (and often to the teacher) that holding and certainly acting on value A may run contrary to value B, also emphasized by the school. Let us take an example from the Singapore situation. From the author's own observations (Thomas, 1992b, 1994a) and those of Chew (1994), it appears that a value such as cooperation is given a high profile in the values education programmes of secondary schools in the republic. However, this value is perceived by teachers and pupils to be at variance with the pressure exerted by the school and especially the parents for their children to achieve and compete with their peers at all costs, so as to ensure a successful future. Here we have a dilemma in which the state, through the school curriculum, is exhorting a collectivism against a competing need for an individual to express intensely his or her individualism through academic achievement. In this context, to exhort cooperation while at the same time promoting individualism through competition in company with the self-same peers is not only a dissonant influence but one which is highly ambiguous and confusing for the pupils.

However, a much more disturbing scenario is one where a values education programme contains political motives dressed up as moral values. This causes an inner conflict within the person between official and private. Observations by a number of educators from the People's Republic of China have commented on how values education in schools and colleges since 1977 still has strong political overtones (Lin Peilin, 1980; He Doungchang, 1988; Li Maosen, 1990). The message, it seems, is that values education in China in the

1990s is really for the benefit of the government (i.e. the collective will). Until this situation is changed, both teachers and pupils will have considerable problems of cognitive dissonance in resolving their private values and those of the collective.

## Consensus at the price of diversity?

One has only to read the five principles of Indonesia's Pancasila, which is akin to a unifying philosophy of life or *Weltanschauung*, to realize how values are used to marshal a consensus of the many diverse peoples which make up a nation. Briefly, the five principles are a belief in the one and only God, a just and civilized humanity, unity of the nation, communal group decisions and the promotion of social justice. The first two principles and the fifth are clear foci for the development of a core of values. These three principles are supposed to form a basic frame of reference for specific values held by the different ethnic and religious groups.

Education has had a pivotal role to play in strengthening the value system which Pancasila promotes. However, how much does a strongly pervasive set of core values in the form of Pancasila dilute and possibly erode specific values held by the diverse groups? According to Ribera, the maintenance and development of a national identity through the principles of Pancasila has been achieved, and the problem now is for the future: 'Indonesia now faces the next big step which is the enforcement of the national identity in all aspects and dimensions of national life' (Ribera, 1990, p. 175). The word 'enforcement' sounds rather strong and, if taken literally, may mean that specific values held by different groups are likely to be subordinated to a consensus.

The dilemma embracing consensus and diversity was also experienced by those who were given the task of developing the various programmes for values and moral education in Singapore (Thomas, 1992b). On the one hand, the population of

Singapore is made up of three ethnic groups (Chinese, Malay and Tamil Indians), and any programme of values education needs to reflect this diversity. On the other hand, the government sees as a first imperative that a Singapore identity is forged and maintained. To achieve this, much store was placed on the design of values education programmes. By the end of the 1980s, it was clear that most of the programmes had failed (Eng, 1989). To ensure that values reflecting a national identity (consensus) were maintained, rituals such as daily flag-saluting ceremonies, activities for the defence of the country and the promotion of values such as service to the nation, good conduct, discipline, self-respect and respect for one's elders were strongly reinforced during school hours. In order to meet the needs of the diverse religions in the republic, the authorities introduced religious education in schools for each of the main religious groups. There is a clear admission here that consensus has its limits and that room must be made for diversity in the transmission of values in the education system.

The introduction of the Integrated Curriculum for Secondary Schools (ICSS) during 1989 in Malaysia also reflects the dilemma of consensus and diversity. Malaysia, like Indonesia, has its national philosophy, which is further elaborated as a statement of national education philosophy. Of the seven principles of ICSS, two specifically mention the word 'values' and one cites the word 'spiritual'. One reference to values is linked to the word 'inculcation', and another reference is linked to the phrase 'emphasis through incorporation'. The word 'integration' is linked with the word 'spiritual'. It is clear from reading the ICSS that there is a concerted effort to produce a consensus, not only in the form of a programme which specifically deals with values, but also as values incorporation into the teaching of other subjects in the curriculum, like science and languages.

The dilemma of consensus and diversity is not only about values, it is about identity, and identity does not necessarily mean national identity. Identity can also refer to one's ethnicity, religion, heritage, cultural roots and language. The dilemma of consensus and diversity is also about

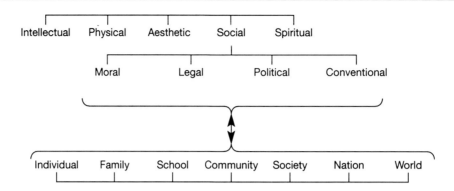

**Figure 21.1**   Content domains of affective development education. *Source*: After UNESCO (1992)

empowerment of one group by another. The inability of societies to tackle satisfactorily this dilemma is probably the single most influential factor in the failure of many programmes of values education. Education, if it has an answer to these problems, is only going to provide a partial one, for there are many other factors (political, religious and so on) that may come into the consensus–diversity equation.

### Contrived universalism versus relative values

In reading through the numerous statements put out by various curriculum centres and institutes in different countries on what values should be included in a programme of values education, one is struck by the long lists that have been compiled, and the meticulous way in which the values have been categorized. Some categories often relate values to national goals, some include values that are thought to be universal and other classifications might include values which are more culture or religion specific.

One gets the impression that educators genuinely want to play a useful role in making values education part of a student's personal development. The results, however, after more than a quarter of a century, have been generally disappointing. Perhaps the most imponderable factor which is related to this disappointment is that educators who have spent much time designing

and teaching values education have never been sure of the outcomes of their efforts. Another issue is that listing, identifying, selecting and classifying values is the easy part. When it comes to values teaching, not only is this a difficult task, but it is often the most controversial as well.

The issues identified above have not gone unnoticed. Recently, representatives from over forty countries located within the Asian region examined alternatives to programmes in values education already in existence in their own and other countries, under the auspices of UNESCO. It was clear from the collaboration between these countries that an alternative in the form of *affective development education* might be an answer. In the production of a guidebook on programmes and practices for affective development education (UNESCO, 1992), an attempt was made to make a dream come true. Reference to the guidebook, which is the result of a workshop on affective development held in Japan in 1989, shows what a difficult task it is to develop a viable programme of values education, and an even more difficult task to provide an alternative. Apart from finding great difficulty in arriving at a meaningful definition of affective development, the authors of the guidebook sketch out a conceptual map which includes domains such as intellectual, aesthetic and social. The social domain is ultimately divided into seven sub-domains, including the family, the school and the individual (see Figure 21.1).

The bringing together of experts from different countries to map out a number of domains, of which one, the social, would include agreed values, is in effect providing a set of values contrived for the purposes of promoting universalistic principles. They are contrived in the sense that a selection and prioritization has been made for the purpose of common reference among the nations of a region, in this case North and South Asia.

However useful this common reference may be for the curriculum of values education, and also for the curriculum of teacher education, there is likely to be a perceived interference, real or apparent, on the part of some member states belonging to a supranational body comprising a grouping of regional governments, or even an organization such as UNESCO itself.

In subjects like mathematics or science, comparisons with other countries are a welcomed feature resulting in the acceptance of common theories and practice. However, in an area such as values education there is a greater degree of what may be called 'cultural sanctity', which reflects not only a particular philosophy of life, but devoutly held religious beliefs and ways of thinking specific to a population. In other words, values education has high value and is an end in itself. Most countries over the past twenty years have been at pains to select appropriate curriculum content and to develop approaches to that end. In countries where there are significant cultural and ethnic differences, the task of developing a national programme of values education has been particularly sensitive, and one which has not been very successful. Judging from the author's experience in Malaysia, Singapore and Myanmar, certain international influences on values education might be seen as making a situation more fraught with uncertainty than it is at present.

It is clear that while an exchange of ideas and practices between countries on values education is to be encouraged, there are real issues to be considered, of which there are at least two. The first issue is one of *ownership* and the second issue concerns *implementation*.

Let us examine first the issue of ownership. It is becoming increasingly important to recognize that schooling is not only the domain of educators and politicians. This is nowhere more obvious than in the area of values. If the school is to be entrusted with much of the responsibility for the inculcation of values, any plans to promote values education

without the close involvement of parents and religious and community leaders are likely to end in failure. This is especially the case with moral values, which are often linked to a national religion and reflected in a values education programme. The community must feel that it has a stake in the process; in other words, it needs to have a say in what is taught and in some cases how it is taught. This stake, or 'ownership', is not easy to achieve. In an area which may be sensitive to the point of sanctity, without attempts to promote the active involvement of all interested groups, values education at a national level will be ineffective and any valuable ideas and lessons learned from other countries will be virtually lost. Whatever values are to be inculcated and in whatever way, it is essential that they are values that are seen to be closely related to that society. In other words, a values curriculum which may be enriched by new ideas originating from outside areas, but has also fully explored effective ownership by the society, will only be achieved if shared and related values are reflected in that curriculum.

The second issue concerns implementation. The curricula for most teacher preparation programmes give little or no place for training in values education, and, where training is given, the subject is presented and taught with a strong emphasis on inculcation, which invariably means large doses of didacticism. Furthermore, if affective development were to replace existing programmes of values education in the countries of Asia, the strongly eclectic and universalistic nature of affective development, coupled with the problem of training and educating teachers to teach it, would be a more formidable task than at present.

Among the many issues that need to be addressed in this dilemma is the development of appropriate pedagogies which incorporate established values within them, while providing invigorating opportunities for discussion and in-depth analysis of newer values which accompany changes in society. It is to the subject of pedagogy that we now turn.

## Facilitating choice through culture-sensitive pedagogies

Initiation and development of a field of study which specifically examines the nature of the teaching process cross-culturally, and which the author calls a *culture-sensitive pedagogy*, is long overdue. There is a small but growing literature relating to practice and research on pupil learning within curriculum development cross-culturally, but little on the related process of teaching. Much of what is written refers to valuable anthropological and interpretative data. A substantial number of quantitative studies about teaching also exist. There is a crying need to draw together relevant qualitative and quantitative cross-cultural research studies on teaching, as a starting point for the development of culture-sensitive pedagogies.

What follows will, I hope, be a start in dealing with the task. There are two main issues that need to be considered when one is developing a culture-sensitive pedagogy in relation to values transmission. The first issue concerns ascertaining needs and analysing the cultural context of a situation. The second issue concerns the theoretical base from which culture-sensitive pedagogies can be developed, and which would provide a framework for the training of teachers in values education.

### Needs exploration and cultural analysis

The cultural dilemmas discussed earlier are essentially all about making choices. Before choices can be made, it is necessary that the needs of parents, pupils, community leaders and educationists (including teachers) are recognized and seen to be taken seriously. Recent research by Aikman (1994), working with the Arakhmut in Peru, and Robert and Jenny Teasdale (1994), working with Australian Aboriginals, has shown how teaching and learning can be improved for these ethnic groups when their needs and wishes are reflected in the school curriculum. Both Aikman and the

Teasdales spent much time exploring the needs of their respective ethnic groups, employing a thorough cultural analysis of day-to-day behaviour patterns, at home and at school. A cultural analysis is an extensive examination of the cultural context of a community. When applied to an educational situation, it is a process which requires rigorous research and study of the background influences and cultural history which pupils bring with them to the classroom. It is also a process that seeks to enrich curriculum planning, through the adoption and adaptation of ideas and practices specific to a particular cultural group, which would, it is hoped, benefit both learner and teacher alike (Thomas, 1994b).

Using cultural analysis, these workers were able to ascertain specific needs which could be built into a school curriculum. A similar approach could be used in analysing salient examples from each of the dilemmas discussed earlier in the chapter.

For instance, in trying to resolve old and new perceptions of certain values, a cultural analysis could be made by curriculum developers researching differing perceptions of filiality among adolescents and parents representing different ethnic groups which make up a society. The analysis would explore current and changing attitudes to this very important Asian value. The outcome of the analysis might result in the development of teaching material which could examine attitudes, old and new, to filiality. The teaching material might also prescribe ways in which adolescents could play out the roles of parents and family under circumstances involving changing filial responsibilities.

A well-designed and effectively conducted cultural analysis is an essential prerequisite for a culture-sensitive pedagogy to ensure meaningful and relevant content.

### A theoretical basis for a culture-sensitive pedagogy?

The subject of pedagogy is not recent: its origin can be confidently traced to the time of the Greeks and probably before that. The notion of pedagogy both as an art and a science has provided its students over the years with plenty of ideas. The sources of many of these ideas have been psychologists such as Bruner (1966), Piaget (1971), Shulman (1986) and particularly Robert Gagné (Gagné and Driscoll, 1988). The work of Schön (1983), Zeichner (1983) and Zeichner and Tabachnik (1983) has added further insights into developments in pedagogy with particular reference to teacher education. Alas, not much in the way of workable theories of teaching has emerged. This appears to hold out little hope for the development of teaching strategies for a culturally sensitive subject such as values education. However, cross-cultural research carried out by Rogoff and Lave (1984), and more recently by Baker Sennett *et al.* (1993), Aikman (1994), Tanon (1994), Teasdale and Teasdale (1994) and Thomas (1994b), examines both content and process in learning and teaching activities reflected by different cultures.

A key feature which comes out from this recent research, although expressed in different ways, is the need to develop good planning strategies which are sensitive to everyday cognition. Another feature is the skill of carefully selecting those culture-specific behaviours which are perceived to improve teaching and learning, and those behaviours which do the opposite. The incorporation of culture-specific behaviour into teaching material can be illustrated by the work of Nunes (1994) with Brazilian street children. The street children can solve day-to-day arithmetical problems using their own street brand of mathematics. Nunes found that the methods these children used were not only faster but also more accurate than those used in the formal school.

An instance where certain cultural features relating to learning and teaching appear to interfere with the development of higher cognitive operations arises from research carried out by Kwan-Terry (1994) in Singapore. She has shown how culture-specific teaching styles associated with rote learning of Mandarin can transfer across to other subjects of the curriculum, probably having a negative effect on the development of creative, original and analytical thinking. The examples discussed above provide useful messages for those who wish to develop a more responsive and inter-

active role for teachers in multicultural classrooms. When a culture-sensitive pedagogy is being devised, whether it is for values transmission or the transmission of any other subject, it is essential that an awareness of current research into the cultural context of learning and teaching is manifested into a pedagogical framework. Such a framework may enable teachers working in multicultural classrooms to promote more relevant and stimulating values education as part of a wider intercultural process.

## Postscript

There is a clear need to translate the increasing importance of the findings from cross-cultural research into workable and culture-sensitive teaching strategies. These strategies may in the long term be the bases from which an adequate theory of teaching might emerge, and for which the current multicultural notion of teaching could provide a sound basis. If this was achieved, it would be a valuable contribution to the development of a cross-cultural pedagogy, which, it is hoped, not only would benefit teacher education and training, but would be pertinent to the focus of the present chapter; namely, the transmission of values and the difficult choices that often have to be made as the result of cultural differences within a society.

## References

Aikman, S. (1994) School curriculum as a forum for articulating intercultural relations with particular reference to the Peruvian Amazon. In E. Thomas (ed.), *International Perspectives on Schooling and Culture: A Symposium Proceedings.* London: Institute of Education, University of London.

Baker-Sennett, J. *et al.* (1993) Planning as developmental process. In H. W. Reese (ed.), *Advances in Child Development and Behaviour, Volume 24.* New York: Academic Press.

Bruner, J. S. (1966) *Toward a Theory of Instruction.* Cambridge, MA: Harvard University Press.

Chew, J. (1994) Schooling for Singaporeans: the inter-action of Singapore culture and values in schools. In E. Thomas (ed.), *International Perspectives on Schooling and Culture: A Symposium Proceedings*. London: Institute of Education, University of London.

Dewey, J. (1963) *Experience and Education*. London: Collier Macmillan.

Eng, S. P. (1989) Moral education in Singapore: dilemmas and dimensions. In *Proceedings of CCU-ICP International Conference, Moral Values and Moral Reasoning in Chinese Schools*. Taipeh: CCU-ICP.

Feiman-Nemser, S. and Floden, R. E. (1986) The cultures of teaching. In M. C. Wittrock (ed.), *Handbook of Research on Teaching*, 3rd edn. New York: Macmillan.

Gagné, R. M. and Driscoll, M. P. (1988) *Essentials of Learning for Instruction*, 2nd edn. Englewood Cliffs, NJ: Prentice-Hall.

Hargreaves, A. (1992) Cultures of teaching: a focus for change. In A. Hargreaves and M. G. Fullan (eds), *Understanding Teacher Development*. London: Cassell.

Hargreaves, D. (1983) The occupational culture of teachers. In P. Woods (ed.), *Teacher Strategies*. London: Croom Helm.

He Doungchang (1988) Speech to the Examination Conference of Ideological Political Teaching Material. *Journal of Political Education*, **1**, 1.

Jackson, P. W. (1968) *Life in Classrooms*. New York: Holt, Rinehart and Winston.

Kluckholm, F. R. and Strodtbeck, F. L. (1961) *Variations in Value Orientations*. Evanston, IL: Row Peterson.

Kohlberg, L. (1976) The cognitive developmental approach to moral education. In D. Purpel and R. Kevin (eds), *Moral Education: It Comes with the Territory*. Berkeley, CA: McCutchan.

Kwan-Terry, A. (1994) Culture and learning: a Singapore case study. In E. Thomas (ed.), *International Perspectives on Culture and Schooling: A Symposium Proceedings*. London: Institute of Education, University of London.

Li Maosen (1990) Moral education in the People's Republic of China. *Journal of Moral Education*, **19** (3), 159–71.

Lin Peilin (1980) *Moral Education 1: Pedagogy*. Beijing: Peoples Education Press.

Little, P. W. (1982) Norms of collegiality and experimentation: workshop conditions of school success. *American Education Research Journal*, **19**, 325–40.

Lortie, D. (1975) *The Schoolteacher*. Chicago: University of Chicago Press.

Luhmer, K. (1990) Moral education in Japan. *Journal of Moral Education*, **19** (3), 172–81.

McPhail, P. (1972) *Social and Moral Education*. Oxford: Basil Blackwell.

McPhail, P. (1982) *On Other People's Shoes*. Harlow: Longman.

Metz, M. H. (1978) *Classrooms and Corridors: The Crisis of Authority in Desegregated Secondary School Classrooms*. Berkeley: University of California.

Nunes, T. (1994) Cultural diversity in learning mathematics: a perspective from Brazil. In E. Thomas (ed.), *International Perspectives on Schooling and Culture: A Symposium Proceedings*. London: Institute of Education, University of London.

Piaget, J. (1932) *The Moral Judgement of the Child*. London: Routledge and Kegan Paul.

Piaget, J. (1971) *Science of Education and the Psychology of the Child*. London: Longman.

Ribera, J. (1990) A national identity in the process: the Indonesian experience. In J. J. Boeren and K. P. Epskamp (eds), *Education, Culture and Productive Life*. The Hague: CESO.

Rogoff, B. and Lave, J. (1984) *Everyday Cognition: Its Development in Social Context*. Cambridge, MA: Harvard University Press.

Rokeach, M. (1960) *The Open and Closed Mind*. New York: Basic Books.

Rokeach, M. (1967) *Value Survey*. Sunnyvale, CA: Halgren Press.

Rotter, J. B. (1966) Generalised expectancies for internal versus external control of reinforcement. *Psychological Monographs*, **80**.

Schön, D. (1983) *The Reflective Practitioner*. New York: Basic Books.

Shulman, L. (1986) Paradigms and research programmes in the study of teaching. In M. Wittrock (ed.), *Handbook of Research on Teaching*, 3rd edn. New York: Macmillan.

Sim, S. H. (1992) Education in morality: a Confucian response. In K. C. Chong (ed.), *Moral Perspectives and Moral Education*. Singapore: Singapore University Press.

Tanon, F. (1994) *A Cultural View on Planning: The Case of Weaving in Ivory Coast*. Tilburg: Tilburg University Press.

Teasdale, R. and Teasdale, J. (1994) Culture and schooling in Aboriginal Australia. In E. Thomas (ed.), *International Perspectives on Culture and Schooling: A Symposium Proceedings*. London: Institute of Education, University of London.

Thomas, E. (1990) Filial piety, social change and Singapore youth. *Journal of Moral Education*, **19** (3), 192–205.

Thomas, E. (1992a) Schooling and the school as a cross cultural context for study. In S. Iwawaki, Y. Kashima and L. Kwok (eds), *Innovation in Cross Cultural Psychology*. Amsterdam: Swets and Zeitlinger.

Thomas, E. (1992b) Moral development, cultural context and moral education. In K. C. Chong (ed.), *Moral*

*Perspectives and Moral Education*. Singapore: University of Singapore Press.

Thomas, E. (1994a) The state, teacher education and the transmission of values. Paper given at the British Association of Teachers and Researchers in Overseas Education (BATROE) Conference, 28–30 March, Institute of Education, University of London.

Thomas, E. (1994b) Schooling and culture: some international perspectives. In E. Thomas (ed.), *International Perspectives on Schooling and Culture: A Symposium Proceedings*. London: Institute of Education, University of London.

Tu, W.-M. (1984) *Confucian Ethics Today: The Singapore Challenge*. Singapore: Singapore Federal Publications.

UNESCO (1992) *Education for Affective Development: A Guidebook on Programmes and Practices*. Bangkok: UNESCO.

Waller, W. (1932) *The Sociology of Teaching*. New York; Russell and Russell.

Wilson, J. (1977) *Moral Education and the Curriculum*. Oxford: Pergamon Press.

Wilson, J. *et al.* (1967) *Introduction to Moral Education*. Harmondsworth: Penguin.

Wittrock, M. C. (1986) *Handbook of Research on Teaching*, 3rd edn. New York: Macmillan.

Yang, K. S. (1986) Chinese personality and its change. In M. H. Bond (ed.), *The Psychology of the Chinese People*. Oxford: Oxford University Press.

Zeichner, K. M. (1983) Alternative paradigms of teacher education. *Journal of Teacher Education*, **34** (3), 3–9.

Zeichner, K. M. and Tabachnik, B. R. (1983) Teacher perspectives in the face of institutional press. Paper presented at the American Educational Research Association, Montreal.

# Reply to Elwyn Thomas

## JOHN WILSON

I find Dr Thomas both illuminating and baffling. He is illuminating inasmuch as he offers a clear and useful description of the 'dilemmas', as he calls them, which arise when some attempt is made at moral education (value education) in particular cultures. Such a description would, obviously enough, be useful for teachers who work in cultures with which they are unfamiliar. Any education must clearly be (to use his words) 'culture-sensitive': one must know where the pupils are coming from. For all this I have nothing but praise, though, coming as it does from someone not well versed in sociology, anthropology or other relevant empirical disciplines, my praise is perhaps not worth very much.

Let me now try to explain why I am also baffled. I do not know – to put the point very briefly and roughly – whether (a) he believes that there is a form of thought or life, perhaps to be termed 'morality' or 'values', which is subject to pure reason and ultimately governed by transcendental and culture-free principles and procedures, a form which pupils of all cultures and creeds can reasonably be encouraged to use (of course, with the teacher being sufficiently sensitive to the culture in which the pupil lives), on the analogy of those forms we term 'science', 'mathematics', 'historical enquiry' and so on; or (b) he does not believe this. Obviously, this has important practical consequences. If I am trying to introduce, say, medicine or natural science into a culture which is based on witch doctoring, astrology and superstitious rituals of various kinds, I shall naturally take account of this; but the *kind* of account I take, the way in which I handle things, will vary greatly depending

on whether I opt for (a) or (b). Thus, if I opt for (a), I shall be governed by the view that medicine and natural science are more reasonable methods of procedure than the methods current in that culture, and I shall endeavour to show this to the pupils. If I opt for (b), I might perhaps think it worthwhile to put medicine and science before my pupils as some kind of alternative to the practices of the culture – perhaps just to broaden their minds in a sociological or anthropological kind of way. But I shall not claim any *merit* for them, and I shall not be disappointed if they stick to their old practices. My aims, and hence my practice, will be importantly different.

If I had to guess, I should plump for Dr Thomas thinking (b). He says, for instance, that 'The community must feel that it has a stake in the process; in other words, it needs to have a say in what is taught and in some cases how it is taught' (p. 255). Again, 'Whatever values are to be inculcated and in whatever way, it is essential that they are values that are seen to be closely related to that society.' And, unsurprisingly, he suggests 'teaching material which could examine attitudes, old and new, to filiality' in Asian contexts (it is 'a very important Asian value'). Suppose now, to make my point in an extreme form, I find myself as a moral educator in Nazi-dominated society in *c.* 1940. I shall very much *not* think that the community should 'have a stake in the process'. What I do as a moral educator will only be 'closely related to that society' in the (odd) sense that it will directly challenge its values; and I may not want to spend much time in examining 'attitudes old and new' to, say, the Jews or other *Untermenschen*, whether or not being

Aryan is a very important Nazi value. Of course, I may get thrown out or sent to the gas chambers. If Dr Thomas actually believes in transcendental and culture-free reason, and is merely indicating a certain amount of realism or low cunning when introducing such reason to various cultures, I have no quarrel. But I suspect him of (b); with the corollary, perhaps, that I have no *right* to make such challenges, since ultimately one set of values is as good as another.

If I here do him an injustice, then he will think that I have this right if, as a teacher, I do in fact have a firmer grasp on what is reasonable in this form of thought and life than the culture does. But then it will be enormously important to be clear about just what that grasp is, what the application of reason is to this form. Thus, to use my example again, it will make a big difference whether we think (a) that there are certain principles of pure reason – the Golden Rule, perhaps, or what Hare (1981) describes as the principle of universalizability (see also Wilson, 1990) – such that a person cannot seriously enter the realm of morality and value unless he or she subscribes to the principles; or (b) that it is just that some cultures follow this principle and others do not. If (a), I could say (at least before being hauled off to the gas chambers) something like, 'Look, if you stop to think, I believe I can show you why it *is* unreasonable to kill Jews.' If (b), I could only say, 'It might broaden your sociological knowledge to be aware that some societies *think* it unreasonable to kill Jews.'

This example is not much more extreme than some contemporary examples: we might think of female circumcision, the subjection of women generally, racial prejudice, even genocide (admittedly on a smaller scale). At this point I must make another distinction clear, since I am again not sure where Thomas stands in relation to it. There will be another big difference to my practice as a teacher – and, therefore, to the kind of research that I shall benefit from – depending whether I think (i) that my job is to sell only the set of rational procedures which (assuming I have got them right) apply to this form of thought, leaving it to the pupils to make up their own minds in the light of these procedures; or (ii) that I have myself directly to challenge the substantive values of that

(or any other) society, that I have the job of selling a particular moral *content*. My own view (Wilson, 1990) is (i): educators (I think by definition) should not, to use Thomas's words, engage in the 'transmission' of values or 'inculcate' them, but encourage pupils to think reasonably about them and act on their decisions. If I stick to that, I may avoid some at least of the blood that might flow from the direct challenge of (ii). In any case, I shall be acting as an educator, rather than as a missionary.

That point is highly relevant to the way in which I shall approach the particular culture in which I work, and to the sociological features which Thomas so clearly describes. For if (i), then I shall say in advance: 'Look, I am not selling any particular moral line of my own. What I shall do is just put before the pupils in your society certain principles of reason which, as I see it, apply to the area of morality or value. I shall not bully them even about these: they may be persuaded or they may not. I am not interested in 'transmitting' anything except some idea – no doubt controversial, and there will no doubt be plenty of argument in the classroom about it – of how reason gets a grip in this general area. Now, if you are not against reason in principle, as no doubt you are not, I'm sure you will welcome this; and you can keep an eye on me to make sure I am not selling a partisan line of my own. I am out to educate, not inculcate or indoctrinate. Of course, the application of reason may, indirectly, cause pupils to question some of your social practices, but that too is an inevitable function of education.'

I am not naive enough to suppose that this sort of advance warning, even if intelligible (even quite sophisticated people often fail to grasp the distinction), would always cut ice. But at least it would be honest, and perhaps enable us to see more clearly just how various cultures stood in relation to the idea of culture-free education – perhaps the most important field for research. In fact, my point should be put more strongly. If I am undertaking research into the best way of teaching or introducing X in a particular culture Y, it will be at least as important to be clear about exactly what X is as to be clear about the state of play in Y. For if I am not clear about X, I shall not know just what features of

Y are *relevant*. 'Value education' and similar terms are names for nothing clear: they might include, for instance, the work of Christian (and other) missionaries, the presence in schools of liberal-minded Europeans, propaganda by feminists displeased with the subjugation of women or almost anything. And obviously the culture's reactions will be importantly different in each case.

So it is, I suppose, a criticism of Thomas's chapter that, although he has given a useful *general* description of how cultures are likely to react in this area, he has not said anything specific enough to be really helpful. It might even be said, perhaps rather nastily, that his general points are tolerably obvious: they amount to not much more than the banal truth that the introduction of new 'values' to a culture is likely to be regarded with suspicion and may be disruptive. The further research for which he rightly calls can only be intelligently conducted on the basis of a much clearer understanding of what 'value education' is supposed to *be*.

Since Thomas has been kind enough to mention (some of) my own work, I should like to add a little more along these lines. Thomas says, 'he uses a problem-solving approach to the inculcation of values. For Wilson there are four basic components to moral education.' What alarms me about this is not that it gives a wrong idea of what I was trying to do (that in itself is negligible), but that I have obviously failed to make clear what must surely be the main crux in value education, something centrally important for anyone who does it or writes about it. The crux is that described above: *either* we take there to be principles of pure reason which govern the area (as they, rather more obviously, govern such areas as mathematics, science, history, etc.), in which case value education will be based on the teaching of these principles (roughly, on *how to do* the subject); *or* we just take, from somewhere or other, substantive values and 'inculcate' them.

Relying largely on the work of Hare (1981), I have defended the former position at length elsewhere (Wilson, 1990) and will not repeat the defence here. That is a matter for moral philosophy, and my view is that we know enough about how reason is supposed to apply to morality and value

for us to be able, tentatively, to educate people in that form of thought and life. But if we do not believe this, what follows? It is not only, as I have said above, that we shall not know how to conduct sociological research about how to proceed in practice; it is, more radically, that we shall have no justification for proceeding in practice at all. For if we are honest, we shall have to say something like, 'We do not know how pure reason applies to values and morality. Nevertheless, we propose to introduce a practice of education in this area to your culture (or to our own culture), which will, we hope, alter the pupils' thinking and behaviour. We cannot say that it will alter them for the better, since to say this would depend upon having a defensible view about the criteria in virtue of which they would count as "better".'

I at least could not say this with a straight face. It would be rather like saying, 'Look, your culture goes in for witch doctoring and myth making, whereas ours goes in for scientific medicine and historical enquiry. We have absolutely no reason to believe that what we call "science" and "history" are any better than your own practices. Nevertheless, we propose to introduce them and encourage your pupils to follow them.' That is not, of course, what we normally believe: we believe, I think rightly, that our practices are better, more reasonable, more justifiable. Of course, we may be wrong, and we must always be open to criticism; but if we do not have this belief, then we have no business to introduce them.

It may be said, not without justice, that (particularly since in some areas the application of pure reason is controversial) we can at least offer the culture some alternatives to its own practices — just for inspection, as it were, for the culture to take up if it wishes. But that will hardly do, for three reasons. First, any such offering will have some practical *effect*: it cannot be wholly *neutral*, it will change things, and we cannot avoid responsibility for that change. Second, the idea of making such offerings, of laying out more options for the culture to choose from, presupposes a liberal ideal of autonomous choice which may be questioned. Some cultures may not wish their pupils to be contaminated by familiarity with these options and, unless we can defend this ideal in terms of pure reason (no doubt we can), we have no grounds for persuading them. Third, the idea of *education* (rather than just 'transmission' or 'inculcation'; Thomas seems unaware of the important difference) implies some change in the direction of *truth* or rationality, not just *any* change.

Briefly, we shall get nowhere in this area — nowhere even from the viewpoint of sociological or other empirical research, let alone of actual practice — unless we first get clear about just what we are trying to do, and how what we are trying to do follows from pure reason. I suspect that this is not a popular (certainly not a fashionable) idea, because of the influence of relativism ('Who are we to impose our ideas of reason on … ?' and so forth). But it seems a necessary idea if we are to make any progress.

## References

Hare, R. M. (1981) *Moral Thinking.* Oxford: Oxford University Press.

Wilson, J. (1990) *A New Introduction to Moral Education.* London: Cassell.

# 22 The Professional Training of Teachers in the Developing World: Who Controls the Agenda?

BILL TAYLOR AND ALAN PEACOCK

## Introduction

One of the first things which strikes anyone who has observed the preparation of teachers world-wide over recent decades is the lack of agreement about priorities, both between countries and over time within countries. Differences exist about whether training should take place predominantly in the schools or in higher education institutions; whether the focus should be predominantly on knowledge of subjects or on pedagogical skills; levels of entry and exit; the balance between initial and in-service training; and the relative emphasis on preparation for primary, secondary, vocational and higher education.

The second thing which strikes an observer is the difficulty of bringing about change in schools and in the institutions which are responsible for educating the teachers who staff them. Many staff now responsible for teacher training around the world were themselves trained by people who went to primary school in the 1940s and 1950s. In the developing world, this means during the colonial regimes and the era of mission schools. It is hardly surprising, therefore, that the ethos of many primary schools and classrooms still reflects a culture different from that which children and teachers inhabit outside the school. Primary education (and particularly teachers' salaries in most developing countries) constitutes one of the largest drains on government expenditure. Changes

with apparently minor cost implications can have a major impact on national budgets.

This chapter seeks to consider some of the pros and cons of involving expatriate resources in the preparation of a country's educational staff. In particular, it is concerned with the involving of personnel from a so-called developed country in the professional development of schoolteachers and administrators in a so-called developing or underdeveloped country. It is based largely on the authors' considerable experience in Anglophone Africa and Asia. The ideas are drawn from our experiences working in initial and in-service teacher education, both in the UK and overseas.

The certification of a nation's professional teachers is a matter for that particular country, yet the routes by which this certification is achieved suggest that, in the past at least, politicians have been more concerned with increasing the number of certificate holders than with looking too closely at what trainees are learning, especially in the hidden curriculum, when expatriate cash and staff are involved. However, there are signs that, in some contexts, concern for quality and accreditation is an increasing priority.

The chapter is divided into two major sections (written respectively by Bill Taylor and Alan Peacock), which view the professional preparation of teachers from differing perspectives: in-country and overseas locations, expatriate and local training personnel, external and internal funding. The concluding section seeks to draw these together, focusing on the potential for resolution of these long-standing concerns.

## External inputs under scrutiny

Half a century after the beginning of the end of Europe's imperial domination of Africa and Asia, many post-colonial nations continue to echo the educational systems they inherited. Many train their teachers in a variety of programmes which rely directly or indirectly on expatriate inputs, often from their former imperial rulers. Oil wealth has enabled countries like Nigeria and Malaysia to participate at both initial and postgraduate levels, in what are claimed to be 'specially designed' UK-based courses, fashioned to meet the needs of the post-colonial independent country, ostensibly identified by that country. But all too often, they are crudely disguised versions of courses created for UK trainees to satisfy UK government requirements for employment in UK schools. Parallels to this can be found in France and the USA. This suggests a *prima facie* form of neo-colonialism. The real cost to the overseas trainee may be much greater than the financial cost of the tuition fee.

While this chapter is based on experience in Anglophone Africa and Asia and with teachers who will work in the primary, secondary or tertiary sectors, there seems to be considerable evidence from educational policies of international agencies and sponsors as well as those of other European imperial nations to suggest that former colonies are psychologically and linguistically, if not financially, partly dependent on their nineteenth-century colonial rulers for increasing their teacher numbers and raising their professionalism, locking their teachers into the cultural imperialism of language, textbook production and the latest educational fad or innovation in the aid-supplying country. The universality of the English language for commercial discourse in part legitimizes this. Teachers who are trained overseas are expected to spearhead innovation on their return home, but paradoxically they can become reactionary forces, in that they can prevent home-grown creativity if it deviates from what they have experienced in the country of their training.

A trawl of the literature, including academic journals, reveals that thousands of articles and books have been written since the 1960s about how educational services have expanded and evolved in the post-colonial world, but little space has been devoted to the preparation of and status of the teachers, and more especially to the involvement of expatriates in this preparation. Sharpes (1988) collected papers by native writers from five continents; these offer descriptive commentaries about teacher education without confronting awkward ideological or theoretical issues, and seem almost relieved to end up saying that the quantity of teacher training has expanded despite the paucity of local resources. King (1991) reported Canadian research about academic investigations in education by scholars in the developing world, but made no link between this and preparation for classroom effectiveness. Graham-Brown (1991) stressed the centrality of teacher education before glossing over it when considering developments in Latin America's schooling, and also implied a self-evident benefit to the region's children if their teachers were trained on American lines. Sharpes's contributors seem sensitive to the caution offered by Englishman Michael Sadler in 1902 about the futility of wandering through the world's educational gardens and picking stems, leaves and flowerheads at random in the hope that by gluing them together and sticking them in some foreign soil they will survive as the embodiment of a new perfection. This caution is as relevant today in the context of teacher education as it was 95 years ago for education in general, and is as apposite for the post-colonial world as it was for the age of imperialism. Yet the simplistic notion survives among many politicians and even professional educators that one particular country can improve by copying the practices of another country. In 1986, the education department of the University of Dar es Salaam introduced comparative education (Taylor, 1986) to master's-level courses for headteachers in an attempt to get them to be less dependent on the educational ideology of the major aid providers. (Tanzania had been influenced by Marxism, not least via East Germany and

China, having been influenced by the British and the Germans in colonial times.) The idea was to encourage a more indigenous response, but the programme was aided and delivered by British aid money, and therefore potentially ran the risk of perpetuating dependence. Watson (1991) offered a perceptive comment on the continuing parochialism of many teacher training courses throughout the world, arguing that cultural and economic interdependence and transnational mobility are increasing and that this would seem to require teacher training to have an international dimension. He does not say whether this internationalizing of teachers can be done without multinational teams of trainers, but if mononational teams suffice in European and American countries why can't they do so in African and Asian ones too?

Two particular programmes, one from the 1970s and the other from the 1990s, the former involving Nigeria and the latter Malaysia, will be used to highlight some substantive points. Both these countries, having strong oil-based economies, want to undertake major educational expansion by getting more students to enrol in formal schooling, from nursery to university levels and in technological and vocational as well as academic education. Both have used their wealth to seek partnerships with foreign countries in order to meet their ambitious targets and to pay for their nationals to study overseas.

Nigeria's Hausa–Fulani northern states had had fewer educational opportunities than the Igbo–Yoruba south, so they sent students to do BEd courses in the UK – just to get a degree in education. A poor command of English and perpetual cash-flow problems (Taylor, 1980, 1984), together with the fact that the Nigerians took precisely the same course as did the British students, choosing their teaching subject (e.g. religious studies, which was mostly Christian even though the students were all Muslims) with a view to securing a pass grade rather than with a view to using it in a direct way on their return to Nigeria, caused countless frustrations for Nigerian and fellow-British students as well as for their university tutors. None the less, degree-holding teachers were rare in northern Nigeria, and so on their return home, the new BEds, unlike their young British equivalents, were not assigned to ordinary classroom subject-teaching posts but were given posts of responsibility as headteachers, inspectors and ministry officials, even though their BEds had not equipped them with the administrative insights and techniques such jobs require. There is circumstantial evidence to suggest that this practice continues. When they were asked about their reaction to being selected by their state ministry to study in the UK, the most common responses from the Nigerian BEd students were personal, social and economic rather than professional or national. They took it for granted that, having been selected, they would succeed academically, and their career success would be guaranteed by pleasing the ministry. When some southern Igbo states began to participate in the programme, inter-ethnic rivalry became an issue in British classrooms. Few British tutors were able or willing to deal with this, and their normal reaction was to ignore it; they concentrated on their trainees as technocrats who had to acquire classroom competence. This ignored the real world in which the graduates would be working on their return home. All too often, British tutors were unable to see overseas students as persons, blinding themselves by the students' nationality or some other huge suprapersonal categorization.

The 1990s programme with Malaysia is much more sophisticated. Details of course content, assessment and ethos have been carefully worked out by ministry and college staff in both Malaysia and the UK. Two years of the four-year BEd programme are spent in each of the two countries. But all teacher training is done in a societal context. If a teacher were merely a walking encyclopaedia with excellent text and illustrations, then training anywhere could ensure that teachers could be authoritative in their subject knowledge and range of pedagogic styles. However, the teaching–learning dynamic is complex and sophisticated, and transferability across cultural–national frontiers of covert and semi-covert agendas can create negative as well as positive consequences. Expatriate teacher trainers may not have given students adequate opportunities to confront this.

The popularity of 'twinning programmes', whereby a Malaysian institution is partnered with an overseas one in order jointly to deliver courses that will result in an overseas academic qualification, is now *de rigeur*. Malaysia is awash with expatriate educational consultants from many countries, and many Malaysians are studying overseas on Malaysian government scholarships. The Malaysian and Islamic contexts are explicitly built into the British BEd programmes. Thirty 20-year-old Malaysian BEd students, training to be teachers of English as a second language, were asked to complete questionnaires in order to provide this chapter with some up-to-date illuminative (not statistical) data; returns were received from 24 of them. The most common answer to 'Why did you apply to get on this course?' was 'to become a better teacher of English in Malaysia'. This dedication to participative professionalism contrasts dramatically with the responses when the question was put twenty years previously to the Hausa students. Asked why they had applied to study in the UK, the Hausas gave the following responses: to ensure a secure job (four); to get a British degree (four); to become an efficient teacher (four); to improve colleagues in Nigeria (four); to learn a variety of teaching styles (five); to become confident in English usage (six); to get better tutoring while training (seven); to become more socially mature (nine).

Singh and Mukherjee (1993), two Indian Malaysians, offer a comprehensive account of educational developments in tri-ethnic Malaysia without making any reference to the preparation of teachers or the career prospects of teachers of different ethnicity. Unfortunately, their bibliography is virtually all from the 1960s. Ministry publications from Kuala Lumpur offer slightly more up-to-date comment on the extent to which teacher training courses explicitly address multiethnicity and equal opportunities (Malaysia Ministry of Education, 1982, 1994). It is courageous of Singh and Mukherjee to deal extensively with the ethnic dimension, since the official line in the country is that legislation ensures inter-ethnic harmony; in reality there is considerable tension just below the surface. The twinning teacher education programmes try to ensure that there are no ethnic injustices in the selection of students, but the extent to which expatriate selectors have any moral right to get even marginally involved in social engineering – taking sides with one politician or another – is dubious, and raises profound questions about whether the programme is only about training teachers of English.

Every 'foreign' student (including, say, a British student in the USA) experiences a culture shock when away from home. There is circumstantial evidence to suggest that the Malaysian student's ethnicity is an important factor in her or his adaptation to British culture. Many of the questionnaires indicated that the students had been strongly influenced by their parents in deciding to apply for a place on the programme. While living and studying in the UK, they experience the normal adjustments any young student does on moving from a rural to an urban environment, from the parental home to self-catering accommodation and to being in a country whose climate and customs pose daily challenges. The young Muslim Malay woman who stops wearing her chador may be making no more a dramatic adaptation than her Indian or Chinese compatriot who develops a liking for fish and chips. Dropping her veil may not mean rejecting her religious convictions. The openly critical atmosphere of a British university coffee bar is far removed from the oppressively polite atmosphere of a country where public criticism is muted or indirect and where tolerance is easily protested as long as no one deviates from agreed norms. No research has been undertaken to determine how students from overseas deal with their memories and experiences when they return home at the end of their overseas studies, but anecdotal evidence from postgraduate students, e.g. from the Middle East, suggests that they need to be diplomatic when they try to apply to their work situations what they have learned while overseas, especially if they consider that some of their most significant learning was from the covert curriculum which had challenged their attitudes and beliefs. This muddle may be too high a price to pay for an overseas degree. Their emotions, beliefs and relationships may have changed irrevocably.

Their political sponsors may or may not be aware of these dilemmas.

'Equal opportunities' has been a central value in British teacher education for decades, and there is a tendency to see this ideology in absolutist rather than cultural-relativist terms. This often is the biggest moral challenge during their BEd training overseas and they have to rely on their personal guile and diplomacy when applying that dimension to their teaching on their return home, as gender roles are defined and redefined more by national tradition than by foreign influence. Presumably, the powerful politicians who initiate and fund overseas study programmes are aware of the power and omnipresence of these complex dynamics, and do not expect their young compatriots to be immune to the socio-ethical environments in which they are studying. Are politicians expecting the returning well-certificated young teachers to revert to their former selves, or be radically different, or demonstrate a range of subtle adaptations? What is expected to be cascaded down to pupils' schools, apart from English accents?

The education process, from pre-school to university and beyond, is a socio-political as well as cognitive dynamic. Its purpose is to improve an individual's understanding of the world. Behavioural modification is an explicit and visible consequence, without which the acquisition of new knowledge would be somewhat arid. The major moulder of this process is the teacher, who filters the knowledge and uses supporting resources to develop students. At a macro level, politicians control many of the resources; at the micro level, teachers are in fact the controllers, as it is they who select what to use in the classroom context. Schools and their teaching staff are therefore at the sharp edge of converting rhetoric and political intention into specific practice, both within classrooms and schools and, less directly, within the individual careers of the school leavers. The teacher determines the nature of the schooling process.

Therefore, is it wise to share the training of teachers with expatriates who are likely to be accustomed to different resources and political controls? The ascribing of worth to knowledge is culturally contextual. Can foreigners participate in this? If developing countries continue to ask for help from developed countries, has colonialism merely been replaced with neo-colonialism? Are ideological creeds like Marxism or American consumerism any less imperialistic than were the religious or the civilizing ones of the nineteenth-century Europeans? Ideology underpins everything a teacher does, as it determines the value put on knowledge. Politicians and religious leaders determine some of these values, but teacher training expatriates are also potential determiners. For centuries, there has been a universal use of mantra chanting as the bedrock of teaching methodology, memorizing as the bedrock of learning methodology and regurgitation as the bedrock of assessment. The crews of eighteenth-century European trading ships taught their new business partners by similar methods, satisfied with establishing minimum accountancy and literary skills that would support their commercial traffic. Later, Christian missionaries believed that a convert's hope of eternal salvation would be greatly enhanced by learning to read the Bible. The nineteenth-century imperial rulers offered only schooling to attainment levels and to the numbers of students they required in order to staff the middle and lower ranks of their civil services. With the virtual end of the imperial age in the 1960s, politicians in newly independent nation states expected that education and therefore schoolteaching would help to nation-build by developing the self-esteem of young citizens. Vestiges of the colonial models of training teachers – very often by expatriate mission staff who were not trained teachers – remain. Various agencies have always funded short in-service courses in developing countries that are staffed by tutors from the developed world, hoping perhaps to update local teachers' knowledge about such things as e-mail and personal computers – even though the chances of such technology being available in the teacher's school are minimal in the foreseeable future. Information technology (IT) is coveted as an essential skill in the modern world, but many teachers in Africa and Asia are working in schools where pupils have no opportunity to acquire IT skills. Even basic utilities such as electricity and running water are unavailable in many schools. Expatriate trainers and training overseas may be similar to training in IT, in that they can offer extra-parochial and futuristic opportunities. There are more immediate educational challenges to confront in the real world of actual schools in developing countries.

Forms of colonial dependence persist in the post-colonial world. Some syllabuses and examinations remain closely linked to those in the former imperial power. There may be a fear of developing new styles of teaching, learning and testing lest they be accused of lowering standards. The view that maths, technology and science are culturally neutral may have deterred the jettisoning of content inherited from overseas. By giving adult literacy centre stage, Tanzania bravely set an educational agenda to address its own priorities, but it relied heavily on expatriate tutors and teaching materials from agencies such as the British Council.

Although there are accusations of incompetence and corruption in Africanized trans-state matriculation examination boards, these bodies have been major curriculum innovators, especially in language and social studies. They have become increasingly involved in adapting most school subjects to incorporate regional culture. But it took decades before the politicians, administrators and teachers who control WASC (West Africa School Certificate) dared to deviate too far from London GCE procedures and syllabuses, the preponderance of expatriate examiners giving the Africans at worst an inferiority complex and a willingness to be passive, at best an impatience to trial their own materials. Even such internationally reputed Nigerian authors as Achebe and Soyinka had to wait impatiently to dethrone Dickens and Wordsworth in Nigeria's English literature syllabus. Teachers therefore need to be trained to be confident enough to participate in the organic adaptation that requires school courses to reflect both local and international scholarship.

It is accepted in most developed countries that a teacher is expected to be 'professional', dedicated to imparting authoritative and worthwhile knowledge to others, to a life-long personal development of insights into the behaviour of learners and their career aspirations, to comprehending his or her young students by knowing more about school –family dynamics and home culture. A developing nation will benefit less, it may be argued, from school leavers who can repeat mantras than from those who are imaginative, confident and creative. Teachers need to be trained to develop these qualities, and this does not necessarily require expatriate trainers. To acquire a counselling postgraduate qualification from some overseas university or to study social education in some foreign country may be more academic than practical in value, as what constitutes normal behaviour and what explains abnormal behaviour in a classroom needs to be understood in its social context. Yet virtually every school counsellor in Nigeria has been trained either overseas or in a local university whose staff have been trained overseas, begging fundamental questions about whether the principles that underlie the practice of counselling in, say, the USA can equally apply to a society whose culture is substantially different from that of the USA.

Few teachers get adequate training in the reflective non-ending process. Small teacher training colleges are usually poorly resourced and poorly staffed and have seldom provided their young trainees with the skills and insights of self-appraisal essential to their professionalism. They offer a culture that is enormously different from that of the teacher training degree-bearing courses in overseas institutions where trainees take for granted an infrastructure which seldom exists in their home context. The sophisticated thinking encouraged by academics in developed-world institutions seldom percolates through to school practice level in developing countries. Students need survival skills to help them to make use of their training and prevent them from becoming overwhelmed by the pressures of the immediate moment. Ideally, teachers should be loyal to their own sense of professionalism and their pupils' needs, but some have to operate within the diktats of religious and political leaders. How many teacher training courses, whether inside or outside the trainee's country, present students with systematic opportunities to examine the ethical dimension of their work? Should this be avoided because it is potentially embarrassing, or is this being cowardly and dishonest?

The answer will depend on the country as well as the individual teacher. If there is no tradition of teacher or institutional development, much of the contemporary ideology underpinning initial teacher training in the UK (as enshrined in DFE circulars such as DFE 9/92, 14/93) will be irrelevant. Indeed, the absence of such opportunities could add to the frustration of overseas students, who would like their home schools to resemble those they have worked in as trainees in the UK. Questions like 'What is best for the child?' are political as well as philosophical, being answered by laws and customs, not by foreign academics. But such questions are often not asked at all. Study at master's level can only be classroom-based or child-focused to the extent that the macro-political context makes it possible, and a doctoral dissertation that satisfies the criteria for a UK degree may not be perceived as having practical or direct value by the power holders in the author's country. If the overall culture in that country is that change occurs in schools only when ministry or external officials dictate it, individual teachers will not be encouraged to think deeply about such matters. Indeed, they may be afraid that comment by them would be perceived as subversive. Many schools in the developing world have no ethos of open discourse. Passivity towards the state's imposed system is the predominant culture. Should education tutors in the UK therefore be fostering in their overseas students a pragmatism, one that will help them to contribute to evolutionary change and reduce their frustration or anger when they try but fail to make radical or immediate innovation? Giddens's (1984) theory of structuration, which locates real power in the principles that a 'system' is built on, demonstrates dramatically how a solitary teacher trained overseas is doomed to have no impact of consequence on any substantive aspect of a school's culture. Systems are more powerful than persons, especially persons in the lower ranks of a hierarchy.

The centrality of the traditional 'ologies' (psychology, sociology, history, philosophy) in the educational studies of teacher training courses, legitimized as a way of providing a secure theoretical base to teachers' work in schools, disappeared in the UK a decade ago but continues to dominate most teacher preparation courses in Asia and Africa. Practice-located learning inside schools is now the preferred orthodoxy for giving the trainee teacher a sense of the value of theory to the development of professionalism (Elliott, 1993). Hence more initial teacher training in the UK is now located inside the schools and the conventional teaching practice is only one of a number of ways in which the trainee learns about the schooling process and the school as an institution. Training the new teacher has become a joint responsibility, schools being full partners with institutions of higher education in identifying and responding to the learning needs of the aspiring teacher. The overseas student who is trained in this milieu may return home to work alongside a teacher who has been trained in a cocooned college with an 'ologies' curriculum and an end-of-course one-term traditional teaching practice. Being trained to think of teaching as keeping a class of about 50 fixed to their desks, working on writing and reading tasks most of the time, is radically different from being trained to be a manager and facilitator of the learning of about 20 children who can chatter and move about the classroom in order to consult reference books and other resources, and produce acceptable work which is not a verbatim reflection of the teacher's dictation.

The substantive issues raised so far could apply equally to courses taught inside the student's home country by expatriates who are invited as distinguished consultants or visiting professors. Neither student nor tutor can divorce theoretical learning from cultural locus when seeking to apply it, and this needs to be central and explicit to training courses in order to make everyone conscious of the importance of the intercultural dynamic. Using as teacher trainers only tutors of the same nationality and ethnicity as the trainees is not necessarily the answer, especially when the expatriate tutor may indeed possess superior substantive knowledge.

## Internal influences

This section draws on case studies from various African states to examine the major influences on change in teacher education, and concludes by focusing on the way such change is currently being brought about in South Africa.

In 1976, Kenya introduced a new and radically different primary school syllabus, supported by new materials for teachers and pupils which had been developed in Kenya with the support of international consultants. At the same time, the primary teaching force was being rapidly expanded to cope with the introduction of free universal primary schooling, and the population growth rate was around 4 per cent per annum. The 1976 report of the National Committee on Educational Objectives and Policies (NCEOP) noted that there were then 35,000 untrained teachers, of whom 12,000 had received only primary or junior secondary education; and that these teachers 'were not trained in methodology and were lacking in content' (Republic of Kenya, 1976). The primary teachers' colleges for initial teacher education were being rapidly expanded with the help of aid funding for both staff and resources, but there was little provision for in-service training. Staff who worked in primary teachers' colleges were almost entirely graduates who had never taught in primary schools themselves and who found the new concepts of child-centred learning, groupwork and problem-solving alien to their culture and experience. Since the 'coffee boom' of the mid-1970s in Kenya, on which much of the expansion was based, the economy has gradually deteriorated through adverse fluctuations in commodity prices and, in popular belief, through corruption and mismanagement, culminating in the early 1990s in a suspension of much international aid to education as a means of pressurizing the government into appropriate action. Prospects for the further development of teacher education are therefore not good.

By contrast, Botswana, the most economically successful state in Africa during the past twenty years, has invested heavily in primary education since independence, increasing its recurrent expenditure from 1 million to 155 million pula in that period. From 1962 to 1988, primary enrolments rose fivefold, from 46,500 to 236,000. The primary teaching force expanded even more quickly in the same period, from 1300 teachers to 7300. Even so, the proportion of primary teachers without training, which reached 41 per cent in 1977, was still 18 per cent in 1988, despite a tenfold increase in the number of teachers in training. During the same period, the number of teachers without a classroom to work in rose from 1815 to 2135 (Republic of Botswana, 1990). Botswana has developed a successful system of in-service training through teacher advisers, and has benefited from curriculum initiatives in universities in neighbouring South Africa, where Setswana, the language of majority, is also a major language. There is thus considerable potential within the country for the further development of teacher education.

Both Kenya and Botswana have been committed to eradicating untrained teachers from primary schools as a matter of national policy. This is a major focus of policy in teacher education in both countries. But in both countries, in the past decade, there have also been other major changes in the structure of education. Kenya adopted the 8:4:4 system, which increased the length of primary education from seven to eight compulsory years. Botswana incorporated the two years of junior secondary education into the compulsory basic phase in the mid-1980s, making nine years instead of seven, with a recent increase to ten years. The agenda in both cases was the upgrading of the quality of education for those pupils (the large majority, in both countries) who would not proceed beyond the primary/basic phase. Departmental heads in ministries thus have key roles in changing teacher education, insofar as they are instrumental in influencing budgets and deciding on allocations. For example, in Botswana, the balance of emphasis between initial training and in-service training appears likely to be decided at this level.

However, there are other less obvious but potentially more powerful influences, such as the international aid community, the economy and employment prospects, the teaching force itself and the historical mind-sets of those who make the training system work. Primary teacher education in Anglophone Africa is nominally a part of higher education. Traditionally, the aid-giving community in the industrialized world has funded higher education extensively. In Kenya, for example, it has been instrumental in establishing the Kenya Science Teachers' College and the Kenya Technical Teachers' College, as well as heavily supporting the work of the old-established universities of Nairobi and Kenyatta. Aid has also funded expatriate staff in core subjects in all the 20 or so primary teachers' colleges. However, following the World Conference on Education for All in Thailand (WCEFA, 1990), most donors accepted the new priority of 'meeting basic learning needs', and made policy decisions to prioritize the basic phase of education, at the expense of funding for higher education. The Overseas Development Administration's (ODA's) latest policy document on aid to education states that 'the weight of recent evidence demonstrates that investment in primary education yields the best economic returns' (ODA, 1990). It goes on to say that teacher education 'lies at the centre of quality improvement'. Yet, in practice, the actual effect of the prosecution of aid policy by the ODA since 1990 has been to reduce aid to primary teacher education in Kenya, as a consequence of reductions in the emphasis on higher education, and an earlier overemphasis on the funding of specialist science and technical schools and training institutions. The agenda is thus in part controlled by those who make decisions about aid funding.

Economic factors influence the agenda in subtle as well as macro ways. For example, in Kenya, the shortage of aid funds has led to a gradual deterioration in the resource base of teacher education, provision of books and journals and payments to staff, to a shortage of vehicles and fuel for visiting schools, to unreliability of telephone and electricity and hence problems with computers and photocopiers. Low wages of academic staff in university faculties of education have led to disputes with government about union representation. Strikes have developed, staff have been evicted from campus housing and teachers involved in mentoring have not been paid for their work; this

at a time when the new BEd programmes mentioned above are beginning to be implemented for a new non-A-level entry from the 8:4:4 system, with the consequent demand on staff for writing of new course materials for a new and much larger student population. The agenda for many local teacher educators is currently more about personal economic and status issues than about curriculum and methods of training.

In Botswana, on the other hand, economic stability and expansion has allowed experimentation with teacher education. Teachers' centres have been established and are used as the bases for workshops run by teacher advisers. An effective structure for classroom support for teachers has been developed. Expansion of the teaching force at the top end of the basic phase has been carried out by recruiting expatriate teachers on competitive salaries. New community junior secondary schools (for Years 8 and 9) have been built, and incorporate design features appropriate to innovative ways of teaching, such as groupwork and resource-based learning. New teachers' colleges have been built. The physical and human resource infrastructure has been high on the national agenda.

However, the administrative structure has been slow to respond to these developments, largely as a consequence of the cultural mind-set engendered by previous colonial administrative methods. A major obstacle in this respect is, for example, the rigidity of the link established between the initial certification of teachers and their subsequent status in the profession. It is a problem common to many Anglophone states in Africa, and seriously inhibits the development of quality teaching, by preventing poorly qualified but expert teachers (usually in primary schools) from progressing into training roles, while ensuring that training remains in the hands of better-qualified staff with little or no primary teaching experience. The reasons behind this rigidity are probably economic. Salaries are linked to initial qualifications, and therefore any change which allows good practitioners with poor qualifications to progress up the career ladder would have serious cost implications. The impact is to prevent good practitioners from being promoted, which diminishes the quality of training.

A crucial example, pointed to by several recent studies in Botswana (Taylor and Sims, 1989; Sutton and Elliott, 1991; Peacock, 1992), is the failure of the ministry to create a career structure for teacher advisers. Many of these highly skilled trainers are having to return to primary schools in order to be promoted; hence their training skills are lost to the system. Even though many of them operate from teachers' centres based in primary teachers' colleges, their links with initial teacher education are minimal, because as good primary practitioners they lack the initial high level of certification which enables them to qualify to work in colleges. Hence cross-fertilization between initial and in-service training is minimal or non-existent. A change would involve at least three departments within the ministry; would have cost implications through the creation of new steps on the career ladder; and, most of all, would imply a different perspective on the notion of how qualifications define the calibre of a teacher.

The idea of accrediting in-service training provided by teacher advisers is still not on the agenda. Aid for accredited training is still largely channelled through the conventional institutions. This suits both ministries and aid providers. The dilemma for aid agencies may well be how to find acceptable mechanisms for channelling aid to primary schools for accredited in-service training of teachers, and similarly to 'training of trainers', without going directly to higher education to provide it. Accreditation will continue to be important, however, since high on the agenda of governments will always be the need to control upward budgetary drift in the salary bill for teachers. Linking salary increases to qualifications seems likely to remain the only acceptable way of doing this in the foreseeable future.

To what extent do teachers themselves influence the agenda of teacher training? In most African states, initial teacher education for the basic phase has been little influenced by teachers, since few primary teachers have ever found their way on to the staffs of teachers' colleges or into the relevant departments of ministries. This is changing slowly in both Kenya and Botswana at present,

through the recruitment of some primary teachers on to BEd programmes in universities. Teacher education is still perceived as being constructed of curriculum subjects taught theoretically, backed up by 'instructional methods' courses and limited school experience, akin to UK courses of thirty years ago. Tutors and students alike place a high value on the academic content of training courses. However, the academic qualifications of trainee primary teachers are often very poor, some having had no more than basic education themselves, and many having difficulties with English. New models of training, and new materials to go with them, are still not on the agenda, even though many teachers openly ignore the requirement to teach in English and revert to vernacular languages.

Teachers influence the training agenda, then, largely by defining negatively what is possible. The level at which teachers are recruited is a key factor in this; yet as long as teachers' salaries and conditions remain poor by comparison with, say, those of other public-sector employees, it will be difficult to foresee a rise in the calibre of the intake (Makau and Coombe, 1994). Motivation to teach better is an essential precursor to benefiting from training. Such motivation is lacking for many teachers, particularly in primary schools and particularly in rural areas. Yet there remain occasional isolated examples of excellence which give inspiration and ideas to trainers and students, such as the work of Githinji (1992) in Kenya. As a primary teacher, Githinji shaped thinking about the use of the school environment for teaching, and this work led directly to the production of new materials for trainers.

Thus what is feasible is influenced by policy-makers, aid providers, ministries, trainers themselves and teachers. What happens when all these agencies have a high stake in the training agenda, as in South Africa at the present time?

South Africa has in many ways a developed-world infrastructure in higher education, research and curriculum development, yet it faces the daunting prospect of creating, almost from scratch, a system of developing-world basic education for the traditionally disenfranchised population. In 1991, in the rural and homeland areas, 69 per cent of children were not in school. There was a shortage of over 50,000 teachers and over 80,000 classrooms. Some 68 per cent of teachers in some homelands were not qualified (Cole and Flanagan, 1994). Such statistics are worse than those in any neighbouring black African states for the same period (Jansen, 1994).

Policy on primary education and training is set out in the White Paper of September 1994 (Republic of South Africa, 1994). This makes clear that there will be ten years of compulsory, free, basic education for all, and that priority will be given to early-years education (grades 0 to 3) as well as to disadvantaged communities, i.e. rural and farm schools and schools in the former self-governing territories (homelands). The intention is to develop a 'culture of active learning' using new modes for teaching and learning; in order to achieve this, the government sees 'teacher education (including the professional education of trainers and educators) as one of the central pillars of national human resource development strategy' (Cole and Flanagan, 1994).

There are currently around 130 government-run institutions involved in teacher education in South Africa, of which over 100 are primary teachers' colleges. These colleges have exceptionally high unit costs (higher than those of universities and technikons), and there are gross disparities in the quality of provision, according to the African National Congress's own research (ANC, 1994). Thus the White Paper expects that methods of financing higher education beyond the compulsory level will have to be reformed. There will need to be an upgrading of the professional skills of teachers and teacher trainers, but at no increase in unit costs over current systems. Partners in the process will have to contribute, by which is explicitly meant the non-governmental organization (NGO) sector, aid donors and students themselves. There will have to be a redesigned approach to both initial and in-service education of teachers, creating flexibility and meeting the need for vastly increased numbers of qualified teachers. Distance learning methods are to be encouraged, and the many NGOs currently involved in in-service provision are also to be encouraged to continue to provide accredited in-service training (INSET). Responsibility for development of this hugely am-

bitious programme will be shared between the Ministry of Education and Training, a National Council for Teacher Education (NCTE) and a new National Qualifications Framework (NQF) (Republic of South Africa, 1994).

The ANC, as the ruling party in seven of the nine regions, has established its priorities for the reform of teacher education. It has been heavily influenced by personnel, many of whom, during the apartheid years, worked in higher education and training in neighbouring black Africa or in the developed world. But unlike many of the national commissions of neighbouring countries, South Africa has made plain its intention to democratize the process of policy development in education and training. The same phenomenon is apparent within NGOs responsible (independently, up to now) for in-service training, where stress has been placed on participatory management and the involvement of teachers; for example, in materials development for in-service work (Raubenheimer, 1994a, b).

Hence the priorities for teacher education in South Africa are being set not only by the organs of the new government, but also by a wide range of vested interests, not least of which will soon be the teachers and students themselves, politicized as they have been by the events of the past twenty years in a way which has no parallel in Africa. Vehicles for the expression of their views are now emerging. Some radical proposals are arising from this process. For example, one proposal for breaking out of the cycle of mediocrity in science and mathematics education involves an expensive plan to provide a free teacher training year to all those who fail science and maths at the last hurdle of matriculation, on the grounds that this well educated resource cannot be justifiably lost to the system (Kahn, 1994).

Contacts between teacher educators and administrators in South Africa and experienced professionals in teacher education in neighbouring states were almost non-existent during the years of apartheid, and therefore the wish to learn from such experiences through new contacts is strong. Such contacts will inevitably contribute to shaping the agenda of reform in the coming years, particularly in the case of the experiences of Botswana, Namibia, Lesotho and Swaziland, with their common linguistic and socio-political backgrounds and their economic links through Southern African Development Cooperation Council (SADCC). Events such as the recent Commonwealth Association conference in Botswana have become important in bringing South African policy-makers and teacher educators into contact with their counterparts in neighbouring countries, often for the first time. Interest is also being shown in other links; for example, between traditional pedagogy and in-service strategies (Peacock, 1994).

Thus a wide range of interest groups is potentially ready to take part in the process of shaping the development of teacher education in South Africa, not least of which are the aid agencies, who will probably be invited to fund a good deal of the expansion and development. Yet many of the difficulties encountered in other African states may also be encountered in South Africa. In a country unused to administering education nationally, a major problem in the short term is likely to be that of obtaining an accurate and comprehensive picture of what is going on. Projects and initiatives developed in the separate regions may well repeat the mistakes of earlier developments elsewhere.

Finally, the teacher education question is bound up with the question of medium of instruction. The currently favoured gradual transition from mother tongue has big implications for the production of materials for use in teacher education, as well as for the schools themselves. As in many other neighbouring states, the 'training of trainers' has been long neglected, and thus the combination of poor-quality trainers working with out-of-date and inappropriate materials is one that cannot quickly or easily be overcome. Distance learning is a much favoured approach for mass delivery of teacher upgrading; but the correspondence course models for this which exist in South Africa are not appropriate to the professional skill development of teachers.

The recent White Paper has attempted to establish clear and widely acceptable priorities, but has had little to say in detail; for example, about INSET. Policy documents emanating from various unofficial sources have attempted to fill this gap,

stressing the importance of early-years education, adult basic education, science and technology education and primary INSET. The effectiveness of any imposed change is always constrained by the willingness and capacity of trainers to implement the changes. The move towards more professional teacher education is inevitably going to be an expensive process, probably involving collaboration with outside agencies. Already, moves are being made by NGOs to develop collaborative, accredited in-service programmes (Glover, 1994). Such programmes at their best are only reaching 10 per cent of teachers at present. Prioritizing a huge increase in emphasis on training trainers will thus be dependent on commitment of funds from central government, regional administrations and donor agencies. Is this the real agenda?

## Conclusion

In looking at the roles played by developed countries in the training of teachers in developing countries, the two contributions in this chapter highlight the tension between policy appearances and practical actuality. For example, the way international aid agencies determine funding priorities which seek to meet their own foreign policy goals can certainly be seen as neo-colonialism. Yet the way in which expatriate professionals employed by these agencies execute their work is often highly context-specific and responsive to local needs. The reasons for sending students overseas for training are often determined by non-educational priorities, as has been shown; their ability to meet local needs on their return is often severely constrained by logistical and environmental circumstances. Vestiges of colonial attitudes are still as often embodied in local staff (now often in powerful positions) who came through colonial or mission schools as they are in expatriate staff. Experience, position and orientation, rather than cultural origin, could be seen as the factors most influencing teacher education.

Many governments in developing countries are thus faced with the dilemma of resolving the need for quality training, as supported by expatriate expertise, with the need for relevance, as defined by local personnel working within the often obvious faults and failings of existing systems. An ethical dilemma implicit in both contributions is evident in the way that some donor agencies continue to provide support to some countries, knowing full well that their inputs stand little chance of being effective on the ground because of local constraints.

The contributions both draw attention to discrepancies in what is seen as valued knowledge. Deficiencies in the older overseas BEd courses, through which African students learned to teach in the way that UK students learned, have been highlighted. But the African students now coming to the UK are much more likely to study management and governance of schools at master's level or to do higher degrees by research which have a substantive focus within their own system. On returning, they will usually occupy academic and administrative roles, while the professional development of teachers and trainers themselves is now largely done in-country, through locally developed programmes. Even where these local programmes are externally funded and supported, expatriate staff involved have typically had many years of experience in a developing-world context, so that in-service is not extra-parochial, futuristic and geared to technical gadgetry, but down to earth and concerned with locally prepared materials and day-to-day problems. The danger, however, is of a separation between the policy-oriented, externally trained decision-makers and the practice-oriented, classroom-based teachers and their trainers, in line with their concomitant differences in value systems.

Our Western view is that teaching is both an art and a craft. Teachers are expected to be imaginative, creative artists as well as skilled, up-to-date technocrats. Teaching is seen as a profession for which teachers are educated rather than trained; hence the dilemma of both authors throughout this chapter in their choice of terminology. Teachers share an ethos, a set of values which commits them to provide social and ethical as well as cognitive and academic guidance. These countless and elusive aspects of professionalism, which relate to

attitudes and expectations, are culturally determined: a national society's own laws and traditions determine what is and is not acceptable professionalism to that society. The updating of skill and knowledge competence can clearly be undertaken successfully by expatriates as well as indigenous staff; but for expatriates to expect ordinary teachers in developing countries to practise a form of professionalism they have been introduced to overseas or from overseas perceptions is to expect at best miracles. At worst, teachers can be expected to become revolutionaries without the drive, status, equipment or conditions to be effective in such a role.

Hence a major concern in terms of the training agenda is the need to address resource constraints (salaries, career structures, class size, provision of materials, classrooms), which are seen by teachers and trainers as the main inhibitors of change. The contextual nature of professionalism for teachers also means that certifying teachers is not simply a matter of minimal competence, but of helping them learn to behave professionally, which is relative, not absolute. Attempts to modify teachers' professionalism may therefore be best addressed by local staff, but in partnership with professionals from varying backgrounds and agencies, so that the resource constraints and policy dilemmas can be simultaneously addressed. It is of paramount importance that the education and training of teachers is more realistic and explicit about the nature and role of professionalism, or there will be tragic repetitions of the all-too-common pattern of passing on Western technocracy and knowledge on the assumption that significant professional change will automatically occur. The fact that specific expatriate input is requested by the developing countries themselves does not in itself ensure that the input will be any less ethnocentrically oriented than it would be if it originated in the aid-giving country, as in the colonial era and in the early years after independence.

It is apparent from both contributions that there is a consensus about what is needed in teacher education. However, as often in developed countries, the economic and political influences on policy-makers are stronger than the educational imperatives. Teachers in most developing countries work in an economic and social environment where most pupils (including those who will become teachers themselves) will never be able to utilize the skills and knowledge valued by the system. The ethos of open discourse itself does not exist in many countries. In countries where the past few years have seen the sudden emergence of the freedom to discuss politics, the impact on education is likely to be great, if the example of the politicization of school students in South Africa over the past twenty years is anything to go by. Here, the children themselves have forced the issue of 'what is best for children' on to the teaching and training agenda.

South Africa's dilemma is particularly problematic. How will a high-technology industrial society, with First World standards in its old-established research and educational institutions, meet the sudden demand for training emanating from a low-skill workforce brought up within a rudimentary system of mass elementary education? How can funds be channelled into the improvement of mass education without destroying or severely diluting the quality of existing higher education? How will a government inexperienced in managing a national system of state education reconcile the competing agendas of external donor agencies and internal pressure groups? Education within South Africa is currently seen as the thorniest of all problems for the new administrations at both national and local levels, and within education, the development of cost-effective training for teachers is the most difficult issue to resolve.

Hence many intractable problems remain. As long as some countries lag economically behind their former colonial masters, there will be a yearning, at least among those with political and economic influence, to re-create the educational systems of these successful countries, which are so often seen (rightly or wrongly) as the key to their success. In this situation, it is difficult to buck the trend at any level, as seen in the decision of newly independent Namibia to go for Cambridge IGCSE as its form of accreditation at the end of secondary schooling, despite the examples of almost half a century earlier in the establishment of WASC in West Africa. Such a decision has enormous and inevitable implications for teacher education, and

it is difficult for any aid agency providing support for teacher education to pretend otherwise. By responding to a request for help in such a context, an aid agency is accepting the agenda of reverse neo-colonialism.

Yet at the practical level, the trend is strongly towards context-related, participatory professional development. Trainers (often themselves seconded teachers) address the concerns of classroom teachers and facilitate teacher collaboration in the development of new materials and methods, developing networks which enable teachers to enjoy mutual support and stimulation.

Such initiatives are often supported by external funding which provides specialist input in such areas as programme evaluation, but which minimally asserts control over policy. This new form of in-service teacher education, most common as yet among primary teachers, is a far cry from older models of didactic '-ology oriented' pre-service programmes, and is being seen increasingly as more cost-effective. Pre-service training in many developing countries has been recognized as being in need of serious overhaul. More than any, it is the area where policy and practice are transparently and disastrously at odds. But perhaps because of the separation between policy-makers and practitioners, the voice of teachers has not yet been heard strongly enough in this debate, and the gulf between in-service and pre-service teacher education, so apparent in many countries, has yet to be bridged.

Ethical questions about the circumstances in which teachers operate, as well as about the needs of children, still have to be brought on to the teacher education agenda in many countries. Such questions are inevitably political. Hence, where teachers are politicized, the issue is at the forefront of the government's agenda for education reform. Recent political openness in many African and Asian countries has been followed by teacher educators demanding a voice and effective representation. However, in many developing countries with predominantly rural populations, there is still no forum for political debate about teacher education. In such a context, ministries abetted by aid agencies are likely to continue to perpetuate the status quo ante with which they are comfortable, rather than risk expensive and politically threatening reform. Participatory management of training may be the rhetoric, but it is still far from being the reality.

# References

ANC (1994) *A Policy Framework for Education and Training.* Johannesburg: African National Congress.

Cole, M. and Flanagan, W. (1994) *A Policy for Quality Primary Education in South Africa.* Midrand: Development Bank of Southern Africa.

Elliott, J. (1993) What have we learned from action research in school based evaluation? *Educational Action Research,* **1** (1).

Giddens, A. (1984) *The Constitution of Society.* Cambridge: Polity Press.

Githinji, S. (1992) Using the environment for science teaching; a teacher's view from Kenya. *Perspectives,* **45**.

Glover, P. (1994) Personal communication from the National Director, Primary Science Programme, South Africa.

Graham-Brown, S. (1991) *Education in the Developing World.* New York: Longman.

Jansen, J. (1994) Inaugural address, National Conference on Primary School Curriculum Initiatives, Durban, July.

Kahn, M. (1993) *Building the Base: Report on a Sector Study of Science and Mathematics Education.* Pretoria: Commission of the European Communities.

Kahn, M. (1994) Science and mathematics curriculum reconstruction in post-apartheid South Africa. Paper presented at the CASTME Conference, Gaborone, June.

King, K. (1991) *Aid and Education in the Developing World.* New York: Longman.

Makau, B. and Coombe, C. (1994) *Teacher Morale and Motivation in Sub-Saharan Africa: Making Practical Improvements.* London: Donors to African Education Working Group, Commonwealth Secretariat.

Malaysia Ministry of Education (Educational Planning and Research) (1994) *Education in Malaysia.* Kuala Lumpur.

Malaysia Ministry of Education (Teacher Education) (1982) *The Philosophy of Teacher Education in Malaysia.* Kuala Lumpur.

ODA (1990) *Into the Nineties: An Education Policy for British Aid.* London: Overseas Development Administration.

Peacock, A (1992) *Botswana: Evaluate the 'Breakthrough to Setswana' Programme.* London: British Council.

Peacock, A. (1994) Primary science in Africa. Paper presented at the Annual Conference of the Southern African Association for Research into Mathematics and Science Education, Durban, January.

Raubenheimer, C. D. (ed.) (1994a) *Proceedings of the Second Curriculum Conference of the Primary Science Programme.* Musgrave: PSP Curriculum Development Unit.

Raubenheimer, C. D. (1994b) Shift in practice, shift in paradigm? *Southern African Journal of Mathematics and Science Education,* **1** (1), 3–20.

Republic of Botswana (1990) *Improving the Quality of Basic Education in Botswana.* Gaborone: Ministry of Education.

Republic of Kenya (1976) *Report of the National Committee on Educational Policies and Objectives.* Nairobi: Government Printer.

Republic of South Africa (1994) *Education and Training in a Democratic South Africa.* Pretoria and Cape Town: Republic of South Africa.

Sharpes, D. K. (1988) *International Perspectives on Teacher Education.* New York: Routledge.

Singh, J. S. and Mukherjee, H. (1993) Education and national integration in Malaysia: stocktaking thirty years after independence. *International Journal of Educational Development,* **13** (2), 89–102.

Sutton, E. and Elliott, N. (1991) *Report on the Principles and Practice of Teacher Advising.* London: British Council.

Taylor, H. J. S. and Sims, K. (1989) *Report on the Education Seminar on Principles and Practice of Teacher Advising.* London: British Council.

Taylor, W. H. (1980) British university BEd courses and the education of Nigerian students. *West African Journal of Education,* **21** (3), 25–37.

Taylor, W. H. (1984) Non-academic pressures on Nigerian BEd students in the UK. *Journal of Further and Higher Education,* **8** (2), 65–81.

Taylor, W. H. (1986) Comparative education – a luxury or a necessity in Tanzania's teacher preparation programme? *Papers in Education and Development,* **11**, 45–60.

Watson, K. (1991) Teachers and teaching in an interdependent world. *Compare,* **21** (2), 107–26.

WCEFA (1990) *Framework for Action to Meet Basic Learning Needs.* New York: World Council on Education for All.

# 23 Teacher Incentives in Botswana: The Debate For and Against

## GAONTATLHE MAUTLE AND SHELDON G. WEEKS

## The Botswana Context

The education profession in Botswana has developed significantly since independence in 1966 (Evans and Yoder, 1991). The educational system has both expanded and striven to improve the quality of schooling at all levels (Swartland, 1991). The primary teacher training colleges have grown in number from two to four and two new colleges of education to train junior secondary school teachers have been established, while the university trains senior secondary school teachers. As a result the proportion of untrained teachers had dropped to 15 per cent in primary schools and 21 per cent in secondary in 1992. The rapid expansion of community junior secondary schools, combined with higher teacher wastage, is the reason for this difference in the proportion of untrained teachers between primary and secondary. The education system expanded dramatically between 1966 and 1992: primary schooling went up more than fourfold (while the population rose only threefold) and secondary schooling increased from 1531 students to 67,167, or by 44 times.

The significant progress that has been made in education in Botswana (see Table 23.1) can be attributed to a number of key factors. One is the government's commitment to develop education. In 1993, 23 per cent of the recurrent budget went to education, an increase from 5.2 million pula in 1976 to 624 million pula in 1993. In addition, in 1993 education received 191 million pula for capital development, or 11 per cent of the budget

**Table 23.1** Development of education in Botswana since independence

|  | 1966 | 1976 | 1987 | 1992 |
|---|---|---|---|---|
| Population[a] | 450,000 | 712,000 | 1,131,700 | 1,357,600 |
| *Primary* |  |  |  |  |
| Schools | 251 | 335 | 537 | 654 |
| Enrolment | 71,546 | 125,588 | 235,941 | 308,840 |
| Teachers | 1,673 | 3,921 | 7,324 | 9,708 |
| Percentage untrained | 43 | 38 | 24 | 15 |
| *Secondary* |  |  |  |  |
| Schools | – | 32 | 73 | 169 |
| Enrolment | 1,531 | 13,991 | 35,966 | 67,167 |
| Teachers | – | 664 | 1,619 | 3,516 |
| Percentage untrained | – | 29 | 26 | 21 |

*Note*: [a] Estimates (there were censuses in 1971, 1981 and 1991).
*Source*: Based on Weeks (1993).

(Simon and Mtekateka, 1994). Political stability and economic development have enabled Botswana to continue to expand the education sector – a unique combination of political will and financial resources that have made possible the attainment of goals. Another factor is the role of the 1976–77 National Commission on Education (Republic of Botswana, 1977). The effort to universalize nine years of basic education as recommended by the commission was largely responsible for the growth in the number of primary (standards 1 to 7), community junior secondary (forms I and II) and senior secondary schools (forms III to V). The rolling six-year national development plans have been rigorous in their analysis of education and enlightened in their commitment to the development of the education sector. There was a second National Commission on Education in 1992 and 1993, which recommended that form III become part of community junior secondary schools, to give ten years of 'basic education'. Most children have access to primary school and approximately 90 per cent of the primary school leavers are able to enter form I in community junior secondary schools, while fewer than a third could continue to a senior school, though the goal of the government is a 50 per cent transition rate.

In Botswana, the expansion of the education system has remained synchronized, with the number of teachers employed growing to match the rise in the number of pupils. For this reason the teacher–pupil ratio in primary schools has averaged 1 to 31 over the past 15 years, while the proportion of female teachers has risen steadily, from 68 per cent in 1976 to approximately 78 per cent in 1992. In the community junior and senior secondary schools, an even better teacher–pupil ratio has been maintained, rising from 1 to 21 in 1976 to nearly 1 to 18 in 1992. The proportion of females in secondary schools has fluctuated around 40 per cent over recent years. While acting to maintain reasonable class sizes, Botswana has also moved to provide improved conditions of service for teachers, including salaries, housing and other benefits. Compared to most countries in Africa the incentives package offered teachers can be claimed to be attractive.

## The need for limits

All education systems face a number of contradictions related to the supply and retention of teachers. The agency responsible for the employment of teachers must balance the attractions offered to recruit and hold teachers against the total number of teachers required and the resources available to cover both material and other incentives. Resources are not finite in any educational system. A trade-off is faced continuously between the number of teachers the system can afford to employ at existing rates and the number required at any given time to maintain consistent coverage of schools and classrooms. This equation is more complicated where the cost of teachers ranges through a variety of dimensions: unqualified, diploma, graduate, master's, citizen, expatriate, school grouping, the school hierarchy and the number of promotional positions in the school, which will vary as parallel progression is implemented (as these additional promotional positions will cost more).[1] These tensions apply equally to an entrepreneur running a private school and to the state running an educational system with thousands of schools. In addition, the resources of the state or employing agency are stretched where they must cover training, allowances, transportation, housing and other incentives that teachers require and expect. States are prone to rely on higher pupil–teacher ratios and unqualified teachers, who are usually 'temporary' employees and cost much less because they have lower salaries and fewer or no fringe benefits (in Botswana the proportion of unqualified teachers has remained high at between 16 and 20 per cent; see Burchfield and Motswakae, 1991).

In many education systems teachers' salaries represent 90 per cent of the recurrent costs (Farrell and Oliveira, 1993). School-based costs, including ancillary staff, school and curriculum materials, external administration, supervision, inspection and in-service training, must all come out of the remaining 10 per cent of the budget to education. Limited resources available to the state have forced the adoption of strategies that pass the cost of education on to the community through fees and other forms of cost recovery, and 'community involvement'. Other strategies designed to recruit and retain teachers all cost something: merit pay to effective teachers; additional increments to specific types of teachers (science, mathematics, Setswana); bonuses for serving in remote areas; and grants to teachers who develop innovative programmes (Murnane, 1993). The World Bank and other international agencies have for years been supporting the creation of cost-effective education systems through reduced teacher–pupil ratios, improved time allocations and reliance on teacher aides to reduce costs, while teachers tend to call for smaller classes, reduced workloads and more professional training to reduce the reliance on untrained teachers.

> What constitutes the optimal mix of human and physical resources to increase school effectiveness? Achievement can be greatly enhanced by increasing the availability of basic inputs such as text books and instructional materials. Other alternatives include increasing instructional time and class size by using differential staffing practices and interactive radio programs. Resources for nonteacher expenditures would help to improve this alternative. Organizational change might also improve achievement, though successful implementation of organizational change requires active participation of teachers, teachers' organizations, and unions.
>
> (Farrell and Oliveira, 1993, pp. 5–6)

The objective of this section (written by Sheldon G. Weeks) is to consider some of the proposals to improve teacher incentives from the perspective of the constraints faced by the state. Most of the literature concerning teacher incentives in Botswana would appear to be pro-teacher and does not give sufficient recognition to the problems faced by the state. The challenge to the state is contained in the choice that needs to be made between differential and uniform incentive policies (Firestone and Pennell, 1993). So far Botswana has tended to follow uniform incentive policies, but should greater consideration be given to differential incentive policies? The move to implement parallel progression in the schools is a step in this direction.

## Attitudes of education bureaucrats

In our interviews with key educational administrators in the government we found that there was a generally held view that teachers in Botswana were well rewarded, serviced and administered, and in most instances did not have grounds for complaint (Mautle and Weeks, 1992). It was felt that teachers were not overworked and had no grounds for claiming additional pay or bonuses for working overtime – preparing and marking student work, supervising sports and other activities after hours, hostel and night study

duties in boarding schools and so on – because teaching was a vocation they had chosen with purpose and dedication, knowing that it entailed these extra responsibilities. They were unanimous in believing that an ombudsman for teachers was not required: if teachers had any grievances they could air them through existing channels and the Teaching Service Commission. Administrators believed that a series of steps had already been taken to shift from outmoded forms of supervision to field education officers, who were colleagues, and advisers, who shared a mutual goal with teachers to improve the quality of education and the outcome as assessed to demonstrate improved learning of pupils.

Perhaps the best quotable example of the view of people in the establishment is from the late Mr Sephuma, former Deputy Secretary, Ministry of Education. When interviewed, he pointed to the tremendous strides that had been made in advancing the terms and conditions of service of teachers in Botswana over the past decade. He then went on to say: 'I really do not know what they [teachers] are complaining about.'

## Previous studies

With support from USAID, there have been a number of key studies of teacher incentives in Botswana since 1991 (Chapman *et al.*, 1991; Burchfield, 1992; Mautle and Weeks, 1992, 1994). The first two of these studies found that primary and secondary teachers favoured monetary rewards for regular attendance, excellence of service, high student achievement and grants to school projects. In addition, customary incentive issues, such as starting salary, salary increments and housing, ranked high. Three non-monetary incentives that ranked high were recognition or awards for in-service training, 'administration's responsiveness to teachers' needs and feelings' and access to Ministry of Education officials.

During 1990, 107 community junior secondary school teachers who had completed a 'quality of worklife questionnaire' were also observed using the Botswana 'classroom observation tool'; this sample was then divided into four clusters that related their attitudes to their conditions of work (incentives), their sense of 'control' over their work and their receptivity to curricular changes (Perry *et al.*, 1995). The authors caution against justifying improved working conditions on the grounds that 'more satisfied teachers may be more receptive to change'.

A number of key government documents that articulate policy on incentives for public servants and teachers have been released since 1991 (Republic of Botswana, 1991b, 1992a, b, 1993b, 1994). The earlier documents have been examined in a previous article (Mautle and Weeks, 1994). The last two have gone the furthest to suggest ways in which the government might act to improve teacher incentives, and will be considered next.

## National Commission on Education 1993 and the White Paper 1994

Since 1989, the state in Botswana has taken a number of steps to improve teacher incentives. Of significance are the variety of studies and commissions mentioned above. The most significant is the report of the second National Commission on Education 1993 (Republic of Botswana, 1993b), which came out in March 1994, and Government Paper Number 2 of 1994, The Revised National Policy on Education, which was released in April 1994 (Republic of Botswana, 1994). In the commission report, on pages 161 to 167, issues of 'conditions of service and teacher incentives' are considered. The commission found that teachers' salaries were favourably related to those in other areas of the public service, and concluded that it did not believe that a general salary increase was likely to have any impact on the quality of teaching and therefore did not support such a strategy. The commission also believed that the gap in salaries between primary and secondary teachers would be rectified following the shift to a diploma in the primary colleges. The recommendations of the commission to improve teacher incentives follow

a strategy of developing a series of non-monetary incentives and that steps be taken to ensure the communication of Ministry of Education decisions to teachers through its own media and annual conferences (see also Recommendation 120 on the Dissemination of Information).

Recommendations 109 to 114 relate to teacher incentives and all but 113 were accepted outright by the government in its White Paper. I will review these recommendations below in detail.

### Recommendation 109: teacher incentives and conditions of service

This recommendation divides into nine parts:

- adequate accommodation on an equal basis with other public servants;
- recognition of participation in in-service training courses;
- clear national training policy and plans with distinct rewards for each level;
- awards to teachers for excellence and commitment;
- an annual 'teachers' day', with awards and recognition to teachers for their service to the nation;
- improved 'schools bulletin' to achieve better communication and flow of information to teachers;
- 'long service' leave after 15 years for 'long, continuous and dedicated service';
- sabbatical leave' and encouragement to further professional development; and
- equal opportunity to serve in all parts of the country, and with equitable rotation.

All nine points are currently under consideration by the government and ways will be found to develop them. The major constraint will be the resources available to pay for them (as long leave and sabbatical leave cost something). The ninth point is expanded in Recommendation 110.

### Recommendation 110: job enrichment and rotational needs

'The Commission *recommends* that as part of the overall development of teachers and as an incentive, attention should be paid to their job enrichment and rotational needs. The goal is to create a pool of experienced professionals for leadership in the various areas such as examinations work, curriculum development, and as resource persons for workshops and seminars' (Republic of Botswana, 1993b, p. 363).

*Recommendation 111: educational study tours*
Teachers should learn from each other, and one way to achieve this is through study tours, both within Botswana and to other countries. This is particularly important for leadership within the educational system to make it more effective. This is a costly option whose implications have yet to be fully considered, though there have been study tours already by teacher educators to Namibia and Zimbabwe.

*Recommendation 112: teacher management and performance appraisal*
There are three key recommendations under Recommendation 112:

- as a consequence of decentralization, management and supervision of teachers should be shifted to the district level;
- to improve advisory and inspectoral services, the cadre of education officers should be increased;
- heads of schools require training in how to appraise their staff.

A number of activities have already helped to move Botswana in this direction, including the enhancement of field education officers and the development of the ODA and Ministry of Education schools management project.

*Recommendation 113: teachers' unions*
The Commission had recommended that the four teachers' organizations should come together in an 'umbrella forum' so as to strengthen their role and impact. The White Paper amended this recommendation because the government felt that it could only play an 'advisory role' – the various teachers' organizations had to take any initiative to cooperate together, not the government.

*Recommendation 114: National Council for Teacher Education*
The Commission wanted the NCTE strengthened, and this conference to be held every year. Teacher educators will have to judge whether this exercise is of sufficient benefit to justify being held annually. The Commission felt that the NCTE 'has a wide scope of teacher education issues to address considering the major developments in education proposed' in the report.

## Summary and conclusion

Although the second National Commission on Education 1993 (Republic of Botswana, 1993b) has come out in favour of non-material incentives over material incentives, the government of Botswana remains committed, through indexing of salaries, to maintaining benefits in relation to inflation, so that all public servants can cope with the rising cost of living. It should be noted that all benefits cost something, even if they have been labelled 'non-material'. Seemingly inexpensive measures, such as recognition of in-service training courses, awards to teachers, 'teachers' day', an improved 'schools bulletin' and other proposals, when implemented, must be organized, coordinated and administered, and this process costs something. The cost implications of all these recommendations need to be calculated, and decisions made as to which ones can be implemented in the short, medium and long run. The provision of adequate housing for all teachers, and long service or sabbatical leave to long-serving teachers, will be costly to the nation, and not achieved overnight. The fair rotation of teachers, though an admirable goal, will not be an easy one to achieve because of social and political constraints. The second National Commission on Education 1993 has pointed the way, and it is of significance that the government has embraced fully all but one of its recommendations that relate to teacher incentives.

## A profession, not a vocation

In 1992, responding to allegations that conditions of service for teachers were still poor, and hence the profession was still unattractive and was chosen by many only as a last resort, the Deputy Permanent Secretary in the Ministry of Education observed: 'Honestly, I do not know what they [teachers] want. Conditions of service for teachers have improved tremendously in the last fifteen years.' The Deputy Permanent Secretary's observation is both right and wrong. It is correct in that an examination of teachers' conditions of service since the 1930s shows a great deal of improvement. But he was also wrong in that a comparison of conditions of service for teachers with those for, say, the civil service shows that the former still lag far behind. This is underscored by the fact that students only choose teaching as a last resort. The science subjects, and mathematics in particular, suffer from a critical shortage of teachers because students who major in science subjects have a number of what they perceive to be better professions to choose from than teaching. Lack of demand for the Post-Graduate Diploma in Education (PGDE) by science graduands led to the suspension of intake of these graduands into the PGDE programme at the University of Botswana five years ago. The other point which the Deputy Permanent Secretary failed to bear in mind is that the real test of the effectiveness of the reforms that had been carried out in conditions of service is how the profession is perceived by teachers and the general public. As this section (written by Gaontatlhe Mautle) unfolds it will become clear that teachers in particular feel that a great deal needs to be done to improve their conditions of service and the status of the profession.

Failure to attract candidates has characterized teacher preparation in Botswana since the establishment of the first government-sponsored teacher preparation programme in 1940. The tar-

get for the first intake into the Elementary Teachers' Training Certificate was 40, but only 20 applications were received (Vanqua, 1992, p. 11). The main reason for this lack of attraction was apparently low salaries, no pension benefits and the absence of terms and conditions of service (Vanqua, 1992, p. 12).

The colonial government made efforts to address the teachers' grievances. For example, in 1943, Dumbrell, then Director of Education, announced that teachers in Bechuanaland Protectorate with training similar to that obtaining in South Africa would be paid the same salaries and allowances as their counterparts in South Africa. And the Rusbridger Commission of 1959–60 recommended common basic salary scales for the same qualifications (Vanqua, 1992, pp. 11, 15).

However, these efforts appear to have had little positive impact. The first post-independence National Commission on Education (Republic of Botswana, 1977) observed that teaching did not command sufficient respect among teachers and members of the public, that it was low on the scale of students' indicated preferences for further training and that teacher training only attracted candidates with low grades who could not gain admission to any other programme. The Commission further observed that trained teachers who could find alternative employment left teaching at the earliest opportunity. This was demonstrated by the wastage of secondary school teachers, at 22 per cent per year from 1972 to 1975, even though not all left teaching permanently. The wastage of teachers at primary level was much lower (about 3 per cent) because of a lack of other job opportunities (pp. 127–8). This is a rather gloomy picture of the teaching profession.

In 1992, a survey was conducted by the authors of this chapter to gather teachers' opinions about their profession. The survey focused on secondary school and tertiary institution teachers. Tertiary institutions included colleges of education, teacher training colleges and vocational training centres. Ministry of Education officials and officers of teacher organizations were also interviewed. The methodology used in the collection and analysis of data was qualitative. Thirty group interviews of 15 minutes to two hours were conducted. Groups varied in size from five to 30. Ministry of Education officials were interviewed individually. Below is a summary of teachers' views on incentives in the teaching profession.

## Teachers' views: enough is not enough

Overall, teachers felt that general conditions of service of teachers were worse compared to those of officers in the civil service. Many of them at the majority of schools and colleges which we visited claimed that their morale was very low owing to poor conditions of service, that teaching is a poor person's job, that it is not respected by members of the public and that it is chosen only as a last resort when the alternative is joining street children. These views are presented below under five specific headings in order to give more details.

### Monetary incentives

The general feeling was that the salary is low largely owing to a lack of promotion opportunities. The starting salary compared to other professions is good but in eight years the top notch of the salary scale is reached, and people are stuck there while counterparts in the civil service get promoted to higher and better-paying positions. Many were sceptical about parallel progression improving the situation, saying that unless criteria for promotion were clearly spelled out it would make very little difference, if any at all. In fact, many feared that promotion would be based on headmasters' recommendations, which would diminish the importance of merit. The failure to recognize and give any compensation for all the hours spent working overtime is a major grievance held by teachers. They feel that when people in the bureaucracy claim that they now get equal pay, they are ignoring all the additional benefits provided to public servants that teachers do not get. The claim that teachers are equal to others in the public service is simply not accepted by teachers (Republic of Botswana, 1993b, pp. 361–3).

College of education staff felt that poor salaries were the major obstacle in their recruitment effort.

They stated that to be recruited as a staff development fellow at a college of education one needed to have taught for a minimum of six years at a secondary school. This requirement was found to be unrealistic given that after three years a teacher could be promoted to head of department with a salary much higher than that of a staff development fellow at a college of education.

### Accommodation

Here teachers were generally satisfied. However, they felt that it was very unfair to require them to pay rent for institutional houses while some other officers occupying the same category of houses stayed rent free; for example, police and army officers. It was noted that staying in institutional houses reduced the chances of teachers buying Botswana Housing Corporation houses, which enjoy government subsidy.

### Job satisfaction

Many teachers reported that they had no job satisfaction, that their morale was low and that they were a frustrated lot. This, it was stated, resulted from, among other things, an excessive workload. Secondary school teachers on average teach 32 periods a week and college lecturers 20 periods. In addition to this, all have extra-curricular activities, such as sport, which are done outside the school timetable and the marking of students' work, which must be done after school. A quotation from one of the interviews is in order:

> We are everything – teacher, counsellor, policeman. Why? In boarding schools, many of us work up to midnight taking care of students; for example, taking the sick to the hospital. Nurses, doctors have night duty allowances, but we do not. Our typical day starts at 6.00 a.m. and ends at 10.00 p.m. and includes extra-curricular activities 4.00 to 6.00 p.m., evening study 6.45 to 8.45 p.m., hostel supervision 8.45 to 10.00 p.m.

More teachers claimed that leisure time is a luxury they are not even supposed to dream about. Thus, they have no job satisfaction at all.

## Further training

The Ministry of Education was reported to have no training plans for teachers (something which has since been rectified). Teachers had the impression that the Ministry of Education view was that the diplomas and bachelor's degrees which they had were sufficient. However, they acknowledged that a few people were sporadically selected and sent for further training. They did not know the criteria used for selecting such teachers. It was observed further that those who went for further training were disadvantaged in that they did not progress in salary while those who remained as teachers in the schools did progress, and ended up with higher salaries than those who went for further studies.

## Ombudsman

There was a strong feeling that the creation of the Office of the Ombudsman was necessary. Two reasons were given for this. First, and more important, the Teaching Service Commission membership includes the Deputy Director of Teaching Service Management, against whose decision teachers would be appealing. It was observed that the presence of the Deputy Director in the Commission makes its impartiality highly questionable. Second, it was stated that teachers were required to channel all correspondence through the headmaster, and that sometimes headmasters did not pass on query letters.

## Gender

The general feeling was that women get a raw deal. Men dominate leadership positions in schools and colleges, suggesting that Batswana believe that only men can lead. Women are given fewer further training opportunities than men and they are given very little recognition, if any at all. It was also observed that women appeared to lack confidence as they do not always apply for senior positions. However, affirmative action was believed to be unnecessary. A strong feeling was expressed against administrative decisions and postings that resulted in the separation of spouses.

## Teaching Service Management

The expressed attitude towards the Department of Teaching Service Management (TSM) was negative. It was stated that there was inadequate communication between TSM and schools, they never ever answered phones and they disregarded teachers' desires when they made postings. It was also felt that the code of regulation contains nothing but threats and that it should be scrapped and replaced with government general orders. However, the president of the oldest teacher association (Botswana Teachers' Union) preferred the code of regulations to the government general order, saying that the latter was more difficult to understand. He added that such documents should be presented in non-legal language.

It was felt that two measures could improve the situation: first, the responsibilities of the TSM should be decentralized to at least 12 districts to make communication with teachers easier; second, tertiary institutions, such as colleges of education, should be made semi-autonomous and be involved in the recruitment of their own staff.

## Discussion

The validity, or lack of it, of teachers' views on their conditions of service must be looked at in the context of steps taken by the government to improve teaching service conditions. A careful examination of the views within this context shows that they are largely valid, even though in some instances teachers complain out of ignorance of their rights. In this instance the author of this section is reminded of primary school teachers' complaints about not being paid subsistence allowance when they had travelled with children to a youth rally on 4B activities. These are Ministry of Local Government, Lands and Housing and Ministry of Agriculture activities. Teachers could not understand the TSM argument that what they were doing was not the responsibility of the Ministry of Education. Teachers seem to be unaware that they are entitled to benefits, such as 14 days' hotel occupancy on first appointment or transfer, hotel accommodation during official trips, leave travel concessions and a car and property scheme. While the employer has the responsibility to ensure that information is distributed to teachers, they themselves must take steps to find information, especially communications relating to their terms and conditions of service.

With regard to the validity of the teachers' claims, it must be noted that the key element in the conditions of service of any employee is salary. It is true that the starting salary of teachers compares favourably with those of other civil servants. However, promotion prospects for teachers compared with those of other government employees are very limited. This has been recognized by both the 1977 and the 1993 National Commissions on Education, and both have made strong recommendations for the creation of a career structure that would enable teaching to compete favourably with other professions. The Botswana government has failed to come up with a career structure that would create promotion opportunities that compare favourably with those available in the civil service. The parallel progression exercise comes closest to doing this. However, it also fails because it ignores the fact that teachers have to make decisions in their individual classrooms whether they hold certificates, diplomas or degrees. It has grouped certificate, diploma and degree teachers as artisans, technicians and group III professionals respectively. This has ensured that teachers' progression opportunities remain inferior to those of people in equivalent professions. For example, a postgraduate teacher whose training takes five years can only progress in salary to senior teacher grade I (non-administrative school position) on the D4 salary scale, whereas a lawyer whose training also takes five years can progress to principal legal draftsman I (non-administrative) on the D2 salary scale (which is 25 per cent higher). This does not improve the competitiveness or the image of the teaching profession.

Other key elements in the general conditions of service have not been attended to by the government. At the core is a different perception of the profession. Bureaucrats view teaching as a vocation that teachers have selected, and assume that teachers are like missionaries who are willing and want to do all the extra work required, because they love being teachers. For example, the teachers complain that they have to work overtime, yet this does not earn any allowance, that they are required to pay rent for institutional houses, yet some other officers staying in institutional houses not only stay rent free, but also have subsidized utilities. Non-monetary incentives have been suggested, but it has been a big mistake to ignore monetary ones. Perhaps the two Education Commissions have misled the government by focusing on the starting salary notches and concluding that teachers' salaries were favourably related to those in other parts of the civil service, rather than considering how slowly teachers rise up the salary ladder.

## Synthesis: The way forward

Taken holistically, the above debate has revealed that while efforts have been made to improve conditions of service for teachers in Botswana, enough has not been done to make teaching competitive with other professions. Fortunately, the first part of the debate suggests willingness on the part of the Botswana government to continue to seek ways of improving the image of the teaching profession. The second part of the debate has identified shortcomings in efforts that have been made so far and has thus pointed out steps that should be taken next in the effort to improve the image of this noble profession. Some specific suggestions are made in the paragraphs below to clarify steps suggested in the debate.

However, before the specific suggestions, it is important to state that we are aware that globally the teaching profession is not as attractive as it ought to be. However, other countries have done much more than Botswana in improving the image of the profession. For example, Botswana is the only country in Southern Africa where junior secondary leavers (nine years of education) are admitted into teacher training institutions. Other countries require a minimum of O-level for training whether it is for teaching at primary or secondary school. It was only recently that a decision was taken to require O-level for admission into all teacher training programmes (Republic of Botswana, 1994).

One step that can be taken to improve the competitiveness of teaching is to extend the career structure of teaching further. This can be done by linking opportunities for upward mobility with the acquisition of additional academic or professional qualifications. For ordinary classroom teachers, the major criterion for promotion to the next level, especially beyond senior teacher, would have to be acquisition of specified additional qualifications. In this way, positions of, say, master teacher II and master teacher I could be created, enabling classroom teachers to progress to the level equivalent to that of principal legal draftsman. Tying upward mobility to additional qualifications would have the added benefit of improving the quality of teaching and, therefore, of learning, as research studies (Campbell and Abbott, 1977; Husen, 1977; Gorman *et al.*, 1988; Nyagura and Riddell, 1992) have demonstrated that additional academic or professional qualification is one of the major factors that lead to improvement in learning. Studies have also shown that: 'The professional and managerial skills of the school head are critical indicators. Heads with higher level skill can produce markedly better results as measured by pupils' test results even though their staff may be relatively less qualified' (Chung, 1992, p. 11).

Thus, for heads of schools and their deputies, upward mobility would have to be tied to additional professional qualifications with a focus on school management and instructional supervision. This would mean abolition of uniform and fixed salaries for heads of schools. It should be noted that some teachers' perception of parallel progression is that it will not lead to a significant change in the progression prospects in the teaching profession (Tlale, 1995). Differentiation of teacher training programmes, teachers' pay scales and teachers' conditions of service according to the age of children they teach should also be eventually abolished. This would remove inferiority and superiority complexes among primary, junior secondary and senior secondary school teachers.

More importantly, it would greatly improve the public perception of primary school teachers.

General conditions of service for teachers must also be reviewed from time to time to ensure that they are competitive with those of other professions as much as possible. Overtime allowance is one area to which serious attention must be paid. How can we justify paying overtime allowance to medical doctors, whose profession is at the top of the professional cadre, who certainly chose medicine voluntarily because they liked it and found it both attractive and prestigious, and not pay the same allowance to people who were forced into teaching by circumstances? Like a medical doctor, a teacher has to work overtime if he or she is to be efficient in the job. Overtime is necessitated by preparation, marking students' work and the so-called extra-curricular activities. Some countries place these activities in the curriculum and train teachers for them. This certainly reduces teachers' overtime.

Finally, implementation of changes in the conditions of service for teachers should always be expedited. The delay in doing this will be most likely to produce negative effects which will be difficult to remove. Parallel progression for teachers was approved at the beginning of 1993 but has not really been implemented. Some teachers are already saying that this delay is causing them great anxiety and is lowering their morale (Ramarotsi, 1995). Taking these measures, in addition to those the government is already committed to implementing, would go a long way to narrow the gap between conditions of service for teachers and those of other professionals. The image of the teaching profession would also be improved considerably.

## Acknowledgements

The authors would like to thank Shirley Burchfield of IEES, and USAID through Florida State University for initiating and supporting our involvement in the study of teacher incentives in Botswana. We are particularly grateful to the Ministry of Education and all the staff in the ministry, teachers' colleges and other institutions who took so much of their time to talk to us. We also wish to thank Daniel Kasule, who helped in the review of documents up to 1991. An earlier paper looking at the preliminary results of our study of teacher incentives was presented at the second Conference of SACHES at Broederstrom in October 1992. We are grateful to the University of Botswana and the British Council for making possible our participation in the Oxford Conference in September 1993, which led to the paper published in the *International Journal of Educational Development* in 1994.

# Note

1 'Parallel progression' is Botswana's unique proposal intended to allow teachers to remain chalk-face artists instead of progressing up through the administrative hierarchy.

# References

Burchfield, S. (1992) *Teacher Incentives in Botswana: Preliminary Findings of Interviews with Teachers, Instructors and Lecturers.* Gaborone: Improving the Efficiency of Educational Systems and Ministry of Education, Republic of Botswana.

Burchfield, S. and Motswakae, R. (1991) Teacher supply and demand: where are we now and where are we going? In M. Evans, H. S. Mogami and J. A. Reed (eds), *The Education of Educators.* Gaborone: National Council for Teacher Education.

Campbell, N. M. and Abbott, J. (1977) Botswana's primary school system: a spatial analysis. In *Education for Kagisano: Report of the National Commission on Education.* Vol. 2. Gaborone: Government Printer.

Chapman, D. W., Snyder, C. W. and Burchfield, S. A. (1991) *Teacher Incentives in the Third World.* Tallahassee, FL: Learning Systems Institute.

Chung, F. (1992) Recent development in research into school effectiveness. Paper presented at a Conference on School Effectiveness, Harvard University, Cambridge, MA, 10–12 September.

Evans, M. and Yoder, J. (1991) *Patterns of Reform in Primary Education: The Case of Botswana.* Gaborone: Macmillan Botswana.

Farrell, J. P. and Oliveira, J. B. (eds) (1993) *Teachers in Developing Countries: Improving Effectiveness and Managing Costs.* Washington, DC: World Bank.

Firestone, W. A. and Pennell, J. R. (1993) Teacher commitment, working conditions and differential incentive policies. *Review of Educational Research*, **63** (4), 489–526.

Gorman, K. S., Holloway, S. D. and Fuller, J. (1988) Preschool quality in Mexico: variation in teachers, organisation and child activities. *Comparative Education Review*, **24** (1), 91–101.

Husen, T. (1977) Pupils, teachers and schools in Botswana: a national evaluation of primary and secondary education. In National Commission on Education, *Education for Kagisano*, Volume 2. Gaborone: Government Printer.

Mautle, G. and Weeks, S. (1992) Teacher incentives – preliminary findings. Paper presented to the Southern Africa Comparative and History Education Society Conference, 29–30 October, University of Botswana, Gaborone.

Mautle, G. and Weeks, S. (1994) The state and the teaching profession: teacher incentives in Botswana. *International Journal of Educational Development*, **14** (3), 339–47.

Murnane, R. J. (1993) Economic incentives to improve teaching. In J. P. Farrell and J. B. Oliveira (eds), *Teachers in Developing Countries: Improving Effectiveness and Managing Costs.* Washington, DC: World Bank.

Nyagura, L. M. and Riddel, A. R. (1992) Primary school achievement in English and mathematics in Zimbabwe: a multilevel analysis. Paper presented at a Conference on School Effectiveness, Harvard University, Cambridge, MA, 10–12 September.

Perry, P. D., Chapman, D. W. and Snyder, C. W. (1995) Quality of teacher worklife and classroom practices in Botswana. *International Journal of Educational Development*, **15** (2), 115–26.

Ramarotsi, C. (1995) The heads did well. *Mmegi*, **12** (24), 7.

Republic of Botswana (1976) *Education Statistics.* Gaborone: Government Printer.

Republic of Botswana (1977) *Education for Kagisano: Report of the National Education Commission.* Gaborone: Government Printer.

Republic of Botswana (1987) *Education Statistics.* Gaborone: Government Printer.

Republic of Botswana (1991a) *National Development Plan 7: 1991–1997.* Gaborone: Government Printer.

Republic of Botswana (1991b) *The Report on the Implementation of Parallel Progression.* Gaborone: Government Printer.

Republic of Botswana (1992a) *Organization and Management Report.* Gaborone: Government Printer.

Republic of Botswana (1992b) *Presidential Commission on the Review of Public Service Salaries and Conditions of Service.* Gaborone: Government Printer.

Republic of Botswana (1993a) *Education Statistics.* Gaborone: Government Printer.

Republic of Botswana (1993b) *Report of the National Commission on Education 1993.* Gaborone: Government Printer.

Republic of Botswana (1994) *Government Paper No. 2 of 1994: The Revised National Policy on Education April 1994.* Gaborone: Government Printer.

Simon, M. and Mtekateka, W. (1994) *A Graphic Look at Botswana Basic Education.* Gaborone: Basic Education Consolidation.

Swartland, J. (1991) *Botswana.* In M. Bray (ed.), *Ministries of Education in Small States.* London: Commonwealth Secretariat.

Tlale, B. (1995) Teachers left in the lurch. *Mmegi*, **12** (23), 6.

Vanqua, T. (1992) Teacher education in Botswana and present trends: 1937–1987. Paper presented to the Southern Africa Comparative and History of Education Society Conference, University of Botswana, 29–30 October.

Weeks, S. G. (1993) Reforming the reform: education in Botswana. Africa Today, **40** (1), 49–60.

# 24 University Affiliation and the Qualitative Development of Teacher Education

A. G. HOPKIN

## Introduction

In relation to the training and provision of teachers for a state system of education, governments are primarily concerned with the supply of teachers, and universities are primarily concerned with the academic and professional standards relating to training programmes. Furthermore, governments do not normally relinquish the control of the supply of teachers or the right to issue licences to those eligible to teach in schools. These two latter factors in the supply and training of teachers relate to matters of control which have political dimensions, and it is understandable that most governments prefer to keep such control within their domain. These two fundamental premises, the supply/quality premise and the maintenance of control premise, are basic elements in this chapter.

The purpose of the discussion is to describe and evaluate the potential of university affiliation in the training of teachers, particularly in matters of quality and standards relating to training programmes. The system used by the University of Botswana for the six teacher training institutions affiliated to the university is considered as a case study. The pattern that has been adopted and adapted is broadly based on those of the University of Manchester (Burge, 1993) and the University of Zimbabwe (Mokgautsi et al., 1988). Particular reference is made to the latter university. It must be borne in mind that Botswana, with a population of about 1.3 million, is a 'small state'. There are about 80 such states (Bray and Packer, 1993), and the experience of Botswana in teacher

training may be directly relevant to them. Furthermore, the lessons – actual and potential – to be gained from this experience could also be of value to larger countries that are developing rapidly, and that face issues relating to the quality of the pre-service training of teachers for state schools.

Matters pertaining to the supply of teachers and the quality of teacher training programmes have been issues in state systems of education since mass schooling was developed for industrial societies (Peters, 1983). The value of universities in these matters has been acknowledged, and the first university departments of education for training teachers were established over a hundred years ago (Thomas, 1990). Since that time, teacher training has been a significant activity in tertiary education in England and Wales. While the activities involved have varied, the assumption that universities should play a directive and supervisory role in teacher education in non-university training institutions was formally acknowledged when universities were given this responsibility within their regions via structures such as area training organizations (Turner, 1990). Through such devices, universities in England and Wales assumed significant degrees of responsibility for the quality and standards of teacher training programmes in their own and a variety of other institutions. These developments are relevant to Botswana because, as in other former British dependencies, practice in England and Wales in tertiary education and teacher training has been a model for its own practice in these fields.

A monolithic structure was not developed in the United Kingdom. For example, in Scotland, university involvement in teacher training has been minimal and the pattern followed has been very different from that in England and Wales (Bell, 1990). Furthermore, in the latter the mode operated differed from university to university, but the basic role of the university remained the same. However, since the early 1980s the role of universities in teacher education has been significantly changed. The locus of responsibility has been shifted and dispersed, the role of universities has been challenged and subjected to increased scrutiny and the state has assumed more responsibility for the quality and nature of the programmes offered.

These developments have been controversial, but the net effects are that responsibility for the quality and standards in teacher training in England and Wales is now shared, and is no longer the monopoly of the universities. These developments, and their advantages and disadvantages, are not the subject of the present discussion. The thesis explored in this chapter is that in countries such as Botswana, given the educational, developmental and political contexts, it is most appropriate that responsibility for the standards and quality of teacher training be delegated to universities, and that governments should concern themselves with teacher supply. A corollary to this thesis is that the most suitable vehicle whereby this responsibility can be discharged is the affiliation of non-university teacher training institutions to universities.

## Basic premises of affiliation

To facilitate and clarify the discussion the following definitions are offered in relation to university affiliation and the way it operates in Botswana. University affiliation is a system whereby affiliated institutions prepare their students for awards that are made under the auspices of a university. Thus the university is the validating body for the awards made by these institutions. Other terms may be used – such as associated or recognized institutions – but the same principle is followed.

This chapter deals with teacher training, which is used synonymously with teacher education. There are no aided, mission or private teacher training institutions in Botswana: all pre-service training takes place in institutions on programmes validated by the University of Botswana, or in the university itself.

Two important components in the system of affiliation used in Botswana are external examining and external moderation. These terms are often used synonymously, but not in the context of the system of affiliation used in the University of Botswana. External examining, an important feature of university education in the United Kingdom and many of its former dependencies, is the process whereby universities take steps to ensure that standards across subjects taught in universities are comparable, and that degrees awarded are of an approximately similar standard. In practice, this entails each university voluntarily employing senior academics from other universities to scrutinize its examination papers, scripts and programmes to ensure that they are comparable with those of other universities. In effect, it is a system whereby standards are subjected to peer monitoring. A second important function is to ensure that the systems of assessment used by universities are fairly administered when classifying the degrees awarded to students (Partington *et al.*, 1993).

This practice, which was developed in a characteristically *ad hoc* fashion in the United Kingdom, has been improved and standardized in the past six years. In the mid-1980s the Committee of Vice-Chancellors and Principals (CVCP) took the significant step of drawing up a code of practice for external examining in universities (Committee of Vice-Chancellors and Principals, 1986). A later report indicated that this code was having considerable influence on practice (Heywood, 1989). Concern had previously been felt that the rule-of-thumb methods that seemed to be used by external examiners would render it likely that the purported aims of external examining might not always be achieved. However, the code of practice referred to above, and the calibre of the academics who have been, and are, appointed as examiners, make it probable that the system does help to maintain standards, and that it ensures fair play for candidates generally. Tacit acknowledgement that the system was, and is, in need of refining and further development was made evident when the code was published. The University of Botswana has benefited to some degree because its programmes are externally examined, often by academics from British institutions.

However – and this will be discussed more fully below – external examining plays a somewhat different and much less significant role in affiliated institutions. Much greater emphasis is placed on external moderation. In the context of the University of Botswana, this process has a very different focus from external examining. In the latter case the relationship is between institutions which are of comparable standing and which award their own degrees. This is not so with external moderating, where the institutions concerned are affiliated to, or are associated with, a 'parent' university, which validates the awards that they make. This means that the university takes responsibility for the standard of the awards which it underwrites.

To effect this, the university has to put in place a moderating system designed to ensure that the programmes and assessment procedures leading to university awards are of the required standard. To do this, the moderators are appointed to act on behalf of the university. Their functions resemble those of external examiners, but the role that they play is markedly different. For example, the moderator, unlike the examiner, reports to the university, an autonomous institution, and not to the institution being examined, which is not autonomous. Some of the implications of this are considered below. To facilitate and clarify the discussion, the term 'external examiner' refers to a person appointed to monitor the courses or programmes offered by a university. The term 'external moderator' refers to a person designated to regulate the subjects offered by an associated or affiliated institution that lead to an award validated by a university.

## Botswana's model of affiliation in practice

There are six teacher training institutions affiliated to the University of Botswana. They consist of four primary teacher training institutions, which prepare students for a two-year Primary Teachers' Certificate, and two colleges of education, which offer programmes leading to a three-year Diploma in Secondary Education, enabling diplomates to teach in the community junior secondary schools (Yoder and Mautle, 1991). At the time of writing, one primary teachers' college is being converted to a college of education preparing students for a three-year Diploma in Primary Education. It is important to note that the government of Botswana has handed over to the university responsibility for academic and professional standards and certification with respect to programmes preparing teachers for the state schools of Botswana. The Ministry of Education, thus shows its trust and confidence that the university has the capacity and willingness to undertake this task competently and in the light of national interests. This trust is important, as without it the potential of university affiliation to underpin the qualitative development of teacher education in developing countries, such as Botswana, could not be realized.

The *modus operandi* of affiliation that has been adopted is a relatively new and simple one, governed by university statutes which permit teaching and research institutions, as well as nurse training schools, to be affiliated. Executive responsibilities are carried out through the Office of the Coordinator, Affiliated Institutions, which is responsible for the six teacher training institutions, and located in the dean's office in the Faculty of Education. The terms of affiliation prescribe that:

> In respect of any affiliated institution the Senate may, if invited to do so and to the extent that it is so invited:
> (a) advise on and assist in the preparation of programmes of instruction;
> (b) validate programmes of instruction, examinations and the granting of certificates and other awards of the Affiliated Institutions.
>
> (University of Botswana, 1991, p. 489)

Responsibilities for affiliated institutions have been delegated to the Faculty of Education and the Office of the Coordinator by the university senate. The mandatory obligation is to ensure that the awards of the institutions are in accord with the academic requirements of the university. This is done by means of moderating the marking and grading of academic and professional courses leading to university awards, with external moderators and examiners being appointed by senate, normally on the advice of the Faculty of Education. The final teaching practice grades awarded by the teacher training institutions are moderated by panels, members of which are appointed by the dean of the Faculty of Education. They are drawn from the Faculty of Education, the Ministry of Education and other peer colleges. The primary teacher training college panel consists of 14 members, who spend two days at each college. A panel of 14 spends four days at each college of education. The Coordinator, Affiliated Institutions, as the chairperson and on behalf of the team, presents a written report to a staff meeting at the conclusion of each exercise (Hopkin, 1993a). About a third to a half of the students are observed, and in the past two years roughly one in five grades have been changed.

Different procedures are used for moderating the final examinations in the primary and secondary colleges. In the former, six subject moderators, each a member of the Faculty of Education, draw up the subject examination papers from questions submitted by a subject panel consisting of two members of staff from each college. The moderator – who is also a member of the subject panel – maintains a bank of examination questions. The papers are processed through the Office of the Coordinator, and confidentiality is maintained prior to the examination. Before 1993, the marking of scripts was done by teams (two members of the staff per subject from each college) over five days under the direct supervision of the moderator. This is no longer the case, and the scripts are now moderated independently after they have been marked and the results submitted. The final results are then processed by the Office of the Coordinator and presented to the Board of Affiliated Institu-

tions for ratification. This board receives reports from the moderators and the Coordinator before releasing the results for publication.

Operational responsibility for the common Diploma in Secondary Education examination taken by students in the colleges of education is in the hands of a joint examinations committee of the Board of Affiliated Colleges of Education. The diploma examinations are drawn up by subject panels made up of staff from both colleges. Draft question papers are then sent for moderation – normally the moderator is from the University of Botswana – and the papers are returned for processing. The examination scripts are marked internally by college staff. Moderation is later carried out in each college over three days. Two external examiners are also appointed, one in humanities and one in science, each responsible for the programmes in his or her respective area. Moderators therefore deal with the subject areas and the examiners oversee their work. Moderators and examiners present verbal reports at the end of the moderating period to the academic board of the college, and written reports are submitted later.

These moderating panels or teams are the vehicles whereby the university maintains the academic and professional standards of the awards made by the affiliated institutions. The more intensive operation used for the examinations set by the colleges of education ensures that the moderators and examiners meet the staff of the colleges, and this facilitates a more effective and thorough moderation procedure than is the case with the primary colleges. Membership of the subject panels enables the primary moderators to keep closely in touch with the staff in their respective subjects. A three-year Diploma in Primary Education is currently being piloted at the Tlokweng primary college, and the recent White Paper on education (Republic of Botswana, 1994) has indicated that this programme will be phased into all primary colleges. Recent experience suggests that the mode for moderating the academic component of the primary certificate will be phased out, and will be replaced by a scheme similar to that used for the secondary colleges (Hopkin, 1994b).

## Advisory and diagnostic aspects of affiliation

Moderation of grades and standards is the mandatory component of affiliation. The provision of advisory services is also an important feature of affiliation. Staff in both the primary teacher training colleges and the colleges of education have indicated that this aspect is important to them. Moderating grades can generate animosity, and dissent is frequently voiced by college staff about the validity of changing teaching practice grades after only one or two visits by moderators. Nevertheless, the feedback offered in the reports made by the examiners and the moderators does seem to be used constructively. This is most evident as, in the meetings held at the start of the teaching practice moderation, a senior member of staff presents the responses made by the college to the previous year's report. Teaching practice reports based on the moderation exercise, written by the chairperson and distributed to all college staff, are derived from the reporting back of members to the moderation panel. Panel members (the panels consist of university staff, nominated representatives from the Ministry of Education and selected college staff) are always experienced educators, and their feedback is perceptive and contains constructive suggestions (Hopkin, 1993a). Overall, the teaching practice moderation exercise is an excellent means of raising standards in this field; more students are observed and the scrutiny is more thorough than is commonly the case with the external examining of teaching practice in universities.

Greater impact has been made to date at the primary level, where moderation procedures have been in place longer. This is one of the effects of the Primary Education Improvement Project (PEIP), which had a significant impact on primary education in its ten years of operation (Primary Education Improvement Project, 1991). Close links between the Faculty of Education's Primary Department, which it helped to set up, and the staff of the primary colleges were developed. The project effected localization of staff in the primary teacher colleges through a staff upgrading policy. The staff of the Primary Department have been

particularly active in the subject panels and in shaping the examinations. The examinations set are generally relevant and appropriate, collaboration has helped to improve college programmes and faculty staff have played key roles. This was further facilitated by the introduction of a self-study exercise in the colleges by the PEIP team, which resulted in a marked improvement in the subject areas offered on the college programmes (Hopkin, 1994a).

Less collaboration and development has been shown to date in the junior secondary area. The USAID project, aimed at improving this level of education, was not remitted to focus on secondary teacher training. In 1991, the university appointed a Coordinator, Affiliated Institutions, and the office activities were extended to the two colleges of education. Rapid development has taken place in the training of junior secondary teachers since then, particularly in the advisory aspects of affiliation. Staff of colleges have increasingly used their moderators to develop their subject areas, and the introduction of more systematic examining and moderation procedures has led to greater collaboration between the staff of the colleges and the university.

The Office of the Coordinator (1994) has facilitated further development through the deployment and pooling of resources. This is particularly the case with workshops and the development of joint working parties. Teaching practice moderation has greatly improved, examination practices are more systematic, common examinations are now set for the two colleges of education and more attention is being given to research in the colleges. Paradoxically, the continued existence of separate boards for the primary and junior secondary institutions has been advantageous. It would appear both logical and beneficial to merge the two boards. However, different procedures have been developed by each, and these have provided useful pointers for improving, strengthening and changing practice. For example, the inadequate teaching practice moderation procedure formerly used for the colleges of education has been replaced by a model based on that used for the primary colleges. The system of moderation for the Primary Teachers' Certificate examinations compares unfavourably with the procedures which have been introduced for the Diploma in Secondary Education. This has been indicated by some moderators, and changes have been recommended to make the process similar to the one used at the secondary level (Mautle, 1994). For these reasons the Diploma in Primary Education programmes, which will be extended to all primary colleges in due course, will be moderated along the lines of the model used for the secondary colleges. While this cross-fertilization has brought benefits, it is probable that the two boards will be merged in future. This will be done to rationalize resources, and also to reinforce the policy of the Ministry of Education in the provision of nine years of basic education for all children (Republic of Botswana, 1994).

Moderation procedures, and the associated reports, are valuable, as they identify symptoms that lend themselves to diagnosis. These reports have been enhanced through the computerized processing, programming and centralization of examination results through the Office of the Coordinator. Computerization has facilitated greater accuracy in processing the results, and an added bonus is that they are published much earlier. Furthermore, the introduction of computer processing of results at the primary (1992) and the secondary (1993) levels has facilitated the establishment of data banks which are available for analysis and research purposes. This is valuable in the Botswana context, as these records are comprehensive. Furthermore, as the student enrolment at the colleges is relatively small (the primary colleges have about 300 to 330 and the secondary about 650 to 700 students enrolled), such numbers do not lend themselves to statistical treatment in terms of significance. If, however, they are aggregated and subjected to meta-analysis, then trends can be discerned and analysis undertaken which are statistically significant (*Economist*, 18 May 1991, pp. 93–4).

The advantages of establishing databases have already become apparent. Analysis of the results at the primary and secondary colleges has shown that the classification criteria enforced on the colleges preclude students from obtaining distinctions, particularly at the primary level, where at

least 10, and as many as 12, subjects are taken. On the basis of the data available, individual members of the boards have been able to present cases for change, and for the introduction of alternative criteria. These well founded arguments have been presented to the boards and to the university senate. To date they have been unsuccessful, and it is clear that the majority of members at both levels have little sympathy towards, or understanding of, cases based on statistical evidence. The words – normally misquoted – and spirit of Disraeli are usually invoked to dismiss the evidence produced ('there are three kinds of lies: lies, damned lies and statistics'). Nevertheless, hard data are essential for such purposes.

The 1994 Primary Teachers' Certificate results caused much concern because of the high supplementation and failure rates (Hopkin, 1994b). Information obtained from the principals of the colleges revealed that the cohort of students was atypical, and that the student enrolment included a large proportion of entrants from an upgrading programme mounted by the ministry for experienced uncertificated teachers. Further analysis showed that the results had been skewed by the presence of this cadre of students, the majority of whom were clearly unable to satisfy the standards required by the university. As a direct result of the moderating procedure, the ministry is reviewing its policy concerning the upgrading of experienced teachers.

A further issue that arose because of these results was that of screening students at the end of the first year of study. This was raised because the results of some students were so poor that it was thought that their inability to reach the required standard should have been diagnosed earlier. In turn, this raised the matter of the external monitoring of college programmes, the facilities at the colleges, assessment procedures and the standards that prevailed. In practice it has become clear that the ministry's decision to replace external inspection by self-study procedures as a means of promoting institutional development and monitoring standards (Hopkin, 1993b) has meant that external monitoring of standards in the primary teacher training colleges has lapsed. At the time of writing, the two colleges of education were undertaking self-study exercises along the lines of those followed by the primary teachers' colleges from 1986 to 1989. This could have deleterious consequences, as the lesson to be learned from the 1994 Primary Teachers' Certificate results is that the monitoring procedures in place at present are inadequate and need to be strengthened. The moderation of examinations and teaching practice caters only for these two areas and is not a substitute for the global monitoring of standards in affiliated teacher training institutions.

From the reports submitted by primary moderators to the Board of Affiliated Institutions (Hopkin, 1994b), it was also clear that the moderation procedure itself was inadequate. Moderators complained, with justification, that they were only able to give a partial assessment of candidates through a perusal of their final examination scripts. The general feeling was that on-site moderation was needed to enable moderators to meet staff and to assess course work done by students. This would ensure that the moderation process would be a holistic one. Furthermore, it also became evident that there was a need for fixed-term appointments to be made for moderators, as some had been moderators for more than five years and had become – albeit unwittingly – enmeshed in the system. The moderators were also responsible for compiling the examination papers, and these had not been subjected to the objective scrutiny that is normally a highly desirable feature of external moderation. In short, the lessons from the moderation procedures for the 1994 Primary Teachers' Certificate indicated that they should be revised and changed when moderation procedures are introduced for the Diploma in Primary Education.

## Affiliation and Institutional Development

Affiliation offers opportunities for teacher training institutions to develop in a number of ways. This is particularly so in relation to academic and professional standards. Moderation reports provide

feedback and guidance for the staff (Hopkin, 1993a). They are able, together with university and other staff, to participate in workshops designed specifically to improve features of the work done by the colleges. For example, a workshop, mounted by the Coordinator, Affiliated Institutions in collaboration with the Ministry of Education, involved lecturers from the colleges of education and the primary colleges (Hopkin, 1992). As a result, a new model for the final teaching practice (an improved version of the one used for the primary colleges) was introduced for the colleges of education. Other workshops have been run by the university's Higher Education Development Unit. One of these concentrated on external examining and moderating. As a result, a code of conduct with guidelines has been drawn up for external examiners and moderators, and this has led to more systematic and improved practice in this field (Hopkin, 1994c).

Affiliation enables the colleges involved to modify some of the restricting practices forced on them by government ministries. For example, the Ministry of Education's stance in some areas, such as allowing students to repeat a year of study, has been amended as a result of pressure from the two affiliation boards and the university. The formation of appropriate committees of the boards has helped to systematize teaching practice and examination procedures, particularly for diploma examinations. There has been little impact on improving the status, the mode of recruitment, or the development of a career structure for teacher trainers in Botswana. This area was also ignored by the National Commission on Education, which reported in 1993 (Republic of Botswana, 1993). A long-term strategy is required to redress these inadequacies, as these aspects of teacher education in Botswana remain notably poor, and localization has been hampered because of these drawbacks. Affiliation does provide the means of addressing these issues. A central feature of affiliation is visitations conducted by the university to establish whether the facilities, the staffing and the academic programmes followed are in accord with the requirements of the university. This process can be used as a lever to exert pressure on ministries of education to ensure that the required criteria can be met (Hopkin, 1994d). To date this feature of affiliation has been neglected by the University of Botswana. If it were more vigorously prosecuted, the standards and practices of the affiliated institutions could be markedly raised and improved, notably the recruitment and professional terms of service of the staff.

Some success has been enjoyed in the field of promoting research in the colleges, and citizens have been participating in this through joint research projects in collaboration with the Office of the Coordinator, Affiliated Institutions, and members of the Faculty of Education (Hopkin, 1993b). Furthermore, in its efforts to stimulate more research by college staff through appropriate workshops, the Ministry of Education has made extensive use of Faculty of Education staff as resource persons. This has been done at minimal cost, and the mutual exchange of expertise on such terms derives largely from the links established through affiliation, which is a system that depends heavily on the availability of university, college and ministry personnel, and the sharing of costs.

Another valuable advantage of affiliation is the opportunity offered to forge international links on the part of the teachers' colleges. Universities are, by their nature, oriented to an international perspective, and the links involved can be extended to the colleges. Connections have been established, through the Office of the Coordinator, between a teacher education institution in the United Kingdom and one of the affiliated institutions. As a result, staff from Trinity College, Carmarthen, ran a successful workshop in Tlokweng in 1994. At the time of writing, the link was in the process of being formalized, other staff and students exchanges were planned and it was hoped that it would be extended to other colleges in due course (Evans and Webster, 1994). One illuminating justification for fostering this relationship put forward by the college involved was that the success of the policy of localization of staff in the primary colleges meant that the current staff profile was a somewhat homogeneous one, in terms of experience, ethnic mix and qualifications. The link being developed was intended to provide an international perspective that had been missing with the withdrawal of expatriate staff from the college. The furthering of an international and developmental perspective in both college programmes was also one of the principal motives of Trinity College staff initiating the link. Affiliation with a university facilitates the forming of such links.

University affiliation in Botswana illustrates the benefits to be gained from taking advantage of scale, as it facilitates the efficient exploitation of available qualified academic personnel and of data. As a small state (Bray and Packer, 1993), Botswana has only nine institutions that train teachers: six of these are affiliated institutions, two others prepare teachers for University of Botswana awards and the other is the Faculty of Education. Establishing and maintaining contacts between staff is relatively easy, and comprehensive data about teacher education in Botswana can be made available. Computerized databases have been set up in the Office of the Coordinator which contain full records pertaining to diploma and primary certificate results for the past four years. The advantages of this have been realized: computer processing of examination results has led to much more rapid publication of results; greater accuracy has been achieved; and the external moderation processes have been improved and enhanced. To take full advantage of computerization all affiliated institutions should be adequately equipped with computers, and there should be a number of staff with computer expertise. A major drawback has been the failure of the Ministry of Education to supply the primary teacher training colleges and the colleges of education with computers and software. Pressure has been brought on the Ministry of Education by the university in this field and plans have been drawn up to equip colleges with the necessary facilities (Teacher Training and Development Department, 1994). When this is done, the prospects for rapid and further development will be good.

There are areas pertaining to affiliation which have not been taken advantage of by the university and colleges. Little has been done until very recently to develop cross-crediting, whereby diplomas and certificates could be used by the holders as credit towards degree courses. This area has been given minimal attention (Prophet, 1991). However, the increasing rigour of the moderation procedures installed, and the recruitment of students with improved entry qualifications to the colleges of education has, from 1996, led to diplomas being assessed for credit towards some degrees offered by the Faculty of Education. Affiliation is also an avenue for raising the status and standards of the programmes offered. The National Commission discounted as premature the notion that the programmes of the colleges of education should be improved so that they could lead to a BEd award (Republic of Botswana, 1994). In the short and middle terms this is valid, but the colleges and university could use the affiliation infrastructure to achieve this in the long term.

Affiliation, in the field of teacher education, has done much to consolidate, extend and link academic communities in Botswana. In the middle term, the university should explore how a ladder could be put in place whereby institutions which are under the umbrella of the university could be upgraded. This has been the practice in the United Kingdom, and is exemplified in the experience of the University of Manchester (Burge, 1993). Different categories of affiliation have to be established, each determined by appropriate criteria. Such a ladder would be an incentive for institutions to upgrade themselves. A change of this nature in the pattern of affiliation in Botswana would be a major one and would necessitate the devising of formal criteria for different categories of association or affiliation. Affiliation could thus be the tool for enhancing the scope of tertiary education in Botswana. There is much work still to be done if the potential of affiliation is to be fully exploited.

## Problematic issues and areas of tension

It has been noted that the interests of the university and of the Ministry of Education are markedly different. The latter is concerned primarily with the supply of teachers for the school system.

The university is primarily concerned with qualitative matters, such as the maintenance of appropriate academic and professional standards. Given these different perspectives, it is inevitable that the colleges are sometimes caught in the middle. Senior staff of the colleges have claimed that the demands made by the two bodies are mutually exclusive and impossible to satisfy (Ministry of Education, 1981, p. 27). The validity of this will be examined below: tensions do exist when those responsible for teacher training are motivated from different perspectives, and this is inevitable when university affiliation is involved.

These tensions do not only arise between the Ministry of Education and the university: they also exist between institutions. An area that promotes tension is the culture of the institutions. Staff in government teacher training institutions work in a very different cultural ambience from those in a university. When individuals manifest these, the clash of cultural styles can cause great offence, even in what might appear to be trivial matters. For example, the attitude of some moderators to time during the moderation procedures is perceived as capricious by senior management in colleges. This is the case when moderators wear casual dress. The Ministry of Education is formal and prescriptive in these matters, and the college staff are obliged to follow ministry directives. These issues have been formally raised at board level, and there have been cases of university moderators and teaching practice supervisors being refused admission to schools on the grounds that they were 'improperly' dressed. University staff have to be discreetly reminded about respecting the dress and time codes of the colleges. However, the culture of the university is inimical to prescription, as this would not be acceptable to individuals. The few who do not conform do not intend offence. Unfortunately, they make an impact out of proportion to their number, and thus cause tension.

Another problematic 'cultural' factor is differing institutional relationships and management styles. Colleges are notably bureaucratic and hierarchical, and approaches to individual staff normally have to go 'through the proper channels'. University staff have difficulty in initiating meetings with individual college staff unless the request is made via the college senior management, or even the ministry. For example, if an individual college staff member has been identified as a suitable collaborator for a research project, or has been invited to a workshop, then the approach has to be made through the ministry and college authorities. On occasions, a different person might be appointed, one who is deemed more suitable by the authorities because of his or her office and assigned duties. University staff operate in a more egalitarian culture where matters such as professional collaboration are concerned, and are accustomed to direct approaches being made on an individual basis. Such conventions can be sources of friction.

Furthermore, it is advantageous that affiliation does not incorporate non-academic regulations and matters. Universities and colleges differ greatly in the way that they attempt to govern – or possibly not govern – how students conduct themselves and/or take on responsibility for their own affairs. The regulations of the Ministry of Education governing students in the colleges are more restrictive, and sometimes even draconian, than are those for students in the university. The college students frequently cite university practices as levers to obtain 'concessions' from the ministry. This again can cause disputes in the management of institutions within a system of affiliation.

The operational procedures and practices of the university compared with those at the affiliated institutions may cause difficulties. An important example of this is the attitude to regulations. Colleges' attitudes to regulations governing academic programmes appear at times to be cavalier. Some ten years elapsed before a satisfactory set of regulations was developed by the Board of Affiliated Institutions (Primary Teacher Training Colleges), and similar difficulties were experienced by the Board of Affiliated Institutions (Colleges of Education). It has taken time for the senior management of the colleges to assimilate the principle that regulations cannot be enacted retrospectively. Another contentious issue is that the university senate and its committees are perceived to be too stringent and inflexible in applying regulations.

The ministry, on the other hand, wants flexibility in the application of academic regulations.

These misunderstandings are the result of the failure of the colleges and the ministry to comprehend and appreciate that the university is a self-regulating body. Regulations governing academic matters in the university are determined by the university itself, through senate. For this reason, university staff, particularly the senators, take great care to uphold and interpret the regulations for which they are responsible. This principle enshrines a basic tenet of university autonomy. College staff are Ministry of Education employees and recruited as such: it is only in academic and professional matters that they enjoy a degree of independence. Even these, to a degree, are subject to and dependent upon the university. When the staff of affiliated institutions are well qualified professionals, as is the case in Botswana, it is not surprising that academic regulations, which are the province of the university, are a source of friction and misunderstanding.

The rights and duties of external moderators and examiners may also be a subject of controversy. With respect to examinations, there has been minimal conflict. However, this is not so with the moderation of teaching practice grades. The basic point at issue raised by college of education staff is that it is unjust for moderators to change the grade of a student on the evidence of one or possibly two visits. The moderation procedure – which has been used by the primary teacher training colleges for a number of years – was introduced only recently in the colleges of education. The injustice is that only a sample of students are seen, and a grade may only be changed if a student is observed by a moderator. This is seen as arbitrary and unjust. However, the common university stance is that this is normal university moderation practice, and that the moderators must have the right to change grades. In effect, moderators are concerned not with justice being done to individual students, but with maintaining university standards and parity between the different institutions. There is little doubt that the college staff have a good case – one which undermines the validity of university practice in moderation and external examining whereby the external decision is invariably accepted as the final ruling.

Contrary perspectives (the concern of the ministry being to supply teachers for schools and that of the university to maintain academic and professional standards) also create problems. Little overt pressure may be exerted by the former to pass students, but devices have been used to reduce non-completion rates. In the late 1980s, there was a large cohort of untrained teachers who had to supplement examination subjects to complete the requirements for the Primary Teachers' Certificate. Pressure from the Ministry of Education and its representatives on the Board of Affiliated Institutions led to the provision of increased opportunities for supplementing candidates to repeat their examinations. Candidates were thus enabled to retake examinations that they first sat more than a decade previously in some cases. Whilst this moratorium has ceased, the fact remains that such devices are of dubious academic and professional merit. In the ministry's eyes they are justified because of the resulting reduction in the number of unqualified teachers in the schools, and the increase in the stock of qualified teachers.

Academic regulations governing examinations have also caused uncertainties. Ministry of Education policy debars students on teacher education courses from repeating a year, but this has not been consistently applied to those on secondary courses. Furthermore, objections have been made by the ministry when examination regulations have caused students to be excluded at the end of a three-year programme. Perhaps the root cause of such conflicts is that the ministry and its officials are unable to accept university autonomy. It is the only autonomous educational institution in Botswana; all other tertiary institutions are subject to the control of the government and such control is rigidly exercised. This is not so on the academic programmes of the affiliated institutions which lead to awards of the university, and this is the source of the difficulties identified above.

Ideological issues also generate tension. The Ministry of Education maintains very formal relationships with the colleges, and these often have paternalistic overtones. This is inevitable in the centralized and bureaucratic educational systems which are characteristic of small states (Bray and Packer, 1993). In these circumstances, efforts by university staff to develop inter-institutional links and programmes can be hampered by the need to go through the 'proper' bureaucratic channels, which involve time-consuming and tedious processes, sometimes resulting in decisions being made on grounds of administrative expediency rather than on educational ones.

The neo-colonialistic attitudes of individual university staff have also raised complications. For example, a move was initiated to make the staff of each primary teacher training college responsible for the marking of the examination scripts of their own students. This received guarded approval from most quarters, as it was seen as a step towards the colleges assuming greater responsibility for these areas. However, some subject staff of the four colleges wished to continue to mark all the papers as a team. This defeated the purpose of the original proposal, and was supported by some of the university moderators. The point made by the latter was that college staff should not mark their own students' work, but had to be brought together under the supervision of a moderator to iron out any problems arising, ensuring that the marking was uniform, and that no colleges would gain an advantage. Furthermore, it was pointed out to the writer that conventional university moderation is not suitable for the Primary Teachers' Certificate examination. Experience to date suggests that the marking of their own students' work by staff has been very professional, and they have marked their own supplementing candidates in the past. Furthermore, a system of examination moderation along university lines has been successfully introduced for the two colleges of education. This latter move should demonstrate that the lack of confidence on the part of some moderators is unjustified. It must also be pointed out that staff in the primary colleges do seem to be very dependent on the university, the ministry and college senior management for guidance. A dependency syndrome prevails that is a legacy of past experience: the university and the Office of the Coordinator are committed to weaning college staff away from it.

An increasingly difficult problem related to affiliation is the recruitment of moderators. At the time of writing, the number of moderators required to service the system of moderation was just over 50, plus two external examiners. In relation to the demands made on it, the resources of the Faculty of Education are limited, particularly those of the Primary Education Department. Very few staff in other faculties or other tertiary institutions in Botswana have the expertise or experience to undertake duties as moderators. This problem will be further compounded when the fixed-term appointments (two to three years) of the current cohort of moderators end. To date, fixed-term appointments have only been used for the teaching practice moderation panels and the moderation of diploma examinations. When the practice is extended to the moderation of all primary programmes, the difficulties experienced in recruiting moderators will be exacerbated.

This problem is not faced by the University of Zimbabwe. The scheme of association is operated by the Department of Teacher Education (DTE), based in the Faculty of Education, which has 14 academic staff, whereas there is one in Botswana. Each of the 15 associated teacher training institutions sets and marks its own examinations, which are moderated by the department (Department of Teacher Education, 1993). However, the department is able to call on the services of the staff of the faculty and the university, and of staff in the associated institutions, as moderators because the examinations taken by each institution follow a common format but differ in content and detail. In the Botswana scheme the colleges take the same certificate or diploma examinations as appropriate. It is therefore not possible to use college staff as moderators for the examinations, as they are involved in the setting and marking of the same examinations. In the case of teaching practice moderation, the use of college staff is feasible, and their participation has enhanced and strengthened this exercise. If an examination format could be devised which facilitated the use of suitably qualified and experienced college staff as moderators, then the reservoir of available moderators could be enlarged.

## University affiliation and quality in teacher training

From the foregoing discussion it is possible to identify the conditions that should be fulfilled and factors that should prevail whereby a scheme of university affiliation could successfully promote the qualitative development of teacher education. The first, and probably the most important, condition is that the country's political climate is a democratic or participative one. It is only in such a political situation that a ministry of education will delegate responsibility to a non-government or parastatal institution for the academic and professional standards of pre-service teacher training. Furthermore, such a climate fosters university autonomy, and the academic and professional freedom that this entails. In turn, the university has to respond to this freedom in a responsible and accountable way, and to conduct its affairs in a way that is responsive to national aspirations and mores. Affiliated colleges would benefit from a spin-off in this, as they would be able to enjoy greater freedom in academic and professional matters than if they were governed by government regulations. Political conditions such as these do not always prevail, particularly on the continent of Africa. Without them affiliation will do little to promote qualitative growth in teacher education.

University affiliation is also easier to promote in states which are relatively homogeneous, because in such states micro-political educational factors are less numerous and obstructive (Archer, 1981). In Zimbabwe, the present system of association has been in existence for nearly two decades, yet the mission and government origins and control of the teacher training institutions still impinge on standards (Hopkin, 1994d). A major factor to be negotiated in current attempts to introduce a scheme of affiliation in Papua New Guinea is that most teacher training institutions are controlled by missions. They are understandably reluctant to hand over their teacher training activities, which they perceive as a major investment in political and educational terms (Weeks, 1994). For a cluster of historical reasons, mission and private activity in teacher education in Botswana has been minimal, and is not present today. One consequence is that education and teacher training is secular and the number of interested parties is limited, thus making it much easier to operate a scheme of affiliation with the university. In a more pluralistic educational context, such schemes are feasible but more difficult to operate.

For similar reasons, schemes of affiliation are more easily established in smaller states. They are also suitable for such contexts because scarce resources can be deployed more effectively. Universities are expensive to set up and run, they normally employ the best pool of high-level expertise in teacher education in the country, and a scheme of affiliation makes that pool more readily available to government teacher training colleges and to the Ministry of Education. In larger states, the same conditions prevail, but should be applied on a regional basis, particularly in developing countries where expertise is in short supply. Equally important is the fact that the academic community is extended through affiliation to a wider 'parish', and the presence of such a community, based on universities, is essential if a healthy ideological and intellectual climate is to prevail (Popkewitz, 1984).

A scheme of affiliation is most likely to be successful in improving the quality of teacher training, or any other field, if it is permeated by a collegiate ethos. To achieve this the management agencies of the teacher training institutions, particularly the Ministry of Education and the senior management and controlling agencies of the colleges, must be part of the decision-making process. This involves full membership of the university boards set up to regulate and control the scheme of affiliation. A guiding principle that should be adopted by the university is commitment to the institutional development on the part of the colleges. Staff of colleges also have to be involved in decision-making related to academic matters. Furthermore, the university has to ensure that every encouragement is given to college staff to be involved in research, workshops and seminars with university colleagues as appropriate.

Much of the above discussion has focused upon external moderation and examining as a means of promoting standards. However, the initiative for

institutional and staff development through affiliation does not rest on the university alone. Universities could encourage affiliated institutions to undertake self-study exercises as a self-directing mode of improving institutional standards and promoting development. Guidelines have been provided by the two self-study exercises undertaken by the primary teacher training colleges and the colleges of education (Ministry of Education, 1987, 1992). These procedures are used in the system of accreditation for teacher training institutions in the United States (Evans, 1991). Accreditation systems feature self-study, in association with periodic reviews by external bodies, as a key to institutional development. This places the onus for development on the staff of the institution, but external moderating bodies are used to ensure that the standards achieved are appropriate and in accord with the goals of the institution (Hutton, 1994).

A variety of factors prevented the potential of the first self-study exercise from being realized (Hopkin, 1993b). If these receive attention and the exercises are conducted periodically, then a major internal impetus will be given to institutional development. Used in tandem with visitations by an appropriate university committee, self-study could become part of the process of monitoring standards and institutional development. To date there has been too much reliance on external examining and moderating to do this. Within their remits these processes have been successful and should always be important features of a scheme of affiliation. To ensure more global institutional monitoring and development it is essential for such schemes to include procedures that are comprehensive and that deal with all academic and professional aspects of the work of affiliated institutions.

## Conclusions

It was noted in the first section of this chapter that in England and Wales in the past ten years there had been a shift away from the universities with respect to teacher training. The theme of this chapter has been that such a shift is inappropriate in the context of developing countries. Indeed, it has been argued that delegating more responsibility to universities through schemes of affiliation would bring about improvements in the quality of teacher training in these countries, as has been the case in Botswana. The benefits, actual and potential, and problems associated with affiliation have been described. Particular emphasis has been placed on the advantages that affiliated institutions gain through attaining greater autonomy in academic affairs than would otherwise be the case. Furthermore, affiliation facilitates more effective deployment of staff and collaboration between institutions. It also makes available the expertise of staff in the 'parent' university and others, particularly from faculties of education.

An important question to ask is whether a unit within a ministry of education could perform a similar function with respect to monitoring and promoting improved standards in teacher education programmes. In the case of Botswana, the Ministry of Education funds the operational costs (but not the salaries) of the Office of the Coordinator, Affiliated Institutions. In theory there is no reason why such a unit could not be set up within the Ministry of Education. However, as such a unit would be an arm of the ministry it is unlikely that it would be able to offer the independent and objective services that must characterize appropriate monitoring procedures. Furthermore, it is unlikely that the staff of the ministry would have either the range of expertise or the time to perform the duties required. While university staff could be utilized for these duties, they could not be employed in the same collegiate spirit as they are with good schemes of affiliation. Any reviews or visitations of the teacher training institutions undertaken by the ministry would be, in effect, 'in-house' operations, and would not have the same status or impact as those carried out through university affiliation. The setting up of such a unit would possibly be more suitable in a political and educational context where the relationships are paternalistic and centralized control is exercised.

In countries undergoing rapid educational expansion and change, university affiliation is one of the strategies whereby standards could be raised in teacher education. This strategy is most suited to relatively small states, and to states where the pattern of government being developed is democratic or participative. University departments of education in the United Kingdom have been the engine rooms for powering change and development in teacher training (Taylor, 1980). In developing countries they should still play this role, and extend it through systems of university affiliation. By raising the quality of the programmes offered in non-university teacher training programmes, affiliation could strengthen the impact made on teacher training by the universities.

# References

Unpublished manuscripts are located in the Office of the Coordinator, Affiliated Institutions, Faculty of Education, University of Botswana.

Archer, M. S. (1981) Educational politics: a model for their analysis. In P. Broadfoot, C. Brock and W. Tulasiewicz (eds), *Politics and International Change: An International Survey.* London: Croom Helm.

Bell, R. (1990) The Scottish university and educational studies. In J. B. Thomas (ed.), *British Universities and Teacher Education.* London: Falmer Press.

Bray, M. and Packer, S. (1993) *Education in Small States: Concepts, Challenges and Strategies.* Oxford: Pergamon Press.

Burge, W. (1993) Visit to Botswana: report on a visit to the University of Botswana and its affiliated colleges. Unpublished manuscript.

Committee of Vice-Chancellors and Principals (1986) *Academic Standards in Universities (1986). Report of a Committee.* London: Committee of Vice-Chancellors and Principals.

Department of Teacher Education, University of Zimbabwe (1993) *A Handbook for the Department of Teacher Education.* Harare: University of Zimbabwe.

Evans, G. and Webster, R. (1994) Report to the British Council, Gaborone, on an academic visit to Tlokweng College of Education May 1994. Unpublished manuscript.

Evans, M. W. (1991) *Selected Issues in Education in Botswana: A Report of a Consultancy.* Gaborone: Government Printer.

Heywood, J. (1989) *Assessment in Higher Education,* 2nd edn. New York: Wiley.

Hopkin, A. G. (1992) Teaching practice workshop: Mochudi education centre. Unpublished manuscript.

Hopkin, A. G. (1993a) Final teaching practice moderation panel: final report. Unpublished manuscript.

Hopkin, A. G. (1993b) Self-study in the primary teacher training colleges in Botswana 1986–9: report to the Botswana Educational Research Association. Unpublished manuscript.

Hopkin, A. G. (1994a) Self-study in primary teacher training institutions in Botswana. *Mosenodi*, **2** (1).

Hopkin, A. G. (1994b) Primary Teachers' Certificate 1994: Coordinator's provisional report. Unpublished manuscript.

Hopkin, A. G. (1994c) External examining and moderating at the University of Botswana. Paper presented at the South African Comparative and History of Education Society Annual Conference, Gaborone, October.

Hopkin, A. G. (1994d) Academic examining at Nyadire Teachers' College, November 17–18, 1994. Chief Examiner's report. Unpublished manuscript.

Hutton, M. (1994) Two approaches to evaluating quality in a university higher education development unit. *Bulletin Number 10*, March. Gaborone: University of Botswana.

Mautle, G. (1994) Primary Teachers Certificate 1994: Moderator's report – social studies. Unpublished manuscript.

Ministry of Education (1981) *Report of the Professional Visits to Teacher Training Colleges: Francistown, Serowe, Lobatse*. Gaborone: Government Printer.

Ministry of Education, Primary and Teacher Training (1987) *A Self Study Guide for Botswana Primary Teacher Training Colleges*. Gaborone: Government Printer.

Ministry of Education, Teacher Education Division (1992) *A Self Study Guide for Botswana Colleges Of Education*. Gaborone: Government Printer.

Mokgautsi, D. O., Tladi, T. and Youngman, F. (1988) Report of a visit to the University of Zimbabwe to study its relationship with external institutions. Unpublished manuscript.

Office of the Coordinator, Affiliated Institutions (1994) Final teaching practice moderation 1994: report of the panel. Unpublished manuscript.

Partington, J., Brown, G. and Gordon, G. (1993) *Handbook for External Examiners in Higher Education*.

Sheffield: Committee of Vice Chancellors and Principals.

Peters, O. (1983) Distance teaching and industrial production: a comparative interpretation in outline. In D. Stewart, D. Keegan and B. Holmberg (eds), *Distance Education: International Perspectives*. London: Croom Helm.

Popkewitz, T. S. (1984) *Paradigm and Ideology in Educational Research: The Social Function of the Intellectual*. Brighton: Falmer Press.

Primary Education Improvement Project (1991) *The Tenth and Final Report*. Gaborone: PEIP.

Prophet, R. (1991) Memorandum to Advisory Committee on Education 7/11/1991. Unpublished manuscript.

Republic of Botswana (1993) *Report on the National Commission on Education*. Gaborone: Government Printer.

Republic of Botswana (1994) *The Revised National Policy on Education: Government Paper No. 2 of 1994*. Gaborone: Government Printer.

Taylor, W. (1980) Problems and solutions in relation to education in comparative perspective: The case of teacher education. In B. Holmes (ed.) *Diversity and Unity in Education: A Comparative Perspective*. London: Allen and Unwin.

Teacher Training and Development Department (1994) Consolidated list of projects (renovations and new constructions) at the colleges of education, teacher training colleges and education centres for 1995/6 and 1996/7. Unpublished manuscript.

Thomas, J. B. (ed.) (1990) *British Universities and Teacher Education*. London: Falmer Press.

Turner, J. D. (1990) The area training organisations. In J. B. Thomas (ed.), *British Universities and Teacher Education*. London: Falmer Press.

University of Botswana (1991) *Calendar 1991–1992*. Gaborone: University of Botswana.

Weeks, S. G. (1994) Report of teacher education program coordination specialist: phase one, 1994. Unpublished manuscript.

Yoder, J. H. and Mautle, G. (1991) The context of reform. In J. H. Yoder and M. W. Evans (eds), *Patterns of Reform in Primary Education: The Case of Botswana*. Gaborone: Macmillan.

# 25 Multicultural Education: Approaches and Practice

LOTTY ELDERING AND JULIA
JOHNSON ROTHENBERG

## Introduction

In this chapter, two authors from two different countries, the Netherlands and the United States, discuss multicultural education in their countries. Both countries have an ethnic-culturally mixed population. Multicultural education can be set up from various perspectives, depending on how ethnic minority pupils are viewed. It can be limited to pupils from ethnic-cultural groups (a particularistic approach) or can be directed at all pupils (a universalistic approach). Multicultural education reflects the social and political context of the schools. Both countries explicitly recognize that they have a multicultural society. This statement, however, does not have the same connotations and implications in both countries.

In the first section of this chapter, the nature of multiculturalism in both countries will be described. The following sections deal with approaches and practice of multicultural education. Our intent is to use the diversity inherent in our two viewpoints of anthropology and education to provide a new framework. Both theory and practice will be examined and expanded. Together, it is our view that policies and practices must be specifically addressed. We also see value in comparing the two countries. The topics within multicultural education are clarified by examining them through the eyes of another culture. In a sense we use a multicultural lens to view each other's strengths and weaknesses.

## Multiculturalism in the Netherlands and the United States

To analyse the nature of multiculturalism in a society, one has to distinguish the following dimensions:

- objective reality;
- ideology;
- official policy;
- practical implementation.

(Fleras and Elliott, 1992)

Multiculturalism as an objective reality concerns the coexistence of different ethnic or cultural groups in a society. These groups often differ in numbers, history, social position, power, culture and ethnic/racial origins. Ethnic-cultural diversity in a society is often the result of (colonial) expansion, slavery or immigration. Each multicultural society has its own genesis and, consequently, its own diversity.

About 6 per cent of the Dutch population are immigrants from former colonies (Surinam, the Antilles and the Moluccan Islands) and from Mediterranean countries (predominantly Morocco and Turkey). Another 2 per cent are immigrants from Western countries (the USA, EU countries, Japan). The character of the immigration has recently changed. About one-third of the 120,000 immigrants coming to the Netherlands each year are refugees and asylum seekers, predominantly from ex-Yugoslavia, Somalia, Iran, Iraq and Afghanistan (Gelauff-Hanzon *et al.*, 1994; Veenman, 1994). The immigrants are mainly concentrated in cities with more than 100,000 inhabitants, particularly in Amsterdam, Rotterdam, The Hague and Utrecht. A similar situation occurs in the schools. Within the big cities, however, a further concentration has occurred over the past years. In the period 1986 to 1992, the number of schools with more than 60 per cent of ethnic minority children nearly doubled (CEB, 1994). For the population in these cities and schools, the multicultural nature of Dutch society is a daily reality, whereas people living in other parts of the country, particularly in rural areas, are only confronted with the multiethnic character of Dutch society by television and newspapers. A relevant issue is what consequences these differences in social context have, or should have, for multicultural education in schools throughout the Netherlands.

Despite the differences in size and scope, the situation in the United States is similar, particularly in the dramatic effects of increased immigration on urban areas. The current immigration patterns in the United States are equal to those at the turn of the century, when Europeans flocked to the United States. Now the immigration is far more global, although the magnitude of Latino immigration (from Mexico, Central America and the Caribbean) is the largest. Immigration was at its highest in 1991, totalling nearly two million people, with the largest numbers of 384,000 from the rest of North America and 357,000 from Asia (US Immigration and Naturalization Service, *Statistical Yearbook*, annual). Immigration to the United States is still concentrated in its border areas. The schools that are most affected are urban areas on the Eastern seaboard, the Southern coasts, Mexican and Canadian borders and the West coast. This is a more specific statement than it may appear, because multiculturalism is not yet at all a major presence in most inland schools, even those, for example, in Massachusetts, New York, Connecticut, Oregon and Washington state.

A second dimension of multiculturalism concerns the ideology with regard to the identity of society and how multicultural differences between groups are dealt with or controlled. The ideology may fluctuate between the extremes of assimilation or pluralism. In the political debate among interest groups, the identity and culture of a society are always the subject of discussion and negotiation (Tomlinson, 1990; Rex, 1991; Eldering, 1996). Views on the identity of a society or the desirable degree of cultural diversity may change in the course of time. Official policy usually reflects the basic values of a society. The ideological discourse concerning immigrants in the Netherlands, for instance, centres on two basic values of Dutch society: equal opportunities for all residents and equivalence of cultures.

Equivalence of cultures (religions), a value with a long tradition in the Netherlands, is the basis of the compartmentalization of the Dutch school system. More than two-thirds of the pupils in the Netherlands currently attend state-funded private (denominational) schools. With the arrival of large numbers of Muslims from Morocco, Turkey and Surinam, the question arises whether a new Muslim 'compartment' ('pillar') will be formed. Although the constitutional right to freedom to establish schools is also given to immigrants, only 4 per cent of pupils with an Islamic background currently attend schools based on Islamic principles. The low numbers of the Muslims and their distribution over the country hamper the forming of a new religious 'pillar' (Eldering, 1993). Official Dutch policy on behalf of ethnic minorities reflects the values of equal opportunities and equivalence of cultures. The Dutch government officially stated in 1983 that the Netherlands is a multicultural society. Although under the 1985 Primary Education Act schools must prepare children for life in a multicultural society, so far no financial aid has been made available for intercultural education. To realize equal opportunities, the Educational Priority Policy came into effect in 1985. Schools with ethnic minority pupils receive extra funds. Further, pupils from Mediterranean countries receive lessons in the language and culture of their country of origin during school hours. This education was originally aimed at preparing the children for return to their home countries. An interesting point for current debate is the compatibility of the culture policy and the equal opportunity policy (Eldering, 1989, 1994a).

In the United States, the discourse is more extreme. Official national policy emphasizes equality of opportunity and recognition of diversity, thereby implying a doctrine of equivalent cultures. However, different states have very different policies and practices. In addition to policy, the currents of debate about varieties of multicultural pedagogy and multilingual pedagogy run strong and deep.

There are areas of most states, such as Iowa, Vermont, Nebraska, Montana, Utah and many others, where Eurocentric cultures prevail to the exclusion of all others. These situations exist side by side with the rising tide of the effects of immigration. California, for example, has designated English as the official language, even though many school districts are more than 90 per cent Spanish speaking, and oriental languages abound in the schools. Similar situations exist in the other states bordering Latino countries. Conflicts among cultures are openly publicized in the United States, and educational practices associated with these conflicts are also debated. Issues such as implicit and explicit racism, multilingual teaching and pluralistic curriculum materials are the foci of policy and educational discussions throughout the country.

One particularly poignant example comes from a current study in a large school system in a state with a high proportion of Latina/Latino immigration (Gonzalez, 1995). The study began because of a panel discussion featuring the chancellor of the state university and the high school principal on the topic of why more Latino/a students did not attend the university. The chancellor said that the university would take any student ready for admission and the principal said that he had 400 students ready. Then and there, the two of them initiated the 'Principal's Pick Program', which included extensive financial help for the students to be 'picked' for admission to the university. The principal found only 14 students who were eligible for admission to the university. The Faculty of Education at the university decided to study possible observable causes of the lack of Latino/a students eligible for university education.

The results of the study were devastating in terms of faculty and student attitudes, expectations, goals and certainly teaching and learning. In a school with 90 per cent Latino/a students, fewer than 1 per cent of each advanced placement class (university level) were Latino/a. On the other end, most of the lowest tracks were totally Latino/a. Teachers openly said that they were preparing such low-tracked students for 'service jobs', such as gardening, cleaning, maintenance, sanitation and the like. This study exemplifies the great complexity of the issues in the United States, from school structure, to racism and classism, to individual issues of psychological development and identity.

Besides the differences in tradition and scale of immigration, the countries share similarities relevant for educational policy and practice. Multiculturalism is publicly, but not universally, acknowledged in both countries, and the implications of both parts of this statement are multi-level. Multiculturalism is a daily reality for the population of urban areas and the students of many schools in the big cities, but a large part of the population experiences multiculturalism only indirectly through the media. A second similarity between the countries is the enormous cultural diversity of the immigrant population. The next sections of this chapter deal with the question of how schools deal with ethnic-cultural diversity.

## Approaches to multicultural education

Multicultural education has many modalities (see Table 25.1). Multicultural education is considered in its broad sense here and is defined as being education which takes into account the ethnic-cultural differences between pupils in some way. The scheme shown in Table 25.1 departs from two principles of order: the target groups at which multicultural education is aimed and the perspective from which this occurs. Multicultural education can be limited solely to pupils from ethnic-cultural groups (a particularistic approach) or can be directed at all pupils (a universalistic approach). Multicultural education can be set up from various perspectives: disadvantage, enrichment, bicultural competence and collective equality. These partly overlapping perspectives differ

**Table 25.1**  Approaches to multicultural education

| Perspective | Target groups | |
| --- | --- | --- |
| | Pupils from ethnic groups | All pupils |
| Disadvantage | Attunement of education to development level<br>Second-language education<br>Bilingual education<br>Culturally responsive education | |
| Enrichment | Monocultural courses aimed at language, literature, geography, religion, history, art | Multicultural courses aimed at language, literature, geography, religion, history, art |
| *Bicultural competence* | Bicultural education | Bicultural education |
| *Collective equality groups* | Private schools | Multicultural curriculum |

*Source*: Eldering (1994a).

according to the position of the minority cultures in the curriculum and the attention paid to individual or collective inequality.

The assumption underlying multicultural education from a disadvantage perspective is that pupils from ethnic-cultural groups have educational arrears in comparison to pupils from mainstream groups. Multicultural education from this perspective is aimed at removing these disadvantages. The catching up on disadvantages occurs with an eye to gaining better school achievement and realizing equal opportunities. The degree to which account is taken of the specific cultural characteristics of the pupils depends on the schools' and teachers' perception and appreciation of cultural differences. Teachers who view children's educational arrears as deficits stemming from their 'backward' home backgrounds pay no attention to the cultural features of the pupils, whereas those that have a more positive attitude towards the culture of the pupils con-

cerned, and perceive educational disadvantages as being a result of cultural differences, tend to use the cultural features of the pupils, such as their native language, communication style and style of learning, as points of departure for 'culturally responsive teaching' (McDermott and Goldman, 1983; Erickson, 1987; Ogbu, 1987). In multicultural education from this perspective, the removal of disadvantage has priority, and the native culture plays only a secondary and temporary role. Different forms of multicultural education can be placed under this heading, varying from the immersion model in which education is exclusively given in the second language, to bilingual education with a transitional character.

The assumption behind the enrichment perspective is that cultural diversity implies enrichment of society and should be given expression in education. Multicultural education from this perspective may be aimed at pupils from specific ethnic-cultural groups ('single group studies'), or at all pupils regardless of ethnic-cultural origins. During the nineteenth and early twentieth centuries, many ethnic-cultural communities in the United States introduced the community's native language, often German, to education (Seller, 1992). Courses based on one culture are set up for a variety of reasons: as an acknowledgment of the language and culture of the ethnic communities ('heritage language courses' in Canada); as a means for making pupils from ethnic-cultural groups aware of the contribution made by their groups to the establishment of society ('Black studies' followed later by 'Mexican-American studies', 'Indian-American studies' and 'Asian-American studies' in the United States); or as a preparation for returning to the country of origin (education in the language and culture of the country of origin for Moroccan and Turkish children in the Netherlands) (Eldering, 1996). The curriculum reflects its origins and focuses on history and literature or language and culture/religion. Multicultural courses are intended for all pupils, irrespective of ethnic-cultural background. The objectives are that pupils from all groups become acquainted with each other's cultures, learn to appreciate them and learn how to relate to each other. This approach is called the 'human relations approach', 'intergroup approach' or 'intercultural education'. The culture elements dealt with in the curriculum mostly concern language, literature, history, geography, religion and art. The basic idea behind this approach is that knowledge of each other's culture would lead to a better understanding and a positive attitude. Multicultural education of this type was developed in the United States during the Second World War, in the period when many African-Americans migrated to the large cities in the North and race riots occurred. It never became an integral part of the curriculum. The report (*Education for All*) of the Advisory Commission set up by the UK Department of Education and Science, for the benefit of education to pupils from ethnic minorities, recommended such an approach for the United Kingdom situation (Department of Education and Science, 1985). This approach, however, did not take root there (Troyna and Edwards, 1993) or in the Netherlands (CEB, 1994; Eldering, 1994b, 1996).

A relatively large amount of teaching materials for multicultural education has been developed by practitioners in this field in the United States. Multicultural education from this perspective has a few serious shortcomings. First, no conceptual and theoretical connection has been sought in psychological theories on intergroup conflicts and the origination of prejudice (Sleeter and Grant, 1987; Vedder, 1993). A second shortcoming is that the cultural content of these courses is usually not based on empirical research on the culture of the specific groups (Ogbu, 1992). Further, research has shown that intercultural education given by teachers not trained in this field works to confirm the stereotype rather than to prevent prejudice (Troyna and Edwards, 1993; Bartolome, 1994).

Multicultural education from the perspective of bicultural competence goes one step further than the previous approaches, and is mainly intended to make pupils from ethnic-cultural groups competent in two cultures by giving them bicultural education. Education in the culture of the ethnic-cultural groups aims at the preservation of the cultures concerned (Banks, 1988). In 1986, the United States Congress ratified the Bilingual Education Act, which provides for the financing of bilingual education programmes. Eighty per cent of these programmes, however, have assimilation as an objective and not an increase in the pupils' bicultural competence (Seller, 1992). In contrast to the approaches discussed so far, multicultural education from the perspective of collective equality acknowledges the collective equality of groups/cultures rather than the equality of individuals. It therefore questions the structure of society, the school system and the mechanisms which support inequality.

Multicultural education has many modalities. These do not occur equally often in practice. Multicultural education is usually aimed at pupils from ethnic-cultural groups. Multicultural education for all pupils still does not properly get off the ground in practice, and is often limited to an ideological discourse. Second, in most cases, multicultural education exists merely as an addition to or as a minor adaptation of the existing curriculum. Multicultural education therefore tends to assimilation rather than to cultural pluralism. This is hardly surprising in situations in which the ethnic minorities are numerical minorities. Recurring points in the public discussion on multicultural education are the questions of how far cultural diversity threatens the unity of society and to what degree cultural diversity hampers or encourages the realization of equal opportunities for all residents (Eldering, 1994b, 1996).

## Multicultural education at school level

We now address a few issues concerning school policy and classroom practice. Multicultural education is almost nowhere the result of a deliberate school policy; it depends on the initiatives of individual teachers and therefore is mostly not an integrated part of the curriculum. A recent survey showed that although more than two-thirds of the Dutch school principals said that intercultural education is important, fewer than half of the schools had discussed this issue in a teaching staff meeting in the past eight years (CEB, 1994). A multicultural school policy, however, is a prerequisite for the successful implementation of multicultural education. This implies that the teaching staff, preferably in close cooperation with parents, discuss and choose the approach and contents of multicultural education.

Multicultural education is predominantly practised in areas and schools with substantial numbers of ethnic minority pupils. Schools with few or no minority pupils have as yet made little effort to revise the curriculum, or develop multicultural policies, dismissing multicultural education as 'not our concern', 'a low priority' or 'stigmatizing' (Tomlinson, 1990; CEB, 1994). Schools in these so-called monocultural or non-contact areas, however, must prepare their pupils for life in a multicultural society too, although the contents of multicultural education will inevitably be different because of the lack of daily contacts with children from other ethnic-cultural groups.

In the past decade a controversy has arisen on the North American and European continents between educators propagating multicultural education and those in favour of anti-racist education. The first emphasize cultural differences, the latter racial differences, between groups. Both approaches require a thorough knowledge and understanding of the underlying principles and theories as well as an open eye for daily reality. Teachers who choose the anti-racist approach need to have knowledge about the social psychological processes of discrimination and racism and to be aware of the genesis of prejudice in children (Vedder, 1993). They also need to be insightful about adult reactions, including their own.

At the end of the comparative section on multiculturalism in the Netherlands and the United States, we noted that immigrants in both countries come from a multitude of cultures. It can be expected neither that teachers have a thorough knowledge of all these cultures, nor that they teach the pupils about all these different cultures. Another problem with emphasizing cultural differences between groups is that cultures are dynamic and not static. Migration to a society with a different culture leads to a process of culture change (acculturation). The rate and direction of the acculturation process depend on the frequency and intensity of contacts and the attitudes of immi-

grants and the members of the mainstream groups (Berry, 1990; Eldering, 1994a). To avoid cultural stereotyping, teachers should focus on the culture of individual families or children rather than on the culture of the group to which they belong. Teachers therefore need to observe the educational and cultural characteristics of their students, and adapt their teaching to these features.

As to the nature of multiculturalism, we conclude that in both countries it is publicly, but not universally, acknowledged, and the implications of both parts of this statement are multi-level. For example, both the United States and the Netherlands still face the difficulty of societies where portions of the population are almost unaware of the issues of multiculturalism. University faculties of education in states in the USA without a major multicultural presence are often concerned about the monocultural backgrounds of their students and have been endeavouring to provide diversity in the classrooms in which they practice teach. For example, students at a Texan university move a long distance from their university, a primarily Anglo institution, to practise teaching in Dallas urban schools that are composed of 90 per cent African-American and Latino/a students (Contreras, 1994). Farther north, at a conservative Lutheran university in Indiana, student teachers also move to urban centres in Chicago and Gary, Indiana, in order to diversify their experiences, travelling long distances to do so.

A further issue of importance for both countries is still in educating and helping people, students, teachers and parents in schools to deal with prejudice. Curricula must be directed towards inclusion and diversity, but probably a more basic and underlying issue is to address what has been called 'dysconscious racism' (King, 1991, p. 133), pervasive attitudes which continue in people's minds even while they deny them. It seems surprising that we must do so, since the topic has been apparently in primacy since the 1960s. But educators are more restricted of mind than we would like to think, and attitudes persist passively. Imagination, social advocacy, transformation of everyday lessons and presentations are necessary; this means a very specific and pervasive form of teaching, which requires both vigilance and planning among educators. We have to plan for social reconstructivism in all our teaching, and ask colleagues to review and critique our teaching work.

In teacher education, the issues of multicultural education must be accepted as a national policy directed towards acceptance of diversity, and move from there. Then, teacher education must direct itself to three crucial levels: first, the teacher's understanding and recognition of his or her knowledge and feelings about diverse people; second, direct and supervised experience with classrooms of diversity; third, the pedagogical skills necessary for teaching diverse students. The third of these, pedagogical skills, is addressed here in more detail.

The knowledge base is staggering. Literature reviews and policy studies regarding the field of multicultural education point overall to the multiple layers of knowledge and understanding necessary for a minimally adequate approach to the multicultural classroom (Appleton, 1983; Lynch, 1986; Sleeter and Grant, 1987; Banks, 1988; Eldering and Kloprogge, 1989; Cummins, 1990). Such knowledge necessarily derives from the fields of education, anthropology, demography, sociology and psychology. The overall reviews also discuss the attendant problem that specific recommendations for educational curricula and instructional practices are often slighted. Although there is a need for the body of work directed to policy directives and broad curricular goals, the pedagogy directed to multicultural classrooms can get lost. In addition, not surprisingly in the United States, cultural diversity has spawned a virtual publishing industry of books about multicultural education. Every day new publications bring studies about the American schooling of the Hmong people from Indochina, the Miao students from China, multiple Latino and Asian populations (for example, Delgado-Gaitan and Trueba, 1994; Trueba and Zou, 1994).

While increasing attention has been paid to teaching and activities for such classrooms, this is probably the area to which the least academic attention has been devoted (Sleeter and Grant, 1988; Sullivan, 1990; Schlene, 1992; Branch *et al.*, 1993; Gormley *et al.*, 1993). In fact, Bartolome

(1994) has specifically described how well-meaning teachers often apply pedagogical strategies that are truly inappropriate for students with varying learning needs and styles because of cultural differences from the students. Teachers need to study their students.

Detailed observations of students by independent observers within their learning environments help to define effective teaching approaches. One can observe the ways in which students make themselves comfortable, attract or avoid attention, use materials, accept or reject praise and criticism, use the structures of the classroom and instruct themselves. During the process of observation, patterns of interaction, rules and understanding emerge that have been used and acted upon but not overtly stated (Mehan, 1979; Edwards and Mercer, 1987). Studies of children from non-dominant cultures in their classrooms can indicate strong pedagogical principles that are necessary for effective teaching, regardless of ideology or policy (Rothenberg and Cassant, 1994).

As a first step, the pedagogical principle of the use of visual learning should be paramount and is apparent for students from a non-dominant culture. Students who do not understand all the language or customs used in the classroom clearly use their visual perception as much as possible in learning and figuring out the environment. Indeed, children are influenced by everything they see around them, whether or not the cues are helpful. Watching one's peers can be misleading, for example, since their actions (e.g. simply marking an 'X' on an answer or a picture) may not be correct. A teaching goal would be to design visual cues so that learning is not accidental or haphazardly contrived by the student's necessity to figure things out. Some work in class could be manifestly shared, so that it would be acceptable for the new student to observe the work of a partner. The teacher could develop routine symbols for situations when it is or is not appropriate to watch what other students do.

For many students, visual symbols or pictures facilitate comprehension of verbal material. To develop or facilitate the use of visual cues, the teacher could recognize and build on group experiences and visual cues. In particular, such work could take the form of including visual materials based on the student's country of origin and language and also becoming more alert to confusing visual cues in class presentations. In one observation, an 8-year-old from Somalia became noticeably distressed when, on 17 March (St Patrick's Day), the duplicated mathematics paper was decorated with leprechauns (Rothenberg and Cassant, 1994). Previously these mathematics assignments had been her daily delight, since she knew the symbol system of numbers and could do well on the arithmetic operations and even understood classroom explanations.

Schoolrooms in the United States commonly demonstrate the symbols of the dominant culture through visual decorations, especially concerning familiar holidays. Such decoration by holiday, it should be noted, is a non-pedagogical use of visual cues, because the holidays are well known by children of the dominant culture. That is, children have no need to learn about the holidays and the decorations are often confusing to children of the non-dominant culture. This can therefore be changed in a wealth of ways with materials from all areas of the curriculum. There are visual materials about other cultures and the arts as well as pictorial symbols in various subjects. Even new representations of material that is already familiar would be appropriate, such as Renaissance art about Christian holidays or iconic representations of Byzantine Orthodox festivals.

Furthermore, the use of visual learning is valuable for all children. Observation by children should be basic in the science curriculum and in other areas, such as art, as well (Duckworth, 1987; Egan, 1988). Egan has pointed out that observing and categorizing often go together naturally and that categories will be introduced by children, if they first do the observing, rather than the other way around. Often in teaching, nominal categories are first presented (rain, snow, ice, mist, clouds) and then children may observe their occurrence and causal relationships. Egan further suggests the encouragement of observation for its own sake, allowing children to be inclusive in what they observe, 'to notice the patterns of [a tree's] branches, the way different kinds of rain run down the leaves, the movement of the branches in different winds' (Egan, 1988, p. 218). Eisner (1993) has also discussed the wide-ranging value of visual understanding and learning.

This principle of using visual cues for pedagogy has been based on evidence derived from the observation of students, but other aspects of the classroom also come into focus through observation (Warren, 1983). This includes neglected or absent features. In many multicultural classrooms, for example, there is little sharing of experiences, academic or otherwise, by any of the children that is initiated by the teacher (Rothenberg and Cassant, 1994). We have observed numerous lost opportunities, in, for example, such simple daily actions as saying hello, please and thank you in the native languages of the students (or others). In order for the classroom to become more of a basis for shared communication among these students, the teacher has to introduce the idea of sharing different languages and the value of sharing culture.

Another area, students' need for structure, has been indicated in observations. Students show a strong concern for rules and for physical structure in their classrooms. For example, in rare acts of initiative, a student from Poland and a student from Somalia pointed out whose turn was next in every appropriate game. In their respective classrooms, each took charge of straightening up the room at the end of the day. They took for themselves the job of making sure that desks and chairs were placed in line with the chairs on top of the desks. Their teachers noted that these students volunteered to check the desks every day. Many students from non-dominant cultures are also clearly concerned about the structure of their classroom materials. Homework and classroom work are often placed in separate folders, and the students repeatedly check these folders and straighten them up. They seem to be concerned for the orderliness of the classroom in general, and to be making a 'community' of their own.

Structure, in such manifestations as rules, time schedules, physical plans and different class groups for different tasks, is already plentiful in most schools and classrooms. It only needs to be made explicit. Reviewing the many elements of structure in the classroom is pedagogically useful to both teachers and students. In addition, implicit, unwritten, structural elements in each classroom should be investigated and clarified, such as the following possibilities: small groups are allowed to work and chat together; students leave their seats when they wish; spontaneous questions are met with positive responses from the teacher; students always raise their hands to ask a question. Such unwritten structural patterns are often difficult to ascertain, especially by classroom members who are unfamiliar with the dominant culture (Mehan, 1979; Kerr and Desforges, 1988).

After investigation and review, teachers can ascertain the necessity for structure for the whole class, as well as for students who are unfamiliar with the dominant classroom culture. Allowing students to be in charge of maintaining order with the desks or other specific items is one way to promote the use of the classroom structure. Using structure effectively is sound teaching in other ways as well, such as making accepted behaviour clear, indicating the times that non-academic transitions occur and when class periods begin and stop (pairing the visual representations on the clock face with verbal designations). Other types of visual cues can also be helpful, such as using international traffic symbols to show students around the school and rooms and using the languages of the students in the school for each symbol.

One intent of observing classrooms has been to direct attention to the use of the pedagogical principles of visual learning and classroom structure in classrooms where students from several cultures are represented. Another intent has been to use observations of children to show the applicability of such principles. On the other hand, visual cues and classroom structures that are not helpful to learning are also important areas of consideration. Those can be misleading distractions or represent confusing cultural symbols or actual biases in the environment. Clearly the students learn from such visual cues, whether by pedagogical design or not. Observations reported here, in addition to others in ongoing classrooms, could lead to a more thoughtful and focused use of the learning environment.

## Conclusions

This chapter explores some educational issues related to the growing cultural diversity in society. By comparing the United States and the Netherlands, we concluded that, despite the differences in tradition and scale of immigration, the countries share similarities relevant for educational policy and practice. These similarities concern the concentration of ethnic minorities in urban areas and the enormous cultural diversity of the immigrant population. A question relevant for education is the way schools reflect the cultural diversity in society. In theory, multicultural education has many modalities, varying from immersion in the second language to complete multicultural curricula. Multicultural education in practice, however, is usually limited to pupils from ethnic minorities and tends to assimilation rather than to cultural pluralism. Multicultural education is almost nowhere the result of a deliberate school policy; it mostly depends on the initiatives of individual teachers and is, therefore, not an integrated part of the curriculum. In schools with few or no minority pupils multicultural education generally has a low priority. A successful implementation of multicultural education, however, requires a multicultural policy on school level and an individual approach to pupils and their cultures. The formulation of a multicultural school policy forces the teaching staff to become aware of the multicultural character of society and the school environment and to choose, preferably in cooperation with parents, the approach and contents of multicultural education. Ethnic minority children come from a variety of cultural backgrounds. After migration, moreover, the culture of the country of origin changes. It cannot be expected that teachers have a thorough knowledge of all these cultures, but teachers can try to assess the acculturation level of their pupils and make them comfortable in their learning environments. We focused here on visual learning to provide an example of a pedagogical approach in multicultural classrooms. Other foci as noted in the scheme would incorporate other modalities and teaching models. These approaches may not be designed *exclusively* for multicultural education, but they have particular relevance in multicultural classrooms.

# References

Appleton, N. (1983) *Cultural Pluralism in Education: Theoretical Foundations*. New York: Longman.

Banks, J. A. (1988) *Multiethnic Education: Theory and Practice*. Boston: Allyn and Bacon.

Bartolome, L. I. (1994) Beyond the methods fetish: toward a humanizing pedagogy. *Harvard Educational Review*, **64** (2), 173–94.

Berry, J. W. (1990) Psychology of acculturation: understanding individuals moving between cultures. In R. W. Brislin (ed.), *Applied Cross-cultural Psychology*. Newbury Park, CA: Sage.

Branch, R., Goodwin, Y. and Gualteri, J. (1993) Making classrooms culturally pluralistic. *The Educational Forum*, **58**, 57–71.

CEB (Commissie Evaluatie Basisonderwijs) (1994) *Onderwijs gericht op een multiculturele samenleving*. The Hague: SDU.

Contreras, G. (1994) Preparing student teachers for diversity. Paper presented at the American Association for Teaching and Curriculum, October.

Cummins, J. (1990) Multilingual/multicultural education: evaluation of underlying theoretical constructs and consequences for curriculum development. In P. Vedder (ed.), *Fundamental Studies in Educational Research*. Amsterdam: Swets and Zeitlinger.

Delgado-Gaitan, C. and Trueba, H. (1994) *Crossing Cultural Borders*. Bristol, PA: Falmer Press.

DES (1985) *Education for All. The Report of the Committee of Inquiry into the Education of Children from Ethnic Minority Groups*. London: HMSO.

Duckworth, E. (1987) *The Having of Wonderful Ideas*. New York: Teachers College Press.

Edwards, D. and Mercer, N. (1987) *Common Knowledge: The Development of Understanding in the Classroom*. London: Methuen.

Egan, K. (1988) *Primary Understanding: Education in Early Childhood*. New York: Routledge.

Eisner, E. W. (1993) The education of vision. *Education Horizons*, Winter, 80–5.

Eldering, L. (1993) Cultuurverschillen in een multiculturele samenleving. *Comenius*, **49**, 9–26.

Eldering, L. (1994a) Benaderingen van multicultureel onderwijs. In S. Miedema and H. Klifman (eds), *Christelijk onderwijs in ontwikkeling. Jaarboek 1994*. Kampen: Kok.

Eldering, L. (1994b) Approaches to multicultural education. Paper presented at the Annual Meeting of the American Anthropological Association, Atlanta, 29 November – 4 December.

Eldering, L. and Kloprogge, J. (eds) (1989) *Different Cultures, Same School: Ethnic Minority Children in Europe*. Amsterdam: Swets and Zeitlinger.

Erickson, F. (1987) Transformation and school success: the politics and culture of educational achievement. *Anthropology and Education Quarterly* **18** (4), 335–57.

Fleras, A. and Elliott, J. L. (1992) *Multiculturalism in Canada: The Challenge of Diversity*. Ontario: Nelson Canada.

Gelauff-Hanzon, C. W., Bilgin, N. S., Bouwer, E. A., Van der Veen, A. and Saija, M. L. (1994) *Nieuwkomers van 12–18 jaar. Schets van een situatie*. PEWA-rapport 3. Leiden: Rijksuniversiteit Leiden, PEWA.

Gonzalez, R. M. (1995) Teachers' roles in the preparation of Latino(a)s for higher education. Paper presented at the American Educational Research Association, San Francisco.

Gormley, K., Hammer, J., McDermott, P. and Rothenberg, J. (1993) Diversity of experienced teachers' book selections. Paper presented at the meetings of the New England Educational Research Organization, Portsmouth, NH, April.

Janzen, R. (1994) Five paradigms of ethnic relations. *Social Education*, October, 349–54.

Kerr, T. and Desforges, M. (1988) Developing bilingual children's English in school. In G. Verma and P. Pumfrey (eds), *Educational Attainments: Issues and Outcomes in Multicultural Education*. London: Falmer Press.

King, J. E. (1991) Dysconscious racism: ideology, identify, and the miseducation of teachers. *Journal of Negro Education*, **60** (2), 133–46.

Lynch, J. (1986) *Multicultural Education: Principles and Practice*. London: Routledge and Kegan Paul.

McDermott, R. P. and Goldman, S. V. (1983) Teaching in multicultural settings. In L. van den Berg-Eldering, F. J. M. de Rijcke and L. V. Zuck (eds), *Multicultural Education: A Challenge for Teachers*. Dordrecht: Foris Publications.

Mehan, H. (1979) *Learning Lessons: Social Organization in the Classroom*. Cambridge, MA: Harvard University Press.

Ogbu, J. U. (1987) Variability in minority school performance: a problem in search of an explanation. *Anthropology and Education Quarterly*, **18** (4), 312–34.

Ogbu, J. U. (1992) Understanding cultural diversity and learning. *Educational Researcher*, **21** (8), 5–14.

Rex, J. (1991) The political sociology in a multi-cultural society. *European Journal of Intercultural Studies*, **2** (1), 7–19.

Rothenberg, J. and Cassant, S. (1994) A watchful eye: observing and learning in multicultural classrooms. Paper presented at the meetings of the American Association for Teaching and Curriculum, Dallas, October.

Seller, M. (1992) Historical perspectives on multicultural education. What kind? By whom? For whom? And why? Paper presented at the AERA in San Francisco, April.

Schlene, V. J. (1992) Teaching about cultural diversity: an ERIC/CHESS sample. *Social Science Record*, **30** (1), 99–102.

Sleeter, C. E. and Grant, C. A. (1987) An analysis of multicultural education in the United States. *Harvard Educational Review*, **57** (4), 421–44.

Sleeter, C. E. and Grant, C. A. (1988) *Making Choices for Multicultural Education*. Columbus, OH: Merrill.

Sullivan, W. R. (1990) A dollar-wise guide to global studies. *Social Education*, **54**, 49–50.

Tomlinson, S. (1990) *Multicultural Education in White Schools*. London: Batsford.

Troyna, B. and Edwards, V. (1993) *The Educational Needs of a Multiracial Society*. Coventry: University of Warwick.

Trueba, H. and Zou, Y. (1994) *Power in Education*. Bristol, PA: Falmer Press.

Vedder, P. H. (1993) *Intercultureel onderwijs vanuit psychologisch perspectief*. Leiden: Rijksuniversiteit, Sectie Interculturele Pedagogiek.

Veenman, J. (1994) *Sinds kort in Nederland. Kenmerken en kansen van nieuwkomers*. The Hague: Directie Coördinatie Minderhedenbeleid, Ministerie van Binnenlandse Zaken.

Warren, R. L. (1983) The application of ethnographic research in multicultural education. In L. van den Berg-Eldering, F. J. M. de Rijcke and L. V. Zuck (eds), *Multicultural Education: A Challenge for Teachers*. Dordrecht: Foris Publications.

# 26 Perception and Reality: Principals' Training Needs and Supply in the UK and Australia

PAUL GANDERTON

Principals must be allowed and required to lead and manage ... In order to devote the highest proportion of their time and energy to instructional leadership, principals must not be distracted from this essential priority by excessive bureaucratic demands and plant maintenance procedures as they are undoubtedly at present. They must be liberated from the minutiae of office management and be emboldened to lead their schools towards real and measurable educational achievement ... Principals need to be freer to develop and proclaim a vision for their schools...

Principals will need additional training in the new educational leadership role envisaged for them, as well as in resource management and accountability requirements.

(New South Wales Government, 1990, pp. 47, 109)

## Introduction

Such fine words, such noble principles! The passages quoted above do much to raise the spirit but offer little to the flesh inured in the daily running of our educational institutions. Yet these are not palliatives offered to a profession by politicians but a real attempt by one educational system to see through the myriad issues facing us and produce a vision of the future. That this vision may be constructed on false premises (or worse, none at all) is an interesting research point but not of much practical help to those running our schools and colleges.

The topic under debate is the notion of leadership and the requirements for the job. Is this something that can be learned by observation, by some sort of educational osmosis, or are we to say that, in the last decade of the twentieth century, it actually requires some training? Let's start with a simpler idea: training is important. This leads us into a series of dilemmas. For example, what is provided, who provides it, what is its basis in theory and practice? Perhaps one should start from an alternative perspective. Rather than dictate what is to be required, why not ask the actual postholders what they see as important and how they view training?

If we do this the debate takes on a new dimension. Training is no longer seen as a linear function (i.e. training in, principal out) but as a dynamic response to a tri-plot of constraints where the principal is in the middle and the three apices are their educational ideals (i.e. the professional mind-set of that generation of educators), the internal constraints of their institutions (finance, staffing, students, etc.) and the external forces (e.g. government regulations, 'market' forces, public expectation, etc). Here are people who deal with a system-as-given but for whom there are genuine constraints to their actions. It is important to examine critically this perspective. What do principals actually see as important to their work, how do they receive training (or more importantly, what do they receive)? Surely this should be central to the training process. There are numerous studies examining the situations facing the principal and other senior staff. While there is much agreement on the fact that change has occurred (e.g. Evetts, 1994) there is less on how it has affected those involved and even less on how staff have seen their situations. Two notable exceptions are Gillborn (1989) and Newton (1993). In his study of English headteachers, Gillborn noted certain common responses: to the external pressures (educational reform) and the need for some support (in this case from peers rather than training). Newton's study emphasized the discontinuity between role conception and personal performance (two elements of the tri-plot outlined above).

The research presented in this chapter aims to address this area and examine the dimensions of the tri-plot as part of this debate on training. Research carried out in the UK and Australia shows both common ground and alarming differences. Despite the small-scale nature of this study (remarkably common in this field; Gillborn, 1989), the implications could be far-reaching. It is argued that there is a dichotomy between the pressures of the state for their new educational perspective and the idea(l)s of the senior staff involved. Further, it is argued that their training is based on insufficient understanding of their needs (and that of the state) and that if true progress is to be made there will need to be a fundamental re-evaluation of the way in which training proceeds.

However, as with any study, there must be a need to ground it in the context within which it is produced; therefore it is important to look at educational changes in the UK and Australia.

## Externalities: changes in education policies, 1988 to 1992

If sense is to be made of the principals' replies it is necessary to study the changes to which they were subjected during this time. In reality, such changes can be seen as part of an ongoing policy progression. This is not just a question of gathering information seen elsewhere or a case of semantics but a practical challenge. It is not what governments (for example) see as important but what is perceived by principals to be important. For example, is all legislation equally important to an individual institution; does the most recent piece

cause undue problems and get undue weighting in a survey?

## *The Australian perspective*

To a certain extent it is disingenuous to talk about an Australian perspective for education: a combination of geography and history has produced not one, but one federal and seven state systems (Clark, 1992). For the purposes of this study the changes in only one state, New South Wales, are described. In many ways this is an ideal case – it is by far the largest education system in Australia and one of the largest in the world (2227 schools with 750,000 students and a A$3 billion budget in 1989 alone; New South Wales, 1990). It could also claim to be one of the more innovative systems, with many of the changes seen elsewhere in the world being developed there.

Although legislation goes back to 1880, it is the most recent changes that have been most keenly felt. The first real moves for change came with the 1987 Education and Public Instruction Act. This was followed up by the state premier, Greiner, who wished to examine some of the chief concerns of state and public alike, notably the centralization of the system, the calibre of management, the accelerating nature of change and the loss of impetus by the NSW Department of School Education. From 1989 to 1992, education in NSW was subject to a series of crucial reports, all calling for reform. Some were state in origin while others were part of a federal initiative to bring unity to a divided system (New South Wales Government, 1989, 1990; AECRC, 1991; AEC, 1992). Although the remits produced a plethora of ideas, they can be crystallized into two thrusts: the need for a responsive institutional system (in terms of finance, staff, buildings, administration, etc.) and a comprehensive curricular structure to meet the present and future educational needs of the people.

Thus, at the time of this survey, principals were faced with a system in almost complete flux. In management terms, they had to go from being headteachers to being management specialists. In curriculum terms, they had to address the need to provide future-oriented, competency-based curricula which both removed the old certainties about their student numbers and put them into competition with 'other providers', i.e. further education and the workplace.

## The UK perspective

Although some of the most important changes in UK education since 1944 took place from 1988 onwards, it is necessary to start by examining the origins of these reforms. The change of government from Labour to Conservative in 1979 was more than just another example of party-switching which had characterized post-war politics: it could be seen as an ideological watershed and an inexorable shift to the right. Up to 1979, one could reasonably talk about consensus politics. From 1979 the dominance of 'free-market' thinking permeated all aspects of government: education was not immune (Lawton, 1992). Lest it should be thought that the whole issue came down to politics, there were many contextual factors (such as demographic trends and an increasing awareness of the low retention rate post-16) that had to be addressed irrespective of government (Chitty, 1992; Lawrence, 1992).

From 1979 to 1988, there was a certain amount of discussion within the Conservative Party and its academic coterie (Lawrence, 1992). In addition, various politicians (e.g. Kenneth Baker) opened up the debate to public discussion (Lawton, 1992). From such discussion flowed the key legislation of the period, the 1988 Education Reform Act, whose key provisions were the introduction of a national curriculum, the setting up of a localized system of school management, the creation of a new tier of schooling (i.e. grant maintained schools and city technology colleges) and the reform of further and higher education funding. The first two elements were paralleled in Australia (see above); the third and fourth remain a purely British solution.

Although they were unaffected by much of this initial reform (which was for students up to age

16), the impetus carried on to sixth-form colleges in the Further and Higher Education Bill of 1991, where there was a call for a separate funding system, 'incorporated' colleges and an assessment of 'quality'.

## Common answers to common problems?

What can we glean from this brief overview of the two systems? Clearly, there are aspects in common: curricular, organizational and financial. The search for a national standard of curricular provision can be seen in both systems. The aims of such provision are similar in that they seek to harmonize currently diverse systems (to allow comparability of standards and cross-boundary transfer of students) and set a base level of provision across the subject range. Organizationally, there is an attempt to devolve power towards the school level while maintaining control at the centre. Financially, there is a desire to give more funding to schools so that they can buy the services they need rather than have them dictated by local or central bureaucracies.

Against such seeming agreement one must pay heed to considerable contrasts. Australian reports are characterized by their highly context-sensitive approach to their analyses; their explicit acceptance of the forces that shaped their current position (Ganderton and Koutouzis, 1995). It is noticeable that the debate is spread wider than in the UK: education debates are common in many forums. Since 1979, the UK approach has been market-oriented. In education one can see that the reforms have been tailored to fit the doctrine rather than explicitly to improve education (see, for example, the microcomputer debate; Ganderton, 1988). Debate is rarely as open to the responses that one can see in Australia. This is not a question of semantics: it reaches to the core of comparative work and should be borne in mind when interpreting the work described below.

Thus, with differences in context but with similarities of goal, principals in the two systems contemplate the future and their training.

## Comparative study

> Comparative studies are not unproblematic. In addition to methodological problems there are conceptual issues.
>
> (Brewster and Hegewisch, 1994, p. 2)

### Methodology

The methodology employed here can be divided into two: a postal questionnaire and participant observer analysis. The questionnaire was sent to a small sample of principals and their deputies in New South Wales, Australia (mainly the Metropolitan West Region) and Hampshire, UK. The aim was to gather reactions to past, present and future events. It was important that no influence was exerted (albeit unconsciously) by restricting the answers to given categories: despite the difficulties it brought to the analysis, all answers were 'free-form', i.e. each respondent could reply in the manner he or she desired. It was further decided to keep the study small-scale. This had the advantage of making the replies easier to analyse (which was important given the nature of the replies), although it would obviously lose the weight of argument that a larger-scale study would give. When suitable senior schools had been chosen, 18 questionnaires were sent out to each system.

The second part of the method, that of participant observer, was to check the systems 'from the inside' – to obtain a perception of the context of that system so that replies could be interpreted more accurately and the implications could be subjected to a greater degree of rigour. The author has worked in the UK system for a number of years, but was on a year's working exchange when the NSW work was undertaken. In addition to being able to observe (but not influence) the changes, he had the opportunity of informally interviewing some senior staff and other education officials to ensure that interpretations accurately reflected changes.

### Results

Of the 18 replies sent to each system, seven were returned fully completed from Australia (six from the UK) with five (six from the UK) returned noting insufficient time to respond. Despite this small reply (not unusual in such surveys), there was certainly enough material to derive some significant findings. The range of answers was considerable: an initial problem was to find some way of both classifying and weighting answers to see which were the most significant. Classification was carried out on a twofold system:

1   To put replies into one of three categories following the ideas put forward by Macpherson (1993), i.e. the realms of 'things' (taken here to mean legislation, funding, resources and competition), 'people' (students and staff) and 'ideas' (curricular matters). From this, key sub-divisions were used, giving a total set of 30 possible response areas.
2   It was necessary to devise a weighting system: one had to be able to give due credit for responses high in the order of replies and also for responses which were given by many respondents. On those questions where a ranking was required, the first response scored four, the second three, etc.

Using both elements it was possible to score replies.

### Analysis

Although the sample size was small, the responses provide much food for thought. Rather than dwell on answers in detail, it is sufficient to highlight the key aspects here.

#### Personnel and establishment
Respondents came from either sixth-form colleges or senior high schools. Experience ranged from 21 to 37 years, with no discernible difference between systems. All staff would have been well

into their careers before the current wave of changes.

### Government policy

Both sets of principals have been very heavily affected by current legislation. Both governments had major pieces of legislation in the late 1980s and both were trying to put the ideas into practice. In addition, the UK legislation was moving heavily towards incorporation (enforced independence), which produced major administrative problems and which also meant that finance was another major worry. Australian replies were less focused on finance, partly because the legislation was not moving in that direction to that extent and partly because the NSW government was trying to move on more than one front at a time, which allowed curricular matters more dominance.

### Educationist policy

Answers were more widespread, with more emphasis given to student, staff and curricular matters. When financial matters were raised, it was usually to comment on the need for more money to implement student/curriculum policies. One interesting result was the Australian emphasis on entitlement and equity. The cultural support for people to have equality of opportunity is fundamental to Australian society.

### Training

With respect to the current position, there was considerable contrast in provision, with UK principals having a series of half-day courses relying on peer group support, while Australian principals undertook more prolonged training courses (with a master's degree fast becoming mandatory for promotion). Satisfaction levels were poorer for the UK (owing to provision?). The training culture was far more highly developed in Australia.

With respect to current government policy, there is uniformity of provision, with both systems responding to policy changes by providing short courses. Improvements were seen as finance-

oriented in the UK and practically oriented in Australia.

### Problems and prospects

UK principals saw the future in more diverse terms, with positive comments on a wider range of issues. This could be reduced to the desires for more funding and the provision of better education to a wider range of students. Australians were far more closely focused, with frequent comments on learning experiences, ethos and school–industry links. Negative prospects showed a greater contrast, with the UK concerned about the realm of 'things' (competition/marketing being the 'winner'), while Australians took concerns about workload and pastoral care (i.e. the realm of 'people') to be paramount.

## Implications

Despite the apparent convergence of the two systems within the context of 'globalization', it is obvious that, although they hold a common position, principals hold different (sometimes radically different) views. While there is some evidence of this within each educational system, the differences are far more marked between systems. One implication is that, although we talk about a global system in theory, in practice the running of our educational institutions is both context-dependent and context-sensitive. Any attempt to use a global training system (such as that espoused by the OECD) would, therefore, be bound to fail. Similar divergences are found when comparing government and educator policies. Even allowing for the fact that the questions demanded differing foci from the respondents, there is little indication that the basic tenets put forward by either government are translated through to students' education. To this extent there is strong evidence to support one of this chapter's original theses, that of differing perceptions of state and person. If the aim of management training is to get a consensus, then the implication from this work is that it is not happening.

The picture is not entirely black. Australian principals often score closer to their government's perceptions than do those in the UK. Education for society is a recurring theme in major reports (e.g. Scott and Carrick – New South Wales Government, 1989, 1990). This is more closely in tune with the prevailing school culture and is thus translated into a consensus. The implication is that compliance comes from working with, rather than against, the prevailing culture. Perhaps Australian satisfaction with both government perspectives and training comes from the degree to which Australians fund (both financially and in terms of carrying the human resource burden) their in-service training. Higher degrees are the rule rather than the exception. However, both groups appreciated the utility of the one- or two-day course. This could be seen as a paradox for the Australians but could also be part of the principals' acceptance of the need for brief, practically oriented training. Short courses give temporary coping strategies but mainstream human resource management (in Europe at least) is moving towards a theory-based training system (Brewster and Hegewisch, 1994). The implication here is that training is not just part of the system but part of the culture. Put bluntly, is there evidence that the school organizational culture is long-term training-friendly?

There is one more area that needs to be addressed here: the relationship between perception and reality. Both governments were putting into place clear educational goals, which, according to the documentation at least, were philosophically and internally consistent (leaving aside their political orientations and practical applications). Government perception pointed in one direction while the reality faced by the principals differed. This was most graphically illustrated by one respondent who stated that he was 'willing to play at shop-keeper' if that was what the government required, but then he was 'going back to being a teacher'. This must be seen as a critical element in training provision, for if the trainees see it as little more than pleasing the trainers/funders, then it follows that there will be little gained from such training.

## Perception and reality: the way forward?

At the beginning of this chapter, the debate was focused on the notion of leadership and how that could be achieved. If training were to be the route then it followed that one element that should be addressed should be the way in which trainees (i.e. principals) viewed their needs bearing in mind the context within which they operated. For the purposes of discussion it was argued that principals operated within a tri-plot of constraints: their own mind-sets, externalities and institutional constraints. The research used in this chapter has highlighted some important issues:

1   Although they held common positions, their responses were constrained by unique contextual sets.
2   The perception of the pressures (externalities and institutional constraints) differed between principals and the government, i.e. both were working on the same programme but with different perceptions of outcome.
3   Given this dichotomy of view, there is little likelihood of the long-term changes required by the governments being met in reality.

Where do we go from here? The most obvious question arising from this is: if the government is going in one direction and the principals in another, what is the role of training? Is it the improvement of the educational service (as both groups purported to support in interviews with the author) or is it more a question of political control by government (see, for example, arguments in Ganderton, 1991)? The research presented here is too small-scale to answer this question, but it is possible to add to the debate by suggesting one possible way forward.

Education, in the UK at least, is notorious for training everyone except its practitioners. The resulting philosophical dichotomy between the education of students and the education of staff is deserving of a wider debate. It is no good looking to the business world for some bolt-on model: there is no equivalent in commerce for that which education globally is urged to emulate. Studies in business training (e.g. Hunt *et al.*, 1988; Mullins, 1993) offer much in the way of ideas but cite virtually nothing from the education sector. The converse is usually true in education writing (e.g. Busher and Saran, 1994). Does this mean that there are two sets of leaders from whom nothing can be gleaned from each to illuminate the work of the other? If this is so, then the whole theoretical basis of these two sets of ideas must collapse under their individual internal inconsistencies.

## *Models of leadership: a critique*

Although there could be more discussion of the point, accept, for the moment, that there are two current sets of leadership model paradigms: business and education. If the implications noted above are given the status of parameters, and this research supports strongly such an idea, then it should be possible to examine key models to see which, if any, are more likely to be valid in training principals. The argument here is that the more consistent the model to the work of the principal, the more likely it is to provide what is required by senior staff and so bridge the divide between perception and reality, which has been a key strand running through this chapter. The literature on this aspect of the subject is vast – only a few examples can be used (Hunt *et al.*, 1988; Wilson and Rosenfeld, 1990; Macpherson, 1993; Mullins, 1993; Busher and Saran, 1994; Fitzsimmons and Peters, 1994).

The authors noted above whose work has been in the educational sphere have identified four models: educative, human capital, structural-functional and cultural pluralist. The 'educative' leader is one concerned with cultural aspects and leadership within a strong participative framework. Strengths of this model lie in its oligarchic approaches, but therein surely lies a weakness given the imposition of current reforms. Human capital models, which base their philosophical perspectives within neo-classical economics, provide a strong theoretical approach but explicitly deny the role of culture and non-rational behavi-our. Structural-functional models assume that one can separate job from person, which helps in the understanding of the nature of organizations but denies the micro-political realities found within all groups of people. Cultural pluralist models take culture as central but have been criticized for their micro-political naivety.

One could attempt the same brief overview of business models (contingency, path-goal, normative, charismatic and transformational are commonly discussed), but that is both to belittle the amount of good research that has been carried out (which is not intended) and to miss the point being argued here. Because of the lack of work in many key areas of leadership, there is no clear perspective. The next section is intended as a discussion that will lead towards such a perspective.

## *Training the education managers of tomorrow: a proposal*

We are urged to see education as a participative activity within a globalist perspective. If participation is a key feature of current management training practice then it is strangely silent when it comes to inward (reflexive) discussion. There is very little in the literature about the feedback from training (one notable exception being Johnson, 1993). If globalization is the key trend then from the research presented here it is clear that the rules of the game have yet to be clearly defined. However, given these caveats it is still possible to suggest ways forward.

The principals questioned for this research have shown a desire to do well, but have felt under considerable pressure, partly because they have not received sufficient training and partly because they have not been given a clear lead from their education ministries as to what is expected of them. If it is desired to train principals and other senior staff effectively, how do we go about it?

We cannot divorce the training needs of principals from those of other people. They might occupy a specific post but so do all employees. If we are going to see a globalist perspective in education, we must have a globalist perspective on training. One way forward has been demonstrated by the wide-ranging Price Waterhouse Cranfield Survey (Brewster and Hegewisch, 1994) – a study of European human resource management (HRM). Training must be seen as part of the broader HRM picture, not just as a brief adjunct to one's job. HRM in education must be tied firmly to the corporate strategy of the institution, thus making training of the trainers as important as training of students. This implies that all staff, and not just principals, see their professional development as a key policy for the effective promotion of education: 'organisations can only achieve their business objectives if the human resources possess not only the appropriate functional knowledge, skills and flexibility, but also personality characteristics considered to be vital for the specific work environment'. (Larsen, in Brewster and Hogewisch, 1994, p. 107). This raises questions of time and finance which need to be addressed. One major difference seen by the author was the importance given to these two factors in Australian and UK institutions. In Australia, professional development was seen as mandatory: school budgets, time allowances, supply (casual) staff and course quality were directed to those ends. In the UK, training (usually very limited and given 'after school hours') has a far lower institutional priority.

If training is to take central place in strategic HRM it must be seen to be effective: research shows that all elements of work must be internally consistent. This means that the importance of the work must be matched by the appropriate micropolitical and financial support. From there, four key strands emerge.

### Philosophy

This research has been conducted from within a phenomenological perspective. The value of such a philosophy has been argued elsewhere (Ganderton, 1991) but the crucial point is not whether one perspective is 'better' than another but that one should place all research within a rigorously argued theoretical–philosophical perspective (see also Hallinger and Leithwood, 1994). Given that comparative studies are valid only for the cultures

in which they are rooted, a theoretical base is the only valid way forward. It would demand a higher level of theory than seen until now, but the benefits outweigh the costs. If we are to discuss the concept of leader, is it defensible to create what amounts to two distinct theoretical bases in 'business' and 'education' leader strategies? There is much that each can learn from the other. New ideas could then be incorporated (e.g. chaos theory; Marion, 1994) without the need to rewrite the texts. Principals need to manage change – the only constant is the theoretical base. They can learn from this and then adopt strategies without recourse to a large number of (very) short courses of dubious value.

### Theory

Like philosophy, theory usually has to take a back seat (Busher and Saran, 1994; Fitzsimmons and Peters, 1994; Hallinger and Leithwood, 1994). Although theory was given a low priority by principals interviewed for this research, it has a utility that should be incorporated into more training. The use of models provides a framework for discussion and, like philosophy, provides one with a base from which to evaluate. The problem related by many answers in this research was not just the lack of a theoretical base but the abilities to judge the utility of a range of courses. Theoretical discussions permit the reconciliation of 'business' and 'education' leader research, to the benefit of both.

### Practice

Generally, training is given a very low status: it needs a far higher status (Erlandson, 1990). Australian principals score far more heavily in this regard than do their English counterparts because of the move towards master's degrees as a prerequisite for promotion. Australians also place a higher emphasis of consultation in the training process (Jenkins, 1985; Gamage, 1992). In European business, HRM is firmly on the agenda – one would hope that it would be so in education. If we require an increasingly sophisticated student output then it follows that those involved in training should also be given the ability to move ahead. In this regard, the Australian concept of life-long education should be considered, but as a planned, three-phase project.

1 Initial training via a master's-level course which stresses the value of theory. The 'educational' MBA seen in increasing numbers could be such a vehicle: the need is there according to this research (see also Daresh and Playko, 1992; Johnston and Pickergill, 1992; Johnson, 1993; Ouston, 1993; National Commission on Education, 1994).

2 A range of short courses focusing on practical management issues, such as the implementation of specific reforms.

3 A formalized network of peer groups for the support of the often-isolated principal and for the dissemination of good practice (see also Sagor, 1992; Walker *et al.*, 1993). The obvious drawback is finance, but if European industry can see it as a key way forward then why should education (which is increasingly asked to follow the business road) be made to think differently?

*Research*

Finally, one must turn to research. Much work is carried out, yet there seems to be a lack of cohesion. Business management strategies can follow a set of key routes through which research can flourish: it should be possible to repeat the exercise in education. Of all the subjects in papers studied for this chapter, lack of research was the most common theme (in addition, see Harber, 1992).

# Postscript

There is a difference between perception and reality: between the ideas of principals and the work they are asked to carry out; between the needs for and supply of appropriate training; between the rhetoric of current government thinking and the supply of resources. As we face the future we must ask ourselves what is required and act accord-

ingly. To do any less is to reduce the quality of the work we do and ultimately to undermine the qualities and abilities of the students we purport to encourage.

I would like to thank the many (anonymous) staff who gave their time to reply to this work. In addition I would like to thank Trish Miller (NSW Department of School Education, New South Wales), Chris Cawsey (St Mary's Senior High School, NSW) and Professor Keith Watson (Reading University) for their help and encouragement during my time in Australia and during the preparation of this work.

# References

Australian Education Council (1992) *Employment Related Key Competencies for Post Compulsory Education and Training (Meyer Committee)*. Canberra: AEC.

Australian Education Council Report Committee (1991) *Young People's Participation in Post-compulsory Education and Training (Finn Report)*. Canberra: AEC.

Brewster, C. and Hegewisch, A. (1994) *Policy and Practice in European Human Resource Management*. London: Routledge.

Busher, H. and Saran, R. (1994) Towards a model of school leadership. *Educational Management and Administration*, **22** (1), 5–13.

Chitty, C. (1992) *The Education System Transformed*. Sydney: Baseline Books.

Clark, M. (1992) *A Short History of Australia*. Harmondsworth: Penguin.

Daresh, J. and Playko, M. (1992) Induction for headteachers: choosing the right focus. *Educational Management and Administration*, **20** (3), 147–50.

Erlandson, D. A. (1990) Performance standards for the principalship: the emergence of a viable model. *School Organisation*, **10** (1), 17–25.

Evetts, J. (1994) The new headmaster: the changing work culture of secondary headship. *School Organisation*, **14** (1), 37.

Fitzsimmons, P. and Peters, M. (1994) Human capital theory and industry training strategy in New Zealand. *Journal of Educational Policy*, **9** (3), 245–66.

Gamage, D. T. (1992) School-centred educational reforms of the 1990s: an Australian case study. *Educational Management and Administration*, **20** (1), 5–13.

Ganderton, P. (1988) Microcomputer repairs: a study of policy and response in an English LEA. Unpublished MA dissertation, Reading University.

Ganderton, P. (1991) Subversion theory: some practical considerations. *Educational Management and Administration*, **19** (1), 30–7.

Ganderton, P. and Koutouzis, M. (1995) Context sensitivity and educational innovation. Mimeo, University of Reading.

Gillborn, D. A. (1989) Talking heads: reflections on secondary headship at a time of rapid educational change. *School Organisation*, **9**(1), 65–83.

Hallinger, P. and Leithwood, K. (1994) Introduction: exploring the impact of principal leadership. *School Effectiveness and School Improvement*, **5**(1), 206–18.

Harber, C. (1992) Effective and ineffective schools: an international perspective on the role of research. *Educational Management and Administration*, **20** (3), 16–19.

HMSO (1991) Further and Higher Education Bill (HL). London: HMSO.

Hunt, J. G., Baliga, B. J., Dachler, H. P. and Schrieshoim, C. A. (1988) *Emerging Leadership Vistas*. Boston: D. C. Heath and Company.

Jenkins, H. O. (1985) Problems in helping head teachers to learn about management. *Educational Management and Administration*, **15**, 35–42.

Johnson, N. (1993) Preparing Australian administrators: an Australian perspective. *Journal of Educational Administration*, **31** (1), 22–40.

Johnston, J. and Pickergill, S. (1992) Personal and interpersonal aspects of effective team oriented headship in the primary school. *Educational Management and Administration*, **20** (4), 239–48.

Lawrence, I. (1992) *Power and Politics at the Department of Education and Science*. London: Cassell.

Lawton, D. (1992) *Education and Politics in the 1990s*. London: Falmer Press.

MacPherson, R. J. S. (1993) Administrative reforms in the antipodes: self managing schools and the need for educative leaders. *Educational Management and Administration*, **21** (1), 40–51.

Marion, R. (1994) Organisation at the edge of chaos. *Management in Education*, **8** (3), 31–3.

Mullins, L. J. (1993) *Management and Organisational Behaviour*. London: Pitman.

National Commission on Education (1994) *Insights into Education and Training*. London: Heinemann.

New South Wales Government (1989) *Report of the Committee of Review of New South Wales Schools (Carrick Report)*. Sydney: New South Wales Government.

New South Wales Government (1990) *School Centred Education (Scott Report)*. Sydney: New South Wales Government.

Newton, E. H. (1993) The secondary headship: perceptions, conceptions, performance and reactions of headteachers in Barbados. *Journal of Educational Administration*, **31**(2), 22–42.

Ouston, J. (1993) Management competencies, school effectiveness and education management. *Educational Management and Administration*, **21**(4), 212–21.

Sagor, R. D. (1992) Three principals who make a difference. *Educational Leadership*, February 13–18.

Walker, A. D. *et al.* (1993) Principalship training through mentoring: the Singapore experience. *Journal of Educational Administration*, **31**(4), 33–50.

Wilson, D. C. and Rosenfeld, R. H. (1990) *Managing Organizations*. McGraw-Hill.

# Name Index

# Subject Index